ATIVE
POLICY

es of Social Choice
in ..... Europe, and Japan

THIRD EDITION

COMPARATIVE PUBLIC POLICY

*The Politics of Social Choice
in America, Europe, and Japan*

THIRD EDITION

ARNOLD J. HEIDENHEIMER
Washington University

HUGH HECLO
George Mason University

CAROLYN TEICH ADAMS
Temple University

ST. MARTIN'S PRESS
New York

Senior editor: Don Reisman
Project editor: Emily Berleth
Production supervisor: Chris Pearson
Graphics: G & H/Soho, Ltd.
Cover design: Darby Downey
Cover art: Lorraine Williams

For information, write:
St. Martin's Press, Inc.
175 Fifth Avenue
New York, NY 10010

ISBN: 0-312-00493-1

Published and distributed outside North America by:

MACMILLAN EDUCATION LTD.
Houndsmills, Basingstoke, Hampshire RG21 2XS and London
Companies and representatives throughout the world.

ISBN: 0-333-52485-3

Acknowledgments
Acknowledgments and copyrights are continued at the back of the book on page 406, which
constitutes an extension of the copyright page.

Table 3.2. Reprinted by permission of the publisher, from *Health and Wealth* by Robert J.
Maxwell (Lexington, Mass.: Lexington Books, copyright 1981, D. C. Heath and Company).
Table 3.10, Figures 3.1, 3.2. Reprinted from J. Rogers Hollingsworth, *A Political Economy
of Medicine: Britain and the United States,* by permission of Johns Hopkins University Press.
Table 6.4. From Joseph Pechman, ed., *Comparative Tax Systems: Europe, Canada and Japan.*
Reprinted by permission of Tax Analysts, Arlington, Virginia. Copyright 1987. All rights
reserved.
Table 7.3. From "Patterns of Income and Poverty, The Economic States of Children and
the Elderly in Eight Countries," by Timothy Smeeding, Barbara Torrey and Martin Rein in
The Vulnerable, John L. Palmer, Timothy Smeeding and Barbara Torrey, eds. Copyright 1988.
Reprinted by permission of The Urban Institute Press.
Table 8.3. Reprinted from *Handbook of Comparative Urban Fiscal Data* by Poul Mouritzen
and Kurt Nielsen, by permission of the authors.

Preface

Our aim in this volume is to utilize our experience in policy observation and analysis and, by tapping many streams of theory and knowledge, compare major tendencies in policy development in Western Europe, the United States, and Japan as they are shaping the world of the 1980s and 1990s.

This Third Edition of *Comparative Public Policy* follows in the path of its predecessor volumes, and is written by the same trio of authors who published the first edition in 1975. At intervals of about seven years we have incorporated our changing assessments of recent policy developments into the previously established framework of comparative analysis.

Do our septennial surveys relate to annual policy reviews in the way that good weekly or monthly journals are related to daily newspaper accounts? Probably not very much. Those policy analysts who write news surveys are more like journalists who give priority to the description of short-term changes. We can be, and have to be, more selective. More importantly, our analyses have become increasingly grounded in a growing body of systematic policy scholarship and theory that has become more comparatively oriented and sophisticated as we have revised our editions. A glance at the bibliographies of the first and present editions will bear this out.

If much of the text and tables of this edition are rewritten, it is less for mere reason of updating, and more because much newly published research has elucidated and refined our understanding of public policy. Comparative policy studies are rapidly filling in the blank boxes where a lack of research had forced reliance on speculation. Penetrating scholarship by many of our colleagues has allowed us to be more confident in describing not only how policies differ, but why they do so, and what some illustrative consequences are.

Whereas our previous focus was primarily trans-Atlantic, we now also seek to tap some policy experiences of developed countries located elsewhere, chiefly Japan and, more selectively, others like Australia. As we did in the second edition, we are also including an additional policy area. Environmental policy is the area newly included, in a chapter mainly written by

Carolyn Adams on the basis of a very extensive and provocative comparative literature in that field.

The universe of national policies which we analyze has experienced some significant changes since the 1970s, and will undergo yet additional ones in the course of the 1990s. The options for pursuing strikingly unique policies have been reduced for many countries, large and small, as the emergence of a world economy has required them to recognize additional constraints. Everywhere borders are becoming more porous. In Western Europe the full implementation of an internal free market within the European Community in the 1990s will require member countries to harmonize their national policies, especially in areas like taxation. But the utility of comparing policies of European countries with each other, as well as with those of the United States and Japan, will continue well into the next century. These nations can be expected to continue to differ significantly in the degree to which their policies emphasize such trends as the privatization of public services and the maintenance of welfare state programs.

* * * * *

We would like to alert readers to a number of conventions and usages employed in this book. First, as to collective labels. Since our book deals with the democratic capitalist systems of Western Europe, it is the residents of that area whom we mean when we refer to "Europeans." Often we use the term for a particular sample of European nations referred to in that particular context. Similarly, since we do not deal with East Germany, we have usually used the term "German" to refer to the West German case. A somewhat parallel practical usage is employed when we use the shorthand "American" to refer to actors and events in the United States.

When we employ monetary measures we often translate pound or mark amounts into dollars at the rate prevailing on the date that the information refers to. But readers will be aware that Western currencies have fluctuated sharply in their exchange value against each other over the past decade. This means that the comparative implications of such data must be read with an additional grain of salt. Whenever possible, we have employed measures, such as percent of GNP, that are less subject to these short-term fluctuations.

Finally, a few words about the chapter bibliographies. For easier reference, these are placed together, so to speak as a bibliographical chapter, at the end of the book. There the volumes referred to in the text are listed by alphabetical sequences of the name of their authors or editors. Also included there are additional titles which are relevant to the subject of the individual chapters.

* * * * *

We have in this edition again both merged and differentiated our efforts. Thus the chapters are usually the fruit of efforts by one, but sometimes by several of us. The responsibility was assumed as follows: One, "The Politics of Social Choice" (Heclo, Adams, and Heidenheimer); Two, "Education Policy" (Heidenheimer): Three, "Health Policy" (Heidenheimer); Four, "Housing Policy" (Adams); Five, "Economic Policy" (Heclo); Six, "Taxation Policy" (Heidenheimer); Seven, "Income Maintenance Policy" (Heclo); Eight, "Urban Planning" (Adams); Nine, "Environmental Policy" (Adams); Ten, "Policy Contrasts in the Welfare State" (Heidenheimer and Heclo).

In the preparation of this edition we have been fortunate in being able to count on the support of many colleagues and other specialists who provided important data or commented on drafts of various chapters. We would like to express special appreciation for such help from Jens Alber, Peter Baldwin, Lawrence Brown, Francis Castles, Gary Freeman, Roger Geiger, William Glaser, Torsten Husen, Richard Jung, Lennart Lundqvist, Lester Milbrath, Akira Ninomiya, T. J. Pempel, Thomas Rohlen, Richard Rose, George Schieber, Manfred Schmidt, Sven Steinmo, Larry Suter, Vito Tanzi, and Ulrich Teichler.

An especially important role in the endeavor was played by Gunther Hega, who made contributions over several years. These ranged from assistance with research to the writing and editing of several chapters, particularly those dealing with environment and taxation policies. His sense of dedication to the enterprise added considerably not only to the information base, but to the consistency and reliability of many parts of the manuscript.

We were very pleased that Emma Dankoski was willing to build on her previous experience to prepare the index for this edition. During the editorial process, the task of coordinating communication between the authors and others involved in the production process was skillfully performed by Emily Berleth of St. Martin's Press, who helped to synthesize the old and the new elements in the book into what we all hope is a readable volume.

We would also like to thank the following individuals who offered St. Martin's Press suggestions for our revision: Stephen C. Brooks, The University of Akron; Brian J. Cook, Clark University; Nicholas Peroff, University of Missouri-Kansas City; Duane H. Swank, Marquette University; Daniel T. Trainer, Edinboro University of Pennsylvania; and Thomas Wilson, Auburn University at Montgomery.

Arnold J. Heidenheimer
Hugh Heclo
Carolyn Teich Adams

Contents

A LIST OF TABLES   xii

A LIST OF FIGURES   xv

1   THE POLITICS OF SOCIAL CHOICE   1
What Is Comparative Public Policy?   3
Crosscutting Perspectives   6
Methods and Means   9
Politics as Choice   12
Choices as Frameworks   15
The Policy Areas   17
The Countries   20

2   EDUCATION POLICY   23
Choices in Education Policy   24
Political Change and Education Development (SCOPE AND
   THRESHOLDS)   26
Reform Modes and Centralization (INSTRUMENTS)   31
Improving Secondary School Opportunities
   (DISTRIBUTION)   36
University Programs and Societal Needs (RESTRAINTS AND
   INNOVATION)   47

3   HEALTH POLICY   57
Choices in Health Policy   58
Public and Professional Controls (SCOPE AND
   THRESHOLDS)   60
Structures for Intervention (INSTRUMENTS)   67
Access to Health Care and Hospitals (DISTRIBUTION)   74
Planning, Competition, and Cost Containment
   (RESTRAINTS AND INNOVATION)   83

4 HOUSING POLICY   **97**
Choices in Housing Policy   98
Governmental Responsibility for Shelter (SCOPE AND
    THRESHOLDS)   99
Interventions into Housing Markets (INSTRUMENTS)   107
Targeting Housing Subsidies (DISTRIBUTION)   120
Political Support and the Future of Housing Programs
    (RESTRAINTS AND INNOVATION)   126

5 ECONOMIC POLICY   **132**
Choices in Economic Policy   135
The Will to Intervene (SCOPE AND THRESHOLDS)   136
Macro- and Micro-Policy Interventions (INSTRUMENTS)   145
Costs and Benefits of Economic Management
    (DISTRIBUTION)   162
Collaborators or Adversaries in Economic Management?
    (RESTRAINTS AND INNOVATION)   170

6 TAXATION POLICY   **183**
Choices in Taxation Policy   184
The Boundaries of Taxation (SCOPE AND THRESHOLDS)   186
Variations in Revenue Raising (INSTRUMENTS)   190
Tax Extraction and Tax Base Erosion (DISTRIBUTION)   199
Tax Reform—Old Whine and New Bottles? (RESTRAINTS
    AND INNOVATION)   207

7 INCOME MAINTENANCE POLICY   **218**
Choices in Income Maintenance Policy   220
Growth of the Transfer Society (SCOPE AND THRESHOLDS)   222
Varieties of Public Provision (INSTRUMENTS)   229
Who Pays, Who Benefits? (DISTRIBUTION)   250
Innovation in a Period of Scarcity (RESTRAINTS AND
    INNOVATION)   255

8 URBAN PLANNING   **267**
Choices in Urban Planning   267
Planning Traditions in Western Europe, the United
    States, and Japan (SCOPE AND THRESHOLDS)   270
Guiding Urban Growth (INSTRUMENTS)   283
Whose City? (DISTRIBUTION)   294
Limits to Public Power (RESTRAINTS AND INNOVATION)   303

9 ENVIRONMENTAL POLICY   **308**
Choices in Environmental Policy   309

Pollution as a Political Issue (SCOPE AND THRESHOLDS)   312
Approaches to Environmental Enforcement
   (INSTRUMENTS)   323
Benefits and Costs of Regulation (DISTRIBUTION)   330
The Uncertain Future of Environmental Controls
   (RESTRAINTS AND INNOVATION)   335

**10   POLICY CONTRASTS IN THE WELFARE
    STATE**   **345**
Welfare State Perspectives   346
Policy Patterns—National, Sectoral, and Temporal   349
Variations in Support for Public Policies   354
Policy Growth and Decline: Towards and beyond the
   Year 2000   359
Recycling Problems, Rescaling Remedies   366

BIBLIOGRAPHY   **372**

INDEX   **407**

A List of Tables

2.1 Proportions of Age Groups Enrolled in Education, 1985–86   30

2.2 Science in Schools: Rank Order of National Achievement Scores for Ages Ten to Eighteen Years   39

2.3 Students' Math Achievement: Do Instruction Time and Teachers' Salaries Help Explain Differences?   42

3.1 The Development of the Public Health Sector in Britain   61

3.2 Public and Private Sources of Health Care Financing, 1982   62

3.3 Public Expenditure as a Percent of Total Health Expenditure, 1960–85   63

3.4 Relative Strength of State Regulatory Intervention, 1980s   71

3.5 Relative Emphasis on General and Specialist Medical Provision, 1984   74

3.6 Hospital Expenditures   80

3.7 Total Expenditure on Health as a Proportion of GDP   85

3.8 Medical Service Fees, 1984 (in U.S. Dollars)   88

3.9 Physician Incomes, 1970 and 1981   89

3.10 Age and Access to Technology: New Kidney Dialysis Patients per One Million Population, 1978   92

3.11 Cost Increases in Two Kinds of Health Systems   95

3.12 Cross-National Rankings of Health Care Expenditures and Measures of Health Status, 1985   95

4.1 Dwellings Completed, by Type of Investor, 1970–85   103

4.2 Composition of Housing Subsidies in Selected Countries   115

4.3 Distribution of Stockholm Households, by Income Group   121

5.1 Inflation, Unemployment, and Economic Growth, 1960–88   133

6.1 Tax Receipts as a Percentage of GDP   187

6.2   Income Tax at the Level of an Average Worker   189
6.3   Tax Sources as Percentages of Total Revenue, 1985   190
6.4   Tax Shares in OECD Countries, 1983, Deviations from
      the Average   196
6.5   Proportion of Taxes Collected by Various Government
      Levels, 1985   198
6.6   Degrees of Self-Assessment in Income Tax
      Administration for Wage and Salary Earners   200
6.7   Changes in National Income Tax Rates   211
6.8   Changes in Numbers of Income Tax Rate Brackets   212
6.9   Growth of U.S. Tax Expenditures, 1967–86   215
7.1   Left or Right Dominance and Welfare Effort for
      Selected Years   226
7.2   Role of Public Transfers in Reducing the Poverty Gap
      among Children and the Elderly, 1979   249
7.3   Percentage of Children, Elderly, and All Persons in
      Poverty, by Family Type and Country, 1979–82   253
7.4   Annual Growth in Social Security Spending, 1965–81   257
8.1   Percentage Population Change during the 1970s in
      Nations and Big Cities   276
8.2   Unemployment Rates in Nations and Big Cities, 1983   276
8.3   Change in Local Government Expenditures, Tax Base,
      and Tax Effort, at 1978 Price Level   277
8.4   Sources of Local Revenue in Seven Nations, 1972–84   278
8.5   Ownership of Passenger Cars, 1970 and 1983   287
9.1   Emissions of Traditional Air Pollutants, 1980   312
9.2   Major Potential Health and Ecological Effects of
      Traditional Air Pollutants   313
9.3   Estimated Forest Damage from Air Pollution, 1986   314
9.4   Index of Concern Expressed by Respondents to
      Common Market Survey, 1982   317
9.5   Political Self-Labeling by Environmentalists and General
      Public in Three Nations, 1982   319
9.6   Distribution of Responses to the Question: "Which
      Should Receive the Higher Priority from Government:
      Protecting the Environment or Promoting Economic
      Growth?"   336
9.7   Government Subsidies for Environmental Research and
      Development, in Millions of U.S. Dollars (at 1980 Price
      Level) and as Percentage of Total R&D Expenditures   343
10.1 Policy Styles in Britain, France, and Sweden   351
10.2 Growth of Public School Expenditure Implied by
      Projected Demographic Change, 1980–2040   364

10.3 Implications of Projected Demographic Change for
      Social Expenditure Financing Burden during Selected
      Subperiods   365
10.4 The Welfare State as "Problem Solver" and "Problem
      Creator"   369

A List of Figures

2.1 The British Educational System   30
2.2 Science Achievement Scores (IEA)   38
2.3 Proportion of Pupils Enrolled in Comprehensivized
Schools, 1950–1980   45
2.4 Higher Education Graduates in the Labor Market, 1976   54
3.1 Centralization as Related to Health Emphases   68
3.2 Policy Orientations of Health Interest Groups   70
3.3 Health Problems and Medical Care Use by Socioeconomic
Groups, Sweden 1980s   76
3.4 Per Capita Health Spending and Per Capita GDP, 1985   86
8.1 Regional Plan for Paris, Showing Twin Axes Proposed for
Future Growth   272
8.2 Plan for the Center of Vallingby, A New Town in
Suburban Stockholm   274
8.3 Randstad ("Ring City") of the Netherlands with Green
Heart at the Center   275
9.1 Acidity of Precipitation, North America and Europe,
1985   341
10.1 The Growth of Social Insurance Coverage   348
10.2 Agenda Support for Housing, Education, and Health
Policies, by Income Group   355
10.3 Performance Evaluation of Housing, Education, and
Health Policies, by Education   356
10.4 Redistribution over the Life Cycle   358

1
THE POLITICS
OF SOCIAL CHOICE

Comparing public policies is a part of everyday life. At election time we often compare one candidate's or party's stands on given policy questions with those of another. We move from one state or city to another and observe how high taxes are here compared to there. We move from cities to suburbs and compare carefully which area has the best schools, the safest streets, or the cleanest environment.

These everyday comparisons of public policies have one important thing in common with more systematic efforts at comparative policy analysis. Both informal and formal approaches seek a deeper understanding than could be gained by looking at only one thing at a time. As Clifford Geertz has observed, "It is through comparison (and comparison of incomparables) that whatever heart we can get to, can actually be reached" (Geertz, p. 233). By assessing one situation against another, we gain a better perspective on our current situation as well as the options and constraints we face. In short, we learn through comparing.

While everyday comparisons generally serve some personal end, the academic study of comparative public policy has a broader agenda. There are basically three reasons for engaging in a systematic comparison of public policies. One aim is to look for guidance in designing better policies. The fact that different countries often adopt alternative strategies for dealing with similar problems represents a kind of natural experiment. Careful comparative research can begin to disentangle those results that may be due to unique circumstances from those that are more generally relevant to

1

other countries. For example, all the developed nations received severe economic shocks from the oil-price increases of the 1970s; however, some nations seemed to handle the strains with less inflation and unemployment than did others. Why? Comparing different ways of coping with similar problems can suggest both positive and negative lessons—guidance on what to do and also what *not* to do. Even if there are no direct lessons, policy comparisons will often throw light on hidden assumptions operating within one's own country and thus alert the observer to latent opportunities and constraints that would otherwise go unrecognized.

A second aim in comparing public policies is to gain a deeper understanding of how government institutions and political processes operate as they deal with concrete problems. The classic questions of politics remain the same: Who governs? How do they govern? What are the results for citizens' lives and welfare? Today the raw material for addressing these questions is increasingly to be found in the expanding policy activities of government. To examine who governs, it is not enough to know who votes or who is elected to office. One must also know what people in government and at its fringes are actually doing to make and remake public policies. As the scale and activities of government have grown, more and more of this "doing" takes the form of making and remaking public policies. One indicator of this growth in scale is that the proportion of gross domestic product passing through the public sectors of the world's nations had risen from about 2 or 3 percent in 1900 to about 30 to 45 percent by 1980 (Deutsch in Dierkes et al).

The third reason for studying policies across national boundaries lies in the growing interdependence that is a hallmark of our times. Problems such as the environment or economic management frequently spill over national borders. Policy strategies adopted in one country often have important impacts on policy-making in other countries. To function successfully in this interdependent world, we need to understand the different problem-solving approaches that nations adopt and the ways they interact with each other.

Hence, comparative policy analysis occupies a middle ground between "pure research" of a theoretical nature and "applied science" directed toward the nuts and bolts of detailed problem-solving. The study of comparative public policy broadens our understanding of particular policy problems and the lessons to be derived from experience. It also helps us test general theories and hypotheses by exposing the varied nature of political decision making as it confronts concrete issues. Above all—and this is the central theme of this book—comparative public policy illuminates the various and subtle ways in which politics works to produce choices of a collective or social nature. Sensitivity to that process helps us to begin seeing beneath the surface of political events in our rapidly changing, interdependent societies.

WHAT IS COMPARATIVE PUBLIC POLICY?

Comparative public policy is the study of how, why, and to what effect different governments pursue particular courses of action or inaction. While this definition may seem straightforward, it contains a number of important conceptual distinctions. It is worth pausing to sort out the major terms in this definition: the study of *how, why,* and *to what effect different governments* pursue particular *courses of action and inaction.*

To ask *how* governments choose to act focuses our attention on what goes on inside and at the fringes of the state. It requires learning aspects of the structures and processes through which governmental decisions are reached. In a general sense, we say that the United States and West Germany are federal states while Britain, Sweden, Japan, and France are more centralized unitary states. Hence, we might expect the policy approaches to differ in the two sets of nations. But when we look closer we see that federalism takes on different meanings, depending not only on the country but also on the policy in question. So too do the connotations of centralization in countries such as Britain and France (Ashford). Hence, if we wish to go beyond clichés regarding federalism and centralization, it is necessary to examine in some detail how different governments and their related constellations of parties, interest groups, and bureaucracies actually work through various policy problems. This approach is pursued in Chapter Two, which deals with the development of national education policies in the six countries just mentioned.

To ask *why* governments pursue particular courses of action is obviously as difficult to answer as it is important to ask. Why has the United States followed Europe in adopting some social policies but preceded Europe in other social programs? Why have some countries preserved their major cities as a national resource while others have tolerated more urban decay? Why is the social security "safety net" a subject of quiet, consensual politics at one place and time and an ideologically charged political issue at other places and times?

Answers to "why" questions such as these can depend on historical developments in the distant past which current policymakers may well be unaware of, on the underlying political culture of a nation and subsections of its population, or even on a changing state of public consciousness that makes something a problem for policy attention rather than simply a condition to be accepted. For example, the French and the Germans may be especially sensitive to policy questions about the uniformity of school curricula because of nation-building experiences that occurred between the sixteenth and nineteenth centuries. Here we cannot trace all of these complicated linkages, nor can we unravel the subtle interactions between political culture and public policy predispositions.

What we can do is keep in mind the importance of these ultimate determinants of policy choices when we discuss the various policy instruments that nations select in areas such as education, health, and economic management. And so we will regularly refer to these background influences even as we concentrate on the more proximate sources of policy development. These closer factors consist of the interactions of politicians, bureaucrats, interest groups, public opinion, program beneficiaries, and any other elements that bear on policy-making. The ideas policymakers present, no less than the power they seek to exercise, constitute the raw materials for explaining why policy similarities and differences occur.

The third element in the definition of comparative public policy—*to what effect*—is for many people the payoff. Apart from political scientists, few people are likely to be interested in studying government for its own sake. But almost all people care about what government is doing to them and for them. In other words, they care about its policies. Studying comparative public policy, rather than comparative government or political behavior, gives special attention to the effects of government action on peoples' lives. Rarely are the results exactly what governments intended when adopting a policy; sometimes, the result is a new round of political debate and choice. Assessing governments' capacity for coping with unintended consequences and learning from different experiences in policy development makes the subject matter both complex and fascinating. And, in our view, an approach that anticipates and explicitly deals with surprises and adaptation leads to more realistic analysis than one which concentrates on deductions based on a few behavioral premises about "rational self-interest."

We are left with two components of the original definition. When we refer to *different governments* we are being intentionally vague, so as not to exclude comparisons that go outside the normal country-by-country approach. Although all the chapters in this volume deal with contrasts among different national governments, it is equally useful to compare public policies among various local units of government. Indeed one can often find as many interesting differences between local jurisdictions of the same country as between different countries (Fried and Rabinovitz). Even more differentiated comparisons can be made by considering voluntary organizations and other private groups that also affect public policy (Sharkansky; Graham).

What is needed, what is seriously lacking in the scholarly literature, is a comparative approach that can span levels of government and public/private sectors, as well as different nations. Interactions among policymakers in the different national capitals are important, but rarely do they tell the whole story. This has become particularly true in recent years as national governments have increasingly sought to cope with their financial problems by shifting policy burdens to local jurisdictions and semipublic groups. Perhaps more than ever before, public policy has become a mosaic pieced together by government authorities at different levels and by private sector actors with public policy responsibilities. The comparisons in subsequent chapters try to capture some of this reality, but there is still much work to be done in the comparative study of subnational policy-making.

That leaves us with the final element of our original definition. A *course of action or inaction* defines a policy. It is not enough to identify this or that decision and how it was made. What matters for purposes of comparative public policy is the string of decisions that add up to a fairly consistent body of behavior sanctioned by governmental authority. In this regard studying comparative public policy is much like trying to analyze weather patterns. The local TV weather forecaster concentrates on a disconnected series of day-to-day decisions about how hot it will be or whether to carry an umbrella tomorrow. But the serious meteorologist, who understands the long-term variations, is more interested in determining whether regions are likely to have warmer temperatures or drier seasons for years or even decades. Making such prognoses means allowing for the introduction of variables such as land clearing patterns or the effects of particular kinds of atmospheric pollution.

Like comparative policy scholars, meteorologists differ about how to weigh and evaluate the factors that produce a colder or warmer winter. But what general weather patterns are to the one, policies are to the other: namely, an *overall configuration of movement and activity.* Both must be flexible observers, concerned primarily with the larger, general trends.

What then about decisions that a government does not make, or issues that it refuses to face? Are these also public policy? Clearly it would be absurd to think that everything a government does not do is *ipso facto* a policy. Few modern governments have made explicit decisions regarding styles of dress between the sexes (Iran and China are exceptions); likewise, no country has decided to impose special immigration quotas on interstellar visitors. This does not mean that the countries therefore have a policy condoning sexist differentiation in clothing or a policy discriminating against earthling immigrants vis-à-vis the interplanetary variety. Yet it would also be absurd to deny that by studied inaction in certain situations governments are expressing something that is just as much a public policy as any big spending decision. Thus, for many years the United States national government did have something of a civil rights policy when it steadfastly refused to intervene in matters of racial discrimination occurring under state laws. Similarly, until the 1960s brought stronger demands for reducing inequalities, U.S. health policy was defined largely by an absence of interference with private enterprise in stimulating and meeting a growing demand for health care.

Government inaction, or nondecision, becomes a policy when it is pursued over time in a fairly consistent way against pressures to the contrary. It is never easy to say just when government passivity begins to assume the characteristics of a public policy, but the growth of controversy is one good clue. Certainly by the 1950s, for example, there was a spreading feeling that by doing nothing Washington was condoning and thus supporting racial discrimination throughout the South. Likewise, by the 1980s it became clear to more and more Americans that by *not* regulating hospital prices, the government was pursuing a public policy of restricting demand by making consumers pay more for health care. In these and other cases, what matters for purposes of identifying "policy in repose" is that the issue be perceived by at least some major participants as being on the political agenda. At that point it becomes possible to compare meaningfully one government's hands-off approach to another government's hands-on approach to the same issue. The discussion in Chapter Three of how the West German government came to institute health cost controls while similar American efforts failed is an example of this kind of comparison.

From the way we have now defined the subject, it should be clear that pursuing comparative public policy studies demands individual judgment, as much as it does skills for measuring objective social conditions. When does a nondecision become a policy? What policy trends should be compared against each other? How deeply should one delve into history and political culture for explanations of differences and similarities? Answers to these and similar questions do not depend entirely on scientific theory or measurement and hence will always be in some degree a matter of interpretation and judgment. In this text we have attempted to be "scientific" in applying careful reasoning to the best available empirical evidence. But the reader should bear in mind that the subject of this book is framed by questions upon which judgments are at least partly, and necessarily, subjective.

Likewise, comparative public policy can never become a self-contained specialized discipline, for the subject draws elements from many different disciplines. The "how" part of our definition draws heavily on work in comparative government, public administration, and political science generally. The "why" portion often extends to topics covered in political sociology, history, social psychology, and political economy, among other fields. The "to what effect" questions are strongly related to implementation analysis, economics, and ultimately—when we evaluate results (as we must) in terms of the kind of society we would like to live in—social philosophy.

CROSSCUTTING PERSPECTIVES

Comparative public policy is located at a busy crossroads in the social sciences. The field has grown in recent years to provide a setting in which political scientists, sociologists, historians, economists, and many other specialists are learning from one another. Policy comparisons have encouraged the premises each discipline brings to the subject to be tested against the perceptions of others. As a result, the last three decades have witnessed a proliferation of competing approaches and methodological refinements. It is worth pausing to take an overview of these recent developments.

Comparative policy studies have an historical background extending much farther than the last several decades. Aristotle dispatched his assistants to collect the constitutions of over one hundred city-states, which he then compared to derive general political principles. Writers in ancient Greece and Rome commonly distinguished systems of government in terms of both who ruled (one person, an elite few, or the many) and the principles by which they actually exercised their power (whether in their own interests or for the good of the whole). It was the principles behind courses of action that separated monarchy from tyranny, aristocracy from oligarchy, democracy from despotic mob rule. In the sixteenth century, Machiavelli combed cases from ancient and contemporary history to expose general principles of power politics and to offer a kind of down-to-earth policy advice to princes. German universities in the eighteenth and nineteenth centuries had the first professorial chairs of "Polizey" science. Efforts were made to systematize the knowledge of domestic policy and administration and to offer guidance in merging the interests of the absolute German monarchies with the welfare of the citizenry (Heidenheimer).

Notwithstanding these precedents, it is fair to say that a clear focus on the systematic, comparative study of public policies has emerged only in the last thirty years or so. In contrast with its ancient ancestors, this modern field of inquiry takes as its starting point the contemporary nation-state and the intellectual framework of twentieth-century social science. Some researchers have concentrated on particular national comparisons—for example, Scandinavian versus Continental European versus Anglo-Saxon versus East-West paradigms. Some have emphasized particular policy fields—for example, health care, taxation, or environmental policy—as the basic focus of analysis. Still other observers have used comparative policy analysis to test more general theories of social and political development. And throughout this intellectual ferment, practical-minded participants in policy-making processes have continued to insist on evidence from this burgeoning cross-discipline as to "what works" and "what doesn't." This development of comparative policy studies has not only vastly expanded the universe of potentially relevant social science observations among diversely trained observers, it has also created diverse efforts to array the empirical policy data along lines that resist any one preexisting theoretical model. We can briefly review the major approaches in this field that have developed in the past thirty years.

The earliest comparative policy studies in the modern era were dominated by what might be called *socioeconomic theories*. The essence of this approach has been to argue that nations respond to the general processes of economic growth and social modernization with basically similar policies (Cutwright; Jackman; Wilensky 1975). Rising levels of economic development and industrialization are seen as creating new economic, social, and environmental dislocations, as well as providing greater financial resources that governments can tap in reacting to these problems. Thus social security and other welfare state–type programs arise and expand everywhere as nations reach higher levels of economic development. This approach perceives a convergence of national policies and a decline of ideological conflict as nations move from traditional agrarian societies and early capitalist excesses into the modernized stage of advanced countries with mixed economies.

After the 1960s, critiques of the socioeconomic model proliferated in the growing circle of comparative policy researchers. Why, for example, had some countries pioneered certain social welfare programs much earlier than their gross level of economic development seemed to justify? Why did the policy efforts (at least as measured in terms of government spending) of some very highly developed countries lag far behind those of other nations? More generally, how could a vision of policy determined by a uniform socioeconomic process account for the significant policy differences that studies showed actually existed among the group of advanced nations?

In responding to the challenge of such questions, diverse approaches blossomed in this young, cross-disciplinary field of study. One school of thought has placed special emphasis on the deeply embedded cultural ideas arising from the distinctive historical experiences of nations (Rimlinger; King; Caim-Caudle). This *cultural values approach* distinguishes, for example, the tradition of laissez-faire liberalism of Anglo-Saxon nations from the statist paternalism of Continental European countries or the familial quality of organizational life in Japan (Dore).

While the socioeconomic paradigm generally dismissed the role of political forces in determining policy outcomes, a whole cluster of approaches soon developed seeking to show "politics matters" (Castles 1987). A *party government* framework has been widely used to argue that policies vary with shifts in the partisan control of government. This approach was used, for example, in some of the earliest comparative policy studies in which American researchers sought to show that welfare policies differed depending upon Republican or Democratic control of American state governments (Key). More recent cross-national work has plunged much more deeply into the complex linkages between parties and policies (Hibbs; Castles 1982).

An influential variant on the party theme is the *political class struggle* model. The fundamental dynamic of policy development is seen to lie in the contest between business forces driven by the imperatives of capitalist accumulation on the one hand, and workers and their representatives on the other (Gough; Offe; Stephens). Typically in these studies, particular emphasis is placed on the political organization of labor through a strong Social Democratic party tied to an extensive union movement. It is the presence or absence of such a political configuration that is said to shape decisively the policy agenda and the government programs that result (Shalev; Korpi; Esping-Anderson).

Yet another approach is the *neo-corporatist* framework. While acknowledging the importance of labor organization, researchers using this framework look to the broader system of interest representation and its linkages to government through institutionalized bargaining. The capacity to frame, coordinate, and successfully implement policy is seen to be dependent on strongly organized interest blocs (labor, employer, professional, and so on) that are continually engaged in centralized negotiations with government on policy matters of mutual interest (Lehmbruch and Schmitter; Wilensky 1976, 1981; Lindberg and Maier). The term *corporatism* expresses the trend toward obliterating public/private sector boundaries in one system of shared responsibilities among the major societal actors.

A final approach that has gained some currency has been termed the *institutional-political process* perspective (Weir et al.). While other frameworks tend to treat policy as the result of outside pressures (socioeconomic, party demands, interest blocs, and so on) on government, institutional analysts are at pains to put the "state" at center stage. In practice this means paying particular attention to at least three things: (1) the distinctive historical patterns through which different nation-states have been formed and their institutional structures distinguished from one another; (2) the way state structures and capacities interact with and affect the prospects of other social actors; and (3) the feedback effects of policy on political alliances, party competition and other features of the policy-making landscape (Heclo; Katzenstein; Skocpol).

Obviously these six approaches are not mutually exclusive or exhaustive, and any serious comparative analysis can easily draw upon several frameworks to account for what is happening. Although we say this is obvious, the fact is that the field of comparative policy studies has at times been agitated by heated intramural arguments about which variable is of primary importance—socioeconomic processes or politics? party control or interest group intermediation? culturally embedded ideas or state-structured institutions? (Wilensky et al 1985; Hancock; Castles, 1982).

METHODS AND MEANS

It is a sign of growing intellectual maturity in the field that comparative studies have increasingly moved away from the search for single-factor, deterministic theories and accepted the need to integrate diverse perspectives in order to produce plausible accounts of policy development. The effort at integration is the approach we have tried to adopt in this book. Some day there may be a unified grand theory of comparative public policy, but that day is not here yet.

Increasing sensitivity to methodological problems is another sign of growing maturity in the field. It is easy to dismiss such problems as matters of mere technical detail, but sensitivity to the difficulties of measuring and empirically testing concepts is essential to drawing any realistic and worthwhile comparisons. Issues of comparative methodology have been discussed at length elsewhere (Przeworski and Teune; Dierkes et al.), but here we shall briefly discuss the major issues.

Elementary though it seems, one key problem in comparative policy studies is the difficulty of finding truly comparable measurements of the same things in different countries. For example, every major nation produces statistics on the distribution of income. However, income is measured differently in different countries; definitions of household versus individual income are often not the same; methods for estimating the underreporting of income in government statistical surveys vary greatly, and so on. Only in the last few years, with the aid of modern computers, has it been possible to go back to each nation's income surveys, create a common accounting framework, and recalculate the millions of individual household income reports on that common basis. Only *then* can we begin to address sensibly questions about the distribution of well-being among the elderly or child poverty and public policy in different nations (Smeeding et al.).

Another persisting methodological problem in comparative policy studies has to do with finding appropriate indicators to serve as usable representations of the more general policy concepts under study. The different conclusions analysts reach are often a function, not of contradictory realities, but of different ways of specifying the important variables. For example, in the 1970s a strenuous argument developed between two schools of thought, one of which argued that level of economic development was "the root cause of welfare state development" (Wilensky 1975, p. 47) while the opposing side argued that the ideology and political power of parties— especially Social Democratic parties—was the crucial factor in explaining welfare state development (Castles, 1978). A closer reading of this debate shows that both sides were really talking past each other largely because of methodological differences. For example, both camps defined welfare state development in terms of "welfare effort" but differed drastically as to how this dependent variable—the thing to be explained—was measured. For Wilensky, welfare state development meant percentage of Gross National Product (GNP) spent on social security programs in each nation; for Castles, it meant a combined index of total government revenues as a percent of GNP, educational expenditures as a percent of GNP, plus infant mortality rates in each nation. Methodological strategies for treating independent variables—the things doing the explaining—were inequally incomparable. For Wilensky, the prevailing ideology behind the policy-making process was measured through 1960s data on elite attitudes toward equal opportunity and the desirability of planning for equality; for Castles, ideology is defined and measured in terms of differences in party systems. Wilensky tested his hypothesis that "level of economic development is what matters" through a sample of nations that spanned the very rich to the very poor; Castles's sample of nations was mainly confined to variations among developed countries. In short, the fine print of methodology matters, especially when reaching for global conclusions.

Another enduring methodological problem is what analysts label the "collinearity of variables." In other words, certain attributes—such as level of economic development, strength of Social Democratic parties, degree of unionization, and so on—often occur together. There are simply not enough national cases available to allow researchers to hold everything else constant while only the one factor being tested varies. Although the aim of comparative studies is to identify variables that have explanatory power across many national cases, the natural science model of compiling huge numbers of observations under *ceteris paribus* ("all others being equal") conditions is usually not practical in comparative public policy. Typically there are too few cases to permit a clear disentangling of attributes clustered with one another. The available "facts" tend to fit not just one theory but several theories.

Yet another difficulty is embedded in the dynamic quality of public policy development. There is no reason to believe that the causes of policy remain invariable over time, even within the same country. Nor should we assume that government policies and programs—even within the same nation at the same moment in historical time—must respond to the same explanatory framework. We cannot even expect that the same general aims will be expressed through similar programs in every context—improving health care may translate into big government spending but it may also find expression in relatively static levels of government spending and tighter requirements on employers funding private health insurance. Similar outcomes may be achieved through a range of policy instruments, while ostensibly similar policies may well be associated with quite different results. Higher government spending on social programs may indicate a thrust toward more egalitarian outcomes, but it may also be a way of maintaining differentials in the status quo. The data refuse to compose themselves into simple answers.

Finally, there is the enduring problem of uniqueness. For comparisons to be possible, we must overlook a great many of the special features that make a country, policy, or decision unique. Every action is part of a particular context, but since every context is different, how can we make comparisons across time or national borders and be sure we are really comparing like with like, apples to apples instead of apples to oranges?

There are no neat shortcuts around these methodological problems. However, the fact that the research community has become more self-conscious in taking account of such constraints on facile theorizing is a hopeful sign. The accuracy and comparability of cross-national data are much more carefully scrutinized than they were thirty years ago. Scholars tend to be more sophisticated in specifying indicators and empirical tests for their theories. In recent years there has been a growing recognition that analysis needs to utilize both broad-scale comparative mapping of similarities and differences *and* contextually rich individual case studies. Comparative strategies, far from being stymied by the problem of uniqueness, can show a versatility depending on the analytic purpose at hand. We can compare apples and oranges, and there is no reason or need to decide in the abstract whether it is the similarities or differences that matter most. If our purpose is to establish better dietary guidelines, the difference between apples and oranges may not matter one bit as long as one of the two substitutes for junk food. If we are trying to make a pie or plant a fruit tree in a northern climate, the differences are all that matters.

POLITICS AS CHOICE

"To govern is to choose." Hidden within this familiar saying lies a profound insight. To appreciate the insight involved in linking politics and choice, we need to pass beyond the image of a few individual governors and encompass many people and groups. We must think not of this or that newsworthy decision, but of many streams of decisions and interactions that cumulate into processes of choice. These are choices made on behalf of society, not because politicians and leaders necessarily act in the public interest, but because the outcomes of such choices authoritatively sanction certain social arrangements but not others. Perhaps, then, we might say that "to be governed is to have choices made for you"; but that statement overlooks one important reality—namely, that leaders do not act unrestrained and that they are continually engaged in reciprocal-influence processes with those they lead. What then does the political-choice process expressed through public policies really look like? Instead of a machine-like churning out of decisions, a more realistic image comes from Hermann Hesse:

> The expedition did not, in fact, proceed in any fixed order with participants moving in the same direction in more or less closed columns. On the contrary, numerous groups were simultaneously on the way, each following their own leaders and their own stars, each one always ready to merge into a greater unit and belong to it for a time, but always no less ready to move on again separately. . . . (Hermann Hesse, *The Journey to the East*)

If this seems unduly abstract, consider some of the collective, or social, choices that have been made through politics over the past one hundred years:

Schooling, at public expense, has grown from a kind of charity offered to relatively few children for a few years to a right provided each generation into adulthood. Selection criteria which used to be most powerful at the entrance to secondary school have been moved "up" the educational ladder to the doors of graduate and professional schools. (Education policy is considered in Chapter Two.)

Health care, once universally thought to be of little governmental concern, has everywhere been elevated to the level of public policy. While in earlier periods of power politics the strength of nations was measured in terms of battalions and armaments, now societal indicators such as infant mortality or the capacity to deal with drug addiction are often perceived as equally or more important. As life spans have lengthened, governments have been drawn more deeply into questions of health care financing generally, but especially for the larger elderly proportion of the population. (Health care policies are dealt with in Chapter Three.)

The shape of cities and the nature of people's housing have always been byproducts of market forces. But whereas they were once thought of as natural and inevitable results of economic realities, they are now regarded as subjects for forethought and governmental intervention. (How Europe, Japan, and the United States have shaped relevant policies is examined in Chapters Four and Eight.)

As societies, we have decided that much of what a person earns shall be taken from him or her in taxes, that certain kinds of income and spending shall be taxed differently from others, and that people will receive various kinds of public income whenever they cannot meet basic needs as we have defined them. (Policies pertaining to these questions are examined comparatively in Chapters Six and Seven.)

Likewise over the years, people in many countries have come to realize that "the environment" is not just the natural setting within which we humans live, but a contingent resource about which collective choices must be made. (Environmental policies are discussed in Chapter Nine.)

These and other topics are dealt with in the subsequent chapters of this book. In 1881 the first great national program of social insurance was initiated by the German Emperor William I. Given the current expansion in the agenda of public policy, we might well call the hundred years since then the century of the welfare state. The data are far from perfect, but the overall trends in Europe and the United States are clear and consistent for the last hundred years: A rising share of total economic resources has been absorbed by taxation and devoted to public spending. Of all public spending, a growing share (except in years of war) has gone to social programs; of all these programs, more and more have involved income security programs (Flora and Heidenheimer). As we shall see, national variations within these trends are important, but the overall movements stand out as long-term themes for every developed nation.

The generation since 1960 has, if anything, seen these same trends become more prominent. Obviously there are many differences among the political systems examined in this text. But for all, the period between 1960 and 1980 may indeed have been a golden age in the long history of welfare state spending and taxation.

But are we really justified in calling these developments examples of collective choice? Surely public spending has grown as a proportion of the economy without anyone consciously choosing what the level or ratio should be; the aggregate patterns have just happened.

Again we must beware of thinking that choices can be made only deliberately by some individual decision maker. Choices can also be made through complex processes of interaction. Politics serves as a mechanism of social choice in much the same sense that markets serve as means of making aggregate economic choices that no individual participant in the market may have intended or decided to make. Changing prices signal the movements in supply and demand and in doing so yield two types of overall aggregate economic choices: namely, choices about how scarce resources will be allocated to produce a desired mix of products from all the possible mixes that could potentially be produced, and distributive choices about who will have the money incomes to purchase these products. This allocation of resources and distribution of income may be seen as the warp and woof of economic life.

For better or worse, political life is even more complex, and deductions based on such political economy concepts take us only a little way toward understanding the complexity of political choice. In the 1970s, for example, many writers used a few simple economic choice concepts to suggest that democratic policy and politics were headed inexorably toward hyperinflation and political disaster. Public demands revealed a preference for government spending but against the taxation to support such spending. The short-term rational choice behavior of politicians interested in reelection inevitably led them to pander to these demands. Reinforcing this tendency was the fact that bureaucrats engaged in the "supply" of public services—and using taxpayers' money—had no "cost" constraint to limit their ambitious programs. Such economic concepts were useful in capturing some general tendencies, but they scarcely offered a full portrayal of political reality. By the beginning of the 1980s, government expansion had slowed down; moreover, hyperinflation and massive government deficits did not develop in most Western democracies during the remainder of the 1980s. Politicians such as Ronald Reagan and Margaret Thatcher won popular followings by promising to reduce government spending and taxation levels. With somewhat different rhetoric and methods, many Social Democrats in Western Europe and Australia similarly acted to cut back public budget trajectories. All of these developments were of course part of the politics of social choice.

What separates a choice from a mere result is the fact that a significant number of people believe that the political process can be managed so as to produce a desired outcome. It is this growing awareness of the possibilities and implications of choice that, perhaps more than anything else, distinguishes our time from earlier periods of policy-making. Thus, a conservative such as Ronald Reagan entered the presidential office with a blueprint, not only for balancing the budget, but also for reducing the federal government's share of Gross Domestic Product (GDP) from 21 percent to 19.6 percent by the end of his first term, for cutting inflation, and for achieving a high and stable level of employment. While economists in his administration differed strongly about how these goals might have been achieved, it was striking that no one questioned the idea that these goals were, potentially at least, within the power of the policy-making process to achieve. Such an assumption would have been regarded as astounding eighty or a hundred years ago. In those days no one could have debated statistics about the size of the government in relation to the economy because only in this century has there been widespread political debate on the concept of managing a national economy; and only in the 1940s were the first reliable measures of economic size and movement (Gross National Product) made. Unemployment and inflation were largely accepted as part of the natural order of things; hard times alternated with good times as a matter of course, just as the weather fluctuated beyond anyone's control.

Once a condition is given a name and accepted as a problem rather than simply as part of the natural order, then it is only a short step to interpreting any unemployment or inflation level as something that government has created through policy or chosen to countenance. That willingness to recognize choices is what marks our times, and it applies to much more than the economy. To grant or refuse federal funding for abortions becomes for many people pro-choice or anti-abortion policy. The area of technological change (nuclear power, chemicals use, natural resources development, genetic engineering, and so on) is especially rich in examples of declining willingness to let developments take their own course and greater willingness to try to control trends—which is to say, to become mobilized in the politics of social choice. Though we cannot hope to cover all these fields in this volume, we shall see this heightened public attention clearly at work in those policy fields we do cover.

CHOICES AS FRAMEWORKS

What choices of a collective nature has politics served to make? Earlier in this chapter, we pointed out that markets make two types of economic choices—allocational and distributive. The possible array in politics is much larger, but in this book we concentrate on four types of choice applicable to each policy area. These four types of choice fall short of the macro-choices between equality and inequality or liberty and security, but they are major choices all the same. And, as we shall see, they are subject to constant negotiation and adaptation.

Choices of Scope

This type of choice concerns whether and where lines shall be drawn between public and private responsibilities. For example, is the purchase of health care strictly a private matter between health care providers and those with the money to pay for it? If the government does take part, how far should it go in setting requirements for doctors and hospitals that provide the service? How much responsibility should the person in need of health care bear? Some scope choices may also exist within public policies themselves rather than between public and private sectors. Should housing policy be concerned mainly with increasing the physical supply of buildings, or should it also be used as part of antipoverty or economic management policies?

Choices of Policy Instruments

Given that government accepts a responsibility to intervene, what structures and tools will it use? Does it want to retain policy-making power at the national level, or delegate the power to subnational levels of government? Does it want to let local or regional governments shape educational or social assistance policies, or does it value homogeneity sufficiently to transfer such jurisdictions to higher levels? Further options relate to specific tools of public intervention. As noted earlier, different instruments can be used for the same end. A government aiming to improve health care or housing conditions may itself build and run a hospital system and housing units. It may grant subsidies to nonprofit or for-profit builders or hospital operators, or it may use government licensing power to assure that some regulatory standards are met. Though such choices are not mutually exclusive, most national systems tend to give priority to some instruments over others. But these choices need not be consistent across policy areas.

Choices of Distribution

Whereas economic markets arrive at distributive choices by letting costs and benefits lie wherever they happen to fall, the political process normally makes such choices in a much more self-conscious manner. Is it fair that children from wealthy families should be able to buy their way into better private schools? Is it fair that their families should have to pay taxes to support public schools their children do not attend? How shall the burden of taxation be distributed between individual income earners and business profits, between income and consumption, between the elderly and families with children?

Choices of Restraints and Innovation

These choices become particularly applicable when significant change in the character of constraints poses questions about how to continue, terminate, or adapt policies which had been implemented in light of the preceding choices. In one direction choices can go toward toughening the prevailing rules regarding the extension or extraction of resources and benefits; in the other they can go toward experimenting with new techniques. Recourse to severity can allow for fewer deviations or loopholes in the administration of prevailing rules, or it can adjust the rules to tighten selection criteria for public assistance, abortions, or housing subsidies.

Without being too ritualistic, we will use these four dimensions of choice to trace the major lines of development in each of the subsequent chapters.

THE POLICY AREAS

The subject matter of these chapters covers a broad field, from education and economic management to the environment. However, the choice of topics is not arbitrary. The public policies which we will be comparing concern government's role in economic and social affairs, for these are the sectors in which national governments have carved out important functions in this past century of welfare state development. The national departments which administer these policies are generally of more recent origin than those that handle the more traditional governmental functions, such as of defense or foreign affairs. Interesting comparative work has begun in defense policy-making (Roherty), but in this book we will confine ourselves to domestic policy.

We begin by examining policies that shape the provision of public services. The services considered in Chapters Two through Four—education, health care, and housing—were in earlier centuries left mainly to commercial and philanthropic agencies. Today these services are often regarded as vital social goods in whose allocation governments must play a key role. In different nations the government role has developed at different times. Germany and Austria preceded Britain and the United States in the introduction of health insurance. Compared to the United States, European nations have generally also been leaders in the provision of public housing. But with regard to the provision of post-primary public education, it was the United States that preceded the major European countries by a generation or more.

In contrast to its lag in the health sector, the United States has been ahead of Europe in the education sector. The American public education policy was first established during the early decades of the twentieth century. In 1890 the United States had proportionately only half as many full-time secondary students in public schools as Germany; by 1899 it had an equal proportion; and by 1930 its secondary school attendance rate was more than three times that of Germany or Britain. During this period in the United States a new public high school was established every day of the year. A 1935 article in the *Encyclopedia of the Social Sciences* noted that education in the United States was still "the only fully developed social service" (Comstock). In contrast to Europe, where academic secondary schools were maintained for a small elite of children from middle- and upper-class families, the American high school by the 1920s came to be attended by children from all social, economic, and intellectual groups.

In Chapter Five we turn to economic policy and look at government influence on the overall performance of the economy. The purpose of this chapter is to examine differences and similarities in the ways that democratic nations have coped with common problems of economic management. Compared to other topics in this book, economic policy is distinguished by widespread agreement, not only on its aims, but also on the specific ways in which progress toward these goals should be measured. Progress toward these goals is everywhere measured in terms of widely accepted statistical constructs: unemployment rates, price indices, and Gross National Product. Policymakers can hence be much more clearly identified with results, even though the underlying economic processes may be largely outside their control. Since no one can deny bad news contained in economic statistics, there is a strong political incentive to engage in or at least appear to engage in problem solving.

In Chapters Six and Seven we turn to taxation and income maintenance policies, two topics that are appropriately grouped together if we think of social policy as being concerned with a distribution of both benefits *and* costs. Income maintenance programs allocate cash payments; taxation distributes tax extractions. In practical terms, a cash benefit received and a tax cost avoided may be indistinguishable in their effect on a family's disposable income. Special tax provisions can support the income positions of some persons by leaving untouched money which would otherwise go into the national tax coffers, while other groups may receive aid from overt cash payments made through social security, public assistance, or other income maintenance programs.

Compared to education, health, and housing programs, these two areas are obviously much more concerned with cash transfers to and from citizens. For a variety of reasons, this difference would suggest that income maintenance and taxation policies are subject to more direct and exclusive government control than any of the other three policies, partially because negotiations with professional groups supplying services and time-consuming capital projects are not normally required for income maintenance and taxation policies.

Though income maintenance programs and taxation are largely monopolistic activities under direct government control, powerful inertia may still affect basic policy change. Moreover, possibilities for change may also be constrained by certain political contexts. A pluralistic political setting with a weak central administration will offer considerable opportunity to specialized groups interested in policy changes. Once a policy is established, advocates of general change are likely to have little leverage compared to that of coalitions of particularized interests. In less fragmented political systems, policymakers, without disregarding the special interests of particular groups, are able to deal from positions of greater strength with those broad policy guidelines affecting everyone in general and no one in particular.

In Chapters Eight and Nine we turn to the role that government plays in promoting the public welfare through the regulation of private activity. Regulatory policies designed to preserve the quality of life for all citizens may bring government directly into conflict with the interests of individual citizens. How governments handle the balance between the collective welfare and individual rights depends on both societal values and institutional arrangements. Even when the nature of the problems and the technological means for dealing with them do not differ greatly among nations, the political presumptions and administrative methods for carrying out regulatory policies can and do differ substantially.

Chapter Eight examines governmental efforts to reduce congestion and to protect open space and amenities in urban regions—a task that involves the sensitive interface between public authority and private property rights. Similarly, Chapter Nine discusses the tension between the preservation of the environment and the rights of individuals and corporations to act in their own interest. In both chapters we will ask whether, in a time of global economic competition, government regulation is taking a backseat to the need for nations to protect their economic competitiveness.

In Chapter Ten we relate our study of policy arenas to a discussion of the dynamics that underlie the expansion and contraction of the welfare state. Here we consider the longer-term perspective through a discussion between two of the politicians who played key roles in the development of the welfare state on both sides of the Atlantic. We also look at patterns of policy change, with special consideration of how much such patterns have varied across nations, across policy sectors, and across different historical eras. How and why support and evaluation of government programs varies by nation and policy sector is then examined cross-sectionally on the basis of survey findings from the 1970s in the United States and three European countries. The factors determining different degrees of voter support for policy expansion or tax reduction are also considered and then related back to the opportunities for social choice in different kinds of Western systems. We conclude by placing in perspective the effective choices facing the Western electorates in the 1990s and beyond, when there is likely to be a growing awareness of scarcity.

THE COUNTRIES

Attention in this volume is focused on the developed nations of Western Europe, the United States, and Japan. Wherever possible we have tried to include information on as broad a range of countries as possible, while looking in much greater detail at the United States, Britain, France, Japan, the Netherlands, Sweden, and West Germany.* Our rationale for this selection is based on economic, political, and historical factors.

The five European countries exhibit overall economic and political profiles similar to that of the United States. They are rather alike in their reliance on mixed economies and in their level of economic development; Sweden and Germany are slightly ahead of the United States in per capita GNP, while the Netherlands, France, and Britain are somewhat behind. Japan of course has grown rapidly in the postwar period to become one of the richest nations in the world. All seven nations' political systems have also remained similar during the second half of this century in exhibiting a continuity of party-based governments selected through competitive elections. During the forty-four years since World War II, their political and economic elites have had to act within parameters bounded by a liberal international economy on the one hand, and by well-organized domestic electorates on the other. It is partly because these characteristics have held true more for the northern-central region of Western Europe that we have chosen to study systems from that stable and prosperous region, and neglected the Mediterranean area. Cavils that might be raised about the exclusion of Italy or Spain might also be raised with regard to Canada or Israel, but our resources were not sufficient to include these somewhat distinctive national policy experiences into our framework in a meaningful way. Even so, we make some references to these countries' policy records, and to those of other small European nations, as well as Australia and New Zealand.

Though we focus in this book on contemporary policy problems, we also concern ourselves with how the historical structures of institutions and roles shape current policy responses. The nations discussed here exhibit basic differences in inherited attitudes toward governmental initiatives and intervention. On the one hand, British and American traditions favor limits on government power, as is reflected both in individualist values and in the sharp borders perceived between private and public spheres. By contrast, in Sweden, France, the Netherlands, and Germany, traditions allow govern-

---

*As already stated in the Preface, we are utilizing the following conventional abbreviations: *Americans* for citizens of the United States; *Europeans* for citizens of Western Europe; *Germany* for the Federal Republic of Germany, or West Germany; and *Britain* for Great Britain.

ments more freedom to devise innovative solutions for problems caused by industrialization, urbanization, and other facets of socioeconomic development. To understand this basic difference between Anglo-Saxon and Continental patterns—as well as the variations that occur within these two groups of nations—one needs to appreciate the way historical development has structured today's policy-making systems (Moore; Rokkan; Dyson).

France, Germany, Sweden, and Japan, despite their many differences, are all countries that entered the modern era with strong carry-overs from the feudal institutions of the past. Living uneasily with the republican impulses of the Revolution, the French aristocracy never quite lost its grip on French society and a large rural sector steeped in traditionalism. The German nation was founded in the late nineteenth century on a Prussian version of feudal authority patterns. Sweden saw itself as a nation organized into four great social estates, a concept that was only gradually abandoned in the late nineteenth century. Japan carried its feudal traditions well into the twentieth century.

These countries each entered the modern era with a well-developed state bureaucratic apparatus that predated both large-scale industrialization and widespread commitment to democratic participation. From the earliest phases of economic and political modernization, the state was an accepted presence and, moreover, an unavoidable independent force in the affairs of each nation. The German and French legacies of statism are undoubtedly the most familiar. Sweden offers another example. After the Crown and local government councils, the national bureaucracy is the oldest Swedish political institution and has played the central role for centuries in linking Crown and *kommune*. Modernized in the nineteenth century according to the model of Prussian bureaucracy (but without the resources or opportunity for territorial aggrandizement), Swedish bureaucracy has played an enduring role in modernizing a nation that was at the beginning of this century still agrarian and pre-democratic. Japan's bureaucracy was demilitarized but largely kept intact by the American occupying forces at the end of World War II. With skill and determination, it quickly turned to the task of rebuilding an economically devastated nation into a world class competitor in the new postwar economic order.

Another common historical strand these nations share concerns industrialization. In each country industrialization occurred after economic modernization was well under way in a growing international economy. Any industrial revolution is of course a complex process with few clear beginnings or endings, but it is important to note that France, Germany, Japan, and Sweden all went from being predominantly agricultural to being predominantly industrial around the beginning of this century. What early industrializers could do with relatively little competition, small amounts of capital, and rudimentary transportation systems was later thought to require collective protection, concentrations of capital, and public investment. The result was a natural mutuality of interest between relatively large-scale business concentrations, banking interests, and a preexisting, well-developed state apparatus that could provide the needed protection and investment aids. A traditionalist, noncommercialized agricultural sector in these countries had no less an interest in state protection.

It would be a very lengthy and probably foolish exercise to try to determine which of these three factors was most important in shaping the domestic basis for current policies. Indeed, economic, political, and historical factors have to form a complex web. The legacy of feudalism carried with it a commitment to established authority patterns and an expectation of coherent status hierarchies. The legacy of statism brought an established administrative apparatus confident of its ability to exercise such authority. And the legacy of late industrialization provided an incentive for concentration of economic power that would work comfortably with an equally powerful public authority.

The contrast of the United States and Britain is striking. Feudal institutions scarcely ever existed in the United States, and in Britain the early commercialization of agriculture in the eighteenth century effectively undercut forever the economic and social base for such authority. The early development of parliamentary institutions in Britain and democratic government forms in the United States represented a severe restriction on the executive power of the state. In both countries national bureaucracies developed afterward and were forced to accommodate themselves to preexisting forms of popular political participation. Relatively early experiences with industrial production and commercial agriculture were seen to demonstrate the virtues of free market approaches and fairly small-scale enterprises.

* * * * *

Comparisons of policies cross-nationally can therefore utilize a variety of conceptual orientations, while trying to stay as close to real-world empirical data as possible. The aims of developing better policies and better theories go hand in hand, especially in an increasingly interdependent world. By comparing, we learn to see better. If we are both methodologically careful in the details and sensitive to the larger meaning of events, we can begin to see how the complex, day-to-day work of policy-making—a mix of ideas and institutions, political expediency and long-standing traditions— adds up to collective choices. The next chapter focuses on education policy, beginning with an examination of governmental roles in education developed in consonance with the emergence of state institutions.

2
EDUCATION POLICY

Citizenship in democratic countries involves obligations, some of which are legally prescribed. Voting in national elections is compulsory in some countries, and nonvoters may even be fined. In other countries the practice of an occupation or profession entails compulsory membership in a chamber of artisans or physicians. But in *all* these countries compulsory education laws require parents to send their children to accredited schools for about a decade of formal education.

Why is it that states have chosen to concentrate their power to compel behavior on adolescents rather than on adults of voting age? Partly because the responsibility for ensuring that youth achieves a certain level of literacy and mathematical proficiency has come to be transferred from the family to the government; partly because governments see schools as an opportunity to inculcate regime values into future citizens when they are still at an impressionable age; partly because future voting rights presuppose a socialization process in which schools play an important part. In these ways adult society tries to legitimize its choices for the next generation and to reduce the opportunities for deviating radically from them.

Extensive state intervention in education can be justified in that the knowledge and credentials achieved in schools broaden the choices that youth can make at later stages of their education and employment. Thus, the choice to "drop out" of education is especially restricted where national goals stress "equality of opportunity"; nations must make sure that youth stays in the education system long enough to be offered this opportunity.

In democratic capitalist systems, social stratification is the main mechanism to implement and legitimize economic and social inequality during adult life. A nation's commitment to allocating "life chances" rests heavily on education, particularly on access to higher education, where the nation's social and professional elites are trained. Some health, housing, and other social policies are also relevant, insofar as poor health or crowded housing may affect a child's development. Most important, however, are the quality of education offered in the various kinds of schools and the equality of access to them.

CHOICES IN EDUCATION POLICY

The Scope of the State Education Monopoly

Although no advanced democracies directly prohibit churches or private groups from operating nonpublic educational institutions, they encourage or discourage them in varying degrees. The techniques with which they implement their education policy choices rest largely on their power to license or charter institutions and to assist them financially. The preponderance of public education varies from nation to nation. The de facto dominance of public institutions is most thorough in Scandinavia. Though only a few Continental countries offer extensive support to private institutions, Britain has a significant private school sector. The largest number of self-supporting religious and other private schools and universities is found in the United States, followed by Japan.

Generally, more than four-fifths of all pupils and students in these countries attend public institutions. Two controversial questions are whether the minority attending private schools should receive public subsidies, and whether it is just for them to get better educations largely because of their parents' higher incomes. The diversity of American practice is illustrated by the fact that in some states—Colorado and Tennessee, for example—no private college students receive state grants, while in others all receive some public support. Such regional differences would probably violate national constitutional rules in West Germany, where few private schools and almost no private universities exist.

The Instruments of Education Policy

How centralized should national education systems be, and how much leeway should local or regional authorities have to make deviating decisions? The polar choices here lie between the strong American local school boards within a decentralized federal system, on the one hand, and the centrally run school systems of unitary polities such as Sweden and France, on the other hand. In the latter countries, powerful national boards enforce similar rules and curricula throughout the nation. Uniformity is lower in Germany, by contrast, because the primary power is exercised from the *Land,* or state, level and not the national level. But Land officials assign teachers and stipulate curricula in ways that would arouse outrage in even the more localized American system.

In Britain local education authorities (LEAs) have inherited stronger traditions of self-government than in Germany, one result of a more pluralist public system. In the United States the emergence of supra-local public school systems has been incremental; in both countries similarity of curricula is still induced indirectly through nationally set examinations, and less through direct bureaucratic prescription. But in Britain under the Thatcher government the power of local authorities has been reduced, and a nationally uniform curriculum imposed.

The Distribution of Educational Opportunity

That goals such as social equality and social mobility until recently held low priority in European countries was reflected in their secondary school systems, which were tripartite in being divided into academic, technical, and general schools. The academic high schools educated only a small elite, selected through what in Britain was known as the "eleven-plus" exam, for rating children at the ages of eleven to thirteen on their abilities. Because the school diploma was something of a ticket to a lifetime journey, the distribution of places was important. As was once said about this system: "The man with the third-class ticket who later feels entitled to claim a seat in the first-class carriage will not be admitted, even if he is prepared to pay the difference" (Marshall, p. 113).

This early selection system limited the number of children from lower social strata who achieved social mobility by graduating from elite schools and going on to the university. In America, greater equality of educational opportunity encouraged broader class recruitment to the secondary schools and universities, causing these levels of schooling to become more universal.

In recent decades in Europe, left-wing parties such as the Social Democrats have sought to reform both the secondary and university systems. Such impulses have coincided with strong expansions of both sectors, so that the proportion of European youth going on to higher education has begun to approach American levels. Whereas about half of American youth now start college, the proportion in Europe is about one quarter.

Restraints and Innovation in Education

Higher education is an appropriate place to examine potential restraints and innovation in education policy, for the variable length and quality of degree courses present complex choices in resource allocation. American students usually study four years to earn an undergraduate degree, British students three years. Over the last fifty years, the length of study in medicine has grown more than that in engineering or social work, reflecting choices by universities and employers about how and where specialized training should be extended. Occasionally, curricular innovations have shortened study time; more frequently they have extended it. But when vastly enlarged numbers of students have coincided with the imposition of fiscal restraints, as has been the case in Europe since the early 1970s, resulting policies have meant restraining educational opportunities for at least part of the student population.

Admission and graduation requirements inevitably color the allocation process. Should "ability" be the sole criterion for allocation, or should allocation be affected by the experience and histories of applicants, or by their capacity to contribute financially to their education? If "ability" must be determined, then by what kinds of previous school or test scores should it be measured? If tuition-paying capacity helps the well-to-do, then should this be balanced by special affirmative action programs for members of "disadvantaged" social or ethnic groups? Should the projected "needs" of labor markets be the chief determinants of how many should study what subject?

POLITICAL CHANGE AND EDUCATION DEVELOPMENT
SCOPE AND THRESHOLDS

Education has long been a concern and responsibility of governments, both local and national. And though education histories tell of no abrupt changes such as the 1946 nationalization of British health care (a takeover that was facilitated by the lack of opposition from the private sector, local governments, and religious groups and that was due partly to special conditions during the preceding wartime period), there have been numerous initiatives for changing and nationalizing school systems. Their implementation, however, has usually been gradually extended over the course of several generations.

Evolution of the Public Systems

In the period of nation building, national governments usually followed several different strategies to increase their influence on private or locally run schools. Two groups who might have resisted governments' actions included educators and church leaders. Educational administrators and teachers often constituted a subsystem whose compliance political leaders could not take for granted. Church leaders also held great power and could retaliate if governments eliminated religious prerogatives in education too abruptly. The way that national governments came increasingly to influence education policy was through financial leverage. (Until the 1960s the United States remained the exception, because conservatives blocked most direct federal aid to education.) With the extension of citizenship and franchise rights in the nineteenth century, moreover, bringing educational institutions more under public control became a prime national concern.

In Europe, churches allied with certain higher social groups had tightly controlled admissions and curricula. Those seeking to erode this quasi-monopoly tended to pursue a *restrictive* strategy of discouraging church schools if they had access to the governing elites and could convince them that religious educational control was politically undesirable. This strategy was pursued in Prussia in the early 1800s, for example.

France, like the United States, has a private school sector which is predominantly made up of Catholic schools, the relationship of which to the state sector has been a long-standing bone of contention between the Right and the Left. In 1984 President Mitterrand's Socialist government prepared a bill which would have strengthened state supervision while expanding public subsidies to these schools. A delicate compromise was upset by amendments in the National Assembly, and subsequent protests against the government bill led to a huge street demonstration in Paris. With polls showing 70 percent of the population in support of survival of the private schools, the bill had to be withdrawn, leading to the resignation of several ministers. The new education minister shifted focus to curricular reforms, particularly aimed at changing the teaching role of mathematics, a notoriously tough screening course in secondary schools.

A *substitutive strategy* of providing alternative education facilities was better suited to reform groups, which were stronger in economic rather than political resources, and could use these gradually to devalue the existing educational monopoly (Archer, Part One). This strategy was optimally pursued in nineteenth-century Britain by middle-class reformers to undermine the stultifying control held by the Anglican Church over schools and universities. Not politically strong enough to legislate large-scale changes, they instead started their own less traditionally oriented schools, which came to compete with the Anglican-controlled schools. In time these plural networks were incorporated into a directly state-run system, though not until 1870 for primary schools and 1902 for secondary schools.

As major school types came to be *unified* within a state-run system, they gradually dropped fees and became increasingly dependent on public financing. Thus, the terms of financing largely determined the long-term viability of church-run or other private schools. In countries where private schools lost state aid, as in Sweden, they eventually became almost extinct. But in countries where religious schools can still qualify for state support on the same terms as secular schools, as in the Netherlands, they still exist. These European systems do not adhere to a U.S.-style "separation of church and state" doctrine. Partly because of this constraint, the American school development pattern followed the substitutive model with an especially strong decentralist bias. This has led to *both* an unusually large public school system and a comparatively large private school and college sector.

Compared to Europe, most American states have remained very permissive in allowing communities and private groups to charter and establish schools and colleges. Due to the rural location of most state universities, with the University of Minnesota one of the few located in large cities, most urban universities founded before 1960 were private.

In order to maintain the unity of culture and standards of professional competence, the French state also monopolized higher education functions within a centralized public system: Private institutions only developed on the periphery by assuming tasks beyond the state's main mission. In Britain the Thatcher government in 1983 made Buckingham University the first chartered non-public university in this century, but it has "yet to achieve a distinctive and prestigious niche in British higher education," and remains a "school of convenience . . . receiving sympathizers" (Geiger, pp. 233–35).

In the more centralized European states, unification of the educational system resulted in tight central control, as manifested in detailed curricula which determine what is taught in schools throughout the country. Thus, French ministers of education could tell that at a given hour fifth-grade *lycée* classes everywhere in the country were reading Livy. In the more pluralist systems, unification came about more erratically as a byproduct of public financial support and legal recognition of school diplomas. Thus, around 1900 the British Education Ministry acted more as a central paymaster than as a ministry, a description that remained apt for the U.S. Office of Education even in recent decades.

The process through which education became anchored in the public sphere reflected the different policy priorities of centralized political systems, such as those of France and Prussia-Germany, and of decentralized ones, such as those of Britain and the United States. In the former, the king and the bureaucracy developed earlier and more complete control over national and local administration, whereas in the latter, national control long remained more circumscribed. French and Prussian-German policy consequences included the tendency to go beyond school system unification to *systematization*, through which types of schools and curricula were made uniform; and the tendency to give priority to *university-level* public institutions, since these were expected mainly to train candidates for the extensive bureaucracy. The more circumscribed national control in Britain meant that it long had fewer universities, and in the United States that the school system remained much more heterogeneous.

Public and Private Schools Today

When systematization was attempted early in democratic political systems, as in some American states, the result was "several systems and subsystems, each comprising institutions of varying degrees of publicness . . ." (Cremin, p. 152). There, attempts to set national standards were repeatedly repulsed. A U.S. federal university was proposed in the early 1800s, but its advocates scared off support by suggesting that its graduates then be the only ones eligible for high federal appointive offices. Since then, "no one has challenged the principle of high academic standards across the whole system because no one has proposed it; there have been no common standards, high or otherwise. Indeed, if Europe's slogan for higher education has been 'nothing if not the best,' America's has been 'something is better than nothing' " (Trow, in Gans, p. 276).

In most countries public schools serve 90 percent or more of the student population. If one automobile manufacturer were to supply cars for as large a proportion of adult drivers as public schools provide education for a nation's youth, it might be deemed a monopoly. But it is only the centralized and systematized school systems with uniform curricula that come close to the monopoly model. Attempts to conceptualize local American high schools as monopolies, because although they offer variegated curricula they smother competing public institutions and offer the same kinds of degrees (Clark 1985), seem more contestable applications of the monopoly model. In the lower school level, pupils are usually assigned to a particular school near home; but their range of choice increases as they progress to the higher levels. At the university level, there is considerable competition among public universities to attract students. In Europe, this has been less overt, tied less to varying rates of tuition than to relative attractiveness of courses, programs, degrees, and locations. As in American public universities, European universities cater to students outside their immediate location, but what is not found in Europe are differential tuition levels, with higher charges for out-of-state students, as exists in the United States. Such variations would violate the equality guarantees of national citizenship in a federal system such as West Germany's, even though German universities, like American public universities, are run by the individual states.

Countries differ considerably in the proportions of youth in various age groups attending school full-time. Since most countries require full-time attendance until age fifteen or sixteen, almost all youths in the six to fifteen age group are enrolled full-time. But national policies differ considerably in the inducements used to keep students in full-time schooling in the upper secondary levels—the sixteen to eighteen age group. In recent years Japan has been most successful in keeping seventeen-year-olds in full-time schooling (91 percent), followed closely by the United States with 87 percent. Canada, the Scandinavian countries, and France follow in that order, with Britain at the bottom of the list (see Table 2.1). In Britain and France a small proportion of seventeen-year-olds combine part-time schooling with apprenticeship, but this model is stronger in Germany and Switzerland. At age twenty-one there are less cross-national variations, but Americans top the list with one-third still enrolled. They also lead among proportions of students in their mid-twenties who are still enrolled in graduate or professional training.

FIGURE 2.1 THE BRITISH EDUCATIONAL SYSTEM

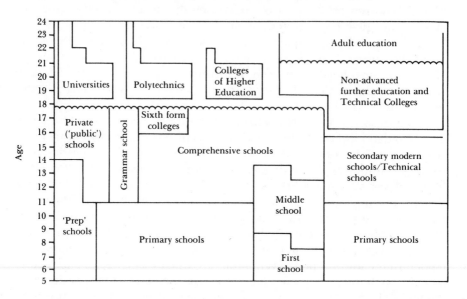

The relative proportion attending private institutions is comparatively high in the United States and the Netherlands, limited in Germany and Britain, and virtually nil in Sweden. In Europe, private institutions become fewer as one ascends the educational ladder, which does not hold for the United States, with its large private university sector. But if we look at direct *public* expenditures on *private* education, the contrast is sharp again. The Netherlands spends about 5 percent of its GNP on such support, whereas Sweden spends only one-hundredth of 1 percent of the GNP. In Japan and

TABLE 2.1 PROPORTIONS OF AGE GROUPS ENROLLED IN EDUCATION, 1985–86

Country	17-year-olds		21-year-olds		Graduate and Professional Degree Candidates
	Full-time	*Part-time*	*Full-time*	*Part-time*	
Britain	30.6	14.4	—	—	4.4
Canada	77.3	—	21.8	2.0	3.9
Denmark	74.5	—	27.3	—	—
France	67.7	10.2	18.5	—	6.2
Germany	51.3	48.4	16.7	8.9	1.4
Japan	90.8	1.6	—	—	1.4
Netherlands	75.3	—	22.2	.5	—
Norway	75.1	1.4	21.7	2.7	8.0
Switzerland	26.8	54.9	13.7	6.9	—
United States	87.3	.7	28.3	4.9	9.8

SOURCE OECD, *Education in OECD Countries 1985–86: Comparative Statistics* (Paris: OECD, 1988).

the United States about one sixth of the private universities' funding comes from public sources.

REFORM MODES AND CENTRALIZATION
INSTRUMENTS

The instruments which governments develop to make and implement education policy are determined partly by the governments' own structures and partly by the traditions of state-school relations. A federal system may tend to entrust education policy to local structures, while unitary systems tend toward centralization of power. But within each category we can identify gradations. Thus, among federal systems, the United States has a more decentralized educational system with more autonomous state and local officials, while Germany has greater homogeneity with less local initiative. Among unitary systems, France's education system is more centralized, and Britain's was less centralized.

In centralized political systems educational policy attention is focused predominantly on national legislation and decrees, because implementation problems are minimal. In decentralized systems the relevant decision-making arena is much broader, since it includes state and local, as well as national, government organs. Moreover, some education policy changes are negotiated autonomously within the educational institutions themselves. This has been especially true in the United States, where some crucial changes in curricula and credentialing have been implemented with little reference to general government. Only when education decisions arouse the ire of outside interests do politicians veto school policies. But those who seek to mobilize protest against controversial subjects or textbooks can do so more easily in the American system than in other decentralized systems, since the responsible policymakers tend to be more accessible and more susceptible to pressure (Church).

"Wherever educational funding is decentralized," an international report concludes, "as in the United States, there tends to be a more or less profound underlying inequality of expenditure among a nation's schools. This renders the task of governments dedicated to equalization of inputs extremely difficult. . . . The problem is compounded when there exists no national salary scale for teachers, for then the poorer local authorities may well be tempted to devote additional resources to raising teachers' salaries rather than concentrating them on the disadvantaged" (OECD 1983b, p. 136).

In 1983 about one-quarter of American white and one-third of American black parents reported some experience with school bussing in their families. Two-thirds of both groups thought the experience satisfactory, but one-third had reservations. When asked about their willingness to have their children attend schools which were one-half black, about one-quarter of white parents had objections. Changes in attitude toward integration had been most marked in the South, but the direction of policy causation was from policy change to attitude change, and not the other way around. That is why within the decentralized American system "it is a rare school district indeed in which majoritarian elections yield policies requiring racial balance. The more perfect the means of popular control, the worse for racial equality" (Hochschild, p. 144).

Even today local policy structures such as U.S. school district boards and British LEAs remain more significant than in more centralized systems. Local officials have power to appoint principals and teachers, which in Bavaria is done by ministry officials in the state capital. French and German systems have no elected school officials at the local level, only appointed ones who generally have civil service tenure. By contrast, American school superintendents usually serve at the pleasure of a locally elected school board, which raises a large part of school finance through taxes which are not only local, but are usually raised separately from the general municipal revenue. The amount of revenue that school boards receive from state and federal sources varies, but is, on the average, lower than in Europe. As British education has become systematized, it also has to rely more on national financing, currently about 60 percent. The British LEAs differ from American school district boards, however, in that their members are local town councillors, are usually elected on party tickets, and have commitments to national party education platforms.

As public education services expanded in the centralized European systems, choices had to be made about which groups in society should get priority. The central government bureaucracy had top priority; next highest priority was given to other political elites; then came lower-status social groups who supported the regime. But as long as resources and institutional capacity were limited, there was a "severe tailing off of educational services to other sections of the population" (Archer, p. 231). Of course this deprivation was in part deliberate, since rulers did not want lower-class children to develop ambitions unsuitable to their future positions in the labor force.

What distinguished American education policy-making in the mid-nineteenth to mid-twentieth centuries from that in most European nations was the greater attention paid to demands from the middling parts of the population. School and college opportunities became so plentiful that even some less affluent American youth could make their way to some college.

In American society at the turn of the twentieth century, class lines were more fluid than in European society, and formal education credentials permitted more members of working-class families to rise to middle-class status. Sometimes, of course, this mobility was costly to the mobile member's own family, as in the case of a Chicago teamster family around 1900. There a working-class father had

. . . encouraged his daughter's ambitions to become a school teacher only to find his own self-respect jeopardized: he was forced first to rent a new flat and buy new furniture; he was then expected to entertain his daughter's status-conscious white-collar friends; what is more, as the result of his added expenses the father was forced to send out his younger children to supplement his now inadequate wages; finally, his teacher daughter threatened, at every sign of opposition from her father, to leave her home for more congenial surroundings. (White, p. 178)

In this American social model, family resources were mobilized to enable the individual of working-class background to acquire the status symbols of the middle class.

In Europe the educational opportunities of the working-class were until the most recent decades low and not rising. In fact, the opportunities of workers' children actually decreased in the course of nineteenth-century industrialization. Growing centralized bureaucratic structures then tended to limit access. Whereas middle-class groups found more of the alternatives they sought, the lower-class children lost some scholarship opportunities which had been more available *before* the systems were unified (Kaelble, in Flora and Heidenheimer).

Proponents of educational reforms often strengthen their positions by relating their structural or curricular goals to broad political ideologies. In earlier European periods dominant ideologies were perfectly consonant with the idea that public universities should serve the interests of the ruling class, but in the present era strong ideological support can be marshaled for arguments that "equality of opportunity" shall also extend, or even especially extend, to the lower classes. Attacks on selective secondary schools have recently been more effective when used with socialist and other egalitarian ideology, for example, to show how retaining Latin as a prerequisite for university study perpetuated the bias in favor of admitting the children of social elites.

Political Change from Within and Without

It is fruitful to examine comparatively how similar changes—such as the adoption of new subjects in the curriculum, or the integration of several kinds of secondary schools—may come to be initiated in several different systems. For example, the *internal initiation* of school policy change—by educators, without reference to political policymakers—takes on a wider scope in decentralized systems. Extra-educational interests such as local businesses or union groups may also be more successful in influencing policy in decentralized systems. Appeals to ideology to promote or oppose change, on the other hand, tend to be weaker in decentralized systems and to come later than they might in centralized or unitary systems. (Some of these concepts are developed in Archer, Part One.)

The initiation of policy change from within the education sector is more feasible in *decentralized* systems because the educators are usually more autonomous and can draw on their own financial resources. The public education sector in these systems usually developed through the integration of regionally and/or religiously diverse local school types. Professional educators benefit from this residual pluralism in that they retain important powers outside the central bureaucracy. Consequently, a new type of curriculum or instructional technique can be tried in a few schools or school systems, then generalized to others without reference to central government. Education leaders can ally with philanthropists, leading to such phenomena as the Carnegie Foundation's tremendous influence on American higher education (Selden). These arrangements have no equivalent in the centralized Continental systems. There teacher organizations are important mainly in negotiating with the central bureaucrats, but they are less able to generate and filter demands from parents, business people, and other consumer groups so as to help structure policy alternatives (Ringer).

Educational change in *centralized* systems arises more from negotiations among political, bureaucratic, and social elites at the national level. For example, reduction, then termination, of public subsidies to private schools in Scandinavia occurred largely as a result of pressure exerted by Social Democrats during the interwar period. This campaign not only led to the virtual elimination of private schools (in contrast to Britain), but also was followed up in the 1950s with efforts to combine parallel secondary schools into a more homogeneous system of comprehensive schools.

Britain experienced a sharp transition from a relatively decentralized to a much more centralized education system as the consequence of the 1988 Education Act. Previously, schools had to prepare students for national examinations, but had retained considerable freedom in shaping their curricula. But the 1988 Act gave the national ministry the power to "establish a complete national curriculum" and to revise this whenever "necessary and expedient." It proceeded to set out programs of study, attainment targets, and assessment tests to be given to pupils at the ages of seven, eleven, fourteen, and sixteen. Initial priority was given to the core subjects of English, math, and science, with later regulations to be issued for other foundation subjects like history, technology, and foreign languages, which are prescribed for elementary and secondary schools.

Policy Choices between Center and Periphery

An observer of the turbulent education controversies of the early 1970s would have been much better able to follow German developments from Bonn than American ones from Washington. Why was this so, since both federal governments played only secondary policy roles to those of the states? It is because German education politics is both federal *and* central-ized. The German Land education ministers' battles were fought out largely on a party basis, with Land ministers confronting one another di-rectly in the national parliament (*Bundesrat*) and the Council of Education Ministers. Changes made in Hamburg schools concerned Bavarians much more than changes made in Georgia concerned Minnesotans. Whether Bavaria would accept the school diplomas from Hamburg concerned the politicians in Bonn much more than any such conflict between regional accrediting associations troubled officials in Washington.

In decentralized systems, such as the American, change occurs all the time; it is constantly initiated, imitated, modified, reversed, and counter-acted at some level in some school district, state, or national arena. Much of it is monitored in Washington by only one bureau of the Department of Education. Many of the changes in curriculum, teacher training, and ac-creditation are negotiated autonomously in one of numerous commissions, which might meet in Cincinnati one year and in New Orleans the next. Not all proposals even have to be passed up to the national level—only those that ask for federal funding or require federal monitoring. In fact, the issues in which federal involvement has made headlines—whether concern-ing free lunches or school busing—have often been quite marginal to the educational enterprise as such. The appearance of federal marshals to force the acceptance of black students at the University of Alabama was seen as high drama, but most decisions affecting access of socioeconomic groups are incremental. A decade later some committee may study the results, and outsiders are often quite surprised to see the trends that have materialized.

In systems which are both centralized and unitary, such as the French, demands for change accumulate over a longer time while awaiting central-ized attention and approval. Since all negotiations involve the all-powerful national ministries, the negotiation process is more distinctively patterned. If teachers in Lyons have salary or curriculum grievances, they have to ask their union representatives to negotiate with bureaucrats in Paris, although this has begun to change in the 1980s. In the German federal system they would go to the Land capital. But if the teachers in one Land get many more concessions than those in another, the issue will soon be raised by a national union or a politician. Uniformity of standards gets much more support in Europe than in the United States, where attempts to require states to equalize funding, so that per-capita school revenue becomes more equal, have not gotten too far, even within one state. Cross-national studies have shown that the difference that particular schools make in effecting achievement varies between the more and the less centralized systems: "The more centralization in terms of uniformity of structure and financial resources, the lower the between-school variability in outcomes." For fourteen-year-olds this variability was found to be three times as high in the

United States than in Sweden, a more centralized system (Husen 1986, p. 131).

IMPROVING SECONDARY SCHOOL OPPORTUNITIES
DISTRIBUTION

Which systems maximize educational opportunities for the majority of their youth:

> The *American* pattern that provides the means to keep the majority of youths in full-time secondary school until the age of eighteen, and supplements legal requirements by social pressure not to "drop out" before the achievement of a high school degree?

> Those like most of the *European* countries that provide comprehensive education through lower secondary, or junior high school, but then provide a variety of options, one of which is the pursuit of a three-year academic senior high school line, but with others constituting shorter and/or more vocationally oriented lines of study, some of them on a part-time basis?

> Or does *Japan* present the optimal model by keeping almost all pupils in full-time schooling until the end of senior high school, but coupling this with intense selection process which directs students at age fifteen to senior high schools of greatly varying quality and prestige?

Views about these options have varied over time as well as between places: "Developments in the 1960s led many observers to believe that at least some European countries would eventually adopt a model of secondary education similar to the North American high school." But this prospect seemed "very unlikely" in 1985, in the view of the authors of an OECD report (Education and Training 1985, p. 83). These authors noted that while some European countries had introduced a common curriculum up to the age of fifteen, they did not try to impose either a common curriculum or a common secondary graduation certificate for the upper secondary schools. Rather, they have developed in their senior high schools coexisting and clearly defined, highly structured lines of study leading to different kinds of graduation certificates.

Thus, while all industrial countries have in recent decades tended to abandon earlier patterns of directing pupils at about the age of eleven or twelve into distinctly different kinds of school, they have differed in the extent to which they have postponed selection. In Europe and Japan, the crucial period has been advanced to about age fifteen, leaving selection largely within the secondary system. In the United States, by contrast, selection is postponed to some point beyond the secondary level, such as the point of entry to college or even to graduate school.

Countries like Germany and Japan utilize tracking by school, the former by placing about one-quarter of pupils into academically oriented *Gymnasien,* the latter by sending them to the more selective senior high schools. Another form of selection involves tracking by subject, as in the French *lycées,* where many able students are directed to difficult math courses. The distinctive aspect of the American high school is that it does not strongly employ *either* form of selection, so that it keeps many of its students together in the same classes most of the time, thus making it both more loosely coupled and more "comprehensive" than the other national high school types.

Why and how does more or less "comprehensivization" of secondary schools matter for the distribution of educational opportunity? And why can we identify different directions of main trend lines, for instance those between the 1960s and the 1980s? In the 1960s many European countries began to move away from the traditional patterns under which some 5 to 10 percent of able students were channeled into selective academic high schools. Partly this was because they wanted to develop more of the potential of the other 90 percent, partly for reasons of social equity, since the previous selection process had been very class-biased. That policy of comprehensivization was pursued with differing intensity and success, as will be shown below in a comparison of the British, German, and Swedish cases. But what kept Europeans, particularly the Swedes who are in some ways more egalitarian than the Americans, from following the American pattern of maintaining a common curriculum throughout senior high school?

Partly it was due to some characteristics of American high schools that came under explicit criticism at home through reports like *A Nation at Risk,* published in 1983 by a presidentially appointed Commission. Europeans, even the more permissive ones, held fast to the idea that pupils should pass from one grade to another if their knowledge warranted it. Those who fail (enough) tests are held back, to repeat some or all of the classes. In American schools such retribution seems too harsh, so most pupils are promoted automatically. "Hence the American embarrassment of having hundreds of thousands of young people graduate from the twelfth grade, the last year of secondary education, while still reading at eighth-grade level or doing mathematics at sixth-grade level. A large subset of students are kept in undemanding programs," making the comprehensive school largely an "educational parking lot" (Clark 1985, p. 314).

The United States did not always expect students to finish high school; that goal developed as a correlate of the trend, from the 1910s to the 1940s, through which the comprehensive high school largely replaced more specialized vocational and technical as well as academic schools. Most teachers for these comprehensive schools were trained in the same state education colleges which trained the primary teachers, with the consequence that America developed a unique "downward coupling" of its secondary to its

primary school systems. In status and income American high school teachers lag those in both Europe and Japan, where secondary teachers are
educated in university liberal arts departments. This contributes to their
regarding their task as teaching students who would be worthy of meeting
university entrance standards, thus exemplifying "upward coupling" (Clark
1985, p. 310).

Cross-National Learning Contrasts

Average test scores can be expected to drop drastically as less gifted
students are encouraged to stay longer in high school and the university. The
key question is whether the most able 1 or 5 percent achieve more highly in
countries that have retained selective school structures. Figure 2.2 shows the
mean scores in science tests for high school seniors to be lower in countries
like the United States and Sweden, where larger proportions of an age group
reach the senior year, than in more selective countries such as Germany. But
if we look at the average grades of the top 1 and 5 percent scorers, then we
find little evidence that the achievement of the most able is held down in
countries that distribute education opportunities more generously.

FIGURE 2.2 SCIENCE ACHIEVEMENT SCORES (IEA)

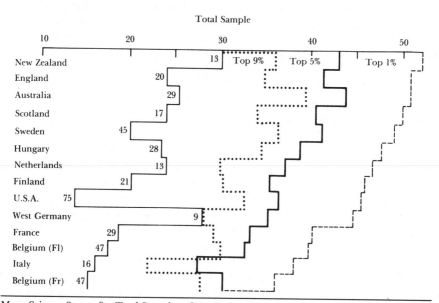

Mean Science Scores for Total Samples of Pre-University Students and for the Top 9, 5, and 1
  percent respectively. For each country the size of the pre-university population as a percentage of the total relevant age group has been indicated.
SOURCE Husen et al. (1973), p. 146.

In the 1980s another set of cross-national tests were administered by the International Association for the Evaluation of Educational Achievement (IEA). Compared to the previous tests, the United States had not increased the proportion of the age group taking advanced high school math, whereas Japan had. Nevertheless, Japanese students got much higher grades on all sections of the math exam, and their scores on geometry and measurement were twice as high as the American ones. French students also outscored American students. Factors that influenced the better French and Japanese grades included more extensive coverage of material in class curricula, and longer school days and/or years. Specialization also played a role, with the British and Japanese test-takers having devoted 20 percent of their school time to math, contrasted to 14 percent for the Americans and Canadians (Garden, p. 61). The international tests led to many undifferentiated references by politicians such as President Ronald Reagan, who used the results to spur critical studies.

The tests for foreign language learning also demonstrated a strong correlation with the duration of study. Thus, both American and Swedish students showed dismal results on the French language tests, mainly because they had studied that language for only about two years, when it takes six or seven years to acquire satisfactory proficiency. As Husen has noted, it has been the "Olympic Games" aspects of the IEA studies that have drawn broad public attention, but the subtler analysis of their results have contributed to answering questions about "how efficiently national policies have been implemented" (Husen 1987, p. 46). Table 2.2 shows the achievement scores of 10, 14, and 18 year olds in a number of countries, and reveals how rank orders in science learning change during school careers.

In the 1980s American high schools were subjected to a degree of

TABLE 2.2 SCIENCE IN SCHOOLS: RANK ORDER OF NATIONAL ACHIEVEMENT SCORES FOR AGES TEN TO EIGHTEEN YEARS

	5th Grade 10 yrs.	9th Grade 14 yrs.	Growth Score*	12th Grade 18 yrs.
Australia	7	6	1.26	5
Canada	5	3	1.18	7
Finland	2	4	0.75	6
Italy	4	7	0.89	8
Japan	1	1	1.06	3
Norway	8	5	1.33	4
Sweden	3	2	0.90	2
Britain	9	7	1.34	1
United States	6	9	0.90	n.a.

*Learning growth fifth to ninth grade, based on standardized scale.
SOURCE International Association for the Evaluation of Educational Achievement, *Science Achievement in Seventeen Countries* (1988), Table A 10, p. 98.

intensive scrutiny which paralleled that leveled at them in the late 1950s after the Soviets took the lead in space exploration. Since most of the American education "establishment," as represented by teachers' unions and education specialists, had developed strong ties to the Democratic party, the Republicans under Ronald Reagan felt fewer constraints in sponsoring searing attacks like those in the 1983 report, *A Nation at Risk*. Though the report exaggerated to draw attention, many other observers, ranging from Burton Clark to Education Secretary Bennett, distinguished high schools from both colleges and primary schools as the weak link in American education, "a segment of education that performs poorly. . . . International comparisons . . . have confirmed some of the harshest domestic evaluations. . . . In the last half of the twentieth century, the development of the American secondary system seems to have gone astray to the point where we can speak appropriately of a distinctive American problem" (Clark 1985, p. 307).

The doubtful attitude toward public high schools on the part of some parents was reflected in a modest reversal of the earlier trend toward a decline in attendance at church-sponsored private schools. In the 1960s attendance at such schools rose again, particularly in "seg academies" which developed in the wake of school desegregation in the South. In the 1970s flight from urban high schools accelerated in many Northern cities, when not only affluent professional parents, but often also upwardly mobile lower-middle-class parents, transferred their children to fee-paying private schools, often run by churches to which they did not even belong. Thus in Manhattan, one-quarter of students attending Catholic schools are non-Catholics. Nationally, there is a close relation between income and private school attendance. In 1982 only 3 percent of families with incomes below $7,500, but 31 percent of those with incomes over $75,000, sent children to private schools (James and Levin, p. 59). Of 21,000 private schools, almost half were Catholic and three-quarters were church-related.

The problems of how to affect the makeup of school populations, and how to equalize resources among school districts of widely varying tax bases, have posed serious questions for theoreticians as well as practitioners. If grass-roots pressure demonstrates parent desires for de facto segregation, how can these decisions be called into question in terms of democratic theory? The peculiar American problem is the weaker position of the American state in guaranteeing social rights at the level of policy implementation. Amy Gutmann argues that de facto desegregation is unacceptable by democratic principles even if supported by democratic politics. But how can principles be translated into practice? Increased federal funding was held to be one answer, and Title I programs did seem to produce some learning gains among those inner-city pupils who did not drop out. But the correlation between educational spending and learning as measured by test results has not been high; and under the Reagan administration such funding was reduced. Its first education secretary, who had prevented the abolition of his department but had to accept a diminished federal role, could only urge the states to make education their number-one priority with the argument that "education is to state government what defense is to the federal government" (Gutmann, p. 159).

Under President George Bush, who had campaigned to become the "education president," a revival of federal initiatives has begun to occur. A federal "merit school" program is planned to provide recognition and money to superior schools, including those that enhance the performance of disadvantaged students. Education Secretary Lauro Cavazos has started to utilize authority to design a test for all eleventh graders. Support is also developing for a proposal to create a new national system of teacher certification, which might diminish the monopoly hitherto exercised by the individual states with regard to public schools.

Japanese Secondary Schools

When compared to the American and European secondary school systems, the Japanese is more like the former in some ways, and more like the latter in others. It is more similar to the American in that the overwhelming majority of pupils are retained in full-time schooling until the age of eighteen, whereas in most European countries only about one-quarter go that far. As in America, most students attend neighborhood schools with similar curricula through junior high school. But at that juncture the Japanese operate a harsh selection system on a universal basis similar to those European countries operate on a more differentiated basis.

The much better average scores of Japanese students than American students on international math and science tests have raised questions as to what it is about school structure and differentiation that can account for them. One evident difference is embedded in the fact that Japanese school districts usually offer five or more senior high schools which are recognized as varying in quality, and as having differing entrance requirements. Thus students of different ability are streamed into differing schools, which teach similar subjects with varying intensity. Only some more progressive school systems, like that in Kyoto, try to adhere to a policy of having all students attend the same kind of school. The tremendous competition to get into the better high schools, and later into the better universities, puts Japanese students under immense pressure. Not only do they go to school for 240 days a year, compared to an average 180 days in the United States (see Table 2.3), but they also devote additional time to tutoring in private cram schools, which prepare them for the rigorous entrance tests through drill based mainly on memorization of vast amounts of material. Most high school students stay the course; only some 6 percent do not finish high school, whereas some 30 percent of Americans earn the invidious label of high school "drop-out."

While scoring points by drawing attention to the lower American average performance, none of the American education reports of the 1980s drew on foreign examples to propose serious change in the comprehensive basis of the American public high school. But in small part there has in fact been some modest convergence. The pattern of alternative secondary schools has found a mild echo in the system of magnet schools which has developed in some American cities, so as to allow students more choice in coupling their interests to different kinds of secondary school curricula. Thus, in St. Louis a court-ordered plan has forced the state to make up for past segregation sins by financing magnet schools that attract both white and black students. Other black inner-city students are bussed to white high schools in the suburbs. This, however, tends to leave only the least able and least motivated in the residual neighborhood high schools.

With regard to one crucial variable, the availability of new and better young teachers, the United States in the 1980s was positioned differently from many European countries. In Germany, for instance, many additional teachers had been given lifetime tenure in the early 1970s. A decade later the combination of declining school enrollments due to a fall in the birth-rate and decreasing number of retirements led to a lack of new positions for young entrants. In America weaker tenure rules and lower salaries led to greater turnover, but the low status and salary prospects led the proportion of college freshmen planning a teaching career to drop from 23 per-

TABLE 2.3 STUDENTS' MATH ACHIEVEMENT: DO INSTRUCTION TIME AND TEACHERS' SALARIES HELP EXPLAIN DIFFERENCES?

		Hours of Mathematics per Year	Days per School Year	Teacher Salary Index*
Higher				
↑	Japan	101	243	2.03
	Netherlands	112	200	2.33
	Canada	126	190	2.14
Math	Britain	130	195	1.69
Learning	Finland	84	190	n.a.
	New Zealand	130	190	2.54
↓	United States	144	180	1.44
	Sweden	96	180	1.37
Lower				

*Index is based on the ratio of average secondary teacher salary to per capita GNP.

SOURCES *The Underachieving Curriculum* (1987), pp. 52–53; *International Comparisons of Teachers' Salaries* (1988), p. 21.

cent in 1968 to 4.7 percent in 1982. Then, business leaders in some states began to put pressure on state legislatures to spend more on education and teacher salaries, as in South Carolina, or to dethrone football players as anti-intellectual high school role models, as in Texas. This began to have some effect on incoming college cohorts, of whom three-quarters felt that being well off financially was a key life goal. Thus by 1987, the proportion planning a teaching career had risen modestly, to 8.1 percent.

Comprehensive Schools as Partisan Issues

Until the 1960s, European students at the secondary level were generally differentiated by tests at about age eleven, with those assigned to the more selective schools receiving a much greater share of teaching and other resources. In practice very few children from working-class families have been assigned to these schools, and in the 1950s some European governments began to reform the prevailing tripartite structure of academic, technical, and general schools in order to provide equal educational opportunity for all children.

Introducing Comprehensive Schools

The first country to initiate such a reform was Sweden, where the Social Democrats "comprehensivized" lower secondary schools. Comprehensivization means that all students are enrolled together in one school, which is created by merging previously distinct school types. The Swedes were able to implement this reform fairly rapidly, for theirs is a centralized system where the Social Democrats long held continuous control of national power.

Just as they had in Sweden, the Social Democrats and Labour supported reform in Britain and Germany, endorsing comprehensivization as a means of overcoming class barriers to educational opportunities and of postponing school selection decisions. Children from their working-class following came from families with lower cultural attainments than did middle-class children. Thus the Social Democrats reasoned that if selection were to take place at age eighteen rather than age eleven, the children from lower social strata would then have had more formal education that might compensate for their family background. Most reformers also thought that keeping youth together in the same classes and schools was socially beneficial. Pro-selection parents disagreed, feeling strong attachments to the selective schools (called *grammar schools* in Britain and *Gymnasien* in Germany), which challenged students with a more demanding curriculum.

To understand fully how these distributional choices were formulated, we must clarify patterns of party control at the national and subnational levels. In Sweden the Social Democrats led the national and most local governments throughout the decades of educational reform, from 1950 to

1970, and by 1976, when the non-Socialists won national government power for the first time since 1932, almost all education decisions had been made. In Germany for the fifteen-year period from 1966 to 1981, all the Länder except for Lower Saxony remained in control of the same party or party coalition. In Britain, by contrast, there was more frequent shift of party control not only at the national, but also at the local level. Thus, many of the 146 LEAs shifted from Labour to Conservative, or vice versa, at least once. Since the British tended to use local elections to voice protest against the party in national power, many local areas had a much more checkered party control than did the German states. Surprisingly, this tended to favor progress toward comprehensivization, because it discouraged Tory attempts to undo what Labour had promoted during its phases in power.

The greater significance of private school alternatives in Britain, compared to Germany, eased the movement toward comprehensives there. Margaret Thatcher was the first Conservative prime minister to have graduated from a grammar school; all her predecessors had been educated at private independent schools (there called *public schools*), most of them at the especially prestigious schools, such as Eton, Harrow, and Winchester, which have for generations educated the sprigs of the English upper and upper-middle classes. Even the 1979 Thatcher cabinet included only two grammar school graduates among a majority of private school graduates. This pattern might be contrasted with the Christian Democratic Union (CDU) leadership, who had all graduated from public institutions, since Germany has only very few prestigious private secondary schools. Indeed, it has been observed that the Conservative leadership had an easier time acquiescing in the movement to make the grammar schools less elite, since members of their social strata could after all afford more selective education for their children outside the public sector.

When Edward Heath, leading the Conservatives back into power in 1970, appointed Margaret Thatcher to the Education Ministry, he did not realize that he was giving national exposure to the woman who would take the Conservative party leadership away from him five years later. Indeed if Thatcher came to win the hearts of the right-wing Tories, it was not because she reversed the ongoing comprehensivization patterns. She did replace her predecessor's Circular 10/65 with her own Circular 10/70, which essentially directed the LEAs to submit comprehensivization proposals if they wanted to, but not to feel compelled to do so. She also scored some points in the private v. public question by cutting back on free school milk and meals. But otherwise she did not try to block any of the pending school reorganization proposals or to veto the additional ones that came to the Ministry from the LEAs. Consequently, the proportion of secondary students in comprehensive schools did not decrease during the 1970–74 Tory period in government, but actually increased from one-third to over one-half (Bellaby, p. 11).

During the late 1970s an anti-comprehensive backlash spread through the conservative parties in both Britain and Germany as a result of economic change. The energy crisis of 1973–74 ushered in a period of low growth, causing the skilled job market to stagnate, which in turn affected the expectations parents held for their children's future. Middle-class parents became less willing to yield accustomed education advantages, and right-wing politicians built on these fears to launch more strident attacks on the "leveling" strategies they attributed to their leftist opponents. In Germany this produced a decline in the number of comprehensive schools to be founded to only about ten a year during the 1974–78 period.

Education and Parties' Reform Capacity

Clearly, Sweden, Britain, and Germany were able to adopt and implement the comprehensive school model at different rates. Sweden was quickest to enact reforms, followed by Britain and then by Germany. Figure 2.3 compares developments in the three countries over the decades following similar take-off points. If Britain did not fully match the Swedish reform pace, it has come reasonably close to approaching it: Fifteen years after reform proposals were first placed on the national agenda, about two-thirds of the students were in comprehensives, and after twenty-five years the proportion rose to between 85 and 90 percent. Germany's implementation pace, however, was much slower than Britain's: After fifteen years only

FIGURE 2.3 PROPORTION OF PUPILS ENROLLED IN COMPREHENSIVIZED SCHOOLS, 1950–1980

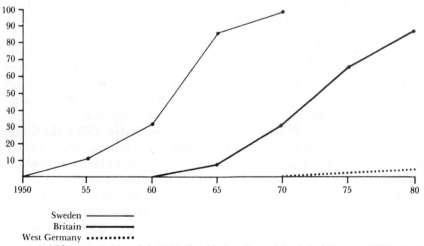

Sweden ————
Britain ————
West Germany ••••••••••

SOURCES *Utbildningsstatistisk arsbok, 1978* (Stockholm: Central Statistical Bureau, 1978). *Statistiches Jahrbuch der BRD, 1979* (Stuttgart, 1979), p. 338. "Schools in England and Wales," *Statistics of Education, 1979,* Vol. 1 (London: HMSO, 1979).

about 2 percent of German secondary pupils were in comprehensives. Moreover, while most British grammar schools were converted to comprehensives in the 1970s, the number of German *Gymnasien* showed no decrease. Rather, they became more accessible to a larger number of students.

To refine our conclusions about party influence on education reforms, we must sharpen our understanding of differences in *context*. In making the distributional choice of whether to comprehensivize or not, what mattered ultimately were the instruments available to national governments to press comprehensivization, and the power allowed to local governments to resist it. The obstacle presented by the great Land powers in Germany's federal system was stronger than the potential obstruction by the British LEAs. Equally important, in terms of the cyclical nature of support for education reform, were factors of *timing*. It was easier for British reformers to marshal ideological support during the affluent and optimistic 1960s than it was for the Germans ten or fifteen years later. Sometimes nations may enjoy certain "advantages of lateness" in policy adoption, but in the pessimistic late 1970s it was the opponents of comprehensive reform who managed to pinpoint and capitalize on the shortcomings of comprehensivization in pioneering countries such as Sweden.

What do these comparisons suggest about the capacity of political parties to carry through education reforms like comprehensivization? The Swedish case illustrates that under optimal conditions a party such as the Social Democrats can provide leadership—for allies in the trade unions, in the bureaucracy, and in other parties—to carry reform through thoroughly in a period of economic growth. In Sweden as well as in Britain, the Left had the advantage of operating within a unitary system, which meant that the national party leaderships held strong positions. Thus, even though local British Conservatives could delay LEA introduction, they did not control arenas which could compete for national attention in the way that the German CDU education ministers did. Moreover, the incremental strategy allowed the center to wear down the hold-out LEAs by waiting until local opponents declined in electoral or financial support. As the number of hold-out LEAs diminished, the Conservative national party tended to lose interest and the issue dropped on the national agenda.

When Thatcher led the Tories back to power in the 1980s, the Conservatives bided their time in education changes, but during their third term in office, in 1988, the government passed a bill that pursued an ingenious strategy involving both centralizing and decentralizing tendencies. It was intended to put great pressure on local districts, many of which were under Labour control, from both above and below. From above the power of the central government was strengthened by the introduction of a national curricula (see discussion earlier in this chapter) and by allowing schools to opt out of local authority control so as to receive direct central government funding. This can be achieved by approval of a simple majority of parents voting on the issue.

The bill facilitated the break-up of education authorities like those in inner London but also elsewhere, and devised ingenious ways in which middle-class parents could help to transfer children out of schools with a social or racial makeup which was not to their liking. It also empowered the boards of individual schools to win control of their budgets. Local education authorities are required to submit mechanisms for accomplishing this decentralization, and if they do not, the minister of education can impose them directly. The bill also transferred control of polytechnic colleges from local to national government. Through this sweeping enlargement of central government power the Thatcher government sharply modified a long-standing Conservative commitment to protect local government powers. In its long-term impact the legislation seemed to pave the way for combining some Japanese-type patterns of competition between schools, with some of the American-type opportunities for asserting preferences of influential groups of parents at the neighborhood level. It was aimed at weakening the ability of teachers, their unions, and other educators—and was in line with a policy using competition to weaken professional groups in favor of business and lay influence. The measure could lead to restratifying secondary education, not by bringing back the unpopular pre-reform system of "eleven-plus," but by creating incentives for the creation of invidious school differences which appear legitimated through initiatives and votes by parents.

As high school education has become more universal, the problem of reconciling universalism and selection has become sharper. Comprehensive education is one way of coping with this challenge, in that it allows selection to occur more subtly and over a longer period of a youth's school life, thus making it more politically acceptable. But the 1990s are experiencing calls for a reversal of the reforms of the 1960s by restoring the earlier tougher forms of selection. "Should they cite the case of Japan, then it would have to be pointed out that the basic building-block of Japanese education is common schooling—it is only the ferocious competition engendered by aspiring parents that distorts it. . . . Even the Japanese are afraid that the products of such schooling lack the creativity which, with all their faults, the British and American systems manage to foster—sometimes" (Timmons, p. 207).

UNIVERSITY PROGRAMS AND SOCIETAL NEEDS
RESTRAINTS AND INNOVATION

From the 1960s, European universities were inundated by greater numbers of secondary school graduates and thus faced questions of how to alter admissions and graduation requirements and, later, how to stretch reduced resources to cover vastly expanded functions. In the name of university reform, all manner of innovations were tried—from the leveling of admission requirements to the imposition of tight quotas even at the department level. Novel allocation mechanisms ranged from centralized national student assignment agencies, as in Sweden and Germany, to the adoption of lottery-based admissions procedures in the Netherlands. At issue were questions also controversial on American campuses—for example, how much admission criteria for medical schools should differ from those for other professional schools. Where high school graduates could enter any faculty of their choice, as in Italy, some faculties were immensely overloaded. But where bureaucrats sought to stem student flow with "limited capacity" arguments, their rules were sometimes invalidated by the courts as infringements on students' rights to train for a profession of their choice (Merritt).

Besides the rapid growth, university problems in Europe were aggravated by the absence of the hierarchies of institutional prestige and tuition levels which served to balance student demand with institutional capacity in the United States. In order to rationalize their selection procedures European authorities tried to introduce qualitative institutional distinctions, but mostly faculty and students warded off such attempts.

Japan's university hierarchy is the most explicit in the world, and it differs from the American one, insofar as the most prestigious universities are public ones like Tokyo University. Some private universities also have high status, but most of them cater to 75 percent of the students who do not pass the entrance exams of national universities (Geiger, p. 30). Some private medical schools charge close to $100,000 in annual fees, even though their students do poorly on the medical examinations which lead to licenses. Japan's women students, who are only one third as numerous as male university students, find it difficult to compete in the public system. In America barriers to women have been largely removed from universities, and in Western Europe a male advantage in university attendance has been reduced from about 2:1 in 1960 to 4:3 by 1980 (Haag, p. 44).

How do working-class students become the first in their families to reach the university? According to those who stress motivations, it happens mainly through the contagious diffusion of aspirations. "Over time, successively lower social strata assimilate aspirations for advancement through schooling" (Anderson 1979, p. 413). While middle-class students may go to the university for cultural motives, those from the lower strata need to anticipate rewards in terms of status and income improvement.

As long as economic growth promised to create more openings for professional workers, governments could choose to promote the contagion of aspirations by lowering financial and psychological barriers to university attendance. Thus in Britain the proportion of university students who came from working-class families increased in the prosperous 1960s to 21 percent in 1969 (Heidenheimer 1977, p. 426). Even in Germany various routes—including the more accessible *Gymnasien*—caused the working-class proportion of university student bodies to increase from 4 percent in 1952 to about 15 percent in the late 1970s. In the United States "affirmative action," meant to compensate for previous exclusion or segregation policies, contributed to a doubling of the number of black students in higher education. Indeed, black high school graduates tended to become *more* likely to attend college than whites. However, with the tightening of student financial aid under the Reagan administration, the proportion of black college students declined significantly in the 1980s.

American graduates of secondary schools can compensate for their weaker academic backgrounds through "second, third and fourth chances in a fashion unimaginable in most other systems of higher education" (Clark 1985, p. 315). They can enroll in colleges with widely varying standards, and move back and forth between them, which in turn conditions their option for professional studies. Students enrolling in community colleges can go on to the four-year state universities, but the proportion using this option vary widely, as between 4 percent in California and 30 percent in Minnesota in 1979. In California the "reverse transfer" option, from universities to state colleges, has actually exceeded the upward transfer rate into the state university system (Boyer, in Jacques and Richardson, p. 20).

In European universities somewhat different conflicts developed between the pressure of student numbers, the anticipated needs of the labor market, and the content and structure of university curricula. In centralized systems such as Sweden's, bureaucrats went furthest in rationalizing university systems against the strong opposition of many students and professors; a radical reorganization of universities has mandated that most course offerings be related to programs leading into the various labor markets. By giving academic credit for work experience, the Swedes caused students to postpone studies to the point where the majority are now over twenty-five years old. And, to reduce the danger of large numbers of unemployed graduates, the Swedish universities in the 1980s extended *numerus clausus* to admissions policies; that is, they set national admissions quotas for the various fields of study and admitted only as many students as planners projected could be utilized in the foreseeable future.

Educational planning based on anticipation of future needs is more difficult to carry through successfully in Western market economies than in the Eastern Communist countries. There long-term plans project economic changes, and the resultant personnel needs can then be translated into the rates at which educational institutions are expected to produce various groups of professionals, thus allowing synchronization. In Western countries the far longer periods required to reach targets compound the problems of unanticipated change which are characteristic of market economies. There "both the total number of job opportunities and its annual variations are time-dependent in barely foreseeable or specifiable ways, with the result that matching input/output coefficients of higher education flows is very difficult indeed" (Sadlak, p. 403).

With student numbers quadrupling in two decades, Europe found itself in an era of mass higher education much more suddenly than had been the case in America. The centralized Continental systems found it difficult to replicate the somewhat subtle American selection mechanisms through which students are not shunted in or out of higher education, but instead are channeled into institutions of varying quality when they enroll in colleges and graduate or professional schools. The highly systematized Continental systems lack the flexibility which makes these informal rankings possible, and hence their bureaucrats were forced to devise generalized rules to deal with problems of student selection. At one extreme was the rule of "open admission" to any university faculty for students who had secondary certificates; at the other was a system of assigning first-year places in all faculties solely according to computerized rankings of high school grades. Operating close to the latter model, central Swedish and German assignment bureaus in Stockholm and Dortmund allocate students to particular departments, often in universities other than the ones students have actually requested (Neusel and Teichler). To study their subject in a university of their preference, students must advertise to exchange places with someone with the reverse preference.

Centralized student assignment systems presume of course that the grade/test ranking criteria further meritocratic equity in terms of societal needs. But is society best served if the high achievers apply disproportionately to high prestige professional schools, leaving to other departments only those with lower scores? In an era of declining research funds, recruitment of the best students to basic science disciplines worsens relative to applied fields. Looking at employment prospects, many abler students decide that they cannot "afford" to study biology or physics and opt for medicine or engineering instead (Neave 1981, p. 148).

Are health care needs really best served if most medical students are selected from the top 5 percent of high school graduates? Will those high achievers make good primary-care physicians, if that is what is going to be needed most ten years later? Some countries think the answer is no and have therefore chosen to allocate medical school places by lottery. The Netherlands operates a weighted system under which all applicants who pass a moderate grade threshold in specified subjects participate in the lottery, but those with higher grades have more entry forms put in for them (Karstanje, in Neave, 1981, p. 205). Germany in 1980 also began to allocate some of its medical school places in this way, responding to a suggestion from its constitutional court that such a selection method might serve to extend the protection of the constitutional right to choose freely a profession or place of training (Merritt).

Sometimes when education ministries try to nudge university professors and students toward the apparent needs of the labor market or of society, the quality of education declines. In 1976 the French tried a variant of the Swedish approach by passing a decree aimed at revamping university curricula so that all programs would have clear outlets into the labor market. Since no additional funds were provided, however, the universities felt pressured to close down programs that were of less vocational relevance. This decree led to the largest French student demonstration since 1968; in contrast to Sweden, the ministry backed down and agreed to continue all existing programs.

Later, when the Chirac government in 1987 attempted to push through changes to toughen entrance requirements and to introduce formal status differences among universities, students again mobilized in protest and were successful in blocking the change. The successful utilization of mass demonstrations to defeat proposals in both non-Socialist and Socialist governments thus continued to distinguish the French education policy arena from among countries surveyed here, where such efforts have seldom had veto effects on the national level.

In Britain, the intended effect of the 1988 Education Act on higher education was aimed at weakening institutions so as to make them more responsive to various outside influences. The University Grants Committee, through which universities had decided on fund allocations collectively, was replaced by a University Funding Council, which lost its predecessor's "right to advise the government on the needs of universities." A parallel body was set up for polytechnics and colleges, thus giving the central Education Ministry sweeping powers to determine funding. This is used to bring about mergers between departments and colleges. Another radical change was one which had been resisted by most Conservatives elsewhere, namely the abolition of academic tenure. It enabled institutions to dismiss university professors for redundancy or any "good cause." Thus junior faculty who had previously enjoyed strong job protection were placed in a more dependent position, while senior professors were also put on limited contracts.

The Fate of European University Innovations

The opportunities and limits for new departures in European university innovations can be illustrated with reference to two such efforts during the 1960s and 1970s—the establishment of the Open University in Britain by a Labour government to allow adults over twenty-one to pursue university courses at special centers and through correspondence courses, and the creation of Comprehensive Universities or *Gesamthochschulen* (GHS) in Germany. According to 1971 Federal guidelines, all the GHS structures were to unify tertiary institutions in the same locality so as to create a coordinated system that would allow credit transferability and to permit meaningful combination of academic study and practical experience. All new universities were supposed to be based on this model. By the time the GHS model was legislated in 1976 it had been diluted so as to gain the support of all Land governments. But in fact no additional foundings ever occurred. The only six German *Gesamthochschulen* were ones founded before 1972, in one of two Social Democratic Party–ruled Länder and in regions where there was an obvious shortage of student places. By the late 1980s they had become isolated outposts in German higher education, and the Kohl government then undertook to phase them out by converting them back to the conventional model.

In Britain by contrast, what had originated as the brainchild pet of a Labour prime minister, Harold Wilson, became in time also a favorite of the Thatcher government, thus receiving better financial nurturance than the traditional universities did in the 1980s. In 1991, after twenty years, the Open University will have taught half a million students.

Why did the German *Gesamthochschulen* fail even more than the comprehensive schools, or *Gesamtschulen*, while the British Open University flourished? One reason for the latter's success lay in the fact that many of the students that it attracted in the first two decades were adults that would not have been eligible to attend universities, and hence were not directly competitive with them. Creating additional routes of access for additional groups, whether based on age or region, proved less threatening to established elites than undermining established prestige and status symbols. The GHS represented potential threats to all universities in a way that the Open University, which was initially headed by a respected Conservative educator, did not. The abortive GHS experiment illustrates that innovators may be "allowed to start, but unless they attach the interests of various groups to their own, persuading potential opponents at least to be moderate in their opposition, they can be tightly bounded—resocialized or terminated as others raise their own level of concern, and increase the bearing of their own weight" (Kerr, in Cerych and Sabatier, p. 266). The GHS and other components of German higher education reforms have been analyzed as having had some crucial differences from other German policy sectors. In this sector more than in others the proposed reforms were nonincremental, and centralized social institutions could not moderate conflict that became polarized along party lines (Katzenstein).

But in overall university access Britain fell behind Germany. Whereas in Germany the proportion of the age group in upper secondary and higher education continued to increase, Britain experienced stagnation or even decline. Whereas the proportion of German eighteen-year-olds who stayed in full-time schooling doubled to 40 percent between 1970 and 1980, the proportion of British students decreased from 17 to 16 percent, just about the lowest in Western Europe after Switzerland. In France as in Germany, the proportion of the age group entering higher education continued to increase toward the 25 percent level in the 1980s; Britain's 1995 target for university entrants is 18 percent, or only about one quarter the 74 percent rate that France plans to reach by the year 2000. Part of the blame has been placed on the lack of governmental action to encourage demand through affirmative action, and part to the fact that "Britain's drive toward mass higher education was not accompanied by a significant change in values and attitudes toward that enterprise" (Neave 1985, p. 357).

In 1984 the Oxford faculty voted against giving Margaret Thatcher an honorary degree, and the *Times Higher Education Supplement* charged that her government had put universities on "the symbolic hit list," along with the civil service and local government autonomy. Reviewing the preceding struggles, a German observer noted "such far-reaching dimensions of intimidation and institutional endangerment" that even a serious provocation like that of Oxford "becomes understandable." Evidently the struggle over university control engendered far deeper partisan divisions than comprehensivization had earlier. In Germany it was the other way around. By the late 1970s the perceived need to avoid further cuts had stimulated reduced conflict and a mood for compromise. The disputes, it was feared, would lead to growing apathy and desperation among youth. German university staff were also protected by the fact that the stronger tenure that most enjoyed made it harder for German governments to "impose major structural changes through radical shrinkage of personnel," in the way that the British government was doing (Gellert, p. 290).

That British universities did not elicit more widespread support in their struggle with Mrs. Thatcher has been partly attributed to their narrower conception of their mission. Not able to resist turning academic standards into a fetish, some academic leaders seemed to perpetuate an underlying elite anti-industrial bias. From an American perspective, the universities had restricted the circle of potential allies by emphasizing selectivity at the cost of diversity. When the chips were down, respect did not convert into political support, and an American friend feared that "British higher education in the foreseeable future will be the object of central government policies based on suspicion and lack of trust, and it faces that grim prospect without many friends!" (Trow, 1988, p. 89).

Degree Value and Career Expectations

How have countries varied in the way they have encountered and coped with an oversupply of university graduates, and what lessons have they drawn from other cases? In 1976 the German Education Ministry commissioned a study of how its situation compared with that of other countries, resulting in the analysis shown in Figure 2.4. It distinguished

FIGURE 2.4 HIGHER EDUCATION GRADUATES IN THE LABOR MARKET, 1976

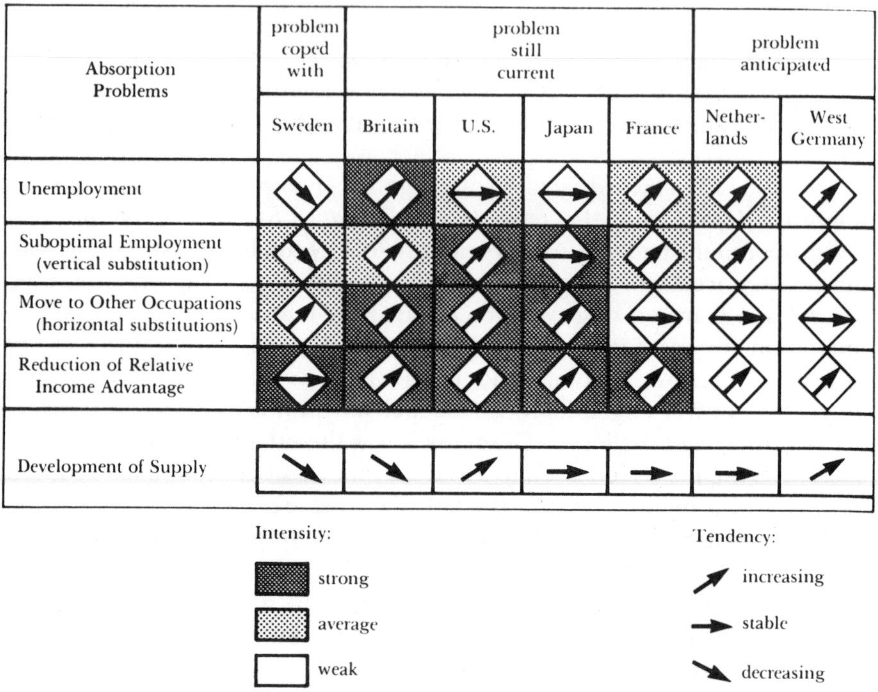

Absorption Problems	problem coped with	problem still current				problem anticipated	
	Sweden	Britain	U.S.	Japan	France	Nether-lands	West Germany
Unemployment							
Suboptimal Employment (vertical substitution)							
Move to Other Occupations (horizontal substitutions)							
Reduction of Relative Income Advantage							
Development of Supply							

Intensity:

◼ strong

▨ average

☐ weak

Tendency:

↗ increasing

→ stable

↘ decreasing

countries which had by then resolved, were then grappling with, and would yet anticipate problems of excess graduates, coding countries on the degree to which they were facing four problems of labor market integration. Sweden was identified as most successful partly because academic unemployment and vertical substitution seemed to be diminishing whereas all other countries except Japan were facing escalation of those problems. Britain and the United States were rated as having serious and intensifying problems in three out of four problem areas, largely as a byproduct of lower economic growth.

In comparing the past employment patterns of their own graduates with those in countries such as the United States, the Germans noted a much higher proportion—about 60 to 70 percent—were going into professional jobs in the public sector. Many of these were teachers, for whom there would be less need because of the smaller number of school-age children in the 1980s. Because of the fiscal consequences of lowered growth and tighter public budgets, they also anticipated many fewer positions developing in other public service areas. They considered cutting back university enrollments, but the unions and other groups protested that this would cause high school graduates to compete for white-collar jobs and simply push unemployment down the skill scale.

Whereas in the Communist countries, and also Japan, entry into a high-status university virtually guarantees a career slot in a public or private bureaucracy, in systems like the American, students assume many more risks because there are many labor markets, each tied in particular ways to the education structure. The options open to young American physicians changed sharply in the 1980s. The demand for various kinds of engineers also fluctuated sharply, partly in response to the ebb and flow of defense appropriations. The pull of better-paying jobs in American industry made it difficult for university engineering colleges to retain highly trained engineers to teach students and pursue research (Kerr and Gade).

But to what extent will there continue to be nationally circumscribed labor markets for professional personnel? The globalization of industries and markets which proceeded so quickly in the 1980s greatly increased the potential for employers to substitute different national work forces. Within the European community it has become possible for professionals licensed in one member country to seek to practice in another one; this has slowly begun to increase the mobility of professionals, and it may do so more in the 1990s. The question is how closely particular professions are tied to particular national cultures. Lawyers are largely confined to practicing within their particular national or even subnational settings, physicians less so, and engineers still less so.

* * * * *

In education policy, then, we can identify some convergence between American and European policies with regard to the distribution of educational opportunities. Institutional policy instruments and selection mechanisms effect considerable national variations in the way that opportunities are allocated and linked to labor market requirements. Variations in demographic patterns and social demands, together with an unusually complex pattern of conflicting interests, help shape strong cyclical patterns in the priority accorded this policy area. But education enjoys relatively strong political agenda support, and is an area where, as further discussed in Chapter Ten, popular satisfaction with public programs is relatively similar in both Europe and the United States.

The 1980s have witnessed a revival of conflicting perspectives about which goals of educational policies should be dominant. Those who saw education as closely linked to the welfare state had to defend reforms aimed at reduction of inequalities against those who urged that strategies be shaped by the need to remain competitive in international markets. The way in which Japan imbued higher levels of numeracy and literacy was linked to its economic success, and the broader competence of its work force was held to be a model for the West. Britain went farthest in abandoning much of its earlier traditions and embracing central controls to reshape its system. In federal systems, such as America and Germany, pluralist patterns more easily allowed simultaneous pursuit of diverse goals, while France moved in a similar direction by decentralizing financial and curricular controls within its education system.

3
HEALTH POLICY

The incidence of illness is different from that of ignorance, and the clients of health care systems are age-skewed in a way drastically different from that of school populations. Whereas one caters predominantly to the young, the other is more concerned with the elderly. In both cases increased supply generates additional demand for services. The provision of more and better secondary education, if accompanied by a "contagion of aspirations," leads to demand for more university places. Breakthroughs in the treatment of disease create additional patient need among those who otherwise would have died at an earlier age.

Families would hate to have to decide that Grandpa should forgo life-prolonging care so that Junior can go to college. In earlier days that choice was usually accentuated by market mechanisms, and sometimes softened by charity opportunities. Then the growing free provision of public services transferred the locus of choices, since demands in both fields were so highly legitimized. Education and health were both among the fastest-growing public sectors when economic growth provided ample public budgets, as in the 1960s. Since then, education expenditures have been suppressed in a way that health expenditures have not, partly because the elderly have become relatively more numerous as both clients and organized voters, and also because governments find it more difficult to implement tough decisions in the health sector.

Of course all age groups have some need for health care, and this has increased the incentive for governments to become financers of last resort at the minimum, and general providers of care at the maximum. Providing health insurance for industrial workers so that medical treatment could help them to resume their productive lives (as Chancellor Otto von Bismarck led Germany to choose in 1883) implied economic benefits for the whole society. Thus national legislation began to transform the mandate which the health system was given by society (Field 1973). No longer were governments content to license certain practitioners to give orthodox medical treatment; now they began to use various incentives and compulsion mechanisms to prescribe where, to whom, and, increasingly, how such care should be provided.

CHOICES IN HEALTH POLICY

Scope and Thresholds

The legislative initiatives as to which social groups in an industrial society should be assured health care have been clearly the results of political choices, not merely the products of socioeconomic development. For example, consider the British introduction of national health insurance of the German model: Had it been determined solely by the pace of industrialization, such a system should have been adopted a half-century before Germany, and not a quarter-century later, as it was. The governments which led public intervention into the health delivery sphere—paternalist monarchies in countries such as Germany and Sweden—sought to anticipate the demands which working-class parties were later to press directly (and to implement when they in turn came to power). In the United States, the relative slowness in public health legislation can be strongly attributed to the later and weaker political organization of labor.

As they function today, the Western European systems reflect different varieties of government intervention due to political choices made in earlier eras. German political leaders from the 1920s to the 1950s transformed their insurance-based arrangements into a *corporatized* system, under which health providers and recipients regulate themselves and one another in accordance with rules prescribed by the state. The British in the 1940s chose to have the national government assume direct responsibility for health care, thus creating a truly *nationalized* system. A more decentralized version of the British model was implemented in Sweden. American decisions to delay intervention produced a *segmented* system, under which several public subsystems—for the poor, the elderly, and military veterans—coexist with a myriad of other privately financed activities.

Instruments of Health Policy

The choice of legislative and administrative health policy instruments has produced varying patterns in different countries. In contrast to the near monopoly of the British National Health Service, Sweden relies on the counties to operate most health facilities as well as to finance them from their own taxes. In Germany hospitals are financed by the state governments, though most health licensing and insurance powers rest with national agencies. In the United States federal legislation has established the larger public programs, while state and local governments have maintained limited roles; some programs, in fact, are jointly financed by federal and state governments, though some states choose to stay out of such arrangements (as Arizona has done with regard to Medicaid, for example).

The constraints on governmental choices are greater where certain kinds of health delivery functions are already being performed by private or subnational public organizations. Although the British case illustrates that national governments can sometimes preempt such activities, in the 1960s the Swedish national government provided a different example, yielding important ground to regional governments.

Governments also make choices, directly or through delegation, regarding which kinds of personnel may provide what kinds of medical care. Should osteopaths and homeopaths be allowed to compete with orthodox medical school graduates? Should primary care be reserved to general practitioners, and specialists limited to practicing mainly in public hospitals?

The Distribution of Health Care

Governmental choices pertaining to the distribution of health care face greater constraints than do those about education. Definitions of illness are subject to interpretation by both doctors and patients, and involve a vast battery of standardized tests. Governments can give priority to research on certain diseases, but delivering the resulting remedies—for example, to those who need it but do not know they do—poses great problems. One thing governments can do is influence the geographical and social distribution of hospitals and physicians' offices.

Let us consider the geographical distribution of doctors. Problems of under-doctoring in rural areas and inferior services in poverty locations are especially evident if private purchasing power is the strongest magnet for hospital and physician location, as in the United States. An instrument like Medicaid, for example, which is targeted only at the poor, invites abuses which are less likely to occur where public funding supports care for both the middle and lower classes. But even in nationalized systems equalized health care access may be a problem, because doctors, more than other professionals, prefer to practice in urban centers and university towns. Whereas in some countries teachers are assigned to both a given school and town, physicians have to be induced, mainly through payment mechanisms, to provide the care that is needed where it is needed.

Restraints and Innovation in Health Policy

How should governments ascertain the efficiency and effectiveness of health services, in both the public and private sectors, and what strategies should they follow to improve deficiencies? These goals and options, which frame a fourth set of governmental choices in the health sector, are complicated by general disagreement over the criteria that determine which patients are getting "too much" or "too little," or "better" or "poorer" health care.

In order to devise more effective and efficient health care delivery methods, planners have suggested innovations ranging from pilot projects to large-scale reorganizations. They have been asked to ascertain where medical resources have been distributed in an ineffective or inequitable manner, and to suggest remedies. Their recommendations have been most easily implemented in the more homogeneous systems such as the British and Swedish ones. In the segmented American system, recommendations about allocation have been more difficult to implement, and hence their effectiveness has been more tenuous.

Proposals for restraints or innovations to bring down the costs of the total health sector have received top priority. Those seeking to improve efficiency by increasing competition have proposed manipulating modes of payment for doctors and hospitals. Planners are dubious that such "a discipline of the market place" can be applied in the health sector; hence, they have focused more on rationing expensive new technology and related specialties in their efforts to keep health facilities more within their budgets.

PUBLIC AND PROFESSIONAL CONTROLS
SCOPE AND THRESHOLDS

The road to revolution may have been paved in some nations' classrooms, but hardly ever has it begun in their hospitals. Partly as a result of the realization that health services are difficult to allocate in accord with uniform bureaucratic rules, nations have varied about whether and how far to transform health systems into public monopolies. The directness of state control—whether it relies mainly on regulation, financing, or actual management of medical care—has varied more in health care than in education.

The Extent of Government Intervention

Though all Western systems have gone beyond mere licensing to assume financing responsibilities, most prominently through compulsory health insurance programs, the scope of their programs varies. Whereas in Britain health insurance was a stepping stone to a nationally managed health service system, in Germany it was not. Even where financing has become predominantly public, some countries have let both financing and management remain at the regional level, as in Sweden. Of the nations we are considering here, the United States has only grudgingly expanded the public finance component, and has shown the least tendency to expand the direct health care delivery role of public institutions.

In Britain, public health jurisdiction developed rapidly and consistently, taking place in three stages, as shown in Table 3.1. Several factors facilitated the establishment of a nationalized public health system there. For one thing, extensive benefit systems were developed voluntarily by trade unions and the Friendly Societies and later utilized by public programs. For another, local public health bureaucracies—similar to the county governments in Sweden or the Sickness Funds in Germany—did not oppose nationalization. Last, the medical profession itself was somewhat divided on the whole insurance issue and so did not present the unified opposition which organized medicine in the United States did.

In 1948 the National Health Service (NHS) Act gave the British government, especially the Ministry of Health, greater direct control of more health subsystems than has been achieved by any other Western government. It made Britain the Western model for a system which was not only collectively financed, but *nationalized;* its components were directly run by the national government. From an administrative point of view, the most dramatic aspect of the British NHS reform was the virtually complete takeover by the national government of voluntary as well as municipal hospitals, and their integration within larger regions that superseded local and county borders. Moreover, the NHS financed the health system largely from general revenue, thus moving away from reliance on insurance contributions.

In twentieth-century America, public health long remained limited to

TABLE 3.1 THE DEVELOPMENT OF THE PUBLIC HEALTH SECTOR IN BRITAIN

Date	Stage of Development	Specific Developments
Late 19th century	Infrastructure growth	Friendly Society insurance for physicians' services Strong local government health responsibilities
1911	Public health financing prototype	Compulsory health insurance—at first only for low-income workers, later expanded
1948	Full National Health Service	Free medical treatment for all residents National operation of all hospitals Standardized remuneration schemes

the predominantly preventive and sanitary preoccupations associated with it in the nineteenth century. Within the segmented system, the public sector ranked low in prestige, scientific interest, and financial support. Public hospitals in the United States continued to cater mainly to the poor, especially in the cities, and public health expenditures increased at a snail-like pace, from 0.4 percent of the Gross National Product (GNP) in 1913 to 0.7 percent in 1932. In 1964 expenditures still stood at less than 1 percent of the GNP. Not until 1965 did the federal government even assume the role of compulsory insurance administrator, which the British government had assumed in 1911 and used as an entering wedge for growing public responsibilities.

The first bitter campaign against U.S. health insurance, in 1918, convinced advocates in subsequent unsuccessful attempts in 1936 and in 1947 to 1948 that "the less identification with Europe, the better." After one debate on Medicare, the British Medical Association's *Journal* deplored "the vulgarity and cheapness of the AMA's past and present attacks upon the National Health Service" (Skidmore, pp. 354–355). Starting early in the 1950s, U.S. health insurance protagonists shifted to an accretionist strategy of relating their proposals to the earlier popular social security programs. Whereas most European countries had initiated health insurance programs by providing coverage for low-income workers, in the United States the initial group was the aged, first covered in 1965 by Medicare. Like Bismarck's original sickness insurance program of 1883, Medicare has operated as a *categorical* program, for which only a small population group is eligible. With a coverage of some twenty million Americans aged sixty-five and over, Medicare insures about 10 percent of the population, a proportion similar to the German one of the 1880s.

How countries differ in their public and private emphasis can be measured in a number of ways. Table 3.2 shows the sources of health financing, though it should be pointed out that some of the public financing may flow through private health care structures. Two of the most public systems,

TABLE 3.2 PUBLIC AND PRIVATE SOURCES OF HEALTH CARE FINANCING, 1982

	Britain	Sweden	Germany	France	Italy	United States
General Taxation	78.0	71.0	14.2	1.8	36.2	
Public Insurance	10.0	18.4	72.5	73.0	45.5	
Total Public	88.0	89.4	86.7	74.8	81.7	43.0
Direct Consumer Payments	8.2	8.6	6.9	21.5	15.0	26.2
Private Insurance	3.8	2.0	6.4	3.7	3.3	30.8
Total Private	12.0	10.6	13.3	25.2	18.3	57.0

SOURCE Bundesministerium für Arbeit, *Gesundheitssysteme im internationalen Vergleich*, Bonn, 1988, p. 225.

Britain and Sweden, finance the bulk of health expenditures from general taxation, relying only modestly on either public health insurance or private sources of any kind (Table 3.3). In the systems which rely primarily on health insurance financing—France, West Germany, and the Netherlands— the dependence on public sources is still predominant, though not as many of the health care facilities are publicly operated in these countries as in Britain and Sweden. The American system, by sharp contrast, draws its predominant financing from the private sector, even though public sources have increased greatly since the 1960s. Its segmented character is reflected in the fact that taxation, private insurance, and direct consumer payments each accounted for between a quarter and a third of revenue, with public insurance like Medicare trailing behind.

The role of both private voluntary insurance systems and of private delivery systems is much more extensive in the United States than in other countries. Though they are not public institutions in the way that German Sickness Funds are, American third payers such as Blue Cross and Blue Shield are becoming similar to these in their functions. Whereas private health insurance plans still loom larger in American health finance, their role in Germany is marginal compared to the role of the publicly mandated systems. The same holds for Japan, where two insurance systems with sharply different benefit options operate within the public sphere. Successive attempts to fuse them have been blocked by vested interests of labor and business, despite support for fusion by organized medicine.

TABLE 3.3 PUBLIC EXPENDITURE AS A PERCENT OF TOTAL HEALTH EXPENDITURE, 1960–85

Country	1960	1975	1980	1985
Australia	47.1	73.0	62.5	74.0
Britain	84.6	90.9	89.5	91.2
Canada	43.6	76.7	74.3	76.2
France	58.1	77.9	80.0	79.1
Germany	68.1	80.8	79.7	78.0
Japan	60.0	73.2	69.7	72.7
Netherlands	33.3	76.6	79.3	78.3
New Zealand	81.8	82.8	83.3	80.0
Norway	78.8	95.5	98.5	96.9
Sweden	72.3	90.0	92.6	90.4
Switzerland	60.6	66.2	65.3	68.4
United States	25.0	42.9	42.4	41.1
OECD Average	60.0	75.4	77.5	76.7

SOURCE OECD, *Financing and Delivering Health Care* (Paris: OECD, 1987); updated by George Schieber.

The Medical Profession and Self-regulation

Of all the major social service occupations, medicine has since the late nineteenth century sustained the fastest rate of scientific and technological improvement. As scientific breakthroughs increased certainty about the causes of contagious diseases and the effects of antiseptics and vaccines, the correlation between physician treatment and patient recovery greatly increased. The doctor's ability to eliminate pain effectively and delay death has helped to rank medicine among the most prestigious professions.

In some American states, medicine was so well entrenched that the medical societies were trusted as the state boards of health. Elsewhere state governors were constitutionally required to appoint health board members from slates submitted by the state affiliates of the AMA. Such provisions were not implemented to the same degree for boards regulating the less prestigious occupations.

Medical claims for self-regulation became stronger as physicians were able to claim a growing monopoly of knowledge of increasingly esoteric and specialized techniques. American doctors for some time did not fully share in this status gain, mainly because of an American lag in phasing out marginal, second-echelon healers and the schools that claimed to train them. In Britain and Germany, improved bureaucratic capabilities had matched scientific advances; rigorous official licensing had helped gradually to raise the standards for physicians.

Scientifically minded American medical leaders for a while supported the idea of giving strong licensing and other powers to the federal government, just as some of them favored following Europe in the extension of public health insurance. Then the alternative of using their own professional association, the American Medical Association (founded in 1847, nationally integrated in 1902), to serve as the key instrument of self-regulation became attractive. Responding to a call from the 1903 AMA convention, medical leaders initiated a vigorous weeding-out process among medical schools on the basis of Abraham Flexner's Carnegie Foundation–sponsored report.

Implementation of the Flexner Report's recommendations, backed up by the "blackballing" powers of the professional elites, led within two decades to a sharp reduction both in the number of medical schools, from 162 to 76, and in the number of doctors, from 157 to 126 per 100,000 (Stevens, 1971).

In some European countries, health care consumers were for a time more effectively organized than physicians. In the nineteenth century, British Friendly Societies organized some three million largely working-class users of health services and exercised strong bargaining power in contracting physicians to treat their members. Germany had similar oganizations, known as Sickness Funds, which became the intermediaries for implementing the first compulsory health insurance for workers in the world introduced by Bismarck in 1883 (Abel-Smith, p. 225).

In Germany the Sickness Funds received better bureaucratic and scientific help from their allies in the trade unions and in the Social Democratic party, and became a prime example of institutionalized *third payers,* which contracted physicians and institutions on behalf of their members. American medical practitioners, on the other hand, successfully combated the creation not only of state-sponsored but even of voluntary third payer groups. Until the 1940s, AMA membership was declared incompatible with treatment of patients under prepaid health insurance plans, and in many instances the use of hospital facilities was denied physicians who defied this rule. In fact, when the third payers Blue Cross and Blue Shield were introduced, they were controlled by hospitals and the medical profession, not by consumers.

Government policies toward the medical profession's claims of autonomy have varied extensively. Sometimes governments have supported medical associations in their quest for tighter professional monopolies. At other times they have undermined the licensing and professional practice rules so as deliberately to place physicians under greater competitive pressure. Since the early nineteenth century, American policies have shifted between the two alternatives more than European ones have.

In Europe the modern governmental tendency has been to recognize and support the attempt of physician associations to share responsibility for health care, but to coopt them by making them instruments of official policies. Means to this end have included compulsory membership in medical associations, granting of franchises to professional associations for certain kinds of care, and recognition of established professional groups as exclusive negotiating partners of governments. At the level of the individual practitioner, this has tended to make the physician less an independent entrepreneur and more a public servant, although subject more to peer rather than to hierarchical pressure.

Thus in Germany membership is obligatory in quasi-public organizations such as the Chamber of Physicians and the Insurance Doctors Association. The physicians who belong to them share legally recognized monopolies in the market for ambulatory medical care, as well as in the formulation and enforcement of rules regarding the practice various groups of doctors can engage in. Office- and hospital-based doctors therefore are subject to quite different constraints. In return for these powers, the medical associations must monitor their members' claims under the health insurance program, and see to it that opportunities for medical treatment are available and publicized at all times. It is this type of system which we label a corporatized one, since it features a deliberate incorporation of public functions with professional and private functions (Heidenheimer 1980).

A comparison with Britain shows that more direct national control of the health system does not necessarily diminish professional autonomy. For since the British national health system has greater financial control than is the case in Germany, the authorities can tolerate greater physician self-control of some conditions of practice. In addition to bargaining exclusively with the British Medical Association over doctors' remuneration claims, the government allows the Association informally to regulate physicians' conditions of practice. But the profession's power to assert itself is limited by direct state management of hospitals, as well as by the general splintering of interests among the physicians. Thus the less prestigious doctors have been able to narrow the income level between themselves and the senior specialists, which has weakened the natural authority pyramids through which the specialists used to exert more distinctive leadership within the profession as a whole (Honigsbaum).

In the United States the monopoly power of the American Medical Association long remained greater than that of its European counterparts because it indirectly controlled the licensing of graduates of AMA-approved medical schools. Leaders of the AMA county affiliates could also determine which doctors were admitted to the staffs of hospitals. Osteopaths and other nonorthodox medical practitioners were denied entry to AMA-recognized hospitals, and so they built their own, though in some states they have come to be blanketed into the AMA after public acceptance made them difficult to boycott. But other potential competitors to physicians, such as chiropractors and optometrists, were combated by the medical association, whose ethics code until recently forbade members from accepting or referring patients from or to these other practitioners (Feldstein, pp. 53–57).

A vigorous attack on the profession's restrictive practices has been pursued since 1975, when the courts ruled that learned professions did not enjoy exemption from antitrust laws. Since then the Federal Trade Commission has sought to strengthen competition between doctors by attacking the legal basis on which medical associations employed ethics codes to prevent doctors from advertising. Also successfully attacked through the courts were the AMA's accrediting powers, the profession's control of some medical insurance programs, and boycotts against physicians who participated in prepaid health systems not approved by the medical societies.

The divesting of the medical association's monopolistic controls was pursued less as an end in itself than as a means of developing potential competitive market pressures. Thus, "If one concludes that antitrust law can in fact be established as a meaningful check on the profession's power to shape its economic environment . . . the entire drift of health policy toward increasingly heavy regulation begins to seem less inevitable" (Havighurst). Though this thrust was consistent with the Reagan administration's aims of dismantling regulations and, instead, seeking to further competition, it encountered strong resistance in Congress.

STRUCTURES FOR INTERVENTION

INSTRUMENTS

Just as countries vary in the structures and techniques they use to implement health policy, so their choice of policy instruments leads in turn to different patterns in different countries. One important element in any nation's health policy is the personnel involved; as we shall see, countries vary also in their policies regarding the training and utilization of physicians.

Policy-making Structures

As the various health care financing and delivering responsibilities assumed by governments suggest, health care is a system to a different extent in different countries. In Europe the agreement of a few ministers and bureaucrats may suffice to set implementable policy goals, whereas in the United States the fragmentation of responsibility requires policymakers to follow carefully considered strategies, with the success of most policies contingent on a long string of conditions. A congressional mandate *may* be implemented, *if* the federal bureaucracies cooperate, *if* they can enlist the cooperation of local officials, *if* the private interests offer support, and so on. Both systems have specialists called health planners, but their ability to implement a program differs greatly.

In Britain once several options crystallize, decisions in the health sector proper can be made rather quickly. If the Minister of Health and the top bureaucrats agree, and if the necessary funds are agreed to by the Treasury, a new set of rules can be issued with some confidence that officials in the health system and local governments will carry them out.

The British and American systems can be used to identify the difference centralized control has on setting priorities for the health system. In the centralized British system, most important budget, personnel, and standard policies are made nationally within the public sector. The American system is decentralized not only because of the division of power at the national level, but also because of the greater role played by diverse private, as well as local and state public authorities, in the shaping of those kinds of decisions. By identifying contrasts drawn from the British-American comparison, one can seek to show what difference greater centralization makes for the relative costliness of health care systems, the degree to which systems permit equality of access to and standards of medical service, as well as other important characteristics of the performance of these systems.

Some of the tendencies extrapolated from this two-nation study, which we can later also try for fit on other groups of national systems, are displayed in Figure 3.1. An apparent advantage of more centralized systems is that they can bring about considerable rationalization of service delivery, thus bringing about greater standardization of health services to different

FIGURE 3.1 CENTRALIZATION AS RELATED TO HEALTH EMPHASES

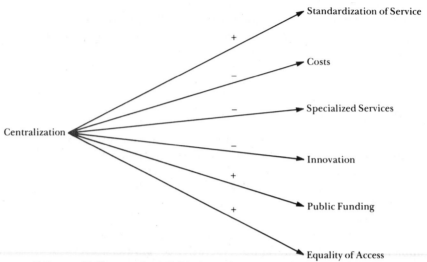

SOURCE J. Rogers Hollingsworth, *A Political Economy of Medicine: Great Britain and the United States* (Baltimore: Johns Hopkins, 1986).

social and geographic client groups. The chances of getting lower-quality health care in the boondocks should also be lower in centralized public than in a decentralized partly private system.

In the British-American example centralization is also associated with high levels of public funding. Does this hold elsewhere as well? Comparisons among other European systems, as between centralized Netherlands and decentralized Switzerland, suggest that it might.

The two above-mentioned tendencies combine to bring about a higher equality of access, for instance among the availability of services in different regions of the country. Thus the interregional differences in the availability of hospitals and doctors may be expected to be lower in nationally run systems than in those where federalism and/or private sectors permit or encourage greater variation, or even overt rivalry.

Decentralized systems, on the other hand, may have the advantage of offering a stronger variety of specialized medical services. Not having to allocate their resources as equally, they can afford to train more specialists than generalists, or to equip hospitals with more intensive care units. By the same token, decision makers in decentralized systems can more easily afford to take the risks involved in the adoption of medical innovations. They can more readily adopt expensive new technologies than can their counterparts in centralized systems, where budgetary trade-offs between standardized and innovative allocations are more direct and apparent.

As regards total costs of the systems: Does the fact that the American health system consumes almost twice as large a share of the Gross National Product as the British one imply that centralized systems are generally less costly? Will this hold even if one controls for the different levels of national wealth? These and other related questions are explored in subsequent sections of this chapter on the basis of a broader range of evidence.

In Germany policy deliberations must include not only the Ministries of Health and Finance, but also the Labor Ministry, which supervises the health insurance system, and all the Land Ministers of Health. On some issues the Chamber of Physicians might claim veto power and, if offended, might resort to the threat of a doctors' strike. Although German health policy has been less party-polarized than its secondary education policy, changes are very difficult to push through the corporatized German decision-making system (Stone 1980, Chapter 2). Thus, to help bring about consensus, the Germans have augmented the official machinery by setting up a broader National Health Conference to set annual health policy goals. Even so, the Germans have made much less progress than the Swedes in projecting and implementing, for instance, a set of medical personnel planning objectives.

In Sweden health planners have been more effective largely because of a policy of *regionalizing* responsibility for the public health delivery systems. The counties were given a virtual monopoly, including jurisdiction over some mental hospitals and district doctor systems which the national government had previously run. Another step was to reduce competition between the twenty-five counties, which meant instituting a uniform national pay scale for all hospital employees and placing all hospital doctors on a "salary only" remuneration basis (Carder and Klingeberg, in Heidenheimer and Elvander 1980). Furthermore, it meant developing a system through which all counties would cooperate to fit their hospital staffing and training policies into one national framework. This scheme was in turn further developed through a "health regionalization" program, through which various kinds of hospitals were assigned duties which carried with them quotas regarding the various medical and other health personnel. Building on this framework, then, Swedish health planners were able not only to announce goals of producing fewer surgeons and more specialists in geriatrics, but actually to implement these goals by coordinating the control mechanisms of hospitals, medical schools, and counties (Heidenheimer and Elvander 1980).

The organized interests in health politics have different policy priorities and leverage opportunities, which tend to be similar across countries. Some of these are shown in Figure 3.2, which identifies some policy priorities of two groups of regulators and providers on the one hand, and users and clients on the other. It suggests how political alliances between provider and client interests have come about. Thus, one frequently finds informal coalitions between government health bureaucrats and representatives of

FIGURE 3.2 POLICY ORIENTATIONS OF HEALTH INTEREST GROUPS

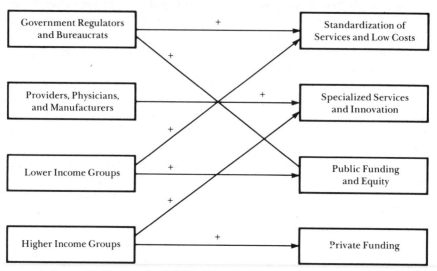

SOURCE J. Rogers Hollingsworth, *A Political Economy of Medicine: Great Britain and the United States* (Baltimore: Johns Hopkins, 1986).

lower-income groups because both tend to favor reliance on public funding, which tends to encourage standardization of services and equality of access. In the United States such coalitions have at times found a home and ideological support in the Democratic party; in Sweden a similar relationship has existed with the Social Democratic party.

Several kinds of health service providers, especially physicians and pharmaceutical companies, have similarly found an alliance potential with the representatives of higher-income groups. Dominant elements in both groups tend to support the priority for scientific-medical innovation and a stress on the development of specialized services. Whether physicians also shared the higher-income groups' preference for private funding has varied more. In the American setting such preferences long formed the basis of an alliance between organized medicine and business, which was backed up by the Republicans. But in many European countries it has been less ideologically attractive or rewarding for the right-of-center parties to espouse private alternatives to predominantly public health systems (Hollingsworth).

Techniques of Intervention

In a nationally administered health system like Britain's, the instruments through which government affects health policy are largely identical with the administrative subdivisions of the National Health Service—for example, ambulatory, hospital, and preventive services. In a corporatized system like Germany's, instrumental powers are more scattered among various public, private, and professional bodies. In a segmented system like the United States', where the national government operates only a few facilities (such as Veterans Administration Hospitals), the government pursues a series of loosely related strategies of intervention aimed at different components of the health delivery system.

U.S. federal health policy of the 1970s was aptly described as a four-ring circus, with four sets of techniques pursued within as many rings (Brown 1978). One technique of intervention tried to determine the quantity, quality, and distribution of medical and other health personnel. Another aimed to support and control the actual health care facilities, including both traditional ones such as hospitals and newer ones such as health centers and prepaid health care centers. A third technique focused on regulating health care services (as in the efforts to control technology described later in this chapter). A fourth technique involved channeling subsidies to groups such as the elderly and the poor. Those involved in health politics find that their options are affected by how loosely or tightly the four rings are interconnected.

In other sections of this chapter we will present analyses of how and why countries differ in the ways they direct and regulate medical markets and health systems. Table 3.4 provides an overview of national regulatory practices and managerial instruments which we will be discussing, as evaluated and coded for simplicity's sake by a knowledgeable OECD official. From it we can see the degree of intensity to which each country employs five selected regulatory techniques as they are applied mainly to hospital-based health care, but also to the degree of intervention in salary bargaining for primary-care physicians.

TABLE 3.4 RELATIVE STRENGTH OF STATE REGULATORY INTERVENTION, 1980s

Country	Hospital Investment	Control over Fees/Prices	Manpower Control	Technology Regulation	Salary Setting
Britain	xx	xx	xx	xx	xxx
Canada	x			xx	x
Denmark	xx	x	xx	x	x
France	xxx	xx	xx	x	xx
Germany	xx		xx	x	x
Netherlands	xx		xx	xx	xx
Sweden	x	xx	xxx	xxx	x
Switzerland			x	x	
United States	xx	x		xx	x

source Pouillier, in A. J. Culyer and Bengt Jonsson, eds., *Public and Private Health Services* (Oxford: Blackwell, 1986).

Physician Training and Utilization

Health policy choices are conditioned by a country's physician-to-population ratio, and also by the proportion of medical students who are trained as generalists or specialists. The difficulty of entering medical training has varied over time and among countries. In the 1960s the United States, like most of Europe, expanded the number of medical students. Yet even with this expansion, admission was more selective than in most European countries, where, apart from Britain, a relatively higher number were allowed to start studies. Often this has resulted in crowding in clinical training, because the number of patients in university hospitals and the number of lab places are limited. This problem has proved severe in Germany, and even more so in Italy.

Starting in 1963, the U.S. federal government began to subsidize both medical schools and medical students heavily in the belief that increasing the number of doctors was the key to improving health delivery. From then to 1973, federal subsidies to medical and other health professional schools acquired a preferred status, since such aid was not given to schools of law, engineering, or business. While first-year enrollments increased from 8,760 in 1965 to 14,500 in 1975, the proportion of medical school income covered by tuition decreased from 17 percent in 1948, to 7 percent in 1960, to 4 percent in the 1970s.

The criteria by which medical students are selected have come to vary cross-nationally. In some countries secondary school grades and entrance test scores count heavily. But high achievers do not necessarily make the best doctors; and so the Netherlands and Germany now rely partly on lotteries to select from those basically qualified. The financial barrier in the United States, where annual tuition fees exceed $15,000, has made family wealth a stronger criterion, with the percentage of students from lower-middle-class families declining as federal subsidies were reduced. Medical school leaders are now concerned that medicine is going to become even more markedly a profession for the rich. In Europe, where fees are not a barrier, more weeding out occurs. Thus France has tightened the test which screens out many after the first year, while in Germany a new second-year multiple-choice test threatened to eliminate 56 percent of the class in 1981. In that case, however, massive student protest led to a revised procedure, and to a lowering of the failure rate.

In most European systems, the crucial role of the "gatekeeper," who determines which patients shall have what kind of hospital care, is played by the specialist, to whom GPs refer patients for more complex diagnoses. Such doctors impose a somewhat higher criterion for hospital admission than would most American physicians, who can arrange admission for their own patients. Once they get to a hospital, the large majority of European patients, in contrast to American ones, are treated by hospital physicians in whose choice they have no part. The relationship of patient to doctor is not a private one, but rather a social one in which the institution takes responsibility for providing the needed medical care. With hospital appointments a mark of great prestige, European hospitals have tended to develop a "closed staff" system, in contrast to the freewheeling "open staff" hospital typical of the United States.

By 1974 American politicians comparing British and American physician distribution noted that in Britain 74 percent of the doctors were primary-care physicians and only 8 percent were in surgery, while in the United States' free-market system about 47 percent of the physicians were in the primary-care specialties (including internal medicine, pediatrics, and obstetrics) and 24 percent were in surgery. As Senator Edward Kennedy asked: "Why do we have the same number of neurosurgeons in Massachusetts, with a population of five million, as they have in England, with a population of forty million? . . . Why do we have twice as many operations in the United States as in England? Could it be because we have twice as many surgeons?" (*National Journal*, 17 August 1974). Yes and no; for American surgeons each perform only half the number of operations as their British peers.

Clearly, the quality of surgery depends on the skill of those who are allowed to perform operations, though the reason for surgery must also be considered. In the United States, for example, surveys have shown a high percentage of unnecessary hysterectomy and appendectomy operations. Half of all American operations are performed by doctors without either surgical specialization or board certification—a function of the fact that individual hospitals set their own standards. Surgeons have also had to accept the fact that health insurers encourage patients to get a second opinion before agreeing to proposed surgery. Studies have shown that in more than one-quarter of cases there was disagreement in the advice given by two surgeons.

While maintaining higher standards for surgeons and other specialists, Britain has also managed to resist the general decline in the supply of GPs. In both the United States and Sweden the proportion of GPs in the total physician population has decreased sharply in recent decades. As Table 3.5 illustrates, these two countries allocate smaller proportions of health resources to primary care, and have relatively fewer GPs. Denmark occupies a somewhat intermediate position in this respect. In America the pull toward specialized practice is reinforced by more marked income differentials, with surgeons enjoying much greater income margins over GPs than in the European countries. The British have prevented the erosion in general practice through both health insurance (from 1911 to 1948) and the National Health Service (from 1948 to the present). These programs have helped to "encapsulate" general practice, protecting it against technological and professional pressures by providing it with a "clearly defined administrative and professional function" (Stevens 1966, p. 356).

The degree of health financing by public insurance has little relationship to a patient's choice of primary physicians. In an insurance-based system like Germany's, patients enroll with a physician of their choice and may change doctors on three months' notice. A similar choice of physicians is available under the British NHS. Affluent American suburbanites have more choice than Europeans in specialist and hospital care; but, for many Americans in rural areas and inner cities, choice is inhibited not only by cost, but by the availability of physicians and medical facilities.

In Britain the distribution of general practitioners is influenced by the various incentives for locating practices in different areas. GPs are offered an additional income for settling in under-doctored areas, while areas with a surfeit of doctors are declared closed to new practices. Even entries into intermediate areas are screened.

The United States' health personnel legislation contained similar incentives, based on the cancellation of student loan debts, for those choosing to practice in under-doctored areas. The hope of guiding medical graduates to rural areas enjoyed little success: Over a ten-year period only 146 of 170,000 loan recipients chose this option.

ACCESS TO HEALTH CARE AND HOSPITALS
DISTRIBUTION

The question of distribution concerns the access that a population has to health care—specifically, to physicians' offices, hospitals and health centers. In formulating health policy, governments have, to varying degrees, con-

TABLE 3.5 RELATIVE EMPHASIS ON GENERAL AND SPECIALIST MEDICAL PROVISION, 1984

	United States	Britain	Denmark	Sweden
Active physicians per 100,000 population	210	168	251	252
General or family doctors among all physicians	14%	46%	25%	23%
Primary health care as share of total health expenditures	18%	25%	25%	15%
Ratio of surgeon's to general practitioner's income	2:1	.9:1	1:1	1.1:1
Ratio of GP income to average per capita income	5.8:1	4.8:1	3.6:1	2.7:1

SOURCE Jonathan P. Weiner, "Primary Care Delivery in the United States and Four Northwest European Countries," *Milbank Quarterly* (1987), pp. 653, 432–33.

cerned themselves with its geographical and social distribution. But distributive issues also remain controversial in Britain, as discussed below.

Inequalities in Health Care Access

A cross-national study of medical care utilization in the United States and Sweden, emphasizing the role of income and class, found that in the early 1960s the utilization of physician services was strongly related to income in the United States—but not at all in Sweden. Whereas the percentage of Swedes seeing a doctor during 1963 was fairly constant for all income groups, in the United States there was a large spread between the low-income group, of which 53 percent had seen a doctor, and the high-income group, of which 72 percent had. Moreover, Americans who carried health insurance were much more likely to utilize both physicians and hospitals than those who did not. In their overall comparison, the authors of the study "judged the accessibility of the population to the Swedish system to be greater than to the system of the United States because the proportion of the cost of services paid by the consumer at time of service is lower in Sweden" (Anderson et al, p. 12a).

A concerted strategy to reduce differences in health status was initiated in the 1980s by the European members of the World Health Organization (WHO) when they set a target of reducing differences in health status by 25 percent between 1985 and the year 2000. Such differences are illustrated in Figure 3.3, which uses age-standardized data for the admission of middle-aged employed men to hospitals in five Swedish counties. It shows that unskilled and skilled workers suffered disproportionately from problems due to accidents and psychological problems, while low-level salaried employees made below-average claims for health care relating to these problems. To reduce such differences the Swedes enacted the Health Policy bill of 1985, which sought to improve the health status—particularly of those groups showing the greatest morbidity due to the cumulative effects of risk factors attributable to occupational and housing status. The bill was supported by all the political parties except the Conservatives, who stated that the distribution of poor health within the population was mainly random, and was due primarily to different lifestyles, which could be controlled by individuals (Dahlgren and Diderichsen, p. 523).

Initially, some students of the British National Health Service argued that, even though there was no cost barrier, medical care benefits were more accessible to the middle class than to the working class. However, studies suggest that the lower-class groups have learned how to take advantage of the benefits to which they are entitled, that they make the greatest use of physicians and in-hospital medical services, and that the care they receive is as good as that secured by the other social classes.

In the United States, the Medicaid and Medicare programs, imple-

FIGURE 3.3 HEALTH PROBLEMS AND MEDICAL CARE USE BY
SOCIOECONOMIC GROUPS, SWEDEN 1980s

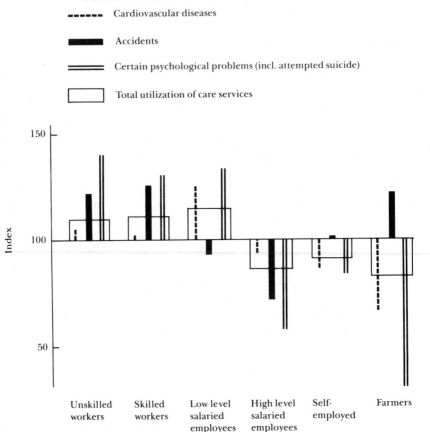

NOTE Admissions in hospitals in five Swedish counties of employed men aged 45–64 years.
SOURCE Göran Dahlgren and Finn Diderichsen, "Strategies for Health: Report from Sweden,"
International Journal of Health Services, 16:4, 1986.

mented in the late 1960s, have increased the access of lower-income groups
to medical care. In 1970, 65 percent of people with incomes below $3000
saw a physician, compared to only 56 percent in 1963. Whereas in 1930
high-income patients averaged twice as many doctor consultations as low-
income patients, by 1970 low-income patients were seeing doctors as frequently as high-income patients, and their hospital admission rate was
higher.

Medicaid is the embattled safety net through which public financial
support reaches the nonelderly poor. In 1981 some 20 million Americans,
including 8 million children, received Medicaid benefits. About 56 percent
of the $31 billion spent under the program that year came from federal

funds, with the remainder coming from the states. Most recipients lived beneath the poverty level, and the median income of Medicaid households (in 1980, $6,100) was barely one-third that of all American households. The trend in the late 1970s was toward a concentration of benefits such as Medicaid and food stamps on the poorest households.

The manner in which national policy styles affect regional differences in the availability of doctors and hospitals has been illuminated through a historical study of developments in Britain and the United States. For a period into the 1930s, the distribution of British doctors was actually more unequal than in America, with many counties having no gynecologists, pediatricians, or psychiatrists. But due to the effects of the National Health Service, the index of regional inequality of doctor distribution by 1971 was only a third as high as it had been fifty years earlier. In America this index in 1971 was twice as high as in Britain, and had not changed significantly over the previous thirty years. In fact, over the same period, the interregional variation in hospital personnel increased rather than decreased (Hollingsworth, p. 200).

Hospitals and Health Care Delivery

Hospital emphasis tends to vary from country to country. In 1975, for example, Britain spent 3.8 percent of its GNP on hospitals, thanks mainly to its highly centralized administration and the virtual monopoly of hospital practice held by a small and hierarchically organized group of specialists, who provided efficient gatekeeping at the hospital door. Sweden, by contrast, spent 6 percent of its GNP on hospital expenditures, twice that of Germany or the United States (Maxwell, pp. 83–86). Sweden constructed some of the world's largest and best-equipped hospitals, which proceeded to rotate world health care records among themselves.

In the United States, the Blue Cross Association, which became the profession's preferred health insurance instrument in the 1940s, was under producer and not consumer control and, until 1972, was linked to the American Hospital Association. Federal grant-in-aid programs also gave overt preference to hospital investment. Thus financing practices, along with fairly lax gatekeeping and the question of physician convenience, made the hospital the organizational hub of medicine in the United States.

While general hospital beds increased markedly in the United States, from 3.3 beds per 1,000 in 1950 to 4.5 beds per 1,000 in the mid-1970s, the ratios in Britain and Sweden declined slightly, though Sweden has long had a high bed-to-population ratio compared to other industrialized countries. In all three countries, however, admissions to general hospitals increased over this period, growing from 110 to 157 per 1,000 in the United States; from 113 to 156 in Sweden; and from 64 to 104 in Britain. The average hospital stay in the United States has declined slightly, to about 8 days; in

Sweden it fell from 16 to 10 days; and in England from 15 to 10 (Anderson and Bjorkman, in Heidenheimer and Elvander 1980, p. 231).

In Sweden one effect of the highly developed and well-financed hospital system was that half of all doctor contacts with ambulatory patients occurred in hospital outpatient departments. When in the 1960s some Swedes questioned whether such a system was either economically or medically justified, health planners gradually leaned toward health centers as less expensive sites for the delivery of health care. By 1970 the National Health Board chairman officially stated that the board "would favor an exodus of specialists from hospitals into health centers," both because this would "relieve some of the need for hospitalization," and because it would "restore the confidence of patients in the health care system by making specialists more accessible" (*The Swedish Health Service System* 1971, p. 209).

A decade later other thrusts toward reducing use of hospital inpatient facilities began to show significant results in the United States. The length of stays in American hospitals was significantly reduced from 7.3 days in 1980 to 5.7 days in 1985, or by almost one-quarter. This reduction was attributed to various incentives to rely more on outpatient treatment, and especially on the introduction of the Diagnosis Related Groups (DRG) method of cost reimbursement (discussed later in this chapter) for Medicare patients. As anticipated, the pressure to reduce stays of Medicare patients, about 40 percent of the total, was transferred also to treatments for privately insured patients, whose hospital stays were reduced almost as much. As a consequence of this trend, American hospital-bed occupancy rates also declined sharply, from 70 to 57 percent. This in turn led to the closing of many hospital wards, and even entire hospitals.

Among those who may have been hurt by this squeeze are patients who had no or inadequate insurance. During the same period, the number of for-profit hospitals, usually organized in national chains operated by corporations like Humana, increased their share of the market. These hospitals especially tended to turn away uninsured patients, as reported by their own doctors in a 1984 AMA survey. Many older patients also had to face larger shortfalls between hospital charges and Medicare payments. Often, widows had to mortgage homes in order to pay the uncovered parts of their dead spouses' hospital bills. They were brought relief through a 1988 catastrophic illness amendment, under which Medicare started bearing all hospital and doctor costs beyond $2,000 for each patient-year. By 1993 this program will also cover 80 percent of prescription drug costs beyond $600 per year.

American critics of the British health care system tend to deplore British priorities as soft-headed, urging them to cut back on ambulances and to invest more in high technology. While admitting that Britain enjoys the service of many more GPs and furthermore that they perform services not always available in the United States—house calls, for example—Americans point out that the British system pays the price. "If community health services seem lavish by American standards, hospital services seem skimpy. Over 750,000 people are now waiting to enter British hospitals". For all eventually admitted hospital patients the waiting lists are not as long; in 1982 only 6 percent were waiting a year, and one-third over three months. But these waiting lists constitute a form of supply rationing which substitutes for the pricing mechanism. Some of those in the queue may opt for earlier service under a privately financed scheme.

How would attempts to transfer equivalents to British budget limits on hospital care work if attempted in American settings? Researchers who investigated this think that doctors and patients would need to be taken into account. The salaried British physicians cope with the resource limits to "preserve what they regard as clinical freedom, the right of each practitioner to prescribe as he or she thinks best in each case." But "American specialists are largely private businessmen who use the hospital as a place for doing business. . . . The norm for hospital care in the United States approximates the maxim, 'if it will help, do it.' Most American physicians gain financially from providing additional care, and medical ethics preclude only the delivery of care that will do harm, not of care that is unreasonably expensive." Also, many American patients are not as ready to accept their doctor's treatment diagnosis as the last word. They tend to "regard doctors as technicians who are periodically called on to repair [their] physical machinery, to be dropped if they are unable to solve the current problem or to be sued if they botched the last one" (Aaron and Schwartz, pp. 7–17).

In some but not all of the specialty services examined, the British services offered were less ample than American ones. Had they been brought up to the American level, this would have necessitated increasing hospital expenditures by one-fifth. The most expensive item which would have had to be added was intensive care units; American hospitals have between five and ten times as many intensive care beds per capita. This reflects their tendency to offer advanced but very expensive specialized care to patients with severe illnesses. A large proportion of such care is given to older patients with severe complications, thus extending life by some weeks or months. Most British hospitals do not offer such options, and this is one reason why they are so much less costly.

Table 3.6 illustrates that American per hospital bed expenditures were three times as high as Britain's per hospital bed, and per day expenditures two and a half times as high as Britain's per day costs. Similar higher cost ratios emerge when comparison is made with Continental countries like Germany, the Netherlands, and Switzerland. Especially low hospital costs are shown by Japan. This seems explained partly by the greater amount of food and nurturing care provided by relatives, and by the fact that some Japanese hospitals cater more to longer-term rather than intensive care patients. Japanese legislation in 1973 made health care virtually free for those over age seventy. This led to considerable cost increases, which were somewhat contained by the reintroduction of some patient cost-sharing a decade later.

Cloning Health Care Structures

During the 1980s, the United States and Britain were ruled by politicians who wanted to contain and/or reduce the public role in health provision. Since most medical terms are standardized, some might have expected the key terms and acronyms being utilized in the health policy debates to have been highly similar in these two English-speaking countries. In fact they were not, for the acronyms tossed around by health policymakers in Washington, terms such as *HMOs, PPOs,* and *DRGs* were not only quite different from those used in Britain, but the structures themselves were in a much more constant process of change. This reflected the different manner in which change in health delivery is brought underway in a primarily private decentralized system, and a centralized system that has been in place for forty years.

The American acronyms mainly represent different types of health delivery and regulation models which were launched by various administrations on different levels of the American system. Several of these had been launched under the Nixon and Carter administrations as efforts to rationalize the way in which health care was delivered for patients under both public and private programs. Some of these structures, like Health Maintenance Organizations (HMOs), were accepted and encouraged by the Rea-

TABLE 3.6 HOSPITAL EXPENDITURES

Country	Amount per Capita	Amount per Bed	Amount per Day	Percent of All Expenditures
	$	$	$	
Britain (2)	320	39,000	140	61.5
Canada	450	65,000	210	41.4
Denmark	490	63,000	220	70.4
France	470	42,000	170	43.0
Germany	370	34,000	110	38.6
Japan	230	19,000	60	32.8
Netherlands	540	45,000	140	59.0
Norway (1) (2)	410	61,000	220	45.3
Switzerland	470	37,000	125	44.4
United States	580	122,000	360	41.8
Mean	410	50,000	170	
High/Low	2.5	6.4	6.0	

NOTES (1) Recurrent health expenditures; (2) Public expenditures only.
SOURCE OECD, *Financing and Delivering Health Care* (Paris: OECD, 1987), p. 63.

gan administration as models through which prepaid health care could be extended on a more economic basis. Other inherited structures, like Health Systems Agencies (HSAs) and Professional Service Review Organizations (PSROs), which represented the type of planning and regulatory models the Reagan administration rejected, were terminated.

In Britain Prime Minister Thatcher initially found it more difficult to dismantle parts of the NHS or to introduce innovations. Scars from the NHS reorganization carried through by a preceding Tory government in 1974 still rankled, and the search for alternative models was stymied. Proposals that Britain experiment with health insurance programs of either the Continental or American types were considered and quickly rejected in 1982 when the cabinet discussed the projections about costs and dislocations involved in setting up viable competitors to the NHS. Unlike the housing sector, where the Tory push for privatizing much of the public housing stock did not engender much middle-class resistance, the NHS had bred support since members of all classes relied on its services and held these in quite positive esteem. So in the early 1980s, the Tories could only attempt to encourage the growth of the small sector of private health insurance companies, which appealed mainly to middle-class patients who wanted to bypass the NHS waiting lists for some noncritical, elective services.

By enrolling in private health insurance, usually as an employment fringe benefit, British patients got access to alternative health delivery systems, even while continuing to use NHS for many services. A Conservative health minister set a goal of having the private sector reach one-quarter the size of the NHS. By 1983 enrollment in private insurance plans had reached 7 percent of the population. But whereas one-quarter of people in the professional class had this coverage, the same rate for semiskilled workers and those over age seventy-five was only 2 percent.

Another instrument used to further the government privatization goals were for-profit American hospital corporations. By 1986 four of the ten largest American for-profit corporations were operating hospitals in Britain. Their niche was facilitated by the reluctance of British capital to invest in this sector, and by the opportunity to cater to prosperous foreign patients, particularly from the Middle East countries.

This sketch of British developments supports the thesis that if a centralized health system is popular and cost-effective it is much more difficult for a government to change or remodel particular parts of it. Thus, although bureaucrats and upper-class consumers share a desire for private alternatives, these can only be instituted at the margin of the dominant public system. Throughout her first two terms, Thatcher assured the voters that she would not tamper with the essentials of the NHS. There were indications that she would back away from this guarantee during her third term.

True to form, Thatcher in 1989 initiated proposals for changing basic ground rules of the NHS which were similar to those she had earlier launched in education. Hospitals were to be given the opportunity to "opt out" of the NHS, just as schools had been given the means of "opting out" from the control of local education authorities. Thus many of the 320 larger acute care hospitals were to be given the opportunity to become "self-governing" by 1991. If taken this route will not mean privatization, but it will engender competition for funds and patients between different kinds of hospitals in the public sector. Similar incentives to increase competition for patients among GP's were introduced by increasing the relevance of patient numbers for doctors' remuneration.

The government plans constituted attacks on the prerogatives of both significant professional and patients groups. By slating medical audits of hospital and physician performance to become operative by 1991, the Tories attacked the tradition under which organized medicine had retained control of accountability within the National Health system. By encouraging patients to "shop around" among doctors, the proposals undermined the almost legendary loyalty which had been perpetuated among British physicians and their patients. While the proposals sought to ally the government with consumers, the questions remained *which* clients would benefit. Critics saw the proposals as moving the system toward the American two-track model, with "better" hospitals and doctors attracting the well-informed, while those with poorer records and/or reputations would be left to cater to the rest of the population.

In America health policy also played an important role in the 1988 presidential and congressional campaigns, but not around any central public vs. private axis, since major alternatives had by then developed along several dimensions which intersected private-public, federal-state, and health subsystem boundaries. Among the major issues were: Was the competition approach halting the rise in health costs? Were federal limits on health care reimbursement charges proving effective? Would states take the lead in mandating employers to provide health insurance as a step to providing coverage for the growing minority who were not covered by any public or private program? Would HMOs become the predominant model for extending health care? Was the cost of operating the various control, accounting, and reimbursement systems growing excessive to the point of drawing resources away from health care itself?

Of the new structures devised to improve the decentralized private health systems, HMOs developed the most impressive record, and retained government backing under Reagan and Bush. Overcoming a slow start, enrollment grew rapidly from 5.7 million in 1975 to 19 million in 1985. A target of bringing enrollment to 50 million by 1990 will probably not be achieved as annual growth rates have again dropped, for by the late 1980s HMOs were being challenged and partly supplanted by new breeds of hybrid health care and financing structures: Independent Practice Associations (IPAs), run from scattered private offices rather than a central

HMO clinic, with doctors remaining self-employed; preferred provider organizations (PPOs), under which a group insurance steers members to particular doctors and hospitals to obtain group discounts; Primary Care Networks (PCNs), under which enrollees designate a member doctor as "case" manager; a fifth of the fee is withheld and put into a bonus fund distributed among doctors at year's end. This cloning of alternatives tended to undercut the emergence of HMOs as the preferred systems, and to impede the transparency of the system which the competition advocates wanted to create for consumers.

With this background it is not too surprising that the most successful of the Reagan health initiatives is also the one which was the greatest anomaly within its overall approach. *Diagnosis Related Groups* (DRGs) formed the core of a 1983 Medicare amendment which provides reimbursement rates predetermined according to an average fee schedule. This schedule is based on average national charges for each of 487 health problem diagnoses. By adopting it for this key federal program, the United States moved much closer to the operating mode of the European public health insurance systems like those of Germany and France. The payment system was intended to force hospitals to be more efficient, and it probably helped to bring down the length of average hospital stays in the late 1980s.

The shifting fortunes of these health care constructs, and the corporations that emerged to operate them, tended to erode the position of the remaining sole practitioners in all but the smallest communities (Starr). Accountants, bookkeepers, business managers, and a host of other professionals were drawn to careers in these new organizations. In the process of improving efficiency, these professionals were adding hugely to the cost of the overall system. But were the results of their combined efforts worth all the bother and expense? One of the aims, that of reducing reliance on expensive hospital care, was achieved as the rate of U.S. hospital admissions declined significantly. But the expectations that outpatient care would cost only half as much as inpatient hospital care were shattered as per visit costs of outpatient care increased a dramatic 88 percent between 1981 and 1987. Consequently, the reduction in hospital inpatient care did not reduce costs significantly.

PLANNING, COMPETITION, AND COST CONTAINMENT
RESTRAINTS AND INNOVATION

One of the most important issues in health policy today concerns soaring health care expenditures. Policymakers fall into two camps: those favoring planning and those favoring competition. The issue at hand is whether costs can best be held down by improving health care planning or by stimulating more market competition.

Controlling Health Costs

The major determinants of the growing health expenditures have been identified as the following: demographic changes involving the increasing needs of aging populations and related changes in disease patterns; advances in medical technology extending the range of particularly acute medical treatment and raising public expectations; and raised skill levels in health sector occupations leading to higher labor costs, which prevailing financing systems, public or private, have difficulty meeting. But management and political control also matter greatly.

At the beginning of the 1980s the proportion of GNP devoted to health expenditures in OECD countries averaged 7 percent. This constituted a vast proportional increase, since only two decades earlier the proportion was hovering around the 4 percent mark. In Sweden the jump was from 4.7 percent in 1960 to 9.5 percent in 1980; in the United States it was from 5.2 percent to 9.2 percent; and the figures for Germany and the Netherlands are similar. In fact, it varied somewhat by calculation method and year just which of these experienced the greatest increase. Systems as distinct as the public insurance-based European systems, the county-based public system of Sweden, and the mainly private American system were all similar in failing to halt the cost inflation. Generally, the wealthier the society, the greater the proportion spent on health care.

Some countries which started with relatively low levels of health provision due to postwar resource constraints, like Japan and Norway, had rates of expenditure increase which exceeded American rates. But a wealthy country like Sweden also increased costs greatly, much more so than Britain, for instance. A less centralized system of political control explained much of this difference. Swedish counties are unique in the degree to which they act as "uniservice health jurisdictions," complete with autonomous taxation powers. Functionally they are similar to American school districts, but can raise tax rates more easily: The average county income tax rate shot from 4.4 percent in 1960 to 12.5 percent in 1978.

But a glance at Table 3.7 will show that during the first half of the 1980s, countries differed quite differently in cost expansion from the previous period. Most European countries were able to stabilize the health costs/GNP ratios, while the United States was the only one to let health costs jump the 10 percent threshold by 1985. By then its health costs/GDP ratio was almost double that of Britain, which retained its record as European low spender. But previous big spenders like Sweden and Germany managed to restrain costs during the 1980s much more than countries like the United States and France, the result of their adoption of new techniques of cost control during the 1970s which began to show some real effect during the 1980s.

To brake the cost increases, the German federal government introduced and passed—over the strong opposition of the medical profession—the Health Care Cost Containment Act of 1977, which created a National Health Conference, in which all major government and private groups engaged in the health sector are represented. It is charged with issuing annual recommendations for ambulatory health development; on the basis of these projections, it fixes annual limits for the total remuneration due to physicians under the insurance system, as well as on total drug expenditures. If the prescription increases attributed to certain doctors grow disproportionately, the excess can be taken out of the funds from which doctors' fees are paid.

In its first year of operation, the Conference got unanimous agreement that payments to physicians should increase by 5.5 percent, of which 2.5 percent was to cover rising prices, and 3 percent was for projected increases in physicians' services. From 1977 through 1979 the rate of health cost increase was kept below the rate of increase of GNP, at about 5 percent. The contributions which employers and workers paid to the insurance fund, which had risen from 8.2 percent of wages in 1970 to 11.4 percent in 1977, were finally being stabilized. Initially it proved difficult to make some of the limits stick, because the Christian Democratic Union and some Länder delayed extension of the controls to the hospital sector.

Though some physician associations strongly opposed the act and were on the brink of strike action in their campaign against the bill, even right-of-center opinion rejected their case. Organized business pointedly refused to back the physicians' struggle; thus physicians also came to participate in the corporatized system, through which negotiation machinery became

TABLE 3.7 TOTAL EXPENDITURE ON HEALTH AS A PROPORTION OF GDP

Country	1960	1975	1980	1985
Australia	5.1	7.4	7.2	7.3
Britain	3.9	5.5	5.7	5.7
Canada	5.5	7.3	7.4	8.4
France	4.3	6.8	7.5	8.6
Germany	4.7	7.8	7.9	8.2
Japan	3.0	5.6	6.6	6.6
Netherlands	3.9	7.7	8.2	8.3
New Zealand	4.4	6.4	7.2	5.5
Norway	3.3	6.7	6.6	6.4
Sweden	4.7	8.0	9.5	9.4
Switzerland	3.3	7.1	7.2	7.9
United States	5.2	8.4	9.2	10.7
OECD Average	4.0	6.9	7.1	7.3

SOURCE OECD, *Financing and Delivering Health Care* (Paris: OECD, 1987); updated by George Schieber.

FIGURE 3.4 PER CAPITA HEALTH SPENDING AND PER CAPITA GDP, 1985

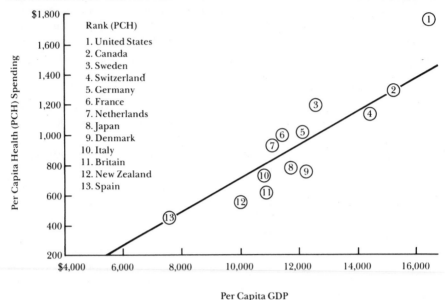

Per Capita GDP

SOURCE   OECD, Social Data Bank.

more centralized. Since 1982 the system has succeeded in holding health expenditure increases at the level of GDP increase, in contrast to the American case.

Some health economists question whether political control factors really matter much, because they see affluence as major determinant of health costs. The more affluent the society the higher its health expenditures: if expenditures in Britain are low—so the argument goes—it is not because of its centralized cost control, but because of its lag in affluence. Figure 3.4 shows the relationship of spending and GNP data: countries are mainly grouped along a trend line which does show them spending larger proportions of increasing GNP. Affluent Canada spends more than twice as large a part of a much larger GNP than relatively poor Spain. But both are on the trend line. The countries that are well *below* the line are several with centrally controlled health systems like Britain, Denmark, and New Zealand. By contrast, Sweden and France are somewhat above the trend line. But in these 1985 data, no country is as far away from the trend line as the United States, with its record high expenditures. (We should note that in these as well as other OECD tabulations used here, national expenditures are converted at so called *purchasing power parity* rates, which make them especially amenable to testing hypotheses such as this one. However, the data will differ from those converted in other ways.)

Physician Payment Systems. Physician payments are a dominant determinant of health expenditures because they constitute the second largest component (after hospital care) of such costs, and because it is mainly physicians who decide what use is made of other care factors, such as technology and pharmaceuticals, and thus determine about three-fourths of all health spending.

Physician remuneration systems can be distinguished according to the payment mode utilized. The *fee-for-service* mode is used for most general practitioners and specialists in the United States, Germany, and France. The *salary* system is used for hospital specialists in Britain and Sweden, as well as for many American medical school hospital staffs. In Britain and the Netherlands, general practitioners are paid on the *capitation* system. Under this system doctors are paid according to the number of patients enrolled with them. How often patients consult them does not affect their income, whereas it does for doctors practicing under the fee-for-service system. In Britain most general practitioners favored the capitation system at the time of the creation of the NHS. German doctors, on the other hand, negotiated a shift from a capitation to a fee-for-service system in the 1960s (Stone 1981).

Payment systems can be deliberately used to influence medical practice. By "weighting" a doctor's income more or less favorably for various services—preventive checkups, drug prescriptions, house calls, and so forth—the payment system can encourage some treatment techniques over others (Glaser 1978). Insurance-based health systems which use the fee-for-service format, such as those in Germany and Japan, have had the highest frequency of doctor visits. The introduction of a compulsory health insurance program does not necessarily trigger basic change in the physicians' remuneration mode, but in time such change may occur. Britain and Sweden are countries where change has taken place, Germany and France where it has not. But in these countries and the United States, fee-for-service levels have become increasingly subject to regulatory constraints.

Table 3.8 presents data on fees for various medical treatments provided by physicians under fee-for-service systems. It shows the average payments received by doctors in 1984 for appendectomies and hysterectomies: The average European payment for an appendectomy was about $124, somewhat more in Japan ($185), but much more in the United States ($1,135). Similarly, the American payments for hysterectomies were much higher than in the other countries. American fee patterns demonstrate discrepancies of five and six to one in what was being charged for the same treatment. These are now being narrowed by application of DRG fee schedules discussed earlier. But it is more difficult to control doctors' profits on diagnostic laboratory procedures. In documented cases physicians have charged insurers four times as much for diagnostic tests as what they paid the laboratories.

Table 3.9 lists some of the results of physicians fee and salary structures by comparing average doctors' incomes across countries and in relation to the average employee income in their own countries, for the years 1970 and 1981. It shows that American doctors' incomes, which approached $100,000 in 1981, were the highest, but were followed fairly closely by those of their colleagues in insurance-based, fee-for-service systems like Canada and Germany. In most of these countries, doctors' incomes were some four to five times those of the average employee in their country. For the Scandinavian countries the ratios are lower, reflecting their ability to use salary controls to narrow income differentials in society generally. It is striking to note the contrast between the American and Italian doctors, who are reported as receiving salaries barely above those of all employees. Partly this is the result of Italian salaries being pegged at a low level at a time of a great physician surplus. But it may also reflect the sizable unreported side-incomes which many Italian doctors received but did not report. In Japan customary gift-giving to doctors above and beyond health insurance fees also generates a considerable amount of unreported income (Steslicke, 1988, p. 185). Until 1979 Japanese doctors enjoyed preferential treatment which permitted a 72 percent tax deductibility of their gross incomes; since then these have been held to more modest proportions.

The relative overpayment of some American specialists was criticized in a study which the Health Care Finance Administration sent to Congress in 1988. It found that doctors had been overcompensated for "invasive" procedures like surgery and diagnostic tests, compared to fees paid under Medicare to internists and family practitioners. It proposed cutting in half the average payment total of $350,000 which surgeons received under Medicare, and upgrading the payments to specialists whose skills were relatively undervalued. Such revisions of inherited "customary fee levels" had been implemented much earlier in countries like Sweden and Britain.

TABLE 3.8 MEDICAL SERVICE FEES, 1984 (IN U.S. DOLLARS)

Service	Germany	France	Switzerland	European (Mean)	United States	Japan
GP home visit	14	13	24	15	31	10
Total hysterec-tomy	151	187	433	235	1,754	300
Appendec-tomy	81	93	258	124	1,135	185
Electroen-cephalogram	32	131	113	60	125	25
Electrocardio-gram	14	15	39	18	45	7
Bronchoscopy	33	56	97	59	413	16

SOURCE OECD, *Financing and Delivering Health Care* (Paris, OECD, 1987), p. 74.

The difference in what doctors earn and the costs of what they prescribe causes American taxpayers to pay about five times as much for the care of each poor fellow-citizen as the British equivalent. One important contributing factor is that "an American doctor will make about ten times as much if he undertakes $500 worth of tests which will give 98% certainty of diagnosing your condition, rather than $50 worth of tests which will give 97% certainty" (Macrae, p. 17).

The high level of American doctors' incomes has driven up total health costs indirectly as well. Their wealth has made them the target of malpractice suits to a much larger extent than elsewhere, leading to much transfer of wealth to enterprising lawyers. These lawyers offer to take cases of disgruntled patients on a contingency fee basis, a technique which European lawyers are not allowed to employ. As a consequence of the enormous increase in many malpractice awards, the amounts which doctors have to pay for malpractice insurance have skyrocketed. For some specialties like orthopedic surgery and obstetrics, the cost of insurance has zoomed (approaching $100,000 a year) to the point where some doctors (particularly older doctors) have chosen to reduce their level of practice, or even to retire prematurely. In 1985 the Government Accounting Office termed the 85 percent increase of per hospital patient/day costs that had occurred over a two-year period "rather shocking." Many doctors, in order to anticipate possible bases for patient complaints, go far beyond what European doctors

TABLE 3.9 PHYSICIAN INCOMES, 1970 AND 1981

	Relative to Average Employee Income		Absolute Amount	
	1970	*1981*	*1970*	*1981*
Australia	4.3	2.5	$25600	$41,500
Britain		2.4		32,300
Canada	5.1	4.1	37800	72,700
Denmark		2.8		38,400
France	4.8	3.3	26600	46,800
Germany	6.4	4.9	40800	76,300
Italy	1.4	1.1	8600	19,600
Japan		4.7		68,200
New Zealand		2.5	21400	33,300
Norway	2.4	1.7	16800	28,500
Sweden	3.7	2.1	25500	35,300
United States	5.4		41800	93,000
Average	3.5	2.8	25800	46,800
High/Low	3.9	4.6	4.9	5.1

NOTE Converted at purchasing power parity.
SOURCE OECD, *Financing and Delivering Health Care* (Paris, OECD, 1987), p. 76.

might order in the way of diagnostic tests, mainly to build up a dossier which might hold up well in court. In Britain the conditions for malpractice suits are much more limited, thus reducing this incentive for possible excessive testing (Rosenthal). At the level of their professional associations, physicians and trial lawyers have been locked in bitter contest when state legislatures have considered legislation which sets malpractice award limits. Whether this struggle between professions has served to increase the quality of care is certainly arguable; that it has served to increase the cost of health care is not (Heidenheimer, 1989).

Technology Control and Health Planning

In the 1960s most health agencies, public and private, were unambiguously in favor of any new medical technology; its cost-effectiveness was seldom in question. By the 1970s, however, uncontrolled technological development and diffusion began to seem less desirable. Some of the new technologies were very expensive, and with third payers absorbing the costs, demand was enormous even when benefit was marginal. Administrators concluded that public agencies had to decide how much of each new, expensive technology could be afforded and who should receive treatment—and then find a way to enforce their allocations.

Scanners. One significant technology issue faced in the 1970s involved the computer tomography (CT) scanner. The CT scanner uses a moving x-ray tube and a computer for a cross-sectional picture of the internal structure of a body or body part. Initially, these scanners cost about $500,000; at full capacity the cost per scan is between $350 and $600. The potential users are almost unlimited. Studies have showed that although CTs can be highly cost-effective, their widespread use could draw funds from other priorities inside and outside the health sector.

Federal standards in the 1970's required that every scanner already in a specified area should be performing a minimum of 2500 scans per year. The actual controls often remained weak, however, as planners learned the hard way that the American local level was the toughest setting in which to try to stem the technological tide. Localism, commercialism, and boosterism combined to overwhelm the controllers.

By 1980, 80 percent of large hospitals had scanners in operation. In 1981 a report by the Office of Technology Assessment concluded that the left hand of the federal government had in effect undermined the curtailment efforts of its right hand. For "the stance assumed by the federal government toward other stages of development and use of scanners has tended to foster diffusion and widespread use . . . through its reimbursement policies it continues to assume an almost open-ended commitment to pay for CT scans" (Office of Technology Assessment, 1981).

The CT scanner has been deployed much less widely in Britain than in the United States, even though it was a British invention, and the original leading manufacturer was British. This can be attributed to an explicit policy of holding down NHS costs, which resulted in strong resistance to the acquisition of anything so new and expensive. Usually the central contracting arrangement, as handled by the Scientific and Technical Branch of the Department of Health and Social Services, made it possible to make restrictions stick. By March 1979 CT installation had been contained in Britain to 1 per million people (compared to 5.7 per million in the United States).

In Sweden there were only two scanners in place and one on order when the national plan for controlling the CT scanner came out. The Swedish preference for broadly supported corporatist decision making led them to early regular consultations with doctors about the scanners and largely precluded major attempts to circumvent the emergent policy. Sweden stressed replacing equivalent, equally expensive, and much more dangerous techniques with CTs, allocating scanners mostly to those regional hospitals already doing a great deal of work in the relevant area.

Germany got a later start at regulating hospital technology, which has allowed the scanner to diffuse much more freely. Hospital purchases are supported with federal or Land funds, though hospitals have financed scanners by holding fundraising drives. In addition, private physicians are permitted to buy the equipment. Consequently, Germany has many more scanners per capita than Britain or Sweden, with 30 percent—an unusually high proportion—installed in the offices of specialists in private practice.

The rule that the British made do with about two-fifths as many scanners as the Germans held into the mid-1980s, when a more powerful replacement device, the *Magnetic Resonance Imaging* (MRI) scanner became available. The same ratio was maintained with the new, even more expensive device, which costs close to $2 million apiece. In America, by 1985, more than half of all hospitals with more than three hundred beds had acquired CT scanners. Those who could not afford them were many large public hospitals, hard hit by Medicaid cutbacks, and serving mainly the poor. The overall initial acquisition rate for the MRIs was similar to the German one. But the reimbursement changes introduced in the preceding years led to a more cautious purchasing policy, since hospitals had to balance reputations as technology leaders against their overall cost competitiveness. Four years after the first U.S. installation, only 108 MRI units were in place compared to 921 CT scanners at the parallel juncture.

Dialysis. Utilization of costly technology dealing with kidney failure, *dialysis*, offers another example of the British innovating treatments, but then restricting access. Table 3.10 illustrates how the stronger British rationing controls led to fewer middle-aged and older patients being admitted for the expensive dialysis treatment—which cleanses the blood of impurities—than in France and Germany. But surprisingly, in this one instance it is just as well to be a patient in America. Due to some opportune lobbying at the time of the 1972 Medicare extension, chronic renal failure is a unique ailment that is generously treated at public expense. Why in this case? It was not incidental that when American hospital administrators and renal specialists became passionate advocates of denying no one access to dialysis machines, Congress responded accordingly. Clearly, patients with end-stage renal failure benefited from this policy, but had the financial rewards not been so substantial for providers, it is doubtful that the pressures would have been generated for Congress to make the treatment so accessible (Hollingsworth, p. 175). Hence, America leads the world in the per capita number of patients on dialysis machines—five times more than in Britain.

Research. American medicine allocates a larger portion of its much larger resources to research. In part this is fuelled by competition for public and private funds between different groups of specialists and patients. The larger interests and more dread diseases can generate commitments like those for the "war on cancer." This leads to innovation and the willingness to try new remedies. Thus, oncologists in America are much more likely to treat solid tumors, partly through chemotherapy. By contrast some British cancer specialists tend to be much more skeptical about these types of treatments, and to believe that "the United States is squandering large sums of money on ineffective treatment" (Aaron and Schwartz, p. 49).

When faced with a new epidemic disease like AIDS, all of the health systems have been hard put to develop innovative responses. Though the United States took a strong lead in pursuing research, its federal government was faulted in 1988 by a presidential commission for being too laggard in coordinating parallel programs of research, prevention, and education. Preventive techniques, like issuing free needles to intravenous drug users to reduce the danger of infection, were put into practice in Britain, Sweden, and the Netherlands before any American public program was willing to try them out.

By 1988 the United States had reported 70,000 cases of AIDS, com-

TABLE 3.10 AGE AND ACCESS TO TECHNOLOGY: NEW KIDNEY DIALYSIS PATIENTS PER ONE MILLION POPULATION, 1978

Age Group	Britain	West Germany	France
35–44	33.1	41.2	34.2
45–54	43.5	58.8	59.8
55–64	22.7	71.3	69.5
65–74	3.5	49.9	56.6
75–+	0	8.6	17.6
All ages	19.2	30.9	30.4

SOURCE J. Rogers Hollingsworth, *A Political Economy of Medicine: Great Britain and the United States* (Baltimore: Johns Hopkins, 1986), p. 175.

pared to 1,700 in Britain and 200 in Sweden. The American incidence rate (237.7 per million) was nearly ten times as high, and it was the only one of the three countries in which the epidemic was strongly linked to poverty and race. In Britain more than half the cases were in three inner London districts, and five out of six involved homosexual or bisexual men. The fact that American victims were also disproportionately found among blacks, Hispanics and drug-users triggered right-wing reactions. But then vigorous initiative was seized by Surgeon General Everett Koop, who insisted that his public health responsibilities outweighed his religious beliefs about sexuality. Thus, although American health institutions were at the start of the epidemic "poorly prepared to take aggressive action" (Fox, Day and Klein, 105), they rallied to the challenge, so that in all three countries the dominant health professional groups came to be firmly in command of evolving strategies to contain the disease.

Competition within and between Health Care Systems

The Reagan administration's health policies centered on dismantling regulation and promoting competition between alternative suppliers of health care. But because medicine has for so long been enmeshed in practices that restrain competition, these policies were very difficult to design. Skeptics continue to insist that the infusion of market forces into health care is limited by the atypical nature of deeply set attitudes in this sector. The pro-competition plans tried to shift the burden of regulation from the providers to the insurers, and critics argue that this merely shifted, not displaced, regulation.

In 1981 the British Tory Social Services Secretary sent several officials to Europe and the United States to examine health insurance models which might be considered as alternative finance models to the National Health Service. The information they returned with was not encouraging for those wanting to devise competitive insurance-based modules in order to begin replacing the National Health Service. In a poll, those who thought that the idea of switching to an insurance-based system of finance was a good idea were outnumbered three to two by those who judged it a bad idea. The idea of privatizing the system, so as to have everyone choosing and paying for the service he or she wants, was rejected by more than six to one.

In the late 1980s the United States made the largest gestures toward furthering competition, but the steps taken in that direction also involved doses of price and income regulation. As one health economist put it in 1988: "Who instituted the freeze on fees paid for hospital procedures for Medicare payments? The Republican who is talking about abolishing the fee-for-service system in favor of paying doctors a lump sum? The Reagan administration. This administration has been tough on doctors. Yet 90% of all doctors will vote for Bush" (*New York Times* 1 November 1988).

The reason why most physicians voted for Bush was they were more hostile to the health policy record of his opponent. In Massachusetts, Governor Michael Dukakis had promoted two important initiatives. One entailed a state law which required physicians to provide service at the fee levels for which the prevailing health insurance systems, like Medicare and Blue Cross, would reimburse. Patients liked that, but doctors did not. The other law passed under his leadership required employers to provide health insurance to their workers by 1992 or pay a tax surcharge of $1,680, or about what health insurance premiums for a family would amount to.

If the Bush administration were to accept the Massachusetts model for a similar federal legislation it would take care of the needs of more than half of the thirty-seven million Americans who are without insurance coverage. Taking care of the others, those who are self-employed, unemployed, or employed part-time, constitutes still another part of the 1990's health care dilemma.

This gap remained in the U.S. health policy mosaic even in the late 1980s as federal health spending was increasing more rapidly even than spending on interest for the ballooning national debt. Total health expenditures— public and private—continued to rise at a rate about twice that of the general inflation rate. As the Bush administration took office it was evident that the combined competition-and-regulation approach of the past decade had failed to slow down the inexorable cost increases. By 1990 health costs are claiming more than 12 percent of GNP, much more than those in other countries examined here.

Why was it that the success of certain programs, like those seeking to discourage hospital usage and stays, did not slow down the rise? In good part it was due to the entrepreneurial spirit of American providers, who tapped new markets for additional outpatient care, diagnostic procedures, psychological services, and drug and alcohol treatments. As one insurance executive put it: "The provider community continues to find ways to increase its revenues. Have you seen the TV ads for hemorrhoid surgery by laser?" In other words, the more new incentives to limit costs, the more counterincentives to expand them in new ways.

Designers of sophisticated pro-competitive strategies, like Alain Enthoven, complained that their plans were adulterated when the Reagan administration compromised on some crucial elements. The government's share of health costs was reduced by only one or two percentage points. This was very similar to the record under the Thatcher government in Britain. Its plans for expanding private sector care slowed down when it became evident that existing private programs could not meet the promise of holding down costs. President Bush came to office with plans to allow older Americans to finance more long-term care for themselves. But these involved tax reduction options, which by increasing tax expenditures would widen the budget deficits.

TABLE 3.11 COST INCREASES IN TWO KINDS OF HEALTH SYSTEMS

| | Elasticity of Health Expenditures[1] | | Ratio of Change 2nd to 1st Period[2] |
	1960–75	1975–84	
National Health Systems i.e., Britain, Scandinavian Countries	2.00	1.24	62.0%
Insurance-based Systems i.e., France Japan Netherlands United States West Germany	1.38	1.43	103.6%

NOTES [1]Elasticities express the ratio of real growth in health expenditures to real growth in GNP.
[2]Elasticity in the later period as a percentage of the elasticity in the earlier period.
SOURCE Alber 1988, Table 6, p. 64.

Looking at a broader range of countries, what seems to correlate with differential rates of success in health cost control since 1975? One analysis identified different cost outcomes for countries with national health systems, and countries with insurance-based systems like those in the United States, France, and Germany. As they were developing their systems in the period up to 1975, the NHS-type countries had cost increases which exceeded those of the second group. But when the national policy shifted to one of giving higher priority to cost control, the NHS-type systems were more successful in containing health expenditure elasticity, as demonstrated and defined in Table 3.11.

* * * * *

There is no consensus about how to assess the benefits that health care brings. With this reservation we nevertheless present figures in Table 3.12

TABLE 3.12 CROSS-NATIONAL RANKINGS OF HEALTH CARE EXPENDITURES AND MEASURES OF HEALTH STATUS, 1985

	Health Care Expenditures as Percentage of GDP	Rank	Patient Access to Specialists	Health Status Indicator: Male Infant Death Rate	Rank
United States	10.7	1	Uncontrolled	12.8	6
Sweden	9.4	2	Uncontrolled	7.1	1
France	8.6	3	Uncontrolled	11.2	4
Netherlands	8.3	4	Referral only	9.2	2
West Germany	8.2	5	Uncontrolled	10.6	3
Britain	5.7	6	Referral only	12.2	5

SOURCE OECD, *Financing and Delivering Health Care* (Paris: OECD, 1987), pp. 36, 55.

which show at least an initial approach with one set of plausible data. This table relates health expenditure rates of 1985 to indicators of health status, as reflected in male-infant death rates, which health care may be presumed to have affected. From them one can extract the following theses for further consideration:

The segmented American system has a relatively poor cost-benefit profile. It leads the other countries in expenditure ranking, and yet exhibits the poorest health status indicator.

The semi-centralized Swedish public system, though also costly, is accompanied by the most favorable health status measure.

The most fully nationalized British system achieves below-average health status through by far the lowest level of expenditures.

Germany, France, and the Netherlands achieve about the rankings in health status that they pay for.

These findings are not conclusive. At the present stage of comparative policy analysis, they must be regarded as suggestive only. Indeed, we must repeat that health status is only partly determined by treatment, and vastly by social conditions affected by other policies. One of the most important of these is housing, to which we turn in the next chapter.

4
HOUSING POLICY

Most people would agree that a roof over one's head is as vital a human need as any of the other goods and services discussed in this volume, including education and even health care. Although housing has not achieved the status of an entitlement in most Western societies, all Western governments have taken some responsibility for assuring that all citizens, including the poor, have access to decent housing. But housing policy, as we shall see in this chapter, is not simply a matter of seeing that every citizen has a roof overhead.

Housing programs have profound effects on a nation's economic health, on individual families' financial security, and on the shape of urban areas. In all Western economies, the construction industry is a major economic sector whose fortunes seriously affect overall levels of employment. By manipulating tax and credit policies and production programs to raise or lower the volume of housing construction, a national government directly influences the jobs of hundreds of thousands of construction workers, suppliers of building materials, real estate brokers, and others who depend on the industry. For many families, buying a house is the largest single investment they ever make. Thus the financial calculations of millions of households are affected by government actions regarding housing. Moreover, unlike some social policies, housing policies have effects that cannot easily be modified or reversed, because they are literally cast in concrete. Housing developments influence transportation, commerce, and the location of many kinds of community facilities for years after they are built.

CHOICES IN HOUSING POLICY

Scope and Thresholds

Despite the similar considerations affecting housing policymakers in the industrialized countries, the choices they have made in formulating national housing programs have by no means been uniform. In establishing the scope of responsibility for housing, national governments face the basic choice of whether or not to limit aid to those citizens who cannot secure even minimally decent housing through the private market. Some governments have supplemented the housing offered by the private market, chiefly to the poor, the elderly, and the disabled, while others have intervened in broader ways by trying to plan and control the provision of housing to all groups in the society. However, even governments that have chosen the broader approach have eschewed the nationalization of housing that has occurred in communist countries. As mixed economies, all the Western nations and Japan maintain strong private housing markets, primarily to serve middle-income households. It has become distressingly clear, however, that private housing markets cannot produce sufficient quantities of decent housing for low-income people. That task has fallen increasingly to the national governments, which typically have worked through either nonprofit producers or local governments to build low-cost housing. In several European nations the nonprofit sector, composed of housing cooperatives, trade unions, and nonprofit corporations, has built most of the low-income housing, in cooperation with both national and local governments. In other nations, local governments themselves operate as builders and managers of low-income housing. The degree to which housing programs faithfully reflect national intent thus depends on the degree of leverage that national governments have over local governments and nonprofit builders. As we shall see, that degree of leverage differs from nation to nation.

Housing Policy Instruments

The selection of policy instruments by national governments presents a choice between two strategies that can be characterized as subsidizing producers versus subsidizing consumers. The balance between these two main types of subsidy has differed in the nations under study, although in the last twenty years a general shift toward consumer subsidies has occurred, as governments have favored policies that rely on the market to build housing and limit the government's role to that of subsidizing market transactions. This shift is generally labeled "privatization." Producer lobbies on both sides of the Atlantic have preferred construction subsidies, and have shown little enthusiasm for subsidies to consumers. Despite producer preferences, however, consumer subsidies are increasing in most Western nations.

Distribution of Costs and Benefits

The distributional issue facing policymakers can be simply stated: Who should benefit from housing subsidies? This issue, as we shall see, is closely related to the choice of policy instruments. Proponents of production subsidies have met increasing opposition from critics who argue that government programs to subsidize producers are ineffective in helping low-income citizens. The filtering effect in urban housing markets has been called into doubt; governments cannot be certain that by enlarging the total housing stock, they are creating vacancies for all income groups in the population. In American cities, residential segregation patterns prevent many families from moving into neighborhoods where better housing opportunities exist. European housing markets have their own built-in rigidities created by rent control. Even when governments subsidize producers to build housing specifically for the poor, it is extremely difficult to ensure that the housing will ultimately be occupied by the intended beneficiaries. Such distributional considerations have certainly contributed to the shift by all seven governments toward direct subsidies to consumers.

Restraints and Innovation in Housing Policy

During the 1950s and 1960s, the massive production programs undertaken by many European governments created a set of institutional relationships and roles that could reasonably be characterized as "corporatist" in nature. Webs of interdependence linking public officials, financial institutions, and housebuilders, both profit-making and nonprofit, developed from government intervention and drove the expansion of housing construction programs. Recognizing that it was the production programs that spawned these powerful government-industry links, we must ask whether the shift toward privatization will threaten those links and ultimately threaten the pace of housing expansion.

GOVERNMENTAL RESPONSIBILITY FOR SHELTER
SCOPE AND THRESHOLDS

Legislative rhetoric regarding governmental responsibility for housing is remarkably similar throughout the industrialized nations. Every national government has produced policy statements pledging its commitment to a decent home for every citizen. Moving beyond the rhetoric, however, we discover important differences in the role that national governments have chosen to play, as well as differences in the extent of local governments' responsibility for, and control over, housing programs.

Public Intervention in the Private Housing Market

Shelter is one of humankind's basic requirements. Yet until the twentieth century the governments of Europe and the United States took almost no direct responsibility for housing their populations. Even the horrifying accounts of working-class living conditions contained in the popular works of writers such as Emile Zola and Charles Dickens stimulated little immediate action by governments. And when, in the late nineteenth century, governments did begin to take action, it was usually in the form of regulations prohibiting slums and requiring tenement owners to upgrade housing on their properties. Governments were not in the practice of building houses, even for the poor. Before 1900, the provision of housing by some local governments in Europe was limited to special-purpose institutions, such as the British foundling homes and workhouses.

The housing sector has, of course, always depended to a certain extent on government economic policies. At a minimum, the functioning of the housing sector requires that government enforce some consistent set of agreements regarding property rights. In addition, government must maintain a stable economic environment in which permanent financial institutions can survive, for housing is a durable, high-cost commodity which requires long-term investment. But before 1900 most direct public involvement in housing was limited to encouraging self-help schemes through cooperatives and unions, in order to build and maintain a limited amount of working-class housing. Even the social reformers of the 1890s tended to agree with the banks, the landowners, and the building industries that government intervention in housing would constitute an unhealthy form of paternalism.

Despite this bias against public intervention in housing which prevailed on both sides of the Atlantic in 1900, the combined impact of two world wars and a major depression in the first half of the twentieth century brought all Western governments into the housing field. While many nations began experimenting with housing programs during the interwar period, it was not until after World War II that most of these programs really "took off" and began to assume their present dimensions. Even up to 1950, many governments assumed that their housing responsibilities were temporary, seeing their role as a response to the emergency conditions created by the war damage, by the 1930s collapse of private capital markets, and by the abnormally high construction costs that stemmed from war-related shortages of material. Once the private housing market was reestablished, governments expected to withdraw.

Several socioeconomic trends, however, conspired to expand rather than reduce government involvement. Postwar demographic changes produced larger populations of elderly people and an increase in marriage rates. These trends, combined with widespread prosperity in the 1950s, led to a greater tendency for households to subdivide, thereby creating pressure on housing markets. In addition to providing greater opportunities for the establishment of separate households, the postwar economic expansion drew large numbers of migrant workers into growing industrial centers, especially in northern Europe. At the same time, governments were recognizing the need to modernize and upgrade much of their older housing stock. Urban renewal on a large scale was thus added to the public agenda. Finally, in addition to all of the problems confronting governments with regard to the housing stock itself, the question of distribution also came to the fore in the postwar period. Governments now intervened to try to reduce the huge disparities in the housing situations of different income groups in the population.

During the 1960s, observers of housing policies in Western Europe and the United States began to use the labels "comprehensive" and "supplementary" to distinguish between policies which aimed at planning and controlling the total volume of housebuilding and policies which aimed only at bolstering the private housing market and providing housing for those groups that could not be served by private builders. Those governments with *comprehensive* policies took responsibility for the housing needs of the entire population; those with *supplementary* policies relied on private industry to plan for the vast majority of the population, while they planned only for the minorities unable to obtain housing on the open market (the poor and the elderly, for example).[1]

Surprisingly, the scope of government responsibility for housing is not necessarily most comprehensive where it is most visible. The presence of large government-owned housing stocks in British and American cities does not mean that government in those two nations takes a greater responsibility for housing. In fact, the reverse is true. Those governments in Europe and Japan which plan for the entire housing market have usually chosen *not* to build government housing, but instead to subsidize private builders of both the profit-making and the nonprofit variety. The scope of governmental responsibility tends therefore to be most comprehensive where it is least visible.

Under this scheme, the housing policies in Britain and the United States are classified as supplementary. In both nations, the growth of the housing stock has taken place very gradually, within the framework of long-established trends toward urbanization and industrialization. In these countries, the building industry and the private credit market have for the most part been adequate to sustain a large volume in construction.

In Britain during the years immediately following World War II the Labour government assumed a very large share of the responsibility for financing and distributing housing. In retrospect, however, that spate of

---

[1]For examples of the use of the labels "comprehensive" and "supplementary," see D. V. Donnison, *The Government of Housing* (Baltimore: Penguin, 1967) and United Nations, Economic Commission for Europe, *Major Long-Term Problems of Government Housing and Related Policies*, Vol. 1 (Geneva, 1966). A more recent study which uses these categories in a modified form is Bruce Headey, *Housing Policy in the Developed Economy: The United Kingdom, Sweden, and the United States* (New York: St. Martin's Press, 1978).

housing activity appears to have been an exception, dictated by the acute postwar shortage, and the 1950s saw the Conservative governments returning to the position that government housing activity should be a supplement to rather than a replacement for the private market.

The history of American housing policy presents an even clearer illustration of the traditional belief that government activity should merely supplement private activity. One commentator on U.S. housing policy even argued that "in a sense, U.S. housing policy is to have no policy and rely on private enterprise" (Headey, p. 175). The cornerstone of federal housing policy is the mortgage guarantee program, which operates through the Federal Housing Administration (FHA) and the Veterans Administration (VA). Far from interfering with private enterprise, the mortgage guarantee program has greased the wheels of the private credit machine so as to promote private transactions. The FHA and the VA furnish insurance on the risks that private credit institutions take in lending money to finance housing purchases; both agencies agree to make good any approved loan if the home buyer should default on payments. By thus allowing private banks and savings associations to lend money to home buyers without bearing the risks involved in normal lending transactions, they have facilitated home ownership.

Nor has American public housing ever occupied a position of competition with the private rental market. So strong were the pressures against undermining the private housing market by building cheap government housing that Congress wrote into the original 1937 legislation an "equivalent elimination provision," which stipulated that for every public housing unit built, a substandard dwelling must be removed within five years, via condemnation or demolition. The anxiety expressed by American housing officials that "the indiscriminate production of new subsidized housing could lead to sharp diminution of the demand for privately financed housing" (Kristof, p. 91) hardly seems justified, given the record of the public housing program. Never since the 1930s has public housing constituted more than 3 percent of the total housing stock in the United States.

In contrast, the housing policies of Sweden, France, West Germany, and the Netherlands are classified as comprehensive, even though none of these governments has directly built as much government housing as Britain (see Table 4.1). All have explicitly committed themselves to a policy of channeling the flow of national resources in the housing field in ways that will maximize the welfare of the entire population. By means of relatively shallow subsidies to a very broad spectrum of housing investors, the governments of these countries are able to exercise significant control over the volume, timing, and even the location of residential building for all income levels and by almost all types of builders.

Sweden presents the most dramatic example of a comprehensive housing policy. Although public programs played a marginal role in Sweden's housing sector up to World War II, the Social Democratic government undertook from 1946 to 1948 a series of measures which vastly extended the government's control. Here the comprehensive approach to housing encompassed planning for all income levels, not just for low-income Swedes. The government's ability to carry out its plans rests on its mortgage loan program, which has expanded so dramatically since 1946 that in recent decades as much as 90 percent of all housing construction in the country has involved government loans.

TABLE 4.1. DWELLINGS COMPLETED, BY TYPE OF INVESTOR, 1970–85

	National, County, and Local Governments	Nonprofits	Private Builders
France			
1970	.7%	32.2%	67.1%
1980	.8	20.6	78.6
1984	1.1	17.3	81.5
West Germany			
1970	2.3	18.4	79.3
1980	1.5	8.6	89.8
1985	.5	7.9	91.5
Netherlands			
1970	16.3	31.6	52.1
1980	2.7	27.7	69.6
1985	4.8	35.7	59.1
Sweden			
1970	4.3	53.9	41.8
1980	2.4	33.3	64.2
1985	2.4	55.1	42.4
Britain			
1970	48.6	3.3	48.1
1980	36.1	11.2	52.7
1985	15.3	6.7	78.0
United States			
1970	2.3	0.0	97.7
1980	.5	0.0	99.5
1985	0.0	0.0	99.9
Japan			
1980	9.2	1.8	88.9
1984	7.1	1.2	91.6

SOURCES United Nations Economic Commission for Europe, *Annual Bulletin of Housing and Building Statistics for Europe 1986* (New York: UN, 1987); and United Nations, *Construction Statistics Yearbook 1984* (New York: UN, 1986).

In West Germany at the end of World War II, there was an undeniable need for the government to take a major role in rebuilding that nation's devastated housing stock. Yet in the postwar climate, officials declined to create a massive government-owned housing stock; instead, they chose to influence the housing supply by providing interest-free loans to any individual or enterprise desiring to build, provided the housing was to be rented at a moderate sum. By this means, as well as with low-interest loans and tax concessions to homeowners, the government was able to bring the nation from a 35 percent housing shortage in 1950 to a national vacancy rate of 3 percent (considered optimal) in 1975 (Hallett, p. 12).

Similarly, France builds almost no housing directly but wields enormous influence over the entire construction industry. All construction is channeled through a government licensing system. And not only does the French government closely control the principal lending agencies, but it manipulates tax privileges on repayment of building loans in order to lure investors in directions it favors.

Japan's national effort to rebuild its damaged cities after World War II involved a massive government commitment, which has produced a very high rate of new construction. Despite the reports of the cramped living conditions suffered by the residents of Tokyo, Osaka, and other large cities, Japan actually spends a higher proportion of its Gross National Product on housing than other OECD countries (OECD 1986, p. 64). And fully two-thirds of the houses built since the war have been constructed with government loans. What is even more surprising is that the ratio of publicly financed to privately financed construction has been increasing since 1965—a trend that runs counter to that in most industrialized countries (Kirwan, p. 353).

Overlaps and Conflicts between National and Local Responsibilities

To produce housing, national governments rely either on local governments as builders or on private producers, both nonprofit and profit-making. One might assume that choosing local governments as producers would give national policymakers more centralized control over the production process than would a decision to rely on nongovernment producers. Such a view would be overly simplistic.

For one thing, many of the nongovernment builders in Western Europe are large, highly professional nonprofit enterprises with far-flung interests throughout a particular country. Working through such companies gives governments more leverage over costs and building standards in a greater number and variety of projects than they could gain by working through local governments. The outstanding example is West Germany's Neue Heimat, which began in the 1920s as a union-sponsored nonprofit builder in Hamburg. As a national and even international organization,

Neue Heimat not only builds an enormous amount of housing but also furnishes planning, zoning, and urban renewal assistance to cities all over the country. This nonprofit has pioneered prefabricated housing technology in Germany, and its computerized information system provides a unique national data base with which to analyze housing market trends. In Sweden, similar roles are played by the two major national housing cooperatives, HSB and Svenska Riksbyggen, and by SABO, the peak organization of the nonprofit corporations. Such national organizations serve to structure what would otherwise be a highly fragmented housing market, and hence they act as coordinating points for housing policy.

Nor is it as easy as it might seem for national governments to control the housing programs of local authorities, even in the unitary political systems of Europe. When local governments take the major responsibility for housing production, they must normally go to the private capital markets for some substantial portion of the investment funds, just as nonprofits and other developers must do. Hence the size and timing of their building programs are affected not only by national priorities but also by the requirements of the private credit market. Furthermore, the partisan complexion of local governments, relative to the national administration, may play an important role in determining local cooperation with national objectives. So, for example, the ability of Sweden's Social Democrats to gain local cooperation in implementing their housing program after the war was undoubtedly related to the fact that the main cities were also controlled by Social Democrats. And in Britain a number of studies have shown that local authorities controlled by the Labour party pursue more vigorous building programs than Conservative-controlled localities (Boaden; Boaden and Alford; Davies).

Normally, local governments can be expected to respond positively to national production incentives when it is a question of housing their own population. It is more difficult, however, for central governments to persuade localities to build housing for people outside their boundaries, especially low-income families. When the prevailing national policy is to promote the movement of low-income households across local government boundaries, then national-local power relationships quickly come into play.

Perhaps the most striking examples are found in American cities. Since its inception in 1937, American public housing has been concentrated in central cities. Under the legislation that created this housing program, localities were free to request federal subsidies to build low-rent housing in their municipality. Small towns and suburbs have been notoriously resistant to any public housing for low-income families. A recent case is that of Yonkers, New York, where a landmark civil rights case filed in 1980 resulted in a judge ordering the city government to reverse its forty-year-old policy of racial segregation and to construct public housing in the community's white, middle-class neighborhoods. Despite escalating fines and threats of jail sentences, a majority of the Yonkers City Council refused to allow the construction to proceed, turning their city into a national symbol of defiance to civil rights. (As of this writing, the Yonkers controversy is still in the courts; not a single unit of publicly financed housing has been built.)

Many suburban communities have turned down federal funds rather than comply with the requirement to include low-income housing. Even if federal officials try to bypass local government to work directly with private developers, local officials can still use zoning laws, building codes, and other local ordinances to obstruct the development. Few profit-oriented developers are willing to sustain lengthy court battles against local governments in order to build low-rent housing in suburban communities.

American cities are not alone in facing suburban resistance against the influx of low-income renters. The city of Stockholm faced a similar problem in the post–World War II era. But in Stockholm's case, the power of the national administration was sufficient to force city-suburb cooperation. Like many other European cities in 1945, Stockholm suffered from a housing shortage. To get the cooperation of the suburbs in tackling this housing crisis, the city launched a vigorous campaign at the regional level, using a double-edged strategy. Socialist city officials persuaded suburban leaders to join in a metropolitan planning agency, the Greater Stockholm Planning Board, to coordinate housing production throughout the region. But, in addition to cultivating the formal cooperation of suburban governments within the planning board, the city also used its land-purchase powers to gain informal leverage over suburban officials.

The city's acquisitions ranged over the entire metropolitan area, some parcels lying twenty miles or more from the city's center. City ownership of suburban property then provided a bargaining edge when the city sought out suburban cooperation in housing production. Numerous bargains were struck, in which suburban governments agreed to accept city building companies as partners in the construction of new housing projects on suburban sites.

However, it soon became apparent that the distribution of these newly built units was a potential source of conflict between the city and the suburbs. One of the great risks run by suburban politicians in cooperating with the city on housing production was that the city could choose to steer large numbers of low-income families to suburban housing units. Since Swedish municipalities gain most of their revenues from personal income taxes, they could not be expected to welcome an influx of low-income residents. The suburbs therefore resisted handing over their power to distribute new apartments to a regional housing exchange.

Their resistance was overcome only when the national government intervened to force an integrated solution to Stockholm's housing crisis. A royal commission created in 1962 to study the question produced a final report which left only two options open to the suburbs: Either they would cooperate voluntarily in a regional distribution scheme for allocating new housing, or the national government would impose a common housing exchange. As a follow-up to the commission's report, the national government announced in 1966 that its loans in the region would henceforth go only to municipalities which were participants in the housing exchange. The impact of that announcement is obvious, if we remember that 90 percent of Swedish housing construction depends on government loans of some kind.

The Trend toward Privatization

Perhaps more than any other policy area treated in this volume, housing policy has been singled out in the 1980s as a target for privatization. Throughout Western Europe and North America, policymakers are increasingly emphasizing private financing, private construction, and private ownership of housing as an alternative to public sector programs. This shift is most visible in countries that have traditionally held to supplementary housing policies. As we shall see, the Reagan and Thatcher administrations in the United States and Britain have gone so far as to begin selling off government-owned housing units to their occupants. And even in countries that had previously pursued more comprehensive housing policies, governments are relying more on private capital markets to finance housing while encouraging higher levels of homeownership.

The high visibility of these policy shifts has led some observers to assume that privatization must inevitably reduce the scope of government support for housing. That is a mistaken interpretation. In fact, privatization does not necessarily mean that governments withdraw from the market, leaving citizens to pay for housing from their private incomes. It does not even mean that governments necessarily reduce their subsidies for housing. It simply means that the nature of housing policy instruments changes. As we shall see in the next section, privatization usually involves large government subsidies to consumers to subsidize their purchase of private housing.

INTERVENTIONS INTO HOUSING MARKETS
INSTRUMENTS

Just as in the delivery of health care each nation has developed its own system for deploying and paying doctors, so different nations use various strategies for producing and distributing housing. Nonetheless, we can broadly distinguish two kinds of strategies: subsidizing producers and subsidizing consumers.

Subsidies to Producers

Offering subsidies to housing suppliers is the most direct method of stimulating housing production. It is therefore the favored strategy for meeting a nation's need for additional dwelling units. The need to stimulate housing construction may arise from a number of different causes, the most obvious being a dramatic population shift. In Sweden the proportion of the population living in urban areas shot up from only 38 percent in 1931 to 73 percent in 1961 (Donnison, p. 160). Naturally, such rapid urbanization created an acute housing shortage in the cities. The Dutch present the clearest case of a postwar housing shortage that stemmed from the effects of demographic change: In addition to very rapid population growth, the Dutch experienced a sharp upturn in the proportion of marriage-age citizens and older people. Such shifts have multiplied the demand for housing units. West Germany's and Japan's postwar shortages were of course related to war damage. For the French, the postwar housing problem was caused less by an absolute shortage of units than by the overcrowded, substandard conditions prevailing in a large proportion of French households. The French lagged far behind most other European countries in such measures as the number of rooms per person or bathroom facilities per dwelling, as well as in the overall modernity of the housing stock.

In the United States the Depression of the 1930s lowered the living standard of a great segment of the population but did not actually create a housing shortage. The federal housing programs created under the New Deal were motivated more by the desire to create employment in the construction industries than by the need to enlarge the housing stock.

The two primary instruments for subsidizing production are: (1) construction programs in which the government builds its own housing for rent, usually to low- and moderate-income people, and (2) subsidies to private producers of either the profit-making or the nonprofit variety. Britain has used the first instrument, public construction, more vigorously than any other Western nation. From 1945 to 1948, Britain moved from a negligible volume of public construction to over 190,000 units of public housing completed in one year (1948). Even under the Conservatives in the 1950s and early 1960s, the annual completion rate never dropped below 100,000. In fact, from 1946 to 1976, Britain built at the impressive rate of 143,000 public housing units per year (Merrett, Chapter 9). Public housing is so prominent now in Britain that it contains a quarter of all British households. Its widespread acceptability is based on the fact that it was not confined to low-income tenants, but open to tenants at all income levels.

Since the early 1970s, however, the view of public, or council, housing held by both the British government and the public has been gradually changing. The largest single step toward change was taken by the Conservatives in the 1972 Housing Finance Act, which forced local government councils to charge higher rents across the board, while instituting special rent relief only for those who could demonstrate need. Defenders of public housing charged that the result would be to force out the more prosperous residents who would find it cheaper to live elsewhere. They invoked the grim images of public housing in America as evidence of the problems that governments encounter when they limit public housing to the poor.

As public housing projects in the United States have been transformed into poverty enclaves in the last thirty years, they have become increasingly unacceptable to even the lowest socioeconomic group. Life in public housing exerts so little attraction that even those families who are poor enough to qualify (maximum acceptable income varies widely from state to state) frequently reject this alternative. As the program's clientele has narrowed over the years, so that now it serves only problem families and the elderly, the reservoir of political support for public housing has shrunk. Labor unions such as the AFL-CIO, which played a key role in the legislative battles over the program in the late 1940s, provide a good example of public housing's political problem. Union enthusiasm for the program has dampened markedly over the years; although union spokespersons still support the program in principle, they have little stake in its expansion. Given their income levels, the skilled and semiskilled members of unions are unlikely to benefit from public housing. On the contrary, in speaking for their members as housing consumers, the unions are much more interested in the expansion of the FHA mortgage insurance program than in large-scale government-sponsored rental programs. The gradual disenchantment exhibited by the program's original supporters, combined with local hostility to the construction of new projects, has meant that "very few people are pushing [public housing] as a vitally important program, the way they were in the 1930s" (Wolman 1971, p. 35).

Rather than building a stock of public housing, most Western European nations and Japan have opted to stimulate production by subsidizing private builders. When offered to profit-making enterprises, such subsidies are commonly restricted to dwellings that will be moderately priced. For example, West Germany's postwar policy of offering interest-free loans to private builders stipulated that the housing constructed with the subsidies must be offered at a prescribed "cost-covering" rent to households that met certain eligibility requirements based on income and family circumstances. Similar restrictions were imposed by the U.S. Congress when it included the Section 221(3) program in the 1961 National Housing Act. This program provided below-market interest rates to private developers who agreed to build or rehabilitate apartments for low- and moderate-income families. In accepting the subsidy, developers committed themselves to limiting rents.

Needless to say, the success of such programs rests on the degree to which they are competitive with other forms of investment that profit-making developers might make instead. In the case of the Section 221(3) program, relatively few units have actually been produced, precisely because profit-motivated developers could earn higher returns by investing in housing for middle- and upper-income families.

Several European governments have avoided this problem by relying more heavily on nonprofit builders. The category of "nonprofits" includes a variety of investor types, from semipublic utility companies whose directorship is part public and part private, to labor unions, housing cooperatives, nonprofit corporations, and associations. Typically, these various nonprofit enterprises sell limited-interest membership shares in order to acquire starting capital, on the basis of which they can then apply for government loans. Once backed by government loans, they are able to secure further loans from private credit sources. Since they are partially backed by low-interest government loans, they extract no profits from their buildings; and, as they usually pay no taxes, they are able to rent their units out at prices below the private market.

Sweden made nonprofit builders the core of its post–World War II housing policy. Unlike Britain's postwar socialist government, Swedish socialists avoided building a large volume of public housing. Instead, they gave favorable treatment to nonprofits, both corporations and cooperatives, thereby helping them to build about two thirds of all postwar housing. As Table 4.1 shows, forty years after the war, Sweden's nonprofits still occupy a prominent position in the nation's housing market.

In France, nonprofits currently represent a little less than one-fifth of building starts. As in Sweden, the HLMs (*habitations à loyer modéré*) are not owned by the government itself but by independent housing societies. They do, however, receive government subsidies in the form of long-term Treasury loans at low interest rates, permitting them to charge rents that are typically only two-thirds the rents on comparable private housing. Another important parallel to the Swedish system lies in the breadth of French subsidies; in recent years, less than a quarter of French construction has been undertaken without some form of government subsidy.

The Shift to Subsidizing Consumers

The second major strategic option available to governments is to stimulate housing demand by subsidizing housing consumers. The two most common instruments used to subsidize consumers are: (1) cash allowances to renters, and (2) tax concessions to owner-occupiers.

The trend toward consumer subsidies began several decades ago when governments no longer faced the severe shortages of the early postwar period. And it began, not with the owner-occupied segment, but with the rental segment of the market. As the housing shortage receded, public debate in many of the nations of Western Europe began to focus on housing affordability as the major housing issue. Inflation and rising construction costs affected all income groups and segments of the market, pushing questions of equity in the distribution of housing costs and opportunities to the fore (Priemus; Heclo and Madsen). Production subsidies gave governments little leverage on these problems of distribution and affordability because they could not be used to target particular types of households. Increasingly, governments turned to housing allowances to supplement construction programs. Sweden, the Netherlands, West Germany, and France all reduced the size of their production subsidy programs in the 1970s, while expanding the coverage of housing allowances (Howenstine 1986).

Virtually all Western European governments now provide housing allowances in one form or another, and the United States has recently begun to experiment with this instrument as well. When they were first introduced, these direct assistance programs were usually structured to meet the needs of particular groups in the population, especially those unable to obtain decent dwellings without subsidy (for example, large families, the elderly, the disabled). These programs take different forms, depending on the target population. In the case of the elderly, governments may channel the recipients of the allowance into apartment units designed specifically for older tenants. But when the target population has been low-income groups, European authorities have seldom encouraged the construction of projects specifically for them. Instead, the most common form of subsidy has been a direct cash transfer, which permits the tenant families to choose among the housing alternatives available on the open market. In some countries, most notably Sweden, the idea of the housing allowance has gradually reached beyond specific target populations to embrace the majority of households in the nation.

The role of allowances has increased markedly in recent years, as the pressure of housing shortages in most European nations has diminished, reducing the emphasis on housing production. Analysts have increasingly perceived difficulties in tying government subsidies to particular buildings rather than to people. In offering production subsidies, governments can never be absolutely certain which households will be the beneficiaries of their largesse. As we have already seen, production subsidies hold down the housing costs of the tenants living in dwellings whose construction has been supported by government loans or grants. Once they are built, however, the government loses control over just how the subsidized units are to be allocated. Families originally qualifying under the established eligibility requirements may experience changes in their circumstances over time; and when their incomes rise or their children leave home, they often opt to stay in the subsidized unit. Without an elaborate, permanent monitoring system, governments cannot guarantee that their stock of subsidized housing will be optimally allocated. Because of the difficulty of targeting the aid to particular kinds of households, production subsidies are a relatively inefficient, and therefore expensive, instrument for meeting the housing needs of particular groups in society. This inefficiency became a more pressing issue for most governments in the 1970s, as soaring construction costs and tighter national budgets forced all Western governments to reassess their spending priorities. An additional criticism of production subsidies is that they restrict residents freedom of mobility: They enjoy the subsidy only so long as they live in a particular unit. British Conservatives have even charged that the practice of attaching subsidies to council houses acts as an impediment to national economic growth, for the subsidized rents and the long waiting lists for council houses discourage British workers from relocating for the sake of job opportunities (*New York Times*, 8 June 1980, p. 1). Yet another objection is that production subsidies have helped to compartmentalize urban housing markets; subsidized tenants are concentrated in certain kinds of buildings in certain parts of a city, instead of being dispersed throughout the housing market.

Conscious of these shortcomings and no longer faced with the severe shortages of the postwar years, European governments have gradually expanded housing allowances so that in recent years they have constituted a growing proportion of national housing expenditures (Howenstine 1975). For example, in 1967 the Netherlands began a process of gradually reducing interest subsidies on its construction loans, while raising rents in subsidized buildings at an equivalent rate. But, to cushion the impact of these increases on low-income families, the Dutch government also introduced a housing allowance. Sweden in 1968 raised interest on government mortgage loans to equal market interest rates. Thus, even though the national government continued to be a major lender, it was no longer subsidizing production with low-interest loans.[2] At about the same time, Sweden began extending housing allowances to cover families with children, pensioners, unmarried mothers and fathers, and finally even single people without children. Similarly, West Germany raised its *Wohngeld*, or housing allowance, in the early 1970s. Housing allowances had been available on a limited basis since 1956, but legislation in 1970 extended them to all housing. They supply the difference between what a family actually pays for its housing and the so-called "tolerable rent" for that same family, based on its size and income. By 1975 such allowances amounted to about half of what Germany was spending on production subsidies (Hallett, p. 33).

As we have said, housing allowances appeal to conservatives as well as to politicians on the left. Britain's Conservative party provides a good example. In their 1972 Housing Finance Act, they took the dramatic step of imposing a "fair rent" scheme on the nation's public housing stock, which said that public housing tenants would henceforth be charged rents which

---

[2]Headey argues that mortgage subsidies were not really abolished by the 1968 measure, because the government took other compensating measures which diluted the impact of this action (p. 84).

were roughly comparable to the rents paid by private sector tenants. The Labour party had introduced a fair rent scheme in the private sector in 1965, designed to assure that landlords would receive no more than a "fair" return on their investments and that all landlords with comparable units would charge similar rents. Contrary to what the Labour government had expected, rents were raised in many buildings, rather than lowered (Headey, p. 152). In the early 1970s, Conservative critics of public housing increasingly argued that the system of rents in council houses was a hodge-podge. Rents differed widely, depending on the age of the building, and many tenants were paying much less than they could afford to pay. In one sweeping move, the Conservatives brought public housing rents up to a fair rent standard, thereby effectively eliminating the benefits to renters of the initial construction subsidies. At the same time, they directed local governments to offer allowances to tenants in both public and private accommodations, according to their income and family size. The Conservatives' intent was to change the subsidy to public housing tenants, from a subsidy attached to the particular building in which they lived, to a housing allowance dependent on their family circumstances. The effect of the change, however, was diluted by the Labour government, which replaced the Conservatives in 1974. Perhaps because of their earlier experience with fair rents in the private sector, Labour repealed the provision that rents in council housing had to conform to a fair rent standard, while leaving in place the system of cash allowances for both public and private tenants.

France's conservative Gaullist party has also enthusiastically advocated the extension of housing allowances. Since its origin in 1939, France's housing allowance has traditionally been linked to the more general family allowance, and both have been systematically manipulated by the government to encourage higher birth rates. As a response to the demographic problems associated with a low birth rate, the French government stipulated that neither allowance was to be available to families with fewer than two children. Since 1971, however, benefits under the housing allowance program have been extended to almost a million more French citizens whose circumstances warranted aid: the elderly, the disabled, single persons, and young couples without children.

The move to extend benefits was part of a housing reform program advanced by the controversial Minister of Housing and Equipment, Albin Chalandon. Like the Swedes, Chalandon had decided that direct payments to families would in the long run provide greater benefits for low-income groups than would government subsidies to construction. The special designation of some housing complexes as low- and moderate-rent units, a practice which fosters social segregation, would be unnecessary, Chalandon argued in 1971, if housing allowances could be increased for those who needed them most. In addition, Chalandon justified greater reliance on the housing allowance as an effort to allocate the nation's housing stock more equitably by eliminating the distortions introduced by production subsidies. A self-styled champion of *désétatisation* (literally, "degovernmentalizing"), Chalandon frequently during his public career found himself at odds with other members of his own party. Far more than most other Gaullist politicians, he wanted to move in the direction of decreased government intervention in the urban economy. In both economic and social ways, he contended, the private market can be made to function more effectively if the government simply provides cash subsidies to help low-income groups obtain standard housing, rather than herding them together in low-rent projects.

A clear preference for housing allowances (*aide à la personne*) to replace production subsidies (*aide à la pierre*) was finally articulated in several major reports published in 1975. The most influential of them, the Barre report, was named for the chair of a government-appointed study commission and future prime minister. France's policy of subsidizing construction, Barre argued, benefited mainly the better-off groups in French society. His conclusion, that market forces should play the principal role in housing provision, was embodied in the Housing Act of 1977, which both reduced government expenditures for construction and channeled subsidies directly to householders through allowances (Pearsall, p. 39).

In the United States, the housing allowance has been promoted recently by conservative Republicans as an alternative to the Democrats' low-income housing programs of the 1960s. Although the allowance idea had been advanced periodically by American social reformers since the 1940s, it was not given serious consideration until the Nixon administration introduced and passed legislation in 1970 which included a $30 million authorization for a nationwide experiment with housing allowances. The trial runs, carried out between 1972 and 1980 in a dozen American cities, were described by HUD officials as a possible vehicle for a radical redirection of the entire federal housing program.

The increased reliance on allowances by West Germany, France, and other Western governments constitutes one form of privatization because it assigns to the private market the responsibility for producing rental housing, while government merely provides a cash transfer to tenants who choose among housing alternatives in the open market. Another important policy instrument to promote privatization is the tax expenditure, which goes to owners instead of renters. Tax expenditures may be defined as losses of tax revenue attributable to provisions of tax laws that allow special exclusions, exceptions, or deductions from gross income, or provide special credits, preferential tax rates, or deferral of tax liability. Normally these tax concessions take the form of government forgiveness of taxes on that portion of income devoted to paying interest on mortgage loans. So widespread is this form of subsidy to housing that it has created what one observer called a "second welfare state" coexisting with the more widely recognized "first" welfare state (Headey, p. 24).

The United States is perhaps the premier example of the use of tax expenditures to subsidize housing. The income tax laws have provided enormous incentives to homeowners, including deductions for interest payments and property taxes, deferral or exclusion of capital gains on home sales, and a decision not to tax imputed rent. As of 1985, tax expenditures comprised the bulk of federal subsidies to housing; homeowner deductions cost the government $49.3 billion (and deductions going to investors another $5.8 billion), while the total direct expenditures for all social housing programs amounted to only about one-fourth as much.

Britain, too, has a long-standing tax policy allowing full deductibility of interest payments on mortgages. In addition, owner-occupiers have been free from capital gains tax and capital transfer tax and, from 1963 onward, free from tax on imputed rent. As in the United States, the subsidy granted to property owners via the tax expenditure is far in excess of direct subsidies to the tenants in social housing. In 1982–83, for example, the average owner-occupier received a subsidy of 366 pounds per year, compared with an average subsidy to council tenants of only 206 pounds (Balchin, p. 239). Among the nations included in this discussion, Britain, the United States, and Japan are normally perceived as the bastions of homeownership. They would therefore be expected to offer the largest tax concessions to property owners, as has Japan. But what about the governments on the Continent? Table 4.2 shows that even in these countries, where homeownership has traditionally been less widespread, tax concessions nevertheless are high. They constitute a sizable portion of housing subsidies, although they do not always go exclusively to owner-occupiers. In West Germany, for example, the impressive tax expenditures go more to the owners of rental properties than to owner-occupiers. For German rental housing, all capital gains remain untaxed so long as they are reinvested in real property.

Yet another sign of the gradual privatization of housing policy has been the withdrawal of governments from the role of primary lender, shifting to private capital markets the responsibility for providing the credit needed to build social housing. Here too, West Germany led other European nations. Immediately after the war, the government took the lead in

TABLE 4.2 COMPOSITION OF HOUSING SUBSIDIES IN SELECTED COUNTRIES

	Housing Allowances	Tax Concessions	Producer	Other
France (1984)	22%	43%	35%	0%
West Germany (1978)	9%	50%	21%	20%
Netherlands (1983)	27%	27%	34%	12%
Sweden (1981)	24%	47%	29%	0%

SOURCE E. Jay Howenstine, *Housing Vouchers: A Comparative International Analysis* (New Brunswick: Rutgers University Center for Urban Policy Research, 1986) pp. 110–111.

making large capital loans and grants to nonprofit builders of social housing. As early as 1956, however, national legislation authorized a shift away from the government's role as banker, and toward government subsidies to assist nonprofits in repaying loans to private credit sources. By 1967 government outlays for this latter type of subsidy exceeded those for government-provided loans and grants. When the legislature extended subsidies to higher-income households in 1967, it employed only the device of subsidizing privately secured loans. "Thus, private capital, now more significantly available, played an ever-increasing role in the housing field, including subsidized housing" (Marcuse, p. 96).

France moved in the same direction, starting a few years later than West Germany. During the 1950s and 1960s most of the funds flowing into the housing market came from government sources. The vast majority of units constructed were government-financed, either as HLMs or as subsidized private dwellings (*secteur aidé*). However, once the French government succeeded in organizing an effective mortgage market in the mid-1960s, banks and other private financial institutions began to take over as the main sources of housing funds. Government activity shifted toward providing subsidies to reduce the interest on loans supplied by private credit sources. By 1975 the banks advanced almost half of the credit used to finance the construction and purchase of housing in France (Bandyopadhyay, p. 167). The Housing Act of 1977 carried this trend even further.

The French have pioneered in the use of mixed-economy corporations (*societes d'economie mixte*) as a device for securing private capital to construct social housing as well as to promote urban development (as noted in Chapter 8). Introduced in the 1950s, these public/private corporations bring together representatives of local government (who usually control 65 percent of the votes on governing boards) with private sector investors holding the remaining shares. Although such organizations can boast considerable success in promoting housing development, they have a less impressive record in achieving their social welfare goals. Their history is one of gradual retreat from their initial mandate to create social housing; increasingly, they have financed middle-income housing and economic development projects instead of low-income housing (Eisinger). The effect on the housing market of the various privatizing strategies outlined above is predictable. As can be seen in Table 4.1, the proportion of units produced by government and by other nonprofit suppliers has declined in recent years.

The vigor with which the Reagan and Thatcher regimes have promoted privatization in the 1980s has led many observers to assume that this is a strategy supported only by neo-liberals. In both the United States and Britain, the most oft-cited example of privatization is the effort to sell public housing units to low- and moderate-income tenants, admittedly a favorite idea of the Tories. Within two weeks of their election victory in 1979, Britain's Conservatives announced that they would offer to sell tenants their council houses at discounts of 30 to 50 percent, depending on the length of time they had lived in them. Labour opposed this new initiative, arguing that the most desirable units would be sold off, reducing the choices for future tenants and moving council housing one step closer to being a last resort. One Labour MP warned in parliamentary debates that Britain's housing problem could not "be solved by easy application of free market forces. Mr. Milton Friedman has only to take a short cab ride from his university in Chicago to see what free market forces have done to some districts of that city" (Katz, p. 464). Despite such dire warnings, the Tories pursued their "Right to Buy" program, selling about 800,000 units of council housing in the early 1980s. Their program became the model for a United States program, launched in 1985 and still in progress, whose goal is to sell public housing units in eighteen participating localities.

However, privatization means far more than selling public housing. It refers to a whole collection of policies that shift away from direct government production or financing of dwellings and toward the private market. Understood in those terms, privatization is a widespread policy trend that predated the ascendence of neo-liberal parties in Europe and the United States. Far from being confined to the Reagan and Thatcher governments, the various policy instruments sketched above have been employed by politicians of both the Left and the Right. Indeed, we can go far in explaining their growing popularity by recognizing their appeal to parties of vastly different ideological stripes. Housing allowances are seen by politicians of the Left as a way to equalize access to housing for their working-class constituents. Politicians on the Right are prone to support allowances because they assign the primary responsibility for house-building to the private market. Much the same analysis applies to tax expenditures for owner-occupiers, which have brought such significant benefits to working-class homeowners that politicians of the Left have consistently managed to overlook their regressive nature, while those on the Right applaud their effectiveness in stimulating property ownership. The political consensus surrounding tax expenditures has been unassailable even in countries with the strongest Socialist parties. Despite the recent partisan conflict in Britain over the Conservatives' effort to sell off council housing, the general pattern in Britain over the past twenty-five years has been one of party convergence on government subsidies to homeownership (McLeay). France's Socialist Party made it clear from 1948 onward that it supported measures to bolster private ownership, largely because the gravity of the housing shortage made virtually all housing schemes acceptable. Ultimately even the French Communist Party abandoned its earlier opposition to owner occupation (DuClaud-Williams, pp. 216, 245). In West Germany it was the Social Democrats who took the initiative in 1977 to extend tax concessions to the purchase of existing houses (as opposed to newly constructed dwellings). Up to that time the government had restricted tax subsidies to newly built housing as a stimulus to construction; the extension by the Socialists in 1977 vastly increased the housing stock to which these incentives apply (Harloe, p. 37).

Interest Group Politics and the Choice of Policy Instruments

One reason the United States lags behind Western Europe in adopting housing allowances is the opposition mounted by the producers' lobby. The National Association of Homebuilders has been joined by the AFL-CIO building trades unions and the National Association of Housing and Redevelopment Officials in resisting any program that would divert federal support from new construction toward cash allowances. Interestingly, two other trade groups have publicly supported the allowance concept: The National Apartment Association and the National Association of Realtors see allowances as an instrument that will increase demand for older units, bolstering rents and increasing property turnovers by giving more tenants and prospective owners the resources to compete in the housing market.

In analyzing the influences shaping housing policy in Europe and the United States, we find some important differences in the roles played by producer groups. All Western governments, whatever the public-private mix in their housing sectors, and whatever their strategic choices as to subsidizing producers or consumers, have had to deal with housing producer groups to implement their policies. In the field of health care, most babies are delivered by obstetricians who are not civil servants; similarly, few construction workers are permanent government employees. By and large, government activity in the housing sector has been channeled through the private house-building industry. But in their dealings with governments, producer groups, as we shall see, have wielded varying degrees of influence over policy.

A reading of the history of national housing policy in the United States suggests that the house-building industry has played the largest single role in formulating the policy. The effort to create a federal subsidy for home-ownership in the 1930s was spearheaded by the major financial institutions connected with the housing industry (the Mortgage Bankers Association, the American Bankers Association, the United States Savings and Loan Association, and the National Association of Mutual Savings Banks), and by the major building industry organization (the National Association of Home Builders). These same lobby groups, along with the Chamber of Commerce and the National Association of Real Estate Boards, organized the vociferous opposition to the public housing program envisioned in the 1937 Wagner Act. Their well-orchestrated attacks forced the Wagner bill's sponsors to limit eligibility for public housing to persons who lacked the resources to bargain for housing on the open market, thus stamping public housing as an assistance program.

This housing industry coalition, formed in the 1930s, has persisted with few basic changes up to the present day, and it continues to operate as a clientele group supporting the FHA and as a veto group opposing public housing in any form. Its continuing influence on federal housing policy is evident, for example, in the drafting of the 1968 National Housing Act (Wolman 1971, pp. 91–92). The role played in that process by a presidential blue ribbon commission on urban housing (the so-called Kaiser Committee) is a classic example of the tendency of the American government to place a major share of policy-making responsibility in the hands of organized groups whose interests are directly engaged by the policy. The total membership of the Kaiser Committee was eighteen; out of that total, nine members represented the construction industry, while three more represented financial institutions. Given that composition, it should have surprised no one that the committee drafted a proposal (which ultimately became Title IX of the 1968 act) based on the assumption that the solution to the nation's housing crisis was for private builders to produce twenty-six million new houses over the next decade. The example of the Kaiser Committee is revealing, not only of the way in which federal policy is formulated, but also of the reasons why federal policy promotes homeownership rather than public housing. One congressional staff member summed up the powerful influence of the building lobby on the 1968 Housing Act this way: "That's why they are builder programs. They are oriented toward housing production—units, starts, and property—with people being secondary considerations" (Lilley in Pynoos et al, p. 37).

Compared with the United States, the more direct control exerted by most European governments over their domestic credit institutions and their larger share of the total investment in residential construction have placed them in a stronger bargaining position vis-à-vis private builders. In fact, we might use the label "corporatist" to describe the strong ties between governments and producer groups that developed during the massive building programs of the postwar years. To achieve their production goals, European governments sought to work through large-scale builders' associations, instead of dealing with thousands of individual builders. Government officials relied on the associations to help them implement their programs, and in return incorporated the groups' representatives into policy-making circles.

Perhaps the most dramatic example of government initiatives to structure the political environment by encouraging industry associations is that of postwar Sweden. In a sense, the Social Democrats actually created Sweden's producer lobby by sponsoring the growth of SABO, an association of nonprofit building corporations, as well as the massive expansion of the cooperatives, HSB and Svenska Riksbyggen. By manipulating interest rates, the Social Democrats moved quickly after World War II to channel private credit away from mortgages and to establish the government as the primary credit source for home-building. In its role as banker to home-

builders, the government proceeded to give preference to nonprofit housing associations in distributing loans and to encourage the formation of
national associations to represent them. According to Headey,

> the nonprofit building corporations, which were in effect created by the
> (Swedish) government, HSB, Svenska Riksbyggen and the construction
> workers' trade union have all gained additional members, resources and
> influence because of central government programmes and municipal con-
> tracts (Headey, p. 81).

France's postwar government was also instrumental in building the
capacity within the construction industry to carry out its postwar program.
Typical of much of French industry, the construction sector in the 1950s
was composed of small, tradition-bound firms which resisted introducing
new building technologies and materials. The national *Ministère de la Construction et du Logement* sponsored research into new construction techniques
and materials, and used its leverage to encourage the merger of small firms
into larger ones as well as to promote the use of modern financial and
management practices by housebuilders (Pearsall). Like Sweden, France
provided low-interest loans to nonprofit housing societies which dominated
construction well into the 1960s.

West Germany's government has played an active role, not only by
bolstering the position of certain industry associations, but by influencing
their internal organization as well. A comparative study of the structure of
house-building associations in Britain and West Germany argued that many
of the important differences observed in the two nations' interest associations could be explained by differing governmental structures and actions
since World War II. Unlike their British counterparts, German national
officials often refuse to talk to individual firms, no matter how large, referring them to their own associations. Naturally this practice enhances the
position of the peak associations in the German system. German officials
have few qualms about trying to mold interest associations in ways that are
useful to the government. British civil servants, on the other hand, generally treat business interest associations as voluntary bodies whose organization is a matter for firms to decide among themselves (Grant and Streeck).

TARGETING HOUSING SUBSIDIES
DISTRIBUTION

The transition from production subsidies to consumer allowances is directly related to distributive issues. Since World War II Western governments have shifted from a focus on absolute housing deprivation caused by
shortages to a focus on equity in the distribution of housing. With this shift
has come an increased determination to use subsidies to improve the relative position of the neediest families in the housing market. Housing administrators have long recognized the difficulty of using production subsidies

to benefit the neediest directly. For reasons discussed in the preceding section of this chapter, the production subsidy is an ineffective instrument for targeting expenditures to specific groups. By 1970 administrators in various European nations were estimating that 20 to 50 percent of all social housing was occupied by households that no longer met the income eligibility criteria that had prevailed when they moved in (Frommes).

Moreover, rising building costs in the 1970s made it more difficult to subsidize construction enough to produce an affordable rent for needy families. Thus, it has been common for housing units supposedly built for the needy to be occupied instead by the not-so-poor, who are more able to afford the rents. For example, German production subsidies have in theory been confined to units built for low- and moderate-income tenants. But in fact the eligibility ceilings rose faster in the 1970s than average incomes rose, so that in one province in 1975 the ceiling on social housing was set high enough to include 70 percent of the province's population (Hallett, p. 34). Needless to say, these increases in eligibility limits were strongly supported by the nonprofit builders, who wanted to improve their chances of collecting a reasonable rent from their tenants.

Another case in point is the Swedish government's growing awareness in the 1960s that while Sweden boasted the highest rate of annual housing production per capita of any Western nation, the construction program was favoring the middle class. Systematic investigations of the tenant population in new units showed that new buildings contained disproportionately large numbers of middle- and upper-class families. For example, a study of four new developments in Stockholm built from 1966 to 1968 revealed the income distribution shown in Table 4.3. Obviously, the units in these new developments tended to go to more affluent families.

As we saw earlier, the Swedish government has since 1967 been gradually replacing the interest rate subsidy to builders with an expanded housing allowance that will single out low-income families for special help. Swe-

TABLE 4.3 DISTRIBUTION OF STOCKHOLM HOUSEHOLDS, BY INCOME GROUP

Household Income (in kroner)	Percentage of Total Number of Households	Percentage of Households in Four New Developments
9,000 and under	16.4%	0.0%
10,000–19,000	26.5	4.3
20,000–29,000	22.8	18.7
30,000–39,000	14.4	27.8
40,000–59,000	13.5	40.4
60,000 and over	6.3	8.9

SOURCE International Confederation of Free Trade Unions, *The Housing Situation of Low Income Groups* (Brussels, 1970, p. 51).

den's experience to date suggests that a housing allowance program is not necessarily less expensive than a production subsidy program. The advantage, however, lies in the government's ability to concentrate housing expenditures on low-income families with children. The amount of the allowance varies, depending on the number of children in a recipient family and on the household income. Thus, although the allowance program provides benefits for a large proportion of Swedish families (an estimated 30 percent of families in 1985), the largest allowances go to the neediest families.

The widespread adoption of housing allowances reflects the fact that housing policy has become primarily an income redistribution issue rather than a shelter issue. Housing allowances are everywhere based on the premise that a family's housing expenses should not exceed some specified percentage of its income, which varies from nation to nation. In Sweden, for instance, national subsidies succeeded in bringing workers' rents down from 27 percent of their income in 1950 to 17 percent of their income in 1974 (Headey, p. 58). This figure climbed back up to 25 percent in the mid-1980s. In a comparison of Britain's rent allowance program and the United States' Experimental Housing Allowance Program, the Urban Institute concluded that "the main effect of the allowance payments in both countries has been a reduction in housing costs relative to income" (Trutko, p. x). In other words, most recipients in both nations have used the allowance, not to buy more housing (by making improvements in their existing unit or by moving to a more expensive unit), but instead to obtain budgetary relief. In short, they have used their allowance as an income supplement. This finding prompted urban economist George Sternlieb to label the housing allowance "an income transfer thinly masquerading as a housing device" (Sternlieb in Sternlieb et al., p. 549).

While it is clear that governments have used housing allowances to target aid to the needy, it would be wrong to identify consumer subsidies in general only with aid to the poor. In fact, the tax concessions to home buyers offered by most Western governments represent a massive subsidy to the middle class. They are regressive in that the size of the benefit increases in rough proportion to the home buyer's income. Dutch tax credits, for example, have been shown to favor high-income groups (Van Weesep). And Japan's tax concessions to homeowners, while they do not appear to have boosted homeownership among lower-income Japanese, have subsidized increased ownership for middle- and upper-income households (Kirwan, p. 353). The higher an individual's income, the higher his tax bracket and therefore the more a major deduction is worth to him. Ironically, the more steeply progressive the tax structure of the country, the larger the proportion of interest payments that is deductible in the higher tax brackets. Even in the category of home buyers, favorable tax treatment has a differential distributive impact on existing owners and new buyers. By stimulating the demand for houses, tax subsidies have inflated house prices to the benefit of those who already own a home and to the disadvantage of first-time buyers (Lansley, p. 136). Only Japanese policies directly address this bias by targeting the most generous subsidies to first-time buyers, especially during the first three years of repayments, when help is needed the most.

Not surprisingly, then, this favorable tax treatment afforded to home buyers is strongly supported by the property-owning electorate. Few politicians in any of the Western nations have dared to suggest limiting or reducing this subsidy. One exception is Sweden's Social Democratic party, which openly addressed the question in 1974, thereby risking alienating Sweden's middle-class electorate. Like other nations, Sweden has allowed home buyers to deduct interest paid on their mortgage loans. Sweden's policy in this regard is actually less advantageous to home buyers than either Britain's or the United States' because it combines the tax deduction of mortgage interest with a capital tax levied each year on the amount of the homeowner's accumulated equity. In the early years of ownership, when the home buyer is accumulating little equity, this tax is small; but as equity grows it grows. In a sense, these capital taxes in later years help to compensate the government for the tax revenue it has foregone in the earlier years. Yet even with this provision, Sweden's steeply progressive tax schedule makes the interest deduction a highly regressive instrument. It was calculated in 1972 that the tax subsidy represented a 33 percent reduction in the cost of the average new home, and that this reduction gave new owner-occupiers a 7 percent increase in their real income (Kemeny 1978, p. 319). In response to a growing controversy over this undeniable subsidy to the middle class, the government in 1974 decided to act. But rather than eliminating the tax concession to home buyers, it offered an equivalent benefit to renters in the form of lower interest rates on the money that builders borrow to construct rental housing. Apartment developers would henceforth pay less interest on their building loans than the rates charged for owner-occupied housing. This would enable them to charge renters less, and the renters would save an amount approximately equivalent to the benefits derived by home buyers from favorable tax laws. This solution to the problem may appear to have been a cowardly and expensive way out of the dilemma, since it cost home buyers nothing and merely provided an increased subsidy to renters. But in fairness it must be acknowledged that Sweden is virtually alone among Western governments in facing this crucial equity issue at all (Headey, p. 88).

By comparison, Britain's Socialists have had much less stomach for the battle over tax concessions to home buyers. This is surprising, since Labour came to power in 1974 on a platform that included a commitment to end "the scandal whereby the richer the person and the more expensive the house, the greater is the tax relief." Anthony Crosland, who was to become Labour's Environment Minister, declared during the 1974 election campaign that "we are determined to stop this situation where the richest men in our society get their houses on the cheap" (Weir, p. 15). Once in office, however, Labour spokespeople got unfavorable press reports every time they raised the issue of mortgage interest relief. But more important in discouraging Crosland from pursuing this election pledge were the conflicts he encountered with the Treasury and with Labour's overall economic strategy in the 1970s. First, the government wanted to hold down housing costs as part of its income policy; raising housing costs by withdrawing the interest deduction would help to stimulate wage demands. Second, the proposal to eliminate tax relief for home buyers in the higher brackets was opposed by the Treasury because it would unnecessarily antagonize Britain's middle-management class, a segment of society whose confidence the Labour government was trying to win. The *Green Paper on Housing* finally issued by Labour in 1977 did not simply postpone reform; it rejected it outright, arguing that the continuation of mortgage tax relief was vital to the growth of homeownership and that its elimination would lead to a decline in investment (Department of Environment).

We have explored the change taking place in housing policy throughout Europe and the United States over the past twenty years—an increasing emphasis on subsidies to consumers and a declining emphasis on subsidies to producers. Without doubt, this shift is related to the gradual elimination of postwar housing shortages, which had obliged Western governments to concentrate on production. As we have just seen, however, the two main forms of consumer subsidies now in use in Western nations are likely to have quite different distributive consequences for housing consumers. In the rental sector, housing allowances have a significant redistributive impact, since the size of the benefit is inversely related to the recipient's income. In contrast, measures to promote homeownership through tax subsidies and programs that increase the flow of credit to home buyers appear more likely to widen the gaps between income groups. Furthermore, neither of these two strategies seems capable of solving the problem of society's neediest citizens, many of whom end up homeless or in illegally squatted properties in London, New York, Amsterdam, and West Berlin.

While policies in these countries appear to have solved the postwar problem of overall shortages, they have not prevented severe maladjustments from occurring, especially in inner-city housing markets. In many of the big cities of Western Europe and the United States, the number of existing units is theoretically great enough to house the urban population. Some of these cities even have significant vacancy rates. Yet there are too few decent, affordable units for the number of low-income households. Particularly at the low end of the private rental sector, many older units that might have served the new homeless have disappeared from the housing stock—demolished to make room for office buildings, rehabilitated and gentrified to house upper-middle-class professionals, or held vacant by speculators who see inner-city revival as an opportunity for profit.

At the same time that cheaper units have disappeared from the inner-city market, a rising share of the cities' residents are childless couples, young singles living independently of their families, the elderly, and single-parent families. Many of the people in such households have low incomes. While they may be eligible for a housing allowance, that does them little good if they cannot even find decent housing units at modest rents. Increasing numbers of homeless people are illegally occupying vacant buildings. Unable to provide alternatives, government authorities have shown themselves to be surprisingly tolerant of these squatters. Officials of several London boroughs, for example, have negotiated agreements with squatter organizations: in return for permission to place squatters in certain vacant buildings, the squatter organizations promise to screen the tenants and manage the property (Adams). The city of Amsterdam has not only relaxed aspects of its housing code but even offered subsidies to help squatters install utilities and rehabilitate their dwellings (Van Weesep, p. 348). And the city government of Philadelphia has established a program to buy tax-delinquent properties and turn them over to squatters.

Housing allowances and other forms of consumer subsidies can never totally solve the problems of the homeless because homelessness is not simply the result of inadequate incomes. It must also be understood as a problem of inadequate supply of low-cost housing. To the extent that national governments in Western Europe and the United States have moved away from directly subsidizing the production of low-rent housing in the inner cities, they have contributed to the problem. The emphasis on privatization only worsens the situation.

The new emphasis on consumer subsidies has emerged in spite of strong producer lobbies in most countries, which have long favored subsidies to production instead. The powerful producer lobby in the United States, for example, was unable to prevent Congress from creating, as a key element of the 1974 Housing and Community Development Act, a new rent subsidy program, called Section 8. This program is a modified form of housing allowance in which the allowance is paid not to the tenant, but to the landlord on the tenant's behalf. Strictly speaking, Section 8 is a voucher program, not a pure housing allowance. It is only a step away from an allowance, however.

Another example of a powerful producer lobby is Sweden's nonprofit builders. Despite their consistent support for government programs to promote the construction of high-rise rental housing, the Swedish government has, through the instrument of the tax concession, subsidized a growing stock of single-family detached housing in the suburbs.

Why would producer groups have resisted the shift away from subsidies to production? Probably because such a shift threatened the close and comfortable relationships they established with government ministries during the years of large-scale construction programs. The political commitment in the postwar years to a massive housing expansion bred a system of negotiation that benefited governments, labor, housebuilding companies, and financial institutions, furnishing a classic example of the way that policy sometimes shapes the political process.

POLITICAL SUPPORT AND THE FUTURE OF HOUSING PROGRAMS
RESTRAINTS AND INNOVATIONS

Political scientists typically concern themselves with the question of how politics affects policy—how the interplay among classes, parties, interest groups, and influential individuals shapes governmental outputs. But governments are more than mere instruments to receive and process demands from their environment. Governments also reach into the environment to mold the configuration of interests in society. Rather than simply responding to demands, public officials shape those demands by legitimizing some interests while excluding others, and by locating different policy processes in particular arenas having their own sets of rules, participants, levels of bureaucratic control, and so forth. (For example, tax policies are made in quite different arenas from social welfare policies.) Governments' choices are not only influenced by, but also influence, the structure of interests in the affected sectors of society.

Recognizing this, we can ask: Will the shift in housing policies, away from direct subsidies to production and toward indirect subsidies to transactions carried out in the market, change the political balance? It would certainly seem plausible that a policy that trades direct intervention for indirect subsidies would require far less institutionalized bargaining between governments and producer groups. One might even argue that privatization embodies a rejection of corporatism in that it seeks to limit government direction of the economy.

Privatization

Privatized policies offer less incentive for producers to organize themselves into peak associations. Under corporatism, the promise of official incorporation into the policy process creates incentives for producers to join peak associations and to accept guidance from sector leaders. But when governments shift to subsidizing consumers (either through housing allowances or tax concessions), then producer groups are no longer assured that direct benefits will result from their collaboration with government. The benefits they receive will come only indirectly, mediated by the market.

Is privatization as a strategy compatible with corporatist arrangements? There is some evidence that the answer is yes. One nation in which corporatism and privatization appear to have flourished together in the postwar period is West Germany. One scholar has described the basic goal of Germany's postwar housing policies as permitting "maximum scope and support to the private housing industry (property owners, builders, suppliers, finance, management) with governmental regulation and subsidy limited to supporting that industry, except for those situations in which other overriding priorities exist" (Marcuse, p. 88). In the years immediately following the war, of course, the government recognized a need to exert strong public control in order to overcome the critical shortages. But as early as the mid-1950s the Christian Democrats began shifting housing policy to the "normal" focus on the private market. Ever since then, with the exception of a brief period of renewed government activism in the late 1960s, an underlying assumption of private sector primacy has guided German policymakers.

Yet its commitment to the private market has not prevented the German government from intervening systematically in the house-building industry, especially to support and protect the small-scale artisan segment of the industry. Artisan firms are represented by a peak association (*Zentralverband des Deutschen Baugewerbes*) which represents about 80 percent of the firms in the industry. Its high level of coverage (impressive for so fragmented an industry) is in part due to the legal and financial assistance it receives from government. A national law regulating artisan firms (*Handwerksrecht*) requires that they employ certified artisans and that they belong to regional "chambers of artisans" which offer training programs and technical assistance to members. The government also subsidizes low-interest loans to help certified artisans set up their own businesses. The overall effect of public intervention is to segment the market and limit competition, all with the intent of protecting these small businesses (Grant and Streeck). The German government also bargains directly with the other important peak association in the industry—that representing large industrial builders, *Hauptverband der Deutschen Bauindustrie* (HDB), though its ties to the HDB are not so close as to the artisans' association.

Even so zealous an advocate of privatization as the Thatcher government in Britain does not appear to find its commitment to free markets an obstacle to preserving some corporatist forms. It was in fact Thatcher's new Environment Secretary who in 1979 formed the so-called Group of Eight to provide ministerial access to representatives of the construction industry. The group's membership included the trade unions, the design professions, and the two major peak associations in the house-building industry, the Building Employers Confederation and the Federation of Civil Engineering Contractors. Unlike earlier governments' consultative machinery, it excluded smaller builders and subcontractors—an interesting move, given the current government's professed support for small business and economic competition.

Even in systems which have strongly favored housing allowances and subsidies to ownership at the expense of direct subsidies to production, we see a universal tendency for producer interests to organize into large-scale associations in order to bargain with the institutions of government. Admittedly, their focus under conditions of privatization seems slightly different: instead of seeking direct subsidies, they lobby for measures that will maximize consumer demand for housing. The locus of activity shifts accordingly to finance and tax policy. But they have not dissolved.

Changing Policy Arenas

Up to this point we have argued that privatization brings about only modest changes in the organization and activities of the key players in the policy process. Housing producers continue to be represented in the halls of government, lobbying now for policies that maintain high levels of demand instead of production programs. Consumer groups continue to play a marginal role, poorly organized and excluded from the policy process; if anything, their influence declines under privatization. And political parties, though they may experience internal conflict between the advocates of private versus collective consumption, typically reshape their programs to accommodate the desire for ownership in all classes.

Let us turn now to an aspect of housing policy-making that *does* change with privatization: the arena in which bargaining occurs. Privatization leads to a gradual migration of housing issues into the realm of finance and tax policy. Obviously, housing policy has never been made in isolation from wider policies of taxation and economic management. But in the current economic climate, tax and finance instruments have become the most important levers on housing expenditures. The reasons are two-fold, having to do with both the economic context and the nature of consumer subsidies.

Throughout the industrialized West there is concern in the 1980s about recapitalizing industries to make them more competitive in international markets. The globalization of the economy, increasing competition from low-wage countries, and high levels of unemployment have prompted policymakers to search for ways to channel investment capital to productive sectors of the economy. Debates on housing policy are focused increasingly on the competition for capital between housing and other more productive investments.

American critics of housing policies charge that they have drawn savings and investment away from more productive uses and thereby jeopardized economic productivity (Tuccillo; Sternlieb and Hughes in Sternlieb et al.; Peterson). Similarly, British economists in the late 1970s began to worry that the privileged position of housing finance had made it too attractive an alternative (Lansley; Kilroy). More recent evidence shows that homeowners are remortgaging their homes to finance other consumer purchases like automobiles, burdening even further the mortgage credit market (Kemeny and Thomas). One particularly outspoken critic charged British building societies with directly contributing to Britain's industrial decline:

> Having wrecked industrial investment in the last decade they [the build-ing societies] should be encouraged to find ways to direct their ten billion a year mortgage disbursement towards it in a massive rescue operation. (Pawley)

A comparative study of the United States and several West European coun-tries has suggested that the nations giving the highest incentives for home-ownership are those with the slowest-growing small business sectors, because the lure of homeownership draws potential entrepreneurs to put their capi-tal into housing (Farmer and Barrell). In several of these countries, econo-mists are pressing government to restrain investments in housing.

Yet the adoption of privatization as a policy strategy has made it harder to control housing investments than it was in the past. This is not solely because responsibility for housing investment has shifted out of govern-ment hands and into the private capital markets. It is also because govern-ments find it harder to restrain their own expenditures for housing. Fund-ing for production programs could be limited by building targets set from year to year. When funding runs out, no new projects would be subsidized. But outlays for housing allowances and tax concessions, distributed as enti-tlements to categories of eligible beneficiaries, are much harder to limit. They are excellent vehicles for encouraging consumption, but less appropri-ate for restraining it. (This is to some extent an unforeseen result of privatization; in fact government policy favoring homeownership has often been perceived as a way of cutting back government support for housing [Lundqvist]. But of course governments have *not* reduced their support for housing, only transformed it from direct subsidy into tax expenditure.)

Given the drawbacks of these major housing policy instruments as levers on housing investment, some governments are turning to the regula-tion of financial institutions as an avenue of influence. In all the advanced industrial countries, governments exercise considerable control over the legal and institutional framework of financial markets and the differenti-ated channels through which credit circulates into the spheres of industrial development, housing finance, consumer debt, and so on. Governments also regulate the amounts of capital flowing into these various channels by fixing interest rates, and sometimes even by direct allocations of credit.

Perhaps the strongest grip on the housing credit market is exercised by the French government, whose main vehicle for influencing the credit sup-ply is the *Crédit Foncier,* a private corporation owned by private shareholders, but run by senior executives who are appointed by the government, according to policies decided in agreement with the government (policies which limit the type, the cost, and the size of housing for which loans are made). The *Crédit Foncier* makes subsidized loans to borrowers (either individual homeowners or builders) for up to 80 percent of the house price, and also controls France's secondary mortgage market. Through its relationship with the *Crédit Foncier,* the French government can limit the total amount out on loan without consulting the legislature—simply by mutual agreement of the Ministry of Finance, the *Crédit Foncier,* and the Bank of France (DuClaud-Williams, p. 221).

As a point of comparison, we note that Britain has historically exercised much less direct control over that country's building societies, the principal providers of housing finance loans. Although they meet regularly together, government officials cannot compel these private institutions to hold interest rates, or to lend to specified types of borrowers for particular types of housing. Yet even without formal leverage over the societies, British officials have drawn them ever closer to government in recent decades. Although they are perceived to be local institutions, the societies have become more concentrated and centralized, keeping their interest rates similar throughout the country through a central association which fits the definition of a peak association. Several times during the 1970s the government advanced large, low-interest loans to the societies in order to ensure a continuous supply of mortgages at stable interest rates (Balchin, pp. 228–29). The societies, in turn, have been responsive to certain government priorities; for example, by agreeing to give favorable consideration to borrowers who are nominated by local housing authorities (Craig and Harrison, p. 83; see also Boddy).

Like many countries, Britain shelters a "special circuit" of finance that directs a portion of the nation's savings to institutions specializing in mortgage lending. Examples are France's *épargne-logement* and West Germany's *Bausparkassen,* both of which are savings societies in which individuals who make deposits according to a specified schedule earn moderate interest and an entitlement to mortgage loans at interest rates below the regular market. Britain's building societies serve the same function, though they operate somewhat differently, paying depositors a more competitive rate of interest and not necessarily guaranteeing each depositor a mortgage loan. In all three cases the government subsidizes the scheme by foregoing all interest earned by depositors. In the United States the savings and loans banks (the so-called thrift institutions) which specialize in mortgage loans have been sheltered both by interest rate regulations and by generous tax concessions to all institutions having at least 82 percent of their loans in mortgages. In all of these systems economic and political pressures are calling into question the sheltered nature of the housing finance system, as other sectors compete for capital (Rosen).

The clearest example to date of this conflict is found in the United States, where the federal government has since 1980 revolutionized the housing finance system, virtually eliminating the favored status of housing finance and subjecting it to the full-market force of credit competition. The Reagan administration essentially transformed the savings and loan associations from specialized mortgage institutions into regular commercial banks (Downs). In other advanced capitalist countries as well, changes in mortgage financing have created heightened competition for limited pools of investment capital (Ball et al). If the American case is any indication of broader trends, then the shift of political bargaining over the national investment in housing—a shift out of the traditional arena of housing policy and into the realm of tax policy and financial regulation—will increase the competition faced by producer groups. For the tax and finance arenas are ones in which many powerful interest groups have long been arrayed. And under current economic conditions, housing producers are by no means guaranteed that they will prevail against competing claimants.

* * * * *

As with health care, policymakers in the housing field are confronted with choices that hinge on the relationship of government programs to private sector alternatives. With the exception of Britain, the governments under consideration here have chosen not to build large stocks of public housing but instead to work through the private market, both by providing loans, grants, and tax concessions to builders, and by offering subsidies to consumers in the form of cash allowances to renters and mortgage support to owner-occupiers. Since World War II the trend has clearly been away from subsidizing producers and toward subsidizing consumers. While this shift has undoubtedly enabled governments to target their aid more directly to the intended recipients, it may also have contributed to an "overinvestment" in housing. Critics charge that like government health insurance, consumer subsidies for housing have inflated prices and encouraged families to consume more housing than they otherwise would. Whether or not we accept this last argument, it serves to remind us that housing policy is closely tied to wider policies of taxation, income maintenance, and economic management, and can never be made in isolation from these other spheres.

5
ECONOMIC POLICY

All of the world's industrial democracies have had to face severe economic problems in the 1970s and 1980s. Declining rates of economic growth, productivity slowdowns, trade deficits, inflation, and higher unemployment have struck Western Europe, the United States, and Japan. In each case, trends that appeared merely worrisome in the late 1960s became much more disturbing in the 1970s and only partially receded in the 1980s.

In retrospect, it seems clear that post–World War II economic development can be divided into two general phases (Feldstein; OECD 1980). From the initial period of reconstruction of wartime damage through the 1950s and 1960s, the industrial democracies enjoyed unprecedented high rates of economic growth amid general price stability. At the end of the 1960s and in the early 1970s, this first phase gradually gave way to a second, as economic fluctuations became more erratic and severe in an increasingly interdependent world economy (Maddison).

There were growing signs of economic trouble well before the first oil-price shock of 1973. Chronic balance of payments deficits in the United States and some other countries contrasted with growing balance of payments surpluses in nations such as Japan and West Germany. Fueled by major U.S. spending in Vietnam without accompanying tax increases, inflationary pressures spread in the international economy. Growing economic imbalances and fluctuations imposed unmanageable strains on the system of fixed international exchange rates for national currencies that had been created at the end of World War II. Unilateral devaluation of the dollar in

1971 quickly led to the collapse of the Bretton Woods system and new instabilities as a booming economic expansion occurred in the Western nations and Japan during 1972 and 1973. Provoked by the declining value of the dollar, international prices of raw materials shot up, and in late 1973 a Mideast war precipitated an oil embargo and quadrupling of OPEC oil prices. The result was a massive redistribution of wealth from oil-importing to oil-exporting nations and a chain reaction of higher prices. National policies seeking to cope with the inflationary pressures in 1974 and 1975 produced the worst economic downturn for most developed nations since the Great Depression of the 1930s. After 1976 came a weak economic recovery, which was followed by more inflation, another oil-price shock in 1979, and another worldwide economic slump from 1981 to 1983. Throughout the 1970s, and contrary to almost all professional economists' expectations, successive bouts of recession and unemployment did little to reverse the inflationary trend. As Table 5.1 suggests, the sharp economic downturn of the early 1980s (once again the greatest since the 1930s) was finally accompanied by a general slowing of inflation. However, economic performance in the 1980s still did not match the robust growth with low unemployment and relatively stable prices of the pre-1974 period.

All in all it was a sorry economic record. At the same time, however, we must consider this period in perspective. Seen against the background of rapid postwar growth during phase one and in the light of economists' confidence that they had finally learned the lessons of economic management, the performance of the 1970s and early 1980s looks bleak indeed. But viewed in relation to the longer history of the last century or more, the recent record is far from disastrous. In their severity and duration, these modern economic downturns have been much milder than the panics and

TABLE 5.1 INFLATION, UNEMPLOYMENT, AND ECONOMIC GROWTH, 1960–88

	Consumer Price Index[1]					Unemployment[2]					Real GDP per Capita[1]				
	1960–68	1968–73	1973–79	1979–84	1984–88	1964–67	1968–73	1974–79	1979–84	1984–88	1960–68	1968–73	1973–79	1979–84	1984–87
Austria	3.6	5.2	6.3	5.1	2.8	2.0	1.4	1.6	2.5	4.3	3.6	5.4	3.0	2.2	1.6
Belgium	2.8	4.9	8.4	7.0	3.0	2.0	2.5	6.3	10.5	11.2	3.9	5.3	2.1	1.3	1.8
Britain	3.6	7.5	15.6	11.3	4.7	2.5	3.3	5.0	9.0	8.5	2.4	2.9	1.5	0.8	2.8
France	3.6	6.1	10.7	11.8	4.3	1.7	2.6	4.5	7.2	10.2	4.2	5.0	2.5	1.3	1.4
Germany	2.7	4.6	4.7	4.9	1.2	0.6	1.0	3.2	4.9	6.6	3.2	4.0	2.5	1.3	2.3
Japan	5.7	7.0	10.0	4.2	1.0	1.2	1.2	1.9	2.3	2.7	9.3	6.8	2.5	3.1	3.5
Netherlands	3.6	6.9	7.2	5.2	1.1	0.8	1.5	4.9	8.7	10.7	3.5	3.7	1.9	−0.1	1.8
Norway	3.9	6.9	8.7	9.8	6.9	1.7	1.7	1.8	2.8	2.6	3.6	3.3	4.4	2.7	3.7
Sweden	3.8	6.0	9.8	10.1	5.9	1.6	2.2	1.9	2.6	2.4	3.6	3.1	1.5	1.6	2.2
United States	2.0	5.0	8.5	8.9	3.5	4.2	4.6	6.7	7.9	6.6	3.1	2.0	1.4	0.0	3.4
OECD Total	2.9	5.7	10.0	9.2	4.0	2.7	3.2	4.9	6.9	7.6	3.9	3.6	1.8	0.9	2.9

[1]Average annual percent change between the years indicated.
[2]Average annual standardized unemployment rate as percent of total labor force (Austrian figures are unstandardized and not directly comparable to other nations; first column for Austria is 1960–68).
SOURCE: OECD, 1988, *Historical Statistics: 1960–1986;* tables 8.11; p. 33; 2.15; p. 39; 2.20; p. 41; 3.2; p. 44.; 1989. *Main Economic Indicators*, pp. 19, 22, 44–45; 1989. *National Accounts 1960–87*. pp. 90–113.

depressions that preceded World War II. And recent inflation, though troublesome, has not expanded into the speculative bubbles that once brought down whole banking and financial systems.

In this chapter we will not try to totally account for different inflation, unemployment, or growth rates among nations. Such differences depend on a highly complex interaction of economic, political, social, and even cultural factors. Instead, we will examine differences and similarities in the ways that democratic nations have coped with common problems of economic management.

Compared with other topics in this book, economic policy has at least two distinctive characteristics. First, there is widespread agreement not only on the aims of economic policy, but also on the fairly specific ways in which progress should be measured. While all people agree that "good" education, "adequate" health care, and "decent" shelter are desirable goals, it is clearly very difficult to decide when and how well these goals are being achieved. Not so with economic policy. Its aims can usually be expressed in terms of full employment, stable prices, and steady levels of economic growth. Progress toward these goals is everywhere measured by the same widely accepted statistical indicators: unemployment rates, price indices, and measures of Gross National Product.

Economic policymakers can thus be much more clearly identified with results, even though the underlying economic processes may be largely beyond their control. Unemployment and inflation rates are watched and reported with great interest. Changes in GNP are scrutinized for signs of recession, stagnation, or recovery. This high visibility—and thus political vulnerability—along with the growing interdependence among national economies, helps explain why, since 1975, the top leaders of the industrial democracies have felt impelled to meet periodically in highly publicized "economic summits" (Shultz and Dam; Putnam and Bayne). Since no one can deny bad news contained in economic statistics, there is a strong political incentive to engage in or at least appear to engage in problem solving.

The second distinction of economic policy is that in every country, a specialized profession has developed to advise on problems of economic management. Professionals in other policy areas, such as educators or doctors, may or may not be consulted for their views on health or education policy; but professional economists are everywhere regarded as legitimate sources of guidance on economic policy matters. This reliance on economists has increased over time, as economics in the postwar period has become more theoretically complex and data-rich (through the advent of computers). The result is that ideas—expressed in the ebb and flow of debate among economists—play a particularly important role in shaping, though never entirely determining, policy choices in economic management. The influence of ideas has been felt throughout the various dimensions of choice in economic policy.

CHOICES IN ECONOMIC POLICY

The various managerial strategies in economic policy can be grouped in terms of the familiar fourfold set of choices; recent economic history has in fact facilitated this kind of comparative policy analysis. The shared economic problems of recent decades, such as the oil-price increases of the 1970s, have provided a natural testing ground, illuminating each nation's particular capacities for political management and economic adjustment.

Scope and Thresholds

Regardless of the party in power, every central government in the industrial democracies is now assumed to have responsibility for overall economic management. There is little question that economic performance in terms of jobs, inflation, and growth is within the legitimate bounds of government activity.

Because it is so obvious, it would be easy to overlook the similarity among nations in this basic commitment to economic management. In every advanced democracy, the government's own taxing and spending policies and its control of the money supply are today considered the key factors involved in managing the economic activity in the private sector. Yet as recently as the 1930s the national budget was regarded simply as a means of paying for the government's own operation, not of regulating overall economic activity. The boundary between public and private sector responsibilities for the economy has thereby become increasingly fuzzy—but fuzzy in different ways in different nations (Lane).

Instruments

Western democracies apply a complex but not wholly dissimilar mix of fiscal and monetary tools in economic management. For example, in response to the 1981–83 recession, government spending and tax policies were everywhere used to prop up domestic demand, while central banks manipulated financial levers such as interest rates to curtail inflationary increases in the money supply. The widespread reliance on these "big levers" of macroeconomic management demonstrates the common influence of economic ideas and the professional economists who expound them. As we shall see, however, the "small levers" of microeconomic management (in the form of industrial policies) can also reveal much about different national approaches to economic choice.

Distribution

The choices of economic policies imply major distributive consequences. Measures to fight inflation can produce significant increases in unemployment. Many persons complaining about inflation are not the ones most likely to suffer from the effects of sustained unemployment. Distributive consequences are also produced by efforts to spur economic growth through increased investment and capital accumulation. Given the existing structure of economic ownership, government incentives to increase investment and savings tend to reward those who are already the largest owners of capital and those with the greatest capacity to accumulate resources for new investment. Thus the debate on "trickle down" theories has followed rather different contours, depending on the distributional sensitivities of the political system in question.

Restraints and Innovation

During the first several decades of the postwar period, a gradual consensus emerged on the role of government in the economy. Essentially, this view was Keynesian: Government must manage aggregate demand so as to assure high levels of stable employment.

Events of the 1970s eroded this consensus without putting any comparable consensus in its place. Each nation has embarked on a search for innovations in economic policymaking, although each has done so in its own way. This recent agitation for economic policy innovation in the midst of constraints provides a good example of what we have termed "structured variation" in public policy.

THE WILL TO INTERVENE
SCOPE AND THRESHOLDS

Since World War II, every industrial democracy has seen the creation of central executive organizations run by personnel with professional economic training to advise on policies for managing the economy. Likewise, in every nation, central government banks nowadays consciously attempt to control the supply of money and other financial aspects of the economy—an endeavor that simply would never have occurred to central bankers before 1940 (Schnitzer and Nordyke; Woolley). As a consequence of these and other factors, the boundary lines between public and private sectors of the economy have become increasingly blurred. With little apparent intention of doing so, modern democratic governments of every political persuasion have effectively converged to blot out the timeworn distinction between government and a self-regulating economy. Private economic relationships and self-managing market mechanisms continue to operate, but they do so everywhere within the larger designs of government economic policy.

Several factors help to explain these overarching similarities. First is the sheer size of today's public sector in relation to the rest of the economy. (The particular categories of spending and taxation are considered at greater length in other chapters of this book.) All of these government commitments have—largely inadvertently—cumulated into a government presence that easily overshadows any other actor in the economy.

In every industrial democracy, government is the single largest purchaser of goods and services (teachers' salaries, school buildings, hospitals, public works, and so on), the single largest distributor of income (through transfers of income maintenance programs), and the single largest borrower of money (to finance capital investment projects and pay for deficits between spending and revenue). Given this presence, it would be difficult for any government to deny responsibility for what is happening in its national economy.

A second reason for the similarity in basic frameworks of economic management concerns ideas. Since its early, scattered beginnings over two centuries ago, the study of economics has evolved in the twentieth century into a professional specialty with its own language and sophisticated models. By and large the basic concepts of economics have been developed in informal dialogue among international networks of economists.

A critical turning point in this dialogue occurred amid the Depression of the 1930s and wartime planning of the 1940s. These events, which struck with stunning impact in all the nations, led economists to a new conception of government's role in managing a national economy. The basic idea that held sway for a generation of Keynesian economists following the Depression was that, left to its own devices, a modern market economy would *not* automatically reach equilibrium at a level of activity assuring full utilization of a country's capital and labor. Keynesianism argued that government should use the tools of fiscal policy—taxing and spending powers—to counter boom and bust cycles and maintain high levels of employment. This meant raising spending and/or cutting taxes when demand was too low and the economy was slowing down, as well as cutting spending and/or raising taxes when the economy was in danger of overheating. From this basic idea and from a general desire to avoid any repetition of Depression-style unemployment, methods were developed to measure national income and GNP (both new concepts in the 1940s), to quantify the impact of government taxing and spending on aggregate economic demand, and to refine indicators of full employment. These ideas and methods of accounting for economic activity took hold among economists throughout the Western democracies and today constitute the basis for most of the day-to-day work in the central economic apparatus of every nation. These ideas come from a way of thinking that, almost by definition, *presumes* general government responsibility for the economy.

During the 1950s and 1960s, another school of economic thought drew greater attention to monetary factors (rather than aggregate demand) and the role of central banking institutions in fueling or controlling inflation. In this view it is monetary policy—the supply of money and the conditions of credit—that is decisive in controlling inflation and the economy. Central banks should set and enforce overall, long-term targets for growth in the money supply and let free-market forces produce the necessary adjustments in prices and wages. Keynesians argued that for a number of reasons prices and wages lack the flexibility stipulated by classical economic models, and that government management of market demand is essential to prevent the huge economic and human costs associated with unemployment. Monetarists replied that any such inflexibility was due to misguided government protections. By promoting expectations that government would guarantee full employment, Keynesian policies simply delayed the necessary adjustment of prices and wages in a self-correcting market and raised the eventual cost of such adjustments (Sawhill; Hoover).

Keynesians and monetarists have agreed on at least one point: that it is macroeconomic regimes (general taxing and spending levels or overall money supply and credit conditions) that matter for economic policy. Two other schools of thought focus on microeconomic (i.e., individual or firm-level) strategies of economic management. "Supply siders" correspond to monetarists in the sense of adhering to the free-market concept. "Industrial policy" advocates can be related to Keynesians in the sense of favoring the managed market concept. Both supply side and industrial policy positions became more prominent and argued more loudly in the economically troubled years after 1973.

Supply-side theorists have emphasized the role of government in restricting the supply of work, savings, and investment. While virtually all economists believe there are some disincentive effects in operation—for example, that income taxes reduce some people's desire to work—supply siders consider there to be huge payoffs for the economy to be achieved by designing cuts in government taxes, regulations, and transfer payments that interfere with free-market processes. Their reasoning is based on the idea that changing people's overall expectations about the returns from work and investment will have a much greater impact than could be predicted by assessing the effects of changing this or that law. The large cuts in U.S. federal taxes in 1981 were predicated on such reasoning (Wanniski).

Advocates of industrial policy have argued that government policy can play a major role in directing the course of economic activity by selectively intervening in particular industries and economic processes. The aim is to work with and shape market forces in key industrial sectors to improve performance and competitiveness beyond what would occur at the hand of blind market forces. This translates into government interventions that are strategically designed to support some firms and economic activities but not others through credit regulations, research support, targeted subsidies, and so on (Barfield and Schambra).

None of these approaches has drawn unanimous agreement among economists, and different governments have given different priority to Keynesian, monetarist, industrial policy, and supply-side theories. But seen as a whole, the ideas of economists have everywhere helped create the presumption that government, by acting or withdrawing in a strategic manner, can decisively affect the course of national economic activity.

One final factor helps explain the universal blurring of public and private sector boundaries. This factor involves the political constraints on the size of the public sector. Governments can and do use a variety of instruments to achieve their policy purposes. But all of the Western democracies are basically market-oriented, private-property based economies, not centrally planned, socialist systems. Thus there are not many economic objectives that democratic governments can accomplish without relying on private or semiprivate groups outside their direct control. In accepting responsibility for economic management, governments are pulled into a web of relationships—consultations, financial inducements, and so on—with the ostensibly independent private sector. Reinforcing this situation is the political incentive everywhere for blurring public and private boundaries. With public budgets looming so large, governments must look for strategies of intervention that do not show up on the budgetary books. Such strategies include the use of quasi-governmental corporations, special credit facilities, various contractual arrangements with private suppliers, and so on. These approaches in effect create a complex set of interdependencies between government and the private economy, so that it becomes very difficult to ascertain where any threshold between the two sectors may lie.

Differences in the Will to Intervene

So far our discussion has focused on overarching similarities in government responsibility for economic management. Yet there are also substantial differences in the willingness of national governments to intervene in economic affairs. Some countries appear to have accepted responsibility unhesitatingly, and indeed show a predisposition in that direction, while other nations seem to act much less deliberately and willingly.

Consider how various countries have responded to common economic problems, such as the OPEC oil embargo and quadrupling of oil prices in 1973 and 1974. In effect these events imposed a large tax on the entire economic product of each oil-importing nation, with the revenues from this oil "tax" going to foreign sources. Every country followed its own course in coping with the resulting loss of national income and in the process evinced its will to intervene in economic affairs.

West Germany. The oil-price shock came at a particularly bad time for Germany. The government had been trying for a year to hold back growth in an economy that showed signs of growing inflation. Wage settlements were reaching historically high levels, adding further to inflation and the likelihood of a profit squeeze on industry. In late 1973 and 1974, Germany was therefore poised on the edge of a major recession (given the huge oil "tax" on top of the government's already restrictive policies) and a major inflationary spiral (given already high wage contracts that could be expected to escalate to catch up with the cost-of-living increases produced by higher oil prices).

The policy debate was short and decisive. Earlier in 1973 the government had begun deploying its economic powers under the 1967 Act to Promote Economic Stabilization and Growth so as to moderate the anticipated recession (see page 159 for details). Investment taxes on private industry were abolished and special tax credits to foster business growth were introduced. At the same time, the powerful Bundesbank, the government's central bank, decisively restricted credit, thereby curtailing the power of firms to pass through the inflationary price increases that had been caused by the high wage settlements and oil-price increases. As it developed, the German recession of 1974 and 1975 was mild by international standards, and inflation (though high by German standards at 7 percent in 1975) was substantially held in check, and then reduced in 1976.

France. The oil crisis dramatized problems that had been emerging gradually for years in France. The French economy was becoming increasingly dependent on international trade, yet there were strong signs that industry was weakening in competition with its foreign counterparts. Moreover, government protection of marginal firms and industries, through price controls, subsidies, and other means, was straining resources and doing little to earn the export revenues that the country needed to pay for imports. Adding to the difficulties of international competitiveness and government subsidization was the fact that French interest rates had traditionally been kept low to aid business investment. Sharp swings in foreign deposits or withdrawals of funds from France—encouraged by a weak export-import ratio—could greatly strain this policy of low interest rates, the value of French currency, and French finances in general. Thus the oil shock of 1973 and 1974 left the country vulnerable to a massive trade deficit through higher import costs, to more demands for subsidizing marginal firms, and to outflows of capital in search of higher interest rates and a stable currency.

French policymakers reacted in 1974 by embarking on a major economic "restructuring" effort. A massive program of accelerated investment in nuclear power was initiated, partly to replace dependence on foreign oil and partly to earn foreign exchange through nuclear industry exports. State investment in the aerospace, armaments, and telecommunications industries increased immensely. A joint public-private sector export drive was launched to reverse the trade deficit. In less than two years, the Bank of France almost doubled interest rates, helping to attract foreign capital and stabilize the currency. The higher interest rates, together with cuts in government subsidization, drove some marginal firms under, while favored areas of production thrived on state investment funds and special credit facilities (Hall 1982).

Sweden. Sweden demonstrated even greater dependence on international trade, yet in late 1973 it appeared to be in a far better position to ride out the oil-price shock than were most other countries. During the worldwide inflationary boom of the early 1970s, the government had deliberately pursued a policy of restricting growth in the Swedish economy. This meant that at the time of the oil embargo, prices and labor costs were rising more slowly in Sweden than among its major trading partners, and a large balance of payments surplus had been accumulated.

Policymakers tried to take advantage of their fortunate position. In 1974 the Social Democratic government quickly launched a "bridging" strategy to protect its economy from the coming recession that the oil "tax" was expected to impose on the Western world. Government job training programs helped to prop up employment, and spending and taxing devices encouraged industry to maintain levels of production, despite the weakening international market. If the German approach was to accept but moderate the combined recession and inflation, and if the French used the 1973–1974 crisis as an opportunity for a major economic restructuring, Sweden elected to use government policy to maintain a fully employed economy pending the next upswing in the international business cycle. Eventually, the worldwide recession was much longer and deeper than expected, and the Swedish government's aggressive strategy proved, as we shall see, somewhat counterproductive.

Great Britain. As extensive media commentary on the "British Disease" might suggest, economic management in Britain has been plagued with difficulties: a growth rate that has lagged behind that of other developed countries, meager increases in productivity, recurring balance of payments crises, and very high inflation rates. The oil crisis could scarcely have occurred at a worse time (Steward; Shanks). By the end of 1973, the British economy was undergoing a major inflationary expansion. Responding to a 1971 increase in unemployment, the government continued to expand its own spending and ease monetary policy throughout 1972 and 1973. Private consumption was rising rapidly as well, creating an excess of imports over exports and a growing trade deficit. Inflation, which had been comparable to that in other nations until 1971, was racing ahead, further weakening Britain's international competitiveness. In addition, the Conservative government was, by the winter of 1973 and 1974, engaged in an ill-tempered confrontation with the trade union movement over demands for large wage increases and a governmental proposal to regulate strike activity. Meanwhile, domestic investment languished.

In February 1974 the Conservatives were turned out of office on the issue of controlling the unions, and the new Labour government faced a severe economic crisis. One portion of its response was to continue accelerating public spending. Another was to dismantle the compulsory restraint on wages, which had been widely disregarded, and to urge voluntary wage restraint through an informal "social contract" between government and unions. At the same time, the money supply was allowed to expand rapidly, with interest rates actually set below the rapidly rising level of inflation.

On the surface, the British response in 1974 resembled Sweden's "bridging" operation to hold up demand during the impending recession. In fact, only the public budget was encouraged to grow, and there was little intervention to shore up industrial production or restrain wage bargaining. Neither did the government undertake any direct measures to bolster employment or prevent the passing through of cost increases to prices. By mid-1975, inflation in Britain was approaching 25 percent, public spending was widely regarded as out of control, the excess of imports over exports had mushroomed, and the international value of the currency was in a nose dive. The government then shifted its stance to restrain public spending and money supply growth. Even stricter deflationary measures were imposed in 1976 as the condition for obtaining desperately needed loans from the International Monetary Fund. These measures, together with the extremely high wage settlements, produced sharp increases in unemployment during 1975 and 1976. The 1974 policies had been a bridge to nowhere.

Japan. As a densely populated, trade-dependent industrial nation with no natural energy resources of its own, Japan and its heretofore brilliant growth record might have seemed doomed by the oil-price increases of the 1970s. In fact, the Japanese economy continued to thrive after 1974 with much better than average OECD rates of economic growth, low unemployment, and relatively little inflation. During the 1950s and 1960s a powerful alliance between government economic ministries and large business firms had nurtured a select group of basic industries (shipping, steel, chemicals) and prepared them for international competition (Tsurumi). Government officials and business leaders eagerly collaborated to find, bring home, and apply leading technologies from the more advanced Western nations; to accumulate and channel investment funds for targeted industries; and to protect domestic firms from foreign competition as they geared up for an assault on international markets.

By the time of the first oil-price shock, joint government/business strategies for economic restructuring to expand the Japanese share of lucrative foreign markets were already well underway. With government guidance, foreign exchange from Japan's first successfully targeted industry—ship-building—had been increasingly funneled to the auto industry. Cutbacks in the ship-building industry now accelerated. Developmental efforts of the government/business alliance intensified to exploit the comparative advantage of small, fuel-efficient Japanese cars in export markets and gain a larger foothold in the rapidly expanding electronics sector. As in some other countries, an expansive fiscal policy produced a troubling government deficit as government spending expanded relative to revenues in Japan (Yashiro). But there was little hesitation in using government to play a vigorous developmental role. This role was clearly aimed at exploiting the more turbulent international economic environment to maintain and expand the market shares of Japanese industry, even at some expense to short-term profits (Dore 1986; Schlosstein).

The United States. Less dependent on foreign oil than any of the other advanced democracies, the United States might have appeared well able to cope with the oil shock. But appearances can be deceiving. Following a large inflationary boom in 1971 and 1972, the U.S. economy was flattening out in 1973. In response to growing inflation, monetary policy turned sharply restrictive in 1973. From 1972 to 1973, food-price increases tripled, in response to agriculture shortages; consumer food prices increased 4.3 percent in 1972 and 14.4 percent in 1973. Federal spending and taxing policy had begun to reverse the economic stimulation of 1971 and 1972, though the rapidly increasing interest rates and food prices were by far the biggest factors in slowing down the economy. Even without the OPEC oil "tax," the U.S. economy in 1974 was clearly headed for a recession (Eckstein).

Complicating the picture was the fact that in 1973 the United States was engaged in an erratic retreat from a system of wage and price controls (Congressional Budget Office; Goodwin). In 1971 President Nixon had imposed a ninety-day freeze on wages and prices; this was followed in 1972 by a second phase of loosely enforced wage-price standards. In January 1973, a third phase instituted a system of voluntary restraints; but, after five months, galloping inflation led President Nixon to reject the unanimous opinion of his economic advisers and to impose a sixty-day price freeze. This in turn created a number of unpopular shortages, and by year's end the whole program was being rapidly dismantled on an industry-by-industry basis.

Thus the oil crisis produced a major transfer of resources from an economy that was already approaching recession, as well as a further boost in price levels that were already rising alongside a disorderly retreat from controls. The American government's response was uncertain and somewhat contradictory during 1974 and 1975. In January 1974 the Nixon administration at first sought extension of authority to use wage and price controls, but quietly dropped the request in the face of conservative Congressional resistance. The program to dismantle wage and price controls was completed in April as inflation reached double digits. As the economy slowed down and went into reverse, monetary policies were tightened further in the first half of 1974 and only gradually relaxed as the recession deepened still more. Government spending, in contrast, was allowed to increase sharply in the first half of 1974 but then held at a constant growth rate and reversed in mid-1975. A public relations campaign to "whip inflation now" was launched to urge voluntary price restraint—to no effect. In

September 1974 the new president, Gerald Ford, recommended a tax increase, but later reversed himself and in the spring of 1975 accepted a major tax reduction passed by Congress. Administration proposals for an immediate decontrol of oil prices were rejected, and efforts to frame a comprehensive energy policy remained on the drawing board. That the U.S. economy did not continue along the road to depression could be attributed more to automatic stabilizers (such as countercyclical unemployment benefits) operating in the economy than to any coherent governmental policy decisions enacted during this period (Eckstein).

An Overview of the Differences

Thus, Germany, Japan, France, and Sweden all responded to the oil crisis of 1973 and 1974 with decisive programs that showed little hesitation in bringing government pressure to bear on ostensibly private economic arenas. The German credit constraint on the power of business to pass through cost and price increases, the French and Japanese attempts at economic restructuring, and the Swedish "bridging" operation to protect the labor market all reflect high government self-confidence in handling any presumed division between the public and private sectors.

In contrast are Britain and the United States. The British response to high union wage demands oscillated between compulsory restraint and an appeal to voluntary self-restraint. More indicative is the fact that the primary British response to the crisis was an effort to manage the economic adjustment solely by manipulating the public budget, with a consequently massive increase in deficit spending. Compared to that of the other nations, British government efforts had little connection with decision making for private investment, labor markets, financial markets, or international competitiveness.

In the United States, uncertainty about the justification for continued wage and price controls, the crosscutting mix of monetary contraction and budgetary expansion in early 1974 and the exact reversal of each after the middle of that year, the directive to Americans to "whip inflation," the attempt at a solution first through a tax increase, then a tax cut—these were signs of a political system deeply ambivalent not simply about the right policy, but even about government's rightful role in the economy. Government policy was defined almost exclusively in terms of moving the "big levers" of the public sector—public spending, taxation, and monetary aggregates—and not as intervention in private investment, labor markets, or finance decisions.

Faced with a fourfold increase in oil prices in 1973 and 1974, policymakers in every country pursued policies based on the policy legacies, group pressures, and institutional capabilities at hand. These were not, however, a random collection of factors but instead fell into fairly intelligible patterns reflecting national predispositions regarding the boundary between public and private sectors of the economy.

Of course there is more to economic policy than implicit choices regarding these boundaries. The nations separate themselves more clearly by their selection of policy instruments for managing the economy. By discussing these instruments we can obtain better feeling for the texture of relationships between governments and their economies.

MACRO- AND MICRO-POLICY INTERVENTIONS
INSTRUMENTS

The leading issue for economic policy instruments was once thought to involve a choice between government ownership and reliance on free markets (Corti; King). In socialist and labor parties throughout Europe, nationalization of basic industries was the key priority in the interwar and immediate post–World War II period (Andrain). Generally, however, the question of government taking over business enterprises has now receded from the forefront of economic policy debate. The leading exceptions are the French Socialist government of François Mitterrand, whose 1981 election program promised extensions of government ownership, and the British Labour party, which has long held a traditional commitment to nationalization. But even in these cases there is considerable doubt as to the efficacy of government ownership in economic management. The Mitterrand government (1981–86) began by pursuing a number of nationalization plans, but after a year in office was forced to de-emphasize government ownership and to rely on familiar austerity measures (higher taxes, lower spending, and wage-price freezes) in an attempt to halt declines in the value of the franc and bring the 14 percent inflation rate under control. In Britain the Labour party split in 1981, with more moderate members breaking off to form a Social Democratic party and a strengthened Liberal Party, both of whom gave little credence to the tradition of government ownership. In 1989 reformers within the Labour Party succeeded in changing the party platform to deemphasize the nationalization of industry.

Nationalization appears to have lost ground as an instrument of economic policy in Europe, even among socialist parties. The basic reason is that government ownership in practice has proven a blunt instrument; changing title to ownership seems largely irrelevant to managing the never-ending adjustments occurring in modern economies. Employees in nationalized industries are no more likely to moderate wage demands than are their private counterparts; and public-enterprise managers may be even less open to the price competition that restrains inflation and promotes efficiency.

The more telling differences among nations relate not to government ownership, nor to the basic ideas of fiscal and monetary policy, but rather to specific policy instruments at the level of particular industries and even firms. Known as *industrial policies,* these comprise government activities designed to influence economic adjustments within and among the various industrial sectors (Diebold; OECD 1975). Certain industrial policies predominate in each country and distinguish one country's policy choices from another's. Closer examination of a few national comparisons will make the meaning of industrial policy clear.

Policy Instruments in France, Japan, and Britain

Industrial policy in France builds on a long tradition of centralized state administration and highly detailed forms of government intervention (Zysman 1977; McArthur and Scott). Many important business decisions are made in small group settings where administrative officials of the central government, industrial representatives, and representatives of a few financial institutions negotiate the terms of economic growth and adjustment. These relationships are formed not simply for the purpose of ad hoc bargaining to deal with particular problems when they arise, but exist as a more or less permanent system of negotiation—a customary way of doing business. Labor unions, covering about 20 percent of the labor force, are weak, fragmented, and essentially excluded from this negotiation system.

Government involvement in business decisions concerning credit, investment, employment, and production is a tradition that goes back many decades in France. It has been facilitated by a central administrative elite with close personal, social, and educational ties to leaders in industrial and financial circles. For purposes of framing economic policy, what has existed in France are not separate, competing institutions, but a common personnel establishment seeking to coordinate government, financial, and business institutions. At the end of World War II, this task was focused by a consensus within the policy elite that the French economy was backward and in need of massive modernization. None of France's economic policymakers doubted the need for or ability of extensive government interventions to push this modernization process forward.

This institutional context helps explain the success of early postwar plans drawn up by the government's official Planning Commission (*Commissariat Général du Plan*). A succession of government plans set out relatively simple goals for vastly increasing the capacity of basic industries, such as steel and electricity, and indicated the coordinate factors—investment funds, demand, personnel, and so on—needed for such goals to be met. More important than the final numbers published in the various multi-year plans was the negotiation process by which government bureaucrats, business representatives, and suppliers of credit formulated expectations about one another's economic behavior. These expectations guided the distribution of government subsidies to particular industries and firms as well as spending for the nationalized industries. A series of semipublic credit institutions was created to guarantee the availability of low-cost loans to priority industries. Also a comprehensive program of price controls was initiated and remained in effect until 1976. But price controls were not instituted to reduce inflation during this period; rather, they served as tools that government could use (or, more often, hint at using) to influence particular companies' profits, investment, and other business decisions.

Industrial subsidies, credit facilities, and price controls have been three important instruments of French industrial policy. The problem is that France has had to adjust its relatively simple postwar goals of modernization in basic industries to a more fluid, post-OPEC environment. Economic planning routines in Paris have become an increasingly meaningless formal exercise offering speculations about the future. The arrival of a center-right government in the mid-1970s under Valéry Giscard d'Estaing (a quintessential member of the policy-making elite) seemed to indicate a turn to pro-market policies. Election of the Socialist Mitterrand government in 1981 pointed in the opposite direction. But political appearances can be deceiving. Given traditions of French microeconomic management, the more things changed the more they often seemed to stay the same.

The Giscard d'Estaing government did dismantle a number of cumbersome economic controls prior to losing office in 1981. Under this program of "liberalization," as it was termed, price controls were ended in 1976, thereby reducing some of the protection of profit margins that less competitive firms and industries had enjoyed. Efforts were made to encourage more competitive conditions in stock and bond markets. A policy of raising interest rates and increasing the international value of the franc was used to put more competitive pressure on less modern, labor-intensive sectors.

In general, however, liberalization did not change the underlying reality: French officialdom continued to take the lead in directing processes of industrial adjustment. The primary instrument has remained a state-orchestrated system for directing the flow of credit and investment funds in officially preferred directions (Cohen, Halimi, and Zysman). Thus the government apparatus directed an infusion of state funds and mergers for over six hundred corporations in danger of failure between 1974 and 1981. In chosen growth areas (for example, robotics and biotechnology), selected firms received special lines of bank credit, government orders, and trade protections in return for official agreements to meet specified performance targets. Government subsidies, mainly through equity loans, continued to dominate industrial research and development. French industrial policy has remained a kind of intricate web. At the center is a bureaucratic core centered largely in the Ministry of Finance where the instruments of fiscal policy, money supply, credit allocation, and industrial analysis are under more or less joint command. Linked to this center is a ring of state-owned enterprises (traditional energy industries, nuclear power, Renault, Air

France, and others), savings funds, and financial institutions under direct control. Farther out is a no less important outer ring of semipublic financial institutions and intermediary groups whose lending and investment activities are indirectly subject to government direction (for example, through preferential regulations depending on the purposes of a loan). Given the narrowness of the Paris stock market and the traditional dependence of French firms on long-term debt for financing, it has been difficult for any major industry in the country to avoid becoming entangled with the economic purposes of the state.

In the 1980s, the Socialist government of François Mitterrand added to and carried forward this interventionist apparatus. A major nationalization program was quickly implemented, largely as a political gesture to satisfy the traditional agenda of the French Left (Hall 1986). State takeover of nine major industrial companies and all of the nation's significant banking institutions (which it had already indirectly controlled in any event) left the French government accounting for roughly one-quarter of the work force, one-third of sales, and 60 percent of all annual investments in the industrial and energy sectors of the economy. This nationalization program, together with increased subsidization and reorganization of declining industries, smoothed the way for the government to pump vast sums of money into the economy and pursue an expansionary Keynesian policy of aggregate demand stimulation as other countries carried out restrictive, anti-inflationary policies in the worldwide recession of 1981–83. However, decades of modernization had left France intertwined with the world economy and the results of this experiment in Keynesianism in one country were quickly felt. Mounting trade deficits and a steep, continuous fall in the value of the franc forced the Socialist government into a series of austerity measures and devaluations beginning in 1982. In subsequent years spending on nationalized industries and industrial rationalization programs was scaled back, and the initial Socialist enthusiasm for large-scale government ownership was replaced by a more selective, market-oriented approach to intervention reminiscent of the Giscard d'Estaing regime. Pressures on nationalized and state-subsidized firms to break even were increased. State-guided rationalization schemes in industrial sectors such as electronics, chemicals, machine tools, paper products, and so on generally reproduced the same basic design for France's economic future: a small number of giant firms specializing in a particular product line, enjoying a near monopoly in the French market and major government support for capital investment and development of new technologies. Rationalization plans in the traditional sector of steel, shipbuilding, and coal projected a loss of 60,000 jobs by the end of the 1980s. In the largest bankruptcy in French history, the Socialist government allowed the giant steel firm Creusot Loire to collapse when its management refused to accept a rescue plan that would have put state banks in effective control of the parent company. Although state aid in the 1980s became more contingent on market criteria, no one could doubt the continuing importance of state-led industrial policies in managing the French economy.

At first glance the tools of Japanese microeconomic intervention appear quite similar to those in France. A cohesive, prestigious, bureaucratic elite staffs a set of interrelated government ministries in which are centralized responsibilities for spending, taxation, money supply, credit allocations, and industrial-sector analysis. As in France, these economic agencies are insulated from short-term political pressures of the parliament. Japanese officials also enjoy discretionary control over vast credit resources. Thus tax laws have exempted substantial amounts of interest on individual savings accounts in postal and commercial financial institutions. By doubling up on these accounts (an average of five such accounts in 1984 for every man, woman, and child in Japan) ordinary citizens gain a device for major tax avoidance and officials gain access to a huge pool of savings. For example, in the early 1980s funds of the postal savings system held in trust and invested by civil servants in the economic bureaucracy were four times the assets of the Bank of America, the world's largest commercial bank (Johnson 1986).

If anything, Japanese procedures for continuous consultation and coordination between government and business leaders are much more extensive and varied than those in France. Labor union representation is not simply fragmented but thoroughly absorbed into the firm-level structure. A narrowly based stock market and traditionally high debt-to-equity ratios throughout industry have helped forge strong linkages between manufacturing enterprises and banking institutions heavily influenced by government guidance.

All of these similarities should not, however, obscure the fundamental difference in the way instruments of industrial policy have been used in the two nations. Interventionist policies in France have typically sought to subsidize and control one or at most two huge companies that would serve as "national champions"—state of the art giants in a given industrial sector that are protected from competition at home to acquire leadership in international markets. Japanese industrial policy has typically sought to structure domestic competition and use marketplace signals to develop the long-term competitive advantage of Japanese products in world markets (Johnson 1986; Cohen, Halimi and Zysman). Thus foreign observers are often surprised to learn that the Japanese government since 1970 has been funding only about 25 to 29 percent of the national spending on research and development (R & D), while in France (as well as the United States and a number of other OECD countries) public subsidies account for 50 percent and more of total R & D spending (Lehner 1987). The difference is explained by the fact that Japan's officials self-consciously avoid long-term subsidies producing dependence on government (rice production and railroads are two political sacred cows that are exceptions). Instead, short-term subsidies serve as seed money and other instruments (tax breaks, loans, trade protection, regulation of financial markets, informational services) are used to enhance the competitiveness of major Japanese businesses in world markets. Both state support and weaning of firms from such support are part of Japanese industrial policy.

Development of the computer industry is a good example (Anchordoguy). In 1960 government and industry leaders decided to promote a domestic Japanese computer industry and hammered out an agreement creating a new public corporation to steer the competitive process. Seven major firms interested in getting into the computer business provided capital for the corporation, while the government channeled low-interest loans (as well as many top economic ministry bureaucrats) to the new body. While the seven firms were left to compete in researching and marketing the fledging computers, the corporation used its funds to purchase those computers that users had agreed to rent. The arrangement allowed the corporation to stimulate a domestic demand by charging artificially low rental fees for the computers it had purchased. It also allowed the producing firms to acquire large amounts of upfront cash as an immediate return on investment, freed them from the costs of having to find a rental market for their computers, and ensured that government aid went to firms whose products were actually in demand.

While the government-controlled computer industry in France focused on state-of-the-art large computers competing with IBM for the technological leadership, the Japanese corporation's committee of industry, academic, and civil service advisers initially used their purchasing power to press firms toward low-priced small computers that could find a niche in the market and not compete directly with IBM. By varying the terms of its purchase and rental operations, the corporation pressed computer makers to cut costs; to use locally produced rather than imported parts; to avoid destructive price wars in domestic markets, to sell at a loss in establishing competition with IBM, and to advance technologically. During the 1970s the government gradually scaled back its financing of computer rentals and dismantled artificial domestic markets as the international competitiveness of Japanese computer firms grew. As dependence on government support declined, the corporation remained an important forum for industry studies and interaction between government officials and business leaders. Thus funds from the state postal savings system have been used by officials in the 1980s to make loans in high-risk areas; for example, development of the fifth generation computer. This in turn has encouraged the banking and business community to mobilize resources for support that would otherwise be unlikely to be forthcoming. The most accurate way of characterizing Japanese industrial policy is, therefore, to say that it is not state-led or private market-led, but both.

The difference between industrial policy in France and Japan on the one hand and Britain on the other is pronounced. Following a period of austerity under the postwar British Labour government, wartime controls and economic planning mechanisms were rapidly dismantled in the early 1950s. Instead of detailed intervention in economic processes, both Conservative and Labour governments of the 1950s and 1960s relied mainly on the general public spending and taxation levels of fiscal policy to manage variations in aggregate demand and cope with recurring balance of payments crises (Steward). Periods of general fiscal stimulus to maintain high employment levels alternated with periods of sharp restraint, as expansion produced an excess of imports over exports and lessened confidence in the value of the pound—the so-called "stop-go cycle." This dilemma was in turn related to the economic interests of Britain's internationally oriented financial institutions (Blank).

Britain's difficulties in economic management have been heavily influenced by inherited institutional features of capital, labor, and the state. The historic process of economic development left Britain with a powerful sector of finance capital vitally interested in defending the international value of the pound sterling and largely separated from domestic industrial enterprises. Unlike France or Japan (or Germany as we shall see), British banks and financial institutions have played a relatively small role in the development or operation of industrial firms (Zysman 1983). Labor has been strongly unionized (about 50 percent of the labor force) but also strongly decentralized, with long-standing divisions among craft unions, and has been suspicious of any interventions threatening the historical autonomy of collective bargaining. Divisions within the structure of state institutions have reflected the separation of an historically independent Bank of England, exercising monetary policy powers oriented to London's international banking center, and the Treasury along with other ministries, operating under the close scrutiny of an adversarial political competition in parliament.

By the 1960s Britain's poor economic performance led many to propose imitating France's apparently successful planning effort; and in 1965 the new Labour government produced a national plan for greatly increasing economic growth over the next five years. But the plan was largely a paper exercise: There was little mutual understanding among government officials, industry, and financial circles as to what should be done to raise the growth rate. In 1966 the plan was effectively abandoned under the familiar pressures of a balance of payments crisis and a swing to the contractionary phase of "stop-go" management so as to restore confidence in the pound.

As noted in the preceding section, the 1970s brought more severe problems to the British economy. Fiscal tools were heavily relied on during the crisis years 1976 and 1977 in an attempt to restrain growth in the public deficit and allow some room for domestic investment expansion. In addition, the Labour government during this period convinced unions to exercise wage restraint in the face of a widely perceived inflationary crisis. Restrictions on aggregate economic demand were relaxed somewhat during 1978 and 1979 with a program of reduced taxes and increased public spending; but lost at the same time was the union commitment to wage restraint, and a series of disruptive industrial conflicts in the winter of 1978 and 1979 eroded the government's standing in the country. In the election of May 1979, voters turned sharply in favor of Margaret Thatcher and the Conservative party, bringing in a radically new set of policy instruments.

It would be wrong to think that during this entire postwar period, British policy was devoid of industrial subsidies, credit controls, and other forms of detailed intervention. Special tax relief to encourage investment was begun in 1945; direct investment grants to the private sector were instituted in 1966; in 1967, government premiums were introduced to subsidize wages in firms located in economically lagging regions. Also, throughout the 1950s and 1960s the Bank of England employed selected credit measures to encourage loans for exports and shipbuilding and to restrict consumer borrowing. In the 1970s the pace of government subsidization quickened in an effort to modernize British industry and so try to achieve high rates of economic growth.

In a formal sense, many of these measures were analogous to French or Japanese industrial policy. However, the British experience differs in three important respects. First, the British approach to industrial policy has been characterized by an arms-length relationship between government officials and the industrial and financial representatives, who are expected mainly to respond to the economic incentives provided by government. No integrated administrative elite exists to bring together bureaucratic, industrial, and financial circles. Indeed, British administrators advance in their careers with little experience in the problems of industry or finance. Despite experiments with joint committees and working groups, the general approach has remained basically "us and them," with an officialdom of self-contained careers that offers investment and other incentives to the "them" who work on the outside with everyday problems of industry and finance.

Second, British programs have been subject to continual chopping and changing to meet the political needs of alternating Conservative and Labour governments. Conservative governments have tended to rely on tax allowances to assist business; Labour governments have typically supplanted these allowances with direct cash grants and special subsidies for employment. In 1972 the Conservative government's Industry Act provided various forms of financial assistance to modernize plants and equipment. These "schemes," as they were known, covered virtually every sector of the economy while Conservatives were in power, but they fell into the background with the succeeding Labour government's Industrial Strategy of 1975. This latter effort involved the creation of three dozen joint working parties of business, labor, and government, charged with setting medium-term objectives for their respective sectors and identifying problems in meeting those objectives. A new government-controlled National Enterprise Board was created to finance key industries in exchange for partial ownership; but the Board soon became the center of a conflict over whether it was simply a means for financially bailing out important firms facing bankruptcy (such as the Rolls Royce and British Leyland companies) or a device for implementing the socialist agenda of government ownership throughout industry (as the left wing of the Labour party wanted). In 1979 the new Conservative government quickly dismantled most of these programs.

Thus, compared to France and Japan, Britain's short-term responsiveness to the demands of partisan competition made industrial policies less predictable, a fact that further encouraged government administrators' natural inclination to avoid close and enduring relationships with private economic decision makers. These factors are related to a third difference. Unlike French and Japanese policymakers, British officials have found it difficult to operate industrial assistance in ways that give strategic priority to some economic activities over others. Industrial subsidies and tax allowances, although called selective, have in practice been very widely distributed, partly because of short-term political advantages and partly because of administrative "fairness" standards that oppose unequal treatment of firms, sectors, and regions. Competing unions and other producer groups have been powerful enough in the workplace and Parliament to block clearly focused strategies in industrial policy but not strong enough to serve as reliable bargaining partners capable of implementing government-supported economic deals.

For all of these reasons, industrial policy as an instrument of economic management is different in Britain (Green; Hall 1986). In Britain it is less predictable, more distant from central decision-making processes, and less integrated with the strategies of industrial and financial leadership. Since industrial policy came as something of an afterthought to the British emphasis on aggregate demand management and is far more open to democratic political pressures than in France or Japan, it might be considered vulnerable to sudden political change. This is precisely what has happened since 1979.

The Thatcher government in 1979 brought a radical shift in the instruments of British economic policy, although it is doubtful if many people voting for the Conservative party at that time realized the extent of the change entailed by their electoral choice. The essence of this change was to abandon fiscal management of aggregate demand in favor of a wholehearted commitment to controlling the aggregate money supply. With this change, most interest in detailed programs of industrial policy was cast to the winds.

It seems remarkable that British policy-making could accommodate such an abrupt shift in the tools of economic management. After all, the British Treasury had functioned for decades as the bastion of Keynesian demand management. But, considered closely, it is easy to see how single-minded monetarism competed with an almost equally single-minded Keynesianism. Both approaches place total emphasis on government control over key economic aggregates—general levels of total demand in the former, and particular measures of money supply in the latter. Concentrating on these "big levers" excused British officialdom from any deep involvement in the details of industrial production and finance. Thus, whereas in France and Japan establishment of a growth rate for the money supply became an opportunity for more extensive *involvement* in the allocation of credit and economic consultation in government, business, and financial circles, in Britain it provided the rationale for government *disengagement* from other economic problems. Thus both Japan's "weaning" of computer firms from state support and France's "liberalization" policy of decontrol went hand in hand with sectoral planning, particularly for export promotion; in Britain decontrol policy was much more single-minded and tended to favor pure market mechanisms freed of government intervention.

During the 1970s a number of countries adopted monetary targets in an attempt to deal with inflation, but it is fair to say that only in Britain was the instrument of monetary policy given primacy over any other aspect of economic policy and pursued so relentlessly through the 1980s (Whiteley). In practice it turned out to be much more difficult than expected to hold growth in the money supply to the government's targets. Even so, the result was a series of disinflationary pressures that saw investment, total manufacturing output, and economic growth stagnate in the five years after 1979. The government cut industrial subsidies, sold a number of state-owned enterprises, and successfully used legislation and a sustained high rate of unemployment to reduce the power of labor unions. Labor, financial, and industrial markets gradually readjusted under the discipline of market forces in the 1980s, but at a high cost of lost potential output and regional imbalances in Britain. At the same time, an overvalued pound—prompted by North Sea oil and favored by the international financial sector—continued to undermine the competitiveness of British goods, and employment subsidies were expanded on a piecemeal basis with little strategy of exploiting comparative advantages in the international marketplace (Alt 1988).

Three Variations: West Germany, Sweden, and the United States

Having considered the choice of economic policy instruments in France, Japan, and Britain, we now turn our attention to Germany, Sweden, and the United States, which offer still other variations.

The situation in the United States is comparatively straightforward.

Only in wartime has the national government been equipped with tools for detailed economic intervention, and the mechanisms, such as wage-price controls and credit allocations, have for the most part been quickly dismantled at the conclusion of hostilities (Wilson; Goldstein). As parts of American industry have faced financial crises (Lockheed during the Nixon administration, Chrysler during the Ford and Carter years), some government assistance has been occasionally forthcoming, but these have been isolated decisions made in response to particular political forces in play at the time and not as part of anything that could be characterized as coherent industrial policy. For example, at the beginning and end of the 1980s U.S. savings and loan associations (which had offered long-term loans at low interest rates and could not attract short-term deposits without paying higher interest rates and taking greater risks in increasingly deregulated financial markets) pressed their case for special federal government assistance. The result was a series of government subsidies, bailouts, and reorganizations. What these actions represented was not a joint government/business strategy to influence the industrial allocation of credit resources but a political expedient worked out between administration and congressional politicians to cope with an emergency financial crisis.

The United States does not lack for interventionist economic programs, whatever the party of the person in the White House. Federal military spending for procurement and R & D financing plays an important part in technological innovations in American industry; on the civilian side a broad range of regulatory, tax, credit, subsidy, and other instruments are in play at the federal and state government levels (Wachter; Heclo; Zysman 1983). The difference is that in the U.S. institutional framework of multiple, competing, power centers, these instruments are rarely used in any sustained, coherent way (Lehner 1986; Hudson). Organized labor is weak (declining from roughly one-third of the work force in the 1940s to less than 20 percent in the 1980s) and relatively excluded from public and private processes of managing economic policy. Business interests are themselves comparatively fragmented in this institutional structure (Weir and Orloff and Skocpol), and a long tradition of government regulation and strong capital markets has prohibited the merging of banking operations and financial institutions with industrial enterprises. Perhaps the closest comparison that can be made is between various American and British programs designed to assist economically hard-pressed regions and cities. Even more so than in Britain, multiple arenas of independent power in the United States impose a political imperative to spread such "selective" assistance very widely. Aid supposedly targeted in the form of grants, special lines of credit, and loan guarantees tends to develop so that most members of Congress, governors, and many mayors find a place at the table of federal assistance (Wachter).

Like the British state structure, the U.S. national government has little capacity to pursue coherent courses of microeconomic intervention and in the postwar era has relied on aggregate demand management and/or aggregate money supply management as its preferred instruments of economic policy. But unlike its British counterpart, the U.S. executive branch must share extensive powers with an independent legislature. And unlike Britain or any of the continental European nations, the United States lacks a senior class of permanent officials with an enduring stake in policy development. Hence consistent and predictable demand management policies have proven especially difficult to achieve in Washington; Congress can easily overwhelm a president's taxing and spending plans, and such plans themselves frequently change as the temporary officials of the presidential staff and the departments come and go.

The situation is different with regard to instruments of monetary policy. The Federal Reserve Board enjoys substantial independence from both the president and Congress. Board members serve long, relatively fixed terms of office and are assisted by a high-level staff of professional economists. In theory this central financial institution can pursue an independent course of monetary policy, but in practice the "Fed" often has little choice but to accommodate the various swings of fiscal policy determined by the president and Congress. For example, in 1966 and 1967 President Johnson first hesitated to ask for higher taxes to pay for increased military spending in Vietnam and then faced further delays in adjusting fiscal policy when Congress debated the proposed tax increase for over a year. The result was a major inflationary movement, which monetary authorities felt forced to counteract by restricting the supplies of money and credit, yielding in turn an unexpected and disruptive credit crunch. Similarly, in 1981 and 1982 the new Reagan administration succeeded against most expectations in gaining not only major federal spending cuts from Congress but also a multi-year program of significant tax reductions. However, increased military outlays and automatic budget increases produced by an unexpected recession had the effect of undermining spending constraints, while the economic downturn reduced revenues even further than foreseen when the commitments for three years of tax reductions were made. The result in this instance was a huge increase in the federal deficit and a severely constrained choice for the Federal Reserve Board: either to abandon the high interest rate policy that had been established to fight inflation, or to keep money tight and risk the supply-side recovery the administration had promised would follow from its tax cuts. In the end, interest rates remained high but were gradually brought down without rekindling inflation. In the meantime, tax cuts, booming military spending, and borrowing from foreign creditors to finance a growing international trade imbalance produced an expansionary fiscal policy of trade and budget deficits during the 1980s that no one had really planned. While the British economy continued to stagnate under consistent policies, U.S. "muddling" was associated with a relatively strong but deficit-ridden recovery in the 1980s.

Thus, unlike Britain, the United States has found it difficult to use its aggregate economic management tools decisively. This may or may not be seen as a disadvantage, depending upon one's confidence in government's ability to recognize the "right" policy and to pursue it consistently. If the U.S. government lacks the French capacity for microeconomic interventions, it also lacks the single-mindedness that would allow anything like the Thatcher government's total commitment to the management of money supply. Certainly the conservative agendas of the Reagan and Thatcher governments had much in common: to reduce government spending, taxation, and regulation; to increase military power; and to rely on private market mechanisms. As actually implemented, however, the Reagan policy could not use one particular instrument (a money supply target, or balanced budget under fiscal policy, or the like) or any policy tool with steadfastness. Navigating its first year's program, the Reagan administration had to make many compromises, retaining ad hoc subsidies (for example, to tobacco farmers) and adding ad hoc interventions into the private markets (for example, tax aids to the savings industry). As unemployment and deficits grew in 1982, the same public opinion that the president had mobilized to pass his original economic program through Congress now filtered into the highly permeable policy-making process of America's divided institutions to demand changes in the original package (for example, new taxes to help reduce the deficit, more help for the unemployed, and so on). By comparison, in the relatively closed environment of British economic policy-making, the Thatcher government could and did march grimly onward along its chosen path.

Germany is also strongly committed to private market mechanisms and has little explicit industrial policy promulgated by the national government. Yet one would be wrong to conclude that Germany resembles the approach of the United States in its instruments of economic management. To be sure, experience with the Nazi-controlled economy lessened the attractiveness of centralized government intervention in the economy. But no one needed to remind postwar German unionists, businesspeople, party leaders, or ordinary citizens about the fatal consequences of class conflict, hyperinflation, and unemployment leading to fascism. Historical experience, not abstract economic theory, taught the value of social partnership, economic stability, and decentralized state administrative power. As a result the postwar German institutional framework became a complex blend of organizationally decentralized government power and procedurally centralized coordination of producer group bargaining (Katzenstein 1987). Dispersed political authority in Germany's federal structure stands in contrast to comprehensive statutes and legal procedures regulating industrial relations between business and labor. Sixteen large, industry-based unions organize workers in one large confederation covering about one-third of the labor force; quasi-judicial collective bargaining regularizes wage settlements that are both enforceable and therefore influential throughout the larger work force. Alongside a historically strong state role in social welfare programs (see Chapter Seven), a politically independent central bank is empowered by the postwar constitution to pursue monetary and credit policies protecting Germans against inflation.

Of course, constitutional requirements could mean little apart from policy choices implementing the mandate for economic stability. Germany is distinguished by its reliance on the instrumental role of a centrally guided banking system to encourage the desired stability amid the destabilizing forces of free markets. Direct government aid to industry is generally limited to tax allowances and research grants at the federal level and loan guarantees at the state and local levels. But government aid is distinctly subordinate to the key instruments of economic management: banking institutions and their links upward to central management of economic aggregates and downward to individual industries and firms.

It is important to understand the extremely close and long-standing relationship between local commercial banks and private companies. Banks possess direct power by owning company stock and sitting on the executive boards of many large firms. In addition, banks exert considerable indirect power as the major source of investment funds and financial information for day-to-day decision making in private companies. These functions occur to some extent among banks in every nation; but the interpenetration of banking and the industrial community is much deeper and more enduring here than almost anywhere else. At the end of World War II, the Allied occupying powers attempted to break up the heavily concentrated banking and industrial sectors; but the leading firms only regrouped in even larger structures as the postwar economy grew. Thus industrial and economic policy began to be interrelated because of overlapping industrial and financial structures (performing something of the same function as that of the interconnected elites of French bureaucratic, industrial, and financial circles). The three dominant German banks sit on no fewer than seventy of the supervisory boards of the top one hundred companies. Industrialists interested in exports and bankers interested in the long-term performance of the firms in which they own or control shares have formed a powerful alliance favoring an undervalued deutschmark and a careful, incremental approach to any industrial restructuring.

These features would be more a hindrance than an aid to coherent public policy without a link to the central processes of government economic policy-making. That link is provided by the single most influential instrument of German economic policy, the *Deutsche Bundesbank* (central bank). The Bundesbank is independent of the government, and its regulatory power extends over virtually every organization capable of supplying credit. Each state of the federal system has its own central bank with direct ties to the Bundesbank. These state units are further subdivided into branches and offices in almost every town of significant size. In all developed countries, central bankers are powerful economic actors; public commitment to a forceful Bundesbank as a stabilizer of German domestic economic policy is, however, more deep-seated than comparable situations in other countries.

And yet, the Bundesbank does not intervene directly in details of industrial finance or decision making. That task is left to local units of the banking system. The task of the central bank is to guide monetary policy and indirectly influence industrial policy by regulating the availability of credit and controlling the stock of money in circulation. In addition, the Bundesbank is depended on to maintain stability in the economy. Within general terms set by the Bundesbank, industries are free to innovate and invest, workers to bargain for benefits, financial institutions to supply credit—in response to signals from market mechanisms. Likewise, politicians are allowed to spend and tax as democratic competition may require. But it is with the Bundesbank's policy framework firmly in mind that they have to undertake their ostensibly free negotiations.

Not surprisingly, the power of the central banking authority has occasionally put it in sharp conflict with governmental, industrial, and labor leaders. So far, the Bundesbank has always prevailed. In 1969 and 1970, for example, inflationary pressures were building in the German economy. Despite urging and quiet pressure from the Bundesbank, first the Christian Democratic government and then a newly elected Social Democratic coalition government resisted pursuing a restrictive fiscal policy, a resistance supported by business and labor. In the end, the Bundesbank imposed stringent constraints on the supply of money and credit, arguing that a fiscal package of spending restraint and tax increases would be much less disruptive to the economy. The government gave way, and as the new fiscal package was passed by the parliament, the Bundesbank announced a phased reduction in monetary restraints.

In 1970 it was the government that had to yield to Bundesbank policy; in 1974 it was business, labor, and government that had to give way. We have already noted the German response to the first OPEC oil shock. The nation's banking authorities were determined to prevent the higher energy costs from causing a surge of inflation. This challenge was intensified when the left-of-center Social Democratic government proposed expansionary measures to fight growing unemployment, and business and labor representatives concluded an extremely high wage settlement averaging almost a 14 percent rise in 1974. The Bundesbank responded by greatly tightening the availability of money and credit, thus making it much more difficult for businesses simply to pass on the higher labor and oil costs in higher prices.

Moreover, bank officials made it clear that this policy would be continued for some time regardless of its effects on business profits and employment. The strategy worked. Restrictive monetary policies forced the government to pursue expenditure cuts and other austerity measures. These included efforts to bolster labor demand by encouraging early retirement and sending home foreign workers (whose numbers, after growing for years, declined from 2.6 million to 1.9 million between 1973 and 1976). Business profits flattened under the pressure of tight money. Realizing that high wage settlements would inevitably restrict profits further, leading to plant closings and more unemployment, labor agreed to moderate its wage demands; and 1975 wage settlements fell back to the 7 percent range, or roughly to the general rate of inflation.

The Bundesbank and banking system can operate in this way because there is general agreement on the importance of stability in German economic development. The Bundesbank is such a powerful instrument of economic policy not simply because of its independence, but because that independence is supported by a consensus against extreme and unpredictable fluctuations in the economy. Without this supporting context, no financial authority could sustain its position in periodic clashes with the short-term pressures of government, business, and labor.

Stability is symbolized by the Bundesbank's relatively autonomous control over monetary policy and its responsibility for preserving the value of the German currency. But its influence extends further; for banking authorities have not acted to try to preserve price stability at all costs if doing so would seriously destabilize other dimensions of the economy, such as employment, investment, and trade. Thus, while Germany was the first major Western nation to announce targets for aggregate growth in the money supply (in 1974), the Bundesbank has never argued for controlling inflation at all costs. It has not, like the French government, used monetary targets as a lever for detailed industrial intervention; nor has it, as in Britain, single-mindedly pursued such targets as the exclusive means of reducing inflation. At times, as in 1978, the Bundesbank has abandoned its monetary targets in favor of achieving stability in other areas of the economy. But it has done so in the name of stable management, not of hitting arbitrary monetary targets. It is an image of predictable management that the Bundesbank adeptly cultivates in its quiet public relations and in its constant interaction with all the major economic interests of the nation.

Swedish methods of economic management share some characteristics of several nations' approaches. Sweden ranks with Germany in its modest extent of direct government ownership in the economy. Like Britain, Sweden has traditionally relied on the management of aggregate demand. Sweden, in fact, was among the earliest nations fully to embrace Keynesian-type concepts of fiscal policy, as the Social Democratic party in power in the

1930s abandoned most of its nationalization promises in favor of countercyclical spending and taxation. As economic problems mounted during the 1970s, the Swedish government was led to copy some elements of French-style detailed intervention in order to cope with troubled industries such as steel and shipbuilding.

However, the more distinctive quality of Swedish economic management lies elsewhere. The familiar tools of fiscal and monetary policy are in place; but the most characteristic aspect of Swedish policy is its heavy reliance on unions as the key element in economic management. Labor unions, particularly the huge central confederation of trade unions, *Landsorganization* (LO), have evolved into the most important instrumentality for determining the success or failure of economic policy. This situation is due in part to the high degree of union organization (covering approximately three-fourths of the labor force—more than in any other country) and in part to LO's long-standing alliance with the Social Democratic party, which held power for over forty years, until the election of 1976. No less important, however, is the fact that two generations of union leadership have made it their business to advance their interests with bold proposals that could be shown to improve the economy as a whole. In the 1940s and 1950s, for example, the unions advanced a so-called "pro-mobility" policy. Through a complex series of government programs and industrial agreements, this policy sought to ensure a rapid adaptability of labor and capital to changes in international competition while maintaining economic security for workers. In the 1960s a union-led campaign was advanced to reduce inequality of living conditions and to rationalize low-paying, low-productivity sectors of the economy.

We might say that the labor union structure in Sweden performs roughly the same instrumental function that the banking system performs in Germany—namely, to provide a fairly coherent link between microeconomic decision making (at the level of firm and industry) and macroeconomic decision making (at the national level). In Sweden, an informal general division of labor developed in the postwar period whereby government maintained a high level of demand, so as to ensure full employment, in return for which trade unions sought to maintain industrial peace and exercise restraint in making wage and other demands on industry.

Of course actual operations have been more complex. As economic problems multiplied in the 1970s, Sweden's much praised system of management encountered severe difficulties. Union-led adjustment processes that had once produced negotiated settlements now yielded a succession of stalemates. Despite some functional similarities, unions and banks are different instruments of economic policy management. An emphasis on stability is fully consistent with conventional banking preferences for maintaining confidence, predictability, and the status quo. The Swedish trade union movement, however, has evolved its own agenda emphasizing redistributions of wealth and power rather than stabilizing the status quo distribution of shares. While the economy grew rapidly, conflict could be avoided by allowing differential gains for everyone. But slower growth meant that gains for some would occur at the expense of others. Such distributive conflicts occurred more often in all nations as postwar growth slowed down after the late 1960s. Swedish dependence on unions as the chosen instrument of economic management made the issues that much more prominent there. Since developments in Sweden as well as other countries during the 1970s and 1980s increasingly revolved around the distribution of scarcities, rather than of affluence, it is to that category of choices that we should now turn.

COSTS AND BENEFITS
OF ECONOMIC MANAGEMENT
DISTRIBUTION

No one can accurately calculate the final distribution of welfare resulting from economic policies. Nor do policymakers in any nation actually try to make these calculations. What matters for policy-making are the *perceived* costs and benefits around which groups become politically mobilized.

During the 1950s and 1960s it became widely perceived that economic management was a largely nonideological, technical exercise. Partisan considerations might of course intrude in the policy-making process, but the basic framework for choice was seen as a matter of applied economic science, not politics. Properly designed policies would produce a regime of sustained economic growth that rendered obsolete the old politics of winners vs. losers, capital vs. labor, producers vs. consumers. With sustained growth, everyone could be a winner.

The unexpected economic troubles of the 1970s and 1980s undercut this consensus and politicized problems of economic policy. The simultaneous occurrence of high unemployment and high inflation in the 1970s (stagflation) and continued sluggishness in economic growth sowed confusion among advocates of traditional Keynesian fiscal policy and supporters of government activism. Free-market economists and conservative political forces took the offensive to argue that economic revival depended on cutting back the role of government in the economy. As economic theory and political interpretation became intertwined, debate centered once again on distributive choices as to who would bear the costs and who would reap the benefits of the economic adjustments being advocated.

Political Cycles and Economic Growth

One interpretation linking economic (mis)management with political calculations of costs and benefits is what has been termed "the political business cycle." In popular press accounts this is usually taken to mean simply that incumbent governments time their efforts at stimulating economic growth (lower unemployment, higher personal income, and so on) so as to improve their chances for winning in election years. More sophisticated versions have sought to explain how, in a postwar regime of Keynesian doctrine and democratic politics, policymakers' sensitivity to the costs and benefits of economic management is asymmetrical. Policymakers in democratic systems are said to compete for favor by enacting benefits for the population; at the same time, they seek to avoid disfavor by deferring any explicit imposition of costs. In practical terms, this means that economic managers are strongly tempted to institute programs of fiscal stimulus, with major increases in spending for government benefits, while refusing to enact the tax increases necessary to pay for them. Deficits grow, producing higher rates of inflation and crowding out resources for investment. Protest against inflation rates also increases, but any bitter medicine to contract the economy (through higher taxes and/or lower spending) will at worst be withheld or, at best, delayed until after the elections that engendered the spending for increased benefits in the first place. Such, in broad outline, is the political business cycle in modern democratic governments charged with economic management (Brittan; Buchanan and Wagner).

How applicable is this interpretation? Various methods of measuring economic policy in relation to swings in the political fortunes of democratic politicians have been used to evaluate this model, and the results give cause for skepticism.

Comparative study of the seventeen advanced democracies between 1960 and 1978 shows no systematic tendency for governments to increase spending and avoid tax increases in line with the electoral cycle. The odds of having a net fiscal stimulus in any election year appeared to be only about fifty-fifty (Cameron 1984a). One careful study of the U.S. experience shows that electorally focused economic expansions have occurred (specifically in 1972 and 1984) but these appear as more the exception than the rule (Hibbs 1987). Moreover, comparative studies have failed to discover any clear evidence of the presumed linkage between big government spending, deficits, and inflation.

Countries with above-average government spending have not regularly experienced large deficits; nor have countries with large deficits necessarily experienced above-average rates of inflation. Countries with particularly high inflation have not necessarily experienced significant deficits or electorally timed policies of fiscal stimulation. Inflation may be a way of concealing costs that would otherwise arise from a more explicit conflict over income shares; but that is different from inflation occurring as the result of some inherent electoral dynamic in economic management (Cameron 1982).

In sum, the political business cycle theory is important because it alerts us to calculations of costs and benefits as democratic policymakers grapple with the ups and downs of modern economies. But it also presumes a degree of consistency, predictability, and control that is very difficult to achieve in practice. Many politicians probably wish they could obtain the kind of strategic control with which abstract theory credits them. But the actual play of political forces in economic management seems too complex for any such fine-tuning to occur.

A much more far-reaching critique has focused, not on cycles, but on the more general trend in relations between macroeconomic outcomes and liberal/leftist political influences. There are many variations, but the essential theme that developed in the 1970s and 1980s—both in economic theory and conservative political offensives—is straightforward: Government policies have interfered with market forces so as to produce deteriorating economic performance. It is a multi-count indictment. Protected by government policies, workers increase their share of Gross National Product beyond what is justified by productivity gains. Redistributional policies and high taxes attenuate the link between personal effort and rewards. Protections demanded by consumer groups, environmentalists, and unions produce excessive regulations and economic rigidities inhibiting efficient reallocations of resources. Work effort and profitability decline, entrepreneurial risk-taking and investment is discouraged, and growth in the economic pie stagnates. In short, the long-term benefits of market efficiency and investment for increased production have been traded off for the mirage of short-term gains in equality and security (Gilder 1981, 1984; Anderson and Hill; Hayek).

Many issues raised by this interpretation depend on philosophical premises and causal relationships that cannot be conclusively proven or disproven (Okun; Campbell). However, researchers have begun examining the record for evidence of some of the gross relationships that are presumed to exist between political interference in the market and economic growth.

Very simple comparisons suggest that the extent of government intervention and redistributive effort in different nations does not appear to be closely related to overall economic performance. If we rank nations according to the real economic growth rate that they have achieved, there is no noticeable correlation between that ranking and the relative magnitude of government transfers, government consumption, or government redistribution through taxes. Countries with low growth often rank low in government transfers and certainly do not seem to make unusually large efforts at redistribution through taxation. Government consumption does seem higher in countries with slow growth, but closer study shows that government consumption of goods and services has been pushed to these heights by military, not social, expenditures. Other studies have found no general tendency for countries with a relatively high share of government in their Gross Domestic Product to turn in inferior economic performances (Saunders). In general, both high and low economic growth countries vary considerably in their degree of government interference in market processes. This is not surprising in view of the fact that national economic growth rates depend on a highly complex set of economic, social, and political factors, many of which appear unmeasurable (Dennison).

More sophisticated studies have tried to probe deeper into the multiple interaction of a large number of factors underlying economic growth rates. One such study examines the economic performance record of twelve OECD nations for the period 1962–83 (Friedland and Sanders). The results suggest that, standing independently, the partisan color of regimes does not affect national economic growth rates. The distribution of political power between right and left in government or in the labor market (i.e., degree of unionization) does not in and of itself relate to differences in economic growth during this period. The influence of politics on growth rates appears to depend, not simply on who is in power, but what they choose to do. Thus policies increasing government transfer payments to households are found to be positively associated with higher growth, while government production of goods and services for households is negatively associated with growth. Government spending on subsidies and other transfers to business firms is associated with slower growth while government production in the form of military spending seems to stimulate growth, possibly because it is concentrated on frontiers of technological innovation.

Other studies have suggested that in the troubled period from 1974 to 1984 leftist control of government needed to be combined with a strong, encompassing union movement in order for growth rates to be affected. But the effect was the opposite of that predicted by the conservative critique. Countries where this combination occurred appear to have done better in managing the post-1973 downward pressures on growth, while strong unions without leftist governments or leftist governments without strong unions had negative effects on growth (Lange and Garrett 1985). These results are affected by the fact that one country with leftist governments and strong unions—Norway—reaped a growth bonanza by having its own sources of North Sea oil (Jackman 1987). Even so, once Norway is excluded from the analysis and degrees of dependence on foreign oil are taken into account, labor dominance in government and the labor market still appears to be associated with somewhat higher growth rates (Lange and Garrett 1987).

Economic growth is a complex phenomenon. In Chapter Seven we will look more closely at the relation between redistributive income-maintenance policies and economic performance—the "tradeoff" between equality and efficiency. No comparative researchers contend that policies of the Left will necessarily produce higher growth rates nor that these are the only regimes capable of turning in good growth performances (Scharpf 1984). What the evidence does suggest is that governments and labor movements committed to managing or interfering with market forces (the choice of terms is a political act) have not been inconsistent with favorable growth rates in recent decades. Policymakers of every political persuasion claim to want growth. The influence of politics on economic performance occurs through the policy strategies that are chosen and nowhere is this more evident than in the distributional choices involving inflation and unemployment.

An Inflation-Unemployment Tradeoff?

We should begin by recalling the two-phase nature of economic developments in the postwar period. Until roughly the end of the 1960s, economic growth was generally rapid, with substantial price stability. In this setting, economic management brought what might be regarded as political good news. A steadily growing economy with minimal price distortion meant that economic policy decisions were mainly concerned with distributing differential gains, perhaps a little more for wages than profits or a little more for public than private consumption. Nevertheless, it was a situation of gain for all with little apparent imposition of costs on any. There was little perception of economic policy as a zero-sum struggle between labor and capital or private and public consumption, in which a gain for one side entails a corresponding loss for the other side. Economic growth meant more for everybody.

The second phase, since the early 1970s, has been a different story. Slower growth, deeper recessions, and unpredictable inflation significantly changed the setting for political management of the economy. New perceptions of scarcity and tradeoffs among mutually incompatible economic goals grew throughout Western Europe, Japan, and the United States. If sustained growth was to be revived, funds for new investment would have to increase; and a tough choice would have to be made between continuing the gains in benefits and wages for workers and shifting resources to private and/or public capital formation. An equally difficult choice was seen between policies for fighting inflation and those for maintaining employment. Both fiscal and monetary approaches counseled that inflation could be countered by slowing down the economy and increasing unemployment. In short, economic management in the 1970s and 1980s has brought the bad news commonly associated with a zero-sum situation.

As inflation rates grew throughout the 1970s, there was a decided shift everywhere toward policies that fought inflation at the expense of full employment. Rarely was this shift explicitly stated as government policy;

but, in each country, there was, in the name of fighting inflation, a willingness to live with unemployment rates that would have been declared intolerable in the noninflationary 1950s and early 1960s. The results of this policy shift can be seen in Table 5.1. In the 1980–83 recession, unemployment rates in the developed democracies reached their highest level since the Great Depression of the 1930s.

This priority shift was so widespread that it must be explained by general, not nation-specific, factors. The most plausible explanation involves the different constituencies affected by anti-inflationary and antiunemployment policies. Rapid and erratic price increases are distributed widely across a nation's population and in every income level, and they are distributed in an arbitrary manner, even within the thinking of each individual. Few persons doubt that they deserve the higher prices as sellers of goods and services, but not many people feel they deserve the higher prices they must pay as buyers of goods and services.

Sensitivity to the pain of inflation is heightened by a certain "money illusion." In an inflationary period income may rise very quickly while purchasing power does not. Although *real* incomes (that is, incomes in constant prices) may grow, many people feel a loss when they consider how much better off they *should* be with so much money. For example, in the United States, real per capita income increased 28 percent in the "dismal" 1970s, compared to 30 percent in the "golden" 1960s and only 20 percent in the 1950s. But it would have been very difficult to convince Americans that they were doing as well as they had been earlier. In the noninflationary 1950s, money income measured real improvements. In the 1970s Americans were more prone to feel dissatisfied because to achieve their 28 percent income growth after inflation, they had experienced a 134 percent increase in money income during the decade. Somehow, one should have felt much richer, even if the increase was in inflated dollars.

In contrast to inflation, the costs of unemployment have tended to be concentrated and predictable. Unemployment tends to fall disproportionately on especially vulnerable groups, such as the young, the unskilled, minorities, and persons in marginal industries. Whereas inflation tends to manifest its costs through widespread disappointment over what inflated incomes will buy, the costs of unemployment are often internalized in various kinds of personal problems—self-reproach for not being able to find a job, mental stress, illness, and sometimes suicide. Thus, for the majority, who have little experience with or likelihood of facing unemployment, retreat on the goal of full employment has often seemed a small price to pay for controlling inflation. In this regard it is revealing that only with the extremely deep slump of 1981–83—when unemployment took on some of inflation's unpredictable qualities and began reaching into white-collar and other occupations unfamiliar with involuntary joblessness—that the anti-inflationary effects of recession predicted by economic theory began to be felt and middle-class opinion moved away from fighting inflation as top priority.

The differential costs and benefits of fighting inflation and unemployment help explain the general shift in distributional priorities that have occurred in the Western democracies in the 1970s and early 1980s. However, nations have displayed varying tolerances for the employment costs of fighting inflation. In recent years students of comparative political economics have devoted considerable effort to trying to unravel the relationships between politics and the unemployment/inflation tradeoff. The results show, not iron-clad laws, but a number of important general tendencies.

The underlying logic linking political partisanship and macroeconomic outcomes is fairly simple (Hibbs 1977). Governments, particularly in recent decades, have been confronted with a policy choice between containing inflationary pressures on the one hand or stimulating the economy to produce low unemployment on the other. The costs of higher unemployment are heavily concentrated on blue-collar or similar occupations and lower-income groups, while higher-income groups perceive—quite accurately—inflation to be the greater threat to their economic position. Since people in the unemployment-averse groups form the core constituency for left-of-center parties and those in the inflation-averse groups form the core constituency for political parties of the right, we should expect the results to show up in economic policies. Governments led by left-of-center parties should give higher priority to fighting unemployment even at the expense of somewhat higher inflation, and governments of the Right can be expected to be more tolerant of unemployment in a more determined fight against inflation.

The economic troubles of the 1970s and 1980s have provided ample opportunity for testing this line of reasoning. A number of studies have supported the general idea that political regimes of the Left have given relatively higher priority to fighting unemployment (Castles 1982; Cameron 1984; Korpi and Esping-Andersen). Of course, unemployment rates depend upon a great many factors, including a country's position in world markets, vulnerability to oil-price increases in the 1970s, and so on. Sophisticated statistical models have been used to see whether partisan control of government makes a difference in unemployment/inflation choices over and beyond what could have been expected once these other important factors are taken into account. One such study for the United States over the period 1953–84 does isolate significant differences in economic priorities and performance between Democratic and Republican administrations (Hibbs 1987, chapters 7 and 8). Other things being equal, Democratic-controlled governments have done more to bring unemployment rates down but have gotten into difficulty with voters over resulting inflation, while Republican administrations have been more zealous in fighting inflation but gotten into trouble because of the accompanying economic slack and unemployment. The American case is important because its economic performance has set the pace for fluctuations in the performance of other developed nations.

Clearly we should not expect that smaller economies more open to international economic forces—whatever the political complexion of their governments—will be able arbitrarily to set their rates of unemployment and real output. Another study refines the analysis by considering unemployment rates achieved relative to the level of demand for a country's goods in the international economy (Alt 1985). In other words, has partisan control of the government mattered, given constraints imposed by levels of international economic activity? A comparative analysis of fourteen Western industrial nations during the period 1960–83 suggests that changes in government favoring parties of the Left have, other things being equal, also been favorable for lower-than-otherwise-projected unemployment, while government by parties of the Right has been associated with higher-than-otherwise-projected unemployment. However, it is also important to note that these effects only clearly occur when economic issues have been salient and parties have made promises to act on those issues—the mere fact of partisan shift in government is not automatically associated with different economic outcomes.

These findings reaffirm the importance of viewing political influences on public policy in terms of strategic contingencies, not mechanistic relationships. Partisan differences in government do not explain why some economies open to international fluctuations sustain low unemployment against world trends (for example, Austria, Norway, and Sweden) while other nations with so-called open economies do not (for example, Belgium, the Netherlands, and Ireland) (Alt 1985, p. 1038). Likewise it appears that, contrary to economic theories of wage-push inflation, countries with high rates of unemployment have often also experienced higher relative levels of inflation in the postwar period (Cameron 1984). The United States, Britain, and Canada are examples. The point is that neither economic theories nor party strategies exist in a vacuum. Both are embedded in a context of constraints created by a nation's position in the world economic order and by its internal structure of power relations. Thus advocates of free-market theories have said that economic policies based on such theories are needed most in countries where the public sector, labor organizations, and other interferences with market mechanisms are most extensive. But it is precisely because of the political realities in such nations that market-oriented strategies have found their warmest welcome in other countries (such as the United States and Britain) where the economic role of government is tentative, union power incoherent, and free-market impulses already strong. It is to this issue of innovation amid constraints that we turn in the next section.

COLLABORATORS OR ADVERSARIES
IN ECONOMIC MANAGEMENT?
RESTRAINTS AND INNOVATION

Management of the economy is a historically recent development. Events of the 1970s undercut much of the earlier confidence that the Keynesian rules of economic management were understood and readily translatable into sustained, noninflationary economic growth. By the 1980s the old sense of mastery over economic developments had receded. National approaches have diverged as economies have become increasingly dependent in a world market. This growing international competition tests not simply one firm against another; it also challenges the comparative capacity of various societies to organize themselves for successful economic performance (Dauderstadt).

The central political problem is one of encouraging powerful groups—whose short-term self-interests can produce inefficiencies, inflation, and unemployment—toward joint action yielding stable growth in the long run.

Such problems of collective action are hardly new in political affairs (Olson 1965). Current economic policy, however, poses the problem in particularly dramatic and inescapable terms. Lacking the surpluses produced by high growth in the 1950s and 1960s, economic policymakers in every nation face the difficult task of imposing short-term costs in order to achieve uncertain longer-term gains. Perhaps the most severe restraint in every developed country lies in the widespread expectations of painless choice built up among consumers, businesspeople, unions, and bureaucrats during the postwar period of high economic growth. Overcoming this inertia of short-term self-interest requires political creativity quite apart from any innovations in economic theory.

All of the countries considered in this book are mature, postindustrial economies. Not only must they compete with each other, but they must also respond to growing pressures from newly industrializing third-world nations where labor is cheap and some developmental shortcuts (for example, copying technologies) are possible. Comparative policy studies are being forced to pay increasing attention to the need for so-called aging economies of the developed welfare states to adapt and innovate if they are to remain competitive in the international marketplace (Kindleberger; Pfaller).

Much attention in recent years has focused on the constraints and opportunities produced by interest groups as they interact with policy-making processes. According to one widely cited interpretation (Olson 1982), mature democracies are characterized by a growing number of interest groups. These groups make claims on the resources of society to satisfy their members but have little or no incentive to consider the cost of their activities on the economy and society as a whole. Only when interest groups are large enough to encompass large segments of society will their calculations of self-interest tend to merge with an appreciation of the overall consequences of their actions. However, small special interest organizations are easier to develop and maintain than encompassing groups, and over time mature democracies can expect to experience a proliferation of special interest groups and coalitions protecting their positions. The result is a series of social rigidities that inhibit innovation, efficiency, and productivity—and eventually lead to economic decline.

Another prominent and more positive view of interest groups has developed under the general heading of *corporatism* (Heisler; Schmitter and Lehmbruch). In the rapidly growing literature on this subject, the term *corporatism* has been conceptualized and measured in a number of different and not always consistent ways (Therborn 1987). Nevertheless, the basic idea is fairly straightforward. While Olson's theory concentrates on the number and size of separate interest groups, writers of the corporatist school emphasize the structural arrangements through which groups interact among themselves and with governments. Even though no one encompassing group may exist, the same regard for larger mutual interests can be achieved through an institutional setting in which the relevant groups and government policymakers regularly collaborate with each other in a centralized bargaining process. Rather than succumbing to a pluralist scramble that pays no attention to the common good, corporatist institutions provide for the development of organizational and government policies in concert. This encourages, it is said, a logic of accommodation that can manage distributive conflict with an eye to shared interests in improving economic performance (Keman and Whiteley; Lehmbruch 1985).

It is easy to understand the attractiveness of the corporatist model for some observers, as economic management has become more difficult. Corporatism suggests a political mechanism for disciplining powerful economic interests by making them jointly responsible for the longer-term results of their actions. Short-term costs of economic adjustment may be more readily accepted in exchange for a continuing part in vital government decisions affecting these groups' interests.

The post-1973 divergences in economic performance among the developed democracies has provided a fertile testing ground for theories of interest group politics and economic policy-making. The results are not as clear-cut as one would predict from either the abstract logic of Olson's interest group model of economic decline or the corporatist theory of accommodation.

A number of studies have failed to find evidence for any simple connection between the growth of special interest groups—especially union organization—and economic decline (Czada; Lehner; Schubert; Colby; Dean). Thus, for example, interest group rigidities and a weak capacity for economic adjustment should be most in evidence where groups are fragmented rather than encompassing and where they have had many years to shape democratic politics through distributive coalitions. In fact, there seem to be few examples of such a relationship. Countries such as Belgium and Denmark have encompassing union interest groups but have done poorly in terms of the wage restraint needed for international competitiveness. Countries such as Germany and the Netherlands have relatively decentralized, less encompassing unions but have succeeded better in adjusting to the more volatile post-1973 economic environment. If a long period of democratic politics and pluralist group organization produces economic decline, Switzerland should be in a deplorable economic condition, but it has actually been one of the best economic performers in the world.

At first glance Japan, with its relatively brief postwar experience in democratic group politics and its outstanding economic record, seems to fit the theory. However, a closer examination shows that Japan fails to fit the theory on several counts. Far from exhibiting the free-market mentality that is presumed to exist before interest group rigidities crowd in, Japanese economic policy has been continuously characterized by massive government intervention in the form of extensive government regulation and protection (Sato; Johnson 1982). Nor has Japan cultivated a system of encompassing interest groups whose huge size merges group self-interest with collective outcomes. Japan's remarkable economic adaptiveness has been achieved through an alliance of government and that segment of business interests represented by large enterprises in technologically advanced industries (Johnson 1986). Groups speaking for small business, low-technology sectors, and workers have played little part in producing economic strategies for the nation.

Examination of the economic context within which interest groups and economic policies must operate yields deeper insights. For example, one study of seven smaller European countries (Austria, Belgium, Denmark, the Netherlands, Norway, Sweden, and Switzerland) suggests how openness to external pressures can provide both constraints and opportunities for political innovation and economic adjustment (Katzenstein 1985). In this account the foundation for corporatist structures and consensual policy strategies was laid in the 1930s and 1940s when the combination of depression and war brought a dramatic awareness of shared vulnerability in a hostile world. The incentives for intergroup cooperation continued in the postwar period as these nations became increasingly dependent on world markets. Too small and too dependent on overseas trade to shield themselves from economic fluctuations, these countries found ways of cushioning groups and citizens from the impact of economic change and limiting domestic conflict on economic issues. The result is said to be a corporatist approach to economic policymaking, in which centralized and concentrated interest groups, sharing an ideology of social partnership, engage in a continuous, informal coordination between their competing objectives and government policies. In those small countries where a strong, international business community faces a weakly organized labor movement (the so-called liberal corporatism of Belgium, the Netherlands, and Switzerland), policies of domestic compensation focus on income transfers to individuals and macroeconomic management with limited state supervision of industry. Where labor is strongly organized and business weak (the social corporatism of Austria, Denmark, and Norway), state supervision of industry is more extensive and compensation tends toward a social wage in which government directly provides free or heavily subsidized goods to the entire population. Sweden constitutes a case in which both labor and business are strong and a broad array of compensations and incentives for economic adjustment are used.

A number of studies found a very general relationship between corporatism and some measures of economic performance both in the subset of small European nations (Katzenstein 1985; Castles 1988) and in the larger group of OECD nations (Bruno and Sachs; Wilensky and Turner 1987; Schmidt 1982, 1987; Castles 1987). Countries with strongly integrated systems of interest group intermediation and government policymaking—ie. corporatist states—did relatively well after 1973 in containing distributive conflict, measured in terms of strike activity (Lehner 1986). Highly corporatist nations did somewhat better in holding down inflation in the 1970s than would have been predicted by their openness to foreign oil shocks, but this performance deteriorated in the 1980s (Therborn 1987). Nor have corporatist regimes been particularly effective in achieving workable bargains for wage restraint in order to cope with the dual problems of inflation and unemployment (Armingeon). In fact the closer one looks at national experiences over the 1970s and 1980s, the more varied and interesting the story becomes (see Table 5.1). Sweden and Norway are small, open economies that have maintained full employment with above average inflation; the Netherlands, a small, corporatist nation even more open to world market pressures, has maintained low inflation with mass unemployment in the 1980s. So-called liberal corporatist Switzerland and social corporatist Austria have achieved both low inflation and low unemployment. So too has Japan—a case that some researchers classify as mid-level corporatism (Bruno and Sachs), others as super strong corporatism, or "concordance" (Lehner 1987), still others as corporatism-without-labor (Wilensky and Turner 1987); and that some refuse to classify at all (Lehmbruch 1984; Schmitter).

Clearly we risk finding ourselves with as many categories of corporatism as there are countries. The most reasonable approach is to consider corporatism as a very rough way of classifying broad groupings of nations with respect to government/interest group collaboration. But we should not expect artificially precise "degrees of corporatism" to be linked in any mechanical way to certain standards of economic performance. For example, high on everybody's list of corporatist countries are Austria, Norway, and Sweden—small countries with open economies, concentrated industrial structures, strongly organized unions, and long periods of Social Democratic rule. At the other extreme are some larger economies in which unions are relatively weak and decentralized, group structures more pluralistic, and conservative parties more dominant—most analysts would count Canada, Britain, the United States, and France (at least before 1981 and after 1986) as among the least corporatist states. And in between, of course, lies a complex tangle of difficult-to-classify countries, such as Germany, Japan, Belgium, Switzerland, the Netherlands, and so on. In looking at the economic adjustments and performance of all these countries, it becomes clear that one needs to tell each nation's story with a richer vocabulary than that supplied by corporatism and interest group theory, or party government models, or class politics, or any other one-dimensional framework. Studies show that unemployment, for example, has been heavily influenced by institutionalized commitments to full employment that have occurred (or failed to occur) in a variety of ways over the years in different countries (Therborn 1986). To understand how countries are adapting to today's economic challenges, comparative policy studies need to assess the particular structures of opportunity and constraint presented to policymakers by a combination of factors.

Despite differences in detail, recent research efforts have produced a kind of rough, *de facto* agreement on what these interrelated factors are (Hall 1986; Therborn 1987; Czada; Lehner 1986; Schmidt 1987; Paloheimo; Weir Orloff and Skocpol). It appears that at a minimum, for each country, one needs to take account of (1) the distribution and organization of power among domestic socioeconomic groups; (2) the structure and institutional capacities of the state; (3) the legacy of historical experiences that has been imprinted, not only on social groups and state structures, but on the public and larger political system as well; and (4) the external economic situation of the country in the world marketplace. A few concluding comparisons may help bring these rather abstract concepts down to earth.

Sweden and Austria are two nations often bracketed together at the corporatist, full-employment end of the policy spectrum. However, the institutional frameworks within which they have adapted to economic crises in the 1970s and 1980s are an interesting blend of similarities and differences.

In Sweden, contemporary configurations of social power began to be shaped decisively in the 1930s when a new Social Democratic government and an increasingly powerful union movement reached an accommodation with business and agrarian interests. While unions moderated their demands, Social Democratic governments reciprocated with countercyclical Keynesian policies to maximize employment. Rather than being threatened by Social Democratic rule, business leaders gradually found the more stable and predictable environment of labor relations and expansionary government policies to be advantageous. Social Democrats willingly promoted conditions under which industrial firms, already a concentrated force in the economy, could prosper—but always in return for measures to enhance employment and expand social welfare programs for the working population. Thus concentrations of industrial capital for export earnings were encouraged, but Social Democrats insisted on controls over financial capital that prevented the emergence of an international business sector and kept investment funds at home for domestic job creation. As the decades of Social Democratic rule went on, the already strong administrative capacities of the Swedish state were further developed in line with the labor movement's full-employment agenda; active labor market policies helped retrain and support workers who otherwise would have officially been counted as unemployed, while expansions in public employment, day-care services, and other social programs further promoted a Social Democratic vision of full employment and social solidarity. Central banking authorities were brought firmly under the political control of parliament and given little freedom to pursue monetary policies contrary to the government's employment goals.

The power of this institutional framework to shape policy alternatives has been amply demonstrated in recent years. A series of right-wing coalition governments were essentially paralyzed between 1976–1982 for fear of appearing to retreat on the labor movement's long-standing employment and welfare commitments. Faced with a deteriorating international economic situation, these governments continued expansionary policies to maintain domestic employment through labor market policies, industrial subsidies, and public sector growth. Sweden's position outside the Common Market made it relatively easy to pursue a series of devaluations to spur exports, but it was only when the Social Democrats returned to power in 1982 that fuller cooperation between government and unions helped a fifth and larger devaluation of the currency achieve major results. Union concessions helped hold down labor costs and tolerated surging profits to spur increased investment and production in export-oriented manufacturing firms. In return, the Social Democractic government accommodated important demands from the powerful labor movement. Against bitter opposition from business and opposition parties, the labor movement after 1982 pushed through a new system of wage-earner funds to increase worker control over investment capital. To gain revenues and encourage moderation in union wage demands, the Social Democratic government also imposed a one-time tax of 7 percent on the total assets of private insurance companies in 1986 and a one-time tax levy of 15 percent on all corporate profits in 1989. The government also made sure that while profits and productivity were increasing in the export sector, wages and employment were generally protected in the nonexport sector with its heavy component of public employment (Martin 1989; Heclo and Madsen; Bosworth and Rivlin).

Austria is a study in overlapping contrasts in terms of social power configurations, state capabilities, historical experiences, and international trading position. Policy adaptations to economic troubles have varied accordingly. In Austria the labor movement never acquired the political and ideological hegemony of the Social Democrats in Sweden. On the contrary, the trauma of Nazi occupation and wartime suffering helped begin a tradition of more or less coequal social partnership among the threatened union, business, and Catholic social interests. The external threat and the incentive for concerted cooperation among domestic groups persisted for years after World War II as Austrian leaders sought to reconstruct the economy in the face of the real danger that Soviet forces might decide to takeover the economic and political institutions vacated by the Nazi regime. Through tripartite negotiations among labor, business, and political representatives, the influence of the already large state-owned sector of the economy was expanded to aid the reconstruction process. Banking and other financial institutions were integrated into the same framework of consensual centralized bargaining among the social partners.

Thus by the 1970s, Austria—like Sweden—had a strongly centralized union movement that was closely tied to a socialist party accustomed to holding office; but unlike their Swedish counterparts, the Austrian labor party governed in intermittent coalition with conservatives and this simply symbolized the underlying fact that policy-making was a continuous process of tripartite bargaining (including a strong Catholic political presence). Like Sweden, Austria had a state structure accustomed to economic intervention and domestic control over financial institutions; but these institutional capacities of government had more to do with a large state-owned sector and less to do with active labor market policies based on a Social Democratic Swedish vision of social solidarity. Both Austria and Sweden were small nations needing export earnings and enjoying a certain freedom of maneuver as internationally minor economies outside the European Community. However, unlike Sweden, Austria is heavily dependent on one nation (Germany) for its trade. With their currency pegged to the value of the German mark and price stability essential to their tripartite bargains on wages, investment, and so on, Austrian policymakers have had little chance of copying the Swedish strategy of devaluation. Instead, Austria responded to the world recessions and unfavorable terms of trade in the 1970s and 1980s by pursuing its own version of expansionary, countercyclical policies. Public investment and state enterprises were expanded. As the balance of payments deficit mounted, policymakers used their dominant leverage in the banking and credit system to create a two-tier financing structure: one paying high interest rates to attract foreign capital and loans to cover the deficit and a second subsidized system of lower rates to meet credit needs of domestic firms. Deportation of immigrant workers, that is, a group not part of the "social partnership," was also used to maintain full employment. In the end, and using different means, both Austria and Sweden have managed to protect themselves against international disturbances and maintain reasonably full employment and real economic growth (Chaloupek; Marin; Martin 1986; Kurzer). However, this was not simply the function of being "Social Democratic" or "corporatist" nations.

The Netherlands is another small, trade-dependent nation that evolved in the postwar period a tripartite bargaining system much like that found in Austria. Dutch unions, too, are strongly centralized and have a long-standing alliance with a Social Democratic party committed to full employment. However, these important similarities have to be seen in relation to other features of the Dutch institutional framework. Sectional divisions, including religious cleavages, among Dutch socioeconomic groups have been strong and labor unions, although centralized, have been far from a dominant force in labor market relations. Tripartite bargaining has in fact been an intricate process of building coalitional compromises among sectional interests. Government institutions have functioned as finely tuned machinery for organizing multilevel, multigroup bargaining and for registering the compromise outcomes. But the price has often been an incapacity for government itself to move decisively in any given policy direction. Thus policies for postwar reconstruction assumed a typical balance of power between Social Democrats and the larger Christian Democratic party, which has itself been a complex coalition of Catholic and secular, pro-social welfare and pro-market forces. The result was a compromise in which the Dutch government developed few of the institutional capacities to be found in Sweden (means for countercyclical fiscal policy, active labor market policy, monetary policy control) or in Austria (state-sponsored enterprises, subsidized investment, monetary policy control). Over the years all parties to the bargaining usually agreed that government should not interfere with their sectoral economic operations but that government social welfare spending should compensate groups for economic hardships they might experience. Constraints on policy have been particularly severe because the Dutch economy—again unlike the case in Sweden or Austria—has historically contained a powerful sector of finance capital and transnational businesses making a livelihood out of international transactions. The interest of this business sector in a strong, stable guilder as an international reserve currency has been reinforced by the power of a central bank that is not only independent of the political bargaining system but is a legal entity of private law rather than a public agency.

The impact of this policy framework was clearly demonstrated in Dutch attempts to cope with the economic challenges of the 1970s and 1980s. The first oil shock found the Social Democrats in power seeking to combat rising unemployment through expansionary policies. But there were few administrative tools in place to pursue such policies, and attempts to create more interventionist programs were delayed and often blocked in the bargaining process with Christian Democratic forces and sectoral interests. An array of powerful forces insisted on defending the international value of the Dutch currency by achieving a continuous balance of payments surplus. These forces included the independent national monetary authorities (who refused a looser monetary policy to validate Keynesian demand stimulation), the internationally oriented business community, pro-market Christian Democrats, and the pivotal Liberal Party, as well as a segment of leading Social Democrats themselves. Thus the Swedish option of devaluing the national currency was effectively closed. Moreover, the Dutch Social Democratic government faced a politically immobilizing balance of power in which working-class interests could not dominate the political scene. The Dutch Socialists swung back toward deflationary policies to restrict domestic demand and protect the balance of payments—doing so with as much zeal as Austrian conservatives ignored balance of payments deficits in favor of domestic expansion (Kurzer; Braun). By the time of the second oil shock at the end of the 1970s, a Christian Democrat/Liberal coalition was in power and pursued a still more severe deflationary program on into the 1980s. The relative ease with which a right-of-center government in the Netherlands could attack public consumption, wage growth, and employment stands in marked contrast to the constraints on the contemporaneous right-of-center government in Sweden. Lacking the threat of a dominant, Swedish-style labor movement as well as the deeper consensus and internationally disengaged economic position of Austria's social partnership, the Dutch government in the 1980s pushed for reindustrialization with little pretense of a commitment to full employment or concerted societal bargaining. Belgium, with an institutional framework much like that of the Netherlands (but a higher degree of unionization and also sharper societal cleavages of a linguistic, religious, and regional nature), followed much the same path in the 1970s and 1980s (see Table 5.1).

The same categories help explain the constraints on policy innovation facing the larger nations we have discussed in this chapter. These categories have to do with social power structures (especially but not exclusively the organization of business capital and labor representation), the organization of state institutions (especially but not exclusively the political control or independence of monetary authorities and capacities for microeconomic intervention by officials), the economic position of a nation in world markets, and finally, whatever has been learned from vivid historical experiences (usually of a disastrous nature, such as war and depression). This institutional framework constrains the field of feasible policy innovations without determining the outcome in some mechanistic way. This becomes clear if we reflect on the economic experiences of the larger nations considered at length in this chapter.

Bitter historical experience left all Japanese fully aware of their vulnerable position as a racially homogeneous but overpopulated nation with no natural resources and almost wholly dependent for its livelihood on what could be sold to foreigners. This shared awareness has endured and colored all efforts at economic modernization since 1945; but it was not written in the stars that a scant forty years later Japan should be the world's second largest economy (bigger than Germany and Britain combined). Bureaucrats in prestigious economic ministries used their vast discretionary powers over micro- and macroeconomic policies to forge alliances with large business firms ambitious for further growth. By no means was the collaboration simple or always harmonious, but it was continuous and always focused on the ultimate goal of competitive success in foreign markets. With the small business sector and labor unions (as understood in the West) largely excluded, this government/ business system of orchestrated policies used the decades of continuous conservative party rule to promote a series of three domestic economic transformations: first, labor-intensive, light industry serving to speed immediate postwar recovery; second, heavy, capital intensive industry; and most recently, knowledge-based, high-technology information industry (Pempel).

As we have seen, the French state has elements of the same centralized institutional capabilities, but its relatively favorable postwar economic position was not one to produce a consensus among the country's many small-scale producers about the need for modernization. In effect France's elite bureaucrats were the entrepreneurs using state power to create and protect a national champion in one industrial sector after another. Industrial sectors grew, not on the basis of their competitiveness in markets, but on the basis of their access to state interventions designed to produce the technological leadership that would pull the remaining unmodernized industries forward. The strategy for innovation seemed to work well in fields where the state controlled markets, competition was weak, and technological (nuclear power, space, energy) changes slow. Where market changes were rapid, competition open and intense, and returns for adaptability quickly felt (as in electronics), the French model of bureaucratic modernization performed poorly.

Germany had much in common with the economic position of Japan in the immediate postwar period: a collapsed economy intensely vulnerable to external pressures and in desperate need for export earnings. As in Japan, the catastrophe of recent history produced a general recognition of the need for social partnership among survivors (Schmidt 1988). And like Japanese modernizers, Germans gained an initial advantage in rebuilding their industries by borrowing advanced technologies from abroad, thus creating a shortcut to catch up with other developed nations. However, unlike in France (or Austria for that matter), collapse of the Nazi regime in Germany destroyed almost all remnants of a large, state-owned sector in the German economy. Likewise, centralized state administrative capabilities of a Swedish nature were unthinkable in post–Nazi Germany with its four occupying powers. As we have seen, Germany developed an institutional framework offering a complex mix of centralization (in procedures for economic bargaining and monetary powers for preserving economic stability) and decentralization (in terms of government power to pursue a centrally mandated economic strategy for industrial restructuring). Unlike Japan, West Germany's institutional framework has permitted incremental industrial change but it has inhibited any extensive transformation of the nation's economic structure. By the end of the 1980s, Germany's industry remained concentrated in the capital intensive, science-based sectors (engineering, chemicals, machinery, automobiles) that have dominated the economy throughout this century (Katzenstein 1987).

As the free world's two leading military and economic powers, Britain and the United States emerged from World War II with little need for a sense of urgency about their economic position in world markets. The difference is that while the United States had the abundant resources and dominant market position to sustain that status for several decades, Britain did not. Economic policy-making in Britain was complicated by an institutional framework that made difficult any consistent or coordinated approach to economic adjustment. Traditionally, labor unions were sufficiently strong to veto major efforts at industrial modernization but sufficiently fragmented to serve as unreliable bargaining parties in policies inspired by hopes of a social partnership. Long-standing division between domestic industrial capital and internationally oriented financial capital was reflected in the division of monetary and fiscal authorities and the perennial government dilemma of spurring growth while maintaining the foreign value of the pound. An adversarial approach was further facilitated by tying the leadership of economic ministries directly to a parliamentary setting designed to produce a constant, bipolar confrontation between the government of the day and a united opposition. After a monumental failure by Labour governments to fashion a workable economic policy based on collaboration with the trade union movement and business, the new Thatcher government responded to the mounting economic crisis in 1979 by pursuing a vigorous free-market orientation. Both public and private industries were put under increasing market pressure to shed surplus workers and modernize. Government subsidies to business were cut; unemployment was allowed to rise rapidly; foreign competition in the British domestic market was welcomed; unions' ability to restrict labor market mobility was curtailed through tough new legislation; and the value of the pound was allowed to fall. Those economically marginal firms, workers, and regions that could not innovate or otherwise adjust to the rough blast of market forces suffered. Surviving sectors of the British economy gradually grew more productive and flourished during the 1980s. By using market forces to break the institutional impasse that had bedeviled British economic policy throughout the postwar period, the Thatcher government embedded Britain in the international economy with a free-market, hands-off approach that was quite different from the no less internationally oriented guided capitalism of Japan, West Germany, and France (Gamble; Krieger).

It is only in recent years, and then incompletely, that Americans have begun to be concerned about their competitiveness in the international marketplace. Historically favored with abundant resources, a huge domestic market, and the productive spur without the physical destruction brought about by twentieth-century wars, the United States has enjoyed the luxury of not having to think very self-consciously about national economic strategies. The 1980s offered a good example of how the fragmented institutional framework in the United States constrained the pursuit of any consistent course of action—whether in a free-market Thatcherite direction or an interventionist guided-capitalism character. As we have noted, interventions of an industrial policy nature have grown piecemeal. Supply side, monetarist, and expansionary Keynesian measures all occurred, usually at the same time. As long as the U.S. economic position remained dominant in the world, the nation's economic policies did not need to be especially effective to maintain a relatively high level of economic performance. By the end of the 1980s, that favored American condition was rapidly fading into history.

* * * * *

Behind international forces and domestic structures lies perhaps the ultimate constraint on and opportunity for political innovation in economic management: the mass of public attitudes, expectations, and behavior that forms the background for economic decision making. Certainly there is no lack of predictions in policy-making circles about what the public will not stand for and judgments about what the people want or should want. But the scattered empirical information suggests that the role of public opinion is more complicated than commonly assumed. People's relative preferences for, say, unemployment versus inflation can and do change, particularly in light of their recent experiences. Expectations about economic performance and the ability of governments to bring about improvements fall as well as rise; some might interpret a fall as a loss of confidence, others as growing realism on the part of the public. People often appear to be capable of distinguishing between their own personal economic circumstances and the state of management in the economy as a whole.

The fundamental question is this: How will a political community of such people organize itself to make the difficult choices posed in economic affairs? Even if we assume decisions will be made entirely by central corporatist bargains among producer groups or by the unfettered play of free-market forces, we still face the problem of how the results can be legitimized and rendered acceptable to the larger political community. In today's world, ordinary people are unlikely to put blind faith in either market forces or a corporatist elite. And dumb acquiescence can hardly be a source of such legitimation in democracies.

Economic theories do not create economic policies. Economic theories are translated into the real world through institutional frameworks that are the product, not of an economist's theory, but of history and politics. And as the struggle over economic choices occurs within and is shaped by this institutional setting, economic policy ideas have to be sustained by powerful political groups if they are to have an impact. Thus politics, which often counsels against clear choices so as to maintain support, and economics, which asserts the necessity for choices amid scarcity, are inextricably linked.

The problem of choice between cooperation and conflict goes deeper than the question of whether or not economic policy must be a zero-sum conflict. Even if a new sense of economic scarcity does mean that what one side wins the other loses, the issue of political choice remains. Zero-sum conflicts can be fought out by the law of the jungle, but they can also be handled in more cooperative, collaborative ways. Economic contestants might agree that if one side wins this year, the other side can win the next; the penalties for losing can be lessened by offsetting compensations; a sense of fair play can be preserved by limiting the rewards of winning; various sides can agree to search for ways to redefine the game itself; and so on. Given everything that can be said about restraints, scarcity, and limited economic options, people still do help create their own economic future. They do it by the way they build and use institutions.

6
TAXATION POLICY

A government's power to tax undergirds to a large degree the scope of the country's activities in the other domestic policy areas. Governments must raise revenue to pay for the services they provide, but they can also finance these by going into debt. These options in turn are related to the state's general economic management, since the relative reliance on taxation and borrowing may affect employment and inflation rates. Taxation policies have come to be powerful instruments of macroeconomic policy; but they are also a means of achieving social policy goals and microeconomic objectives. Taxation policy is thus characterized by a complex interaction between revenue-raising functions on the one hand, and other economic and social policy functions on the other.

Many forces in and out of government try to manipulate taxation policy toward diverse and often conflicting ends. Situations in which one "school" achieves sweeping changes—such as the Reagan tax-cut legislation of 1981—are relatively unusual. Normally, taxation policy is hammered out among tax experts, with the result that the "essence of a tax question moves swiftly from general principles to excruciating legal details. . . ." Even members of the U.S. Senate Finance Committee are expected to follow their staff specialists: When questioning became too prolonged in one session, the committee chairman was said to have remarked in frustration that "if the members insist on knowing what's in this bill we'll never get it passed!" (Shultz and Dam, pp. 44, 63).

CHOICES IN TAXATION POLICY

Scope and Thresholds

The flexibility that legislators enjoy with regard to matching revenues and expenditures may be limited by the nation's constitution. Certain restrictions may forbid a government from engaging in deficit finance or may place limits on certain kinds of taxes. Governments may then choose to accept such constraints or alter them, either by amending the constitution or by encouraging change at the subnational level. The long-term trend has been toward eliminating such constraints, but there have also been some recent tendencies in the opposite direction.

Clearly, the scope of tax extraction is partly determined by how governments perceive taxpayer resistance—are there thresholds beyond which taxation levels should not rise? Governments can regularly increase the ratios of taxation to national incomes, or they can avoid crossing taxation levels of 30 percent, 40 percent, or 50 percent of Gross National Product (GNP). During the period from 1950 to 1975, all Western governments increased these ratios, but they varied in the degree to which they did so.

Instruments

National governments can choose either to monopolize the tax-collecting function, or to allow regional and local governments to collect certain kinds of taxes. The Netherlands follows the first pattern; the second is found in all federal systems, and in many unitary systems as well.

In some federal systems, such as West Germany's, national, regional, and local governments share the proceeds from one jointly administered tax. Elsewhere, national governments may get priority in the use of direct taxes such as income taxes, while state governments must rely mainly on indirect taxes such as sales taxes. Within the overall taxation system, governments differ in their reliance on direct taxes and on indirect taxes.

The more kinds of taxes that a government can rely on, the more marginal tax rates can be kept down. If a taxpayer has to yield to the state $70 of each additional $100 earned, he may decide to substitute leisure for work. If such "substitution effects" are considered undesirable, the government can minimize them by adjusting its reliance on different taxation instruments.

Administrative feasibility is an important factor in a government's selection of instruments. Most European nations, for example, have adopted a value-added sales tax, which is levied at each stage of production and collected disproportionately from larger firms, because it is easier to implement than a retail sales tax. It has been claimed that this must be looked at as a European argument that does not fit in the North American context, however, since those states with retail sales taxes encounter no major difficulty in tax collection (Whalley, 228). Of course, if U.S. state governments choose to increase the sales tax levels from the 5 to 8 percent range to the 15 to 35 percent range found in Europe, they might also encounter greater collection difficulties.

Distribution

In selecting taxation instruments and directing them at the various income groups, governments attempt to act with regard to concepts of fairness. Thus the principles of *vertical* equity pose choices as to whether the rich should pay smaller, equal, or larger shares of their income than should the average income earners and the poor. If emphasis is placed on across-the-board sales taxes, the taxation system may increase income inequality; if emphasis is placed on progressive income taxes, the system may decrease after-tax income inequality.

If the social goals of taxation policy have priority along with revenue-producing and other economic goals, taxation systems tend to have greater redistributive effects. In Sweden, the linking of social, revenue-producing, and macroeconomic goals led to a taxation system that altered the incomes of the top 20 percent of households in relation to the bottom 20 percent from about 7:1 to 6:1 in 1972. In the United States taxes had a much smaller effect in reducing the 9:1 advantage of the well-to-do. And in France it had no effect on an 11:1 advantage of the rich over the poor, mainly because the French taxation system is largely based on sales taxes (Sawyer, p. 14).

When tax legislators choose to apply different instruments or rules to income derived from different sources, they engender problems of *horizontal* inequity. That is, taxpayers who earn the same income may be taxed at very different rates, depending on whether they pay taxes on the gain on appreciated property or wait to pay only after they sell their property.

Restraints and Innovation

Prior to the mid-1970s, governments could avoid many tough choices because economic growth and modest inflation levels produced automatic revenue increases—often to the point where revenue-producing was not even perceived as a major problem of taxation. But the "stagflation" of the 1970s, which combined low growth with high inflation, led to a situation where tax extractions rose more quickly than real incomes. As a result, the disposable income of an average family of four in most countries grew more slowly than its gross earnings. Such families suffered a 15.6 percent relative loss in Britain, a 6.4 percent relative loss in France, a 3.5 percent relative loss in Sweden, and a 2.3 percent relative loss in the United States between 1972 and 1976 (OECD 1978).

Governments could pursue several policy options in response. One option was to apply corporatist instruments to distribute the costs of belt-tightening in an equitable manner. Another option was to shift emphasis among taxation instruments, perhaps from the more visible to the less visible. Another option was to increase tax extraction by tightening up on existing tax collection. Attempts at increasing restraints on tax avoidance and tax evasion had varying effects, among them encouragement to various tax protest movements and parties. Other options included proposals to "index" tax levels. Indexation ties tax levels inversely to price levels, thus mitigating the automatic rise inflation causes in money incomes and tax extractions, and hence the automatic fall in real after-tax incomes.

In the 1980s the major thrust of policy innovation in Western countries was aimed at tightening up on what might be thought of as the fiscal equivalent of urban sprawl. The sprawl developed as manifold tax incentives and deductions led to erosion of the tax base, in turn making higher nominal rates necessary, particularly for income taxes. The 1986 U.S. reform led the way in seeking to end various distortions so as to broaden the tax base and to lower tax rates to levels not seen in fifty years. Consequently, "by the end of the 1980s the developed world will have lower individual and corporate income tax rates and fewer tax preferences, particularly incentives for investment, than at the beginning of the decade" (Pechman 1988, p. 13).

THE BOUNDARIES OF TAXATION
SCOPE AND THRESHOLDS

In recent decades the per capita amount of taxation has risen in all nations, partly because of increased government activity and partly because of inflation. In all countries, the scope of taxation is at least partially defined by taxpayers, whose resistance (or potential resistance) needs to be balanced against the revenue needs of governments. In this section we discuss the scope and thresholds of taxation policy, focusing on the evolution of tax systems, the differences in various national tax levels, and particular factors affecting tax limits.

The Evolution of Tax Systems

The ancient world and medieval Europe relied on direct taxation of subject classes and territories, and of products of the agricultural economy. Indirect taxes became a major revenue source only when commerce and industry became more important. Customs tariffs and levies on luxury and other consumption goods then augmented property taxes and other traditional tax forms. In an absolute monarchy, the aristocracy and other privileged groups were often exempt from taxation; but with the broadening of political representation, high-income groups became less immune. As middle-class groups won political influence, some countries, such as Britain (in 1842) and Austria (in 1849), introduced proportional (or flat-rate) income taxes on a permanent basis.

In nineteenth-century Europe, possession of the franchise was linked to the payment of property taxes, so that the lower classes who owned little real property had no legislative representatives who could effectively protest the governments' reliance on regressive indirect taxes. When the lower classes won the right to vote, the parties that represented them pressed for greater reliance on direct taxes, as well as on an "ability to pay" doctrine (Ardent): This implied changing income tax structures from the principle of *proportionality*, according to which all taxpayers paid equal proportions of their incomes, to the principle of *progressivity*, according to which the larger income earners paid at higher tax rates. A taxation system is defined as progressive if the average tax rate rises as income rises. It is regarded as *regressive* if the tax burden on lower incomes is greater than that on higher incomes. In 1909, when he sought to finance new welfare programs, Britain's Lloyd George made the tax more progressive by introducing rising marginal tax rates (Sabine).

How National Tax Levels Vary

As welfare, education, and other public sector programs have grown, so the proportion of GNP collected as tax revenues has risen. In the mid-1950s this proportion approached 25 percent in some "low tax" countries and 33 percent in some "high tax" countries.

By the mid-1980s most of the developed countries had tax ratios in the range of 35 to 50 percent of GDP. But the United States along with Switzerland and Japan remained below these thresholds. Of these three countries

TABLE 6.1 TAX RECEIPTS AS PERCENTAGE OF GDP

	1965	1975	1985	1965–85 Increase in Percentage Points
Austria	35	39	42	7
Britain	31	36	39	8
Canada	26	33	34	8
Denmark	30	41	49	19
France	35	37	46	11
Germany	32	36	38	6
Italy	27	29	41	14
Japan	18	21	27	9
Netherlands	34	44	45	11
Sweden	36	44	51	15
Switzerland	21	30	32	11
United States	26	30	29	3
Unweighted Average	27	33	37	10

SOURCE   OECD, *Taxation in Developed Countries* (Paris: OECD, 1987), p. 62.

it was the United States which increased its tax load the least between 1965 and 1985. Table 6.1 allows us to identify some other countries which exhibited similar patterns of relative change. The Scandinavian countries and the Netherlands were among the leaders in 1965, and Denmark and Sweden retained those relative positions by 1985. Among the larger European countries, Britain and Germany had very similar development patterns, whereas France left both behind in the early 1980s. In the same period Italy also overtook Germany to join Austria among those countries with ratios above 40 percent.

In most countries the tax share increased more in the years 1965–75, because this was a period when strong economic growth engendered automatic increases in the fields of many taxes. Japan, as a latecomer in developing many public programs, was an exception insofar as its growth was greater during the 1975–85 period. Still, the difference in the tax ratios of the highest and the lowest countries, Sweden and Japan, changed very little over the twenty-year period.

Differences existed also in the average levels and starting points of income taxes. In 1985 the average tax rate for a worker's family of four with average earnings ranged from zero in France to 34 percent in Sweden and Denmark. However, the French family paid much more in social security contributions than did the Swedish one. In Denmark, Sweden, and Britain, the tax threshold, that is, the income level at which a citizen starts paying income tax, is quite low, contributing to the higher tax burden of an average worker in these countries (see Table 6.2). When Margaret Thatcher's Conservative government took over in 1979, it raised the minimum threshold and lowered the basic income tax rate, compensating for revenue losses by significantly raising an indirect tax, the value-added tax, from 8 to 15 percent. With 95 percent of the British taxpayers now being taxed at a common marginal rate of 27 percent, the average income tax burden in Britain, as compared to Denmark and Sweden, has slightly declined between 1981 and 1985, although not as much as did the comparable United States figure for the same period. Including social security contributions, however, a British two-child family with average earnings still pays a much higher rate than its equivalent in high-threshold countries like Japan or France. For a low-income family with two children, and average earnings of about $10,000, the gap is even wider, with a marginal income and social security tax rate of 32 percent in Britain compared to 28 percent in Italy, 14 percent in France, and 11 percent in Japan (*Economist*, March 19, 1988).

Factors Affecting Tax Limits

Economists have argued fiercely over whether there are limits beyond which tax extractions can have destructive economic consequences. Some hold that such limits may vary over time and between countries, and they have tried to identify the factors that cause this variation.

Historically, tax legislators have tended to defy the pronouncements of theorists. In the late nineteenth century, it was argued that taxes amounting to 15 percent of national income were generally excessive. At the conclusion of World War II, when tax rates were rising in all countries, the British economist Colin Clark urged that tax ratios be held to peacetime levels of below 25 percent lest inflation and other harmful economic consequences ensue. Nonetheless, by 1980 the tax ratio in some countries had exceeded 50 percent.

Some scholars have argued that wars displace attitudes toward taxes, insofar as the public gets accustomed to high taxes during wars, and thus becomes willing to support higher postwar spending. British experience after both world wars seems to fit this pattern, but American experience does not. "Postwar spending fell off more sharply in the United States than elsewhere. . . . Prewar ideological orientation toward competitive individualism did not change; indeed, reaction against wartime expansion of central government enhanced postwar public pressure to cut it down to size" (Webber and Wildavsky, p. 445).

Certainly tax escalation has been accompanied by both inflation and taxpayer resistance. But there has been no clear cause-and-effect relationship. Countries with the highest tax ratios, such as Sweden and the Netherlands, have not suffered from either excessive inflation or inordinate tax protest. So the political limits on tax extraction have seemed to depend on how people fared individually. If purchasing power declines, people have tended to become more sensitive to high marginal tax rates. Thus the

TABLE 6.2 INCOME TAX AT THE LEVEL OF AN AVERAGE WORKER
(Expressed as a percentage of gross earnings)

| | Single People | | Two-child Families | |
Country	1981	1985	1981	1985
Austria	10.2	10.2	7.6	7.6
Britain	23.4	22.3	19.8	17.9
Canada	19.0	19.4	10.6	10.2
Denmark	37.8	40.0	32.6	34.3
France	8.6	7.4	0.5	0
Germany	16.4	18.1	9.7	10.9
Italy	14.1	n.a.	10.8	n.a.
Japan	8.5	8.8	2.8	2.8
Netherlands	13.5	11.0	11.2	8.1
Sweden	36.1	35.6	33.7	33.9
Switzerland	11.6	11.2	7.2	6.4
United States	23.5	22.8	14.4	15.3

SOURCE   OECD, *The Tax/Benefit Position of Production Workers* (Paris: OECD, 1986), p. 50.

avoidance of steep progressivity has recently become a principal concern in taxation policy.

In the early 1980s most Western nations faced policy consequences by lowering the tax rates applicable to the upper-income brackets. They differed considerably, however, in how they implemented this plan.

VARIATIONS IN REVENUE RAISING
INSTRUMENTS

There are several categories of national tax emphasis: redistributively oriented systems; broad tax base systems; traditional, noncentralized systems; and systems that minimize direct taxation. Within any taxation system, governments differ in their reliance on direct and indirect taxes. Whereas some countries consider it advantageous to rely more heavily on the less visible indirect taxes, others choose to diversify their revenue sources by relying on a variety of both direct and indirect taxes. In this section we will discuss the different tax systems and their reliance on direct and indirect taxes as well as their use of another important instrument, revenue sharing.

Direct and Indirect Taxes

Governments employ both direct and indirect taxes. They differ, however, in the extent to which they rely on direct rather than indirect taxes, in how they develop, then eliminate, various taxation instruments, and in the extent to which national governments monopolize tax extraction or share that power with local and state governments.

Table 6.3 illustrates the pattern of similarities and differences among eleven nations. France differs significantly in its lower degree of direct

TABLE 6.3 TAX SOURCES AS PERCENTAGES OF TOTAL REVENUE, 1985

	Direct Taxes			Indirect Taxes			
Country	*Personal Income*	*Corporate Income*	*Employees' Social Security*	*Employers' Social Security*	*Sales and Consumption*	*Property and Wealth*	*Other*
Austria	23.1	3.3	13.2	15.9	32.6	2.4	9.5
Britain	26.0	12.9	8.1	8.8	31.6	12.0	0.6
Denmark	50.2	4.8	1.9	1.9	34.2	4.3	2.7
France	12.7	4.3	12.2	28.2	29.4	4.6	8.6
Germany	28.7	6.1	15.8	19.0	25.6	3.0	1.8
Italy	26.7	9.2	6.8	24.8	25.4	2.5	4.6
Japan	24.8	21.0	10.7	15.4	14.0	9.7	4.4
Netherlands	19.5	7.0	19.0	17.5	25.8	3.5	7.7
Norway	22.5	17.0	5.6	14.3	37.5	1.7	1.4
Sweden	38.5	3.5	0.0	23.7	26.4	2.3	5.6
United States	35.7	7.1	11.1	17.3	17.7	10.1	1.0
OECD Average	31.5	8.2	7.9	13.9	30.1	5.0	
Lowest OECD Country	12.7 France	2.7 Greece	0.0 Sweden	0.0 Australia	14.0 Japan	1.7 Belgium, Norway	
Highest OECD Country	60.0 New Zealand	21.0 Japan	19.0 Netherlands	30.9 Spain	44.5 Ireland	12.0 Britain	

SOURCE   OECD, *Revenue Statistics of OECD Member Countries 1965–1985* (Paris: OECD, 1987) p. 85ff.

taxation; but its lower income tax receipts are made up for by higher sales and excise taxes and social insurance taxes paid by employers. Another apparent difference is that Britain and the United States rely more on property taxes than do the Continental countries. Japan derives a large share of its tax revenue from personal and corporate income taxes, but has moved in 1988 with the introduction of a sales tax to shift the tax burden more towards indirect taxes. Austria, France, Germany, and the Netherlands derive more of their tax income from social security contributions. What are the reasons for these differences?

In France, the oldest centralized bureaucratic system in Europe, citizens have developed legendary wiles for avoiding direct taxes (for example, deliberately maintaining a dilapidated facade on their houses). Consequently, the state has developed sophisticated indirect taxes, particularly the *value-added tax* (VAT), through which a tax is collected at each stage of production and distribution. In this way businesspeople are forced to monitor one another on how they forward taxes to the state. In order to equalize conditions in the emerging Common Market, other members of the European Community (EC) have adapted their sales tax systems to the VAT model; sales taxes are now levied at fairly similar rates by all EC member states. In countries such as Germany, Austria, and the Netherlands, on the other hand, social security taxes have grown rapidly without much controversy. This is probably the case because these taxes contribute to popular health and pension programs.

In Britain and the United States, property taxes are more important because of local government taxation powers. Other countries gradually reduced or eliminated these local taxes as their national systems became more uniform. But where local government prerogative remains strong, property taxes remain in force, even though they are more difficult to assess fairly and collect. Local politicians in the United States hate to give up the favors which property assessment power allows them to distribute. In a centralized system such as the Dutch one, where even city mayors are appointed by the national government, local party machines do not demand such lubrication.

Richard Rose has examined patterns of taxation over the past thirty-two years to determine whether countries are converging in their use of various tax instruments. Some data seem to point in that direction. Thus in most OECD countries, four kinds of taxes account for over four-fifths of all revenues. Also, the taxes that vary most among countries are those that account for relatively small amounts of revenues, such as customs and property taxes. But most detailed calculations show that there was in fact practically no convergence in the period from 1955 to 1982. Rose's explanation for the fact that after a generation of active international collaboration and trade the degree to which countries diverge from the mean is virtually the same lies in the force of inertia. "At any point in time, policy-makers are risk averse. . . . Politicians refrain from repealing established taxes. . . . Nor do they wish to introduce new taxes . . . which can be expected to have a large and unfavorable impact upon the electorate. In the short term the logic of the situation is clear: do nothing" (Rose 1985, p. 307).

Political factors also help explain why income taxes are such prominent tax sources in Britain, the United States, and the Scandinavian countries. During much of the past half century, the governments of these countries have been controlled by left-of-center parties, which have tended to prefer income taxes because of the possibility of imbuing them with progressive components. Thus the tax rates of the highest brackets reached 90 percent in the 1960s. In the 1970s they were 80 percent in Britain and 70 percent in the United States, before they were sharply lowered in the 1980s. Among the factors leading to a search for alternatives to steeply progressive rates was the concern "expressed by many about the possible effects of high and rising marginal tax rates at moderate income levels on money wage claims" (Cnossen 1983, p. 8).

By contrast, countries which have had more centrist and right-wing governments have tended to rely more on social security contributions (which tend to be levied at flat, or proportional, rates) and on sales taxes than on progressive income taxes. U.S. federal income tax rates rise consistently for each income class, but right-wing administrations have tended to flatten the tax curves. In 1977, a four-member family with a $100,000 income paid federal income taxes at three times the rate (30.8 percent) that a $10,000-income family paid (10.2 percent). But the Reagan tax cuts implemented from 1982 through 1984 reduced this progressivity considerably: The tax rate for the higher-income family in 1984 was only twice as high (30.6 percent) as that of the lower-income family (13.6 percent) (*National Journal* 18 August 1981).

Political reasons also explain why countries do not always distribute taxation efforts among a greater variety of instruments. For example, let us consider why the United States has not adopted a value-added tax. Various administrations and members of Congress have supported such a measure, but strong local interests have made it difficult to get such a bill through Congress. State politicians oppose it because of the competition it would create for sales tax proceeds.

The need to tap additional revenue to close the budget deficits of the 1980s has led some to predict that the United States is only one president away from the adoption of a value-added tax. But there are numerous hurdles, apart from President Bush's campaign promises, because such a measure would constitute a significant policy change for the United States. In Europe, the VAT is levied at different rates for different kinds of luxuries or essential goods; in the United States, these differentials would be difficult to achieve again because legislative party cohesion would probably give way to the pressures of special interests.

The Japanese have also considered a value-added tax for some time. However, several administrations who backed its introduction suffered setbacks when parliament would not go along. In 1987 an unsuccessful proposal suggested a 5 percent VAT to compensate for a reduction of the top individual income tax rate from 70 to 50 percent. The VAT proposal again failed to pass in parliament, mainly because its opponents feared (as in the United States) that a VAT would greatly expand the scope of government and create disadvantages for large firms. Intraparty opposition in the ruling party and walk-outs by the opposition were the major parliamentary barriers. However, by the end of the eighties a consensus among the ruling party and two opposition parties emerged. In 1988 the Liberal Democrats engineered an unusual split in the opposition and thus were able to push through the lower house of the Japanese parliament a package of six tax bills. The main aim was to cut direct taxes, which accounted for an overwhelming 73 percent of tax revenues, and to shift the revenue-raising burden to indirect taxation. The slight 3 percent sales tax is seen as a first step toward the introduction of a full value-added tax needed to collect the revenue to pay for the medical and pension costs of Japan's rapidly increasing elderly population.

Corporate income taxes, as compared to other tax sources, are more prominent in the English-speaking countries and Japan. Their above average importance for revenue in Japan, Britain, Australia, New Zealand, and Canada is matched on the Continent only in Norway and Italy (Steinmo 1986). Many countries have moved to integrate their individual and corporate income taxation, so as not to impose double taxation on dividends. Sweden, the Netherlands and the United States are the exceptions which still employ separate taxes for both. U.S. stockholders must pay a "double tax" on dividend income; that is, the corporation pays as well as the individual stockholders. In Europe, tax harmonization trends are to give stockholders tax credits for the corporate taxes paid by their companies (Bracewell-Milnes, Ch. 8). Thus the lower personal income taxes paid by high-income Americans have sometimes been partly offset by the higher corporate income tax rates.

A 1989 study commissioned by the German Economic Ministry found that formal rates for taxing corporations are not of key importance for the actual tax burden of firms. Rather, the two countries with the highest formal corporate tax rates, Sweden and Germany, had the most favorable provisions for corporate tax deductions. The seven-country study concluded that only in Italy and Britain is the total corporate income tax burden lower than in Germany.

Britain followed a new path with the introduction of a poll tax, which markedly changes the way British local authorities raise tax revenues. Property taxes on homes and businesses are to be replaced in April 1990 by a locally set, flat-rate poll tax on adults, and a nationally levied uniform business rate on commercial enterprises, which is to be redistributed from a national pool in proportion to the adult population. The strategy behind this tax was to discourage poor electors, who paid no taxes, from voting for local councils who promised to spend lavishly the revenues contributed by better-off rate payers, and by local businesses. The government therefore argued that everybody should pay the same tax for the same set of local-authority services, regardless of income and wealth. Though the concept was slightly eroded in the case of "welfare" families, "a student nurse on £4,500 a year will still pay the same charge as Lord Moneybags in the same borough" (*Economist* 3 September 1988). This inequity led to an unsuccessful revolt of Tory backbenchers, who supported an amendment which would have introduced a crude link between a voter's income and the poll tax level. In Scotland, a 1988 poll found that 42 percent of all Scots would support a campaign to encourage people to withhold tax payment.

Sales and Excise Taxes

Excise taxes apply to specific categories of consumer goods (for example, liquor and tobacco); *sales taxes* apply to all unexempted categories. Their merits depend largely on how one evaluates the substitution effects they engender. Welfare economists view excise taxes with disfavor, because, without raising any more revenue than a direct tax, they reduce consumers' freedom by pushing them from a taxed to a nontaxed commodity. However, some groups want governments to use taxation powers precisely in this way to induce consumers not to purchase items that are "bad" for them, such as alcohol and tobacco. In Scandinavia, tobacco taxes are much higher than in the United States, in good part because tax rates have been deliberately increased to discourage use. As two tax experts noted, "It may well be that an essential part of the tax 'constitution' in modern states is the fiscal castigation of legalized 'sins'!" (Head and Bird, in Cnossen 1983, p. 21).

Historically, general sales taxes have tended to replace excise taxes on specific goods. The reason for this shift lies principally in the ease of administration. Numerous excise taxes are difficult to administer, because of the diversity of products and the many retail outlets involved. Most value-added sales taxes, however, can be collected more systematically from larger manufacturers and wholesalers.

Sales taxes can levy higher rates on less essential or luxury goods; thus they can be progressive, in the sense that they can extract more from the higher-income groups. This potential progressivity diminishes in the developed industrial countries, however, where there are fewer consumption pattern differences between the rich and the poor, and where there is a higher degree of commercial integration. Where the lower middle class buys cheaper replicas of the same goods enjoyed by the upper class, it is difficult to design sales taxes which will extract more money from the rich purchasers.

Automotive taxes were mildly progressive as long as it was part of upper-middle-class social style to drive expensive Cadillacs and Mercedes-Benzes, but since small cars have become fashionable that no longer holds.

Value-added and excise taxes play a prominent role in transforming the economies of the European Community into a single market without internal frontiers by 1992. Given the significant divergence in levels of indirect taxation among European countries, prices differ greatly on each side of any border. This provided incentive for those in highly taxed countries, such as Ireland and Denmark, to buy their goods in neighboring low-tax countries.

Until 1992 a system of remission of tax on exports and taxation of imports ensures that the tax will accrue to the country where goods are finally consumed. A Europe without fiscal frontiers, however, must find other ways of guaranteeing that taxes on goods are paid where they are due. Only a closer approximation of the different national VAT rates and excise duties makes it possible to eliminate fiscal barriers.

How close will the approximation have to be? The example of the United States shows that one nation can have different tax rates from state to state without border controls between them. In other words, American evidence suggests that it is not necessary to go as far as having identical rates of taxation; differences up to 6 percentage points, even between neighboring states, do not appear to distort trade or affect competition significantly. Hence in regard to VAT, most EC nations agreed on a proposal for a two-rate system, which leaves individual countries free to fix their own rates within a band of 14 to 20 percent for the standard rate for most goods and services, and 4 to 9 percent for the reduced rate for basic necessities.

Only Britain sees no need for harmonizing value-added taxes or excise duties, and would rather leave it to market forces to determine what taxes governments can get away with. To meet British demands, the European Commission has proposed to drop the bottom of the reduced VAT rate to zero and to compromise on a minimum VAT rate of about 15 percent. It seemed to largely abandon attempts to harmonize excise duties on alcohol and cigarettes. In seeking to reconcile big disparities in duties (e.g., Denmark's tax on drink is 75 times Greece's), the Community will probably resort to measures rather similar to those used in the U.S. (i.e., tax bands or stamps on packets and bottles) in order to prevent commercial bootlegging out of low-tax countries.

Although broad-based consumption taxes such as VAT and general sales tax have long been favored over narrow-based excise taxes by tax experts, selective excise taxes might in the future come to play a more prominent role in tax policy if designed to internalize such negative externalities as environmental pollution and congestion (Head and Bird, in Cnossen 1983, p. 21).

The panorama of choices which governments have include numerous tradeoffs and compensatory relationships among the various components of their taxation systems. For instance, social security systems and consumption taxes are more interrelated than is apparent at first glance:

> The income redistribution role of consumption based taxes may probably be related to the scope of a country's social security system. If that scope is limited, then the attempt might be made to achieve as much progressivity in tax design as possible, basically through the exemption of necessities and the higher taxation of luxuries. If a country has a highly developed income transfer system, however, it might be argued that even necessities should attract the standard rate of sales tax, because the transfer system can adequately compensate for the relatively greater degree of regressivity which this may entail. (Cnossen 1977, p. 115)

Grouping National Taxation Systems

An analysis of how countries deviate from the average of all OECD countries is shown in Table 6.4. Regarding both the size of the tax share to GNP, and the reliance on five major kinds of taxes, we offer the following typology:

> *Heavy social security tax countries.* These systems, such as Germany, Austria, and the Netherlands, garner from one-third to two-fifths of reve-

TABLE 6.4 TAX SHARES IN OECD COUNTRIES 1983, DEVIATIONS FROM THE AVERAGE
(Percentage Points)

Country	Social Security	Personal Income	Corporate Income	Property and Wealth	Sales and Consumption	Tax/GNP Ratio*
Austria	+ 12	− 9	− 5	− 3	+ 2	+ 4
Britain	− 6	− 4	+ 2	+ 8	0	+ 3
Denmark	− 23	+ 21	− 5	− 1	+ 8	+ 7
France	+ 19	− 20	− 3	− 1	+ 1	+ 7
Germany	+ 10	− 4	− 3	− 1	− 3	0
Italy	+ 21	− 8	0	− 2	− 4	+ 3
Japan	+ 4	− 6	+ 12	+ 5	− 14	− 10
Netherlands	+ 16	− 9	− 1	− 2	− 5	+ 9
Norway	− 5	− 8	+ 9	− 3	+ 6	+ 11
Sweden	+ 4	+ 8	− 5	− 4	− 5	+ 13
United States	+ 2	+ 5	− 1	+ 5	− 12	− 6
Tax Shares, All of OECD	26	33	8	5	29	100

NOTE   *Based on the ratio of tax revenue to GNP 1981.
SOURCE   Joseph Pechman, ed., *Comparative Tax Systems: Europe, Canada and Japan* (Arlington, VA: Brookings Institution, 1987), p. 88.

nue from social security, and are below average in their reliance on almost all other kinds of taxes.

Unbalanced, low income tax countries. Countries such as France and Italy rely on social security for close to half of their tax receipts, but are far below average in their reliance on income taxes.

Low (sales) tax countries. The United States and Japan are farthest below average on tax shares, and also very below average in reliance on sales and consumption taxes.

High but varied tax reliance countries. Sweden and Norway are highest in their tax shares, which they raise with broad reliance on tax sources which do not deviate too far from patterns elsewhere.

Revenue Sharing

In addition to choosing which kinds of taxes to levy, national governments choose how to share revenue-raising powers with their own states, counties, and local governments. The choice depends on whether state and local governments are entitled by the constitution to raise their own taxes, as is the case in federal systems, and on the degree to which traditions of local self-government reinforce their own taxing powers. If they do have such powers, mechanisms may exist to prevent the disparity of resources among local and state governments that results in regional divergences in the quality of public service, which may diminish the guarantees of "equality of access" with which the constitution endows national citizenship.

The proportion of the total taxation which is raised by state and local governments is higher in federal systems, between one-third and one-half in Canada, Germany, Switzerland, and the United States. Among unitary systems the variation is greater, from almost nothing to around 30 percent, as Table 6.5 illustrates. In the Netherlands and Italy, subnational taxation amounts to only a small percentage of the total.

The composition of state and local taxes differs from the all-levels-of-government composition, though in various ways among groups of countries. Sales taxes are disproportionately utilized in the federal systems, as are property taxes, especially in the English-speaking countries with stronger traditions of local government.

All governments have programs of intergovernment revenue cooperation to assist poorer sections, but they vary in the techniques that they emphasize. The U.S. federal government relies heavily on complicated programs of grants-in-aid and some revenue sharing, but each level of government maintains distinct tax-raising powers and machinery. Germany offers a contrasting model, where two-thirds of the total tax revenue directly raised by the national and *Land* (state) governments is derived from taxes whose proceeds are directly shared by two or all three levels of government.

In the United States the federal government, most states, and some cities collect income taxes, but they are levied separately and differ in their degree of progressivity. Under the German system the income taxes collected from individuals and corporations are shared among the federal government (43 percent), Land governments (43 percent), and local governments (14 percent). Proceeds from the value-added sales tax are divided thirty–seventy between the federal and Land governments. Administration of these taxes is integrated, with the Land finance ministries collecting on behalf of the other levels of government. Canadian provinces also levy their income taxes as a proportion of the federal rate, but in the United States only two small states, Vermont and Rhode Island, utilize this option.

In Germany as elsewhere, wealth and income levels differ considerably. A poor Land such as the Saar can expect only about three-fifths the revenue from the same tax rate applied in a rich Land such as Baden-Württemberg. According to the American model of federalism, the poorer Länder (states) might be expected to pay lower teachers' salaries and to maintain schools of lower quality than those of the richer Länder. The Germans consider differentials of this kind intolerable in view of their interpretation of constitutional "equality guarantees."

The near equality of per capita revenues of Länder is maintained through various equalization techniques, which operate in a much more fundamental and sustained manner in Germany than in the United States.

TABLE 6.5 PROPORTION OF TAXES COLLECTED BY VARIOUS GOVERNMENT LEVELS, 1985

	Supranational[a] Percent	National[b] Percent	State or Provincial Percent	Local Percent
Federal Countries:				
Austria		76.1	13.1	10.7
Canada		54.6	36.0	9.4
Germany	1.0	68.1	22.3	8.5
Switzerland		60.7	22.5	16.7
United States		69.1	19.0	11.9
Unitary Countries:				
Britain	1.2	88.6		10.2
Denmark	0.7	71.0		28.3
France	0.6	90.7		8.7
Italy	0.6	97.0		2.3
Japan		74.0		26.1
Netherlands	1.5	96.1		2.4
Sweden		69.8		30.2

NOTE   [a]Supranational taxes are those collected by the European Community.
 [b]National tax totals include social security taxes.
SOURCE   OECD, *Revenue Statistics* (Paris: OECD, 1987), p. 204.

Through the *vertical equalization* program, a portion of the jointly collected revenues is earmarked to help bring the tax income of the poorer states close to the average. Another important instrument for equalizing financial capability among the Länder governments is the program of *horizontal equalization,* which requires the richer Länder to subsidize the poorer ones. Because their economies are less developed, the normal income tax receipts per capita of Länder such as the Saar and Lower Saxony would be 20 to 30 percent lower than that of the average of all Länder. But through a combination of horizontal equalization and other programs, their tax income is brought up to at least 95 percent of the Länder average. With some 25 percent of the population, the four poorer Länder have been receiving about 24 percent of total final Länder tax revenues (Bennett).

TAX EXTRACTION AND TAX BASE EROSION
DISTRIBUTION

The complex sets of rules, organizations, and enforcement techniques through which governments extract tax revenue from their citizens exemplify national differences in administrative style, political culture, and enforcement strategy. For example, in the United States income taxes are self-assessed, whereas in Europe for the most part citizens report their income sources and officials then assess the taxes due. If one calculates the cost of the income tax collection as a percentage of the total tax revenue, then a vigilant and intrusive taxation bureaucracy such as the German one is relatively expensive, with costs of about 4 percent.

The British, who also use official assessment, employ 4 times as many officials as the United States does, and spend over 2 percent on collection expenditures. In the mid-1970s there were 30 U.S. federal tax officials per 100,000 population, compared to 70 in Canada. On both national and regional levels, there were 100 in Sweden, 130 in Britain, and 175 in Germany (Barr et al., p. 150). The U.S. collection costs were only .5 percent of income tax revenue, whereas those of Sweden and Canada were about 1 percent.

In the European systems which do not practice self-assessment, the tax bureaucracies tend to distribute their personnel to achieve wide coverage at the examination level. The U.S. authorities, in contrast, concentrate on a more intensive review of a relatively small sample of returns. Only 2 to 3 percent of returns are examined in the United States, and only about 1 percent are subject to internal review.

Income Tax Assessment

Under the self-assessment system in the United States, 97 percent of the income tax returns lead to an adjustment at the end of the year, usually in favor of the taxpayer. In Britain this occurs in only about one-seventh of the cases, since withholding is adjusted during the tax year. Because they want year-end refunds, most American taxpayers resist lowering their pay-roll deductions, even though the interest foregone in overpayment actually raises their tax rates. The same prospect of a refund motivates a timely completion of returns. Proposals to introduce self-assessment in Britain have had to contend with the problems of educating the taxpayer and adjusting the taxation system. As Table 6.6 makes clear, British citizens do not at present practice self-assessment in any way. The table shows how Britain compares with the United States and other countries in the degree to which taxpayers, or those hired to prepare their taxes, carry out practices which elsewhere are carried out by state tax officials. Sweden in 1987 joined the rank of countries, which also includes Japan, where assessment is car-ried out completely by officials. A shift to such a "return-free" system was also briefly considered by the U.S. Treasury Department in the 1980s.

Although self-assessment may allow the taxpayer to cheat marginally, from the government's point of view, it has the compensating advantage of "shifting a lot of the cost of tax collection from the civil service to the individ-ual citizen." One economist argued in 1971 that "the American system seems to be effective in inducing the vast bulk of middle-class taxpayers to pay their taxes promptly . . . and fairly cheerfully," whereas self-assessment might be offensive to Europeans accustomed to more emphasis on "individual equity and the policing of individual cases." He described the period prior to April 15 in the United States "as a sort of rueful national festival and collective penitential experience justified by the subsequent sense of relief and accom-plishment" (Johnson, pp. 79–84).

Compared to their European equivalents, U.S. tax authorities present the public with quite elaborate tax rules. The U.S. tax code's substantive income tax provisions extend to over 1,000 pages of text, which makes them ten to twenty times as long as that of most European countries. How-ever, while the U.S. Treasury must foot a larger printing bill, it supports fewer tax-collecting agents and gets by with less elaborate examining and auditing procedures for most taxpayers.

TABLE 6.6 DEGREES OF SELF-ASSESSMENT IN INCOME TAX ADMINISTRATION FOR WAGE AND SALARY EARNERS

Standard Practice of the Taxpayer	Britain	France	Sweden	Canada	USA	Germany
Adds own income sources	No	No	No	Yes	Yes	No
Computes deductions	No	No	No	Yes	Yes	Yes
Calculates tax payable	No	No	No	Yes	Yes	No
Sends tax due with return	No	No	No	Yes	Yes	Yes
Sample checks by administration	No	No	No	Yes	Yes	Yes

SOURCE Nicholas A. Barr, et al., *Self-Assessment for Income Tax* (London: Heinemann, 1977), p. 153. Supplemented by additional data.

In France, where citizens generally manifest low civic consciousness in their income-reporting behavior, the state feels obliged to monitor taxpayers at the grass-roots level. In Paris, for example, this means that each of the twenty *arrondissements* is divided into four quarters, with sixty-seven tax offices covering the various sectors of the city. Inspectors conduct an annual building-by-building census of their sectors. In Sweden inspectors can refer cases for scrutiny by local tax boards—one for each area of 2,000 inhabitants—whose members will be knowledgeable about their neighbors' lifestyles.

In some European systems certain categories of taxpayers are subject to periodic scrutiny. In Germany all small businesses can expect to be audited every third year. In Sweden tax authorities used to select a different professional group every year for a thorough review of the tax returns of all its members. French tax authorities sample returns of various occupations to identify patterns in the underreporting of incomes. Shoe repairers, taxi drivers, and jewelry makers have been found to have reported only about half their real incomes. Among professionals, lawyers led physicians in underreporting, while engineers tried fewer such techniques (Pechman 1987, p. 207).

Tax Extraction Intensity

According to cross-national studies of the processes and norms of tax collection, the intensity of bureaucratic scrutiny is directly proportionate to success in tax extraction. The costs of confrontation between taxpayers and collectors, manifested in control, inspection, and appeal processes, were assessed in terms of the resources they absorbed and in terms of the negative feedback leading to increased tax resistance. The British system was found to be less than fully effective but relatively inexpensive, the German one very effective and also very expensive, and those of France, Italy, and Spain were found to be expensive—and ineffective (Schmoelders).

The researchers found that the success of the German system is characterized by more frequent visits from the tax inspector and more time spent in checking tax declarations. Thoroughness is deemed necessary because an official assessment notice becomes final within one month. Among small businesspeople in Germany the more frequent confrontations with tax officials have fed an undercurrent of hostility, with the officials themselves complaining about the difficulty of enforcing overly detailed regulations (Struempel, p. 74). Moreover, prosecutions there are relentless. In Britain prosecution through the courts leads annually to about 300 convictions for tax evasion, compared to about 6,000 in Germany. German taxpayers greatly overestimate the infallibility of tax offices. Indeed, the vast majority think it impossible to file a misleading return without being caught (Grunow et al., pp. 204–211).

By contrast, the British system has been found to treat "businessmen and professionals with great caution," dispensing with most administrative auditing, offering a wide variety of loopholes, and imposing fewer obligatory accounting procedures than are required in Germany. The British Inland Revenue Office was once chided by a Royal Commission for having been "led by a laudable anxiety to protect the subject from any needless official imposition to overestimate the extent to which certain simple requirements for the filing of returns could fairly be resented by the general public." Noting that total penalties had scarcely increased while the tax volume had tripled, economists observed: "The informal penalties employed in Britain may provide a more gentlemanly method of encouraging compliance than methods used abroad, but the greater use of more formal penalties might be more effective" (Shoup, p. 196; Barr et al., p. 41).

The French system of tax collection, on the other hand, assumes that several of the most important non-salaried groups subject to income tax— the well-to-do, small businesspeople, and professionals—will not declare their real incomes no matter what the law says. Small businesspeople and professionals whose annual turnover is less than 500,000 francs ($100,000) are entitled to use the "agreed income," or *forfait*, system, under which taxes are individually negotiated on the basis of sales and expenditure estimates. Those who use this option (approximately one million taxpayers, 80 percent of those eligible) do not even have to keep records of their sales. Because tax level is bargained out with the tax inspector according to the flimsiest evidence, this system allows great potential for personal influence. It is not surprising that the vast majority of workers and employees, who *are* taxed on their real incomes, believe that the French tax system is unjust.

In the United States tax officials are subject to relatively substantial public scrutiny. Rulings by U.S. tax authorities have in recent years become more accessible, and now any taxpayer is entitled to see any written Internal Revenue Service (IRS) determination, as well as file documents relating to it. Earlier one of Ralph Nader's groups submitted twenty-two identical tax reports to as many IRS offices across the country and received tax determinations varying from a refund of $812 to a tax due figure of $52. Another review of IRS procedures found that the higher the tax deficiency the IRS initially claimed, the lower the percentage it finally accepted in settlement. The Federal Administrative Conference suggested that this was due to the ability of rich taxpayers to hire lawyers, who then negotiated more favorable settlements.

Compared to their American equivalents, tax officials in the German Finance Ministry exercise much discretion in issuing administrative ordinances. These ordinances are binding on the Länder even though they have never had legislative approval. American authors comment that "such administrative autonomy would be anathema in the United States. Indeed the U.S. federal code's intricacy is in part related to the public's desire to constrain discretion in the IRS" (Webber and Wildavsky, p. 538).

National tax systems differ enormously both in the number of tax loopholes based upon permitted deductions and exemptions of categories of income or expenditure and in the prevalence of illegal but tolerated forms of tax evasion. Both of these factors contribute to massive erosion of the income tax base. France incurs tremendous erosion prior to the income-reporting stage by accepting massive legal and quasi-legal non-reporting of certain kinds of income. Britain and the United States achieve a fairly high income disclosure rate, but then permit taxpayers to take advantage of numerous deduction possibilities. Consequently, the proportion of personal income which is finally subject to tax is usually about half the total reported in national income accounts.

Tax Avoidance

Since American legislators have allowed a variety of loopholes, exemptions, and "write-off" privileges, most clever or well-to-do taxpayers have no need for clearly illegal forms of tax evasion. Instead, they can hire specialized assistance to help them avoid taxes legally. Ingrained libertarians can vent their hostility to the tax system by spending their free time in finding loopholes with which they can outsmart the tax officials.

As concern for economic growth has become more predominant among economists and politicians, equity of tax distribution has often had to take second place. The instrument which most easily permits the wealthy to hold their tax rates down is the special treatment of capital gains. Until 1970, gains on assets held more than six months were taxable at a maximum rate of only 25 percent. Then the rate for individuals was raised to 35 percent, only to be lowered again in 1978 to 28 percent. Finally the issue was brought to solution through the 1986 tax changes which removed the distinction by bringing the rates for all kinds of income down to roughly the level that had been levied on capital gains. This provision currently allows upper-income American taxpayers to avoid half or more of the income taxes they would otherwise have to pay. In fact, the effective rate of taxation on the rich and the upper-middle classes declined in the years between 1952 and 1967, and has again dropped considerably in the 1980s.

The prevailing undertaxation of capital gains constitutes the most important inequality in the treatment of various income sources. Although France and Canada have recently begun to levy this tax, most Western countries tax realized gains only lightly, and unrealized gains not at all. In Germany gains from assets held for more than six months escape taxation altogether, a practice which contributed significantly to the concentration of ownership in the postwar German economy and to the unusually high rate of capital investment. Sweden taxes declining proportions of capital gains as the holding period lengthens, but adjusts for inflation in a way the United States does not.

As more taxpayers have become liable to more taxes, and at the same time have been able to take advantage of many complicated loopholes, a private "tax minimizing industry" has expanded at a rapid rate—much faster, in fact, than the public tax bureaucracy. This industry has long been prevalent in the United States. As early as the 1950s one observer noted that "the minimizing art in the United States has been carried to a degree of perfection," and that "tax avoidance in Britain is rapidly approaching the degree of refinement now common in the United States" (Shoup, p. 195). Thus there exists a certain lopsided adversarial relationship between the "tax minimizing industry" and the public tax bureaucracy.

Tax Evasion

How much national income evades taxation altogether, because it is blatantly unreported, is politically a hot issue that concerns both tax administrators and policymakers. One aspect of this issue concerns how much income derived from perfectly legal activity is lumped with profits from illegal criminal activity under the umbrella of the "underground economy." This label has come to be applied to all income which evades taxation because it is non-reported. The examples range from a carpenter who does a small private job for cash payment, which he never declares on his income form, to a drug dealer who might hide vast sums.

In a report on both the legal and illegal components of income in the United States in 1976, the IRS listed their quantitative significance as a proportion of all unreported income:

Self-employment (legal)	30–33 percent
Wages and salaries (legal)	20 percent
Drug traffic (illegal)	16 percent
Gambling and prostitution (illegal)	8–9 percent
Dividends and interest (legal)	7–10 percent

The total estimated unreported income corresponded to between 6 and 8 percent of GNP. Estimates of similar magnitudes were published by authorities in Britain, Italy, Sweden, and other countries.

Some economists have made indirect calculations suggesting that the magnitude of the "underground economy" might be even larger, constituting as much as a quarter or even a third of GNP in the United States and other Western economies. This analysis for the most part blames high marginal income tax rates, which are assumed to drive some perfectly legal activity into the barter or moonlighting corners of what has come to be called the "underground" or "informal" economy.

Other estimates of the hidden economy are based on discrepancies between income and expenditures data at the national level. Studies in France and Belgium showed unexplained differences of about 20 percent of GNP, while recent ones in Scandinavia have produced estimates more in the 4 to 6 percent range. In comparative studies some relatively low-tax countries, like Italy, the United States, and Spain, have been shown to have larger underground sectors than the Scandinavian countries, leading to the conclusion that "it is quite implausible that the tax rate is the only determinant of the size of the hidden economy" (Frey and Pommerehne, in Tanzi 1982, p. 18). Rather, they point to the structure of labor markets and to attitudes toward tax morality and the public sector as other crucial factors in explaining cross-national variations in the magnitude of the underground economy.

The creation of the EC's internal market by 1992, with a free flow of capital across borders without exchange controls, highlights problems of tax avoidance and evasion concerning income from capital. France, with its weak income reporting system, has been a strong proponent for the EC-wide withholding tax on interest payments in order to avoid French capital flight to low-tax neighbors such as Germany or Luxembourg. In January, 1989, the Germans went along and introduced a 10 percent withholding tax on interest payments, to be deducted at the source, i.e., by the banks. But taxpayer resistance and German capital flight abroad pushed the German government to repeal the new tax only six months after its introduction. However, critics maintain that tax evasion is already high and could only be curbed by an European withholding tax, together with an improved, cross-national monitoring system of bank accounts.

Taxpayer Resistance

Perceived inequities in the tax system or hostility toward tax increases do not often become the central issues in an election campaign; but when they do, they can generate massive voter shifts. In the United States such shifts have recently occurred at the state and local levels through referenda initiatives, as in the case of California's Proposition 13 in 1978. In Europe, where subnational government has fewer tax-setting responsibilities, taxpayer protest has sometimes led to the sensational rise of national "flash parties" led by colorful antitax crusaders. In the early 1970s a Danish tax lawyer, Mogens Glistrup, generated an astonishing protest vote with an antitax platform that drew half a million voters away from the established parties, permitting him to emerge the leader of the second-largest party in the Danish parliament. Attacking the expansion of the public bureaucracy,

Glistrup's Progress party won twenty-eight seats in the December 1973 national elections, while both the Social Democrats and the established bourgeois parties lost more than a third of their seats.

Considering developments in the 1970s, we might ask: Why were the highly taxed Swedes more reluctant to form tax protest parties? How should one compare the American tax protest movements, such as the Proposition 13 movement in California, with the European examples? Can one draw any generalizations about which negative effects of the tax policy-inflation-low growth syndrome are most likely to lead to voter retaliation?

The fact that tax protest varied can be partly explained through a comparison of the *rate* of tax expansion in the two Scandinavian countries. Average tax levels from 1965 to 1971 were higher in Sweden than in Denmark, both absolutely and in relation to GNP. But the Swedish buildup had been gradual since the early 1950s, whereas the revision of Danish income taxes led to a sudden 22.1 percent increase in 1970. An increase of one-third in tax extraction over a three-year period prepared the ground for Glistrup. During these years, no less than three-quarters of the GNP gain was being soaked up by increased taxes.

Also, potential for a tax revolt was especially great among groups such as small shopkeepers, who were more than twice as prevalent in Denmark as in Sweden. Indeed, Glistrup received much larger support from the urban petit bourgeoisie than any other group (Esping-Anderson, pp. 157, 422).

Compared to the United States, where self-assessment and tax preparers have allowed taxpayers to use loopholes, Danish taxpayers' high tax morality had assumed that an honest administration treated all taxpayers with equal severity. Therefore, when Glistrup boasted on Danish television that he had exploited loopholes in the new tax legislation to avoid paying any income tax at all on his large income, he caused much more of a sensation than he would have in the United States.

Although the Glistrup success triggered something of a European "wave," tax backlash parties elsewhere clearly were not able to replicate Glistrup's initial success. A similar party in Norway made a modest splash in the early 1970s, then weakened but returned to parliament in 1981. In Germany the antitax Citizens party was founded in 1978 by none other than the former chairman of the Tax Officials Association. But it also disintegrated before it could mount a serious challenge to established parties who combated it vigorously.

In California, by contrast, the tax reduction movement met with little strong party resistance. Surprisingly, Democrats were equally willing to support Proposition 13 and to join in bringing a two to one victory for the measure. The Democratic governor, Jerry Brown, even reversed his position to endorse radical tax cutting, which weakened all liberal resistance.

The immediate impact was startling. Within a few years California dropped from third-ranking state in per capita tax burdens to twenty-third. Other states which relied on progressive state income taxes and had above-average state tax burdens also experienced moves to set tax limits, usually by initiative. Of the ten states with the most redistributive tax systems, all but three (Wisconsin, Minnesota, and Alaska) adopted tax or expenditure limitations in the period between 1976 and 1980.

Often the object of tax resistance has been the local property tax, which, according to surveys in the 1970s, was the most unpopular American tax. Dissatisfaction with the unfairness of this and other taxes and increased distrust of government, as in Denmark, provide ideological support for the tax protest movement. When Ronald Reagan and other conservatives then traded on this sentiment at the national level, more of the ire came to be directed at the federal income tax, which in 1980 replaced the property tax as the one regarded as "worst and least fair." Important components of the backlash are the quality of public service and the differences in income between public servants and private-sector workers. A key target of Glistrup's attack in Denmark was the fact that civil servants' incomes had been increasing while private-sector earnings had been decreasing (Hibbs and Madsen, p. 428). Governments elsewhere were wise enough not to let this happen. Jealousy of public officials generally has not caused backlash provided voters were satisfied with the quality of services being offered.

Although the vast majority of Swedes thought that taxes in the 1980s were too high, only about half supported the notion of a tax protest campaign. Well over a third said they would have voted for a party like Glistrup's in Denmark, and a large majority said they would vote for lower taxes if a referendum gave them an opportunity. But in the same survey, two-thirds of the Swedes opposed introducing referenda to determine tax levels, and said that these kinds of decisions should be made by the politicians. Thus they were saying that the politicians should be entrusted with the necessary power to carry out high-quality public services (Hadenius, p. 73).

TAX REFORM—OLD WHINE AND NEW BOTTLES?
RESTRAINTS AND INNOVATION

Changes of their countries' tax systems have been high on the agendas of many governments in recent years. But does what has been called the "tax revolution of the 1980s" really constitute something very different from major tax reforms of earlier decades? Are the tax revision programs which are occurring simultaneously in many countries driven by the almost universal recognition of the distortions and inequities of existing tax codes, as has been claimed by the reformers, or is this rhetoric simply a disguise of the imaginative efforts of lawmakers and administrators when it comes to meeting their current and future revenue needs, as has been the case so many times throughout history?

Tax Indexation

Tax indexation was one new thrust. Tax protests in Denmark and elsewhere taught governments a lesson about the political costs of allowing inflation to increase tax ratios automatically. Policy attention was thus turned to devising techniques which would relieve reductions in real incomes caused by the simultaneous impact of consumer price increases and escalating tax withholding from take-home pay. Countries with low economic growth and above-average inflation were identified as prime settings for voter retribution against incumbent governments. The possibility that national governments could go "bankrupt"—not in a literal sense, since they could always print more money, but in the sense of losing credibility with their voters—was raised dramatically by some social scientists (Rose and Peters).

The more farsighted leaders of some of the smaller welfare states anticipated and developed techniques to cope with some of these problems. One such technique, implemented in Sweden from the early 1970s, was the adaptation of wage and salary bargaining from a pre-tax to an after-tax basis. Thus, the government bargained about its tax changes just as employers and unions bargained about wages and, to some extent, prices.

Another innovation was tax rate indexation, through which tax levels come to vary with levels of prices or wages. Tax indexation keeps real levels of taxation from rising with inflation, just as indexing social security benefits keeps real levels of pensions from falling as prices rise. The Netherlands introduced such a scheme in 1971. Denmark followed, and then Canada introduced the most complete and automatic indexation program in 1974. Previously, the Netherlands had made three major adjustments of tax rates between 1956 and 1971; since 1971 it has made annual adjustments. Using an indexation formula reduces the government's decision-making powers, but it also allows the finance minister to cancel, or disregard, up to 20 percent of the tax adjustment. Denmark also did not tie taxes automatically to inflation, but tied the tax rates to wage rather than to price levels. It worked this way: In 1975, the national income tax yielded 22.2 billion kroner. Without indexation it would have risen to 28.1 billion in 1976; through index limitations the rise was held to 25.3 billion (OECD 1976).

Income tax indexation was introduced in the United States in 1985. Tax levels are now insulated against inflation so that future rates will apply to real incomes. This model follows the Canadian practice of introducing price escalators and calling for full, automatic, annual adjustments. To bring this about, tax brackets, exemptions, and deduction figures will be increased annually at a rate equal to the inflation rate, as measured by the Consumer Price Index.

It is not clear that European experience is a good basis for predicting the consequences of American indexation. Neither the Danish nor the Dutch case provides full, automatic indexing, and in France indexation only operates when inflation passes a given threshold. The Canadian case seems more relevant. In Canada income tax revenues inched up from 10 to over 15 percent of GDP in the nine years before indexation. Since 1974 income tax receipts have stabilized in the 14 to 15 percent range. But in Canada (as well as in Australia), the reduction of revenue produced fiscal problems which caused strong calls for eliminating the indexation experiment.

The adoption of indexation by a 57–40 vote in the U.S. Senate (moved without hearings and without a separate role call in the House) surprised some observers who had not believed that Congress would surrender its power to legislate semiannual "tax reduction" adjustments, which will henceforth come automatically. The voting lineup was not wholly in line with ideology. Some liberals were opposed, because indexation potentially limits expenditures on social programs, but others were in favor, because it gives protection to lower-income groups that have tended to be hit hardest by "tax bracket creep." However, such protection may be undercut if there is a simultaneous shift to unindexed indirect taxes, which are generally more regressive. One of the costs of indexation is that it deprives policymakers of the ability to target tax cuts for micro- or macro-policy purposes.

Another argument against indexation is that it may undermine resistance to inflation by cushioning some of its impact. In some heavily indexed economies, inflation-fighters have sometimes had difficulty lining up public support, because many people were protected against some of the effects of inflation. Somewhat characteristically, these ramifications had scarcely been explored when Congress acted precipitately in 1981—even though its own legislative research machinery had suggested that "although indexation makes it easier to live with inflation, evidence is conflicting as to whether or not it is effective in lowering the rate of inflation" (U.S. Congress).

Tax Coherence

Innovation in tax policy, which will be judged successful by both experts and most taxpayers, is much harder to carry from drawing board to implementation than in most other policy areas with considerable redistributive impact. This is partly due to the fact that the intense interest negotiations on which any bundle of tax policies are built often make them hard to alter or replace in a large-scale way. So it seldom occurs that large-scale tax system adjustments take place nearly simultaneously in many Western countries. But the late 1980s, when many countries dramatically broadened their base and lowered many income tax rates, was one such period of relatively far-reaching change.

But how did this period of tax system changes compare with other significant periods of postwar tax changes? Answers to this question vary considerably between American and European observers. Particularly those Washington movers and shakers who helped prepare the buildup for the 1986 tax act rank this endeavor the most significant. One reason for this is that in many respects the Americans led the way in this effort at increased tax coherence, with the European countries in part following their pattern. Another reason is that in the context of American tax reform history the 1986 Tax Reform Act was unique in the degree to which bipartisan consensus among tax policy actors led to a surprising ability to ward off the efforts of many powerful lobbyists.

However, from a European comparative perspective, the American tax system changes of the 1980s, consisting mainly in reductions of the highest marginal income tax rates and the corporate tax rates, in conjunction with some base-broadening measures, seem less overwhelming. When compared with other postwar tax system changes such as the introduction of social security taxes, the adoption of the value-added tax, or the introduction of corporate-income-tax integration to relieve the double tax on dividends in many European countries, the American reforms appear rather as a correction of the previous extensive reliance on tax expenditures and deductions, and thus as minor tax reforms (Cnossen, in Pechman 1988).

Similarly, the recent history of corporate taxation in the United States and Great Britain indicates that major changes in individual nations' tax systems are not rare events but occur with surprising frequency: each country saw about eight major reforms of corporate taxation since the mid-1960s (Atkinson and Leape). A look across countries also reinforces the view that tax reform is a common, not rare, phenomenon.

In 1989 Sweden, the country with one of the world's highest tax burdens, announced that national income tax will be phased out for 90 percent of the country's taxpayers. This would leave most Swedes paying only 30 percent, in the form of county and municipal income taxes, while the top marginal national income tax rate will drop to about 50 percent.

Moreover, a proposed corporate income tax reduction from 58 to 30 percent, together with a broadening of the tax base, the closing of loopholes, and the increase of capital taxes, constitutes somewhat of a U-turn in Swedish tax policy, which for long has relied on high income taxes combined with favorable tax treatment and extensive deductions for firms and capital owners.

Table 6.7 shows the changes in marginal income tax rates at the national level over the last two decades: Concerning the lowest marginal tax rates, there appears to be no clear pattern across countries over time. Some countries decreased them slightly in the earlier years, while others raised them to make up for revenue losses and deal with the "fiscal crisis of the state" in the early 1980s, leading to a fairly constant average over time.

However, a general trend in all countries seems to be the substantial reduction of the highest rates, from an average of 68 in 1975 to 50 percent in 1990. The trendsetters were the English-speaking countries and Japan, with Britain and the United States leading the way with reductions of 43 and 42 percentage points, respectively. In comparison, the reductions in the central European countries remained below the average reduction of 18 percentage points. Denmark, the Netherlands, and Germany decreased their top rates only slightly. On the other hand, in France and Italy reductions have approached the average.

How are these differences in magnitudes to be explained? Obviously, much depends on where a country started from in terms of tax levels, tax structure, enforcement and compliance. In countries where income taxes account for a higher percentage of total tax revenue, and where tax compliance is high, such as the northern European countries, even small rate reductions lead to large revenue losses. In the southern European countries, where tax evasion has been traditionally high, reductions do not have such major effects and might actually lead to less resistance to tax enforcement and, eventually, better compliance.

Reductions in high marginal income tax rates have been accompanied by selective base-broadening measures, such as attempts to cut tax expenditures and reductions in the number of tax brackets in several countries

TABLE 6.7 CHANGES IN NATIONAL INCOME TAX RATES

Country	1975 Tax Rates		1985 Tax Rates		1990* Tax Rates		Changes in Top Marginal Rates 1975–90
	lowest	highest	lowest	highest	lowest	highest	
Australia	20	65	30	60	24	49	−16
Belgium	17	60	24	72	24	60	0
Britain	35	83	30	60	25	40	−43
Canada	9	47	6	34	17	29	−18
Denmark	50	73	50	73	50	68	−5
France	5	60	5	65	5	50	−10
Germany	22	56	22	56	19	53	−3
Ireland	26	77	35	65	35	58	−19
Italy	10	72	18	65	11	56	−16
Japan	10	75	10.5	70	10	50	−25
Netherlands	20	71	16	72	40	70	−1
New Zealand	19.5	57	20	66	24	33	−24
Sweden	32	85	35	80	30	50	−35
United States	14	70	11	50	15	28	−42
Average	21	68	22	63	24	50	−18

NOTE *1990 Tax Rates are proposed or already legislated.
SOURCES OECD, *Personal Income Tax Systems* (Paris: OECD, 1986), p. 34; Vito Tanzi, "The Response of Other Industrial Countries to the U.S. Tax Reform Act," *National Tax Journal* 40:3 (Sept 1987), 344.

(Table 6.8). Here again the English-speaking countries led the way early on, by cutting the number of brackets by half or more. Sweden, the Netherlands, Belgium, and Italy have followed this trend, whereas other Western European nations such as Denmark and Germany had a small number of tax brackets to begin with. Thus the other countries followed the leaders in their claim that a smaller number of brackets simplifies the income tax, a claim that is justified from an administrative point of view. But this may seem less apparent to the individual taxpayer, who usually relies on tax tables and to whom the number of brackets may matter less (Tanzi 1987, p. 346).

Does simplification of rate structures explain the outstanding reductions of the highest rate in Britain and the United States? In both countries rate flattening was accompanied by sharp reductions in the number of tax brackets—from fifteen to two in the United States; from eleven to two in Britain—a measure intended to broaden the tax base and thus to increase revenues.

The considerable American and British top rate reductions were possible in these two countries, particularly in the United States, because there was more room for base broadening to finance significant rate cuts than in other countries (Witte). In both countries, the closing of tax loopholes and the cutting of tax expenditures was to compensate income tax cuts, a goal, however, which proved difficult to achieve. Hence Britain's additional reliance on a substantial increase in consumption taxes to correct for revenue

TABLE 6.8 CHANGES IN NUMBERS OF INCOME TAX RATE BRACKETS

Country	1975	1985	1990
Australia	6	5	4
Austria	11	10	5
Belgium	21	14	4
Britain	10	6	2
Canada	13	10	3
Denmark	3	4	3
France	13	10	10
Germany	4	5	5
Italy	32	9	8
Japan	19	15	6
Netherlands	10	9	3–4
New Zealand	22	5	2
Sweden	11	16	2
United States	25	15	2
Average	14	10	4

SOURCES   Vito Tanzi, *The Individual Income Tax and Economic Growth: An International Comparison* (Baltimore: Johns Hopkins Press, 1987), p. 346; OECD, *Taxation in Developed Countries* (Paris: OECD, 1987), p. 84.

losses in the early 1980s helped to prevent the huge budget deficits of the American type (Waltman and Studlar). In Japan, where the central government was running large deficits in the early 1980s, the Finance Ministry proposed the introduction of a new consumption tax rather than base-broadening measures to raise revenues. In the continental European countries, both rate and bracket reductions appear to be less significant. This might point to the "quasi-constitutional nature of tax systems" in these countries—that is, their reluctance to "put the existing and often hard-won compromise on cost-sharing and the income distribution up for grabs" (Head and Bird, in Cnossen 1983, p. 5). On the other hand, the Reagan and Thatcher administrations of the 1980s were much more willing to use tax policies as major instruments to increase productivity according to their supply-side philosophies.

Hand in hand with the top rate reductions of the personal income tax in the United States and Britain went the reductions in the basic corporate income tax rates from 46 to 34 and from 45 to 35 percent, respectively, which made the two countries those with the lowest corporate tax rates in 1989 (Tanzi 1987, p. 348). Canada also reduced its tax rate for corporate income slightly from 46 to 43 percent by 1989, and lags again, as in the case of personal income tax reduction, behind its two closest allies.

Corporate tax rate reductions, however, are not general. In some countries, such as Australia and New Zealand, the rate actually increased. This might indicate that corporate tax cuts are more difficult to implement politically, since they are publicly regarded as benefiting only the "rich" shareholders. In Germany, where corporate taxes are relatively high and the goal to reduce them in order to maintain competitiveness in the world market was high on the agenda of the Kohl government, a cut of the basic corporate tax proved difficult. Only when the government agreed to reduce the lowest personal income tax rate from 22 to 19 percent were relatively small cuts in the corporate tax rate (from 56 to 50 percent) and the top income tax rate cut (from 56 to 53 percent) considered acceptable. Still, as one student of German tax reform noted, "seldom has a government that cut taxes by so much received so little praise" (Krause-Junk, in Pechman 1988, 140).

One reason for this might be that income tax cuts in Germany were accompanied by tax hikes for gas, alcohol, and cigarettes. This shift of revenue-raising burden from direct taxes to consumption taxes can also be seen in countries such as Britain, New Zealand, Sweden, and Japan, where income tax cuts were followed swiftly by a raising of old, or the introduction of new, consumption taxes. The Spanish government in 1986, accompanying its entry to the European Community (EC), replaced a complex set of excise taxes with a comprehensive value-added tax, and in 1988 proposed across-the-board income tax cuts including a reduction in the top marginal rate from 66 to 56 percent. The other new EC member countries Greece and Portugal also reduced direct tax burdens by changing the tax mix through the introduction of VAT in 1985–87.

In the United States, where a national sales tax has long been disputed, more reliance on excise and consumption taxes by the Bush administration to curb the inherited budget deficit seems likely. Even a European-style value-added tax is coming under scrutiny by Bush advisers as a possible deficit-reduction measure.

Tax Expenditures

Following the example of the United States, Britain, Canada, and Germany, an increasing number of national governments began in recent years to focus more systematically on revenue losses due to the exemptions, deductions, and tax credits written into tax codes, especially those for the income tax. These special provisions have come to be seen as *tax expenditures,* which might be scrutinized as closely as normal budget expenditures since they in effect constitute government expenditures made through the tax system.

Tax expenditures are commonly defined as "departures from a normal, benchmark or generally accepted tax structure" which involve a revenue loss and are designed to achieve certain economic and social objectives (OECD 1984, p. 168). However, there exists a major definitional problem of drawing a clear dividing line between the basic tax structure on the one hand and such special tax reliefs on the other hand. For instance, are tax allowances for children part of the benchmark tax system or do they constitute a tax expenditure? In practice, tax expenditures can take a variety of forms:

Tax exemptions. Income or sources of income which are excluded from the tax base.

Tax allowances. Amounts deducted from gross income to arrive at taxable income.

Tax credits. Amounts subtracted from tax liability which may or may not be allowed to exceed tax liability.

Special rate reliefs. Reduced rates of tax built into the schedule, which are intended to benefit special groups or activities (OECD 1984, p. 9).

Other distinctions that can be made refer to tax expenditures which reduce the amount of tax paid (for example, non-taxation of a benefit) and those which defer the payment of tax (for example, deductibility of pension contribution). "A tax expenditure which takes the form of the non-taxation of an item of income is the equivalent of a direct transfer, whereas a deferral provision is the equivalent of an interest-free government loan" (Owens, in Cnossen 1983, p. 175).

In the United States, some of the most costly types of tax expenditures were introduced during the first several decades of this century. Tax subsidies were then considered simpler and more efficient than government spending programs, a belief that was often linked to a preference for private initiatives which might be spurred by tax incentives. Thus the exclusion of tax payments for pension plans and medical insurance was initiated at a time when no public programs existed. Later, in the 1930s, benefits from the social security programs were also excluded from taxation.

Since the 1950s, the income tax has become even more a "social workhorse," providing indirect subsidies for a variety of special activities which some lobbies or reformers persuaded Congress to further. This form of promotion is often chosen because tax expenditures enjoy the support of "a peculiar alliance among conservatives, who find attractive the alleged reduction in the role of government that would follow from the extensive use of tax credits, and liberals anxious to solve social and economic problems" (Aaron, p. 5).

As Table 6.9 makes evident, in the two decades between 1967 and 1986 tax expenditures in the United States grew from a total of 36.6 to 424.7 billion dollars, or from 23.8 percent of federal revenues in 1967 to 55.3 percent in 1986. However, tax expenditures have a longer history. A significant expansion took place over the several decades after the passage of the first income tax law in 1913, with about half of a list of ninety-one provisions originating between 1913 and 1945, and the other half between 1945 and 1982. Thus in terms of numbers, the growth of tax expenditures has been relatively steady, although the rate of growth may have increased slightly in the last two decades. Moreover, most of the major revenue-losing provisions were introduced prior to 1945.

Expenditures through the tax system vary considerably across countries and policy areas. Tax expenditures do sometimes exceed direct expenditures and, in some cases, may even entirely replace direct expenditures.

TABLE 6.9 GROWTH OF U.S. TAX EXPENDITURES, 1967–86

	1967	1975	1981	1986
Tax expenditures				
Totals (billions of dollars)	36.6	92.9	228.6	424.7
Percentage of federal revenues	23.8	33.1	37.9	55.3
Percentage of total federal outlays	20.5	28.5	34.6	42.9
Percentage of income tax receipts	n.a.	40.7*	65.9	103.0
Percentage of GNP	4.4	6.3	8.0	10.0

NOTE   *1973

SOURCES   Stanley S. Surrey and Paul R. McDaniel, *Tax Expenditure* (Cambridge, MA: Harvard University Press, 1985), p. 35; Sven Steinmo, *Taxes, Institutions and the Mobilization of Bias. The Political Economy of Taxation in Britain, Sweden and the United States* (Doctoral Thesis) (Berkeley: University of California, 1986), p. 411.

But more often they complement these programs—for instance, by excluding from the tax laws the benefits paid under them.

Generally in European countries the ratio of tax expenditures to direct expenditures in selected areas of social policy seems not to approach the American levels. U.S. tax expenditures are particularly high in areas where the United States lags the European nations in terms of comprehensive programs, such as sickness benefits. The same holds for Canadian old-age and disability tax expenditures, whereas high French tax expenditures to assist families might partially explain the low revenue generated by the personal income tax in that country. In practice, for each country the choice is posed of whether the use of the tax route, rather than the direct expenditure route, is more likely to achieve social and economic impacts in the desired directions. The choice between tax expenditures and direct expenditures as an instrument of policy is influenced by factors such as administrative effectiveness, equity, and the transparence of the redistribution of resources.

Who benefits from tax expenditures? People in all income groups pay lower taxes because of them, with even those in the lowest group able to claim deductions like those for such things as interest on consumer credit. Thus in 1977 and 1978 American families with incomes of less than $10,000 had 54 percent of their taxes discounted through tax expenditures. At the other end of the income scale, those with incomes over $50,000 escaped 41.6 percent of taxes they would have had to pay were there no tax expenditures. However, the middle-income groups were less fortunate, experiencing below-average savings on their tax bills due to the effects of tax expenditures. A study of the impact of Canadian tax expenditures shows a very similar distribution pattern (OECD 1984, p. 36ff).

Why have governments not developed more explicit criteria to govern the choice between direct and tax expenditures? An answer is suggested by the American continuation for housing interest deductions in 1986. Public opposition to this would have been too great because of recognition that there could not be a direct expenditure, but there can be, and is, a tax expenditure. This illustrates why politicians do not want to be bound by explicit criteria, but to consider alternatives on an ad hoc basis.

* * * * *

Tax policy, then, is a product of contending political forces interacting with contending economic paradigms. While the Keynesian paradigm and economic growth prevailed, all Western governments increased their tax ratios. But since the mid-1970s, manifestations of tax resistance have combined with monetarist and supply-side paradigms to exert pressure for policy reversals. Income tax systems have lost much of their progressivity as top rates have been lowered, especially in Britain and the United States. And as middle-income groups realized that they were benefiting less from tax expenditures than either the lower- or higher-income groups, politicians responded by once again seeking new tax models which would be both simpler and fairer.

The viability of a taxation system lies ultimately in its administrative implementation. What matters is not how many more or less progressive taxes are legislated, but how toughly, cunningly, and thoroughly the extractions are carried out. Tax evasion is a common problem, and the question is how well civic values, political ideology, and administrative ingenuity can serve to contain its corrosive effects on revenue receipts. We have seen how much national political culture and citizen-bureaucracy relations differ in these respects. Tax burdens of similar magnitude may elicit very different reactions depending on how deprived some taxpayer groups feel in relation to others.

Countries as different as Sweden and Japan have moved to shift the tax burden from visible direct income taxes to less visible indirect consumption taxes. The lowering of marginal rates and the reduction in brackets, together with the broadening of the tax base and the closing of loopholes, follow a similar logic.

All these measures are geared to increasing economic incentives for those who work and invest, rather than defusing the distributional conflict between those who have and the have-nots. However, it remains to be seen to what degree they will meet not only the revenue needs but also the political needs of governments, national and local, which in the future will have to face an increasing number of people depending on income maintenance payments: the elderly, students, and single parents.

7
INCOME MAINTENANCE
POLICY

The origins of the welfare state in the nineteenth century were accompanied by expectations—fears among conservatives and hopes among socialists—that a government-led expropriation of private property was about to occur. In the past one hundred years, however, events have taken a different turn. Instead of a "nationalization of the means of production," in a traditional socialist sense, the trend has been toward what might be termed a *nationalization of the means of consumption*. In other words, national governments in advanced capitalist societies have not taken over extensive ownership of private enterprise, but government policies have become a major force in determining the distribution of disposable income among citizens. Contemporary welfare states perform this distribution function most directly through the combined impact of two activities: taxation policies that distribute extractions from people's income and income maintenance (or income transfer) policies that distribute payments to augment people's income.

Of course this reshuffling of income by government is not just a simple matter of paying taxes or receiving cash transfers in accord with government policies. Complex public policy influences are at work in *both* the primary (private sector) distribution and the secondary (government sector) distribution of income.

Suppose, for example, we wished to account for the flow of income between private households and the public sector. We might begin with wages and salaries from private employment, but we should not neglect the impact of public policies in the form of minimum wage laws, collectively sanctioned wage bargaining, government purchase of goods and services, and so on. Obviously, income from direct public employment should be added, as well as public transfers both in terms of cash and "in-kind" (for example, food stamps, health services, and so on) benefits. The income of some people is also increased by interest, rents, and dividends, as well as by inheritances and charitable gifts, but all of these are also significantly influenced by public policies (such as inheritance and charitable tax deductions, rent controls, business regulations, and so on). Deductions from income would have to include direct income taxes, social insurance contributions, indirect taxes on consumption, and tax-subsidized savings programs. Accounting for all these possible interactions is extremely difficult (Reynolds and Smolensky; Lampman).

These considerations should remind us that similar goals, such as individual income security, can be pursued by quite different policies and policy instruments. National patterns can vary considerably, and sometimes change over time. Despite these national differences there is one underlying similarity in this policy field. In every developed nation, income maintenance programs have grown immensely over the course of this century. This remarkable growth has institutionalized a redistribution of resources that is of profound economic and social significance. Through such programs spending power is transferred from the employed to the unemployed, from the healthy to the ill, from working-age persons to the young and the elderly, from the affluent to the poor—and also at times from low-income to higher-income groups. Virtually everyone living in modern societies can expect to be touched by such programs at various points in their lives.

Income maintenance programs are also important because of the growing economic and political problems associated with this policy area. Following World War II cash transfers for income maintenance were vastly expanded (from 6.7 to 14.3 percent of GNP between 1950 and 1975 in the major industrialized democracies). During this period of rapid economic growth such programs accounted for at least half of the progressive redistribution of income accomplished by all government taxing and spending (Hicks and Swank, p. 108). As the economic pie grew more slowly in the 1970s and on into the 1980s, problems of financing these generous provisions mounted, but public expectations about entitlements to such benefits changed slowly if at all. Thus even under the stringent budget regimes of the Reagan administration in the United States and the Thatcher government in Britain, income maintenance programs in the 1980s remained the largest single component of national government spending in these two countries as in other OECD nations (OECD 1985).

Complicating the short-term economic problem is a longer-term generational difficulty as the European, American, and Japanese "baby boom" generations approach retirement age after the end of this century and a smaller working-age population must strain to pay for their social benefits. Fears of an evolving crisis in social insurance and a growing conflict between the needs of the young and the old are becoming a more prominent part of the policy conversation in advanced capitalist societies.

In this chapter we will try to gain some sense of the reasons for similarities and differences in the way nations try to address the common human desire for economic security.

CHOICES IN INCOME MAINTENANCE POLICY

Scope and Thresholds

It is possible to imagine a "pure" market system in which government income maintenance policies were nonexistent. The flows of income would seem to be determined by strictly "private" arrangements among employers and workers in the marketplace and among family members in private households. (We should recall that even in this situation government could still be important in the distribution of income by building highways or defense facilities in one area rather than another, by using judicial powers to define and enforce private property rights, by hiring more soldiers or more teachers, by trying or not trying to regulate the prices of food and wage labor, and so on.) In such a world the effects of government on people's income would be more or less an accidental byproduct of its other activities.

This sort of society was approximated in the nineteenth century among what are now called the developed countries. It was in response to the economic and social insecurities produced by market forces that a third element to the welfare mix was added—a direct and more or less self-conscious government involvement in the distribution of economic resources alongside the role played by markets and families (Polanyi; Rose). Government transfers in advanced democracies now amount to anything from one-fifth to one-third or more of all income earned through wages and salaries (OECD 1981). Yet today's welfare states have stopped well short of trying to substitute public transfers for all market-determined outcomes. How have these choices of public versus private boundaries in income distribution been made in different nations?

Instruments

Comparison reveals a general cross-national similarity in income maintenance policy, with every country using the same basic program instruments. The first and most dominant instrument, in terms of its costs and the number of people benefiting from it, is *social insurance*. Through the payment of specially earmarked taxes (sometimes called "national insurance" or "social security contributions"), an entitlement to certain cash benefits is acquired.

Commonly, such programs cover risks of income loss due to old age or retirement, sickness, industrial accidents, widowhood, and unemployment.

The second basic instrument of income maintenance policy is *public assistance*. Such programs characteristically rely on some form of income test to determine need and usually entail a good deal of administrative discretion in dealing with individual clients. Benefits are given not only in cash, but also "in-kind," for example, food stamps, medical services, day care for children of mothers on welfare, and so on. Unlike social insurance entitlements, public assistance benefits typically place a considerable stigma on the recipients in the eyes of the general public.

These instruments can take different forms and be arranged in different ways. Continental European nations, for example, have typically organized social insurance in such a way as to reflect differences among occupational groups. Britain, on the other hand, has emphasized a system of more uniform payments for all recipients. In Sweden the mix of insurance and public assistance is heavily tilted toward generous insurance entitlements, while in the United States public assistance programs are more prominent.

Distribution

The thresholds and instruments of income maintenance policy clearly have important distributive consequences. The general trend in the past fifty years has been away from the assumptions of individual equity in strictly insurance-type programs—that is, one's benefits correspond to one's contributions—and toward emphasis on the social adequacy of benefits—benefits should meet basic income needs. Entitlement to income security has become less individually earned and more a social right of citizenship (Marshall).

However, one should not exaggerate this commitment to redistribution in the name of social citizenship. Some income maintenance systems tolerate more or less inequality among the elderly, greater or fewer disparities between the elderly and working-age population, more or less poverty among children. Moreover, the harsher economic climate of recent years has tended to raise new questions about the limits of social citizenship— even in countries that have given greater emphasis to redistributive goals than have other countries.

Restraints and Innovation

Social insurance was a historic social innovation, offering an ingenious means of pooling economic risks across the population while recognizing individual circumstances and doing so without the stigmatizing effect of traditional public assistance. As the social and economic dislocations of modernization increased, social insurance provided a timely political compromise between the respective demands of collectivism and individualism (although, as we shall see, the timing varied considerably among nations).

Economic and social dislocations of the 1970s and 1980s were certainly less severe than those much earlier in this century; nevertheless, recent economic troubles and demographic changes have generated debate in many countries about the need to make tough choices in income maintenance policy. Indeed, the difficulties of policy innovation may be even greater today than they were during the origins of the welfare state, mainly because current expectations of what public policy can do are so much higher and the momentum of existing social programs is so much greater and thus more difficult to arrest.

The emerging policy debate suspends income maintenance programs between two perspectives. One perspective stresses the smaller margin of resources, produced by slower economic growth, left to pay for transfer programs. Questions are also asked about the effects of public income maintenance on private savings, investment, and work effort, thus raising the specter of a downward spiral to even lower growth.

The second, and opposing, perspective stresses the increased insecurity being produced by the rapid pace of economic and social change. Growing competitiveness in the international economy is seen to make workers and their dependents more vulnerable to impersonal economic forces. Changing family structures and increasing participation of women in the labor force are accompanied by calls for expanding, rather than cutting back, income maintenance programs.

Whatever the intellectual arguments, the debate on income maintenance policy must also be carried on within a political environment that is extremely sensitive to the popular outrage that can be created by any intimation of cutting government benefits. What taxpayer resistance is to taxation policy, anticipated beneficiary backlash is to income maintenance policy— namely, a profound constraint on policy innovation.

GROWTH OF THE TRANSFER SOCIETY
SCOPE AND THRESHOLDS

Students of comparative public policy have devoted considerable energy to trying to unravel the effects of economic and political variables on public policy. Nowhere is this more true than in income maintenance policy. In fact it is the creation of such income security programs that most observers consider the birth of modern welfare states. Comparative policy studies have become increasingly refined in trying to account for this development. The effect has been to supplant fairly simple, deterministic models with a more complex understanding of the interaction of economic and political forces that are at work in social policy.

The Logic of Industrialization

A number of studies have described the tendency for the social welfare commitments of governments—and income maintenance spending in particular—to increase with levels of economic development (Cutright 1965, 1967; Wilensky and Lebeaux; Pryor; Jackman; Wilensky 1975). The typical way of denoting this relationship has been to show that social spending (primarily income transfers) as a proportion of national product is greater in rich nations than in poor nations and has tended to grow as economic development progresses in any given nation.

Early attempts to explain the development of welfare states argued, in effect, that government income maintenance programs were inherent in the logic of industrialization. The process of economic development carries with it huge upheavals in the way people lead their lives. These changes include the loss of traditional support from extended families and community relationships in agrarian settings. Industrialization leaves parents and their children dependent on wages and salaries controlled by impersonal market forces in an ever-increasingly specialized system of economic production. At the same time that economic development raises general levels of income (and thus expectations about minimum standards of material well-being), it also makes the growing cadre of industrial wage-earners more vulnerable to economic insecurity produced by sudden income losses due to unemployment, illness, accidents at work, and retirement. The economic and social transformation entailed in industrialization creates both a growing demand for government programs to support groups in need and a growing supply of revenue resources produced by economic growth to meet those demands.

There are significant variations on this theme that industrialization produces income maintenance policy. One school of thought, dubbed *functionalism,* sees nationally organized social programs as a functional response to the common problems of insecurity and instability that occur in every country undergoing the modernization process (Kerr et al.; Bendix). The development of statutory social policy is seen to be a trend toward which all industrial nations converge regardless of their economic or political systems. Another school of thought derives from the Marxist tradition. Far from being politically and socially neutral, income maintenance policies are said to reflect the needs of capitalist systems to sustain their legitimacy. Human labor becomes a commodity that is bought and sold for the profit of the owners of capital. Left unchecked, the forces of capitalism destroy the bonds of social community and drive workers and their families into more desperate, marginal living conditions. Income maintenance policies are a palliative serving to defuse worker unrest and support the mass consumption needed to keep the processes of capitalist accumulation working. Thus government social policies stabilize the underlying

capitalist order, at least temporarily, until public appetites for income transfers outrun capitalist needs for saving and investment (Miliband; O'Connor 1973; Offe).

Interpretations of social policy based on the logic of industrialization
have been attacked on many grounds in recent years, and a rough consensus seems to have emerged. Most observers agree that at a very general
level there is a correlation between economic development and social policy
responses. Certainly processes of industrialization and social modernization
create problems demanding attention, and obviously, rich nations have the
resources to devote to social welfare programs that poor nations do not.
However, careful empirical studies do not support the proposition that
levels of economic development and industrialization somehow determine
the creation or scope of different nations' social welfare policies.

First, it is clear that nations initiated major income transfer programs
at quite different levels of industrialization, from the late nineteenth century onward (Collier and Messick; Flora and Alber). Thus the world's first
and most industrialized nation, Britain, lagged behind Imperial Germany
in the nineteenth century; the agrarian, monarchical nations of Scandinavia were inexplicably doing more than they "should" in the early twentieth
century while the United States, even then one of the world's industrial
leaders, was doing little to institute social insurance and other modern
statutory social measures.

A second problem with the industrialization thesis is that it cannot
explain major policy variations that exist among advanced industrial nations. An immense economic gap separates the cluster of developed countries from the group of less-developed nations, and it is not particularly
surprising that when all these states are analyzed together social welfare
spending turns out to be correlated with measures of economic development (Castles and McKinlay). The contrast between poorer and richer
nations suggests some very general relationship between economic development and social spending, but it does not account for differences, for
example in social spending, that exist among the capitalist democracies.
Thus by seeming to explain everything about the relationship between
socioeconomic change and public policy responses, both functionalist and
Marxist theories leave us at a loss to understand the varying experiences of
developed welfare states.

The consensus among many comparative studies would appear to go
something as follows: Industrialization, and its accompanying social
changes, set in motion the necessary preconditions for contemporary income maintenance policies. However the timing and content of those
policies remain heavily influenced by political processes. Exactly how that
influence works has been a topic of considerable comparative research in
recent years.

Class Politics, Parties, and State Structures

Income security programs are not a politically neutral, technical by-product of industrialism. They are part of a struggle for power in which those who would benefit from increased security and equality must fight to prevail over forces of the status quo. It seems reasonable to suppose that, as many analysts have argued, working-class movements and their political representatives have been particularly important in extending the scope of these social policies (Shalev).

At a general level and with some important qualifications, this idea of a political class struggle over the expansion of social programs has acquired a good degree of empirical support in recent years. The studies in question usually aim at explaining differences among the eighteen or so most developed democracies, and the variables being measured do vary somewhat from author to author. Nevertheless, the overall thrust of the findings shows that where unions are extensive and well organized, and particularly where they are allied with a powerful Social Democratic party that consistently wins office, welfare state benefits are generally more extensive (Stephens; Korpi; Esping-Andersen). Others have argued, for example, that with greater working-class power in the state, public pension entitlements take on more of the aspects of a "citizen wage" based on principles of adequacy, equality, and social solidarity (Myles 1984; Hedstrom and Ringen).

While working-class political mobilization and control of government can be an important factor, particularly in expansive Scandinavian welfare states like Sweden, it would be a mistake to extrapolate this fact into a single-cause theory of welfare state development. Comparative policy research has produced more refined findings to suggest other factors that also need to be taken into account. And as always it is important to be clear about exactly what dependent variable is being explained—timing of the introduction of income security policies, or rates of spending growth, or levels of resource commitments in relation to the economy or total budget, or adequacy of programs in relation to need, and so on.

One way of introducing many of the refinements that need to be made to the political class struggle thesis is to look at Table 7.1. In this table the dependent variable is the one most commonly used in such comparative policy studies: social security expenditures as a percentage of GNP, or "welfare effort," as it is often called in the literature. (Ideally analysts would like to have a set of spending statistics based on a broader concept of "welfare effort" for the entire twentieth century, but it is only in the latter post–World War II period that reliable comparative data on even social insurance spending is available.) Countries are arrayed into five groups, depending on (1) how extensively the working class is politically mobilized (that is, degree of unionization and average votes for Social

TABLE 7.1 LEFT OR RIGHT DOMINANCE AND WELFARE EFFORT FOR SELECTED YEARS

Working Class Mobilization & Control*	Average Vote for Major Party of the Right		Average Social Security** Expenditures as Percentage of GNP/GDP			
	1958–72	*1973–86*	*1960–67*	*1968–73*	*1974–79*	*1980–86*
High mobilization, stable control						
Austria	45	42	14	16	18	20
Norway	19	26	9	12	14	15
Sweden	15	19	9	12	16	18
High mobilization, unstable control						
Belgium	16	19	12	14	19	22
Britain	45	40	7	9	11	14
Denmark	19	23	8	11	14	17
Medium-high mobilization, low control						
Australia	45	47	6	6	8	n.a.
France	35	28	16	17	21	n.a.
Italy	40	37	11	13	15	16
Low mobilization, partial control						
Netherlands	12	19	n.a.	18	24	27
Switzerland	22	21	7	9	13	13
West Germany	46	47	12	13	17	17
Low mobilization, political left excluded						
Canada	37	38	7	8	10	12
Japan	52	46	4	5	8	11
United States	48	53	5	8	10	11

*Political "mobilization" here is determined by the degree of unionization and average votes for Social Democratic parties or other parties of the Left. Indications of "control" reflect the proportions of cabinet and parliamentary seats held by parties of the Left as well as the duration of such government participation.

**Social security is defined as social security benefits for sickness, old age, family allowances, etc., plus social assistance grants and unfunded employee welfare benefits paid by general government.

SOURCES   Korpi, Table 4, p. 312: Castles and McKinlay, Table 1, p. 158; OECD, *Historical Statistics 1960–86*, Table 6.3, p. 63; Thomas Mackie and Richard Rose, *The International Almanac of Election Statistics*, 2nd ed. (New York: Facts on File, 1982); *The Europa Yearbook* (London: Europa Publications, 1987, 1988); Colen Hughes, *A Handbook of Australia Government and Politics, 1975–1984* (Sydney: Australian National University Press, 1985).

Democratic parties or other parties of the left) and (2) how often working-class parties have participated in minority or majority control of the government (proportions of cabinet and parliamentary seats held by parties of the left and duration of such participation in government). Also shown is the extent of popular electoral support for parties of the right. Thus we can identify nations where working-class mobilization has been high and control generally stable (such as Sweden and Norway) and nations where mobilization has been high but control sporadic (as in Britain) or low (as in Australia).

As both this table and a number of other studies suggest, the relationship between a powerful labor movement and a high level of social insurance spending is far from perfect. Countries such as the Netherlands, West Germany, and France appear to have developed quite substantial spending patterns without an unusual degree of dominance by the political left. Some scholars have argued that for certain countries (for example, the Netherlands, Belgium, West Germany, Austria) the presence of a strong Catholic party competing for power has played an expansionary role similar to the dominant Social Democrats of Scandinavia (Wilensky 1981).

Political dominance by the Left may not be a necessary condition for high levels of social spending, but dominance by parties of the Right does seem to help account for the relatively low levels of spending found in some wealthy democracies. Using data from the postwar period, a number of authors have found that in countries in which right-of-center parties have remained in control of government and labor has been poorly mobilized (Canada, Japan, the United States), both levels and rates of increase in welfare effort have remained comparatively small (Castles 1982; Hicks and Swank; O'Connor 1988).

Extremely low levels of transfer spending can also be found in countries where labor is highly mobilized but usually excluded from government office (Australia and New Zealand). The historic pattern in these nations has been to rely, not on large income maintenance programs, but on wage regulation and other forms of protection to provide income security to workers (Castles 1985, 1988).

Interpretations based solely on working-class struggles against the forces of capitalism and the political right obscure the importance of other groups that are active in shaping social policy. For example, observers have long noted the tendency for income maintenance spending to rise in response to the changing age structure of an industrialized society (Wilensky 1975). With a larger elderly population, there are obviously more pension benefits to be paid while smaller family sizes may leave the younger population feeling less able to support their parents within the family (Entwisle and Winegarden). However careful, multivariate studies also show that even after controlling for these demographic changes, the trend has been to increase pension spending and to do so especially in association with increases in political democracy (Pampel and Williamson; O'Higgins 1988). For a program such as pensions, age politics may well be more important than class politics.

The need to expand our explanatory framework becomes even more evident if we switch attention from levels of spending to the timing of shifts from strictly private distributional systems to the more public redistribution of income maintenance programs. In fact, one of the most consistent findings in the literature is that the level of current welfare spending is closely associated with the length of time particular social insurance programs have been in existence (Wilensky 1975; Cutright 1965; Pampel and Williamson). Why did some countries cross the boundary between public and private so much earlier than others?

Examining the historical origins of social insurance programs does not suggest that these programs were introduced as various nations attained certain levels of economic development. Austria, Sweden, and Norway initiated their programs at relatively low levels of economic development, whereas Britain did so only at a very high level of economic modernization. Nor is there much evidence to support the idea that these programs were introduced as nations reached high levels of political mobilization among the working classes (even though early social insurance legislation was concentrated on industrial workers). Depending on the country and the program, legislation was initiated when working-class parties received as little as 0 percent and as much as 50 percent of total votes (Flora and Heidenheimer, pp. 65–68). Many of the oldest—and thus today most expensive—income security programs were introduced in countries where the political right was firmly in control and democratic institutions weak (Germany, France, Scandinavia). Compared with nations at a similar level of economic development, such non-parliamentary regimes often faced a greater need to legitimate their power than did more democratic regimes such as Britain and the United States. Moreover, these rightist governments also had strong paternalistic bureaucracies in place to facilitate the creation and implementation of a policy innovation as complex as social insurance. As we shall see in greater detail later in this chapter, such institutional arrangements of the state are also an important force shaping social policy development generally and the origins of social insurance in particular (Weir, Orloff, and Skocpol). Without understanding how state structures continually interact with party struggles over policy as well as class and other social divisions, the varying patterns of income maintenance policy are incomprehensible.

If nothing else, these considerations should help us realize that there is not likely to be a single cause or one grand theory for explaining the development of "the" welfare state (Carrier and Kendall). Nor can we even assume that the causes of policy remain unchanging over time. Usable accounts of public policy need to be pitched in a middle range between universal socioeconomic laws and country-specific experiences. It is in this range that uniqueness can be identified by comparison and generalizations can be brought down to earth to distinguish among cases. Far from being in competition with each other as the "real" source of social welfare programs, economic and political variables are in constant interaction amid the historical experience that constitutes public policy development. It is from this perspective that we shall examine the choices of instruments in income maintenance policy.

VARIETIES OF PUBLIC PROVISION
INSTRUMENTS

It is important to begin by recognizing the historic significance of social insurance. In one Western nation after another, the invention and diffusion of this income maintenance technique in the late nineteenth and early twentieth centuries eventually freed large sections of the population from dependence on charity, local poor laws, and the ubiquitous stigma surrounding means-tested assistance. In practice, a test of means typically entailed a degrading examination of all one's personal circumstances so as to prove to some local official that there were no viable means of support from work, family, or friends. The advantages of the new insurance technique were immense. Decisions regarding eligibility were now automatic, since they were based on nationally standardized rules rather than on the discretion of local poor-law officials or private charity workers. Degrading investigations into a family's means were unnecessary in a system in which beneficiaries had earned the right to support by virtue of past contributions. Focusing insurance on certain contingencies or accidents (industrial disability, widowhood, unemployment, loss of earning power with old age, and so on) also meant that administrative decision making could concentrate on whether or not a particular contingency had actually occurred and not on the moral character of the claimant. Moreover, the political costs were less apparent, inasmuch as this new system could be paid for by "contributions," rather than by more visible taxes on the population. After centuries of reliance on medieval poor laws, the advent of social insurance was a great watershed in the history of social welfare policy.

Despite this underlying similarity in the conceptual significance of social insurance, nations have, in using the technique, varied considerably in rationale and emphasis. Current policies reflect their histories; and this is certainly true with regard to the slow-changing contours of income maintenance policy. In no nation have the choices been made in exactly the same way. However, in every nation, fundamental decisions taken early in the development of income maintenance policies did much to shape the patterns evident today.

Policy Legacies

If industrialization was the precondition generating demands for increased income security, particular combinations of economic, social, and political factors supplied the historical materials for dealing with (and in some cases anticipating) those demands in each nation. The development of social insurance programs occurred within an existing context of social cleavages, typically represented in the organization of working-class, agrarian, religious, and sectarian interests. These social divisions interacted in turn with inherited structures of state power shaped by the varied mixtures of bureaucratic and democratic development that characterized different nations. Out of this complex process came early policy choices that were then influential in shaping the assumptions and political resources for later policy development. Perhaps the best way of making sense of these generalizations is to consider the comparative policy histories that unfolded in a number of different countries, specifically with regard to the choice of social insurance as an instrument of income maintenance policy.

Although lagging behind Britain in economic development, Germany in the last quarter of the nineteenth century experienced all the social problems of rapid industrialization. National social insurance programs (for industrial accidents, sickness, and old age pensions) were introduced in the 1880s as a defensive innovation designed to counteract the growing socialist movement and to ensure the loyalty of the new industrial working class. In making this effort, the prime movers behind German social insurance—certain elements of the government bureaucracy, large-scale industrialists, some academics, and Chancellor Bismarck himself—drew on a long tradition of state paternalism for artisans, craftsmen, coal miners, and other workers that had developed during the preindustrial period of German history.

At the same time, policymakers had to accommodate the fact that Imperial Germany was a society with strongly institutionalized status distinctions in the labor force. (Agricultural interests were dominated by the powerful Junker class of large landowners; little thought was given to including farm workers in the new insurance schemes.) The industrial working class was itself a collection of divided, status-conscious groups. When Bismarck (largely on grounds of administrative convenience) sought to establish uniform flat-rate insurance benefits, workers' representatives protested loudly against the injustice that would be done in lumping skilled craftsmen with day laborers. In the end, lest skilled workers become disgruntled and even more prone to socialist influence, German social insurance took form as a system of differential benefits closely tied to prior earnings.

Bismarck's plan to pay for the new system also had to accommodate certain political realities. His hopes for major state subsidies encountered stiff resistance in a wide variety of quarters, particularly by groups worried that they would be paying to subsidize benefits to which only working-class people were entitled (Baldwin). The result was a system of worker contributions (to teach thrift), employer contributions (to express a joint interest in maintaining the social and economic order), and a modest state subsidy confined to the old-age portion of social insurance (in Bismarck's view to demonstrate the state's interest and responsibility for workers' welfare).

Social Democrats and other socialists were generally hostile to social insurance and fearful of its paternalistic state intervention in workers' lives. At this early stage of policy development Germany's working-class representatives preferred pushing for British-style legislation to regulate working conditions (hours, safety, and so on). In Bismarck's Germany, however, the Left and its views could be and were effectively excluded from the policy debate.

The German social insurance programs of the 1880s and 1890s established a curious mixture of state centralization (with a new Imperial Insurance Office compelling membership and compliance with rules) and intermediary organizations (accident insurance associations, sickness insurance funds, and the like), which were co-opted into, but also highly influential within, the state social insurance structure (Mommsen).

In view of the vast upheavals in twentieth-century Germany, it is remarkable how much of the basic social insurance structure has remained intact. The Nazi government reshaped many intermediary insurance organizations (particularly those with a trade union, Jewish, or socialist presence). But not even the Nazis could prevail against the well-entrenched power of bureaucrats and social groups defending the traditional social insurance system. Nazi promises of a tax-financed, noncontributory system of pensions for all citizens eventually shriveled into yet another separate plan of compulsory contributory insurance for artisans, independent workers in skilled trades conventionally regarded as members of the middle classes.

At the end of World War II, the Allied occupational forces in cooperation with some West German reformers proposed the creation of a single, comprehensive program of national insurance modeled along the lines of the Beveridge system that had been instituted in Britain in the 1940s (see p. 238). This proposal came to little in the face of intense opposition from bureaucrats and insurance fund officials, who had helped their programs survive the political turmoil of previous decades; from self-employed and higher-paid workers, who insisted on a separate identity for their social insurance funds; and from leading politicians of the new Federal Republic, who discounted any need to rely on foreign models of a policy technique that the Germans themselves had invented. Postwar policy, despite the much higher benefits and wider coverage, would have looked familiar to a citizen of Bismarck's Second Reich: a complicated system of funds for accident insurance, paid for entirely by employers; an even more complicated arrangement of sickness insurance funds, paid for jointly by workers and employers; and a system of state-subsidized public pensions, differentiated among categories of workers and closely attuned to differences in workers' earnings.

A number of other continental European nations bore a family resemblance to the German policy experience, but with outcomes that were often shaped by even stronger social divisions and weaker central structures of state power. Unlike the situation in northern Europe, the Catholic Church in southern Europe was a deeply rooted institutional structure (charity organizations, schools, hospitals, and so on) that inhibited any complete takeover of responsibilities for the poor by secular public authorities. As demands for economic security grew, it became a common practice to publicly subsidize Catholic institutions, and as democratization proceeded in the early twentieth century there frequently developed strong clientele relations between political parties and these intermediary welfare structures (Flora). At the same time Catholic influences were important in the early attempts to pay particular attention to family policy and income needs of families with children (Kamerman and Kahn 1981).

In a band of nations across the middle of Europe, the religious, ethnic, and other social divisions formed a more variegated set of forces that affected and were in turn affected by different state structures in the policy process. The Netherlands, for example, had to cope with the problem of income security in a society so riven by religious divisions that they carried through to the political constitution of the government itself. The introduction of social insurance in 1913 left the mandatory contributions for retirement and disability to be run by semipublic boards of employers and employees in each industrial sector, with most sectors containing Calvinist, Catholic, and "independent" boards (Cox). This arrangement helped delay the introduction of comprehensive old-age insurance for all citizens until 1957. Tiny Switzerland, with its three language groups, provides the extreme example of political decentralization. In this setting of city-confederations, local control by citizens (that is, males who were mainly small land-owning farmers) over the funding and delivery of social welfare provision flourished, mutual benefit societies and other forms of self-help associations became entrenched, and national (federal) income maintenance policy languished.

France is an instructive case from this socially heterogeneous band of countries. Industrialization proceeded much more slowly than in other leading European nations. Even when it occurred, industrial operations often retained a semirural status with workers retaining ties to the countryside and drifting in and out of wage labor. As the debate on social insurance intensified throughout the developed world in the late nineteenth and early twentieth centuries, France was a mixture of fragmented and contradictory political movements and social impulses. Overlaying this mosaic was a French state that had acquired—through wrenching swings between radical republicanism and conservative counterattacks—a thoroughly ambivalent status for purposes of social policy-making.

Catholic influences were important but far from monolithic. The strength of Catholic charitable institutions meant that the assumption of responsibility for the poor by local public authorities was slow in coming compared with Britain or the nations of northern Europe; hence, unlike these countries, the state's poor-law policy provided no focal point against which reformers and social insurance advocates could easily react. Although the substantial political influence of Catholic liberals plummeted when the Second Empire was replaced by the secular forces of the Third Republic (1875–1940), their ideas about the Church's social mission resonated with the conservative attributes of French society and the ambivalent legitimacy of state authority. Key among those ideas was the need for protecting the sanctity of the family and reproducing its bonds of solidarity throughout the communal associations of society and industry (Ashford).

French agriculture was dominated by a mass of peasant proprietors whose families had wrested control of the land from the aristocratic state during the French Revolution. Their concerns for security and independence blended into the village and small-town life of an extensive lower middle class—a petit bourgeoisie of self-employed shopkeepers, artisans, small-scale employers in rural industries—together with such local notables as lawyers, doctors, and notaries. These clusters of localism dominated the social and economic scene and provided the political base of support for vigorous but incoherent parliamentary democracy of the Third Republic. Their hostility to strong national efforts at social reform, much less compulsory social insurance, was an extremely important force. At the same time, the French urban working class was a significantly smaller presence than in Britain or Germany, but the issue was much more than a mere matter of numbers. As with the land-owning peasants, French industrial workers had good historical reasons—the crushing of the 1848 labor revolt and of the Paris Commune in 1870—to doubt the benign influence of state power. In a labor movement splintered along craft, religious, and geographic lines, the central tendency of French socialism was a kind of industrialized version of rural and petit-bourgeoisie independence—which is to say, a syndicalist approach to socialism that sought solutions to the problems of industrial society through communal association outside the reach of centralized government authorities (Baldwin).

It should come as no surprise then that national income maintenance policy in France occurred at a halting pace. The historic bureaucratic capacities of the French state were willingly used to subsidize communal efforts at social protection (with state encouragement, the number of voluntary, mutual-aid insurance societies grew from 2,438 in 1852 with a quarter million members to 13,677 societies in 1902 with 2 million members), but any nationally directive policy was stalemated (Ashford, pp. 88–89). A weak pension law of 1910 covering rural and urban wage earners was effectively crippled when many employers, upheld by the courts, refused to make the necessary wage deductions for contributions. As the mutual-aid societies became more financially hard-pressed in the gradually industrializing French society, a series of public insurance laws were passed in the 1920s and 30s. While the left wing of the labor movement continued to attack contributory social insurance as a capitalist ploy and denial of workers' rights, state support splintered into a variety of schemes based on unions, employers, mutual-aid societies, agricultural pursuits, and religious organizations. For those left out of this montage of social provision, more purely state-organized social insurance funds helped to mop up any remaining sources of discontent—all this behind a state system of tariff barriers and related protections that shielded French society and social policy from the need to adapt to external economic forces for change.

Shifting our geographic focus again, this time farther to the north of Bismarck's Germany, we encounter Sweden, where the level of industrialization lagged well behind that in France (much less Germany or Britain) during the earlier part of the twentieth century. But here again, the interaction of economic, political, and social forces shows itself to be more complex than any single-factor theory of welfare state development can comprehend. Like France, and unlike Germany, Swedish agriculture (at this time the bulk of Swedish economic life) was in the hands of peasant proprietors. However, lacking a violent French-style revolution against the established landed aristocracy, Swedish agriculture represented a more mixed system of small, medium, and large farmers. Moreover, the historical experience of Swedish farmers was one of obtaining independence through an alliance with enlightened monarchs and their strong central bureaucracies against the power of landed nobles. State power was not necessarily something to be feared, and this became especially true as democratic reforms in the late nineteenth and early twentieth centuries gave the numerous middle-class farmers a growing voice in Swedish government.

Like France, Sweden's industrial working class was tiny by German or British standards, but differences in economic resources and position in world trade helped give that emerging class a different character than in France. Sweden's main resources for underwriting the industrialization process—timber and mining—tended to require larger-scale operations and a more extensive, self-contained body of wage labor than did France's semirural system of small employers. The need for the small Swedish economy to organize these products for export (often to comparatively huge German firms) helped push toward a distinctive class of wage laborers. Thus when Stockholm reformers began taking up the issue of social insurance—and although their country lacked anything approaching Germany's urban concentrations of industrial workers—they did so with distinctly Bismarckian overtones of anti-socialist paternalism. Like German policymakers, they could rely on a strong central bureaucracy to develop and implement this new policy innovation. Like the German model they studied, Swedish reformers proposed a compulsory social insurance system confined to the working class—full-time workers with incomes below a certain level. (It was presumed that some nonindependent farm workers would also earn entitlement.)

However, Sweden differed from Germany in two important ways. First, Swedish agricultural interests had an independence and social importance that could not be simply dismissed in this new era of social policy reform. There was good reason why middle-class farmers and their families should be interested in this innovative social insurance technique that was being touted as a means of relieving the need for reliance on a degrading poor law. Like other non-Catholic nations, public authorities in Sweden had long been responsible for relief of the poor, and processes of agricultural and industrial change were stretching the capacities of this premodern system of secular charity to the breaking point. The problem was particularly acute in the Swedish countryside where a combination of huge emigration to America and considerable longevity in the rural population that remained produced an abundance of old people needing support (with twice the number of residents over seventy as in Britain or Germany and 15 to 20 percent more than in France) (Baldwin, p. 160). Agriculturalists had a vested interest in some third option to the two main alternatives that were available for dealing with the situation: further strains on intergenerational family support or the disgrace of public charity.

In the second place, the elite politicians and administrators of Stockholm presided over a much more open policy-making process than did their German counterparts. In Sweden, social insurance as a statutory social policy evolved in a freer political climate involving parties, interest groups, political and bureaucratic reformers. Consequently, much time was lost between the first proposals by liberal parliamentarians at the end of the 1880s and the final enactment of social insurance for the aged in 1913. But, for the purposes of building a broad-based political consensus, the time was well spent. It is easy to forget that at this time Sweden was wracked by intense social divisions and economic conflict. Powerful agrarian interests, national administrators, academics, businesspeople, unions, socialists, and laissez-faire liberals all disputed the advantages and disadvantages of social insurance. However, two important features must be pointed out: that Sweden's political process drew these disparate groups into active and continuous participation in the policy-making system, and that it did so early, before the participants became too firmly locked into opposing positions. Gradually, a series of official investigations, commissions, legislative proposals, defeats, renegotiations, false starts, and reinvestigations moved the participants toward agreement.

After two decades of debate, the final plans were worked out in an investigative commission led by national civil servants but also composed of representatives from the major political parties, business, agrarian, and working-class interests. Unlike those in Germany, Swedish agricultural interests recently empowered through democratic reforms were able to insist successfully on being included in the new form of statutory income protection. It was largely because of this insistence that in 1913 Sweden—one of the poorest, most agrarian nations in Western Europe—adopted the world's first essentially universal contributory social insurance law covering virtually the entire population (Baldwin).

For their part, union and socialist representatives of the young Swedish working class were subordinate players in this policy-making process. But the accommodations they were led to make in these circumstances were portentous for later developments in Swedish social policy. During the early stages of the long debate on social insurance, Swedish Social Democrats followed orthodox socialist thinking by supporting social insurance measures limited to urban industrial workers and paid for entirely by employers as a worker's right. However, as Social Democrats joined with liberals in successfully pressing for electoral reform, there was no denying the immense presence of agrarian interests in the newly democratized electorate that had emerged by 1911. Sharp divisions within the labor movement produced a reformist majority in the Social Democratic party willing to broaden appeals to the farmers and support the 1913 law, along with a more doctrinaire left wing opposed to including workers with farmers and other self-employed groups.

The 1913 law was far from a panacea for Sweden's elderly but the process of its creation did yield a broad-based political consensus around essential principles. Above all, coverage would be universal to include all groups in the same system. Instead of employers' contributions in a program limited to industrial wage earners, tax-financed state subsidies from the population at large would have to play a major role. To help pay this large bill and create a true entitlement to benefit (as opposed to the degrading charity of the Poor Law), individual contributions would also be required. To balance the low contributions the rural population could afford and the high benefits urban workers felt were required, administrators devised a three-tier system of income groupings. The lowest level of contributions and benefits embraced the rural population and most women, the second was for most industrial workers and self-employed of modest means, and the third covered the most affluent wage earners and independent workers. In effect, Swedish history had constructed a context in which the state could interact with—and not simply reflect—the demands of powerful social groupings. Sweden could create and administer a truly national social policy without kindling entrenched fears of state repression (as in France) or expecting passive acquiescence to the government's will (as in

Germany). In subsequent years this approach became the model for other social policy developments. The long tenure (1932 to 1976) of the Social Democratic party, again in alliance with the farmers' party, did much to expand social insurance as a comprehensive tool of income support organized for the entire population. The concept of individually earned private insurance was gradually laid to rest in favor of more uniform basic benefits with major financing from general revenues.

Compared to Germany, France, or Sweden, Britain was a thoroughly industrialized nation by the end of the nineteenth century. Britain's central administrative resources were relatively weak compared with leading continental powers but its democratic institutions—male suffrage, political parties in meaningful competition, parliamentary powers—were markedly strong. At the same time, gaining a first-start in the industrialization process meant that Britain's industrial working class was extremely important in terms of sheer numbers and institutions of industrial labor were well established. In fits and starts, Britain created a universal system of income security to be sure, but it was one aimed at creating a minimum level of support and not, as would develop in Sweden, a nationally organized and guided system of income distribution across social strata. And as we shall see, this difference in the meaning of universalism has continued to the present day.

During the last quarter of the nineteenth century many proposals for contributory social insurance were made by British middle-class reformers but they ran up against three major obstacles. First, many key participants, including civil servants themselves, were doubtful of the administrative capacities to run a contributory program, and were committed instead to advancing administration of the British poor law (which was more centrally controlled than that of any other nation at this time). Second, liberal and conservative politicians as well as the popular media generally objected that social insurance of the German type would involve a state regimentation that would be "un-British." But by far the major practical obstacle was the entrenched power of the workers' own organizations, the Friendly Societies, which already collected workers' contributions for disability and death benefits; these societies feared state competition. Employers, some of whom pointed out the advantages of social insurance as a disciplining device and aid to industrial peace, were far too fragmented to assume any coherent position pro or con the new initiatives.

Britain's first statutory pension law (1908) was a non-contributory system responding to demands, mainly from labor groups and liberal reformers, for an alternative to the degrading poor law. Unlike Germany, there was no intention of enhancing the security of the industrial working class, and hence pensions were universal in the sense of being available to any elderly person falling below a very low income level. But this provision of a minimum for the indigent was also something different from the Swedish universalism that was produced by accommodating the demands of a powerful sociopolitical group for inclusion in a public income security system for mainstream workers. British pensions remained a meager substitute for poor relief. Dependent on general government revenues rather than workers' contributions, the system faced political resistance from middle- and upper-class income taxpayers. Efforts to contain costs by restricting the number of people eligible meant relying on a means test that aroused persistent criticism from labor and heightened the similarity between the new pensions and the old poor law.

Faced with this stalemate, and having studied the German example more closely, reform-minded liberal ministers and their civil service advisers worked out plans for contributory social insurance largely outside the domain of public debate. In 1911, against labor opposition to contributions and with rather passive acquiescence from other parties and interest groups, the liberal government introduced the world's first national unemployment insurance program. At the same time a limited scheme for workers' health insurance was instituted, giving the Friendly Societies the responsibilities and financial rewards of the program's administration. Thus, by the interwar period, the British policy process had produced one false start (noncontributory pensions) and an ad hoc mixture of two other insurance programs, one run by the state for particular categories of workers and one heavily influenced by the private-sector societies.

In general, Britain's pragmatic arrangement lacked the coherence and authoritarian rationale found in Germany and the positive consensus for contributory state insurance found among the interested parties in Sweden. As Friendly Societies' finances continued to deteriorate and the 1908 pensions proved increasingly inadequate, a modest contributory program of old-age insurance for workers was introduced in the 1920s.

World War II and its accompanying sense of national solidarity against the Nazi onslaught provided an opportunity for more comprehensive social insurance reform. The basis for a postwar consensus on income support policy was laid by William Beveridge, who as a civil servant had helped create the 1911 unemployment insurance plan, and a committee of government civil servants. Now there was close consultation with trade union leaders who were essential to the war effort. Having experienced the degradation of the "dole" that followed the financial collapse of unemployment insurance during the late 1920s and 1930s, labor leaders were now much more receptive to the value of insurance contributions as a means of establishing a right to benefits and providing a sound financial basis for income support. Developed as the war-weary nation sought a symbol of postwar hope, the Beveridge plan was eventually accepted by all parties by the end of World War II.

The new reform created one comprehensive national insurance program applicable to all citizens, with flat-rate benefits and contributions as well as modest subsidies from state revenues (in order to keep the uniform contributions within reach of the lower paid). While a dramatic move, the inclusion of all citizens in a single framework of social insurance was not particularly controversial. This was partly because there were relatively smaller groups of independent workers to be absorbed in Britain compared with continental nations and partly because the paying of equal contributions for uniform benefits meant there was no significant redistribution among income groups (Baldwin). In fact a number of middle-class persons could expect inclusion to be economically advantageous. The Beveridge plan aroused much attention internationally as an embodiment of the welfare state ideal of social citizenship for all. However, it is important to recognize that this new system of all-in insurance, embraced by labor as a way to abolish the hated means test, was much more within the social policy traditions of British liberalism than it was the outgrowth of working-class demands or socialist appeal for solidarity. Social insurance benefits were set at a uniform subsistence minimum level in order to leave room for individual self-help and private provision above that poverty threshold. It followed that if all were to receive the same benefits, there would be immense political difficulties in asking contributors to pay different amounts for their state insurance—hence uniform contributions. This relatively simple system of insurance unrelated to the different earnings of different groups also fit well with a state administrative structure that was lacking the capacities for detailed intervention in economic affairs found in continental bureaucracies. These ideas—comprehensive coverage, uniform treatment, and minimum income levels to avoid destitution—were Britain's essential policy legacy in the postwar period.

The interactions of economic development, social cleavages, and state structures can also help us understand patterns of income maintenance policy in developed countries beyond Western Europe—for example, the so-called laggards in welfare state spending such as Australia, Japan, and the United States—that appear in Tables 7.1 and 7.2.

Australia is an interesting case of a country that was, at the beginning of this century, widely regarded by European reformers as a leading innovator in modern social policy (Castles 1985). In fact Britain's 1908 pension act was more or less modeled after old-age pension laws in New Zealand and Australia that had come into effect eight to ten years earlier. The explanation of this puzzling change from early welfare state leader to laggard is a powerful example of the importance of policy legacies and how they are created.

At the beginning of this century, Australia ranked as one of the most economically developed, modernized nations in the world (Castles 1988). Being a new nation created through overwhelmingly British immigration in the nineteenth century, Australia lacked the entrenched religious, ethnic, and cultural divisions that characterized much of Europe. Australia's agricultural sector was a modern economic sector of large-scale, capitalistic production that bore little resemblance to the peasant societies of rural France or Sweden. While lacking the concentrated industrialization of Britain or Germany, Australia's labor force exhibited the qualities of a modern, integrated economy (an estimated 76 percent of the work force were wage or salary earners, and rates of urbanization were among the highest in the world). With a growing world demand for the exports of Australia's efficient agricultural sector and with labor in short supply, wages reached very high levels by international standards. It has been estimated that during the last third of the nineteenth century Australia was probably the richest country in the world in terms of GDP per capita (Castles 1988).

The political framework within which social policy developed also set Australia apart from the nations of Europe. Democratic institutions came significantly earlier in the form of universal male suffrage shortly after 1850, and the establishment of parliamentary government and competitive political parties. At the same time the political mobilization of labor through unionization and a viable socialist party for workers was proceeding at a pace that could scarcely be matched in Europe. This became particularly true after a violent depression in the 1890s gave the comparatively affluent Australian worker a new awareness of the vulnerability of being an isolated wage earner. By 1906 socialist parliamentary representation stood at 35 percent in Australia, compared to 10 percent or less of seats in such countries as Britain, Sweden, and most of the continental nations. While not in control of the government, working-class political representatives were clearly in a pivotal position to seek concessions in the form of measures for social protection in an economy exposed to uncontrollable swings in international markets. But what sort of protection?

There were few doubts about the capacities of the Australian state to stand in the way of an activist approach. The fact that the colonial government had already taken the lead in helping create a new nation out of the continental wilderness left no room for the laissez-faire theories of hands-off government prevalent in the British mother country. During the nineteenth century the Australian state had subsidized immigration, secured foreign loans to build the physical necessities for an integrated export economy, and accounted for approximately 40 percent of domestic capital formation between 1860 and 1900. Few Australians could doubt that the government was, and should be, a leading force to address the security concerns of the nation's wage-earning population. By the same token, Australia had been spared the historical experiences that had taught oppressed groups in Europe, as well as rebellious colonials in America, to distrust state power.

In this historical context, the Australian labor movement sought vigorous government intervention to protect and preserve the largely favorable economic conditions that the mass of wage-earners already enjoyed. The great depression of the 1890s had been a traumatic experience; memories of the depression-induced strikes that had devastated both employers and unions were still fresh. At the beginning of the twentieth century—while European nations debated new ideas about social insurance—business and worker representatives in Australia gradually converged in support of a series of measures that would use government power to safeguard more directly their respective desires for economic security. In essence, this meant combining tariff protection for industry with wage protection for workers. A system of compulsory government arbitration in labor disputes set legally binding wage norms designed to assure workers a "living wage." This minimum wage payable for unskilled labor became applicable in all wage awards and was indexed against inflation. At the same time, labor representatives succeeded in gaining immigration controls that prohibited non-whites from permanently entering the country. This helped both to satisfy racist sentiments and prop up wage rates by reducing the potential number of unskilled workers.

Using a strategy of labor market regulation to attain income security carried important implications for the development of social policy. The focal point of income maintenance policy became the adult male worker shielded from external shocks to employment and earning a state-regulated wage sufficient to support a family. (State arbitration boards consistently ruled that women's wages should be lower than men's since they had no dependents to support.) Any idea of a general program of contributory social insurance was overshadowed by the expectation that male wage earners, assured of a living wage through state labor regulations, could make their own provisions against income insecurity through private savings and enrollment in the huge number of Friendly Societies that existed in Australia. This left the problem of providing for persons who were not protected by such a wage system, mainly the elderly and infirm. Public income support programs were therefore oriented toward the destitute, using means tests to establish eligibility for benefits. The results were those typical of all means-tested public assistance programs. The examination of personal financial resources required by such state charity continued to arouse resentment and shame. Benefits financed from general revenues for an isolated category of needy persons—even means-tested pensions for the elderly—remained stingy. This historic pattern of policy development, based on protecting workers' wages rather than establishing contributory social insurance, meant that for decades to come Australia would rank near the bottom of the national charts used by social scientists to compare levels of welfare state spending.

As we have seen, Japan often joins Australia at the bottom of these charts. However, the historically weak development of social insurance as an instrument of income maintenance policy in Japan has quite different roots. These roots extend deep into a cultural history that was markedly different from the experience of European nations and their colonial off-spring in America and Australia. Even before the industrial revolution, European society was distinctive in the world for its dominant pattern of the nonextended, nuclear family, a human grouping especially vulnerable to the insecurities generated by rapid economic change (Laslett and Woll). By contrast, Japan could cushion the impact of industrialization over the last one hundred years with a more extended, intergenerational pattern of family support and employment conditions.

Even though Japan industrialized quite rapidly after the mid-nineteenth century, social insurance as an instrument of income security came late to the nation. A modest health insurance program for workers was begun in the 1920s and extended to the self-employed in 1938. The first national pension program for old age, disability, and survivorship was initiated in 1942 for male factory and mine workers; in 1944 this coverage was extended to office employees and female workers. It seems fair to say that these early efforts were mainly motivated by the desire of Japanese leaders to enhance the physical and social strength of an increasingly militarized population (Maruo). Major development of social insurance programs came only in the post–World War II period and even then coexisted with strong elements of traditional social organization. Thus although three-generation households have been becoming less common in recent years, it was still the case that in the early 1980s, over half of all elderly Japanese were living with a married son or daughter (comparable figures for the United States, Britain, and France are 3, 2, and 9 percent, respectively) (Maruo).

The policy legacy for contemporary Japan has therefore had a peculiarly dual nature. More than any of the other developed nations, Japan entered the postwar period with a largely clean slate in terms of formal social insurance programs. Since existing commitments were small and new programs were slow in building spending momentum, Japanese social security spending consistently ranked low in postwar international comparisons. At the same time Japan entered the postwar period with a heavy legacy from the past in terms of traditional systems of income support within the extended family. Paternalistic relations between employers and employees also remained strong as a carryover from the prewar cultural history of Japan. As we have seen in Chapter Five, postwar Japan took off from this base of managed paternalism to produce a brilliant record of economic growth (registering a sevenfold increase in real per capita income between 1950 and 1980). It was in the context of this rising affluence that the struggle to shape Japanese social insurance took place.

The United States has a longer tradition of democratic politics than any of the other nations we discuss in this chapter, but this probably did more to hinder than promote the introduction of contributory social insurance. The United States lacked the centralized administrative institutions found in any number of European countries at the turn of this century. This reflected a deep popular distrust of government power, which inhibited development of any compulsory programs in Washington to deal with the social insecurity accompanying industrialization. Morever, having witnessed the expansion of Civil War pensions as a kind of political pork barrel in the last quarter of the nineteenth century, many U.S. reformers doubted that a federal government so open to political pressures could responsibly run a coherent social insurance program (Orloff). There was the further problem that America's fragmented structures of political authority and pluralistic system of interest group politics provided an abundance of possible veto power in the states, courts, and Congress for opponents of social insurance. News of social insurance experiments in Europe reached a turn-of-the-century United States in which the counterpoint to a fragmented labor movement suspicious of government power was a strong, self-assertive business community that had succeeded in identifying private enterprise with the tradition of American individualism.

In this setting, social insurance programs of national scope were not only relatively late to arrive, but came imbued with an individualistic rationale, and—paradoxically—were less adaptable through open political processes. So rarely did any general program pass through the many screens of particular interest, and the unease about government power that there was great incentive to leave policy guidelines alone rather than risk further political debate. Once the basic concept of social insurance was accepted, incremental improvements, often of profound significance, passed largely into the hands of program bureaucrats and other policy experts (Derthick).

The movement for social insurance in the United States was represented by the American Association for Labor Legislation, a private pressure group organized in the beginning of this century and led by academicians, social workers, and some civic and labor leaders. Workers' compensation could be clearly shown to be favorable to industrial efficiency, and laws soon were instituted in most states. But this was not viewed by business as social insurance, and reformers seeking more far-reaching sickness, old-age, and unemployment insurance did not find similar support from either business or labor. Leaders of unions were particularly opposed to sickness and unemployment insurance, largely for fear of weakening union influence over workers and increasing workers' dependence on the government. Lacking any political or mass backing, the association found its educational activities frustrated throughout the first third of the twentieth century. The fragmented American system did offer an opportunity for the social insurance lobby to gain a foothold at the state level, and by the end of the 1920s eight states had old-age pension programs, typically with strict eligibility conditions to direct aid only to the neediest. But the competitive subunits of American federalism hindered income support policy more than they advanced it. Unemployment insurance, for example, aroused very little state action because of fears that the insurance contributions would drive businesses into other states without such costs.

Only the Depression and the arrival of the Roosevelt administration created those exceptional circumstances necessary to overcome the inertia. By then unions had reversed their opposition to pensions and unemployment insurance, and mass agitation for free pensions (the Townsend movement) threatened politicians as never before. Roosevelt had already, as governor of New York, become convinced that social insurance offered the necessary alternative to degrading poor-law relief. The essentials of the 1935 Social Security Act were worked out by administrative experts who showed that social insurance could be interpreted within the American liberal tradition of individual self-help. Typical European distinctions between manual and other employees had no place in their perspective, but neither did coherent nationwide planning for income security programs. Only in the contributory old-age pensions were uniform national standards established; conditions and benefits of unemployment insurance and public assistance were largely left to the vagaries of state discretion. Administration policymakers judged health insurance to be politically too controversial for action. As for contributory pensions, emphasis was clearly on the individual's contractual right to an earned benefit. Thus there were no government contributions from general revenue, a low ceiling on the wages from which an individual's contributions could be deducted, a large spread (depending on earnings records) in monthly benefits, and no national floor on minimum benefits. Absence of a national administrative structure had hindered the drawing up of social insurance plans, but the very newness of the enterprise meant that framers of the policy could set up a new administrative apparatus that would be firmly committed to the new insurance doctrine and would insulate the basic policy approach against future interference from pluralistic politics. The doctrine of individually earned insurance clearly separated from inferior, public assistance–type welfare programs became firmly imbedded in both the 1935 Social Security Act and the new Social Security Administration.

While maintaining doctrinal adherence to individually earned benefits and no support from general government revenues, American social insurance in practice nevertheless has changed substantially. In 1939, for example, "unearned" benefits for dependents were introduced, the large fund of individually contributed accounts was abandoned, and pension payments were begun far earlier than could be justified by recipients' contribution records. Yet this major change occasioned little public debate. It was supported by business interests fearful of a large public insurance fund and program bureaucrats and liberals eager to provide more adequate pensions. Major liberalizations occurred in subsequent years, usually with the agreement of both parties and little public controversy, as rapid postwar growth provided seemingly endless financial resources. In practice, the insurance concept has been characterized not by individuals earning their own benefits with their own contributions but by an intergenerational contract in which today's pension benefits are financed entirely by payroll taxes paid by today's workers. Paying the growing social security bill has been politically easier with these less visible taxes than with higher income taxes. Moreover, avoiding subsidies from general revenues has helped maintain the impression of "getting what you paid for" in social security. This doctrine can be found in the history of social insurance in many countries, but it has persisted with particular strength in the United States.

Our brief survey of the introduction of social insurance suggests why it is rather unproductive to debate whether general patterns or national subpatterns are ultimately more important for understanding the choice of income maintenance tools. From a general perspective we can see that social insurance grew in importance everywhere during this century. There has also been a pervasive tendency to shift from a strictly insurance-based relationship between contributions and benefits to more generous attention to benefit adequacy. But within these common trends are different national features. Both the general patterns and the national subpatterns are essential to any full picture of the structured variation that exists.

Contemporary Patterns

Many of the policy differences visible today are related to historical trends. To live in Germany or Sweden, which committed themselves early to contributory social insurance, is to be part of a comprehensive system of public transfers that may seem almost as routine as a paycheck. In countries that embraced income entitlements more hesitantly, such as Australia or the United States, the distinctions between those who have and who have not earned their benefits are sharper, and one's feelings as a recipient might be rather different.

Among all of the industrial nations, the long-term pattern during this century has been one of expanding the ambitions of income security programs. The focus has moved from simply protecting the most vulnerable against destitution to providing a system of income replacement allowing the mass of the working population to maintain their living standards, especially during a newly invented stage of life called retirement (Perrin; Myles 1988). But as we might expect from the discussion of policy legacies, there have been quite important differences within this general pattern.

Although provisions have become more uniform in the post–World War II years, the West German social insurance system consists of a series of administratively separate funds organized by occupational group with benefits based heavily on past economic performance. This approach prevails across much of continental Europe. Social insurance protection is supplemented by a variety of income support measures such as maternity benefits, help with housing costs, family allowances for children, and child support (a supplemental child allowance paid when the support from an absent parent to the child in a one parent family falls below a given level).

In Sweden, the social insurance system covers all citizens more uniformly and aims at providing a high level of income protection more or less equally to all regardless of occupational status or past economic status. A uniform basic pension is paid to all persons from age sixty-five. To this is added a pension benefit related to prior earnings and for those with a limited earnings record an income-tested supplement is automatically attached to the basic pension. The surrounding array of child benefits, housing allowances, and so on are also more broadly available to families and more generous than counterpart programs in continental nations. Sweden's approach is dominated by a strategy of common entitlement whereby all citizens participate in the same programs (while benefit taxation, income-related fees, contributions, and so on vary the extent to which different people are subsidized).

A third general strategy has been to focus income support quite explicitly on programs geared to those with demonstrated economic hardship. This is most clearly the case in Australia, where public pensions and unemployment benefits have traditionally been based on satisfying a test for low income rather than a record of social insurance contributions. In the United States the social security program is the dominant entitlement program that is not targeted on the needy. However, in comparison with West Germany, the U.S. social insurance system offers a more redistributive benefit formula to shore up retirement income of low-wage workers and relatively low level of maximum benefits to avoid any competition with the private pension market that focuses on higher income earners (Esping-Andersen, Rainwater, and Rein). Other parts of the U.S. income transfer system (such as the AFDC public assistance program and food stamps) are even more clearly focused on particular categories of needy persons.

These three strategies based on occupation performance, universal entitlement, or selective support for the needy are obviously only rough approximations of very complex patterns of income maintenance policy that exist within each nation. However, these categories are sufficient to denote major differences in national emphasis when it comes to income transfers. Japan, for example, finally developed its postwar social insurance system in such a way as to fall clearly within the general category of past occupation–based programs.

Amid a period of rapid economic growth, Japanese social reforms in the 1950s and early 1960s established social insurance coverage on a nationwide scale, but with programs clearly divided along lines of employment status. Alongside six smaller specialized public pension funds (for employees in national and local government, public corporations, private schools, maritime trades, and agricultural corporations) are two huge public social insurance programs each covering approximately 45 percent of all households. People's Pensions *(Kokumin Nenkin)* created in 1961 are for all persons (mainly self-employed, including farmers) not covered by one of the employee pension plans. Modest flat-rate contributions are supplemented by a 33 percent government subsidy, and uniform benefits varying only by years of contribution are paid at age sixty-five. The second major system, with a longer history, is the Employee Pension program *(Kosei Nenkin)* covering wage and salary workers in private firms with five or more employees. Earnings-related contributions with a 20 percent government subsidy are used to earn entitlement to earnings-related benefits at age sixty. Benefits per beneficiary have been roughly five times higher than under People's Pensions (Preston and Kono). The lack of uniformity in protection has been accentuated by provisions allowing firms with over one thousand employees, generally the more prosperous industries, to contract out of contributions and benefits beyond a minimum pension level and establish a more generous earnings-related pension system with a 17 percent government subsidy (Lee). All pension contributions are pooled in a reserve fund which, together with funds from the huge postal savings system, is under the discretionary control of government bureaucrats to use for economic development purposes (see Chapter 5). As in the United States, most participants believe their benefits are paid by accumulated contributions, but in fact pensions are largely financed by transfers from current workers; in the Japanese case it is a transfer to retirees who are relatively wealthy since the benefit structure offers more transfers to people with higher past earnings (Noguchi). In this setting, small-scale programs of income-tested public assistance and very modest child allowances for low-income families (since 1972) are a minor part of the Japanese system. By comparison a traditional and very extensive system of lump-sum payments by employers to employees ceasing work is encouraged by favorable tax laws; a person who has been with a firm for thirty-five years (not unusual among successful firms) can typically expect a payment equal to thirty-five to forty-five times his or her monthly salary. In addition a minority of employers, usually larger firms in leading industrial sectors, offer lifetime job security to workers.

Unfortunately there are severe data limitations that make it difficult to compare income transfers actually received by people in different nations. However, where careful research into comparative income statistics has been carried out in recent years, the evidence is consistent with the overall patterns of entitlement, means-testing, and so on that we have been discussing for different nations. Thus a three-nation comparison of family well-being found that in the early 1970s the proportion of all non-aged families receiving some means-tested transfer payments was not greatly different in the United States (7 percent of such families), Sweden (9 percent), or Britain (8 percent). What did differ markedly among the three nations was the

extent to which the bulk of the population with earned income also participated in more entitlement-like public transfers. In Sweden over 90 percent
of non-aged families at every income level received some government transfer payment. In Britain, with a legacy we earlier described as a more minimum subsistence approach to universalism, the percentage was 60 to 77 at
every income level. In the United States, only the bottom sixth of families in
terms of earned income had as many as 50 percent receiving government
transfer payments; above that, participation dropped sharply to around 10
percent or less in middle- and higher-income groups (Rainwater, Rein, and
Schwarz).

The most thorough effort at income comparison has recalculated the
detailed national statistical surveys in a painstaking attempt to derive truly
comparable income data for a limited number of countries (Smeeding,
Torrey, and Rein). The results give us one of the first clear pictures of
income distribution across nations using a common set of definitions and
measurement techniques. In Table 7.2 the official U.S. definition of poverty
is used and translated into a comparable poverty line for seven other developed nations. The focus here is on the *poverty gap* in each country. This gap
is defined as the difference between, on the one hand, the economic resources a family has (before receiving public transfers or paying taxes) and,
on the other hand, minimum income needs for physical subsistence. Minimum income need is defined in terms of the official U.S. poverty line
converted into each nation's currency (using the international purchasing
power parities developed by the OECD) and adjusted for family size (that
is, the poverty line is set proportionately higher in each nation for a family
with two children than one with one child, for a family with two adults than
a family with one adult and one child, and so on). Thus the figures in the
first column show, for different family types, what proportion of the poverty gap is filled by public transfers going to those families in each nation.
The next columns show how much different kinds of transfer programs
contribute to whatever filling of the poverty gap occurs.

Although there are important limitations in the data (which apply to
only one year for each nation between 1979 and 1982), the results provide a
usable overview of basic policy patterns. We see that all the countries more
than fill the aggregate gap between pre-transfer income and basic needs for
elderly families; this does not mean that there are not poor elderly people
in these nations, only that the total resource gap for all such families is more
than filled by total public transfers. For all these countries except Australia
the dominant instrument accomplishing this result is contributory social
insurance, but Britain does least well in this regard. This is probably related
to Britain's historical commitment to spreading minimum flat-rate insurance benefits broadly with relatively less emphasis on earnings-related public transfers. For all nations, the poverty gap remains larger for families
with children than for the elderly, but here there are significant variations

in policy instruments that tell an important story. Those countries that leave the largest poverty gap for families with children—Australia, the United States, and to a lesser extent Canada—are those that have concentrated on income transfers through means-tested programs rather than social insur-

TABLE 7.2 ROLE OF PUBLIC TRANSFERS IN REDUCING THE POVERTY GAP AMONG CHILDREN AND THE ELDERLY, 1979

Family Type and Country	Percentage of Poverty Gap Reduced by Public Transfers[a]	Percentage of Total Poverty Gap Reduction Accounted for by:			
		Social Insurance	Means-tested Program	Child Allowances	Total
Families with children					
Australia	0.71	—	87	13	100
Britain	1.17	38	38	24	100
Canada	0.85	38	48	14	100
Germany	1.06	68	11	21	100
Norway	1.05	86	3	11	100
Sweden	1.76	52	37	11	100
Switzerland	0.91	93	7	—	100
United States	0.65	29	71	—	100
Single-parent families					
Australia	0.71	—	88	12	100
Britain	0.90	15	63	22	100
Canada	0.75	19	69	12	100
Germany	0.84	67	16	18	100
Norway	1.13	83	4	13	100
Sweden	2.03	45	45	10	100
Switzerland	0.78	92	8	—	100
United States	0.58	7	93	—	100
Elderly families					
Australia	1.30	—	100	—	100
Britain	1.10	91	9	—	100
Canada	1.61	94	6	—	100
Germany	1.56	99	1	—	100
Norway	1.24	99	1	—	100
Sweden	2.42	94	6	—	100
Switzerland	1.92	95	5	—	100
United States	1.48	93	7	—	100

NOTE   [a]This rate is calculated by dividing total public transfers to the pretax/pretransfer poor by the total poverty gap.

SOURCE   Timothy Smeeding, Barbara Torrey, and Martin Rein, "Patterns of Income and Poverty, The Economic Status of Children and the Elderly in Eight Countries," in Palmer, Smeeding, and Torrey, eds., *The Vulnerable* (Washington: Urban Institute, 1988), p. 111.

ance strategies. Reliance on social insurance may not in and of itself guarantee closing the poverty gap (see, for example, the figures for single-parent families in Germany and Switzerland), but countries that succeed in filling the income-to-needs gap for families with children clearly use social insurance as a major component in policy patterns linking such entitlements with means-tested programs and child allowances (Britain, Germany, Norway, Sweden).

Here as in other policy areas the choice of instruments is not simply a technical, value-neutral problem of finding the most efficient means to accomplish given ends. Means shape ends.

It is reasonable to think that the spread of entitlement-type benefits among many persons, almost as a right of citizenship, creates a much smaller constituency for an antiwelfare backlash, especially compared to the "us-them" patterns that develop in nations where means-tested benefits are concentrated on a small and distinctively poor fraction of the population.

WHO PAYS, WHO BENEFITS?
DISTRIBUTION

It would be simplistic to think that there is any single clear egalitarian goal associated with income maintenance policy. Some income support programs do pay particular attention to the needs of the poor and, in that sense, are devoted to an egalitarian ideal. But many programs, particularly in the area of social insurance, are intended to meet the income security problems of people before they fall below any given poverty line. Furthermore, it is never easy to determine who pays for the costs of income transfers. Financing transfers through general revenues is considered by some to be more egalitarian than the use of payroll taxes earmarked for social security, but this conclusion rests on at least two assumptions that are difficult to prove: (1) that general revenues, especially income taxes, are actually distributed according to the ability to pay—that is, they are progressive; and (2) that income support programs detached from their own earmarked tax sources, such as social security contributions, could compete successfully with all the other spending programs that bid for shares of general revenues.

Thus, although government income transfers clearly are redistributing immense sums of money, it would be wrong to think that this redistribution necessarily results in, or was ever intended to be, a thoroughly *egalitarian* redistribution of income.

Taking a broad historical view, there appears to be little doubt that absolute poverty—the want of economic means for basic physical survival—has been greatly reduced in the countries covered in this volume (Kelley). This is due mainly to the high levels of economic growth in the Western nations during the twentieth century, but it is not unreasonable to think that expanding public transfers have helped ensure that the dividends of such growth have been more widely shared than they might otherwise have been.

Statistical studies of income inequality in advanced capitalist societies for the period 1975–80 suggest that the political complexion of governments has mattered in terms of distributional consequences (Muller 1989). During this economically troubled period, countries with strong socialist parties have, other things being equal, experienced a smaller gap in disposable income between the richest and poorest income groups (with no apparent effect on the gap between the upper- and middle-income groups). Likewise, in contrast to those (mainly Scandinavian) nations, the government strength of conservative parties has been unrelated to the size of the disposable income gap between rich and poor but appears to have a very strong positive effect enlarging the gap between upper- and middle-income groups. (Regardless of partisan control of government, smaller trade-dependent economies are more egalitarian in their income profiles than large democracies that are less dependent on international trade.)

And yet taking a longer historical perspective, there is also general agreement among in-depth national studies that since the end of World War II the overall shape of household income distribution has not undergone a massive transformation. Amid a general rise in real income standards at all income levels, the differentials between levels have not undergone a radical egalitarian shift. This is a paradoxical result. Although immense sums are transferred in any one year and do raise many low-income families above poverty levels, the overall shape of the distribution of final incomes (after taxes and transfers) does not appear to have changed greatly during the postwar years in the countries for which reliable information is available (Levy; Roberti; Sawyer).

Three reasons for this paradox lie close at hand. First, income maintenance policies—and, indeed, the entire tax-transfer shuffle of disposable income—are only partly aimed at producing a greater equality in income distribution, however that term is defined. Providing income security frequently means securing differences in living standards acquired throughout the course of people's working lives. Hence, insuring against economic insecurity often means insuring for inequality. Second, government transfer payments, large as they are in every country, are still small and relatively inflexible compared to the immense scale and adaptations of a national economy. In a sense, income maintenance policies are always in the position of playing "catch-up" against the power of national economies to generate inequalities. Finally, the redistributive effect of income maintenance policies has been subject to a law of diminishing returns as coverage has become more comprehensive. At the early stages of welfare state development—when only a relatively few people may be receiving benefits and a few people paying—a comparatively small amount of income transfers may have rather large effects on the shape of income distribution. At later stages—when huge numbers of people are both receiving benefits and paying taxes—many of the overall redistributive effects may be mutually offsetting (Klein 1980).

Even within a stable or at most slowly changing overall profile of income distribution, there can be significant shifts in the relative shares and positions of particular groups. As we noted at the outset of this chapter, the income maintenance policies of modern welfare states make little effort to shape the primary distribution of income produced by occupational and earning differentials of the "private" market. But income transfer programs can and do affect the disposable income of people over and beyond whatever distribution has been decreed by the labor market. In recent years, as a demographic aging of the population has gathered pace in all developed nations, new interest has focused on distributional choices regarding two groups generally outside the purview of labor markets: children and the elderly.

A common interpretation of recent trends is that government policies have benefited the elderly relative to the young. The more extreme charge can also be heard that improvements in the economic security of the elderly have been occurring at the expense of children, in large part because of the greater voting power and political clout of the elderly compared to the latter group (Preston). A comparative examination of the economic status of the two age groups throws considerable doubt on this argument as a general description of distributional tendencies in countries with aging populations. Table 7.3 presents information from a recent period for the eight nations where comparable income statistics have been developed. Again the official U.S. poverty line is used as a need standard. While there are problems in using this or any other absolute measure of low income, the overall picture and ranking of countries would not change appreciably if, instead of the U.S. poverty measure, we substituted a relative poverty standard such as the proportion of families falling below one-half the median income in each nation (Smeeding, Torrey, and Rein, p. 96).

There is no general tendency for all children to experience higher poverty rates than all elderly persons in all or even most of these developed nations. The figures show Australia and the United States have quite high rates of child poverty (by 1987 in the U.S. the figure was up from 17 percent to 20 percent), but both nations also have comparatively high incidences of poverty among the elderly as well. Children in single-parent families have a hard time escaping poverty, but so too do elderly persons living alone in a number of countries. Sweden has best succeeded in preventing high poverty rates for either age group. Britain stands out for its high rate of poverty among the elderly, even those who are not living alone.

Of course there are many factors that might account for these differences among nations, but it turns out that policy choices—the structures of income maintenance programs that have been created—seem to play the largest role in determining the patterns of poverty both within and among these nations. Thus there is no consistent relationship between the relative size of the elderly population or the child population and the age-specific poverty patterns in each country. Family structures differ among the nations, but both Sweden and Norway have higher proportions of children in one-parent families than the United States and much lower child poverty rates. The United States is more racially and ethnically diverse but this does not fully explain the broad poverty differences among nations; the child poverty rate among United States white children only is still high (11.4 percent) compared with the general population in a number of other countries. Nor does the degree of income inequality within these nations correlate strongly with poverty rates.

In the end, to understand the distributional outcomes within and between age groups we need to understand the differences in policy patterns and their surrounding politics. The high minimum benefits and broad entitlement approach of Sweden is consistent with filling the poverty gap and lowering poverty rates among not only children and the elderly in general but also for the most marginal income groups within each age group (children in one-parent families, elderly living alone). The more minimum, uniform level of income security in Britain left a number of children and many more elderly persons in poverty. Whereas in Germany income support is oriented more to reflect the differentials of occupational status, overall poverty rates can be fairly low, but those who are in the economically marginal conditions of single-parent families or elderly persons alone may find themselves left behind. The two nations with the highest poverty rates for children—Australia and the United States—have relied

TABLE 7.3 PERCENTAGE OF CHILDREN, ELDERLY AND ALL PERSONS IN POVERTY,* BY FAMILY TYPE AND COUNTRY, 1979–82

	Children			Elderly				All Persons *(Percent)*
Country	Single-Parent Families *(Percent)*	Two-Parent Families *(Percent)*	All Children *(Percent)*	Male Living Alone *(Percent)*	Female Living Alone *(Percent)*	Married Couple *(Percent)*	All Elderly *(Percent)*	
Australia	65	12	17	40	48	6	19	13
Britain	39	10	11	55	70	24	37	12
Canada	39	7	10	6	9	2	5	7
Germany	35	5	8	19	24	9	15	8
Norway	22	4	8	32	31	0	19	9
Sweden	9	5	5	7	3	0	2	6
Switzerland	13	4	5	9	11	1	6	6
United States	51	9	17	26	31	8	16	13

NOTE *Poverty defined in terms of the official U.S. poverty line converted to other currencies using OECD purchasing power parities and adjusted for family size.
SOURCE John Palmer, Timothy Smeeding, and Barbara Torrey, eds., *The Vulnerable* (Washington: Urban Institute, 1988), adapted from Tables 5.2, 5.6, and 5.8.

most heavily on means-tested, selective strategies for providing income security for children. Thus a greater targeting of income maintenance resources on particular categories of needy people does not necessarily imply more adequate income support for those who are assisted. In fact, the opposite more often seems to be the case. Countries with more comprehensive programs of income maintenance also seem to do the most to help raise those at the lower income levels.

Consistent with these generalizations is the fact that the one universal entitlement program in the United States—social security—is also the income security program with the greatest impact on reducing poverty. It is largely because of the continued improvement in the real value of social insurance benefits in the postwar period that the economic status of the low-income elderly in America has so greatly improved, particularly since the mid-1960s. Dependent only on private income, some 47 percent of American elderly would have been poor in 1986; after government transfers, mainly through social insurance, the poverty rate was actually only about 12 percent. To be sure, significant numbers of American children do benefit from aspects of the social security program (approximately three million children as survivors of insured workers or children of disabled workers). But the fact remains that income support programs for American children are essentially categorical (means-tested, confined to certain categories of the poor, and contingent on public judgments of the worthiness of parents mainly outside the labor force) while income support for the elderly occurs through a basically universal approach transcending income classes. It is this difference in policy structure—and not some general tendency for aging societies to transfer income to the old at the expense of the young—that underlies the peculiarly American divergence in poverty rates for these two age groups after 1979 (the year of comparison shown in Table 7.3).

Lacking better comparative data, it is difficult to define with precision the distribution of benefits and costs in income maintenance policy. But the problem goes beyond mere matters of technical measurement. The deeper normative problem involved in constructing a net balance sheet to show who pays and who benefits is the most revealing fact of all about income maintenance policy. Income security is distinguished from other policy areas by a common unit of measurement—cash—that should, in theory, facilitate a clear identification of distribution choices. However, real-world fact is that tax and transfer programs always interact with each other in complex ways. The very concept of costs and benefits is constructed out of social perceptions of reality. It is not self-evident that a taxpayer, even one receiving no direct government transfer payment in return for taxes paid, is a net loser—considering the costs one might otherwise incur to support aged parents or the problems of social disorder that the taxpayer may have to live with—and bequeath to his or her children—because of the economic insecurity of others.

INNOVATION IN A PERIOD OF SCARCITY
RESTRAINTS AND INNOVATION

After a long postwar period of economic growth and relative calm in the expansion of income maintenance policies, the policies again became a focus of major controversy in the 1970s and 1980s. The specific arguments are complicated, but the general reason for growing controversy is not: new perceptions of economic scarcity in relation to the growing cost of government transfers. Those charged with economic management worried about "disincentive effects," social insurance officials projected the higher costs of supporting an aging population, working-age people became sensitive to the effects of social security taxes on their take-home pay—and all formed a new constituency for questioning the momentum of income maintenance policy. It is a constituency that scarcely existed in the more confident and economically buoyant 1950s and 1960s; now it can be found in every developed nation (Rosa).

Harmonizing Economic and Social Policy

The central issues are encompassed by the term *harmonization*. Harmonization refers to the reconciliation of income maintenance policy with the perceived needs of economic management in ways that do not incur disastrous political costs.

Prominent harmonization problems can be considered in four interrelated categories. First is the need to reconcile income maintenance policy with the need for *flexible economic management*. Early in the adoption of Keynesian economics, there was considerable discussion of using government transfers countercyclically to help stabilize economic fluctuations. Forms of income maintenance such as unemployment insurance have an automatic stabilizing effect by increasing during recessions (thus adding to aggregate demand) and receding during economic upturns. But the largest categories of income maintenance policy—pensions, health insurance, and so on—are not so automatic. No economic managers have seriously considered reducing pension checks or health insurance payments in order to stabilize the economy. Increasing transfer entitlements may be economically justified and politically easy in bad times (as long as higher taxes can be deferred), but decreasing entitlements in good times is everywhere regarded as politically impossible.

The main problem facing economic managers is one of controlling the inbuilt momentum of transfer spending. During the 1950s and 1960s, one nation after another adopted some formula for indexing social insurance benefits to price changes, wage changes, or a combination of the two. Today income maintenance programs have become so prominent in every nation's budget that it is very difficult to make fiscal adjustments without dealing in some way with this sector of spending. Politically, it is unwise to try and alter existing entitlements to transfer payments; economically, it is difficult to find any maneuvering room in national budgets without touching them.

A second and related problem in harmonizing economic and social policy arises from the *demographic aging* of the population. Virtually all developed nations can expect to experience a growth in the proportion of older people in the population during the coming decades. Under existing social insurance commitments and expectations surrounding social spending for the aged, these larger cohorts of retiring baby boomers will represent a major claim on economic resources.

The third problem of harmonization involves *disincentive effects,* a worry that government income transfers have grown to the point of inhibiting national economic performance. Economists, particularly in the United States, have argued that the existing system of income redistribution produces significant disincentives to work, save, and invest (Danziger, Haveman and Plotnick). The result may be to retard economic growth, particularly if poorly designed government interventions misallocate scarce economic resources from more productive to less productive sectors.

The evidence on many of these points is inconclusive. Disincentive effects clearly exist but efforts to study the magnitude of effects on work effort, savings, and investment have produced mixed and generally modest results (Haveman). Weighing against the economic costs of income transfer are also certain gains to the economy and society more generally that need to be taken into account—for example, improvements in human capital, reductions in economic uncertainty, greater social cohesion, and so on. Nor does the scale of government transfer spending and redistribution correlate neatly with higher or lower rates of economic growth among developed nations in recent decades (Burtless; Navarro).

Likewise demographic developments, while important as a constraint on policy, should not be exaggerated to suggest an unmanageable future. Demographic projections suggest that the total dependency ratio (the population under age fifteen plus those sixty-five and over compared to the working age population) will not change significantly in the decades ahead. Moreover, in terms of workers available to support the elderly, the demographic future for a country like the United States in 2020 is no different from the situation already prevailing in Sweden in 1980, and as we have seen, this situation has not precluded the virtual elimination of poverty for the elderly and children in that nation.

In other words the future of income maintenance policy, like its past, will depend not on abstract laws of socioeconomic development but on the political dynamics and coalitions that produce policy choices. The problem of coordinating income security programs with economic policies poses a serious challenge for policymakers in democratic regimes. Income maintenance policy constitutes a political system of income distribution outside the market discipline of mixed capitalist economies. Does this represent an impending "crisis of the welfare state" as economic forces of production clash with social demands for redistribution (OECD 1981)? Or does the challenge amount to a modest disequilibrium pointing toward a new round of piecemeal adjustments? For some clues we can consider the actual responses of various countries.

The Crisis in Practice

The generic problem of the welfare state may be stated as follows: First, government must be capable of disciplining private market forces; then, the government must be capable of disciplining itself. Since the mid-1970s, a search for self-discipline has become the abiding theme in many countries—without leading to the dismantling of major income maintenance programs. As Tables 7.1 and 7.4 suggest the general trend in more recent years has been a slowing down in the rate of spending increases that characterized social security programs in the 1960s and early 1970s. This slower growth has continued into the 1980s.

The overall tendency has been one of "tinkering" with the gears of income maintenance policy without scrapping the basic machinery. In most developed countries, this tinkering has taken the form of avoiding exten-

TABLE 7.4 ANNUAL GROWTH IN SOCIAL SECURITY SPENDING, 1965–81

	Percentage Growth		
	1965–70	*1970–75*	*1975–81*
Australia	5.3	15.6	2.8
Austria	6.4	5.8	4.6
Belgium	9.1	10.5	5.1
			(1975–80)
Britain	5.3	6.3	3.9
Canada	11.5	12.9	3.3
Denmark	9.0	6.6	4.5
Finland	10.7	9.5	5.5
France	5.0	6.6	7.4
Germany	5.5	8.6	2.0
Italy	8.2	6.5	3.9
Japan	10.4	12.3	8.6
Netherlands	11.6	8.3	4.5
Norway	15.3	8.0	6.2
Sweden	10.2	9.6	4.4
Switzerland	8.9	10.4	2.7
			(1975–79)
United States	9.3	9.9	3.7
Average	9.4	9.2	4.6

SOURCE Therborn, G. and Roebroek, J. "The Irreversible Welfare State," *International Journal of Health Services*, Vol. 16, No. 3, 1986, Table 5, p. 328.

sions in coverage or introduction of costly new programs, adjusting downward the indices by which transfer benefits are increased, and trimming the imbalance between future benefits and revenues (Simanis; Copeland; OECD, 1988a).

In Britain the Thatcher government carried through a number of measures aimed at restraining the growth in public spending but stopped well short of attacking the basic structure of income security programs (Krieger 1987). The basis for annual updating in the value of social insurance benefits was altered to provide a less than full adjustment for price increases. Earnings-related components to basic unemployment and sickness benefits under national insurance were abolished. Eligibility conditions for unemployment benefits and public assistance were made more restrictive. As unemployment lingered at record-high postwar levels, new programs for unemployed youth cut cash transfer payments but sought to guarantee them, as well as all persons unemployed more than six months, access to government retraining and work-experience services. Public sector housing experienced substantial spending cuts, representing a shift from direct government provision of council housing to income-related supplements for poor families under the social security program. On the whole these changes left social security spending rising more slowly than would have otherwise been the case (up 28 percent in real terms between 1979 and 1985). At the same time there is evidence that income transfer programs also have done much to continue checking the increased inequality that would otherwise have escalated under the pressure of market forces (O'Higgins 1985; Judge).

In Sweden, the non-Social Democratic governments first elected in 1976 and reelected in 1979 proceeded more cautiously, but by the early 1980s they too had begun to tinker with the gears of automatic growth in the nation's elaborate system of income transfers. In 1981 the government instituted an adjustment to the basic index for calculating almost all transfer payments; the effect was to withhold increases in benefits due to higher prices insofar as such price increases were caused by higher energy costs or indirect taxation.

Other austerity measures favored by Swedish conservatives have included higher contributions from workers for unemployment insurance, reduced sickness cash benefits from 90 percent to between 60 to 80 percent of prior earnings, and reintroduction of a two-day waiting period for receipt of such benefits. The Social Democrats won office in 1982 and remained in power throughout the rest of the 1980s, profiting greatly from charges that their opponents sought to dismantle the Swedish welfare state. However, the Social Democratic leadership itself responded to the tighter economic conditions by arguing for a strategy of "consolidation" as opposed to either dismantling old or introducing major new social welfare programs. In practice this has meant withholding any new money and requiring that social reforms be financed by reconstructing existing programs. Thus some small improvements in transfer benefits were made (higher child allowances for families with three or more children); other ideas aroused too much opposition and were dropped (the introduction of fees for hospital maternity and proposed income-testing for certain widows' benefits); still other restrictive measures have succeeded (the reduction of eligibility and benefit levels for part-time pensions). As a result, the 1980s saw Swedish social expenditure continue to rise but not accelerate as no major improvements in benefits occurred (Olsson).

In France the 1980s provided an interesting test case for welfare state development under an explicitly Socialist series of governments following twenty-three years of rule by a center-right political majority. During its first two years in office the new Mitterrand government hoped for a burst of economic growth (see Chapter Five) to finance a host of expanded benefits. Child allowances, housing allocations, and old-age pension minimum benefits were raised substantially (the latter by 62 percent in two years). The retirement age was reduced to sixty. When this economic growth failed to materialize, the Socialist government reverted to the kind of marginal economizing measures familiar in any number of other welfare states in the 1980s (Ross). In the name of promoting profitability in business, the government raised social insurance contributions proportionately more on workers than employers. Growth in the purchasing power of social benefits was cut back and more vigorous cost controls reined in expenditures on the margins of different income maintenance and other social programs. Unemployment benefits were restructured to separate insurance-based benefits from a less generous unemployment allowance paid from general revenues. As the government pushed its strategy for economic modernization, and unemployment in traditional industries (steel, coal, shipbuilding, among others) rose after 1984, new schemes were initiated for training programs, job creation, early retirement, and youth employment at subminimum wages. While Mitterrand continued to hold the presidency for the Socialists, a new center-right coalition government in 1986–88 proceeded in the same direction of marginal trimming.

By the end of the 1980s French social security was facing the largest deficits in its history while there was little evidence of popular support for any major retrenchment in social spending. All the contending political parties lived in hopes that committees of experts and bipartisan commissions might prepare public opinion for a more affordable social insurance system.

West Germany has displayed a considerable commitment to holding down public spending, moving from the top ranks of welfare state spenders in the 1950s to the middle ranks in the 1970s and 1980s (Katzenstein 1987). The first major step in this direction came with the economic crisis of the mid-1970s. It was then that the Social Democratic government under Helmut Schmidt shifted from a pro–social reform stance to a strategy of public spending restraint and (like the Swedish Social Democrats and French Socialist government later in the 1980s) consolidation of existing approaches rather than initiation of major new reforms. Generous pension increases based on optimistic economic forecasts in the early 1970s were gradually cut back as automatic pension increases were decoupled from changes in prevailing wage rates. Lower rates of economic growth combined with sharply higher levels of unemployment. Eligibility for unemployment benefits was narrowed, the value of unemployment benefits and retraining services was diminished, and pressures on recipients to take less desirable job offers were increased.

The second major step occurred with the 1983 victory of the center-right coalition of Christian Democrats and Free Democratic parties. Through the remainder of the 1980s, the government of Helmut Kohl continued the same no-growth, consolidation approach with even greater rigor. Spending restraint in income maintenance programs generally hit lower income groups the hardest, while the proportion of recipients on long-term welfare support increased. The indexation of pension benefits was changed from gross earnings to net earnings. The effect of this seemingly minor adjustment will be to progressively reduce the growth rate of benefits as social security contributions rates increase. With those on the Social Democratic left and Green (environmentalist) party arguing for a universal approach of uniform income security coverage and those on the political right urging a more selective, means-tested targeting of resources, the central consensus in Germany upheld the basic structure of segmented social insurance based on occupational status (Markovits and Halfmann; Katzenstein 1987). Roughly the same strategy of spending restraint, pro-market industrial adjustments, and a trimming of fragmented programs dividing recipients along occupation lines characterized center-right governments in the Netherlands during the 1980s (Braun). As a result, Germany and the Netherlands have stood out as the two OECD nations where real social spending grew more slowly than the economy (measured by Gross Domestic Product) during much of the last ten years (Alber; O'Higgins 1988).

Japanese income maintenance policy, like other welfare-oriented domestic policy initiatives, has followed a somewhat erratic course, expanding vigorously as pressures threatening the ruling party system's long preeminence have mounted and decreasing as pressures subside and financing problems take center stage (Calder). During the 1960s Japan's complex structure of differential pension coverage was put into place amid acrimonious controversy among the political parties and occupational interests. Demands for improvement culminated in the early 1970s when the government responded by declaring 1973 "the first year of welfare in Japan" and initiating major boosts in pension benefits, free medical care for the elderly,

and higher standards for public assistance and child allowances. Unfortunately it was also at this time that the OPEC oil-crisis ushered in a long
period of slower economic growth in Japan; as the government put the
finishing touches on reforms creating a strong momentum for higher social
spending, the first signs of a postwar decline in Japan's economic growth
rate began to appear. Between 1971 and 1981 social security spending as a
percentage of Gross National Income more than doubled from 6 percent to
13.5 percent, the bulk of the increase being due to pensions and health
care. With worries about the continued growth of the government deficit,
the approaching depletion of the pension reserve fund and an aging population projecting vastly higher state spending for social security (doubling
to 25 percent of GNI in the year 2000 and 31 percent in 2010), Japan's
conservative government slowly took action in the 1980s (Lee; Maruo).
Health insurance contributions and cost-sharing by patients were increased
significantly, albeit from a very low base (the patient's share rose from about
$1.50 per day of hospitalization to 10 percent of cost up to a maximum of
$200 per month). In 1982 the free medical care system for the elderly,
begun in 1973, was eliminated. By far the greatest challenge to the government has been one of moderating the looming financial imbalance as much
larger numbers of Japanese reach old age and public pension system commitments from the 1970s mature. Government policy calls for gradual changes
that will only partially offset these forces but that should help reduce the
drain on government budget resources. In 1986 public pension programs
were integrated to the extent of offering every pensioner a minimum basic
pension regardless of employment status; above this more leeway for
earnings-related benefits will be offered to the private sector and by 1995
financing will switch from the current modified pension reserve to a direct
pay-as-you-go system. Of greater financial significance is that over the years
1990 to 2010 the eligible age for receiving pensions will be raised from 60
to 65 (that is, Employee pensions will match the age for People's pensions)
and contributions will be gradually raised. Even so, these changes are projected to reduce the cost of public pension benefits (as a share of national
income) from only 13.8 percent to 12.6 percent in the year 2000 and from
17.1 percent to 15.3 percent in 2010—compared to 4.8 percent in 1981
(Noguchi). Within these totals, the basic structure of income security programs divided along occupational class lines shows little sign of changing.

Like the Japanese record of the 1970s and 1980s, recent Australian
experience is striking testimony to the enduring power of policy legacies
amid economic constraints. After twenty-three years out of power, the Labor party finally won office in 1972 and pledged, under its new leader
Gough Whitlam, to a vigorous program of social welfare reform bearing a
somewhat universalistic, Scandinavian flavor. Some benefit improvements
had already begun under the electorally hard-pressed rightist coalition
government, but the Labor government now pushed for much larger in-

creases in pensions, unemployment and sickness benefits, and further liberalizations in the means-testing that pervaded Australian income maintenance policy. A national health service (Medibank) was created, a new cash benefit for supporting mothers was introduced, and plans laid for the nation's first contributory and earnings-related public pensions. In the brief span of three years after 1972, social expenditures (though still low by OECD standards) shot up from 13 percent to 19 percent of Gross Domestic Product (Castles 1988). Just as these spending increases were being implemented, the international economic crisis precipitated by OPEC oil-price increases began to hit Australia, devastating the optimistic economic assumptions on which the Whitlam reforms had been based.

With inflation and unemployment running at the highest rates in forty years and economic growth almost flat, the Whitlam government was dismissed in late 1975 and replaced by the rightist coalition under Malcolm Fraser. Pursuing a clear-cut monetarist policy, the new government launched a vigorous attack on public spending that included abolition of Medibank and a number of other Whitlam reforms. In practice, spending cuts were typically offset by the additional costs of higher levels of social dependency produced by rising unemployment and economic stagnation in the years 1976 to 1983.

The years following 1983 were crucial for reaffirming the Australian social policy tradition. With inflation down from 15 to 10 percent but unemployment doubled to 10 percent of the labor force, the Fraser government was replaced in that year by a new Labor government. The fact is that many within the labor movement had never embraced the more universalist reforms of the Whitlam era, preferring instead the historic approach of regulating the primary distribution of income rather than contributing to comprehensive public programs of income redistribution (Castles 1987). During the remainder of the 1980s, the Labor government reaffirmed this preference through its policy actions (with the one exception of reinstituting universal health insurance under the new name of Medicare). Pledging not to increase taxation, public spending, or the deficit as a percentage of GDP, the Labor government immediately introduced an assets test as a component of the means-test for receipt of old-age pensions. Previously universal pensions for persons over 70 were also made subject to an income test. In 1987 family allowances, the country's one existing universal transfer benefit, were made subject to a means test to restrict eligibility to low-income families. Through these and other steps, the Labor government pursued its goal of targeting income maintenance benefits on the poor and held down such spending below the rate of increase in GDP and public expenditures as a whole (Jamrozik). Thus by the end of the 1980s, Australia's approach to income transfers remained flat-rate, income-tested, pegged at subsistence levels, and financed from general taxation. Unlike all other OECD welfare states (with the exception of New Zealand), Australia had no contributory social insurance linking benefits to contributions or income entitlements to prior income. And with income maintenance programs limited to a needy subpopulation set apart from middle-class taxpayers (who pay the bills but are excluded from benefits), Australia remained at the bottom ranks of OECD tables on social welfare spending.

Recent developments in the United States are in some ways the most interesting of all. We have seen the tendency for major social policy initiatives to occur later, and subsequent expansions to occur more hesitantly, in the United States than in other developed democracies. Yet, in the past ten years, American policymakers have found it particularly difficult to restrain income maintenance policy in the light of changing economic conditions. Attempts by Presidents Ford, Carter, and Reagan to trim even small portions of the social security program encountered floods of political opposition and were quickly abandoned. (Among the proposals were a 5 percent ceiling on cost-of-living adjustments for social security benefits under Ford, a cutback in some dependents' benefits under Carter, and a reduction in future benefits for early retirees under Reagan.)

Particularly during its first four years, the Reagan administration was somewhat more successful in cutting back those programs for low-income persons that lay outside the social security entitlement system. During the 1981–84 period, Congress enacted 8 percent cuts in the projected costs of means-tested income transfer programs (the administration had proposed 28 percent cuts) and 43 percent reductions in expected costs of other low-income programs (social services, public employment, compensatory education, and so on) as opposed to Reagan proposals for 60 percent cuts (Palmer and Sawhill). Still, these changes generally represented a tightening of eligibility requirements to focus resources on the neediest rather than the working poor. Even the most ardent White House advocates of a Reagan revolution were eventually forced to admit that there was little public support for a wholesale dismantling of welfare state programs in the United States (Stockman). In 1988 a bipartisan political coalition enacted a major reform in public assistance based on a consensus that income support, especially for younger persons and single parents, needed to be combined with work requirements, training, and day-care services. How these federal requirements would actually be implemented was left to a good deal of state government discretion in the 1990s.

All of these developments were a reflection of the inherited presumptions underlying income maintenance policy in the United States and the historically clear demarcation between social insurance and welfare programs. So thoroughly has the concept of contributory "insurance" benefits permeated the politics of social security that any alterations in the program in the name of economic policy—even alterations involving cutbacks to generous benefits not payable until the next century—arouse severe complaints about tampering with individually earned rights to income. By contrast, public assistance programs enjoy no such legitimacy based on claims of individual equity and rights, and this small portion of income maintenance spending has proven much more vulnerable to demands for cuts. In effect, the nation's largest antipoverty program—social security—has remained politically untouchable even in a more conservative, budget-cutting era; others in the poverty population who are not aged have not been so well protected and have had to bear a disproportionately large share of the economizing pressures.

Given the immense political constraints on any changes in social insurance programs in the United States, policymakers have frequently felt compelled to resort to the rhetoric of "crisis" as a device to force change. Since the mid-1970s, in the United States perhaps more than in any other nation, the policy debate has tended to revolve around a series of impending crises in social security financing. This appears to relate less to the actual state of social insurance accounts in the United States vis-à-vis other countries than to the political imperatives facing anyone attempting to tamper with social security spending amidst a policy psychology of individually earned rights.

It was in such a crisis atmosphere that a bipartisan commission and political negotiating team put together a major social security reform package in 1983. Like that of other developed countries, the United States social insurance system has faced a short-term financial problem (stagflation and the problem of paying for benefits geared to keep pace with higher prices out of revenues from wage contributions and taxes that have not risen as fast as expected) and a long-term financial problem (entitlement commitments to a proportionately larger elderly population as baby boomers retire). The 1983 reforms sought to address both problems without generating controversy or even open public debate. Current pension beneficiaries were protected from any major cutbacks (to help with immediate finances, a one-time delay in a scheduled cost of living increase was imposed, and one-half of social security benefits going to the richest 15 percent of retirees were made subject to income taxation). Other changes were of longer term significance. Starting in the year 2000, the age for acquiring full social security benefits will gradually rise from 65 to 67 years. To build up a reserve fund that will help pay for retiring Baby Boomers after 2015, an increase in worker and employer contributions was pushed forward to the years 1988 and 1990. Fearful of a public backlash that could result from charges either of doing nothing or of tampering with social security entitlements, Republican and Democratic leaders in Washington enacted these reforms by severely restricting congressional debate and public discussion (Light).

In reviewing the record of innovation among the developed nations as a whole, one finds that the general tendency in recent years has been an attempt to adjust or fine tune the inherited structures of income maintenance policy to new perceptions of economic scarcity. Contribution rates have been raised, projected benefit growth trimmed, eligibility tightened, politically vulnerable programs cut at the margins, employment emphasized over income support—especially for the younger working-age population. Nowhere in the developed OECD nations is it possible to find evidence of any major dismantling of the basic policy structures. To supporters of the welfare state model that has developed in this century, this commitment to incremental change may be a hopeful sign. To critics, it is a confirmation of the political infirmities that prevent major policy adjustments corresponding with economic rationality. However one evaluates this situation, it is clear that the gradual growth of income maintenance policies has redistributed significant amounts of economic resources without posing a stark or ultimate political choice as to what is the "right" amount or purpose of the redistribution. Such a bald confrontation on the issue of redistribution would have the most unsettling political consequences in any nation. Indeed, in considering the total population of rich and poor democracies, there is evidence through time that it is progress in reducing income inequality, and not economic development as such, that is most important in preserving the stability of democratic institutions (Muller 1988). Critics of welfare state transfers face the reality that income maintenance policies have themselves become part of the prevailing distribution of income within developed nations. Any effort at major change will now be widely regarded as a fundamental venture into income redistribution.

* * * * *

Income maintenance policy is a good example of structured variation on comparative public policy. Each nation has clearly crossed the border between public and private distributions of income, some more hesitantly, some more decisively, but no country has tried entirely to replace market-determined distributions of purchasing power. Common policy tools in social insurance and means-tested assistance are used, but in different combinations and with different emphases. The shift in insurance concepts from individual equity to social adequacy has been a long-term trend in every Western democracy in this century. But the United States has maintained a stronger belief in individually earned benefits than have other nations, and countries with the strongest base of working-class politics seem to make the greatest efforts at conscious redistribution. Still, no government transfer system is committed to thoroughgoing egalitarianism with uniform outcomes. This is because the normal course of democratic politics in advanced capitalist nations permits no easy or final choices between those who claim a right to differential rewards and those who claim a need for fairer distribution, between economic and social conceptions of rational policy. Thus income maintenance policy, broadly understood, endorses neither equality nor inequality as the supreme principle of social organization.

The result is an ongoing series of ambiguous compromises between competing values. Today's policy compromises, no less than those accompanying the introduction of social insurance a hundred years ago, involve a complex interplay of economic and political forces. And for tomorrow, as more economic resources are allocated through the political mechanism of government transfer policies rather than through the traditional market mechanisms of capitalist production, the fundamental question remains the same: Have income security policies gone too far or not far enough in equalizing life chances? Does the politics of social protection threaten to undermine capitalist economies, or are programs for improving individual economic security more essential than ever to legitimize the very existence of democratic capitalism?

8
URBAN PLANNING

During the last hundred years, growing government responsibility for education, health, housing, income maintenance, and a host of other public programs was inextricably tied to the expansion of cities as the centers of economic growth in the West. Japan, with a more ancient urban tradition than the countries of Western Europe or North America, also experienced a boom in city growth during the nineteenth century, due largely to Japan's opening to Western trade and influence. In the twentieth century Japan's levels of urbanization and industrialization are far closer to those of the West than to those of other Asian nations. With advancing metropolitan growth throughout these societies, particularly after World War II, public authorities have been increasingly challenged to exert some control over the urban physical environment, which for most people plays as important a role in determining the quality of life as do social services and benefits. In this chapter our subject is the choices available to governments to influence urban development.

CHOICES IN URBAN PLANNING

Scope and Thresholds

How much responsibility should government assume for the physical development of cities? This question highlights, as clearly as any policy question posed in this volume, the conflict between public welfare and private interests.

There can be little doubt that the quality of life in urban areas constitutes what economists call an "indivisible good." That is, a safe, well-ordered, and unpolluted environment is a benefit enjoyed, not just by a few, but by virtually all of a city's inhabitants. Nor can there be any doubt about the important link between the physical environment of cities and their ability to generate economic growth. Given these facts, it is not surprising that the physical development of urban environments has become a concern of governments. Inevitably, government intervention in urban development brings public authorities into conflict with private interests. When they exercise their constitutional right to purchase land owned by private parties (the right of *eminent domain*), or restrict the ways in which a private owner may use his or her own property, governments are asserting the primacy of the collective welfare over the rights of individuals. They are, in short, using the coercive power of the state to promote the public interest.

In most cities of Europe and the United States, this power is largely in the hands of appointed, rather than elected, public officials. Typically, city planning commissions and planning departments are staffed by professionals whose vision of the city has been shaped in schools of architecture and engineering, rather than in political party caucuses. But their ability to translate that vision into concrete reality depends heavily on their relationships to local politicians and interest groups. As we will see, urban planners in Europe have been both more ambitious in their vision and more aggressive in confronting private interests than have their American counterparts.

Instruments

Urban growth is shaped by thousands of individual decisions made by developers, builders, homeowners, renters, and commuters. How far planners can go in influencing these private decisions depends on the instruments at their disposal, which may be broadly classified as either subsidies to promote growth in desired directions ("carrots"), or regulatory measures to prevent undesirable development ("sticks"). For example, public authorities may offer low-interest loans or tax concessions to encourage developers to build in neglected areas, while forbidding development in other areas to be preserved as open space. Similarly, transportation planners who want to reduce downtown traffic congestion may opt to subsidize fares in order to make mass transit a desirable option for commuters, or they may prefer to institute sufficiently strict controls on driving and parking to discourage motorists. Obviously, the balance among these instruments depends on the resources available to planners to offer as carrots, and the political costs incurred by encroaching on the rights of property owners and motorists. The problem of balancing public and private interests is especially apparent in the variety of different types of mixed public-private enterprises that have been formed in recent years to lead urban development efforts. In theory, they reflect the common ground between government and business, but many critics have seen them as a sign that governments are "selling out" to developers.

One important determinant of the leverage enjoyed by planners is the pattern of intergovernmental relationships, particularly the degree of coordination among local governments. Many of the problems addressed by urban planners involve entire metropolitan regions, containing dozens of local jurisdictions whose actions must be reconciled. Land-use patterns, transportation systems, water supplies, and air pollution are examples of planning issues which cross jurisdictional boundaries and are therefore tackled most effectively at the regional level. How is regional planning to be achieved? One way is through voluntary cooperation among the various jurisdictions; another is through coordination imposed by a higher level of government. As we will see, policymakers in Europe and the United States have differed significantly in the extent to which they acknowledge a *national* responsibility for urban planning.

Distribution

In 1970 a British urbanist wrote a book whose title perfectly expresses the distributive choices facing urban planners: *Whose City?* (Pahl). The question is how government actions influence the distribution of urban space among the many groups and activities competing for a place in the city. Public policy in both Europe and the United States since World War II has contributed to decentralizing manufacturing jobs—and many workers along with the jobs. At the same time, planners have promoted many alternative land uses, including office buildings, hotels, shopping complexes, expressways, and residential developments of various kinds. Not until the late 1960s did public interest begin to focus on the distributive consequences of this postwar trend, particularly on the effects of the construction boom on the low-income residents whose neighborhoods were often damaged by the new development. By the mid-1970s, the growing incidence of one- and two-person households, the accelerating costs of new suburban construction, and the sharp rises in energy prices had increased the appeal of central cities as residential areas, thereby intensifying the conflict for space. In many European and American cities, planners must balance the city's need to develop land in ways that attract private investment and generate tax revenues against its commitment to housing an increasing share of society's elderly and poor.

Restraints and Innovation

To a great extent, cities are shaped by forces beyond their control. The way that space is used in a city is strongly influenced by trends in national and even international economic markets—for example, the types and cost of energy available for production, transportation, and housing; the decisions by industrial capitalists about where to locate their investments; and the fluctuations in global demand for the goods and services produced in the city. During periods of high growth, policy choices generally involve the degree to which the private market is to be regulated, and its impact on the city mitigated. As we have already observed, European planners have shown a much greater willingness than their American counterparts to take measures which restrain the private market.

Not surprisingly, the current era of economic stagnation has led American policymakers to talk about reducing what is already a comparatively limited effort at regulating private market forces in the cities. More noteworthy, perhaps, is the fact that this trend is being seen in Europe as well. Economic conservatism in Britain has prompted a similar impulse toward easing land-use and environmental regulations in cities, and using public power to adapt the city to the requirements of business, rather than forcing business to adapt to planners' requirements. Even continental cities with long traditions of strong planning are exhibiting similar responses to slowed growth. Planners' increasing tendency to accommodate to private investors, along with the growing reliance on public-private partnerships to finance development projects, weakens the government's ability to channel growth. Private developers, it appears, are being accorded greater latitude to "pick their spots," even if that means concentrating new growth in already congested areas.

PLANNING TRADITIONS IN WESTERN EUROPE, THE UNITED STATES, AND JAPAN
SCOPE AND THRESHOLDS

The use of public power to regulate urban growth was common in Western Europe much earlier than in the United States, and so the scope of public intervention in land use, transportation, and housing is today considerably wider in European cities. Although the need for some form of government regulation in urbanization is presently acknowledged on both sides of the Atlantic, Europe's longer experience with such regulations, as well as the existence there of certain cultural and government patterns especially conducive to planning, has given European city officials greater power.

The Planning Tradition in Europe

Many European cities still bear signs of the town planning carried on in medieval times. The winding streets that connect churches, marketplaces, and homes may give the impression of spontaneous, unplanned growth, but urban historians tell us that impression is false: "The esthetic unity of the medieval town was not achieved any more than its other institutions without effort, struggle, supervision, and control" (Mumford, p. 311). Later, in the Baroque period, monarchs undertook monumental building projects in many capitals to reflect their power and tastes. But perhaps the greatest spur to public planning in Europe was industrialization, whose advance in the nineteenth century brought pollution, crowding, and general deterioration to city life. In response, municipal socialists of the late nineteenth century carved out public parks, upgraded water and sewer systems, took over private transportation companies, and built workers' housing projects. By the early twentieth century, many cities had adopted "master plans" to guide such activities.

Moreover, some European planners looked beyond the overgrown industrial centers, to advocate the creation of healthier and more efficient new towns. These brand new "garden cities" would contain all necessary basic services, along with industrial plants to employ residents, but would be designed on a small town scale. The first such garden city was Letchworth, England; established in 1903, it became the model for new towns developed a half century later in Britain, France, Sweden, and several other European countries.

Both in preserving their aging urban centers and in creating brand new towns, European governments have benefited from a much older planning tradition than exists in the United States. Land is considered a resource which is subject to strong government regulation, a view that can be traced all the way to feudal times, when all land tenure was enmeshed in a hierarchy of rights and obligations descending from the sovereign to the peasants. This tradition has bred a degree of public acceptance of government intervention in and regulation of land use that is far greater in Europe than in the United States. It is hardly surprising that Europe's planners have taken advantage of this hospitable climate to launch planning ventures that are bold by American standards.

To an American observer, the most striking characteristic of European urban planning is the scale at which it has been undertaken since World War II. In most of Europe's big cities, planning initiatives have been focused on the entire metropolitan region rather than confined within the boundaries of individual municipalities. In postwar Britain, for example, the response of policymakers to rising traffic congestion and deteriorating living conditions in London was to place a limit on the size of the city. They did so by creating the "Green Belt," a permanent girdle of open space about five miles wide around London's built-up center, to prevent indefinite sprawl. Recognizing, however, that setting up the Green Belt would not halt population growth in the southeast region of England, Parliament also provided for construction of complete new communities of moderate size beyond the open space. From 1946 to 1949, eight new towns were established within a radius of thirty-five miles from central London. To minimize commuting across the Green Belt, planners designed the communities to be reasonably self-sufficient, with services, shops, and even a large number of industrial jobs. In the late 1960s, three more new towns were created in the Greater London region, fifty to eighty miles from central London—the greater distances were an effort to guarantee that they would not become commuter towns. Together, the new towns and the Green Belt comprised a comprehensive regional plan for the decentralization of people and jobs from London.

In Paris, as in London, postwar planners drew up a master design for the entire metropolitan region. Adopted in 1965, the plan designated open space, projected a series of new towns to be built from scratch, and selected several older suburbs for development into higher-density nodes. The new towns program was undertaken in 1966, and by 1975 five new towns were functioning within twenty miles of Paris. In addition, three major nodes of development have been built up closer to central Paris, at La Défense, Créteil, and Bobigny, in an effort to siphon some office development away from the central city (see Figure 8.1). The long-term goal of the plan was to

FIGURE 8.1. REGIONAL PLAN FOR PARIS, SHOWING TWIN AXES PROPOSED FOR FUTURE GROWTH

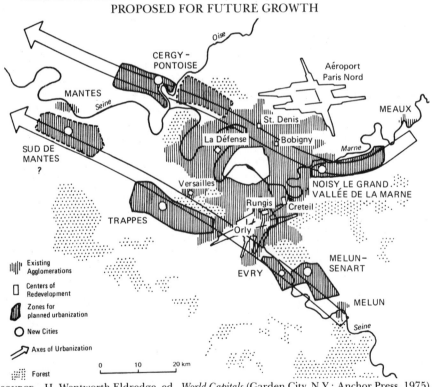

SOURCE   H. Wentworth Eldredge, ed., *World Capitals* (Garden City, N.Y.: Anchor Press, 1975), p. 84.

redress the growing regional imbalance between employment, which was concentrated in central Paris, and new housing, which increasingly was being built in the suburbs. Besides causing a tremendous strain on the region's transportation network, this imbalance threatened eventually to make Paris unlivable.

Among professionals, one of the best-known examples of comprehensive planning for a metropolitan region is Stockholm. Although occasionally criticized on social and esthetic grounds, the well-ordered suburban communities that ring Stockholm are widely acknowledged to be among the best-planned in the world. The 1952 General Plan for Stockholm proposed an entire system of these communities, and by 1970 twenty-seven of them had been completed. While economically dependent on the central city, each of these suburban centers (called "satellite cities") has its own shopping, recreational, and cultural facilities, as well as basic social services and health care. Unlike new towns around London, Stockholm's satellites are not expected to be self-sufficient; instead, the central city is assumed to continue as the major employment center of the region. Figure 8.2 shows the plan for the city center of one such town.

One final example will suffice to illustrate the ambitious scale at which European urban planners have operated since 1945. This is the case of the *Randstad,* or "ring city," in the western Netherlands. A metropolitan region in the shape of a horseshoe, about thirty miles long and thirty miles wide, the Randstad connects Rotterdam, The Hague, Amsterdam, Utrecht, and a number of smaller cities (see Figure 8.3). Dutch planners after World War II saw that these growing cities might actually sprawl outward to meet one another, eventually swallowing up the open space in the center of the horseshoe. Starting in 1949, Dutch authorities began charting a regional plan which evolved through several stages (Hall, p. 111), finally to encompass both the preservation of an existing "green heart" as open space, and the channeling of future growth along a few transportation arteries extending outward from the horseshoe. As in Stockholm, much of the land between the arteries was to be preserved as open space.

The Randstad planning scheme, like the others described above, was an ambitious response to the prospect of postwar metropolitan growth that would overcrowd the traditional urban centers and consume the open space around them. Within the last decade, however, European planners have been forced to respond to a rapidly changing urban picture. No longer do they need to worry about discouraging growth in the city centers, whose populations are now declining and whose industries are leaving. After decades of postwar growth, about half of the larger European cities lost population during the 1970s. (See Table 8.1.) And like U.S. cities, they began to lose their appeal to industry, as high land prices and congestion outweighed their economic advantages. By the early 1980s, unemployment was disproportionately concentrated in Europe's largest cities. (See Table

8.2.) British cities offered the closest parallels with American urban trends, but similar declines were widespread in the core cities in continental Europe (Van den Berg et al). For example, in the Netherlands, unemployment in some inner city districts had climbed to over 30 percent (OECD 1987, p. 16).

One might assume that a loss of urban population would mean that city governments' expenditures would be reduced proportionately. But no such losses have occurred. In fact, local governments throughout the Western countries and Japan spent increasing amounts in the early 1980s. (See Table 8.3.) In part, this is because the population loss from many cities was balanced by a growth in the *number* of households: While the size of urban households was shrinking, the number of households continued to in-

FIGURE 8.2. PLAN FOR THE CENTER OF VALLINGBY, A NEW TOWN IN SUBURBAN STOCKHOLM

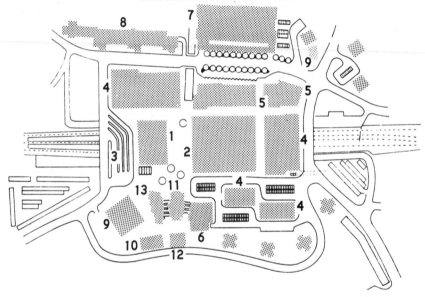

1	transit station	8	apartment building
2	commercial building	9	churches
3	bus platforms and taxi stands	10	library
4	commercial buildings	11	cinema
5	stores	12	youth center
6	residence hotel	13	community hall
7	600 stall parking garage		

NOTE   Transit station, department stores, and shops are incorporated into a system of pedestrian streets with the transit line beneath. Parking facilities are at approaches to the center and in a parking garage on the northern side. Multistory housing development is on both long sides of the center.

SOURCE   David Pass, *Vallingby and Farsta: From Idea to Reality* (Cambridge: MIT Press, 1973), p. 100.

FIGURE 8.3. RANDSTAD ("RING CITY") OF THE NETHERLANDS WITH
GREEN HEART AT THE CENTER

SOURCE Peter Hall, *The World Cities* (New York: McGraw-Hill, 1966), p. 98.

TABLE 8.1 PERCENTAGE POPULATION CHANGE DURING THE 1970s IN NATIONS AND IN BIG CITIES

	Nations (Percent)	Big Cities (Percent)
Japan	12.9	2.3
United States	11.4	−5.7
Netherlands	8.0	−14.4
France	3.1	−4.7
Sweden	3.0	−11.0
West Germany	1.5	2.2
Britain	.5	−8.1

SOURCE   OECD, *Revitalising Urban Economies* (Paris: OECD, 1987), p. 14.

crease, as youths, the elderly, and other single persons formed independent households. For many types of local services, cost is a function of the number of households served, rather than the number of persons served. Furthermore, the urban centers of Europe and the United States contain a disproportionate share of society's elderly, poor, and others who depend heavily on public services and benefits.

Thus, in most of the nations under study here, the cost of running local government has increased at a faster rate than local tax bases have expanded. National subsidies to local government (known as "transfers") have remained steady or even declined as a revenue source. (See Table 8.4.) Facing stagnant tax bases and national transfers, local governments have been forced to step up their local tax effort; that is, they have increased the levels of tax collection, relative to the size of their tax bases (again, see Table 8.3). This greater dependence on the local tax effort in many cities has prompted local politicians to emphasize programs that will build the tax base by drawing commerce and industry into their towns.

Instead of dispersal, the new emphasis among urban planners is on the economic development of Europe's urban centers. For example, in 1982 the city of Amsterdam proposed abandoning the policy of controlled dis-

TABLE 8.2 UNEMPLOYMENT RATES IN NATIONS AND BIG CITIES, 1983

	Nations (Percent)	Big Cities (Percent)
United States	9.4	12.6
France	8.3	10.1
West Germany	8.2	7.8
Netherlands*	8.6	9.8
Britain*	9.0	11.9

*Figures are for 1981.
SOURCE   OECD, *Revitalising Urban Economies* (Paris: OECD, 1987), p. 11.

persal and focusing instead on revitalizing the city's economy, by luring suburbanites back to the city. To insure jobs for city dwellers, the provincial authorities even decided to allow factories, offices, warehouses, and other firms to locate in "the highly accessible fringe areas" of the green heart, thus sacrificing open space (Levine and Van Weesep, p. 319). Similar reversals of policy can be found in other parts of Europe as well, even in nations whose cities are relatively better off. By 1985, 150 Swedish municipalities

TABLE 8.3 CHANGE IN LOCAL GOVERNMENT EXPENDITURES, TAX BASE, AND TAX EFFORT,* AT 1978 PRICE LEVEL

	1978	1981	1985
France			
Expenditures	100.0	111.2	130.1**
Tax base	100.0	101.6	113.2**
Tax effort	100.0	108.8	119.0**
Netherlands			
Expenditures	100.0	110.1	129.3
Tax base	100.0	103.9	114.5
Tax effort	100.0	109.2	118.2
Sweden			
Expenditures	100.0	114.2	127.2
Tax base	100.0	102.7	105.2
Tax effort	100.0	97.3	96.8
United States			
Expenditures	100.0	102.5	110.9
Tax base	100.0	104.4	111.9
Tax effort	100.0	94.2	95.9
West Germany			
Expenditures	100.0	110.3	117.9
Tax base	100.0	93.6	103.0
Tax effort	100.0	105.6	106.7
Britain			
Expenditures	100.0	97.9	97.7
Tax base	100.0	95.3	108.3
Tax effort	100.0	119.8	106.4
Japan			
Expenditures	100.0	115.5	125.6
Tax base	100.0	106.3	114.4
Tax effort	100.0	113.9	131.7

NOTES *"Tax effort" is defined as total taxes collected, divided by the total tax base. **Figures are for 1984.
SOURCE Poul Mouritzen and Kurt Nielsen, *Handbook of Comparative Urban Fiscal Data* (Odense, Denmark: Odense University Danish Data Archives, 1988).

had adopted economic development programs, compared with only 50 in 1975. As the OECD recently warned its member countries: "policies designed to contain or restrict urban development need to be reassessed." They must give way to policies aimed at reinforcing urban centers, and that means supporting the private sector as the engine of growth (OECD 1983). This "new pragmatism" brings European planners closer to American notions about the role of urban planning, which has always functioned to support private economic activity.

The Tradition of Privatism in the United States

In his historical study of Philadelphia's growth, Sam Bass Warner identifies "privatism" as the single quality which best characterizes America's urban inheritance. In Warner's view, it has been private institutions and individuals that have been responsible for guaranteeing the productivity and social order of American cities (Warner, p. 214). The emphasis on private interests in urban development reflects the commitment to individualism and limited government that have characterized so much of America's political tradition.

No collective commitments such as those that the medieval city had spawned in Europe restrained the private pursuit of wealth in the newer, faster-growing American cities. In the expanding capitalist economy of the nineteenth century, liquid assets were at a premium, and profits from real estate speculation depended primarily on frequent turnover. The pursuit of profits therefore encouraged the continual destruction of older urban structures and their replacement with new ones yielding higher rents.

Even today American public authorities remain relatively powerless to intervene in the cycle of decay, clearance, and reconstruction that proceeds in the nation's cities. That process is dominated by market forces. In fact, urban redevelopment programs actually perpetuate the cycle, by their reli-

TABLE 8.4 SOURCES OF LOCAL REVENUE IN SEVEN NATIONS, 1972–84

	Direct Taxes (Percent)			Indirect Taxes (Percent)			Transfers (Percent)		
	1972	1978	1984	1972	1978	1984	1972	1978	1984
France	19	21	25	24	26	31	47	41	35
Netherlands	2	2	3	4	4	4	81	80	80
Sweden	58	59	56	2	2	1	27	31	30
United States	17	19	21	57	51	53	23	26	20
West Germany	26	27	28	34	33	32	32	33	33
Britain	0	0	0	36	31	35	50	54	54
Japan	20	21	25	36	31	33	42	46	40

SOURCE   OECD, *National Accounts of OECD Member Countries, 1972 to 1984*, Vol. II (Paris: OECD, 1986).

ance on private capital for construction on renewal sites. Redevelopment projects, whether they are undertaken by individual investors or by large firms such as Prudential Insurance, may generate favorable publicity for investors, but such benefits are of secondary importance, compared with the primary objective of such undertakings: to provide shareholders with a reasonable return on their investment. Thus the choice of sites to be cleared and redeveloped must be made to suit the investors who supply the money to build on them. In 1981, when General Motors agreed to consider building a new Cadillac plant in Detroit, the city's redevelopment officials had to find an acceptable location. Determined to secure the plant, Detroit offered GM a 456-acre site that included a Polish neighborhood of 3500 people. Ignoring protests and even fighting a lawsuit, the city argued that this massive urban renewal project involving $320 million in government subsidies would serve a public purpose by providing jobs for Detroit's ailing economy. It was necessary therefore to demolish the aging neighborhood in order to accommodate the corporation's requirements for space.

The government role in planning American suburbs has been even more marginal than in the redevelopment of inner cities. Granted, federal housing and transportation policies after World War II were instrumental in facilitating suburban growth; but the United States has no parallels to the regional planning efforts mounted in Europe's metropolitan centers in the 1950s. On the contrary, suburban growth in the United States is the result of private planning by commercial developers. And while the minimum standards for constructing houses and even entire subdivisions are established by local building codes and subdivision regulations, public authorities have almost no control over the timing and the scale of new development within their boundaries.

Nor is there any parallel in the United States to the systematic creation of new towns in the metropolitan regions of Europe. After a half-hearted eight-year experiment with a program to encourage new towns, the U.S. Department of Housing and Urban Development (HUD) in 1978 gave up the effort. At its close, one commentator called the program "a disaster whose magnitude surprised even the program's harshest critics" (Evans and Rodwin, p. 90). Never did this experiment put the kind of public power or public money behind the new communities that European governments have committed to their new towns. Instead, like the urban renewal program, it relied on private developers. Federal support for the program was limited to backing the bonds that builders sold to raise the money they needed.

Launched in 1970, when the housing market was still booming, the new towns program ran into problems that are typified by the example of Newfields, one of the federally assisted new towns started near Dayton, Ohio, by a millionaire housing developer. He assembled the 4,000-acre tract and secured federal backing for his borrowing in late 1973. The next year construction started, but it quickly became clear that the developer's sales revenue simply could not keep pace with expenses. Because it was built from scratch, Newfields tied up vast amounts of money and a large tract of land for a long time before it could begin to generate revenues. Prospective buyers were not eager to invest before they actually saw the community taking shape. Moreover, the housing boom slowed down in the mid-1970s as interest rates rose, and federal housing subsidies were curtailed by the Nixon administration. By the time the developer abandoned the project in late 1975, he had borrowed $18 million—loans for which HUD was ultimately responsible. The government had no choice but to take the project into receivership, scale it down, and look for another developer to buy it.

Public Ownership of Land

Surveying the historical contrasts between European and American city planning, we must note the tremendous importance of the different attitudes toward public land ownership on the two continents. Owning large tracts of land enables public officials not only to decide how specific parcels should be developed, but also to time development so that it fits with the provision of public services. European municipalities have vigorously pursued this course of action in order to control urban growth; American cities have not.

Stockholm has the largest land bank of any metropolitan area in Western Europe. At the turn of the century, the Stockholm city council embarked on a program to purchase outlying land for future expansion. Ironically, the impetus for the initial decision came not from the Social Democratic party, but from a Conservative party banker and financier on the city council. In 1904 the council began buying large areas of farm and forest land on the open market. Gradually, the city's holdings grew, with the greatest period of acquisitions in the 1960s. The city's acquisitions, totaling 138,000 acres since 1904 (Strong, p. 43), now range over the entire metropolitan area, with two-thirds of the land lying outside Stockholm's city limits, within suburban jurisdictions. Once acquired by the city, these lands are almost never resold; rather, private parties who wish to develop the tracts must negotiate long-term leases with the municipal government. In negotiating the leases, the city requires that any development conform to the town plan. The extent of municipal ownership in the region thus provides city officials with significant control over new development. Furthermore, Stockholm's leasing system is a money-making proposition; the city earns more than enough from its leases to pay off the debts it has incurred in buying the land (Ratzka).

Dutch municipalities began land banking even before the Swedes, with Amsterdam's first purchase in 1896. In the Dutch case, as in the Swedish, initial support for land banking came from the business community. The completion of the North Sea Canal in 1874 brought rapid growth in shipping and industry to the major cities of the Randstad, and the merchants who dominated the powerful Liberal party viewed public land acquisition as the only way to build housing fast enough to accommodate the migrants flooding into the cities (Strong, p. 103). Traditionally, it has been relatively easy for Dutch cities to acquire surrounding agricultural land for planned urban expansion; municipalities could do so at a price only slightly above the existing use value.

Within cities, however, authorities have had more restricted powers of expropriation. In city centers expropriation could at first be used only to condemn "unfit" housing or to make room for public projects, not to gain land for resale to private developers. However, the war damage suffered in several Dutch cities brought modifications of this rule. In the years immediately following World War II, cities were given exceptional emergency powers to acquire large tracts of war-damaged land within their boundaries in order to rebuild. This special authorization was granted to several municipalities, some of which (Rotterdam, for example) opted to sell the land back to private entrepreneurs once it had been cleared. Amsterdam, on the other hand, acquired land, prepared it for rebuilding, and then leased most of it out on long-term contracts. This policy may be accounted for, at least in part, by the fact that the Amsterdam city council in the late 1940s and early 1950s, having Labor and Communist party components, leaned further to the left than other Dutch city councils.

The success of the postwar programs, along with a growing sense of urgency regarding urban renewal, led the national government in the Physical Planning Law of 1965 to ease restrictions on municipal expropriations. The 1965 legislation provided that a municipality could expropriate any land in the city center with the approval of the crown, so long as the site was included in an approved development plan. Thus, local governments are no longer prevented from acquiring any city tract, although they are restrained by a cumbersome appeal process, generous compensation provisions, and the problem of relocating displaced tenants. By the early 1970s the scope of the Dutch cities' acquisitions was so great that in one year 83 percent of new development was on land bought or leased from municipalities (Strong, p. 106).

Although only a small proportion of public purchases in the Netherlands is by eminent domain, the issue of land expropriation is politically sensitive. In fact, a dispute over expropriation procedures actually toppled the national government of Prime Minister Joop Den Uyl in March 1977. The five-party coalition, which had been in power since 1973, fell apart over the issue of how much money local governments should have to pay owners whose land they expropriated. The leftist Labor party argued that the more centrist Catholic People's party wanted to give too much protection to landowners, while the centrists accused the leftists of seeking to give local governments too much power over compensation.

From the American perspective, one of the most interesting European cases is the French adoption of land banking policies in 1958. France came to land banking much later than its neighbors, largely because its political tradition places a strong value on private property ownership. In the words of Albin Chalandon, Gaullist minister of public construction,

> The principal enemy of urbanism is the Frenchman's attachment to own-
> ership of land. . . . A "municipalization" or, more precisely, a "collectiviza-
> tion" of land of a progressive and rational sort, which is the only definitive
> solution of the problem, is too utopian to wish to realize instantaneously.
> (Strong, p. 140)

As a compromise that would be acceptable within the framework of French political culture, the Gaullists devised an intriguing system based not on large-scale public purchase of land, but rather on a limited amount of public acquisition supplemented by a public *option* to purchase. According to this system, a local government anticipating new development in a particular area can designate a specific tract of land as a zone for priority urbanization (ZUP) and establish a detailed plan for its development. The locality may then acquire a small portion of the zone through eminent domain. But, rather than buy all of the land outright, the local government reserves for a period of four years its option to buy any of the land within the zone that might henceforth be offered for sale. Thus, if an owner declares an intent to sell his land for development that violates the munici-pal plan for the zone, the municipality can buy him out first in order to prevent that development. Since the price to be paid by the municipality is fixed on the date when the zone is first designated, the landowner is likely to get less from the municipality than from a private buyer. This circum-stance gives authorities considerable leverage over development, even though the bulk of land transactions remains in private hands.

How widespread is the use of land banking by American municipali-ties? Despite a lively interest in the idea among planning professionals, its use is extremely limited. Public landownership in the United States is heav-ily concentrated in remote areas; very little public land lies within major metropolitan areas. There has been virtually no suburban land banking by public authorities that could seriously influence development patterns. Within cities, municipal governments have often used their power of emi-nent domain for urban redevelopment, but only to assemble individual project sites which are then sold to private developers as quickly as possible. Typically, a city expropriates land not to restrain or control development, but rather at the behest of a private developer who has selected a specific site for investment. In return for the much needed investment, the city acts as the developer's agent, assembling the site for the developer by using its power of expropriation. Normally, the only land parcels remaining in municipal ownership are those for which no private buyer can be found.

Only the Japanese government appears as reluctant as United States authorities to expand public land ownership in the interest of controlling development. In fact, the most common method of assembling land for development, either inside cities or at the fringes, is an arrangement known as *kukakuseiri,* or "land readjustment," that does not involve any public purchase at all. Japanese law makes it possible for groups of private property owners to pool their holdings temporarily in order to develop an area according to a mutually acceptable plan. Once the project is completed, the temporary cooperative association disbands, and each owner receives an equitable share of the project (which may or may not correspond to the tract the individual owner originally owned). The technique, borrowed from the Germans in 1899, has been widely adopted by Japan's local planners. Not only are they relieved of the need to purchase land for development; they normally do not pay for the cost of roads and service installations, which are borne instead by the private association. The local and national governments provide only partial grants or loans for infrastructure, and private banks supply the rest of the capital. While it saves money for public authorities, the disadvantage of "land readjustment" is that it does nothing to inhibit sprawl, a major planning problem in Japan's metropolitan areas (Hebbert; OECD 1986).

GUIDING URBAN GROWTH
INSTRUMENTS

What are the instruments wielded by European planners in exercising their formidable influence over urban growth and development? In this section we will examine the main regulatory devices available to them, and contrast these with the weaker planning controls in the United States. Probably the most important characteristic of Europe's more successful planning efforts is its combination of land-use planning with transportation planning. Government actions in one sector reinforce those in the other.

Most local governments in Europe are responsible for drawing up plans that project land-use patterns in their communities, and for monitoring all construction to see that it conforms to such plans. Residential neighborhoods, industrial plants, recreational areas, and all public infrastructure are subject to municipal control, and the linkages among the various types of land use are considered in issuing building permits. Local government regulates both the density and height of new development, as well as the particular use to which the land is devoted. Officials take more or less restrictive approaches to regulation, depending on the political culture. While Dutch planners, for example, place a great deal of emphasis on drawing up "structure plans" that project future development in detail,

British land-use plans tend to be vaguer and to give planners more flexibility in making operational decisions about how the plan will be applied (Thomas et al). (Note the similarity to the description in Chapter 9 of the flexibility in British environmental regulation, relative to the continental European systems.)

So far, this description of European cities sounds very similar to municipal responsibilities in the United States. Most American communities, especially large ones, have developed land-use plans which are expected to guide public decisions on building new infrastructure and issuing permits for private construction. However, because they lack the advantages of land banking, public planners in the United States have had to rely on the *zoning ordinance,* a device that has very limited utility either for planning new development or for controlling development that is already underway. The zoning ordinance, a statute which restricts the types of construction that are acceptable on a particular parcel of land, is a classic example of a reactive instrument. Clearly, the aim of the zoning ordinance is to encourage conformity with already existing use patterns; though zoning may prevent unacceptable structures, it cannot provide an adequate framework for planning new developments.

Moreover, it would be difficult to argue convincingly that zoning really constitutes an expression of "public purpose" in American cities. Although the zoning ordinance is adopted and enforced by public officials, the nature of the device is such that it operates on the urban fringe to enforce conformity to a set of private decisions made by commercial developers. Large-scale builders frequently plan a development which violates existing zoning codes. Then they launch a campaign to persuade the local zoning board to permit the development, chalking up the legal fees involved in obtaining the variance to their development costs. A study of the massive land-use planning apparatus operating in suburban Suffolk County on New York's Long Island concluded that it had practically no impact at all on the county's growth: "The over-all land use pattern resulting from this process is one that would occur if there were practically no zoning at all" (Gottdiener, p. 104).

Controls on Land Speculation

One of the main factors in any kind of new development—public or private—is the cost of the land, which normally inflates as soon as news of the impending development is made public. A long-time property owner may thus reap tremendous profits, not because he or she has improved the property, but simply because the land he or she happens to occupy is desired for some new development. This phenomenon of massive price inflation preceding development is an accepted feature of the land market in the United States and Japan. Even when government expropriates land in the American system, it must pay the owner a "fair market value" which takes into account the land's development potential. Japan's land prices in metropolitan regions are notoriously high, and constantly inflating. They now contribute about 35 percent of the cost of housing, compared to only 15 to 20 percent in other advanced industrial nations (OECD 1986, p. 50). While Japanese law provides an impressive body of planning controls for local authorities, they are rarely invoked against politically powerful landowners. What is worse, tax laws actually assist land speculators to hoard their properties by assessing agricultural lands, even those that lie well within metropolitan areas, on their agricultural rents and not on their potential value to developers.

European governments, in contrast, have intervened actively in urban land markets to reduce the potential profits of speculation. They have had two primary purposes for doing so: (1) to capture for the public treasury some of the inflation in land values that occurs in improving areas, and (2) to ensure that when local governments buy land for public purposes, they do not have to pay prices that have been inflated by speculation. We will examine in turn the instruments most commonly used to pursue each of these goals.

The device used to accomplish the first purpose is a "betterment tax" levied on the difference between the value of a property in its present use and its value if it is used in a more profitable way. For example, West Germany's 1971 Urban Development Law stipulated that when local governments completed urban renewal projects, the property owners in the renewal district would have to pay a betterment tax equal to the difference between the original site value and the new site value. This is known as a 100 percent levy, because it amounts to the entire profit that the owner would otherwise realize from the inflation of his property. Compared to some other European betterment taxes, Germany's is quite limited in scope, as it applies only to urban renewal districts where it is reasonably certain that government investments caused the inflation to occur.

In 1975 the Social Democratic party (SPD) actually moved to extend the betterment tax to *all* unearned increments in land value, not just those occurring in renewal districts. The SPD's initial proposal was for a 100 percent levy, but opposition arose from the Free Democratic party (FDP), the socialists' coalition partner in the government. Not only did the FDP balk at the 100 percent figure, but also the government anticipated strong resistance from the *Bundesrat,* the conservative upper house in Germany's parliamentary system. As a compromise, the proposal was changed to a 50 percent levy, but even this diluted version met resistance. Ultimately, the government withdrew the proposal altogether.

The most determined proponent of the betterment levy in Europe is undoubtedly Britain's Labour party. Three times since World War II—in 1947, 1964, and 1974—Labour governments have experimented with mechanisms to obtain some of the profits of land development for the public treasury. And each time, the succeeding Conservative government has scrapped the betterment levy, on the grounds that it placed too great a restraint on private capital, with the result that the activities of private developers were severely hampered.

The second purpose of European government intervention in land markets has been to relieve governments themselves of the necessity to pay inflated prices for land. The most imaginative approach to this problem is that of the French "zones for deferred development" (ZADs). This device was created by the French parliament in 1962 to complement the already existing ZUPs. Under the law, a municipality, a regional prefect, or a national ministry can designate a tract of land lying in the path of development as a ZAD. Having created the zone, public authorities then enjoy a fourteen-year option to buy any land within its boundaries that is offered for sale. The cost to the public authority is usually fixed at the value of the land one year *before* the creation of the ZAD. So appealing to public authorities was this anti-inflationary instrument that as of 1974 about 1 percent of the nation's land area had been placed in ZADs, about a third of it in the Paris region (Strong, p. 243). No one expects that all of this territory, or even most of it, will be government-owned, but the option to buy gives French municipalities and other public authorities extraordinary power over the land market, while at the same time assuring them that they will be able to buy land for public projects at uninflated prices.

The massive inflation in land costs in Japanese cities in the late 1960s led that country's government to introduce a price control system that relies much more on notions of consensus and social conformity than on laws. In 1974 Japan's national government decreed that all buyers and sellers of lots over a half-acre in urban zones must report their transactions to the prefectural governor, who can *recommend* that the transaction not go ahead if the price is out of line with established guidelines. If the buyer and seller choose to proceed with the sale against the government recommendation, their names are published. Out of nearly 40,000 transactions registered in 1982, about 1,500 went ahead after the price was "corrected"; 2,500 were withdrawn; and the rest were approved at the reported price (Kirwan).

Transportation Planning

The single most important influence on urban form in the twentieth century has been the automobile. At the edge of growing cities, the automobile has facilitated low-density suburban sprawl, because it has freed residents of the necessity to live near mass transit lines. Within the central city, the growing dependence on the automobile since World War II has enlarged the amount of space devoted to automobiles—for roadways, parking garages, service stations, automobile dealerships, and so on—and has increased congestion in central business districts.

The first of these two effects—suburban sprawl—is much less advanced in Europe than in the United States, where car ownership rates surpass those in Europe (see Table 8.5). The second effect—central city congestion—is more pronounced in Europe, despite lower car ownership rates. That is because the shape of many European cities even today reflects medieval configurations. The spatial limitations imposed by early fortress walls resulted in densely built-up areas with narrow streets radiating from a central market district. Consequently, many European cities have even worse traffic problems at their centers than those which plague American cities. Furthermore, European town centers frequently contain historical sites considered worthy of preservation, so that planners are reluctant to bulldoze through the central city to develop expressway networks that would speed auto traffic.

We have seen that several national governments in Europe have intervened to guide suburban growth in their major metropolitan regions. Recognizing that any movement of people and economic activities outward from the center increases the demand for transportation, planners in some nations have tried to coordinate transportation investments with land-use planning. The leading example is Sweden, where Stockholm's expansion program has been integrated with transportation planning since the 1940s. In fact, the initial impetus to suburban planning came when the transit company began developing plans to extend the subway into the suburbs. The so-called finger development that resulted from spacing suburban communities along the public transportation lines was intended not only to promote high-density development and preserve the open spaces between the lines; an equally important goal was to ensure that the transit lines, once constructed, would have a ready market to serve—a market of commuters living at sufficient densities to make it financially feasible to offer high-quality rail service.

In addition to helping guide suburban growth, mass transit is of course

TABLE 8.5 OWNERSHIP OF PASSENGER CARS, 1970 AND 1983

	Cars/1000 People		Percentage Change
	1970	*1983*	
United States	434	556	28
Sweden	285	361	27
France	254	351	38
West Germany	223	402	80
Britain	211	286	36
Netherlands	173	334	93
Japan	85	220	159

SOURCE Calculated from United Nations, *Statistical Yearbook,* 1974, 1983/84 (New York: United Nations, 1975, 1985).

an important tool in minimizing auto traffic in central cities. If commuters can be persuaded to leave their automobiles at home and travel to work by train, subway, or bus, central cities will have less congestion and less need to devote space to roadways, garages, and other facilities.

In an effort to influence the cost-benefit calculations made by motorists, most European governments had begun imposing heavy costs on private driving even before the fuel crisis of 1973 and 1974, usually in the form of high taxes on gasoline, automobiles, and auto accessories. Another approach to influencing motorists' calculations has been to inhibit the use of cars in cities. The British and Dutch governments since World War II have increasingly moved toward restricting auto use, with the British government meeting far stronger opposition from pro-auto interests.

Conflict over urban transportation problems emerged in Britain in the early 1960s, centering on the question of how far public authorities should go in limiting the use of the private automobile in towns. Neither Labour nor the Conservatives wanted to appear an enemy of the motor car. To Conservatives, measures to restrict motoring appeared to place intolerable restraints on individual freedoms. Labour politicians feared that increased restrictions on owning and driving cars would tend to freeze existing ownership patterns; such an outcome would clearly violate the party's concern with an equal distribution of goods in British society. The "restrictionists" therefore found no strong support in either of the major political camps.

In 1963 a national commission appointed to review the growing problem of auto traffic in towns concluded that British motorists would not tolerate serious restrictions on their driving, and that urban congestion could be tackled only by building road networks that would accommodate increased traffic while segregating high speed traffic from secondary traffic by the use of tunnels, bridges, and barriers. The report, in short, advised massive reconstruction of British cities to accommodate automobiles, warning against trying to curtail motorists' freedom:

> A car-owning electorate will not stand for a severe restriction. And even if a severe restriction could be got on to the statute book, it would be almost impossible to enforce. It is a difficult and dangerous thing in a democracy to try to prevent a substantial part of the population from doing things that they do not regard as wrong; black markets and corruption are the invariable fruit of such attempts at prohibition. (Buchanan et al., p. 3)

When planners in London tried to apply the policies outlined in the commission's report, however, they discovered that adapting the city to the automobile in this way entailed costs, both financial and political, that were too high. In line with the commission's conclusions, both Labour and Conservative majorities in the GLC supported the construction of a massive system of four ring roads successively farther from the center of the city, combined with a series of radial arteries to bring traffic from the ring down into the city. Yet the strong opposition from community groups against the enormous construction projects, coupled with the tremendous cost of the enterprise, finally led to the plan's abandonment. Instead, the GLC settled for the much less ambitious—and far less expensive—alternative of increased parking restrictions to discourage motorists from driving into town.

The Dutch have been especially sensitive to the problems presented by the automobile. Given that the Netherlands is the most densely populated nation in Western Europe, it is not surprising that the Dutch were among the first to recognize the devastating consequences that the automobile could have on city centers (Valderpoort), and to take measures to restrict auto traffic. In 1972 the national government cut highway expenditures by over $20 million, in spite of the politically damaging 15 percent reduction in road construction employment. Then, in 1973, the government introduced legislation to require a deposit of about $90 on each new car sold in the Netherlands. The deposit, which was to be refunded upon receipt of proof that the car had been scrapped, was obviously intended to discourage people from abandoning old cars; in addition, however, it was expected to inhibit the growth of automobile ownership. The figures on Dutch automobile ownership in Table 8.5 suggest that the latter goal was unrealistic. No Dutch city has yet banned cars entirely, but more than a dozen have set up large pedestrian zones within which automobiles are prohibited. Most of these zones are in commercial districts; the most celebrated example is probably the Lijnbaan, a shopping mall in central Rotterdam.

In the United States, the greater reluctance of local governments to impose restrictions on motorists must be understood in the context of the more limited systems of mass transit. In most American cities, motorists simply do not have the option of public transit that is convenient and reasonably priced. Like their European counterparts, some of the older cities on the east coast of the United States (for instance, Boston, New York, Philadelphia), which had assumed their urban character before the advent of the internal combustion engine, do possess functioning rapid-rail transit systems. In New York, which has by far the most extensive subway system of any American city, over half of all persons entering and leaving the downtown area for work each day travel by mass transportation. New York, however, is the exception rather than the rule in American urban transportation; it is one of only six American cities now operating rail transport networks. The more common pattern has been the degeneration and finally the phasing out in the 1930s and 1940s of once viable street railway and rapid transit systems. In fact, collective transportation in American cities was at its peak at the turn of the century, when most major cities had several competing transit companies. Numerous factors—including increased operating expenditures, massive indebtedness incurred in mergers, and legal constraints requiring fixed fare schedules—contributed to the financial squeeze on street railway companies that began about 1910. In addition, transit holding companies bought out streetcar lines with the intention of replacing them with passenger buses. Many cities lost their street railway networks through such private business agreements in the 1930s and 1940s.

Even in cities where mass transit systems survived, they faced increasing competition from the automobile, encouraged by massive highway construction in and around cities after World War II. Between 1950 and 1970 the annual vehicle miles of service provided by buses and trolleys dropped by over 30 percent nationally. By 1970 almost three-quarters of all mass transit passengers in the United States were concentrated in only the twelve largest metropolitan areas (Gorham and Glazer, pp. 283 and 293), and residents of the vast majority of American cities did not even have a realistic alternative to the automobile.

The Role of National Governments in City Planning

Compared to American public authorities, European governments have more numerous and more powerful instruments at their command to influence urban development. In particular, we have noted their ability to discourage speculation in urban land and their methods of discouraging automobile traffic in towns. But how is it that European planners have been able to use tools which are so seldom used by their American counterparts? Are European local officials simply more aggressive and more enlightened in pursuing the public interest?

Of course, the answer is no. In Europe, as in the United States, local officials tend to view problems from a local perspective, which is strongly colored by the views of their local constituents. Because their first concern is with the welfare of their own community, issues of regional and national balance remain secondary. They are as little disposed to contain development or to restrain automobile use as are American city officials.

The great difference lies in the much stronger role in urban planning played by the national governments in Europe. In most European nations, the responsibility for urban planning is shared by authorities at the national and local levels. Typically, city officials devise a comprehensive land-use scheme for which they must seek the approval of the appropriate national ministry. Obviously, European cities obtain significant financial and political support for this comprehensive planning effort from the national governments, many of which have formulated national urbanization policies.

Compared to national officials in the United States, European national policymakers have the obvious advantage of operating within political cultures which are much more conducive to public planning than is the American milieu:

> Hierarchical social and political systems, where the governing class is ac-
> customed to govern, where other classes are accustomed to acquiesce, and
> where private interests have relatively less power, can more readily evolve
> urban and regional growth policies at the national level than systems
> under the sway of the market, local political jurisdictions, or egalitarian
> political processes. (Berry 1973, p. 180)

How is this national interest in urban development reflected in European policy? First, national governments have intervened to try to restrain competition among cities and regions, and to redress some of the imbalance created by that competition. The well-known cases of regional planning for Europe's metropolitan areas (for example, London, Stockholm, Paris) have typically been stimulated by *national* initiatives. Some national governments have gone so far as to pass legislation discouraging localities from competing with one another for business by offering tax concessions to firms to relocate their plants; Germany is an example (Boesler, p. 218). The greater leverage which European governments exercise in promoting cooperation among localities has much to do with the larger national subsidies to local governments.

Money is also the key to national influence on the land-use and transportation decisions made by local governments. Obviously, the ability of local governments to acquire large tracts of land depends on having the necessary funds. National governments may influence local land acquisitions not only by direct lending, but also by their authority to control local borrowing. In the Netherlands, for example, municipalities in theory have the responsibility for managing growth, including the acquisition of land. But since localities cannot borrow money for such purchases without provincial and national approval, their plans must take account of national planning objectives.

National initiatives have been crucial to building and preserving mass transit systems as well. Stockholm's metropolitan transportation authority would never have been established without national intervention in 1965. It was the national government's pledge to furnish 60 percent of the funds for the new subway extensions that persuaded the city and suburban governments to cooperate in transportation planning (Anton, p. 109).

The contributions which the national governments in Europe have made toward solving the burdensome problems of local traffic congestion have not been confined to handing out subsidies to city administrators. National administrators have also played more active roles at the local level. At a minimum, they have acted as mediators in deadlocked local disputes. On other occasions, however, they have promoted schemes that, because of political implications, could not reasonably have been promoted by local officials. An illustration of active national concern for local traffic problems is found in Paris. Even though it is one of the most intensively used subway systems in the world, the Paris métro still suffers from financial problems. Studies of both the bus and subway systems in Paris showed that during the 1960s mass modes were constantly losing ground to the private automobile. By 1970, passenger fares were covering only about half the cost of maintaining public transportation, the deficit being made up by government funds, with a full 70 percent of that operating deficit being shouldered by the French national government. National concern was heightened by the observation that Paris's elected city council was showing reluctance to take unpopular steps against private car owners, even in the face of what is perhaps the worst traffic congestion in the world. For example, the first parking meters appeared in Paris only in 1971, and many city streets still have no parking meters.

Parisian city officials not only appeared to lack the political will to confront their car-driving constituents; they were also making little visible progress toward improving subway facilities, despite periodic public declarations about future plans. Finally, in February 1970, the national transport minister seized the initiative on the question of mass transit by supporting the controversial *tax d'équipement*. This was a proposal which had initially surfaced in the National Assembly several months earlier under Communist sponsorship. The premise was a simple one: Collective modes of transportation provided benefits for Parisian businesses by enlarging both the labor and consumer markets on which they could draw; therefore, businesses ought to contribute to financing mass transit. Transport Minister Raymond Mondon was uncertain as to the best method of imposing the obligation on business—whether to base the assessment on the amount paid in salaries by an employer, the volume of business, or the number of employees. Nevertheless, Mondon saw the *taxe* as "simple and at the same time productive." The proposal was immediately denounced by Paris merchants and manufacturers, but the national government continued to pursue the idea under its new transport minister, Jean Chamant, and in July 1971 Parisian businesses employing nine or more people began paying a tax that was equivalent to 1.7 percent of their firm's payroll to help put mass transit back on its feet. In June 1973 the law was extended to cover eight provincial cities with populations of 500,000 or more. The *taxe d'équipement* was a controversial measure whose promotion depended on national political "muscle"; in all likelihood the tax would never have been introduced by the city council on its own. Thus it illustrates the important role played by national officials in urban transportation decisions.

Public-Private Partnerships

As we noted above, urban planners throughout the United States and Europe are increasingly concerned with reinforcing the economic strength of central cities, as opposed to dispersing population and economic activities away from the center. As a result, they are relying more on the private sector to generate the economic growth that has been receding from the older cities. One analysis of recent British planning characterized the shift as replacing a high level of public intervention and expenditure with a more market-oriented approach to regeneration (Moor, p. 57). The main vehicles to involve private investors in publicly sponsored redevelopment schemes are various types of "partnership" arrangements in which representatives from government and business act as codirectors.

The approaches that governments take to such partnerships vary. In some instances, governments take only an initiating role, offering grants and low-interest loans to developers who pledge that they will bring jobs and economic activity back to the city. That is the approach taken by the U.S. government with its Urban Development Action Grants (UDAGs) from 1977 to 1988. The federal government awarded UDAGs to cities for projects that drew at least $2.50 of private investment for every public dollar invested and generated new employment. Although the program has since been eliminated in the United States, it has been copied in Britain's Urban Development Grants (UDGs), where the Department of the Environment subsidizes locally administered grants and loans to developers who create jobs in declining urban areas.

Often partnerships take the form of special-purpose authorities whose boards of directors include both government and business representatives. They are charged with carrying out specific development projects or programs and are chartered to act in the public interest. Yet because they operate outside the boundaries of government, they need not be responsive to popular political pressures. Such development authorities have been widely used in American cities since the 1960s, and their popularity is spreading in Europe. In some instances, they are formed to oversee the development of specific neighborhoods, such as the Zeidjik in Amsterdam or the Marais in Paris. Or their purpose may be to promote a specific type of development. So, for example, the North-Rhine Westphalian Center for Innovation and Technology, cosponsored by the Länder government and a group of banks and other businesses, promotes the adoption of new technologies by small and medium-sized companies. Or they may have as narrow and specific a task as the construction and maintenance of a specific facility, like a sports stadium or a convention center. Whatever their mission, these authorities are expected to reconcile public and private interests in the pursuit of economic development.

A good example is the Urban Development Corporation (UDC) created in 1981 by Britain's Conservative government to develop London's "docklands," stretching eastward down the Thames River from the Tower of London. Modeled on the development corporations that have built British new towns, the Docklands UDC was charged with regenerating almost nine square miles of decaying wharfs, warehouses, abandoned factories, and dilapidated housing. To accomplish this task, the UDC was granted substantial funds and extensive powers to acquire, hold, manage, and dispose of property and to negotiate with private investors. Its plans to transform the waterfront, which include exhibit halls, malls, offices, and upscale housing, have drawn vigorous protests from residents, who charge that the government's main motive in setting up a special-purpose authority was to insulate the scheme from local political constituencies. In a part of London that is traditionally dominated by Labour, the Docklands UDC virtually bypasses local government. The UDC's chief executive openly acknowledges his goal of "inviting the private sector to take the lead in investment," and promoting "a market-led response in place of a conventional planning response" (Ward, p. 207). Critics have complained that quasi-public authorities like the Docklands UDC threaten democratic accountability for development planning and shift the balance-of-power toward the private interests involved in the process.

In France, the same criticisms have been made about the public-private companies (*sociétés de'économie mixte*) that manage most large-scale urban development projects. Their loans come primarily from France's Central Savings Bank. Typically, 65 percent of the capital invested in these public-private development companies comes from government sources (Underhill, p. 32), and control over the companies tends to be exercised by national officials in collaboration with lenders. Out of the public eye, these quasi-public planning agencies "repeatedly adapt their goals for urban renewal to the needs of private investors" (Webman, p. 125).

Several Labour-controlled local governments in Britain have pioneered an alternative approach to public-private partnerships in the 1980s—one that guarantees greater democratic control. They have established "local enterprise boards" whose purpose is to foster development by investing public funds in private companies. Unlike the more traditional instruments of subsidies and loans, the enterprise boards' investments establish part-ownership in the companies, so that local government becomes a partner in the business operation itself. In London, the Greater London Enterprise Board was the offspring of a Labour-controlled Greater London Council (the regional-level government in London). Like its fledgling counterparts in four other cities, it is having difficulty surviving in Britain's neoconservative policy climate (Cochrane).

WHOSE CITY?
DISTRIBUTION

Urban planning is by definition an activity with strong distributive overtones; its purpose is to influence the distribution of people and economic activities across the urban landscape. Stated slightly differently, urban planners are concerned with the allocation of urban space to different socioeconomic groups, different firms, and different land uses. Viewed from this perspective, the activities of European and American planners have had rather different effects.

During much of the period after World War II, European planners concentrated their efforts on shifting population and economic activities away from congested central cities to planned suburban communities, or even to distant regions of the country where development was lagging. If we look at the kinds of economic activities and the kinds of people moving away from central cities from 1945 to 1975, we see that they were predominantly manufacturing firms and blue-collar workers. Britain's new towns program presents the best example. The jobs provided in new towns have tended to be manufacturing jobs. And since getting a house in a new town was normally tied to getting a job in the community, the residents of Britain's new towns have been, disproportionately, skilled industrial workers. Suburban and new town development around Paris has followed the same pattern; the factories located at the edge of the city are surrounded by working-class residential developments. In fact, the industrial suburbs of Paris are sometimes called the city's "red belt," because of the support they deliver to communist candidates.

It proved much more difficult for public authorities to decentralize office jobs away from the central cities. Powerful forces in the 1960s combined to increase the growth and concentration of corporate management, banking, insurance, finance, marketing, and advertising in central cities. In the late 1960s Paris tried to tighten its restrictions on the construction of office buildings in the city, but proved unable to stem the tide (Sundquist, p. 138). Britain's national government in 1964 tried to impose controls on office development in London and then in Birmingham similar to the controls that had helped decentralize manufacturing from London. Would-be developers were required to obtain a permit from the national government as well as the normal planning permission from the local authority. This permit system proved ineffective, however, because the ministry dispensing the permits had great difficulty distinguishing between offices that needed a central location and those that did not, and so gradually the system was dismantled (Sundquist, p. 76). The Netherlands has had a similar experience—greater success in luring manufacturers to suburban developments than in luring office developers.

So pronounced was the trend toward the dispersal of manufacturing by 1980 that several Western European governments began to question whether their policies to promote decentralization had gone too far. British policymakers were the first to reverse direction, after it became apparent that the accelerating exodus of manufacturing jobs from the central cities was creating, not just slower growth than in the suburbs, but an absolute loss of population (Drewett, p. 51). Continental European centers have not emptied out so quickly as British and American cities, yet the signs of similar trends are unmistakable.

Observers of these widespread trends argue about whether to attribute them to government policies that have encouraged the dispersal of industry. Some evidence suggests that public policy had little to do with the suburbanization of manufacturing, which would have occurred anyway. Studies in France and Britain, for example, show that the residential outflow to the suburbs actually *preceded* the decentralization of employment, as did suburbanization in many American metropolitan areas. Employers were, in effect, following the work force to the suburbs. There is further evidence that whole regions have begun declining, as population and employment have shifted away from the largest cities, and into small and medium-sized towns. The OECD reports that within its member nations, towns having populations between 50,000 and 100,000 grew by 30 percent during the 1970s, three times the rate of big cities with half a million or more people (OECD 1987, p. 16).

Even for Sweden, the least likely case, recent research has demonstrated that contrary to the impression of Swedish policymakers in the 1960s and 1970s, the cities were undergoing much the same process, albeit at a much more gradual rate. Population within the metropolitan regions was dispersing to the periphery; and over the country as a whole, population was growing faster in many small towns than in the metropolitan centers. Furthermore, Swedish research concludes that since regional development policy was not enacted early enough to have had a real impact on these trends, "an explanation of interregional shifts of the population must ultimately be based on an explanation of the structural changes in the economy as a whole" (Falk, p. 750). Thus the apparent breadth and depth of these trends throughout the postindustrial economies raise doubts about how large a role was played by public planners.

Why do these trends disturb policymakers? After all, dispersal of both people and economic activities was their goal through much of the post–World War II period. The problem is that migration out of the city centers has been highly selective. Younger, better-educated, more employable people have left, while more disadvantaged groups have stayed behind in the inner cities. The population shift has brought dramatic disparities between cities and suburbs, and even between regions.

The most striking example of such disparities is, of course, the United States. Suburban communities in the United States have been built primarily for middle- and upper-middle-class residents, while central cities are home to the society's working class and unemployed poor. The contributions made by public policy to this distribution pattern are well known; the FHA program, which exerted a strong influence over postwar housing development, favored middle-income buyers and suburban locations. The federal public housing program, on the other hand, concentrated its low-rent projects almost exclusively in central cities. The Interstate Highway System encouraged movement to the suburbs, by providing cheap transportation between outlying communities and central employment districts. Even the federal tax code increased the appeal of the suburbs to middle-income taxpayers, who could deduct both interest payments and property taxes paid on new suburban homes. As suburbanization continued through the 1960s and 1970s, more working-class Americans migrated to the suburbs, following the outflow of manufacturing jobs. Large residential districts in aging inner cities, especially in the Northeast and Midwest, have become the exclusive preserve of the unemployed poor. Gradually over the postwar period, the central cities have become business districts, dominated by skyscraper office buildings and ringed by decaying neighborhoods populated by those who could not afford to "escape" to the suburbs.

A large proportion of the people left behind were, of course, minorities. The very large concentration of blacks, Hispanics, and other minorities in the inner city has complicated planning issues in the United States compared with Europe. Moreover, there can be no doubt that racism accelerated the flight of many residents and businesses out of the inner cities. As large districts became identified as minority areas, they lost their appeal to white residents. But, having come to dominate these areas of the city, minority communities found that they had gained little except control over deteriorating houses and dying businesses.

Among the European countries, only Britain has experienced comparable racial problems. In the large cities there, growing numbers of immigrants from Britain's former colonies are clustered in inner city neighborhoods, including blacks from Africa and the West Indies and Asians from India and Pakistan. Currently, Britain's population of 56 million includes 2.2 million nonwhites. These people began migrating to British cities after World War II to work on subways and buses, in textile mills and hospital laundries, and on sanitation crews; as their numbers increased, they became more visible in urban neighborhoods and aroused growing concern—both from leftists who worried that they were taking jobs from British workers, and from conservatives who worried about law and order and, in the words of Margaret Thatcher, about "being swamped by people with a different culture." Especially during periods of economic hardship in Britain, racial tensions have broken into open street fighting. As in the United States, minorities in Britain tend to live in the most economically depressed parts of the city.

Other European countries have experienced similar difficulties, though on a smaller scale. In France, some of the Algerians who were granted French citizenship following Algerian independence in 1962 still live in run-down shacks at the edges of the large cities. Of all French cities, Marseilles has the largest number of immigrants living in these *bidonvilles,* or shantytowns.

Other French cities have reduced the squatter settlements by relocating immigrants in public housing. Better living conditions, however, have not eliminated the segregation and discrimination against North Africans. For example, one sprawling housing complex outside Paris, La Courneuve, includes two bleak towers called *Le 4000 Nord* and *Le 4000 Sud*, each of which contains four thousand apartments occupied mostly by immigrant families. Parisians advise visitors not to enter the complex, for fear they will be robbed or attacked. Of France's population of 54 million, about 1.4 million are North Africans, whose families came originally in the 1960s to work in expanding factories. Second-generation Arabs have found it harder to get employment in a slower-growing economy. One of the largest demonstrations in recent French history took place in December 1983, upon the arrival in Paris of seventeen sons and daughters of North African immigrants who had marched 750 miles from Marseilles to protest against racial discrimination and violence. Entering Paris, the marchers drew over ten thousand spectators for their final leg, suggesting how serious an issue racism has become for French urbanites.

In some Dutch cities, immigrants from Turkey, Morocco, and Surinam confront similar problems. Unlike the "guest workers," or foreign laborers, who flooded into France, West Germany, and other European countries in the 1960s, immigrants now face an economy in which urban unemployment is often twice as high for them as for Europeans. And their numbers are growing rapidly. In Rotterdam, for instance, birth rates for immigrant groups are three to five times higher than the Dutch birth rate. Alarmed by this rapid growth, the right-wing *Nederlandse Volksunie* party has called for the expulsion of all nonwhite immigrants and foreign workers. Even in peaceful Sweden riots broke out in August 1982, as gangs of Stockholm youths attacked a gathering of young Turkish immigrants, chanting, "Keep Sweden for the Swedes." The growth of unemployed, untrained, and poorly educated immigrants presents a challenge to the urban social order in Europe that increasingly resembles the challenge presented by America's urban underclass.

Another similarity in urban demographic trends on the two sides of the Atlantic is the growing proportion of elderly in the inner cities. Often living alone, they require a high level of services; yet they have disproportionately low incomes, with little to invest in improving their homes. As a result, the urban elderly are often concentrated in deteriorating districts.

The picture we have painted of urban decline must be qualified in one important respect: *some* neighborhoods of *some* big cities have undergone dramatic upgrading, even as the areas around them were emptying out. Of course, Europe's central cities have always housed significant numbers of middle-class and upper-middle-class residents and have retained them even during the recent decades of suburbanization. Indeed, inner-city residential districts in some European capitals like Paris are the most desirable locations in the region, and therefore populated by affluent professionals who can afford the high rents. The less affluent must be content to live at the edge of the city. One outspoken critic of Parisian urban planning labeled the workers who inhabit Parisian suburbs "the victims of commuting and of the dormitory suburbs" (Harloe, p. 152).

By contrast, most American inner cities were abandoned by the middle and upper-middle classes after World War II. In some of the most blighted neighborhoods, however, middle-class whites began to reclaim whole blocks in the mid-1970s. The persistence of white-collar employment in central business districts, along with soaring fuel and housing costs in the suburbs, led them back to the city. Typically, the influx of the new "gentry" into these neighborhoods was accompanied by large investments in the rehabilitation of houses and in improvements to community facilities. As a consequence, housing values and rent levels in "gentrified" areas rose markedly and the lower-income residents often found themselves displaced by newcomers who were able to pay the inflated prices.

In effect, this process has redistributed space in central city neighborhoods, taking it away from long-term residents and allocating it to more affluent newcomers. The trend was observed in the 1970s in both British and American cities (Laska and Spain; Hamnett and Williams), and by 1980 it had been documented as well in cities on the continent, especially Paris, Amsterdam, and Stockholm (Gale 1984, pp. 119–40). Critics have charged that in many cases the actions of local government actually contribute to the redistributive process. Public grants to home buyers for rehabilitation and public investments in community improvements make such neighborhoods more attractive to the middle class. Local governments' increasing reliance on private investors to finance renewal will probably exacerbate the trend toward gentrification, as developers prefer to build shops, offices, or *residences de grand standing*, rather than low- and moderate-income housing.

Criticisms of and appeals to government to intervene to prevent displacement of the poor have provoked very little response from local officials. The reason is obvious. The vitality of the local economy and by extension the vitality of the local tax base are improved by an influx of middle-income residents. Thus it is simply not in the interest of local officials to discourage such an influx. On the contrary, they have everything to gain by encouraging the trend, if necessary by investing public money to attract middle-income residents. Only in a communist-controlled city like Bologna in the 1970s could one find a local government that deliberately discouraged gentrification in the city center in order to avoid displacing lower-income residents.

The gentrification of urban neighborhoods is only one illustration of the undeniable convergence of the interests of city government and those of the city's dominant economic groups. City governments throughout Europe and the United States depend in some measure on tax revenues generated from profitable businesses and from middle-class residents, and city officials must therefore put a high priority on attracting and retaining those groups in the city. But how far should local governments go to accommodate the preferences of key businesses and affluent residents?

One school of political scientists in Europe and the United States—the so-called neo-Marxist school—has portrayed public planners as the agents of the dominant economic classes in cities, and urban public policy as simply an extension of the interests of those classes (Castells; Harloe; Harvey; Walton). In many ways this case is more easily made for the United States than for Europe. Few observers of urban development policies in American cities would dispute neo-Marxist claims that the key function of local government in the American system has been to influence the distribution of economic growth (Molotch), and that the main impact of land-use planning in American cities has been to adapt land-use patterns to the needs of production and exchange (Mollenkopf). The direct influence of developers and business interests on urban policy is in fact institutionalized in the policy process, for the legal and political frameworks within which American city planners operate require that they constantly consult and accommodate the important private development interests in the city. In fact, American public planning can be seen in large part as a mechanism for facilitating and protecting private development activity (Barnekov and Rich).

The argument that public planners operate simply as tools of the city's dominant economic interests is not so convincing for European cities, mainly because their planning process is somewhat different. Typically in Europe, the activities of public planners have very low visibility in the urban community, and so planners do not experience the same degree of pressure from either powerful private interest groups or from citizen lobbies that American planners must continually confront. And, since conflict over planning issues is often confined to debate within and among administrative bodies, the European city planner is typically less responsive to external pressures. This has been particularly true in continental Europe, where municipal bureaucrats (as distinct from elected officials) enjoy very high status and play the dominant decision-making role. But even in Britain, where local politics more closely resembles the American scene, the Chamber of Commerce, labor unions, and other organized economic interest groups have much less influence on land-use and development planning than in the United States (Elkin).

The relationship between local governments and local interest groups is strongly influenced by the extent of national intervention in local affairs. Because European national governments supervise many of the activities of the local governments, local officials often take on the additional role of agent for the national government in the community. While it may limit their administrative options, this link to national agencies may also provide a political "backstop" for local officials in their dealings with local pressure groups.

The political economists who employ a neo-Marxist framework do not necessarily presume that there is overt, direct manipulation of local officials by the capitalist class. Their analysis posits instead the existence of an ideology shared by planners with the capitalist class. The ideology, which reinforces class power, need not even be consciously recognized by the public officials who apply it. An example of this analytical perspective is Manuel Castells' criticism of the Parisian urban renewal program for its emphasis on office development as opposed to housing. Castells does not claim that developers exerted direct influence over public planners. Rather, he asserts that the view which public officials held of their own interests coincided almost perfectly with the interests of developers (Castells, pp. 317–20).

The neo-Marxists' model of urban politics, in which the interests and priorities of capitalists are translated almost mechanically into public policy, no matter who is in power, is consistent with the findings of much research on local politics done in the 1960s and 1970s. Studies of the factors influencing urban policy have overwhelmingly concluded that the political orientation of the group in power in local government is not an important determinant of policy outputs (Fried).

Given the failure of most researchers in the field to establish linkages between party politics and local policy, should we conclude that local politics is moribund in the cities of Europe and the United States? Such a conclusion would be premature. Instead, we see local political conflicts increasingly fought outside the bounds of traditional party politics. The phenomenon of the single-issue citizens' protest group, unaffiliated with any established party and formed on an ad hoc basis, has long been a feature of American local politics. Such groups have recently become common in Europe and Japan as well. Typically, they take the form of territorial coalitions of residents whose space is threatened by government action. In Germany, for example, civic action groups known as *Burgerinitiativen* have sprung up in virtually every big city in response to public redevelopment projects. In Munich such groups have been formed to protest demolitions of housing and to stop the Land government from building on the grounds of a city park. In Hamburg groups have protested against the disruptions caused by new highway construction, and against the planned construction of a nuclear power plant north of the city (Sorensen, p. 7). After a celebrated, decade-long struggle in London, citizens' groups finally forced the GLC to abandon its plan for a massive new road network (Hart, Thomson). In Amsterdam the city's urban renewal program has engendered resistance from dozens of campaign committees carrying such determined names as "Stay Out of Our Neighborhood" and "The Strong Arm" (Heinemeyer and Gastelaars). As we mention in Chapter 9, local environmental disasters in Japan prompted the formation of victims' associations, which evolved into large-scale citizens' movements. By the early 1970s there were an estimated three thousand such groups (Pempel, p. 237)—a significant departure from the traditional politics of consensus in Japan. Even in Sweden, where public protests against government actions have been exceedingly rare, there were in the 1970s signs of citizen unrest. In Malmo, for example, a citizens' protest movement forced the abandonment of a plan to build a one hundred-foot-wide road through the center of the old city (Wiedenhoeft).

In the case of the United States, the abundance of such citizen action groups has often been explained as arising from the weakness of local political parties. American political commentators have often expressed envy of European systems, because by comparison local parties in the United States "are neither ideologically oriented nor do they have a sustained social program" (Aiken, p. 111). Consequently, they do not aggregate collective interests in a social program that is sustained by an ideology.

But how do we explain the proliferation of single-issue groups in Europe, where political parties at the local level are directly tied to ideological, programmatic, national parties? Local party competition in most European cities is structured around the same party organizations and ideologies that compete at the national level. Yet the presence of strong local party organizations in Europe does not necessarily help to structure political conflict on *local* issues. Voters tend to select their party identification based on the various parties' stands on national issues rather than on local issues. Consequently, the local party organizations play a weaker role in mediating local conflicts than we might expect. In fact, it may be that these national/local linkages, so envied by Americans, actually contribute to the growing incidence of political activism outside the bounds of party politics. That is the intriguing suggestion made by one recent study of British local politics. Examining the dominance of national parties on the British local scene, the authors noted that voters tend to vote for local candidates on the basis of their party affiliation. Local issues in fact have little influence over electoral outcomes. That being the case, local politicians do not consider their electoral fortunes tied to their decisions on local issues and, as a consequence, may easily become less responsive to constituents' opinions on those issues. The authors' conclusion was that "national partisanship impedes responsive governance at the local level" (Peterson and Kantor, p. 198).

The rising tide of citizen activism in European cities can be read not only as a show of dissatisfaction with local party politics; perhaps even more significant is the implication that citizens are dissatisfied with the planners and technicians who make the important decisions. With increasing frequency, citizens' groups are asserting that the decisions made by the planning bureaucracy represent more than technical solutions to problems— they represent distributional choices about whose property is expropriated, whose street is widened for heavier traffic, and whose neighborhood is changed. These questions must ultimately lead to challenges to the political authority that planners have historically wielded (Susskind and Elliott).

LIMITS TO PUBLIC POWER
RESTRAINTS AND INNOVATION

One of the major policy concerns of urban planners throughout Europe and the United States in the 1980s is the extent to which they can and should influence the distribution of people and economic activities within metropolitan regions and among the various regions of the country. With increasing frequency in the United States and Britain, doubts have been voiced about the wisdom of trying to combat or even restrain the operation of market forces in urban areas. The political tide in both countries has turned in favor of giving private enterprise a freer hand to shape the economy of the nation, of cities, and, by extension, of the urban physical environment.

One reason for the emerging free-market bias is increased awareness in the late 1980s of the competition that Western countries are facing in the world market, and the consequent emphasis on productivity. The pressure on the Western economies to compete with Third World economies, where goods can be produced more cheaply, has brought the issue of economic productivity to the forefront. This trend is crucial for urban policy because it weakens the case for policies aimed at containing and redistributing growth to achieve an optimal distribution of population and economic activities within the national land area. Planning for balance and containment of urban growth is perceived by many policymakers as incompatible with an all-out effort to maximize productivity. Advocates of pro-growth policies are likely to want to give private entrepreneurs free rein to make locational decisions that maximize their productivity, regardless of whether those decisions conform to government planners' notions of the optimal distribution of people and firms. Considerations of this kind have already led the United States and Britain to shift their urban policy emphases.

In reality, this shift requires no dramatic change in U.S. policies, for American urban planning has always operated essentially to support rather than to control private market forces. The "public planning" done by city renewal authorities in the United States consists largely of furnishing support services for private real estate interests: selecting sites which the authorities believe will be attractive to private capital, acquiring the sites through condemnation or purchase, and clearing them in order to resell to private developers. Local public authorities have not only provided a service to private developers in assembling redevelopment sites, but the national government has subsidized the purchase of the land by private enterprise, through the device of the "write-down." Under the 1949 Urban Renewal Act the local authority, after purchasing and clearing a site, could resell it at a price far below what they paid for it; the national government then paid the city between two-thirds and three-fourths of the difference between the city's expenditures (in buying, clearing, and developing the tract) and the price charged to the private developer. Frequently, this provision allowed private developers to purchase prime city lots with several million dollars worth of federal subsidies. This subsidy system operated on the premise that the urban renewal program had to compete with other forms of investment for the developers' interest and that renewal opportunities must therefore be made particularly attractive to private capital. As one federal official observed in 1960, urban renewal in the United States was "in essence private real estate development with a brief interval of government intervention" (Brownfield, p. 737).

In the 1970s the role of public planning as a complement to, and support for, private capital began to receive increased emphasis. The 1974 Housing and Community Development Act and subsequent legislation in the community development field (such as the Urban Development Action Grants) emphasized the obligation of city officials to use public development funds to "leverage" private investments in cities. If this "leveraging" is to occur, then private investors must be given a central decision-making role in virtually all housing, commercial, and industrial development planning for cities. In the late 1970s, the Carter administration reinforced this trend by basing its urban policy on the premise that urban decay results from a decline in the overall economic position of central cities in the national and world economy. Programs to aid cities therefore must focus primarily on encouraging economic growth in cities. Only weeks before he left office in 1981, President Carter received the report of his blue ribbon Commission for a National Agenda for the Eighties. Its controversial recommendations on urban policy went even further than the administration itself had gone in stressing economic growth: "The federal government's concern for national economic vitality should take precedence over the competition for advantage among communities and regions" (*Report of the President's Commission*). At a time when successes are so few and public resources so meager, the commission argued, it is futile to try to restrain the flow of private capital from the inner cities of the Northeast and Midwest to newer suburban centers and to the Sunbelt. Instead of wasting government resources trying to prop up deteriorating cities, public policy should subsidize the migration of unemployed people to locations where jobs are available. The priorities and preferences of private capital, in short, should be given free rein, regardless of the cost to the nation's aging industrial centers.

Even some of the most outspoken free marketeers in Washington, such as Republican Representative Jack Kemp of New York (subsequently named Secretary of Housing and Urban Development by President Bush), balked at the harsh recommendations of the Carter commission, preferring to see local governments make an all-out effort to attract private investors through a device known as the "enterprise zone." Cities would designate these zones in certain distressed sections, and would offer to potential business investors a package of financial incentives in exchange for their locating in the zone and hiring local workers. The incentives would include a variety of federal tax breaks—a cut in capital gains taxes, a reduction in business taxes, a huge reduction in Social Security payroll taxes, and accelerated depreciation allowances on plant and equipment. In addition, the businesses would be exempt from a range of government regulations ranging from health, safety, and environmental regulations to the minimum wage. Local governments would be expected to follow the federal example by reducing local taxes and regulations in the zone. The hope was that dramatic reduction of the burdens imposed by government taxes and regulations would lure wary investors back to the urban core. Originally put forward by conservative Republicans, the idea was endorsed by President Reagan, but also by liberal groups including the NAACP and the Urban Coalition.

American conservatives did not invent the enterprise zone idea; they borrowed it from British Conservatives. In 1978, while still in opposition, Conservatives formulated a proposal which was later implemented when the Thatcher government came to power in 1979. Although the version ultimately inserted in the March 1980 budget fell short of the original proposal, it maintained the basic principle that areas would be designated in British cities where businesses would benefit from fifteen years' exemption from corporation tax, complete freedom from Britain's development land tax, and increased capital allowances. At the same time, the Thatcher government moved to reduce the government's role in urban land-use planning. In distinct contrast to Labour policies, the Thatcher Conservatives sought "to limit the state's role to providing basic unremunerative infrastructure and the facilitation of private development" (Cox, p. 276). They even signaled a willingness in the mid-1980s to relax land-use controls in the green belt surrounding London (Ambrose, pp. 200–13). The Tories' pronouncements that more development would be desirable, even if it meant sacrificing some open space, met quick and determined resistance from the Greater London Council (GLC). The Labour-controlled GLC countered with a statement that if the lower-level borough governments proved too weak to resist development pressures, then the GLC itself would undertake "positive intervention at the strategic level" to preserve the open space (GLC, p. 8). The GLC's spirited opposition to further development of the green belt may be one reason why the Thatcher government decided in 1986 to dismantle the GLC, which it labeled an unnecessary and obstructionist layer of government between Whitehall and the town halls.

The Thatcher government also imposed significant cutbacks in the regional programs which had been accepted by both parties since 1945. Throughout the 1970s the national government had attempted to redistribute economic activity in the nation by giving blanket aid to lagging regions and discouraging expansion in already-congested regions. The Conservatives under Thatcher abolished the Regional Economic Planning Councils, dramatically reduced the amount of aid to lagging regions, and cut back on the scope of industrial location controls.

As in the United States, the shift away from urban policies designed to constrain private market forces toward policies which support and stimulate the private market is supported by a broad spectrum of political groups. The perception is widely shared in Britain that the cities are in trouble because of the country's declining economic fortunes, and that to rebuild them one must first address the larger economic question. Even the prestigious Town and Country Planning Association (TCPA), long an advocate of government control over land development, has come to the conclusion that trying to prevent the forces of decentralization at work in Britain's metropolitan areas is futile and costly. Instead, the government should support private enterprise in its move to decentralize (TCPA; see also Lawless, pp. 224–25).

It would be a mistake to attribute this tendency to accommodate the private sector entirely to the emergence of neoconservatism in national politics, even though such accommodation is a well-known tenet of both Thatcher and Reagan. Other factors are at work as well that prompt local officials (of many different political stripes) to defer increasingly to the needs of private entrepreneurs and developers. An informative case study of one inner London borough in the mid-1970s illustrated why so many local authorities have elevated economic development to a higher status than physical planning. When a major employer threatened to leave, the council's chief concern became job development instead of housing and amenities, and the borough's Industrial Development Officer gained increasing power. After several years of squabbling over whether a valuable riverfront tract would be used for much-needed housing or for industrial development, the Labour-controlled council finally abandoned its preference for housing and amenities, and sided with the economic development lobby. The borough's 1977–78 budget contained the council's first capital allocation for industrial development, £250,000 (Young and Mills, pp. 101–22).

Everywhere in Europe one sees signs of the priority that local authorities are placing on stimulating economic growth in the older city regions. The signs range from more sympathetic responses to industrial building applications, to greater efforts to assemble and service industrial land. Some local governments have relaxed planning bans on nonconforming uses, while others have played down environmental constraints on commercial and industrial development. Planners face a complicated set of trade-offs when they abandon planning controls in order to stimulate development. Giving some private firms more freedom to develop their land as they see fit may create environmental problems for others—disamenities that could ultimately deter new firms from locating within the city. Since residential and work choices seem increasingly to be made on amenity considerations, some basic protection of a community's quality of life is vital to its future economic development.

More and more, local governments perceive the campaign for new development as a zero-sum game, in which one city's gain is another's loss. A good example is the competition among Dutch municipalities to offer prospective employers the lowest price for cleared industrial land. Technically, Dutch cities are not supposed to dispose of industrial land for less than it costs them to expropriate and redevelop the site. So hungry are many towns for new development, however, that they find ways to set the lowest possible prices, sometimes below their own cost. One technique is to push some of the costs onto other municipal accounts. Moreover, instead of insisting on disposing of the land through long-term leases, most Dutch cities are now selling their properties outright to industrial buyers, even though that relinquishes control over future land-use (Needham, pp. 303–05). Summing up the change in Dutch planning controls in the late 1970s and early 1980s, one commentator observed that "to encourage business growth, government had to be more tolerant in allowing business and housing developers to locate new facilities where they chose, whether or not such decisions contradicted established spatial planning policy" (Levine and van Weesep, p. 321).

Despite this widespread tendency among planners in both Europe and the United States, we should expect continental governments to practice the free-market approach more cautiously than their British and American counterparts. Even among conservatives on the Continent there is greater reluctance to abandon public controls altogether. This is so because most conservative parties in Europe contain not only the kind of "neo-liberals" who advocate a laissez-faire approach to business, but also statists who see the need for firm government guidance in the economy and society.

* * * * *

Urban planning, then, is one of the most visible activities of government, both because it affects the physical circumstances in which people live and because it frequently brings government into direct conflict with the rights of citizens. When conflicts have arisen between private property and the interest of the community as articulated by public authorities, European planners have prevailed more regularly than American planners. Blessed with a cultural tradition that accepts public regulation and ownership of land in the city, and backed by national subsidies, local planners in Europe have not been limited to projects that generate immediate payoffs. Hence, they have been better able to balance economic gains with other considerations such as the architectural value of historic districts and the equitable distribution of the benefits of development. Their latitude of choice may well be narrowing, however, as the need to revitalize declining urban economies forces them to accommodate the needs and preferences of private sector entrepreneurs and developers.

9
ENVIRONMENTAL POLICY

Of all the concerns of governments that we analyze in this book, environmental pollution is the most recent. Not that pollution itself is a modern condition. Far from it. Beginning in the thirteenth century, British citizens protested against the smoke and odors that emanated from coal fires. In the New World, historical records tell us that Los Angeles had a smog problem as early as 1542, when Spanish occupiers suffered from a thermal inversion that trapped the smoke from native American fires. At least since the Renaissance, Western societies have viewed the conquest of the forces of nature as a necessary part of humankind's productive and creative activities. After centuries of conquest, it is clear that the damage we have done to the earth's ecological balance ultimately threatens us as well.

While we can trace back centuries and find episodes of pollution, the most dramatic deterioration in the environment took place with industrialization, which brought widespread use of internal combustion engines and petroleum products. As the earliest continents to industrialize, Europe and North America first fell victim to air pollution arising from factories' use of fossil fuels for energy, from elaborate transportation networks and the growing use of the automobile, and from tons of industrial waste which found its way into rivers, streams, and even the groundwater at industrial sites.

Although industrialization magnified the threat from environmental pollution, national governments in Europe and the United States did not respond systematically to that threat until the middle of the twentieth century. Many observers attribute the environmental awakening of national politicians to a general shift in values in Western societies—a shift that Suzanne Berger has characterized as "an explosion of doubt about the quality and direction of life in advanced industrial societies" (Berger). By the 1960s Western societies no longer doubted the economy's ability to provide growth and material prosperity. What they questioned was the all-too-evident success of the economy and the price it extracted in other realms of life. With surprising swiftness, government leaders added "quality-of-life" issues to the political agenda.

A distinctive feature of environmental policy is the technical and scientific nature of its central questions. No doubt this discourages some citizens from following environmental debates as closely as they would other policy areas. Yet for all their scientific and technical apparatus, environmental policies have immediate and far-reaching consequences for the average citizen's daily life and livelihood.

Unlike most other chapters in this book, this chapter focuses on *regulatory* policies designed to influence the private decisions and behavior of millions of householders disposing of trash and garbage and driving automobiles, and business owners whose factories, utilities, oil companies, and mines generate tons of pollution in the course of production. Typically, environmental policy involves government decisions that must be implemented largely by nongovernment actors, either as individuals or in private sector firms. Thus, its acceptability to the citizenry depends on deep-seated beliefs and values regarding the role of government in society.

CHOICES IN ENVIRONMENTAL POLICY

Scope and Thresholds

Government intervention to protect the environment is largely a post–World War II phenomenon. In a virtual explosion of activity since the 1950s, national authorities have developed a vast corpus of legislation to restrain citizens and corporations from recklessly fouling the air, land, and water on which they depend for life and health. These initiatives fall into four broad categories: (1) regulation of emissions into the air, (2) regulation of discharges into water, (3) treatment and disposal of solid wastes, including toxic wastes, and (4) treatment and disposal of nuclear wastes. This last category has been regulated separately from other wastes, including other hazardous wastes. Because it is produced and regulated so differently from other pollutants, nuclear waste will be excluded from the discussion in this chapter.[1]

---

[1]Nuclear waste is produced by only a limited number of generators in much smaller quantities than other hazardous wastes, and is transported in a small number of consignments to only a few treatment and storage facilities. Compared with other polluting industries, the nuclear-power industry has few centers of decision, control, and responsibility. It is typically a mo-

We associate environmentalism with the burgeoning of grass roots citizen participation in the 1960s throughout the Western countries. As motivating issues, nuclear power and other environmental concerns were second only to the Vietnam War in their power to mobilize middle-class citizens. Yet once mobilized, the environmental movement had difficulty incorporating itself into national politics, largely because its goals and style did not fit that of traditional party politics. The environmentalists' banner has therefore been carried by newly formed ecology parties throughout Europe.

Environmental Policy Instruments

As with most regulatory policies, this one raises questions about the extent to which governments should employ coercion to obtain compliance from citizens. The most basic choice that governments make in selecting instruments and techniques to protect the environment is between confrontation and collaboration as ways of approaching polluters. This is both a philosophical question about the proper relationship between public and private sectors and a practical question. Which approach is likely to achieve the greatest reductions in pollution?

Interestingly, the government of the United States, whose political and legal culture is the most protective of private property rights, takes the most confrontational position toward private polluters of any nation under study here. Its laws are the strictest, giving administrators the least discretion in their dealings with industry. But the strictness of laws and procedures in the United States has not necessarily produced better results than in other countries that take a more conciliatory stance toward industry.

Pricing systems, which exact a fee from polluters based on the volume of emissions from their plants, have recently gained popularity on both sides of the Atlantic. The fee forces a company to pay for its pollution, thereby encouraging the owner to minimize emissions. Such instruments have attracted adherents on both the political Left and Right. Conservatives like them because they operate by market principles, as opposed to more coercive uses of government power. At the same time, politicians on the Left applaud this public statement that corporations should pay more of the real cost of producing their goods, instead of expecting the public sector to absorb the cost of cleaning up their waste.

---

nopoly industry and therefore not subject to the kind of competition that influences the regulatory environment in other industrial sectors. Government regulators are an integral part of industrial design, planning, and decision making. Political questions about the appropriate level and type of government intervention—so central to the politics of pollution in other spheres—are virtually non-issues in the nuclear industry. These features of the nuclear waste problem lend themselves to analysis separate from other industrial wastes. See Kasperson, Surrey, Wynne.

Distribution of Costs and Benefits

Increasingly, policymakers in the environmental field are adopting cost-benefit analysis to decide which environmental controls should be imposed. Despite some methodological disagreements, the general principle that the social benefits of regulation should equal its costs is gaining acceptance as a framework for thinking about environmental policy.

There are some serious weaknesses in this approach from a political, if not an economic, standpoint. It fails to take into account the most fundamental distributive question: Who reaps the benefits and who pays the costs? Politicians can seldom afford to operate on calculations of the aggregate benefits and costs of any given policy. What is important to their constituents is how the benefits and costs are allocated. One of the most common obstacles to environmental improvement is the asymmetry of costs and benefits. For example, while the benefits of pure water are widely distributed, the disadvantage of having a massive new water treatment facility built next door is borne by a single neighborhood. Citizens who bear such costs may be expected to mobilize immediately against the policy or project, while those who enjoy the broader benefits may feel less inclined to become active in defense of the program.

Restraints and Innovation

The above observation about the asymmetry of benefits and costs has led some observers to conclude that environmentalism has no dedicated political constituency, yet strong political enemies (Schnaiberg et al., p. 231). Particularly when they endanger the livelihoods of particular groups of workers, or threaten particular industrial sectors or regions of the country, environmental policies excite opposition. The heightened sensitivity to unemployment throughout the Western world in the 1980s seems to have produced a more cautious brand of environmentalism that balances ecological and economic goals.

Government officials at all levels, from municipalities to nation-states, face the fact that they cannot control all of the factors that impinge on the quality of the environment within their borders. Pollution travels easily across artificial political boundaries. Moreover, the growing interdependence of the global economy means that more and more, the governments of different municipalities, provinces, and countries compete against one another for investment. Corporations are far more mobile than ever before, and they can choose to locate wherever they find the most hospitable economic and political conditions. Among those conditions is the regulatory climate—and this fact alone may discourage some jurisdictions from strengthening environmental standards.

The combined effect of cross-national spillovers and increased capital mobility has been to heighten efforts at international cooperation. The

United Nations, the Common Market, the Organisation for Economic Co-operation and Development (OECD), and numerous other international organizations have placed environmental concerns near the top of their agendas. If it has spawned few hard-and-fast agreements among nations, their work has at least encouraged cooperation on research and technological development.

POLLUTION AS A POLITICAL ISSUE
SCOPE AND THRESHOLDS

A 1960 report prepared for U.S. President Dwight Eisenhower and titled *Goals for America* identified the fifteen most important goals for national government attention and action in the coming decade. That report did not even mention addressing environmental problems as one of the fifteen. Yet less than five years later, environmental concerns had emerged in a position very near the top of the list of concerns for national legislators. In other Western societies as well, at a similarly rapid pace, national governments moved to protect the air, water, and land from damaging pollution.

To illustrate how environmental issues thrust their way onto national political agendas in the 1960s and 1970s, let us take the problem of air pollution as an example. From 1950 to 1980, worldwide use of fossil fuels quadrupled, led by the economic expansion and the rise in auto ownership in Europe, North America, and Japan (Brown et al., p. 11). The effects of this steep rise in air pollutants began to appear first in Scandinavian lakes, whose aquatic life disappeared when acid rain contaminated the water. Dying lakes multiplied across Europe and North America. Not many years later, it became apparent that the same kinds of air pollutants also damaged forests, especially mountain forests. Produced primarily, though not only,

TABLE 9.1 EMISSIONS OF TRADITIONAL AIR POLLUTANTS, 1980

	Units Emitted per Person (kg/capita)				Units Emitted per Person (kg/TOE)			
	SO_x[a]	*Part.*[b]	NO_x[c]	CO[d]	SO_x	*Part.*	NO_x	CO
United States	102	37	89	334	17.8	6.4	15.6	58.3
Japan	11	1	11	—	4.8	.5	5.1	—
France	66	5	48	97	24.8	1.8	17.9	36.2
West Germany	52	12	50	146	16.0	3.6	15.4	44.7
Italy	67	3	27	71	35.9	1.9	14.6	38.1
Netherlands	31	11	35	97	8.7	2.9	9.7	26.6
Sweden	58	20	39	150	14.0	4.9	9.5	36.3
Britain	83	8	34	92	33.9	3.2	14.0	37.3

NOTE   [a]Sulphur oxides; [b]Particulate matter; [c]Nitrogen oxides; [d]Carbon monoxide.
SOURCE   OECD, *Environmental Data Compendium* (Paris: OECD, 1987), p. 19.

TABLE 9.2 MAJOR POTENTIAL HEALTH AND ECOLOGICAL EFFECTS OF TRADITIONAL AIR POLLUTANTS

Pollutants	Effects on Human Health	Effects on the Natural Environment
Carbon monoxide (CO)	Can affect the cardio-vascular system, exacerbating cardiovascular disease symptoms, particularly angina Can affect the central nervous system, impairing physical coordination, vision and judgment	
Nitrogen oxides (NO_x)	Nitrogen dioxide (NO_2) can affect the respiratory system Nitrogen monoxide (NO) and nitrogen dioxide (NO_2), where they play a part in photochemical smog formation, may contribute indirectly to increased susceptibility to infections, pulmonary disease, impairment of lung function and eye, nose and throat irritations	NO and NO_2 can contribute significantly to acid deposition, damaging aquatic ecosystems and possibly other ecosystems such as forests; NO_x has also a fertilizing effect on forests
Sulphur oxides (SO_x)	Sulphur dioxide (SO_2) can exert effects on lung function	SO_2 and other sulphur oxides can contribute significantly to acid deposition causing impairment of aquatic and possibly other ecosystems Sulphates can affect the perception of the environment by reducing visibility even at low concentrations
Particulate matter	Fine particulate matter may be toxic in itself or may carry toxic (including carcinogenic) trace substances Fine particulate can penetrate deep into the respiratory system, irritating lung tissue and causing long-term disorders	High dust and soot levels are associated with a general perception of dirtiness of the environment Fine particulates, in the size range of the wavelength of visible light, can significantly reduce visibility

SOURCE OECD, *Environmental Data Compendium* (Paris: OECD, 1987), p. 18.

in the industrialized nations, air pollutants from fossil fuels built up quickly to a point at which their devastating effects were visible over vast stretches of water and woodlands.

Pollution control became a growth industry which employed about 1.25 million people in the European Community by 1978. This total, which includes workers engaged in manufacturing equipment, operating and maintaining equipment, and providing services and public sector administration, amounts to about 1 percent of the work force in the European Community (JURUE/ECOTEC). Not only does the industry service the European market; it also provides exports. As a whole, the European Community is a net exporter of pollution control and waste treatment equipment, West Germany being the largest supplier.

If we review the results of this flurry of legislative activity on environmental issues from the late 1960s, we conclude that the content of environmental policies differs little among the nations of the West (Knoepfel et al. 1987, p. 174). That is not to say that national policy profiles are indistinguishable from one another. There are, for example, striking differences in the disposal of solid waste and hazardous waste in Western Europe and the United States. Europeans possess only limited amounts of vacant land for disposing of garbage and toxic wastes. Moreover, they depend heavily on groundwater for drinking; in some nations as much as 90 percent of the drinking water comes out of the ground. Confronted by these physical limitations, the Europeans have chosen to dump very little of their waste into landfills—particularly toxic waste. Instead, they employ high-temperature incinerators to reduce the volume of waste drastically before it is disposed of. For example, West Germany sends 85 percent of all its waste to treatment facilities; very little goes to landfills. German law makes the treatment and disposal of waste primarily the government's responsibility, al-

TABLE 9.3 ESTIMATED FOREST DAMAGE FROM AIR POLLUTION, 1986

	Total Area Damaged (000 hectares)	Percent of Total Forest Area Damaged
Netherlands	171	55
West Germany	3,952	54
Britain	979	49
France	4,043	28
Sweden	3,434	15*
Italy	416	5

NOTE   *Coniferous forests only.

SOURCE   International Cooperative Programme on Assessment and Monitoring of Air Pollution Effects on Forests, "Forest Damage and Air Pollution: Report on the 1986 Forest Damage Survey in Europe" (United Nations Environment Programme, Nairobi, 1987). Mimeographed.

though government may choose to delegate some tasks to private industry when that is appropriate. The Dutch Parliament, while avidly supporting waste treatment instead of mere landfilling, has gone even farther. Their 1976 Chemical Waste Act prohibited dumping a wide variety of toxic wastes, and even prohibited the manufacture of certain goods that generate wastes which are "impossible or very difficult to dispose of." With this measure, the Dutch government secured the ability to circumvent the disposal problem by preventing the wastes from being generated in the first place.

The U.S. government, by contrast, neglected the toxic waste problem during the flurry of air and water pollution legislation in the 1970s. (This, despite the fact that processes for cleaning up the country's air and water themselves produce toxic residues which must then be disposed of.) While Congress did take steps in the late 1970s to upgrade the condition of America's landfills, it was not until 1982 that the Environmental Protection Agency got around to writing regulations to control the dumping of toxic wastes into landfills. California was the first state, and one of only a few, to restrict landfilling as a way to encourage treatment and incineration (Piasecki and Davis, pp. 71ff). The United States continues to dump about 80 percent of its hazardous wastes into landfills.

European public authorities are more involved than their U.S. counterparts in managing hazardous wastes, especially by operating public treatment facilities. As early as 1968, the Länder (State) and local governments in the West German state of Bavaria joined to create the world's first hazardous-waste treatment center. Together with private investors, the two levels of government financed the facilities, with the Länder owning 40 percent, municipal cooperatives owning 30 percent, and fifty industrial corporations owning the remaining stock. As part-owner in the venture, the Bavarian state government has negotiated treatment and collection rules with industries and with citizen groups to encourage businesses and householders to bring their waste to the treatment facility (or to collection sites that are scattered throughout the state). By 1980, five out of ten German states had formed similar joint venture companies with private investors to handle waste treatment. Most American localities, while they assume responsibility for disposing of household trash and garbage, do not provide disposal services for businesses that generate waste. In fact, businesses are specifically excluded from many municipal waste disposal systems, and must contract with private haulers.

Why is the content of some environmental policies (air and water) so similar on the two sides of the Atlantic, while the content of other environmental policies (toxic waste) differs substantially? One possible explanation lies in political culture. Since air and water pollution are mostly emitted from discrete sources, those sources can be identified and emission standards applied to them relatively easily at the point of dispersal into the environment. But toxic wastes may travel great distances, undergo chemical and physical transformations, and be handled by several different agents before they are finally dispersed into the environment. Controlling such wastes requires even closer knowledge and control of the production process than is required to police air and water emissions. Government authorities need information, not just on the pollutant at the point of emission, but also on where and how it was produced and what path it took to a final disposal site. Just to secure that information, much less force private producers to modify their processes, government must intrude in a way that "runs counter to strong traditions of private property in the U.S., where the sanctity of an industrial process is not under the purview of government" (Piasecki and Davis, p. 10).

How Important Is Public Pressure?

To what extent was the "explosion" of environmental regulation in the 1970s due to citizen pressure on political leaders? We have already mentioned the detectable shift in public opinion in Western societies during recent decades—a shift away from economic growth and toward quality-of-life concerns. This shift has been described by Ronald Inglehart as the ascent of "post-materialism," a constellation of values elevating personal empowerment and participation and life-style issues over material well-being and physical security (Inglehart 1977). Inglehart hypothesizes that an individual's economic circumstances during upbringing play a crucial role in shaping his or her values. A period of sustained prosperity following World War II brought about a fundamental intergenerational shift in value priorities within Western societies. Citizens became less preoccupied with basic material needs and began to place higher priority on the quality of their lives. This value shift appears to have been most pronounced among people in white-collar and service occupations—a growing segment of all Western populations. Inglehart's post-materialists place particularly high value on protection of the environment and a life-style that is high-quality but simple.

Public anxiety about pollution runs high throughout the advanced industrial nations. A Common Market opinion poll taken in 1982 revealed acute and very widespread concern among Europeans about the deterioration of the environment, even on the part of respondents who did not suffer from particular nuisances in their own surroundings. (See Table 9.4.) No single pollution problem appeared to be decidedly more salient than others, though respondents expressed slightly more concern about chemical wastes and damage from oil tankers than about the others. In Japan as well, public opinion strongly favors environmentalism. However, Inglehart questions whether in fact the nonmaterialist values expressed by Japanese respondents are necessarily reflections of a genuine post-materialist culture. He speculates instead that some of these value positions may in fact be remnants of Japan's preindustrial culture (Inglehart 1982, p. 469).

How readily does popular sentiment favoring environmentalism translate into popular pressure for environmental controls? Research shows only a weak link between people's attitudes about environmental issues and their political behavior. In a three-nation study, respondents in West Germany, Britain, and the United States voiced a generally high level of urgency about environmental problems, yet these sentiments did not translate effectively into action (Milbrath, p. 85). This observation, of course, could be applied to any number of areas of political life, not only environmentalism. However, those who seek to mobilize citizens around environmental issues carry some additional handicaps.

First, environmental policy debates are typically conducted in the discourse of scientific and technical experts, discouraging amateur activists. Many policymakers assume that the alternatives must be debated by persons of advanced training. Despite the obvious impacts in communities, politicians do not naturally turn to local constituencies for advice. Rather, the debate over regulatory structures and techniques is usually carried on within government, particularly within administrative arenas.

Second, as economists point out, environmental quality is essentially a "public good" whose benefits are diffused widely throughout the population. Those benefits cannot readily be channeled to certain classes of people

TABLE 9.4 INDEX OF CONCERN EXPRESSED BY RESPONDENTS TO COMMON MARKET SURVEY, 1982*

	West Germany	France	Ireland	Italy	Netherlands	Britain
Pollution of rivers/lakes	2.20	1.97	1.85	2.17	2.25	1.76
Damage to sea life & beaches by oil tankers	2.25	2.24	1.91	2.21	2.38	2.19
Air pollution	2.15	1.87	1.67	2.19	2.11	1.59
Disposal of industrial/ chemical waste	2.25	2.14	1.95	2.15	2.45	2.16
Disposal of nuclear waste	2.16	2.17	1.97	2.07	2.40	2.23
Pollution from other countries (acid rain, etc.)	2.19	2.02	1.84	1.95	2.49	2.02

NOTE   *Scale from 0 (not at all worried) to 3 (worried a great deal).
SOURCE   Commission of the European Communities, *The Europeans and Their Environment.* (Brussels: CEC, 1983), pp. 45–54.

and denied to others. The classic example is cleaner air—if it is available to one citizen, it is available to all. Political science theory tells us that it is more difficult to mobilize individuals to lobby for such collective goods than for benefits accruing to specific segments of the population. Citizens are likely to sit back and let someone else invest the time and resources in political activity, knowing that if the effort succeeds, everyone will enjoy its fruits—even the nonparticipants.

One important exception to this generalization is the relative ease with which citizens can be rallied against *localized* environmental threats to their own communities. One of the most successful citizen movements in history is Japan's citizen movement protesting environmental contamination. In a traditionally deferential political culture, the size of this protest movement increased tenfold from 1970 to 1973, "spurred solely by outrage against threats to daily life" (Krauss and Simcock, p. 188). So significant was this citizen movement that it has been labeled "the most outstanding development in the postwar period" (Krauss and Simcock, p. 274) with consequences reaching well beyond the arena of environmental politics.

Japan's environmental movement was catalyzed by a series of tragic episodes in the 1960s known as the "Big Four" pollution incidents: mercury poisoning in Minamata and Niigata that killed and crippled many people; air pollution causing bronchial asthma in Yokkaichi; and cadmium poisoning in Toyama prefecture, resulting in bone diseases. The protests began as victims' movements, then expanded to more general environmental concerns. Their ultimate impact was considerable: beginning with a session of the Japanese Diet in 1970, called "The Pollution Diet," the national government passed more than a dozen laws involving pollution control, created an environmental protection agency, and fixed fines and jail terms for polluters.

Another case of environmental disaster galvanizing citizens took place in the small Dutch village of Lekkerkerk in 1979, when a handful of citizens obtained documents showing that their local government was allowing chemical wastes to be dumped without appropriate permits. Armed with evidence that 1,650 drums of paint and industrial waste had been dumped in their neighborhood, the citizens went to local newspapers. The news that their local government officials had retroactively issued a disposal permit, without a public hearing or comment, so enraged the protestors that they took their case directly to the national government. Even though it lacked any clear legislative mandate for doing so, the national government responded to their appeal with astonishing measures: it shipped bottled drinking water, evacuated residents and bought their homes at market value, even providing money for child care during the evacuation and funds for the citizens to hire attorneys to assist them. (One leader of this Lekkerkerk citizen effort expressed sadness at learning how much less sympathetic the U.S. government had been to the victims of the Love Canal incident (Piasecki and Davis, p. 191).)

Political Parties and the Environment

As important as such citizen protests have been in calling public attention to intolerable local situations, they typically lack technical expertise and the capacity for sustained political efforts that are needed to influence policy. That is the task of the political parties. Within the party structures of all Western countries, parties of the left have been more sympathetic to environmental concerns than parties of the center or the right. That is not surprising, since there is a modest tendency for persons who favor environmental protection to be left-leaning (Buttel and Flinn; Wiegel). Table 9.5 shows that environmentalists tend to cluster on the "middle left" to a greater extent than the general public in the United States, Britain, and West Germany.

Among members of the U.S. Congress, Democrats are more likely to support environmental policies than Republicans (Dunlap and Allen). Admittedly, the regulatory expansion of the 1970s in the environmental field enjoyed bipartisan support, rather than being carried by Democratic votes alone. However, that bipartisan support rested on other considerations than environmental quality. For example, in passing the federal Water Pollution Control Amendments of 1972, politicians representing the various states were moved as much by the promise of $18 billion to be allocated to the states for public waste treatment, as by a sense of urgency about the nation's water supply (Mann). When environmental issues are considered on their merits alone, Republicans have tended to place more emphasis than Democrats on the costs of cleanup, compared to its benefits—a calculation that frequently leads them to reject environmentalists' demands.

TABLE 9.5 POLITICAL SELF-LABELING BY ENVIRONMENTALISTS AND GENERAL PUBLIC IN THREE NATIONS, 1982

	Strong Liberal Left *Percent*	Middle Left *Percent*	Center *Percent*	Middle Right *Percent*	Strong Conservative Right *Percent*	NA *Percent*
United States						
Environmentalists	24	43	14	15	2	2
General public	3	17	27	34	7	11
Britain						
Environmentalists	12	35	17	20	8	8
General public	5	13	22	25	11	23
West Germany						
Environmentalists	22	32	18	11	1	17
General public	3	17	33	24	6	17

SOURCE   Lester Milbrath, *Environmentalists: Vanguard for a New Society*. (Albany: SUNY Press, 1984), p. 127.

A particularly dramatic example of the clash between Democrat and Republican approaches to such questions came in the transition from the Carter administration to the Reagan presidency. In one of its last initiatives, the Environmental Protection Agency (EPA) under Carter issued procedural rules requiring industrial polluters to employ the "best available technology" to treat discharges into sewers and surface waters. As soon as Reagan's new conservative EPA administrator took office, she took steps to reverse Carter's "best available technology" rule, which she said amounted to "treatment for the sake of treatment." Industries should be pressed to spend only as much on cleanup as is required to produce acceptable environmental conditions—a standard that may not require the *best* available technology.

It would be a mistake, however, to rely exclusively on the categories of "Left" and "Right" to predict party responses to environmental issues. The Left-Right continuum in Western politics has only limited applications to environmental policy. Those labels have traditionally been used to differentiate beliefs about the economic management of society—beliefs that do not correlate highly with views concerning the government's rightful role in solving environmental problems. Thus, although nuclear power became a highly divisive political issue in Western Europe in the 1970s, the debate was not reflected in splits along traditional party lines. Rather, traditional parties of all stripes lined up against the ecologists (whom Suzanne Berger has called the leaders of "anti-politics" because they have renounced the methods of traditional parties). In Japan as well, environmentalism was the exception to postwar political issues, most all of which were characterized by a division between the conservative coalition on one side and the opposition camp on the other: "the Japanese environmental problem was one that political parties were incapable of dealing with in established ways" (Pempel, p. 237). Instead of leading to realignments among the mainstream parties, the ecological debate has simply added another cleavage to politics in Western Europe and Japan: ecologists versus supporters of economic growth (Lauber).

Environmentalists are not necessarily more welcome in left-of-center parties than they are in conservative parties. Left-wing parties, traditionally committed to material and economic goals, sometimes find it difficult to champion environmental causes. For example, throughout the 1960s and most of the 1970s, Italy's socialist and communist parties generally rejected that country's conservation movement, which they labeled a bourgeois attempt to protect the capitalist system (Paccino). Only when opposition to nuclear power surfaced in Italy in the 1980s did the Italian Left incorporate environmental issues into its platform (Reich).

Instead of aligning themselves with traditional parties of the Left or the Right, environmentalists have tended to form new "green" parties, which now exist in West Germany, Belgium, France, Ireland, Sweden, the

Netherlands, and Britain. Their membership tends to be the young, well-educated, secular, and urban members of the new middle classes, especially people who work in public service (Boy; Burklin; Logue; Muller-Rommel). By far the largest and most successful of these new parties is West Germany's *die Grunen* (the Greens), formally constituted in 1980 out of a collection of regionally and politically diverse sections: remnants of the student movement, citizen groups, and an environmental movement that was divided into a conservationist wing and an activist wing opposing nuclear power. Their motto is "We are neither Left nor Right; we are in front."

In March 1983 the Greens captured 5.6 percent of the total vote in German national elections, entitling them to twenty-five seats in the federal Bundestag. This was the first time since the establishment of the three-party system in the 1950s that a new party had drawn enough votes to enter the Bundestag. In January 1987 the Greens increased their presence by winning 8.2 percent of the national vote. Compared to other European ecology parties, the Greens scored earlier successes. (For example, Sweden's Environmental Party did not enter the national parliament until 1988, when they won twenty seats and became the first new legislative party in the Riksdag since 1917.) The explanation for the Greens' gains may lie in West Germany's federal structure, which offered the newcomers smaller-scale arenas in which to test their popularity and build their strength.

The Greens' presence in the federal legislature and the legislatures of a half-dozen Länder does not guarantee their influence in shaping public policy. For one thing, their numbers are too small. For another, they disdain traditional bureaucratic, centralized party structures. The party exercises little discipline over officeholders. In fact, Green candidates do not even have to be members of the party, so long as their ideas coincide with the party's. The Greens have consciously opted for openness and informality in running the party organization, sacrificing the discipline that might help them to establish a cohesive presence in the legislatures. "Because the open, fluid participatory process in ecology parties rarely leads to definite choices, parliamentarians have to make crucial political decisions on their own" (Kitschelt, p. 148).

Nor are the green parties of Western Europe building strong mass-membership parties on the traditional European model. Even the West German Greens had a membership in 1985 that comprised only 1.3 percent of Green Party voters. (By comparison, the other three major West German parties counted over 5 percent of their voters as party members.) Instead of building mass-membership parties, the ecologists have formed personality-centered coalitions that are more electoral alliances than cohesive political machines with disciplined party workers and professional politicians. One commentator has accused the ecology parties of "Americanizing" European politics (Kitschelt, p. 148).

In sum, while citizen movements and ecology parties have played a role in increasing public consciousness about environmental problems, they have seldom shaped policy directly. That shaping takes place largely through the interaction of administrators and well-organized, technically sophisticated interest groups representing environmental causes and industrial interests. The administrators' discretion and control are particularly evident in Britain, Sweden, and Italy. British administrators hammer out regulations with industry groups in private administrative domains, rather than through public appeals processes, media publicity, or legal challenges. Bureaucrats set environmental standards, grant effluent discharge permits, and establish performance standards; conversely, the public's right to information is circumscribed by law. For example, the 1974 Control of Pollution Act gave neither the British public nor adjacent property owners the legal right to know the details of any polluting discharge. Similarly, Sweden's regulation of chemicals is determined by the Worker's Protection Board, which consults with peak organizations, but not the public at large. In air pollution control as well, Swedish administrators consult with industrial and technical experts and virtually dictate policy to politicians (Lundqvist 1980). France's regulatory process is firmly in the hands of administrators and the *Conseil d'Etat,* the court with jurisdiction over administrative affairs. Even in the United States, which nominally has the most open policy-making process, the administrative/interest group axis is dominant. Where once interest groups lobbied Congress as their chief target, now interest group participation in the administrative process is as important as, if not more important than, their legislative efforts. The EPA is strongly influenced by business lobbies (Haskell; Ackerman and Hassler). And public interest groups have been officially incorporated into the decision-making process at the EPA (Lowi, pp. 141–42).

Even more than in other policy domains, environmental legislation tends to be written in vague and general statements, to be fleshed out by the experts in the bureaucracy, industry, and the environmental lobby. Commenting on the overwhelmingly important role played by experts in environmental policy-making, Lowi has remarked that "we no longer even pretend that the expert will be relied upon to know what Congress wanted. We depend upon the scientist and technician to tell us what there is to want" (Lowi, p. 139).

Yet the ubiquitous presence of scientists in the policy-making process does not mean that their expertise is always the determining factor. In fact, there are those who argue that scientific knowledge only determines policy when political structures have already mobilized to favor particular approaches (Schnaiberg, p. 350). On the whole, the U.S. government seems to rely much more heavily on scientific evidence than do European regimes. From a large and diverse scientific community, decision makers obtain extensive and broad-based research, which may take the form of commissioned studies, expert testimony at hearings before the Congress or regulatory agencies or in judicial proceedings. Yet American science loses some of its power to shape policy simply because there are so often conflicting scientific opinions submitted to decision makers. In fact, the structure of many congressional and agency hearings is such that scientists with rival interpretations become adversaries for different policies (Wildavsky, p. 73). When all sides find their own experts, the credibility of scientific evidence is weakened.

The governments in Western Europe and Japan tend to rely far less on expertise. When they *do* seek scientific opinion, it usually comes from a small number of leading scientists who speak for the research community. Fewer in number and trained in only a few leading universities, the national scientific communities in Europe and Japan tend to exhibit more consensus of opinion than their American colleagues. In Wildavsky's terms, the governments of Europe and Japan use consultation to camouflage scientific uncertainty, while U.S. agencies reduce uncertainty by an adversarial process that is presumed to produce the best available knowledge. In neither case could we say that scientific truth is the sole guide to policy-making. That seems appropriate, especially since scientists themselves remain uncertain.

APPROACHES TO ENVIRONMENTAL ENFORCEMENT
INSTRUMENTS

As we observed earlier, the content of environmental policies across the advanced industrial nations is remarkably similar. On the other hand, the various governments' approaches to implementing policies offer some interesting contrasts. What separates the national approaches from one another is the relative balance they adopt between enforcement-through-consultation and enforcement-through-coercion. Judged by this standard, Britain and the United States represent two extreme ends of the spectrum, with the continental European nations and Japan falling somewhere in between.

The implementation process in the United States is by far the most formalized, rule-oriented, and adversarial—in a word, confrontational (Wildavsky). Regulations are based on collected evidence marshalled by the contending sides and interpreted according to specific procedures that are open to appeals and legal challenges at all stages. The rule-making process is typically long and contentious, often ending in litigation. The United States is unique among the countries in this study in the key role it assigns to the courts in implementing environmental policies. In almost all federal environmental laws Congress has incorporated broad opportunities for judicial review of the EPA's practices, authorizing any citizen to file suit against administrators, either for performing their duties too aggressively or not aggressively enough. Motivated by Congress's desire to open up the regulatory process to groups other than the regulated industries, these provisions have placed the courts in a position, not merely to enforce policies, but to make them (Melnick).

The frequent confrontations engendered by this arrangement are not confrontations between the two sides that most disagree—industry and environmentalists—but rather, confrontations pitting each of these groups against governmental authorities. Environmentalists constantly sue the regulatory agencies to secure stricter regulation, while business groups sue to get standards relaxed. The two principal adversaries seldom meet in the same courtroom. Environmentalists have tended to concentrate on challenging regulations with national applicability, while businesses have tended to focus instead on source-specific regulations. In individual enforcement cases, district court judges have decided on compliance schedules and sanctions by balancing society's interest in a clean environment against the industries' claims of hardship. The results of this system have been "lengthy litigation, lenient schedules, and few fines" (Melnick, p. 354).

Britain provides the most dramatic contrast with the American style of implementation. British environmental officials operate through consultation and compromise in setting the standards that polluters must meet. Since 1847 British environmental laws have compelled business owners to employ "the best practicable means" to prevent emissions of noxious substances into the atmosphere. Britain's leading environmental agency, the Alkali Inspectorate, was created in the 1860s to control pollution from the manufacture of alkalis (used in the production of glass, textiles, paper, and soap). It pioneered the approach embodied in the phrase "best practicable means," which describes not so much a standard as a process of close personal consultation between government and industry. In regulating pollution, British officials made only limited use of emissions standards or environmental quality, or compliance deadlines. The Alkali Inspectorate considered every case on its own merits, eschewing hard-and-fast rules. Each factory's situation was evaluated with regard to its size, local conditions, age of equipment, and financial strength, and a tailor-made plan for reducing pollution was agreed upon by inspectors and owners. The tone set by nineteenth century inspectors has underpinned virtually the entire pollution-control effort in that country. An observer in the early 1970s remarked about the Alkali Inspectorate that it still "likes persuasion; it dislikes compulsion; it detests prosecution" (Bugler, p. 11). The relationship of the British inspector to the polluter has been "more like that of a doctor getting the patient's cooperation than a policeman apprehending a culprit" (Ashby and Anderson, p. 136).

Given the very close connections linking Japanese government to business, it is not surprising that Japanese regulation too is produced through a process of consultation rather than confrontation. It is commonplace to observe that in response to stricter environmental standards, American businesses have hired more lawyers while Japanese businesses have hired more engineers. Perhaps that is because government policy in Japan is typically the product of an alliance between national government ministries and peak associations, like employers' organizations and industrial federations. Through an elaborate network of joint institutions, industries' interests are incorporated into the policy-making process, and in turn the peak associations act as an aid to government, disseminating information and encouraging members to cooperate with regulatory standards.

The continental European states also fall somewhere between the extremes of consultation and confrontation in their approach to enforcing pollution controls—more formalized than the British, yet less adversarial than the U.S. system. Sweden's regulation of air pollution is the subject of continuous negotiations between government officials and the affected firms and workers. Rather than setting goals that are beyond available technology, Swedish regulators select their goals on the basis of the available means (Lundqvist 1980, p. 61). In West Germany as well, formalized consultations are held between government officials and peak organizations, producing regulations that industries usually find acceptable (Knoepfel and Weidner; Schneider). The French government gives industry a somewhat less privileged position in the policy process. French civil servants rely more on a variety of technical and advisory bodies than industry associations. In the regulation of toxic waste, virtually all of the continental European systems engage in extensive arbitration with various groups about the alternatives before promulgating any rules. Industry tolerates more government involvement than in the United States, while at the same time government takes more of the responsibility and liability for managing hazardous waste than does the United States (Piasecki and Davis, p. 225).

Does the incorporation of industrial representatives into the rule-making process result in weaker rules? Americans tend to assume so. Hence, American regulatory procedures tend to limit business representatives to highly formal routes of appeal and litigation. The assumption is shared by some critics of Britain's informal system, who have complained about the government's "leisurely implementation" of standards, its "abhorrence of bringing offenders to court," and its "benign policy of cooperation with industrialists" (Frankel). Yet defenders of the consultative mode question whether strict rule-making and inspection practices produce any greater benefits than their negotiated approach. A zeal to prosecute, they argue, only leads to more resistance among manufacturers and in the long run defeats the goal of an improved environment. Their contention is supported by at least one study that showed Britain achieving a higher degree of compliance with emissions standards than other governments because of the close cooperative relationship between regulatory agencies and polluters (Knoepfel et al. 1980).

Apart from a government's strategic choice between consultation and confrontation, implementation involves choices among specific policy in-

struments. Pollution control policies can be broadly classified in two categories: (1) outright prohibition of certain kinds of behavior (like driving an
automobile without emission controls or dumping industrial pollutants into
streams), and (2) pricing systems that increase the cost of polluting behavior
without prohibiting it outright (known as the "polluter-pays-principle").

Regulation as Prohibition

In the traditional approach to regulation, sometimes called the
command-and-control approach, government curbs pollution by setting
standards which private individuals or firms are expected to meet. If they
fail, they are subject to court-mandated compliance schedules, fines, or
prosecution. This sounds like a simple, straightforward exercise. But as soon
as we begin to think about how to set such standards, complications arise.
Should the standards dictate what kind of technology polluters must install
in order to minimize their effluents? That is called a "technology-based
approach." Or should standards specify the minimal acceptable quality of
the receiving medium (air or water) and limit polluters to that level of emissions that is consistent with keeping the receiving medium acceptably clean?
If this latter approach, known as the "media-quality-based standard," is
adopted, then government sets a ceiling on emissions from a particular
factory, leaving the owners to determine the most effective way to comply.

Politicians in both the United States and Europe have voiced a preference for media-quality-based standards. One recent OECD study concluded that because of the complex, constantly changing nature of technology, public policies should not make reference to specific pollution control
technologies. In fact, it argued, the less the regulations concern themselves
with technology, the more they stimulate technological improvement. Governments may actually inhibit technological advances by imposing ready-
made solutions on industry. "What might be called 'technological flexibility'
is in our view a fundamental policy rule" (OECD 1985a, p. 91). The U.S.
Congress displayed a similar preference for media-quality-based standards
in the Clean Air Act of 1970. When Congress directed the EPA to set
ambient air quality standards for specific pollutants, it specifically barred
the agency from considering the costs of attaining those standards. What
was important was to achieve a quality of air that prevented new injuries or
the aggravation of preexisting injuries to the health of Americans.

Yet, despite the widespread preference for media-quality-based standards, enforcement systems commonly shift toward technology-based standards. For example, when pressed by the EPA to set air-quality-based
standards for their own jurisdictions, the states often prescribed technology-based regulations. In a similar fashion, the effort to improve water
quality during the 1970s shifted away from media-based to technology-
based standards. Why? Probably not because the regulators held some

fundamental objection to implementing media-quality-standards, but because they proved too difficult to administer. They required a calculation of the approximate contribution that a particular plant's emissions were making to the total regional pollution problem—a very difficult calculation. Furthermore, the fact that different polluters contribute different amounts to the total problem means that regulators will have to impose unequal performance standards—a politically sticky proposition (McGarity, p. 208).

Among some European environmentalists, the choice among different pollution standards carries strong ideological overtones. Some Dutch socialists, for example, castigate the government technocracy for promoting media-quality-standards. This the more radical environmentalists see as condoning the poisoning of the environment within certain acceptable limits rather than challenging the fundamental economic order that produces pollution. It diverts public attention away from the polluters and toward the effects of pollution. "The most important threat to politically progressive environmentalism," they assert, "is not formed by right-wing reactionary currents within the environmental movement, but by the technocratic governmental approach" (Wams, p. 32).

Only the British have resolved this dilemma. Their solution is not to set fixed standards that are either technology-based or media-quality-based. Nor do they hold to strict deadlines or impose sizable penalties for noncompliance. In the negotiating process, regulators are authorized to extend deadlines, reduce the stringency of standards, and eliminate fines or legal actions for past violations. And they refer to the courts only the most serious cases of noncooperation.

Pricing Approaches

Pricing mechanisms are meant to modify the behavior of polluters by manipulating the costs of pollution. Rather than flatly prohibiting the discharge of effluents, advocates of pricing prefer to increase the price that polluters pay for the privilege of discharging wastes. This can be accomplished in two ways.

First, government regulators may set a price on pollution and let the market determine the quantity of emissions discharged into the environment, based on how much polluters are willing to pay for the privilege. This amounts to attaching an additional cost to the production process and relying on the natural desire of producers to minimize their production costs wherever possible. Efficient producers, it is presumed, will make their best effort to reduce their total emissions or change their location or clean up emissions before they will pay such fees.

Second, regulators may fix the quantity of pollution that is allowable in the environment and let the market determine the price to be paid for the privilege of polluting. Regulators decide how much effluent the environment can safely absorb within a geographical area and then auction off permits-to-pollute, each permit entitling the owner to emit a specified quantity of effluent. The permits are auctioned off to the highest bidders, which may then create an exchange market in permits as businesses proceed to sell and trade among themselves. Still, government officials are assured of maintaining a predetermined quality of air or water because the total number of permits in the market is fixed.

Economists favor pricing mechanisms because economic theory holds that such mechanisms offer the least costly way for society to abate pollution. Why? The cost of pollution removal differs from firm to firm. Governments will achieve pollution abatement at the lowest cost if they exact the largest reductions in pollution from firms whose removal costs are the cheapest. A pricing mechanism accomplishes just that. Firms that can reduce pollution cheaply will naturally engage in more abatement, in order to avoid paying the cost of emissions. Firms that can only reduce pollution at considerable cost to themselves will probably opt instead to pay for the privilege of discharging (Kneese and Shultz, p. 19).

Many government officials also favor pricing mechanisms, not because they are persuaded by such economic theory, but because this approach is consistent with the ideological currents favoring market-based policies and because it promises to generate revenues (OECD 1980, p. 21). In 1972 the Council of the OECD adopted the polluter-pays-principle as a guiding principle of environmental policies in its member countries. The OECD reasoned that economic efficiency would be promoted, and distortions of international trade minimized, if each nation required polluters to incur the full cost of controlling pollution. That way, abatement costs would be reflected in the prices of goods marketed throughout Western Europe and North America.

Governments like that of the Netherlands have used the revenues generated by emissions charges to pay for the costs of cleanup. The Dutch Pollution of Surface Waters Act of 1970 established a system of effluent charges, with the revenues being used to finance purification. Since the law was adopted, the fee charged for each unit of pollution has risen sharply, from $4 in 1971 to between $15 and $20 in 1980 (depending upon the region of the country). In 1980 these revenues totaled about $300 million (Downing and Hanf, p. 144).

In the United States, although Congress has never really embraced pricing mechanisms, EPA administrators have quietly begun to shift toward pricing systems, particularly in the realm of air pollution control. As we have already observed, the Clean Air Act of 1970 called for setting up strict ambient air quality standards for a collection of pollutants: sulfur dioxide, nitrogen oxides, carbon monoxide, ozone, hydrocarbons, and total suspended particulates. The primary responsibility was to lie with the states, but progress in the states was extremely slow. As the deadline for compliance in 1977 approached, virtually every major city in the United States remained in violation of standards (and remained so for ozone and carbon monoxide by the 1987 deadline).

Legally, the EPA could simply have declared that no new polluting firms be allowed in regions that had not yet achieved compliance. Rather than take that drastic action, the EPA issued a ruling in 1976 that allowed for the building of new polluters, *provided* that they be equipped with the best available pollution controls *and* that the emissions from the new polluter could be offset by reductions elsewhere in the region, so that the overall quality of the air would not degenerate. By implication, the EPA was creating a new exchange market in permits. Newcomers can buy permits from existing firms whose abatement costs are low. Subsequent modifications by the EPA allow firms to "bank" emission rights: If they can do better than they are required to do in the present, they receive credits that can be used later on to increase emissions, or can be sold to other firms to offset their pollution.

The EPA's transformation of the Clean Air Act from a command-and-control approach to a marketable permit arrangement is an excellent example of bureaucratic officials' ability to create discretion for themselves where there appeared to be none. They shifted, *not* because their client groups demanded it. In fact, there appears to have been little pressure for pricing systems from industry. Instead, the change came about because EPA administrators needed to reconcile environmental policy with the generally conservative policy climate of the 1970s favoring economic growth as the nation's top priority. Rather than using pollution regulations to impose curbs to growth in the nation's metropolitan regions, the EPA devised a compromise that would allow new firms to come into the market (Meidinger, pp. 158–59).

Emissions trading, like emissions charges in general, has drawn criticism from staunch environmentalists. They decry the fact that businesses think that by paying emissions charges, they purchase an entitlement to pollute. Critics also challenge the real-world efficiency of pricing mechanisms in minimizing pollution. Like all market-based models, emissions charges assume conditions of competition that would force polluters to minimize their costs by minimizing their pollution. But since perfect competition never exists in real markets, there may be many situations in which producers in monopoly or near-monopoly conditions can decide simply to pay the price of discharging large amounts of pollution and pass the costs on to their customers. Utility companies might be an example of firms who enjoy enough of a monopoly to take this attitude. If consumers are unable to shift their demand to cheaper alternatives, then they will continue to buy the pollution-generating goods at higher prices. Government will not have succeeded in minimizing pollution by imposing emissions charges (Nagel;

Braithwaite; Neiman). Other arguments against using pricing mechanisms to control pollution are based on logistical considerations. For example, how can government employ the polluter-pays-principle to clean up the contaminated industrial sites that dot the older urban centers of Europe and the United States? Often, it is impossible to trace the parties responsible for the contamination, which may have taken place years earlier. And the most caustic criticism of all comes from those who believe that market models eliminate the notion that government is pursuing a public purpose by promoting environmental quality:

> Market-derived terms like "interest" and "incentive" dominate the contemporary policy-making vocabulary, depriving it of the very language needed to think about public purposes. Market imagery transforms the public's view of itself from one of an active, deliberate citizenry to one of a gaggle of consumers shopping for policies from shelves stocked by government experts. (Landy and Plotkin, p. 8)

BENEFITS AND COSTS OF REGULATION
DISTRIBUTION

In 1969 a leading British Labour party official who carried special responsibility for environmental pollution phrased the distributional question this way:

> There is virtually no form of environmental pollution that we do not know how to control. It is just a question of economics. . . . How much prosperity, and for whom, shall be sacrificed for how much environmental purity, and for whom? (Lord Kennet, quoted in Johnson, p. 106)

His formulation aptly points out that the two major distributive features of environmental policies—their benefits and their costs—must be analyzed separately because they are likely to accrue to entirely different groups in society.

Who Benefits from Environmental Controls?

The benefits of environmental quality are often cited by economists as the classic example of "public goods"—that is, goods that accrue equally to all citizens of a particular community. When the air or water is cleaned up, all residents enjoy the outcome equally. Such an analysis might lead us to conclude that there is little to say about the distribution of benefits from environmental policies. Such a conclusion, however, would be mistaken.

Those who suffer the most from the damaging effects of pollution are, logically, the greatest beneficiaries of effective pollution controls. There is a good deal of evidence to show that the poor suffer the most when environments deteriorate (Berry; Baumol and Oates). The poor are least able to protect themselves against environmental degradation.

The most dramatic illustration of this principle is in the Third World, whose ecology has suffered damage from many of the commercial and industrial processes that sustain Western economic growth. Urban industrial waste from the United States, much of it containing arsenic, lead, mercury, dioxins and other toxics, has found its way to dumpsites in many Third World nations. Western commercial agricultural interests have used pesticides on crops they grow in the Third World that would be illegal in their home countries. The demand by Western consumers for beef has induced Latin American herders to destroy vast amounts of tropical rain forest in order to grow beef for export (it is estimated that to produce only a quarter pound of beef for export, Latin American herders must convert 55 square feet of rain forest to grazing land). Even when Western nations attempt to assist Third World governments with resettlement schemes, hydroelectric dams, and agricultural projects, they sometimes wreak environmental havoc. An example is the World Bank project to settle Brazilian farmers in the northwestern province of Rondonia, which has destroyed pristine tropical forests and prompted armed conflict between the settlers and indigenous Indians living in the forests (Cahn 1985, p. 140).

Over the past century, the concentration of carbon dioxide in the earth's atmosphere is believed to have increased almost 25 percent, mostly due to the burning of fossil fuels and deforestation. The advanced industrial nations of Western Europe and North America are responsible for about two-thirds of the world's carbon dioxide emissions (OECD 1982, p. 10), but the climatic impacts are worldwide. The waste gases from industrial production have built up in the earth's atmosphere where, like the panes of glass in a greenhouse roof, they allow the sun and its heat to pass in, but then trap the warmth on the earth's surface. This is the so-called greenhouse effect, which scientists predict will lead to an average global warming of three to nine degrees within the next century. Weather patterns throughout the world will shift, and sea levels may rise by as much as four feet, swamping many coastal areas.

A Third World trend that exacerbates the greenhouse effect is the deforestation of the world's equatorial rain forests, found primarily in Latin America, south Asia, and Africa. Tropical forests act as filters, removing large amounts of carbon dioxide from the earth's atmosphere. About twenty million acres of tropical forest are destroyed every year for logging, farming, and pastureland. At a 1988 United Nations debate on worldwide pollution, representatives from the industrialized nations urged concerted action to preserve what Norway's ambassador called the earth's "green lungs." Mexico's representative to the United Nations Economic and Finance Committee protested against the assumption that all nations must share equally the costs of fighting pollution. He questioned whether Third World countries should be asked to forego development and limit energy consumption to correct a problem created by the industrialized nations' unbridled use of fossil fuels. Should peasants who need farmland be told not to clear it because of international concerns about tropical forests? "What are we supposed to do?" he inquired. "We should postpone our hunger?" (Jaffe).

Another invisible group of relatively defenseless victims is the next generation of the earth's inhabitants. Those who are not yet born are, of course, utterly powerless to oppose the polluting practices of the current generation. Philosophers have constructed arguments defending the principle that future people have rights in the present (Sikora and Barry), and public opinion in several Western nations has been shown to favor conserving resources now to benefit future generations (Milbrath, p. 29). Yet, when it comes to specific policy questions, consideration for future generations is rarely a determining factor.

If we look for the victims of pollution closer to home, we find that especially in the area of toxic wastes, society's burden is unequally distributed. In Western Europe, contamination from toxic wastes tends to be concentrated in the economically declining regions that once contained the Continent's industrial infrastructure—for example, parts of the Ruhr region and Nord Pas de Calais in France—and the West Midlands in Britain. Industries that have long since shut down left behind a legacy of hazardous waste. In the United States, it appears that minority communities suffer a disproportionate share of the damage from uncontrolled toxic waste sites, which tend to be located in the urban areas where blacks or other minorities are concentrated. Large commercial hazardous waste landfills are disproportionately found in rural communities in the Southern "blackbelt" (USGAO). Presumably, this pattern arises from the inability of poor black communities to resist the placement of such facilities in their backyards. The advantages of a vigorous policy to clean up hazardous waste sites would appear to accrue to just such communities.

Sometimes, alert politicians can manipulate the distributive impacts of pollution controls to benefit their own geographical constituencies. An interesting example is the pattern of support in the U.S. Congress for strong new-source emission controls under the Clean Air Act. That act differentiated its treatment of already-existing polluters and new sources of pollution that may enter the marketplace. While existing-source standards were largely the states' responsibility, the new-source standards were to be made by the EPA at the national level. All new firms have had to meet uniform national standards, which are more stringent than those that the states have devised for existing firms.

The effect of this distinction is to increase the costs of pollution control in the southern and western states, which contain the largest proportion of new facilities. Control costs per dollar of output there are higher than in the northeastern and north central states. For example, the paper industry in the sunbelt carries abatement costs that are roughly four times greater than in the frostbelt ($11 per $1,000 of value added, compared with $2.58). It is hardly surprising that the legislators most likely to vote for strong new-source controls were from declining states; they saw the controls as a way of discouraging industrial migration to the sunbelt (Crandall, Chapter 7).

Similarly, when a proposal came before Congress in 1975 to force western utility companies to employ extensive emissions control equipment even for low-sulfur coal, some of the strongest proponents of the controls represented eastern coal producers who were concerned about the loss of prospective markets for their high-sulfur coal. The champions of vigorous enforcement reasoned that if western utilities could avoid abatement costs by burning low-sulfur coal, the market for eastern coal might be threatened (Haskell). Ultimately, the EPA's ruling called for scrubbing 70 percent to 90 percent of sulfur content from the coal burned. Critics charged that this ruling needlessly cost billions of dollars to achieve environmental goals that could have been attained more cheaply, more quickly, and more surely by other means (Ackerman and Hassler).

Does the inordinate burden that pollution places on those who are economically and politically disadvantaged mean these groups are the most likely to support environmental policies? Not at all. In fact, as we observed earlier, those groups in society most likely to support the environmental movement and green parties are the middle- and upper-middle-class educated professionals. How do we explain the fact that the groups who would probably benefit the most from cleaning up the environment are the least active in promoting it? One explanation is of course that disadvantaged populations tend in general to participate at lower levels than more affluent citizens. But even more fundamental than the differences in levels of participation are the differences in priorities among different groups in society. Some analysts have concluded that the poor and minority groups place a lower value on environmentalism than middle-class whites. For example, most studies that have examined the relationship between race and environmentalism show that American blacks are less environmentally oriented than whites (Hershey and Hill). And some economists have asserted that when governments introduce environmental controls, they typically supply the poor with more environmental quality than they would have been willing to pay for, given a choice (Pearce). In our estimation, theories about the differing preference structures of the poor and the middle-classes are inadequate to explain their differing levels of political support for environmentalism. More to the point is an examination of the relative costs of environmental controls that are paid by different segments of society.

Who Pays the Costs of Pollution Control?

Political commentators on both the Left and the Right have asserted that the costs of imposing environmental regulations fall disproportionately on low-income citizens, who must pay more for consumer goods and services, whose wages are dampened, and who risk unemployment due to plant closings. A significant body of economic research suggests that environmental policies have regressive effects on the distribution of personal incomes (Zimmerman, pp. 95–96). This is the reason why environmentalism is often labeled an "elitist" movement. Some have even gone so far as to claim that elite backing for regulations and controls reflects a deliberate attempt by the affluent to use environmental policies to protect and improve their class position (Frieden; Tucker).

Like the poor and minorities, industrial workers share disproportionately in the costs of regulation. And within the category of industrial workers, some are far more affected than others. In the advanced industrial countries of the West, about 80 percent of the total cost of pollution controls is borne by a handful of industries: iron and steel, pulp and paper, chemicals, electric utilities, and nonferrous metals (Potier, p. 254). In the United States, the EPA estimated that from 1971 to 1983, 155 plant closings, with 32,899 job losses, were environmentally related. Of these, 55 percent were the result of state actions; 14 percent were caused by federal actions; and 7 percent resulted from local regulations (Potier, pp. 262–63). Moreover, environmental controls have sometimes forced delays, postponements, and even the abandonment of large construction projects like dams, nuclear power plants, and heavy industrial facilities.

In a number of the policy areas treated in this book, labor unions have been among the most powerful forces for increased governmental activism. As progressive organizations, labor unions should be inclined to sympathize with environmentalists. Yet their presence is not nearly so strong in environmental politics as in other areas. Naturally, differences exist among unions in their degree of support for environmental causes. Among American labor unions, the United Auto Workers (UAW) furnish a good example of a socially progressive union, known for its strong environmental record. The UAW has subsidized environmental groups, lobbied for environmental legislation, and sponsored conferences to bring together labor and environmental activists. Yet even the UAW compromised its commitment to environmentalism in the 1980s, when the automobile industry was facing a recession. In congressional debates about weakening the national ambient air quality standards that had been established under the Clean Air Act, the UAW advocated relaxing some of the more stringent emissions controls in order to salvage the failing United States auto industry. Another large union that had initially supported air pollution controls—the United Steelworkers of America—changed its position in the early 1980s. In an aboutface, the steelworkers came to favor extending the deadlines for compliance because the steel industry in many parts of the country remained in violation of air quality standards (Siegman).

West German unions have similarly shifted their attitudes toward strict controls. In the early 1970s the German Federation of Trade Unions (DGB) took a leadership position in environmental politics, strongly supporting the polluter-pays-principle. The DGB remained dedicated to this position during the period of full employment and economic growth. But at the height of the recession in 1975, labor representatives reversed themselves dramatically, opposing pollution controls even more stridently than did German industry (Ewringmann, p. 334).

From time to time workers and environmentalists have joined forces on specific issues. West German coal miners have aligned themselves with antinuclear activists to fight the expansion of nuclear power. In Britain and Sweden, labor and ecological interests have combined to lobby for the workers' right to know about environmental hazards that may exist in their workplaces. In general, it may be said that in nations where unions have banded together into peak federations that have no vested interest in the welfare of particular companies, labor leaders can afford to be more pro-environment. But in nations like the United States and Japan, where unions bargain with individual employers, it is difficult for labor to take a strong anti-industry stance (Krauss and Simcock, p. 220). They may work assiduously on environmental problems within factories, but not on problems outside the plant.

THE UNCERTAIN FUTURE OF ENVIRONMENTAL CONTROLS
RESTRAINTS AND INNOVATIONS

Political Resistance from Threatened Sectors

What we have just observed about the distributive effects of environmental regulation suggests that policymakers who favor the expansion of controls may encounter serious resistance from some political constituencies, particularly those who see their livelihoods threatened. Granted, opinion surveys in the West have shown that when asked whether they believe that environmental protection should take precedence over economic growth, most respondents will agree that it should. (See Table 9.6 for responses to a Common Market poll.) Milbrath reports that in 1980 polls, the preference for environmental protection outweighed that for economic growth by three to one in the United States and West Germany, and by five to one in Britain (Milbrath, p. 27).

However, some commentators are unconvinced that the pro-environment attitudes of the early 1980s will last. If the post-materialist values that have supported environmentalism are, as Inglehart says, a product of the affluence of the 1950s and 1960s, then they may not have been transmitted to youths who grew up in the 1970s and 1980s. This younger cohort has a different set of experiences and expectations, including the very real possibility of unemployment. We know that the constituency for ecology movements and parties in Western nations is predominantly among younger citizens. Thus, any signs of rising unemployment among youth may mean that young voters shift to more conservative viewpoints and candidates. There are some indications that green party politicians have recognized this possibility. The West German Greens, for example, have moved closer to the positions of the labor movement, endorsing some union demands (Kolinsky).

Several studies conducted by the OECD challenge the belief that environmental regulation has had a negative impact on the levels of employment in the Western countries. That unemployment rose at the same time as environmental controls were increasing does not necessarily mean the two were connected. Environmental regulation was coincident with unemployment, but did not cause it to happen (Meissner 1984; OECD 1985b). Even though regulation may cause the loss of some jobs in polluting industries, the new jobs created by investment in pollution control tend to offset such losses. In fact, because pollution control is a labor-intensive activity, government expenditures for the environment tend to create more jobs per dollar than other types of public spending (Meissner 1986, p. 46). The OECD has therefore concluded that environmental and economic goals are compatible and interdependent, and that the benefits of environmental protection outweigh its costs. A similar conclusion was reached by the U.S. Congress's Joint Economic Committee, which reported in 1980 that "the aggregate effect of environmental regulations on overall employment, though perhaps negative, is not very severe. The impact is likely to be positive when there is substantial investment in pollution control technologies" (Joint Economic Committee).

Knowing that the aggregate effects of regulation are positive does not allay the fears and resistance of workers and business owners in the specific sectors targeted by regulators. The consequences for their firms or regions may be distinctly unfavorable, even though the overall economy remains unaffected. These threatened sectors have found comfort in the antiregula-

TABLE 9.6 DISTRIBUTION OF RESPONSES TO THE QUESTION: "WHICH SHOULD RECEIVE THE HIGHER PRIORITY FROM GOVERNMENT: PROTECTING THE ENVIRONMENT OR PROMOTING ECONOMIC GROWTH?"

	Percent Favoring Environment	Percent Favoring Growth	Percent Don't Know	Total (percent)
West Germany	64	21	15	100
France	58	30	12	100
Ireland	29	58	13	100
Italy	67	20	13	100
Netherlands	56	34	10	100
Britain	50	36	14	100

SOURCE   Commission of the European Communities, *The Europeans and Their Environment* (Brussels: CEC, 1983), p. 38.

tory stance taken by conservative politicians in the United States, Britain, and several other Western countries. Their opposition constitutes one important restraint on the expansion of environmental policies.

Another restraining factor may be taxpayers' unwillingness to pay the cost of cleaning up the environment. In 1989 the Prime Minister of the Dutch government tested the limits of political support for new taxes to pay for environmental programs, and his coalition government quickly became the first Western government to collapse over an environmental issue. Prime Minister Ruud Lubbers, a Christian Democrat, could not get agreement from his coalition partners on how to pay for an ambitious plan to cut pollution 70 percent by the year 2010. The liberal People's Party for Freedom and Democracy, a junior partner in the government coalition, strongly objected to the Prime Minister's proposal to raise the required $3.5 billion a year through new taxes on automobiles, gasoline, and property, as well as taxes on industry. The People's Party, complaining that Dutch taxpayers and auto drivers simply could not be burdened further, withheld their cooperation and thereby forced the Prime Minister's resignation.

Moving Policy to Higher Levels

It is commonplace to observe that pollutants recognize no political boundaries. Wastes that are discharged into a river in one locality may threaten the public health in other towns along the waterway; wind currents may carry the effluent produced in one state into the airspace of other states or even other countries. Toxic wastes produced by one community's factories may be trucked to treatment facilities or landfills at great distances. The spillover effects of pollution present one of the thorniest problems for environmental policymakers, whose jurisdiction extends only to the boundaries of their particular municipality, province, or nation. Their frustration has pushed environmental policy to higher and higher political levels.

Historically, local governments carried most of the burden for disposing of wastes. The traditional municipal housekeeping functions included sewage, trash removal, and street-cleaning. Now more than ever, municipal officials have reason to pursue environmental objectives, because the quality of life in localities figures centrally in business location decisions. High-tech industries in particular seek environments that include natural amenities and leisure opportunities for their employees. Yet local government can only take partial responsibility for that environment. Like economic development planning at the local level, environmental planning is influenced by a great many factors that local officials do not control. One of those factors is the mobility of some industries, whose owners may threaten to move their businesses elsewhere if local environmental regulators become too zealous.

The French have a vivid description of this practice: *chantage au chomage*, or "blackmail by unemployment."

It might be supposed that nations with strong unitary governments would give businesses fewer opportunities for such blackmail by unemployment, simply because investors who face more uniform standards from one locale to another would have fewer opportunities to escape regulation by moving. Lundqvist's comparative study of Sweden and the United States, for example, concluded that unitary states have advantages in imposing strict environmental regulations. More decentralized systems, he argued, resulted in more lenient standards (Lundqvist 1974, p. 140). However, it is possible even within strongly unitary nations for industries to exert influence over local officials. A case in point is Marseilles, a heavily polluted industrial port on the southern coast of France. Even though serious pollution control efforts were underway during the 1970s in France, Marseilles' most flagrant polluters were hardly touched by the campaign. The explanation lies in the political alliance between local industrialists and the mayor, Gaston Deferre, who concurrently held important positions in the national government. Deferre committed himself to shielding the mainly small and medium-sized firms in iron and steel, metals, and chemicals against the environmental push by regional authorities. Rather than confront Marseilles' powerful mayor, the regional authority chose to focus its attention instead on less critical problems in the sparsely populated area of Fos-Etang de Berre-Martigues (Knoepfel, pp. 374–75).

Even the provincial or state level may not be high enough to preclude the possibility that businesses will escape regulation by moving. Many American states, for example, have adopted the practice of levying fees on businesses that produce hazardous waste, in order to help pay for cleaning up after industrial accidents or leakage from uncontrolled waste sites. But the amount of the fees has remained too low to dissuade any polluters from discharging wastes. Why? Because state governments are afraid that high fees will scare away new firms and will induce existing firms to move out of the state (Hirschhorn, p. 133). The pressures against strict controls are particularly strong in states experiencing economic decline. For example, Michigan workers, organized in the Michigan Committee for Jobs and Energy, have lobbied against regulation by state agencies, arguing that the state's hard-hit economy will erode even further if Michigan imposes stricter standards than other states.

The states' reticence in dealing with polluters has led federal authorities to assume more and more responsibility. While the earliest federal laws of the 1950s and 1960s emphasized the role of states and local governments in setting standards and enforcing them, the Congress has reacted to state delays by shifting authority upward to the federal level. Given the mediocre record of state enforcement, some critics of the Reagan administration in the United States concluded that the conservative Republican's push to restore state and local responsibility for environmental policy was a deliberate attempt to weaken regulations.

Nation-states as well have sometimes displayed reluctance to crack down on polluters, particularly during a period of intensifying economic competition. The same OECD studies that documented the employment gains from pollution control programs also showed the negative effects of regulation on consumer prices and on exports (OECD, 1985b). Unless the polluter-pays-principle is adopted universally, nations that impose charges on polluters or force them to invest in emissions control equipment have to sell their products overseas at a slight disadvantage, and multinational corporations have an incentive to relocate in countries with more lenient regulations (UN Centre on Transnational Corporations). No doubt that is why the ministers attending an OECD meeting in 1979 concluded that international cooperation on pollution control must be strengthened:

> Without such international cooperation, governments may be reluctant to develop and apply environmental design and product standards for fear of affecting the international competitive position of their national industry. (OECD 1980, p. 16)

Even a trading giant like Japan worries about the impact of regulation on industry's ability to produce competitive goods for overseas markets. The great expansion in regulation in Japan came between 1970 and 1975, when environmental activism actually seemed to advance Japan's position on some international markets. The most important was the automobile market. Japanese emissions standards forced the automobile companies to develop new technologies that helped them to sell to American and European markets as well as the domestic market. But the backsliding on regulation since the economic recession of 1975 shows that Japan's conversion to environmentalism was "not exactly analogous to the reformation of the Prodigal Son or the conversion of St. Paul" (Pempel, p. 233). The Environmental Agency has lost ground to the economic ministries, as Japan's leaders have become more concerned about protecting the country's international economic position.

Surveying the problems that governments at all levels have in maintaining strict environmental standards in a world of economic competition, one understands why many national politicians now look to international cooperation as the ultimate remedy. Many of the most urgent environmental problems have worldwide impacts and cannot be addressed within the political framework of nation-states. The growing awareness of the earth's fragility has spawned a number of important international agreements in the last decade: the 1978 Protocol Relating to the International Convention for the Prevention of Pollution from Ships (ratified by 45 nations), the 1979 Convention on the Conservation of Migratory Species of Wild Animals (ratified by 34 nations), the 1982 United Nations Convention on the Law of the Sea (ratified by 136 nations), the 1985 Vienna Convention for the Protection of the Ozone Layer (ratified by 27 nations), and the 1987 Protocol on Substances that Deplete the Ozone Layer (ratified by 34 nations).

The last two on this list, both concerning the depletion of the earth's ozone layer, illustrate the kind of tradeoffs that must be built into international accords to accommodate the differing agendas of the industrialized countries and the Third World. Both agreements focus on a group of chemicals known as "chlorofluorocarbons," 90 percent of which are produced in Western countries to be used in solvents, refrigerants, automobile air conditioners, fast-food packaging, and aerosol cans. When dispersed into the atmosphere, these chemicals deplete the ozone layer which shields the earth from the sun's ultraviolet rays. Scientists have estimated that between 1969 and 1986, the ozone layer over the northern hemisphere eroded by as much as 3 percent, and over the southern hemisphere by as much as 5 percent in some regions. The results range from increased skin cancer to damaged crops, fish populations, and other natural systems the world over. Third World nations, although they produce and consume only a fraction of this menacing substance, must share its effects. This imbalance was explicitly recognized in the 1987 Montreal Protocol, an international agreement to limit the production of chlorofluorocarbons around the world. The Western signatories agreed to limit their production drastically. DuPont Corporation, which produces nearly 25 percent of the world's chlorofluorocarbons, announced it would phase out all production by the year 2000. Third World countries, on the other hand, were allowed to increase their annual production slightly, if it would help their economic development.

Cooperation is exceedingly difficult to establish, even among neighboring countries. As an illustration of the difficulties, let us return to the problem of acid rain, a form of pollution that we discussed near the beginning of this chapter. It results from a complex chemical change that occurs when oxides of sulfur and nitrogen in the air are exposed to sunlight and water vapor. The resulting solution, a diluted form of acid, falls to the ground as rain or snow and forms acid fogs that corrode buildings, kill fish, and stunt forests and crops. The Canadian government has complained repeatedly about the environmental damage inflicted by acid rain produced in the Great Lakes region of the United States. But United States and Canadian authorities cannot agree on how to apportion the blame for the sulfuric and nitrogen oxides that cause the acid rain.

Even more complicated are the relationships among European nations as generators and recipients of this pollution. The Swedes have been especially concerned about the severe environmental damage inflicted on their country by acid rain from other nations. Since 1976 the Swedes have managed to cut their own sulfur emissions in half, and by 1995 they expect to have reduced the volume to only 20 percent of its mid-1970s level. That will

FIGURE 9.1. ACIDITY OF PRECIPITATION, NORTH AMERICA AND EUROPE,* 1985

North America (pH units)

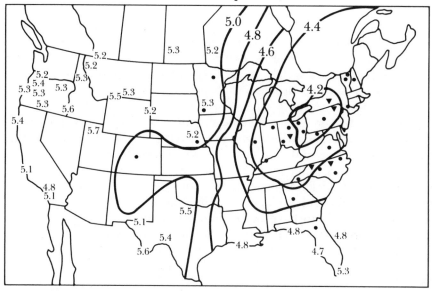

Europe (pH units)

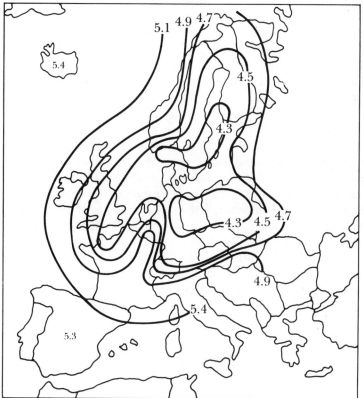

NOTE *The pH scale is used to measure acidity or alkalinity. Neutral solutions have a pH of 7, while acid solutions have a pH less than 7. Each decrease of one unit in pH represents a ten-fold increase in acidity. For example, rainfall with pH 4 is 10 times as acidic as rainfall with pH 5 and 100 times as acidic as rainfall with pH 6.

SOURCE World Resources Institute, *World Resources 1988–89* (New York: Basic Books, 1988), p. 337.

offer considerable relief to Finland, Norway, and the U.S.S.R.—the countries that receive acid rain from Sweden. Yet Sweden's own environment will continue to suffer acutely, because it imports such large quantities of acid rain from Britain, West Germany, and Eastern Europe. It is estimated that of the total amount of sulfur that rains on Swedish territory, only 10 to 15 percent is produced within the country (Aniansson and Hagerhall).

How likely is it that Britain will cooperate in cutting emissions for the sake of the Swedes? As long ago as 1973–74, an OECD study showed that 60 percent of Britain's large volume of sulfur dioxides was exported to other countries. Yet the British were not suffering particularly from sulfur emissions themselves, and their government gave emissions controls a relatively low priority. Despite Sweden's complaints, the British took the position that the costs of scrubbing coal emissions would be too high to justify the benefits (Ashby and Anderson, p. 150). Of course, their estimation of "benefits" was likely to have been quite different from the Swedes'. To create and enforce an effective international agreement, all the signatories must see that they gain as much as they give in the bargain.

New Ways of Thinking about Waste

Some of the most promising new approaches to improving environmental quality involve new ways of thinking about waste. Traditionally, policymakers have concerned themselves with treating wastes as they come out of the polluter's pipeline. Increasingly, however, they are focusing on new ways to avoid producing the waste in the first place, thus minimizing the costs and the risks of treating pollutants. Research and development are targeted on the production process, investigating the parts of that process that produce waste, and identifying alternative manufacturing processes and substances, as well as alternative raw materials.

In the United States, Minnesota Mining and Manufacturing (3M Corporation) has one of the best-established programs to reduce waste—the "Pollution Prevention Pays" program launched in 1975. The company reports having cut its waste in half since then. According to the EPA, already-existing techniques, such as those applied by the 3M Corporation, could reduce the total industrial waste stream in the United States by 15 to 30 percent (USEPA). Similar methods are being introduced by some European manufacturers, such as the Astra pharmaceutical company in Sweden, which cut toxic wastes in half by improving in-plant recycling and substituting water for solvents; and the Duphar pesticide company in Amsterdam, whose new manufacturing process cut toxic waste per unit of chemical produced from twenty kilograms to one kilogram (Brown et al., p. 131).

Not surprisingly, the countries in which governments have taken a consultative approach to industry are the same ones whose governments offer substantial support for technical assistance, technology transfer, and educational programs to encourage industries to reduce their waste streams. Particularly important in Western Europe are subsidies for new products and new processes to control pollution (see Table 9.7). In France, for example, the "Clean Technologies Unit" within the Ministry for Environment distributes financial aid to support industrial research and development of nonpolluting technologies. In both France and West Germany, the governments provide 50 percent or more of the financing for large-scale research programs in energy conservation and pollution control. The Netherlands launched a special subsidy program for clean technologies in 1975. There, as elsewhere in Europe, it is common for research and development to be carried out by semipublic bodies financed jointly by government and industry—for example, TNO in the Netherlands or the Water and Air Pollution Research Institute in Sweden. Such joint institutes can be especially helpful to small and medium-sized businesses that could not afford to operate their own research and development programs.

By comparison with these European models, the U.S. government spends relatively little on waste reduction. The EPA's 1988 budget request for activities to minimize waste amounted to only $398,000, or .03 percent of its operating budget, and less than it had spent for the same purpose in 1986 (U.S. Office of Technology Assessment). Only a handful of American states have waste reduction programs, despite the fact that a modest investment in the development, demonstration, and transfer of waste-reducing technologies could significantly lower the costs of waste management as well as public opposition to siting new facilities. Far more common is the levying of fees on waste generators to pay the costs of cleanup and presumably to encourage polluters to minimize the waste they generate. Here, as in

TABLE 9.7 GOVERNMENT SUBSIDIES FOR ENVIRONMENTAL RESEARCH AND DEVELOPMENT, IN MILLIONS OF U.S. DOLLARS (AT 1980 PRICE LEVEL) AND AS PERCENTAGE OF TOTAL R&D EXPENDITURES

	1975		1979 ·		1983		1985	
	$	%	$	%	$	%	$	%
United States	$235.6	.9	$308.5	1.0	$171.6	.5	$198.2	.5
Japan	62.6	1.5	81.3	1.6	80.4	1.4	—	—
France	44.0	.8	64.7	1.1	26.3	.3	39.0	.5
West Germany	65.8	1.0	144.3	2.1	201.5	2.8	236.4	3.1
Italy	7.4	.6	19.0	1.1	64.1	2.1	33.9	1.0
Netherlands	—	—	—	—	—	—	40.8	3.1
Sweden	12.2	1.3	18.8	1.6	20.4	1.6	19.6	1.5
Britain	32.0	.5	51.6	.8	71.6	1.1	76.4	1.1

SOURCE   OECD, *Environmental Data Compendium* (Paris: OECD, 1987), p. 301.

other areas reviewed in this chapter, U.S. policymakers appear more intent on punishing those who do not comply, while European authorities seem more inclined to try to help industries comply.

* * * * *

This review of environmental policy serves to remind us that in some policy areas, governments distinguish themselves from one another more by their choice of implementation methods than by their choice of policy content. The national governments of Western Europe, the United States, and Japan have adopted legislation that is remarkably uniform in its content. Authorities in all these nations have set roughly the same standards for similar groups of pollutants. But when it comes to implementing legislative mandates, administrators have taken quite different paths to secure compliance from private individuals and corporations. The EPA in the United States uses an open and highly formalized process to set the standards and fix the penalties for noncompliance—a process that produces the highest environmental standards in the world, but also the highest rates of appeal, postponement, and litigation. Japanese and European regulators consult more fully with industry before setting standards which, while usually less ambitious, stand a better chance of being realized. The British system stands alone in the extent to which it affords regulators wide discretion to negotiate with individual firms rather than setting uniform standards for large classes of polluters. These distinctions correspond generally to the distinctions among nations made in the chapters on economic policy and housing policy, based on the degree to which their policy processes conform to corporatist models.

10
POLICY CONTRASTS IN THE WELFARE STATE

Assessing policy options in a cross-nationally comparative context became a widespread pastime in the course of the 1980s. Politicians and journalists have joined policy scientists in pointing out how much the adequacy of national programs is contingent on what other nations do. The discussion about research and industrial policies after the election of President Bush in 1988 was a case in point. There was much comment that civilian research and development expenditures constituted about 1.8 percent of GNP, while the Japanese and West Germans were investing about 50 percent more. "Why does this country's research policy remain so incoherent, while Japan targets one high-tech industry after another and wrests dominance from American competitors?" asked the *New York Times*. It complained that the concentration of American spending on space and military research was luring the best scientists and engineers away from research with commercial application, and called upon Bush to stem the "erosion" of America's technological preeminence (*New York Times* 6 December 1988). Noting that "the absence of an industrial policy is a policy too," the *Times* attributed the American phenomenon to the fact that "American economists believe that the governments rarely improve on the wisdom of the marketplace." A few years earlier the *Times* had itself inveighed against the attempt to shape an industrial policy in America, by arguing that it would merely lead to pork barreling. But how does one distinguish innovative "policies" from pork barreling "politics"; and how differently are the notions expressed? The title of that editorial had been "Industrial Policy = Industrial Politics" (*New York Times* 23 January 1984).

How would the complex notions embedded in that title be translated into other languages and political cultures? When it was submitted to officials of the German, French, Spanish, and other embassies, the resultant translations varied tremendously. One reason was that the way other languages express the negative connotation of the term *politics* varies. Another reason was that the distinction between the concepts of "politics" and "policy" cannot readily be expressed in most of the continental European languages. One consequence of that, in turn, was that political scientists in Germany and elsewhere came to import the English term *policy* into their professional writings (Heidenheimer 1986).

Thus, if the relationship between the concepts of "policy" and "politics" remains ambiguous in English, the problem is even compounded in French or German terminology. The title and sub-title of this book, for example, would be difficult to express in French or German without redundancy.

But problems of terminology have fortunately not inhibited the growth and convergence of an international body of scholarship dealing with cross-national policy comparisons (Heidenheimer 1985). The bibliography at the end of this text attests to the vigorous body of literature which grew in quality and quantity during the 1980s. The availability of this literature is one reason why the contents and shape of our volume have changed rather considerably from edition to edition.

Another reason for the extensive revisions is that we attempt to keep readers abreast of the changing contextual and historical contexts under which contemporary policy-making occurs. More theoretically oriented approaches to comparative policy studies have tended to ignore portions of the context in order to achieve the parsimony which permits the weighing of a limited set of quantified variables in the explanation of policy variations.

As a leading practitioner of more theoretical and quantitative policy studies has recently written, a contextual or historical approach is important "because it allows us to bring back into the policy outcomes arena a whole area of causation which is systematically ignored in much of the current, theoretically-inspired literature of comparative policy studies; namely the complex and evolving interactions of political actors—whether governments, parties, classes, groups or individuals—whose capacity to influence public policy development is conditioned, but by no means wholly determined, by their own understanding of the historical restraints within which they operate" (Castles 1985, p. 22).

WELFARE STATE PERSPECTIVES

How might historical actors place the policies which they helped shape in the context of preceding or subsequent periods? What kind of questions would two important figures in the development of the British and American welfare states, David Lloyd George (1863–1945) and Harry Truman (1884–1972), raise if they were to look at the policy choices of the 1980s in contrast to those of earlier periods? Below is a sample from an imaginary dialogue. It commences with response to a question about how British and American welfare state development compared with that in Germany.

Lloyd George: Well, if you identify the welfare state with the four basic social security programs, three of which Germany initiated in the 1880s under Bismarck, then you can say that we British initiated them about a quarter-century later, around 1910, and the Americans about a half-century later, in the 1930s. For a while in the 1940s, British programs led other countries in coverage against illness, accident, and unemployment, and in old age protection (see Figure 10.1), but then we were overtaken by the Scandinavian countries. The United States approached our protection levels, but remains significantly behind, mainly because they still don't have a general health insurance program. The British loss of leadership may be related to relative economic decline, but I don't quite understand why the Americans haven't caught up more.

Truman: Well, it may be due to the fact that our lower-income citizens are less organized, and vote less frequently, than do lower-income Europeans. When they have gotten mobilized—in the 1930s and 1960s, for example—we have put through and expanded our basic legislation. However, most of the time our institutions—from the Representative who disregards party loyalty, to the private T.V. station that allows fat cats to buy political time—favor those who beat the drums against Big Government. They sure hit me for a loss when I tried to introduce public health insurance in the 1940s. And even LBJ had to settle for a partial program in the 1960s. So, relative to the task of moving a whole, diverse continent, not a homogeneous medium-sized country, our policy instruments have somewhat limited capability most of the time.

Lloyd George: One question in the 1980s seems to be whether the trend toward increased inequalities—held necessary on economic stabilization grounds—can be effectively resisted. Left-of-center parties in both the United States and Britain seem to be in greater ideological disarray than in Germany or Sweden. What with in-fighting among party leaders, and declining party loyalty among voters, the framework through which policy commitments can achieve progressive results seems more fragile than at any time since the 1930s.

Truman: Here's something that's been puzzling me: Why do government policy responses seem to be so different in the 1980s from what they were in the 1880s? After all, both are decades of economic downturn after a longer preceding period of growth. Yet, in the former, we see Bismarck expanding the role of the state and increasing the "cash value," if you will, of national citizenship by providing public benefits. In the 1980s, we have seen Reagan

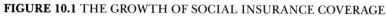

FIGURE 10.1 THE GROWTH OF SOCIAL INSURANCE COVERAGE

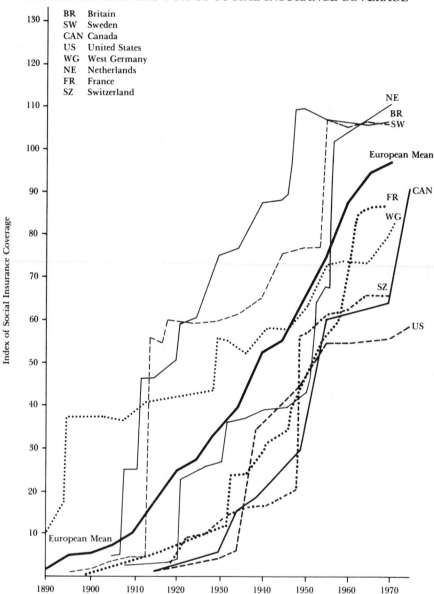

BR	Britain
SW	Sweden
CAN	Canada
US	United States
WG	West Germany
NE	Netherlands
FR	France
SZ	Switzerland

SOURCE   Peter Flora and Arnold J. Heidenheimer, *The Development of Welfare States in Europe and America* (New Brunswick: Transaction), p. 55.

348

and Thatcher trying to diminish the scope of state intervention and reducing the protection against extreme inequality which comes as a civic entitlement. We hear so much about this return to market mechanisms—is it a product of tight economic times, or rather a relapse in precisely those countries where the principles of competitive individualism were already more dominant a century ago?

Lloyd George: Perhaps the explanation is that in prosperous times the policy thrusts of capitalist democracies tend to converge, whereas in periods of economic decline they tend to diverge. If you look at periods of relative growth and prosperity, such as the decade before 1914 or the decades up to the mid-1970s, you see a lessening of differences among national policy packages. Most of Europe got social security in the former period, and the cross-national differences in education, health, housing, and other public benefits were lessened in the latter period.

In the depressed 1880s governments reacted quite differently. Germany gave priority to social security, the United States to education; other countries relied just on tariff protection. In the 1980s, we have again seen governments all trying to control budget growth, but in strikingly different ways. France, Sweden, and other continental countries are not willing to subordinate social policies to military ones, but are willing to go into debt to maintain the social benefits their citizens now regard as theirs by right. Britain, by contrast, is reducing its level of social and education benefits, even forcing its local governments to sell public housing.

Truman: Bismarck would have been surprised to look at Reagan's budget for 1983. Not only did it propose ending construction of low-cost housing units and sharply trimming rent and heat subsidies, but it moved to eliminate summer meal programs for children and reduce food stamp distribution. Federal job-training programs were to end, and day-care centers were to be reduced. Federal funds for improving the schooling of educationally deprived children were to be cut by one-third. The White House claimed that these cuts would not really hurt the poor; but not even the Republicans in Congress believed this. In thinking about the welfare state, I think you have to take the long view. Developing social programs can be a slow and off-again, on-again process—as in the case of American health insurance, for example. Maybe I'm old fashioned, but I don't think liberals have to believe in big spending or big bureaucracies. What we do have to believe is that government has a duty to do what's right and what's fair—and that often means attacking privilege, whether it be in the private or the public sector.

POLICY PATTERNS—NATIONAL, SECTORAL, AND TEMPORAL

The affluence and temper of an era have potent impact on policy development. One writer predicted in the early 1970s that the welfare state "rides the wave of the future," and that apart from some "marginal" American groups, there were "no signs of dispositions to curb it" (Girvetz, p. 520). A decade later the picture was quite different; but the impact of the expenditure crunch had varied greatly in the policy areas. Education and housing had been cut back much more than health; there are many more unemployed teachers than physicians. At the same time, the distribution of resources among sectors and subsectors varied considerably from nation to nation. How, therefore, can we analyze the impact of time periods, national settings, and policy sector characteristics on the content of policies? To answer this question, we must examine how they interact in good *and* bad economic climates.

Let us approach this broad subject by drawing on studies which have examined the shaping influences of national system variables, on the one hand, and policy sector variables, on the other. We have identified many discrete differences among nations' handling of various challenges; but to what extent can these habits and experiences be subsumed under consistent national models of policy-making? Are these models applied similarly in most policy areas, or do the various sectors develop their own policy-making characteristics? If national institutions help shape national "styles," do the styles remain constant as long as the institutions don't change? To what extent can national policy styles explain why some countries might be more successful in some policy areas than in others?

Some political scientists thus have directly characterized national styles. The British style has been identified with a tendency toward extensive consultation, an avoidance of radical policy changes, and a disposition against actions which would challenge well-entrenched interests. The French style, by contrast, is said to exhibit a greater willingness to enforce radical policy change even against the resistance of strong sectional interests. The Swedish style has also been noted to have a capacity for radical policy innovation, but with widespread consultation and great efforts to wear down and convert opposing interests (Gustafsson and Richardson).

Building on such characterizations, another political scientist developed the extended typology shown in Table 10.1. He ranked three countries on six dimensions. Sweden ranked highest on four of the dimensions. Its policy-making was the most consultative and also the most open. Its policy processes were most deliberative but most radical in their proclivities toward sweeping change. The British were ranked lowest on all but two of these dimensions. The French ranked lowest on consultation and highest on centralism and level of conflict. This general policy model was then applied to the area of higher education policies to see if the pattern would hold.

The author found a "high degree of fit" between the generalized national policy style models and the particular case of higher education. In eight of the eighteen cells of the table, the rankings were in full consonance; in four of the cells, the rankings were reversed; and in six cases, the fit was indeterminate or arguable (Premfors). But one could also interpret the data to show that the policy area characteristics probably produced the significant deviations that the author noted.

Analysts of health politics have also examined whether national political systems or policy sector characteristics have had stronger effect on policy-making. An influential early study of British medical interest groups concluded that the major determinants of policy in the health sector were functions of the national political system (Eckstein). Other authors argued that the crucial nature of their services gives physicians in all Western countries overwhelming political resources and that national contexts are comparatively insignificant as determinants of political influence (Marmor and Thomas). A subsequent study of German health politics concluded, more in line with the first study, that "much of the political power of physicians can be accounted for by characteristics of the political system and by political decisions, rather than by the technical nature of medical care or by ideological beliefs and values about health care" (Stone, p. 18).

Another political scientist has examined rule-making in the area of occupational safety and health, considering American and Swedish practices to see how institutions embedded in dissimilar political systems handled almost identical problems. For example, how did administrative agencies set tolerance levels for noise, chemical pollution, and construction industry standards? By and large the contents of these regulations turned

TABLE 10.1 POLICY STYLES IN BRITAIN, FRANCE, AND SWEDEN

	Britain	France	Sweden
Policy Change	Non-radical (3)	Occasionally radical (2)	Radical (1)
Centralism	Less centralized (3)	Highly centralized (1)	Centralized (2)
Consultation	Quite extensive consultation (2)	Limited consultation (3)	Extensive consultation (1)
Openness	Secretive (3)	Quite secretive (2)	Open (1)
Conflict Level	Quite low (2)	High (1)	Low (3)
Deliberation	Not very deliberative (3)	Quite deliberative (2)	Very deliberative (1)

SOURCE   Rune Premfors, "National Policy Styles and Higher Education in France, Sweden and the United Kingdom," *European Journal of Education* 16:2 (1981), pp. 253–62.

out to be "surprisingly similar" (Kelman, pp. 51 and 81), even though the legislative processes varied enormously and the values of the bureaucrats were very different in the two national settings. In this instance the characteristics of the policy sector, when combined to some extent with the reform ethos of the period in which the rules were made or changed, outweighed the differences of the national settings.

The findings were quite different when the same political scientist examined the implementation processes of the same rules in the same countries. The enforcement methods applied by health and safety inspectors in similar industrial settings displayed striking differences of style, with much heavier reliance on fines and other punitive methods in the United States. These national characteristics are attributed to the greater reliance in the United States on adversarial relationships and institutions in both the political and judicial systems. Although differences of national style might have been expected to affect *both* rule-making and rule implementation, they left a much sharper imprint on the latter (Kelman, Chapter Five).

The fact that subnational differences in political cultures may affect policy implementation as strongly as cross-national ones has been illustrated epigrammatically and empirically in a study of nursing-home regulation in England, New York, and Virginia. The researchers had come across the following epigram:

> Question: How many Virginians, New Yorkers, and Englishmen does it take to change a light bulb?
> Answer for Virginia: Three. One to change the bulb, two to talk about how good the old one was.
> Answer for New York: Thirty-seven. One to change the bulb, and a 36-member law firm to sue for damages under the product liability laws.
> Answer for England: Only one. But he won't do it because the bulb has always worked in the past.

They proceeded to see whether empirical research would bear out the epigrammatic model.

The size of each regulatory staff assigned to check on nursing-home standards began to supply an answer. New York had more than twice as many regulators as England and Virginia put together. The story of New York's "exceptionalism" was based on a long history of nursing-home scandals, which caused the industry to be treated with aggressive suspicion, leading to complex regulations and close supervision of the inspectors, to conform to a "no-nonsense deterrence" model linked to threats of litigation and punishment. In both England and Virginia, by contrast, they found compliance models based on a "deliberate emphasis on building up trust relationships with the facilities, with no apparent sense that this may risk regulatory capture by the industry" (Day and Klein, p. 328). The great contrast in regulatory styles for the same industry between the two American states calls into question the role played by a national style, and stresses the need to better understand why the actors in the two American states interacted so differently from each other.

One might also compare the relative fit of sectoral patterns to generalized national models. One would scarcely expect to find many situations in which the strength of the national policy style is completely overwhelmed or reversed by the factors peculiar to any one policy sector. After all, many of the key actors, from parliamentarians, to finance ministry officials, to government auditors, serve to extend homogeneity among the policy sectors. However distinct some policy subsystems are—due to the privileges of a dominant profession as in health or due to the varying autonomy of regional governments or such institutions as central banks—most characteristics of national policy style are likely to be strongly reflected in the individual policy areas.

Up to now there have been very few systematic attempts to compare functionally different policy areas cross-nationally. One could seek to determine, for instance, whether policy processes in housing conform more to general national policy styles than do those in economic management. One difficulty here would be agreeing how to select and measure the relevant indicators. Another would involve the fact that national policy styles change over time. Thus, when many new groups entered into the policy process in Sweden in the late 1970s, some of the differences between Swedish and British policy-making that had been clear-cut a decade or two earlier were diminished (Gustafsson and Richardson, p. 33).

Another comparative approach identifies policy experiences as either very successful or very unsuccessful, and then asks whether this was because of, or in spite of, the national policy style. Such an inquiry into the recent failures of British economic policy noted that Britain failed to replicate both the links between public and private sectors and the bargaining machinery that weighed social benefits against inflationary debits (instruments used, for example, in France and Germany). These shortcomings were said to reflect some yet more general attributes "embedded in institutional and constitutional rigidities that serve politicians well, but serve the country poorly" (Ashford, p. 121).

Recent attempts to harmonize national policies in such larger supranational political entities as the EC have added more interest to the question of how "nations matter." Is it more through their historically determined set of institutions or by the cultural orientations of their elites and mass publics? Or do both translate equally into national styles, serving as the "missing link" between institutional and cultural preconditions and policy outputs (Feick and Jann)? What role does the long-time rule of one dominant party and its past policy performance in countries like Sweden or Japan play in determining present national variances (Pempel, 1988)? In other words, do past policy successes or failures through a political learning process shape the ideas and values of the elites and mass publics about future policy choices, bringing about some "dominant rule system" in a nation (Verba et al., Heclo and Madsen)?

VARIATIONS IN SUPPORT FOR PUBLIC POLICIES

How does citizen support for government initiative and activity vary cross-nationally and by policy area? We expect variations, and the results of a 1974 survey administered in four of "our" countries confirm that expectation. Respondents were asked to consider such policy issues as "looking after old people," or "providing a good education," or "supplying adequate housing." They were asked how important these issues were to them, and how much responsibility government had toward that problem. By combining the ratings from these responses, the authors of *Political Action* calculated indices of "agenda support" for public activity in various policy sectors. We will discuss their findings for five policy areas: education, health care, housing, old age security, and employment. On a 1 to 5 scale, the average ratings were (Farah, Barnes, and Heunks in Barnes and Kaase, p. 413):

	Britain	Netherlands	United States	West Germany
Education	4.4	4.5	4.1	4.2
Health Care	4.6	4.3	3.9	4.4
Housing	4.3	4.2	3.3	3.7
Old Age Security	4.3	4.0	3.9	4.3
Employment	4.2	4.1	3.6	4.3

Neither the highest ranking—that for health care in Britain (4.6)—nor the lowest—for housing in the United States (3.3)—should come as a surprise to readers of the preceding chapters. Agenda support in the United States was consistently below that in the European countries. While the gap was smallest in education, it was largest in the areas where the norms of free enterprise support for private initiative come into play most directly—housing and employment. Among the three European countries, we note relatively strong German agenda support for old age security and health care (public programs initiated by Bismarck in the 1880s), and somewhat lower support for education than in Britain and the Netherlands.

We might expect support for public activity to vary by social class. Figure 10.2 confirms this with regard to five income groups. Support in Europe for public housing programs declined slightly among the middle- and higher-income groups, but a much sharper decline occurred in the United States, where lower-middle- and middle-income groups probably perceived their own benefits from government policies less clearly.

Similar agenda support figures in health care and education show some contrasts. British upper-income group support holds up better for the more universal National Health Service than for housing programs. The largest cross-national differences are found in housing, the lowest in education. In these service areas we do not find the Anglo-American vs. continental contrast which was identified in the economic policy chapter. Here the two continental systems are bracketed on the high side by the British, on the low side by the Americans. On balance, these patterns are consonant with the finding that on questions regarding the scope of government intervention, "the mass of citizens express views that match their government's behavior" (Wilensky in OECD 1981, p. 188).

How did *satisfaction* with government performance vary across nations and policy sectors? This can be discerned through analyses of responses to the question, "How well do you think government has been doing?" regarding the various policy sectors. In all three European countries health care was most positively evaluated among the ten policy areas included in the original survey. In the United States, by contrast, public health efforts ranked only fourth, behind education policy and two other areas (Farah et al., p. 419). Also striking is the high degree of satisfaction among the British

FIGURE 10.2 AGENDA SUPPORT FOR HOUSING, EDUCATION, AND HEALTH POLICIES, BY INCOME GROUP

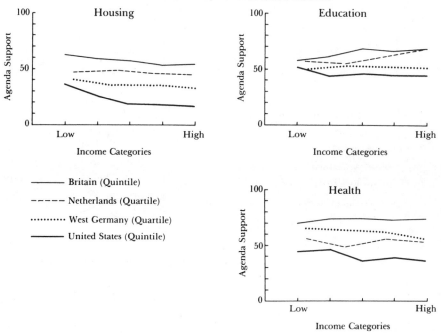

SOURCE   Samuel Barnes and Max Kaase, eds., *Political Action* (Beverly Hills: Sage, 1979).

with their National Health Service, which ranked far ahead of the health programs in Germany and the Netherlands.

We are also able to analyze how the evaluation of public policy performance varies among groups with different educational attainments. This information is presented in Figure 10.3, where Group 1 includes respondents who have only elementary education, and Group 5 includes those who attended institutions of higher education. We might expect the more highly educated to be more critical, because of both their expectations and their information sources, and because they tend to belong to higher-income groups and are therefore resistant to equalizing tendencies.

The graph on health policies bears out this expectation. The higher the education level, the less likely that people would grant that the government was doing well. Compared to similar strata in Europe, the least educated American group was notably negative. Also distinctive was the stability in the evaluation of the British National Health Service among all except

FIGURE 10.3 PERFORMANCE EVALUATION OF HOUSING, EDUCATION, AND HEALTH POLICIES, BY EDUCATION

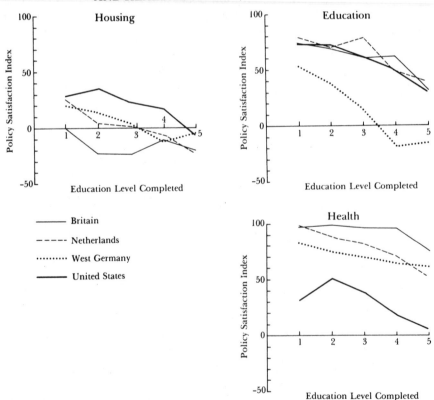

SOURCE   Samuel Barnes and Max Kaase, eds., *Political Action* (Beverly Hills: Sage, 1979).

the university group. The decline was sharper in the Dutch and German insurance-based systems, where white-collar workers seemed to perceive that the system was not serving them as well. But both the lowest satisfaction levels and the highest intergroup declines were found in the United States, where both white-collar and professional groups criticized public health programs in whose benefits they largely did not share.

The results are both similar and different when we turn to education policy. Again the more highly educated tended to be more critical. But here it is the Germans who differ sharply from the others. The sharper and more prolonged controversies over reform policies, such as school comprehensivization and university reform, probably contributed to the unusually sharp slope of the German curve. It is interesting to compare the slopes of the second, third, and fourth groups in Germany and Britain. The British medium-education groups regarded recent policy changes fairly positively, whereas the university graduates, whose children were most likely to be attending grammar or private schools, deviated sharply from the evaluations of other groups.

Housing policy in all countries is the area where government generates the most dissatisfaction. At first glance it might appear curious that Americans are less dissatisfied than the Europeans. But the especially negative British response provides the clue: There, government has been most directly involved in actually running, not just subsidizing, a large housing sector. Governmental policies thus become a more likely target for blame in Britain, compared to countries where nonprofit or private developers are more significant.

Conservatives who argue in favor of a diminution of state power through privatization of many public services were heartened by strong initiatives in this direction taken by Margaret Thatcher's governments in the 1980s. During this decade about one million public housing units were sold to the people who occupied them, thus pushing the proportion of British homeowners from 54 to over 60 percent. A French writer hailed this, because "if the state gives up its millions of dwellings, it will rid itself of a function that other institutions could probably fulfill better." He called for a similar move to privatize university expenditures, arguing that "a privatized system of higher education is possible, as the case of the United States attests, and it could be adopted in other advanced pluralist democracies" (Dogan, pp. 264–67).

Yet during the same period the British government could not go much beyond raising one previously existing institution to full university status. Its major initiative in this direction went in the direction of substituting loans for grants given to university students, thus increasing the share of private financing. But when this bill was debated in Parliament, a revolt of Conservative backbenchers—a rare occurrence on this scale—forced the government to withdraw the proposal. This reflected resistance from middle-class parents. But it also showed that the dynamics of privatization cannot easily be transferred from one policy area to another. Nor has the flourishing of private universities in the United States and Japan helped similar initiatives to bear fruit in Western Europe.

There may be something to the argument that the quality of services will decline as society makes a determined effort to widen access to them quickly.

Will consumer disappointment be greater in cases of personal consumer goods for which the individual pays directly, or in the case of services paid for indirectly through taxes? Direct payment should make the consumer more critical of quality received. "On the other hand the very fact of payment often sets up the presumption that one must have received an adequate countervalue, so that people will tend to blame themselves (and remain silent) if the outcome of the transaction is considered unsatisfactory. It is perhaps in part because of this strange psychological mechanism that publicly financed services are much more frequently and strongly criticized than those rendered on a private basis" (Hirschman, p. 44).

Politically significant, too, is the fact that the costs and benefits of public services are distributed very asymmetrically over an individual's life-cycle. Figure 10.4 illustrates how the impacts of publicly provided benefits and publicly exacted taxes have differing incidence as an individual progresses from childhood to old age. Children draw many benefits, and pay no taxes themselves. As some enter the work force during the late teens, they begin to pay various kinds of taxes, which then outweigh the benefits

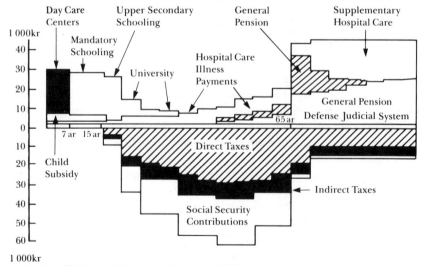

FIGURE 10.4 REDISTRIBUTION OVER THE LIFE CYCLE

SOURCE   Swedish Central Bureau of Statistics, 1985.

they receive and which peak in middle age. After retirement at about age sixty-five, benefits in the form of pensions and health care again begin to exceed taxes. The degree to which working people have to bear burdens for the other two age groups is becoming more of a political issue in developed nations as longevity increases and birthrates remain at or below replacement levels. Generational conflict among age groups is a possibility in the future of the welfare state. But so too—depending on the political choices made—is generational solidarity (Heclo 1988). Each of us who lives a normal lifespan is, after all, a member of every age group.

POLICY GROWTH AND DECLINE: TOWARDS AND BEYOND THE YEAR 2000

To what extent is the *scope* of government social policies the product of underlying socioeconomic determinants? To what extent do policies reflect political choices? These questions dominate much of the literature in comparative public policy. Some argue the predominant power of the forces of economic development and its demographic and social correlates; they are opposed by those who maintain that "politics matters." The latter argue that such factors as the party composition of governments do have an identifiable effect on social policy.

> The vehemence of the "politics matters" debate, and the fact that it is frequently tied in with the conflict of sociological functionalists and Marxist structuralists, on the one side, and the pretensions of a political science discipline premised on the exercise of human choice on the other, suggest that the issues are fundamental, relating to the extent to which the structured socio-economic processes of contemporary societies leave room for conscious agency in reshaping policy and institutional arrangements. (Castles 1981, p. 119)

Those who contest the shaping influence of political processes have utilized cross-national studies to demonstrate that per capita GNP and the age structure of populations suffice to explain social security extension, and that one can leave aside discussions of party programs and ideologies (Wilensky 1975). Analyzing similar data differently, their opponents have come to very different conclusions (Cameron 1978, Castles 1981). Economists have asserted that economic and structural variables were predominant in determining such policy output indicators as the cost of health systems, the shape of educational systems, and the nature of urban planning devices. They, too, have been rebuffed by those who believe politics, or social choice, affects policy outcomes.

This debate has further stimulated the array of intellectual challenges which have attracted scholars of different backgrounds to comparative policy studies. Recently, however, one notes tendencies toward some synthesis in the battle of paradigms. Thus a Marxist scholar still holds that those who dominate the institutions of the state are constrained by the imperatives of the capital accumulation process, but he grants that "within these constraints there is room for maneuver, for competing strategies and policies. There is scope for the various organs of the state to initiate policies, to reverse them, to make choices and to make mistakes" (Gough, pp. 43–44). There has been some convergence toward examining policy outcomes by focusing on varying policy patterns and the structural relationships which underlie them. This trend has been viewed as "congenial to the practitioners of a comparative approach to politics and policy for whom an understanding of structured variation is the very essence of their discipline" (Castles 1981, p. 229).

How strongly macroeconomic conditions affect public sector growth has been amply demonstrated over the past decade. Where the public sector had attracted increasing proportions of national incomes in all Western countries up to about 1975, there have been standstills and declines since then. But within these strong structural constraints governments have made very different kinds of choices. In Britain and the United States right-wing governments have made heavier cuts in many social policy areas, and used political muscle to force a reprivatization of certain sectors such as public housing. More than their continental partners in NATO, the United States and Britain have reallocated resources from social welfare to military expenditures. Similarly, they have moved beyond retrenchment to the abolition of programs and agencies which had provided the poor with legal and organizational means to assert their interests (Piven and Cloward).

* * * * *

How important are the linkages between political, economic, and social systems in conditioning choices of policy *instruments?* The argument that significant differences exist among the Western democracies in the nature of choice-making capacities at the macro level has led social scientists to assess instrumentally the political-economic systems themselves. Some view many European systems as "corporatist democracies" which have relatively greater ability to adapt social policies to economic constraints with less political conflict. This capacity is attributed to three of the countries examined in this volume—the Netherlands, Sweden, and Germany—and also to Austria, Belgium, and Norway. There, consultative relations between employers, workers, governments, and other organized groups are seen as facilitating relatively equitable distributions of costs and benefits. By contrast, the less coordinated political economies of Britain and the United States are seen as being much less able to inhibit conflictual challenges to a political consensus (Wilensky 1975).

Our comparative micro-level discussions of the policy areas strengthen our ability to evaluate the utility of these system-level models, or characterizations. Our probings may suggest that they are more applicable in some areas, such as health and incomes policies, than in others, such as education and urban planning policies. Within a policy area like health corporatist characteristics may be exhibited more where the private sector is still significant, as in Germany, than where it no longer is, as in Sweden. But the contrast between Germany's handling of health cost control and the United States' suggests that corporatist predispositions can help produce different outcomes—in this instance, in good part because of the different positions taken by organized business.

If the so-called democratic corporatist systems were clearly more successful than the others in adapting policies, the discussion might be less extensive than it has become. As is pointed out in Chapter Seven, the record of the democratic corporatist systems in the policy area which provides them greatest opportunity to display their structural advantages—incomes policy—has been at best mixed; even Sweden has recently faltered in its attempts. There the equilibrium between organized labor and business has been threatened by the unions' claims to sharing collectively in the ownership of industrial enterprises, a demand which went beyond the labor participation in management found in Germany (Heclo and Madsen). It remains to be seen, however, whether the higher cooperative potential of the more corporatist systems will engender greater success in meeting Japanese and other Asian competition on international markets than most British and American industries have so far been able to achieve.

When we turn from production to allocation of costs and benefits, the "democratic corporatism matters" thesis is more persuasive. In 1982 and 1983 the officials who manage social services such as education and housing in the "corporatist" systems were in many cases given less ample budgets than they had been a decade earlier. Still, these countries seemed to avoid the widespread—not diminution, but *abolition*—of public agencies, regulatory and social programs, and university-level colleges and departments, which was so prevalent in Britain and the United States during the same years.

But conservatives argue that "neocorporatism leads slowly to state capitalism. The growth of public expenditures—and consequently of various forms of taxation—has been continuous and more or less cyclical. . . . Several European countries already seem to be travelling this path, particularly Austria, the Netherlands, Sweden, Norway, and to a lesser extent, West Germany, but obviously they cannot do so indefinitely." Reversing the pattern of state intervention might engender, this author admits, "a serious risk of partial delegitimation of the political regime in the poorest sectors of the population. Some people will see such an attempt to reduce state intervention as a social regression . . . but what if it was simply a reaction against the hypertrophy of the bureaucratic state?" (Dogan, p. 271). Some have been surprised that the cutbacks of the 1980s have not produced more powerful signs of protest or regime delegitimation. But, on the other hand, there has also not been a very broad and widespread movement of grass roots resentment against bureaucracies.

As we discuss in Chapter Six, it is striking that those democratic corporatist systems with higher tax levels had much weaker antitax movements than Britain and the United States did with their relatively lower tax levels. Tax protests like those of the Danish Glistrup party, the Proposition 13 movement in California, and similar phenomena in other American states were scarcely present and never markedly successful in those continental countries with stronger corporatist structures. In none of these countries did the right-wing parties go as far in implementing broad income tax reductions as the Tories did under Thatcher and the Republicans under Reagan. In part this can be attributed to their different traditions of responsibility for economic management. But it is also due to the fact that the organizational web underlying the societal consensus was better able to convey to potential middle-class tax protesters what they too stood to lose from lowered social safety nets.

In a study of the interdependence of industrial, labor market, incomes, and social policies in eight countries, Wilensky and Turner contrasted policy patterns of pluralist and more corporatist systems. They found that in the more corporatist systems bargaining structures gave the bargaining process a more "rational-responsible" bias, with linkages fostering tradeoffs "that reduce conflict and create consensus and thereby make policy implementation more effective." By contrast Britain and the United States showed "most policy segmentation and least policy continuity." Even if they had wanted to, governments could scarcely use labor federations or trade associations to formulate and implement national policies in areas like industrial, occupational health, and social security policies. They conclude that "structures count: types of political economies predict the kinds of policies governments adopt; even more, how effectively and persistently policies are implemented" (Wilensky and Turner, pp. 49–50).

* * * * *

The conservative British and American governments made more drastic *distributive* choices in allocating social and economic costs than did the continental systems. To what extent this pattern is attributable to differences in corporatist structures, and to what extent it is due to broader historical factors, which we discussed at the end of Chapter One, is still difficult to assess. But it is evident that the continental countries did not experience to the same degree the recent vilification of bureaucrats, and the delegitimization of public services which have been prevalent in the English-speaking countries ever since the Keynesian paradigm was dethroned. Much more discontinuity was generated in Washington between the time that President Nixon declared, "We are all Keynesians now," and when President Reagan tried to enthrone the Laffer Curve, than in the continental capitals.

But in an analysis of macroeconomic policies in four European countries—Austria, Britain, Germany and Sweden—Scharpf found that "neo-corporatist institutions are of relevance to macroeconomic policy only as long as the Keynesian game is being played." As soon as monetarist policies replace Keynesian ones, thus allowing unemployment to rise, "there is no reason to assume that decentralized and fragmented union movements should be any less 'docile' than highly centralized and disciplined corporatist unions are said to be" (Scharpf, p. 253).

In Britain and the United States, politicians were able to carry out more extensive budget-cutting because they were less constrained by agreements with unions and interest groups, and thus could more fully exploit changes in public moods. Because the mood of the war on poverty had passed from the American scene, job-training programs fell victim to more severe cuts than in countries where the programs of the 1960s were more firmly entrenched. The Swedish non-socialist government of the early 1980s engendered vast deficits rather than reduce such programs. If policy fashions change less quickly in democratic corporatist countries, it is not only because their bureaucracies are more legitimated, but probably because the organizational density tends to perpetuate a stronger sense of recent history. The memories of the unemployment of the 1930s were retained more vividly in the Netherlands and Sweden than in California, where a former union leader, Ronald Reagan, could persuade his more mobile audience that the policy lessons drawn by the preceding generation could be stood on their head with impunity.

Studies show that during a period of budgetary decrementalism, such as the 1980s, those groups whose esteem in public recognition and moods has been least consistent are disproportionately hurt. Among social groups this has meant that the working poor were more easily permitted to slip back under the poverty line than were the elderly, whose claims to social insurance pensions had become more firmly anchored in the English-speaking countries as well. So pensions and health care have not been deeply hurt in the decrementalist era; but it has been different in the case of education. In the 1950s new conceptions of the benefits of educational expansion led to "an astonishing story of public, political, and administrative commitment to, or at least acceptance of, the expansion of service whose products are wholly indirect and invisible." But this was followed by the "erosion of confidence in education's social and productive functions," and the swift deceleration of growth (Kogan in Hood and Wright).

For many who espouse a politics of redistribution, "the 1980s became a decade of wasted opportunity. The reserve army of the unemployed was not used to remove the warts that disgraced affluent societies—whether it was slum housing and decaying urban centers, polluted rivers and forests rotted by acid rain, or old and disabled people with grossly inadequate care and even less adequate social contact."

But the consequences were much worse for the developing countries, where living standards dropped sharply in areas like Africa and Latin America, which had very little in the way of social security programs to cushion the impact on the poor. "Some poor countries were forced to devote up to a third or half of their export earnings to servicing their debts. With their budgets loaded with the prior charge of interest payments, social programs had to be cut. Less could be spent on education, health and social welfare. Thus many doctors in Africa were deprived of the tools to do their job and transferred their skills to the richer nations" (Abel-Smith, p. 281).

What then can be said about the future of today's welfare states? Powerful demographic forces are clearly shaping that future, but not in any deterministic manner. As we have seen in Chapter Seven, all the developed nations can count on an ageing of their populations, even though the elderly's exact share of the population depends partly on uncertain trends in fertility rates in the twenty-first century. Table 10.2 shows the projection of social spending implied by this demographic shift, assuming simply that real per capita benefits for the various age groups remain constant at 1980 levels. Since there will be relatively fewer young people, spending on education and family benefits is projected to decrease or (for the United States, Canada, and Australia) grow slowly. This will account for only a fraction of the increase in health and pension costs that can be expected due to the larger number of elderly people, yielding a net increase in social expenditures of approximately 30 percent because of demographic change over the

TABLE 10.2 GROWTH OF PUBLIC SOCIAL EXPENDITURE IMPLIED BY PROJECTED DEMOGRAPHIC CHANGE,[a] 1980–2040
(1980 = 100)

	Education	Family Benefits	Health	Pensions	Total Social Expenditure[b]	Total Population	Population 65+
Australia	128	126	240	288	207	168	346
Belgium	71	74	99	134	102	92	139
Britain	85	86	121	130	110	103	141
Canada	103	110	218	304	187	146	345
Denmark	58	61	95	124	88	77	131
France	80	83	119	172	128	104	170
Germany	53	60	90	126	97	74	131
Italy	62	64	108	134	107	85	152
Japan	79	77	146	229	140	102	255
Netherlands	70	69	137	160	121	98	210
Sweden	83	84	117	123	109	95	126
United States	102	114	178	215	165	136	238

NOTE [a]Cumulative growth rates assuming constant real per capita expenditure by age within each program.
[b] Including education, health, pensions, family benefits, unemployment compensation and, in the case of Australia and the Netherlands, other cash benefits and welfare services.
SOURCE OECD 1988, p. 42.

next fifty years for these OECD nations as a whole. However, these demographic pressures will not occur evenly over this entire period or simultaneously in different nations. Moreover, in those subperiods when expenditure is rising due to the ageing of populations, the number of working-age people available to finance these costs will be growing slowly or even declining in a number of countries. This suggests a significant increase in the financing burden per worker during certain "crunch periods."

Table 10.3 shows how these periods will vary in timing and magnitude among nations. Japan, for example, will face the demographic crunch soonest. Assuming benefits based on 1980 levels, after 1990 Japanese social expenditure can be expected to be boosted 24 percent as a result of demographic forces while the working-aged population 15 to 64 decreases by 17 percent. The table also shows that the financing of the additional social outlays implied by population ageing in this period will require a 49 percent increase in real earnings per working-age person (or an average yearly growth rate of 0.8 percent) in Japan. Britain and Sweden will face smaller financing problems and face them later than Japan. The strains will be somewhat greater in the U.S., Canada, Denmark, and Germany. The growth rates required in productivity and workers' earnings are within the range of past precedents in postwar economic performance, but the efforts needed to keep pace with demographic change will still be substantial.

TABLE 10.3 IMPLICATIONS OF PROJECTED DEMOGRAPHIC CHANGE FOR SOCIAL EXPENDITURE FINANCING BURDEN DURING SELECTED SUBPERIODS

		Projected Compound Growth (Base Year = 100)		Growth in Real Earnings per Worker Required to Cope with Pure Demographic Effect	
	Period	Social Expenditure	Population Aged 15–64	Compound Growth (Base Year = 100)	Average Annual Compound Growth (%)
Australia	2010–40	142	111	128	0.8
Belgium	2015–40	103	85	121	0.8
Britain	2020–40	105	96	109	0.4
Canada	2005–40	143	102	140	1.0
Denmark	2015–40	96	75	128	1.0
France	2010–40	111	87	128	0.8
Germany	1995–40	98	63	156	1.0
Italy	2005–40	101	76	133	0.8
Japan	1990–40	124	83	149	0.8
Netherlands	2005–40	108	78	138	0.9
Sweden	2010–40	108	88	123	0.7
United States	2010–40	133	100	133	1.0

SOURCE   OECD, 1988, p. 36.

Of course, these figures are simplistic projections, not predictions. Everything will depend on policy choices made or not made in the years ahead. Demography influences but it does not determine that destiny. Consider only a few examples of the choices that will be required.

We can be sure benefits per head will not be pegged at their 1980 levels, but how will health care and pension benefits be allowed to grow in relation to real earnings?

We know that political problems and institutional rigidities will prevent any simple diversion of resources from programs serving the young to programs serving the elderly but what generational tradeoffs, if any, will be made to set social priorities?

It is clear that projections based on employment conditions in 1980 misrepresent future labor markets but what choices will be made to affect unemployment or the labor force participation of women, youth, foreign workers, and the elderly themselves?

Changing age structures clearly mean that a larger share of national resources will be channelled to the elderly, but will this mean a greater or lesser role for the private sector in providing social benefits and services?

While the future of the welfare state may be unpredictable, we can be sure that it will flow out of the way these and a host of similar choices are made through political processes.

RECYCLING PROBLEMS, RESCALING REMEDIES

The tendency to view politics as a means of collective social change is likely to grow, not diminish, in the years ahead. There is the obvious sense of growing scarcity in economic and natural resources as well as in the tax revenues to support government programs. Scarcity forces us to be aware of starker choices; some of one thing must be given up to have more of another. This situation has been played out most dramatically in budget-cutting exercises throughout the Western nations in recent years. This setting has clearly evoked another factor in policy options—namely, the size and power of nations.

The United States, as a world power, has pursued a higher level of armaments expenditures at the same time that it has cut the growth of federal expenditures in many domestic policy areas. In this it has differed from the middle-sized nations of Europe. In earlier periods, size of military effort generally has not been strongly related to size of social policy effort (Wilensky 1975). In the 1990s, however, the tradeoffs between these spheres may become more direct. This pressure toward new priorities, from the promotion of individual security through social policy measures to the bolstering of national security through military and strategic measures, engendered considerable uncertainty in Europe, Japan, and the

United States. Considering proposals in NATO countries in the early 1980s that "renewed military effort must be financed from declining economic resources," one Dutch writer assessed the chances that popular opinion would support such a shift, concluding that while such support had earlier been generated during the "coldest" stage of the Cold War, signposts for the 1980s indicated "less popular consensus and support for stressing warfare priorities than for fighting unemployment and preserving welfare programs" (Keman in Castles 1982, p. 217).

By the early 1990s, profound changes were shaking once-settled Cold War assumptions about the shape of international, domestic, and national security policies. From the reformist turmoil in the Soviet bloc, symbolized by Mikhail Gorbachev, to the Chinese students of Tiananmen Square, policymakers in Europe, America, and Japan were being challenged to rethink their positions in a moment of historic transformations.

Just as the traditional welfare state agenda is feeling the strains of scarcity and a changing Cold War context, so its so-called post-materialist goals are also expanding. While public concerns about jobs, schools, and health care remain high, the younger generation seems more interested in seeing other equality-related concerns added to the agenda of political choice (Barnes and Kaase 1979). Quality-of-life issues—such as the meaningfulness of one's work and opportunities for contributing to the preservation of one's environment—do not appear to be replacing traditional bread-and-butter policy topics; but they are lengthening the list of criteria by which public policies are debated and judged in every nation.

Comparative studies of public opinion show that despite conservative electoral successes and tax backlashes in the 1970s and 1980s, public support in the United States as well as throughout the affluent democracies remains solidly behind an active, welfare state role for government. What appears to have occurred are various marginal shifts in preferences that represent a consolidating of the modern welfare state rather than a movement toward dismantling its components (Shapiro and Young, p. 65). But this support is hardly unconditional or unambiguous. After an exhaustive study of the attitude surveys in the United States and Europe, the most thorough book on this subject to date sums up the results in this way:

> ... enough evidence currently exists to lend some credibility to the notion of a distinctively "modern" system of mass attitudes, opinions, and beliefs associated with social policy development. The characteristics of this system include, as we have seen, widespread public acceptance of the general principles of the "social rights" of citizenship, entailing positive governmental efforts to promote individual security and social equality, with a simultaneous allegiance to individual freedom, the "free market," and individual responsibility for success or failure in a competitive economic order. In addition, the data firmly establish that some types of social

welfare programs are invariably popular in modern society (e.g., old-age pensions), while other categories of programs may be universally problematic (e.g., public assistance). (Coughlin, pp. 155–56)

In other words, public opinion appears to be as inconsistent in its commitment to social policy principles as the welfare state itself. And here we find a key to understanding how democratic politics could create the modern welfare state without satisfying the reasoned requirements of economists or the preferences of ideological purists. Political processes, like public opinion, involve choices that avoid the "big choice" between individual liberty and social equality, between the inequality and insecurity generated by market mechanisms and the flattening equality implied by distributive concepts which arise from uniform definitions of social needs.

By the strict canons of economic reasoning, a democratic welfare state should be impossible. In a brilliant analysis, the economist Kenneth Arrow offered proof that a consistent summation of individual preferences into a collective welfare choice could not be achieved (Arrow, Mackay). Making a number of fairly reasonable assumptions about the distribution of welfare preferences and other constraints, Arrow was able to show the internal contradictions that were bound to arise in any effort to define a democratic social welfare function.

By the less strict, but emotionally charged, canons of ideological reasoning, the welfare state should also be impossible. It fails to satisfy socialist criteria for production organized around social needs rather than profit motives. In fact every Western welfare state is highly ambiguous about how social needs are actually to be defined and who defines them. Yet the welfare state also fails to satisfy conservative criteria for maximizing individual liberty. It does not leave people, as Milton Friedman put it, "free to choose," and it neither fully accepts nor rejects market mechanisms. In terms of ideological clarity, the welfare state is incoherent.

But one need not therefore jump to conclusions about a "system breakdown" or political "overload," for engineering concepts may be no more applicable than economic concepts. Rather, we need to recall that the management of such contradictions is precisely what the politics of social choice is about. If the political choice process had been required to yield a consistent ordering of objectives, the modern welfare state as we know it could never have come into existence.

* * * * *

The momentum of the *welfare state* expansion in the 1960s engendered an almost unconditional belief in its "problem solving" capacities. It was seen as an instrument for such diverse purposes as resolving class conflicts, deflecting tendencies towards anomie and alienation, while enhancing demands to control economic cycles. But since the sobering period of the 1970s, sharper

TABLE 10.4 THE WELFARE STATE AS "PROBLEM SOLVER" AND "PROBLEM CREATOR"

	"Problem Solver"	"Problem Creator"
1. Political Dimension	secures citizens' loyalty organization of class compromise defuses interest conflicts relief of private sector due to lesser strike frequency inhibits converting economic crises into political crises	engenders new distributional conflicts (i.e., tax revolt) promotes selfish competition undermines traditional civic virtues political inflexibility/ ungovernability
2. Social Dimension	higher protection against poverty threat comprehensive state protection of living standards deflects anomic tendencies marginalizes deprivation and opposition reduces gender inequalities	turns old and new inequalities into persistent issues undermines individual initiative and personal freedoms and responsibilities creates new forms of handicap destabilizes class structure (loosens traditional bonds) dependency of daily life
3. Economic Dimension	built-in anticyclical demand enhancement social peace as productive factor assured reproduction and training of labor incentives for (labor saving) technological modernization (securing adaptive capacity of the economy) countries with strong welfare state handle crises as well as or better than countries with weak welfare state	cost burden on business with negative effects on achievement and job creation strain on work force threatens performance and work morale migration into shadow economy overburdens public budgets distorts or inhibits the adaptive capacity of the economy ineffectiveness and inefficiency of public social policy

SOURCE   Manfred G. Schmidt, *Sozialpolitik. Historische Entwicklung und internationaler Vergleich* (Opladen: Leske und Budrich 1987), p. 187.

attention also came to be focussed on the manner in which the welfare state programs could also engender problems of their own. In Table 10.4 various competing perspectives on the welfare state as both a problem "solver" and problem "creator" are presented in a form which permits a synoptic overview of attributes which social scientists of various persuasions have identified with the welfare state under both broad rubrics.

Manfred Schmidt, the German political scientist who constructed this conspectus, thus perceives the securing of citizens' loyalty and the constraints on converting economic crises into political crises as among the problem-solving capacities of welfare states. But also recorded are the views that welfare states undermine such traditional civic virtues as self-reliance, or that they engender new kinds of distributional conflicts, as manifested in the tax revolts against the allocation of public burdens. Enlarged claims to benefits are also seen as contributing to political inflexibility as elected governments may hold back from making some necessary reallocations of resources.

Social problems which welfare states are seen as creating or aggravating include the destabilization of class structures and the engendering of new inequalities as persistent issues. Thus the provision of subsidized public housing created new kinds of resentment and jealousy among various groups of renters and homeowners, even as the breaking up of old working-class neighborhoods contributed to an increasing dependency on bureaucratic interventions in daily life. But as against these drawbacks, welfare state programs are seen as sustaining standards of living, reducing deprivation, and lowering levels of gender inequality. Other problem-solving and -creating attributes of enhanced government programs are also identified as they relate more directly to economic consequences. Table 10.4 makes no attempt to assess the degree of agreement or disagreement as to the relative impact of these characteristics.

Most analysts would agree that the welfare state is to some degree both a "problem solver" and a "problem creator." Which tendencies are stronger may be seen as varying with time and place. But if one speaks generally for the countries discussed here, we can agree with Schmidt that the capacity of welfare states as problem "solvers" continues to outweigh and counterbalance the additional problems which it may have served to engender.

The countries for whom a too-zealous pursuit of welfare state goals brought insolvency have been in the other parts of the world. Earlier in this century, Uruguay became a "basket case." Presently, small out-liers like New Zealand are having to struggle to maintain exemplary welfare programs in the face of sharply altered world markets. But no European or North American government has bankrupted itself by welfare spending. The scaling back of entitlements which has been part of the effort to stabilize public budgets has selectively increased some inequalities. But there are few cases of return to a *status quo ante,* that of 1928 or even of 1958. The capacity to use public budgets to transform inequalities has been reduced, but not maimed.

At the same time, world market trends have pitted some poor workers of Alabama against the poorer workers of Mexico. So what can politics do to complement markets? Do again what was done earlier: export the welfare state model to Mexico, to Korea, then to Bolivia, and then maybe later even to Bangladesh. The trend in the collectivization of risks which the welfare state represents has in the course of a century of adaptation become part of the self-image of Western civilization. Piecemeal export of its techniques has become part of what in earlier days the French might have called a Western *mission civilisatrice*. Margaret Thatcher and some like her have somewhat retreated from this mission. In the process, some corrections have been made.

The welfare state may or may not emerge strengthened from what has been heralded as its "crisis." But more than parliamentarism, militarism, or other -isms, the welfare state, late twentieth-century model, may well provide instruments for equilibrating destabilized world economic regions.

BIBLIOGRAPHY

This bibliography serves the dual purpose of providing reference information on sources referred to in this volume and listing some additional cross-national studies relating to the policy areas covered. It is intended to provide an easily accessible overview of the relevant literature, with emphasis on recent English-language publications. Some general references are included in the sections for Chapters One and Ten.

Reference items are generally listed by senior author. Articles in edited volumes are occasionally cited in the text by the author of the article and editor of the volume: (Smith, in Jones). To find reference information in the bibliography you should look under the name of the editor, Jones.

Certain journals are referred to with abbreviations, as follows:

AJS	*American Journal of Sociology*
APSR	*American Political Science Review*
BJPS	*British Journal of Political Science*
Comp Ed Rev	*Comparative Education Review*
Comp Pol St	*Comparative Political Studies*
Comp Pol	*Comparative Politics*
High Ed	*Higher Education*
Int Jl Urb & RR	*International Journal of Urban and Regional Research*
Int Jl Hlth Svc	*International Journal of Health Services*
Jl Hlth PP & L	*Journal of Health Politics, Policy and Law*
JPP	*Journal of Public Policy*
Law & Con P	*Law and Contemporary Problems*

Mil Mem Q   *Milbank Memorial Quarterly*
Pol Anal   *Policy Analysis*
Pol & Pol   *Policy and Politics*
Pol Stud   *Political Studies*
Sc Pol Stud   *Scandinavian Political Studies*
Tijd E & S Geo   *Tijdschrift voor Econ. en Soc Geografie*
Urb Aff Q   *Urban Affairs Quarterly*
West Eur Pol   *Western European Politics*

CHAPTER 1. THE POLITICS OF SOCIAL CHOICE

Ashford, Douglas E., ed. 1978. *Comparing Public Policies: New Concepts and Methods.* Beverly Hills: Sage Publications.

Caim-Caudle, P. R. 1973. *Comparative Social Policy and Social Security.* London: Martin Robertson.

Castles, Francis. 1978. *The Social Democratic Image of Society.* London: Routledge and Kegan Paul.

———, ed. 1982. *The Impact of Parties.* Beverly Hills: Sage Publications.

———. 1987. "Comparative Public Policy Analysis: Problems, Progress and Prospects." In *The Future of Party Government*, Vol. 3: *Managing Mixed Economies*, edited by Francis Castles et al. New York: DeGruyter.

Comstock, Alzada. 1937. "Expenditures, Public." *Encyclopedia of the Social Sciences.* Vol. 6. New York: Macmillan. 5–10.

Cutwright, Phillips. 1967. "Income Redistribution: A Cross-National Analysis." *American Sociological Review* 32:180–90.

Dierkes, Meinolf, Hans Weiler, and Ariane Antal, eds. 1987. *Comparative Policy Research: Learning from Experience.* Aldershot, Eng.: Gower.

Dore, Ronald. *Taking Japan Seriously: A Confucian Perspective on Leading Economic Issues.* London: Athlone Press.

Dyson, Kenneth. 1980. *The State Tradition in Western Europe.* New York: Oxford.

Esping-Anderson, Gosta. 1983. *Politics against Markets: The Social Democratic Road to Power.* Princeton: Princeton University Press.

Flora, Peter and Arnold Heidenheimer, eds. 1981. *The Development of Welfare States in Europe and America.* New Brunswick: Transaction.

Fried, Robert C., and Francine F. Rabinovitz. 1980. *Comparative Urban Politics.* Englewood Cliffs: Prentice-Hall.

Geertz, Clifford. 1983. *Local Knowledge.* New York: Basic Books.

Gough, Ian. 1979. *The Political Economy of the Welfare State.* London: Macmillan.

Graham, Helen. 1977. "Implementation through Bargaining." *Public Policy* (Fall).

Hancock, M. Donald. 1972. *The Politics of Post-Industrial Change.* Hinsdale: Dryden Press.

Heclo, Hugh. 1974. *Modern Social Politics in Britain and Sweden.* New Haven: Yale University Press.

Heidenheimer, Arnold. 1986. "Politics, Policy and Polizey as Concepts in English and Continental Languages: An Attempt to Explain Divergences." *Review of Politics* 48:1, 3–30.

Hesse, Hermann. 1956. *The Journey to the East.* New York: Farrar, Straus & Giroux.

Hibbs, Douglas. 1977. "Political Parties and Macroeconomic Policy." *APSR* 71:1467–87.

Jackman, Robert. 1980. "Socialist Parties and Income Inequality in Western Industrial Societies." *Journal of Politics* 42:135–49.

Katzenstein, Peter. 1985. *Small States and World Markets*. Ithaca: Cornell University Press.

Key, V. O. 1942 and 1959. *Politics, Parties and Pressure Groups*. New York: Crowell.

King, Anthony. 1973. "Ideas, Institutions, and the Policies of Governments: A Comparative Analysis." *BJPS*. 3 (July/October), 293–313, 409–23.

Korpi, Walter. 1983. *The Democratic Class Struggle*. London: Routledge and Kegan Paul.

Lehmbruch, Gerhard, and Phillipe Schmitter, eds. 1982. *Patterns of Corporatist Policymaking*. Beverly Hills: Sage Publications.

Lindberg, Leon, and Charles Maier, eds. 1984. *The Politics and Sociology of Global Inflation*. Washington, DC: Brookings Institution.

Luebbert, Gregory. 1986. *Comparative Democracy: Policymaking and Governing Coalitions in Europe and Israel*. New York: Columbia University Press.

Moore, Barrington. 1966. *The Social Origins of Democracy and Dictatorship*. Boston: Beacon.

Offe, Claus. 1982. *Structural Problems of the Capitalist State*. London: Macmillan.

Przeworski, Adam, and Henry Teune. 1970. *The Logic of Comparative Social Inquiry*. New York: Wiley Interscience.

Rimlinger, Gaston. 1971. *Welfare Policy and Industrialization in Europe, America and Russia*. New York: Wiley.

Roherty, James, ed. 1980. *Defense Policy Formation: Towards Comparative Analysis*. Durham, NC: Carolina Academic Press.

Rokkan, Stein. 1974. "Cities, States and Nations." In *Building States and Nations*, edited by S. N. Eisenstadt and Stein Rokkan. Beverly Hills: Sage Publications.

Shalev, M. 1983. "The Social Democratic Model and Beyond: Two Generations of Comparative Research on the Welfare State." *Comparative Social Research* 6:315–51.

Sharkansky, Ira. 1979. *Wither the State? Politics and Public Enterprise in Three Countries*. Chatham, NJ: Chatham House.

Skocpol, Theda. 1980. "Political Response to Capitalist Crisis: Neo-Marxist Theories of the State and the Case of the New Deal." *Politics and Society* 10:2, 155–201.

Smeeding, Timothy et al. 1987. *Should Medical Care Be Rationed by Age?* Totowa: Rowman and Littlefield.

Stephens, John D. 1979. *The Transition from Capitalism to Socialism*. London: Macmillan.

Weir, Margaret, Ann Orloff, and Theda Skocpol, eds. 1988. *The Politics of Social Policy in the United States*. Princeton: Princeton University Press.

Wilensky, Harold. 1975. *The Welfare State and Equality*. Berkeley: University of California Press.

———. 1976. *The New Corporatism, Centralization and the Welfare State*. Beverly Hills: Sage Publications.

———. 1981. "Democratic Corporatism, Consensus and Social Policy." In *The Welfare State in Crisis*, OECD. Paris: OECD.

Wilensky, Harold et al. 1985. *Comparative Social Policy: Theories, Methods and Findings*. Berkeley: University of California Institute of International Studies.

CHAPTER 2. EDUCATION POLICY

Ahier, John and Michael Flude, ed. 1983. *Contemporary Education Policy.* London: Croom-Helm.

Anderson, C. Arnold. 1979. "Societal Characteristics within the School: Inferences from the ISEA Study." *Comp Ed Rev* 23:3 (October) 408–421.

———. 1985. "Social Class and Education: Comparative Perspectives." *Encyclopedia of Education Research* 4614–17.

Archer, Margaret S. 1979. *Social Origins of Educational Systems.* London: Sage Publications.

Bellaby, Paul. 1977. *The Sociology of Comprehensive Schooling.* London: Methuen.

Ben-David, Joseph. 1977. *Centers of Learning: Britain, France, Germany, United States.* New York: McGraw-Hill.

Bereday, George Z. F. 1977. *"Social Stratification and Education in Industrial Countries."* *Comp Ed Rev* 21: 2 (June–October), 195–210.

Boudon, Raymond. 1974. *Education, Opportunity and Social Inequality.* New York: Wiley.

Brickman, Ronald. 1981. "The Comparative Political Analysis of Science and Technology Policy." *Comp Pol* 13:479–96.

Burn, Barbara, ed. 1978. *Admission to Medical Education in Ten Countries.* New York: Interbook.

Cerych, Ladislav, and Paul Sabatier. 1986. *Great Expectations and Mixed Performance: The Implementation of Higher Education Reforms in Europe.* Stoke-on-Trent: Trendham.

Clark, Burton R. 1983. *The Higher Education System: Academic Organization in Cross-National Perspective.* Berkeley: University of California Press.

Clark, Burton R., ed. 1985. *The School and the University: An International Perspective.* Berkeley: University of California Press.

Clarke, Alex M., and L. Michael Birt. 1982. "Evaluative Reviews in Universities: The Influence of Public Policies." *High Ed* 11:1 (January), 1–26.

Church, Robert L. 1976. *Education in the United States.* New York: Free Press.

Coombs, Philip H. 1985. *The World Crisis in Education: The View from the Eighties.* Oxford: Oxford University Press.

Cremin, Lawrence A. 1980. *American Education: The National Experience 1973–1976.* New York: Harper.

Cummings, William K. 1980. *Education and Equality in Japan.* Princeton: Princeton University Press.

Eckstein, Max A. 1985. "Comparative School Achievement." *Encyclopedia of Education Research* 323–29.

Eurich, N. 1981. *Systems of Higher Education in Twelve Countries. A Comparative View.* New York: Praeger.

Flora, Peter, and Arnold J. Heidenheimer, eds. 1981. *The Development of Welfare States in Europe and America.* New Brunswick: Transaction.

Fomerand, Jacques, J. van de Graaff, and Henry Wasser. 1979. *Higher Education in Western Europe and America: A Selected and Annotated Bibliography.* New York: Council for European Studies, Columbia University.

Garden, R. A. 1987. "The Second IEA Mathematics Study." *Comp Ed Rev* 31:1.

Geiger, Roger L. 1986. *Private Sectors in Higher Education: Structure, Function, and Change in Eight Countries.* Ann Arbor: University of Michigan Press.

Gellert, Claudius. 1985. "State Interventionism and Institutional Autonomy: University Development in England and West Germany." *Oxford Review of Education* 11:3, 283–93.

Goldschmidt, Dietrich. 1976. "Participatory Democracy in Schools and Higher Education." *High Ed* 5:2, 113–33.

Gutmann, Amy. 1987. *Democratic Education.* Princeton: Princeton University Press.

Haag, Daniel. 1982. *The Right to Education: What Kind of Management?* Paris: UNESCO.

Hearnden, Arthur. 1973. *Paths to University: Preparation, Assessment, Selection.* London: Schools Council/Macmillan.

———. 1979. *Education in the Two Germanies.* Boulder, CO: Westview.

Heidenheimer, Arnold J. 1977. "Achieving Equality Through Educational Expansion: Problems in the Swedish Experience." *Comp Pol St* 10:3 (October), 413–32.

———. 1974. "The Politics of Educational Reform: Explaining Different Outcomes of School Comprehensivization Attempts in Sweden and West Germany." *Comp Ed Rev* 18:3 (October), 338–410.

Hochschild, Jennifer L. 1984. *The New American Dilemma: Liberal Democracy and School Desegregation.* New Haven: Yale University Press.

Hughes, M. G. 1988. "Comparative Educational Administration." In *Handbook of Research on Educational Administration,* edited by Norman J. Boyan. New York: Longman.

Husen, Torsten. 1977. "Academic Performance in Selective and Comprehensive Schools." In *Power and Ideology in Education,* edited by J. Karabel and A. H. Hasley. New York: Oxford University Press.

———. 1980. *The School in Question.* New York: Oxford University Press.

———. 1986. *The Learning Society Revisited.* New York: Pergamon.

———. 1987. "Policy Impact of IEA Research." *Comp Ed Rev* 29–46.

Inglehart, Ronald. 1981. "Post-Materialism in an Environment of Insecurity." *APSR* 75:4 (November), 880–900.

Jacques, David, and John Richardson, eds. 1985. *The Future for Higher Education.* London: NFER-Nelson.

James, Henry, and Henry M. Levin, eds. 1988. *Comparing Public and Private Schools.* Philadelphia: Falmer.

Kaelble, Harmut. 1981. "Educational Opportunities and Government Politics in Europe in the Period of Industrialization." In *The Development of Welfare States in Europe and America,* edited by Peter Flora and Arnold J. Heidenheimer. New Brunswick: Transaction.

Katzenstein, Peter J. 1987. "University Reform." In *Policy and Politics in West Germany.* Philadelphia: Temple University Press.

Kazamias, Andreas, and B. G. Massialas. 1985. "Comparative Education." *Encyclopedia of Education Research,* Vol. II. 309–317.

Kerr, Clark, and Marian Gade. 1986. "Response to Decline and Change: The USA Experience." *European Journal of Education* 21:1, 67–79.

Kogan, Maurice. 1979. *Educational Policies in Perspective: An Appraisal.* Paris: OECD.

Levin, Henry M. 1978. "The Dilemma of Comprehensive Secondary School Reforms in Europe." *Comp Ed Rev* 22:3 (November), 434–51.

Mallinson, Vernon. 1980. *The Western European Idea in Education.* Oxford: Pergamon.

Marshall, T. H. 1963. *Sociology at the Crossroads and Other Essays.* London: Heinemann.

McKnight, Curtis C., et al. 1987. *The Underachieving Curriculum: Assessing U.S. School Mathematics from an International Perspective.* Champaign, IL: Stipes.

Merritt, Richard I. 1979. "Opening up the Universities: The Courts, the Universities and the Right of Admission in the Federal Republic of Germany." *Minerva* 17:1 (Spring), 1–32.

Neave, Guy, ed. 1981. "Changing Links between Secondary and Higher Education." *European Journal of Education* 16:2, 141–253.

Neave, Guy R. 1985. "Elite and Mass Higher Education in Britain: A Regressive Model." *Comp Ed Rev* 29:3, 346–61.

———. 1988. "Education and Social Policy: Demise of an ethic or change of values?" *Oxford Review of Education,* 14: 3, 273–83.

Neusel, Ayla, and Ulrich Teichler. 1982. "Comprehensive Universities in the Federal Republic." In *Compleat University,* edited by Harry Hermanns, Ulrich Teichler and Henry Wasser. Rochester, VT: Schenkman.

Organisation for Economic Cooperation and Development. 1981 *Education Statistics in OECD Countries.* Paris: OECD.

———. 1983a. *Compulsory Schooling in a Changing World.* Paris: OECD.

———. 1983b. *Educational Planning: A Reappraisal.* Paris: OECD.

———. 1984. *Educational Trends in the 1970s.* Paris: OECD.

———. 1985. *Education and Training after Basic Schooling.* Paris: OECD.

———. 1987. *Adolescents and Comprehensive Schooling.* Paris: OECD.

———. 1988. *Education in OECD Countries 1985–86: Comparative Statistics.* Paris: OECD.

Oxenham, J. 1985. "Policies for Educational Equality." *International Encyclopedia of Education.* Vol. 3. 16:7, 1689–98.

Paulston, Rolland G. 1968. *Educational Change in Sweden: Planning and Accepting the Comprehensive School Reforms.* New York: Teachers College Press.

———. 1977. "Social and Educational Change: Conceptual Frameworks." *Comp Ed Rev* 21:2 (June–October), 370–95.

Pempel, T. J. 1982. *Politics and Policy in Japan.* Philadelphia: Temple University Press.

Postlethwaite, T. Neville, ed. 1986. *International Educational Research: Papers in Honor of Torsten Husen.* Oxford: Pergamon.

Premfors, Rune. 1980. *The Politics of Higher Education in a Comparative Perspective: France, Sweden, United Kingdom.* Stockholm: Political Science Department, Stockholm University.

Ringer, Fritz. 1979. *Education and Society in Modern Europe.* Bloomington: Indiana University Press.

Rohlen, Thomas P. 1983. *Japan's High Schools.* Berkeley: University of California Press.

Röhrs, H., ed. 1987. *Tradition and Reform of the University under an International Perspective.* Frankfurt: Lang.

Sadlak, Jan. 1986. "Comparing Higher Education Planning Approaches in Western and Eastern Europe." *European Journal of Education* 21:4, 397–408.

Selden, William K. 1960. *Accreditation.* New York: Harper.

Stahl, Abraham. 1987. " 'Closing the Educational Gap': Inferences from the Educational Experience of European Jews." *Comp Ed Rev* 23:2, 145–59.

Taylor, William. 1987. *Universities under Scrutiny*. Paris: OECD.

Teichler, Ulrich. 1976. *Das Dilemma der modernen Bildungsgesellschaft*. Stuttgart: Klett.

———. 1988. *Wandel der Hochschulstrukturen im internationalen Vergleich*. Kassel: Zentrum für Hochschulforschung.

Timmons, George. 1988. *Education, Industrialization and Selection*. London: Routledge and Kegan Paul.

Trow, Martin. 1979. "Aspects of Diversity in American Higher Education." In *On the Making of Americans*, edited by Herbert J. Gans et al. Philadelphia: University of Pennsylvania Press.

Trow, Martin. 1988. "Comparative Perspectives on Higher Education Policy in the UK and the US," *Oxford Review of Education*, 14:1, 81–94.

Watson, Keith, ed. 1985. *Key Issues in Education: Comparative Perspectives*. London: Croom-Helm.

Weiler, Hans N. 1983. "West Germany: Education Policy as Compensatory Legitimation." In *Politics and Education*, edited by R. Murray Thomas. Oxford: Pergamon.

White, Dana F. 1969. "Education in the Turn-of-the-Century City: The Search for Control." *Urban Education* 4:2 (July), 169–82.

CHAPTER 3. HEALTH POLICY

Aaron, Henry J., and William B. Schwarz. 1984. *The Painful Prescription: Rationing Hospital Care*. Washington, DC: Brookings Institution.

Abel-Smith, Brian. 1972. "The History of Medical Care." In *Comparative Development in Social Welfare*, edited by E. E. Martin. London: Allen and Unwin.

Altenstetter, Christa. 1974. *Changing National-Subnational Relations in Health*. Washington, DC: National Institutes of Health.

Altenstetter, Christa. 1978. *Innovation in Health Policy and Service Delivery: A Cross National Perspective*. Cambridge: Oelgeschlager.

Anderson, Odin W. 1972. *Can There Be Equity?* New York: Wiley.

Anderson, Ronald, Bjorn Smedby, and Odin W. Anderson. 1970. *Medical Care Use in Sweden and the United States: A Comparative Analysis of Systems and Behavior*. Chicago: Center for Health Administration Studies, Research Series 27.

Bates, Erica M. 1983. *Health Systems and Public Scrutiny: Australia, Britain and United States*. New York: St. Martin's Press.

Berg, Ole. 1980. "The Health Services System: the Interaction of Medical, Socio-Cultural, Economic and Political Logics." *Sc Pol Stud* 3:3, 209–234.

Berki, S. E., and B. Kobashigawa. 1978. "Education and Income Effects in Use of Ambulatory Services in the United States." *Intl JL Hlth Svc* 8:2, 351–65.

Bjorkman, James W. 1985. "Who governs the health sector? Comparative European and American experiences with representation, participation, and decentralization." *Comp Pol* 17:399–420.

Blanpain, Jan. ed. 1978. *National Health Insurance and Health Resources: The European Experience*. Cambridge, MA: Harvard University Press.

Brown, Lawrence D. 1978. "The Formulation of Federal Health Care Policy." *Bulletin of the New York Academy of Medicine* 54:1.

———. 1981. "Competition and Health Cost Containment." *Mil Mem Q* 59:2 (Spring), 145–89.

Carrier, John. 1986. *In Defence of the Welfare State*. Manchester, Eng.: Manchester University Press.

Culyer, A. J., and Bengt Jonsson, eds. 1986. *Public and Private Health Services*. Oxford: Blackwell.

Dahlgren, Göran, and Diderichsen, Finn. 1986. "Strategies for Equity in Health: Report from Sweden," *Intl Jl Hlth Svc* 16:4, 517–537.

Döhler, Mariah, "Physicians' Professional Autonomy in the Welfare State," Freddi and Björkman, ed. *Controlling Medical Professionals*, pp. 178–198.

Enthoven, Alan C. 1980. *Health Plan*. Reading, MA: Addison-Wesley.

Feder, Judith, Jack Hadley, and Ross Mullner. 1984. "Poor People and Poor Hospitals: Implications for Public Policy." *Jl of Hlth PP & L* 9 (Summer), 237–50.

Feldstein, Paul. 1977. *Health Associations and the Demand for Legislation*. London: Ballinger.

Field, Mark. 1973. "The Concept of the 'Health System' at the Macrosociological Level." *Social Science and Medicine* 7:10 (October), 763–85.

———, ed. 1988. *Success and Crisis in National Health Systems A Cross-National Approach*. New York: Routledge and Kegan Paul.

Fox, Daniel M. 1986. *Health Policies, Health Politics: The British and American Experience, 1911–1965*. Princeton: Princeton University Press.

———, Patricia Day, and Rudolf Klein. 1989. "The Power of Professionalism: Policies for Aids in Britain, Sweden and the United States," *Daedalus*, 118:2, 93–112.

Freddi, Giorgio, and James W. Bjorkman, eds. 1988. *Controlling Medical Professionals: The Comparative Politics of Health Governance*. London: Sage Publications.

Fuchs, Beth C. 1987. "Health Policy in a Period of Resource Limits and Conservative Politics." In *Political Economy*, edited by Jerold L. Waltman and Donley T. Studlar. Jackson, MS: University Press of Mississippi.

Garpenby, Peter. 1989. *The State and the Medical Profession: A Cross-National Comparison of the Health Policy Arena in the United Kingdom and Sweden 1945–1985*. Linköping: University of Linköping.

Glaser, William. 1978. *Health Insurance Bargaining: Foreign Lessons for America*. New York: Halsted.

Glaser, William D. 1987. *Paying the Hospital*. San Francisco: Jossey-Bass.

Goodman, John C. 1981. "NHS: An Ill for All Cures?" *Policy Review* 17 (Spring).

Ham, Christopher. 1988. "Governing the Health Sector: Power and Policy Making in the English and Swedish Health Services." *Mil Mem Q*. 66: 2, 389–414.

Havighurst, Clark C. 1980. "Antitrust Enforcement in the Medical Services Industry: What Does It All Mean?" *Mil Mem Q* 58:1, 89–124.

Heidenheimer, Arnold J. 1980. "Organized Medicine and Physician Specialization in Scandinavia and West Germany." *West Eur Pol* 3:3 (October), 373–87.

Heidenheimer, Arnold J., and Nils Elvander, eds. 1980. *The Shaping of the Swedish Health System*. New York: St. Martin's Press.

Himmelstein, David U., and Steffie Woolhandler. 1986. "Socialized Medicine: A Solution to the Cost Crisis in Health Care in the United States." *Intl Jl Hlth Svc* 16:3.

Hollingsworth, J. Rogers. 1986. *A Political Economy of Medicine: Great Britain and the United States*. Baltimore: Johns Hopkins University Press.

Honigsbaum, Frank. 1979. *The Division in British Medicine: A History of the Separation of General Practice from Hospital Care, 1911–1965*. London: Kogan Page.

Jaspers, Frans. C. A. et al., eds. 1983. *Health Manpower Planning*. The Hague: Nijhoff.

Kelman, Steven. 1981. *Regulating America, Regulating Sweden: A Comparative Study of Occupational Safety and Health Legislation Policy*. Cambridge, MA: MIT Press.

Klein, Rudolf. 1983. *The Politics of the National Health Service*. London: Longman.

Legge, Jerome S. 1986. "Abortion policy: an evaluation of the consequences for maternal and infant health." *The Journal of Politics* 48 (November), 1095–97.

Leichter, Howard M. 1979. *A Comparative Approach to Policy Analysis: Health Care Policy in Four Nations*. New York: Cambridge University Press.

Light, Donald W., and Alexander Schuller, eds. 1986. *Political Values and Health Care: The German Experience*. Cambridge, MA: MIT Press.

Lockhart, Charles. 1981. "Values and Policy Conceptions of Health Policy Elites in the United States, The United Kingdom, and the Federal Republic of Germany." *JL Hlth PP & L* 6:98–119.

MacRae, Norman. 1984. "Health Care International." *Economist*, 291 (28 April) 17–20.

Marmor, Theodore. 1983. *Political Analysis and American Medical Care*. New York: Cambridge University Press.

Maxwell, Robert J. 1981. *Health and Wealth: An International Study of Health Care Spending*. Lexington, MA: Lexington Books.

Maynard, Alan. 1975. *Health Care in the European Community*. Pittsburgh: University of Pittsburgh Press.

Organisation for Economic Cooperation and Development. 1985. *Measuring Health Care, 1960–1983: Expenditure, Costs and Performance*. Paris: OECD.

———. 1987. *Financing and Delivering Health Care: A Comparative Analysis of OECD Countries*. Paris: OECD.

Office of Technology Assessment. October 1981. *The Implications of Cost-Effectiveness Analysis of Medical Technology*. OTA Background Paper 4. Washington, DC: Office of Technology Assessment.

Raffel, Marshall W., ed. 1984. *Comparative Health Systems: Descriptive Analyses of Fourteen National Health Systems*. University Park, PA: Pennsylvania State Press.

Rinehart, Sue T. 1987. "Maternal Health care policy: Britain and the United States." *Comp Pol* 19 (January) 193–211.

Rodwin, Victor G. 1984. *The Health Planning Predicament: France, Quebec, England and the United States*. Berkeley: University of California Press.

Roemer, Milton I. 1977. *Comparative National Policies on Health Care*. New York: Denner.

Rosenthal, Marilynn M. 1988. *Dealing with Medical Malpractice: The British and Swedish Experience*. Durham: Duke University Press.

Saltman, Richard B., ed. 1988. *International Handbook of Healthcare Systems*. New York: Greenwood.

Sapolsky, Harvey M., Drew Altman, Richard Greene, and Judith Moore. 1981. "Corporate Attitudes toward Health Care Costs." *Mil Mem Q* 9:4 (Fall), 561–85.

Skidmore, Max J. 1970. *Medicare and the American Rhetoric of Reconciliation*. University, AL: University of Alabama Press.

Starr, Paul. 1982. *The Social Transformation of American Medicine*. New York: Basic Books.

Steslicke, William E. 1987. "The Japanese State of Health: A Political-Economic

Perspective." In *Health, Illness and Medical Care in Japan*, edited by Edward Norbock and Margaret Lock. Honolulu: University of Hawaii Press, 24–65.

Stevens, Rosemary. 1966. *Medical Practice in Modern England*. New Haven: Yale University Press.

———. 1971. *American Medicine and the Public Interest*. New Haven: Yale University Press.

———. 1976. "The Evolution of the Health-Care Systems in the United States and the United Kingdom: Similarities and Differences." *Priorities for the Use of Resources in Medicine*. Bethesda, MD: Fogarty International Center.

Stone, Deborah. 1977. "Professionalism and Accountability: Controlling Health Services in the United States and West Germany." *Jl Hlth PP & L* 2:32–47.

———. 1980. *The Limits of Professional Power: National Health Care in the Federal Republic of Germany*. Chicago: University of Chicago Press.

———. 1984. *Disabled State*. Philadelphia: Temple University Press.

The Swedish Health Service System. 1971. Chicago: American Hospital Association.

Townsend, Peter, and Nick Davidson, eds. 1982. *Inequalities in Health: The Black Report*. London: Penguin.

Vladeck, Bruce C. 1981. "The Market vs. Regulation: The Case for Regulation." *Mil Mem Q* 59:2 (Spring), 209–223.

Weiner, Jonathan P. 1987. "Primary Care Delivery in the United States and Four Northwest European Countries." *Mil Mem Q* 65:3, 426–58.

Wilson, Graham K. 1985. *The Politics of Occupational Safety and Health in the United States and Britain*. New York: Oxford University Press.

CHAPTER 4. HOUSING POLICY

Adams, Carolyn. 1986. "Homelessness in the Postindustrial City: Views from London and Philadelphia." *Urb Aff Q* 21:527–49.

Balchin, P. 1985. *Housing Policy: An Introduction*. London: Croom-Helm.

Ball, M., M. Martens, and M. Harloe. 1986. *Mortgage Financing and Owner Occupation in Britain and West Germany, Progress in Planning*. Vol. 26. Oxford: Pergamon.

Bandyopadhyay, P. 1984. "The State, Private Capital and Housing in the Paris Region." *Science and Society* 48:161–91.

Boaden, Noel. 1971. *Urban Policy-Making: Influences on County Boroughs in England and Wales*. Cambridge: Cambridge University Press.

Boaden, Noel, and Robert Alford. 1969. "Sources of Diversity in English Local Government." *Public Administration* 47:203–33.

Boddy, Martin. 1980. *The Building Societies*. London: Macmillan.

Craig, P., and M. L. Harrison. 1984. "Corporatism and Housing Policy: The Best Possible Political Shell?" In *Corporatism and the Welfare State*, edited by M. L. Harrison. Aldershot, Eng.: Gower.

Davies, Bleddyn. 1971. "Comment on Nicholson and Topham." *Journal of the Royal Statistical Society* 134:311–13.

Department of Environment. 1977. *Housing Policy—A Consultative Document*. Cmnd. 6851. London: HMSO.

Donnison, David. 1967. *The Government of Housing*. Baltimore: Penguin.

Downs, Anthony. 1985. *The Revolution in Real Estate Financing*. Washington, DC: Brookings Institution.

Duclaud-Williams, R. H. 1978. *The Politics of Housing in Britain and France.* London: Heinemann.

Eisinger, Peter. 1982. "French Urban Housing and the Mixed Economy: The Privatization of the Public Sector." *Annals of the American Academy of Political and Social Sciences* 459:134–47.

Farmer, M., and R. T. Barrell. 1982. "Entrepreneurship and Government Policy: The Case of the Housing Market." In *Policy Studies Review Annual,* edited by R. Rist. Beverly Hills: Sage.

Frommes, Robert. 1970. *Problems Raised by the Individual Subsidization of Accommodation.* The Hague: International Federation of Housing and Planning.

Grant, W., and W. Streeck. 1985. "Large Firms and the Representation of Business Interests in the UK and West German Construction Industry." In *Organized Interests and the State,* edited by A. Cawson. Beverly Hills: Sage Publications.

Hallett, Graham. 1977. *Housing and Land Policies in West Germany and Britain.* London: Macmillan.

Harloe, Michael. 1981. "The Recommodification of Housing." In *City, Class, and Capital,* edited by M. Harloe and E. Lebas. London: Edward Arnold.

Headey, Bruce. 1978. *Housing Policy in the Developed Economy: The UK, Sweden, and the U.S.* New York: St. Martin's Press.

Heclo, Hugh, and H. Madsen. 1986. *Policy and Politics in Sweden.* Philadelphia: Temple University Press.

Howenstine, E. J. 1986. *Housing Vouchers: An International Analysis.* New Brunswick: Rutgers University Center for Urban Policy Research.

——. 1975. "The Changing Roles of Housing Production Subsidies and Consumer Housing Subsidies in European National Housing Policy." *Land Economics* 51 (February), 86–94.

Katz, Robert. 1979. "Is Public Housing Going Out of Business in Great Britain?" *Journal of Housing* 36:9 (October), 461–64.

Kemeny, James. 1978. "Urban Home-ownership in Sweden." *Urban Studies* 15:313–20.

Kemeny, James, and A. Thomas. 1984. "Capital Leakages from Owner-Occupied Housing." *Policy and Politics* 12:1, 13–30.

Kilroy, B. 1978. *Housing Finance: Organic Reform?* London: LEFTA.

Kirwan, Richard. 1987. "Fiscal Policy and the Price of Land and Housing in Japan." *Urban Studies* 24:345–60.

Kristof, Frank. 1966. "Housing Policy Goals and Housing Market Behavior: Experience in the United States." *Urban Studies* 3:2.

Lansley, Steward. 1979. *Housing and Public Policy.* London: Croom-Helm.

Lundqvist, Lennart. 1984. "Housing Policy and Alternative Housing Tenures: Some Scandinavian Examples." *Policy and Politics* 12:1, 1–12.

McLeay, E. M. 1984. "Housing as a Political Issue: A Comparative Study." *Comparative Politics* 17:1, 85–106.

Marcuse, Peter. "Determinants of State Housing Policies: West Germany and the US." In *Urban Policy under Capitalism,* edited by N. Fainstein and Susan Fainstein. Beverly Hills: Sage Publications.

Merrett, S. 1979. *State Housing in Britain.* Boston: Routledge and Kegan Paul.

Organisation for Economic Cooperation and Development. 1986. *Urban Policies in Japan.* Paris: OECD.

Pawley, M. 1983. "Reform," *Roof* (January/February).

Pearsall, J. 1984. "France," In *Housing in Europe,* edited by M. Wynn. London: Croom-Helm.

Peterson, George. 1980. "Federal Tax Policy and the Shaping of Urban Development." In *The Prospective City,* edited by Arthur Solomon. Cambridge: MIT Press.

Priemus, Hugo, ed. 1983. *Who Will Pay the Housing Bill in the 80s?* Delft: Delft University Press.

Pynoos, John, et al., eds. 1973. *Housing Urban America.* Chicago: Aldine.

Rosen, K. 1981. *A Comparison of European Housing Finance Systems.* University of California Center for Real Estate and Urban Economics Working Paper 81–37. Berkeley: California.

Sternlieb, George, et al. 1980. *America's Housing Prospects and Problems.* New Brunswick: Rutgers University Center for Urban Policy Research.

Trutko, John, Otto Hetzel, and A. David Yates. April 1978. *A Comparison of the Experimental Housing Allowance Program and Great Britain's Rent Allowance Program.* Washington, DC: Urban Institute.

Tuccillo, John. 1980. *Housing and Investment in an Inflationary World.* Washington, DC: Urban Institute.

Van Weesep, Jan. 1984. "Intervention in the Netherlands: Urban Housing Policy and Market Response." *Urb Aff Q* 19:3, 329–53.

Weir, Stuart. 1978. "How Labour Failed to Reform Mortgage Relief." *New Society* 5 (October), 14–16.

Wolman, Harold. 1971. *The Politics of Federal Housing.* New York: Dodd Mead.

CHAPTER 5. ECONOMIC POLICY

Alt, James. 1985. "Political Parties, World Demand, and Unemployment." *APSR* 79:4, 1016–40.

———. 1988. "New Wine in Old Bottles: Thatcher's Conservative Economic Policy." In *The Resurgence of Conservatism in Anglo-American Democracies,* edited by Barry Cooper, Allan Kornberg, and William Mishler. Durham: Duke University Press.

Anchordoguy, Marie. 1988. "The Public Corporation: A Potent Japanese Policy Weapon." *Political Science Quarterly* 103:4, 707–24.

Anderson, Terry, and Peter Hill. 1980. *The Birth of a Transfer Society.* Stanford: Hoover Institute.

Andrain, Charles. 1980. *Politics and Economic Policy in Western Democracies.* North Scituate, MA: Duxbury.

Armingeon, Klaus. 1987. "The Compatibility of Economic, Social and Political Goals in Income Policies." In *Coping with the Economic Crisis. See* Keman, Paloheimo, and Whiteley.

Banting, Keith, ed. 1986. *The State and Economic Interests.* Toronto: University of Toronto Press.

Barfield, Claude, and William Schambra, eds. 1986. *The Politics of Industrial Policy.* Washington, DC: American Enterprise Institute.

Berger, Suzanne, ed. 1981. *Organizing Interest in Western Europe.* Cambridge: Cambridge University Press.

Blank, S. 1973. *Government and Industry in Britain.* Farnsborough, Hants.: Saxon House.

Bosworth, Barry, and Alice Rivlin, eds. 1987. *The Swedish Economy.* Washington, DC: Brookings Institution.

Braun, Dietmar. 1987. "Political Immobilism and Labor Market Performance: The Dutch Road to Mass Unemployment." *JPP* 7:3, 307–35.

Brittan, Samuel. 1977. *The Economic Consequences of Democracy.* London: Temple Smith.

Bruno, M., and J. Sachs. 1985. *The Economics of Worldwide Stagflation.* Oxford: Oxford University Press.

Buchanan, James, and Richard Wagner. 1977. *Democracy in Deficit.* New York: Academic.

Cameron, David. 1982. "On the Limits of the Public Economy." *The Annals* 459, 6–62.

———. 1984a. "Social Democracy, Corporatism and Labor Quiescence." In *Order and Conflict in Contemporary Capitalism. See* Goldthorpe.

———. 1984b. "The Politics and Economics of the Business Cycle." In *The Political Economy. See* Ferguson and Rogers.

Campbell, Colin, ed. 1977. *Income Redistribution.* Washington, DC: American Enterprise Institute.

Castles, Francis, ed. 1982. *The Impact of Parties.* Beverly Hills: Sage Publications.

———. 1985. *The Working Class and Welfare.* Winchester, MA: Allen and Unwin.

———. 1987. "The Politics of Labor Market Policy." In *Managing Mixed Economies. See* Castles, Lehner, and Schmidt.

———. 1987a. "The Politics of Economic Vulnerability: A Comparison of Australia and Sweden." *Thesis Eleven* 16:112–21.

———. 1988. *Public Policy and Economic Vulnerability: The Australian Experience in Comparative Perspective.* Sydney: Allen and Unwin Australia Pty.

Castles, Francis, Franz Lehner, and Manfred Schmidt, eds. 1988. *Managing Mixed Economies.* New York: deGruyter.

Chaloupek, Gunther. 1985. "The Austrian Parties and the Economic Crisis." *West Eur Pol* 8:71–82.

Cohen, Stephen, Serge Halimi, and John Zysman. 1986. "Institutions, Politics, and Industrial Policy in France." In *The Politics of Industrial Policy. See* Barfield and Schambra.

Colby, Peter. 1983. "The Organization of Public Interest Groups." *Policy Studies Journal* 11:1.

Congressional Budget Office. 1977. *Income Policies in the United States.* Washington, DC: US GPO.

Corti, G. 1979. "Perspectives on Public Corporations and Public Enterprises in Five Nations." *Annals of Public and Co-Operative Economy* 47.

Czada, Roland. 1987. "The Impact of Interest Politics on Flexible Adjustment Policies." In *Coping with Economic Crisis. See* Keman, Paloheimo, and Whiteley.

Dauerstadt, M. 1988. "Free Markets vs. Political Consensus." *Intereconomics* 22:1.

Dean, J. 1984. "Interest Groups and Political X-inefficiency." *European Journal of Political Research* 12:2, 191–212.

Dennison, Edward. 1967. *Why Growth Rates Differ.* Washington, DC: Brookings Institution.

Diebold, William. 1980. *Industrial Policy as an International Issue.* New York: McGraw-Hill.

Dore, Ronald. 1986. *Flexible Rigidities: Industrial Policy and Structural Adjustment in the Japanese Economy 1970–1980*. Stanford: Stanford University Press.

———. 1987. *Taking Japan Seriously*. Stanford: Stanford University Press.

Eckstein, Otto. 1978. *The Great Recession*. Amsterdam: North Holland.

Esping-Andersen, R. Friedland, and M. Zeitlin, eds. *Political Power and Social Theory*. Vol. III. Greenwich, CT: Jai Press.

Feldstein, Martin, ed. 1980. *The American Economy in Transition*. Chicago: University of Chicago Press.

Ferguson, Thomas, and Joel Rogers, eds. 1984. *The Political Economy*. New York: M. E. Sharpe.

Friedland, Roger, and Jimmy Sanders. 1985. "The Public Economy and Economic Growth in Western Market Economies." *American Sociological Review* 50:4, 421–37.

Gamble, Andrew. 1988. *The Free Economy and the Strong State: The Politics of Thatcherism*. Durham: Duke University Press.

Gilder, George. 1981. *Wealth and Poverty*. New York: Basic Books.

———. 1984. *The Spirit of Enterprise*. New York: Simon and Schuster.

Goldstein, Walter, ed. 1975. *Economic Planning and the Improvement of Economic Policy*. Washington, DC: American Enterprise Institute.

Goldthorpe, John, ed. 1984. *Order and Conflict in Contemporary Capitalism*. New York: Oxford University Press.

Goodwin, Crauford, ed. 1975. *Exhortation and Controls*. Washington, DC: Brookings Institution.

Grant, W., ed. 1985. *The Political Economy of Corporatism*. New York: St. Martin's Press.

Green, Diana. 1981. "Promoting the Industries of the Future: The Search for an Industrial Strategy in Britain and France." *JPP* 1:3, 333–51.

Hall, Peter. 1982. "Economic Planning and the State." In *Political Power and Social Theory*. See Esping-Andersen, Friedland, and Zeitlin.

———. 1986. *Governing the Economy: The Politics of State Intervention in Britain and France*. New York: Oxford University Press.

———, ed. 1989. *The Political Power of Economic Ideas*. Princeton: Princeton University Press.

Hayek, Fredrich. 1976. *The Mirage of Social Justice*. Chicago: University of Chicago Press.

Heclo, Hugh. 1986. "Industrial Policy and the Executive Capacities of Government." In *The Politics of Industrial Policy*. See Barfield and Schambra.

Heclo, Hugh, and Henrik Madsen. 1987. *Policy and Politics in Sweden*. Philadelphia: Temple University Press.

Heisler, Martin. 1979. "Corporate Pluralism Revisited." *Scandinavian Political Studies* 2:3.

Hibbs, Douglas. 1977. "Political Parties and Macroeconomic Policy." *APSR* 71:1467–87.

Hibbs, Douglas, Jr. 1987a. *The Political Economy of Industrial Societies*. Cambridge, MA: Harvard University Press.

———. 1987b. *The American Political Economy*. Cambridge, MA: Harvard University Press.

Hochmuth, Milton, and William Davidson, eds. 1985. *Revitalizing American Industry*. Cambridge: Ballinger.

Hoover, Kevin. 1984. "Two Types of Monetarism." *Journal of Economic Literature* 22:58–76.

Hudson, William. 1985. "The Feasibility of a Comprehensive U.S. Industrial Policy." *Political Science Quarterly* 100:3, 461–78.

Jackman, Robert. 1987. "The Politics of Economic Growth in the Industrial Democracies, 1974–80." *Journal of Politics* 49:202–12.

Johnson, Chalmers. 1982. *MITI and the Japanese Miracle*. Stanford: Stanford University Press.

———. 1986. "The Institutional Foundations of Japanese Industrial Policy." In *The Politics of Industrial Policy*. See Barfield and Schambra.

Joint Economic Committee of Congress. 1981. *Monetary Policy, Selective Credit Policy, and Industrial Policy in France, Britain, West Germany, and Sweden*. Committee Print, 97th Cong., 1st sess. Washington, DC: US GPO.

Katzenstein, Peter. 1985. *Small States in World Markets*. Ithaca: Cornell University Press.

———. 1987. *Policy and Politics in West Germany*. Philadelphia: Temple University Press.

Keman, Hans, Heikki Paloheimo, and Paul Whiteley, eds. 1987. *Coping with the Economic Crisis*. Beverly Hills: Sage Publications.

Keman, Hans, and Paul Whiteley. 1987. "Coping with Crisis: Divergent Strategies and Outcomes." In *Coping with the Economic Crisis*. See Keman, Paloheimo, and Whiteley.

Kindleberger, Charles. 1978. "The Aging Economy." *Weltwirtschaftliches Archiv* 113:3.

King, Anthony. 1973. "Ideas, Institutions and the Policies of Government." *BJPS* 3:409–23.

Korpi, Walter, and Gösta Esping-Andersen. 1984. "Social Policy as Class Politics in Post-War Capitalism." In *Order and Conflict in Contemporary Capitalism*. See Goldthorpe.

Krieger, Joel. 1987. *Reagan, Thatcher and the Politics of Decline*. New York: Oxford University Press.

Kurzer, Paulette. 1988. "The Politics of Central Banks." *Journal of Public Policy* 8:1, 21–48.

Lane, James, ed. 1985. *State and Market: The Politics of the Public and Private*. Beverly Hills: Sage Publications.

Lange, Peter, and Geoffrey Garrett. 1985. "The Politics of Growth: Strategic Interaction and Economic Performance in the Advanced Industrial Democracies, 1974–1980." *Journal of Politics* 47:792–827.

———. 1987. "The Politics of Growth Reconsidered." *Journal of Politics* 49:256–73.

Lehmbruch, Gerhard. 1984. "Concertation and the Structure of Corporatist Networks." In *Order and Conflict in Contemporary Capitalism*. See Goldthorpe.

———. 1985. "Neocorporatism in Western Europe: A Reassessment of the Concept in Cross-national Perspective." International Political Science Association XIII Congress. Paris. (Reproduced).

Lehner, Franz. 1986. "The Political Economy of Distributive Conflict." In *Managing Mixed Economies*. See Castles, Lehner, and Schmidt.

———. 1987. "Interest Intermediation, Institutional Structures, and Public Policy." In *Coping with the Economic Crisis*. See Keman, Paloheimo, and Whiteley.

Lehner, Franz, and Manfred Schmidt. 1987. *The Political Management of Mixed Economies*. Beverly Hills: Sage Publications.

Maddison, Angus. 1982. *Phases of Capitalist Development*. New York: Oxford University Press.

Marin, Bernd. 1985. "Austria—The Paradigm Case of Liberal Corporatism?" In *The Political Economy of Corporatism. See* Grant.

Martin, Andrew. 1986. "The Politics of Employment and Welfare in Advanced Capitalist Societies." In *The State and Economic Interests*. See Banting.

———. 1989. "Sweden: Restoring the Social Democratic Distributive Regime." *Center for European Studies Working Paper*. Harvard University.

McArthur, John, and Bruce Scott. 1969. *Industrial Planning in France*. Cambridge, MA: Graduate School of Business Administration, Harvard University.

Okun, Arthur. 1975. *Equality and Efficiency: The Big Tradeoff*. Washington, DC: Brookings Institution.

Olson, Mancur. 1965. *The Logic of Collective Action*. Cambridge, MA: Harvard University Press.

———. 1982. *The Rise and Decline of Nations*. New Haven: Yale University Press.

Organisation for Economic Cooperation and Development. 1975. *The Aims and Instruments of Industrial Policy*. Paris: OECD.

———. 1980. *Main Economic Indicators: Historical Statistics 1960–1979*. Paris: OECD.

———. 1988. *Historical Statistics, 1960–1986*. Paris: OECD.

———. 1989a. *Main Economic Indicators*. Paris: OECD.

———. 1989b. *National Accounts, 1960–1987*. Paris: OECD.

Palmer, John, ed. 1986. *Perspectives on the Reagan Years*. Washington, DC: Urban Institute.

Paloheimo, Heikki. 1987. "Explanations of the Economic Crisis and Divergent Policy Responses: An Overview." In *Coping with the Economic Crisis. See* Keman, Paloheimo, and Whiteley.

Pempel, T. J. 1982. *Policy and Politics in Japan*. Philadelphia: Temple University Press.

Pfaller, Alfred. 1987. "Are the Western Welfare States Still Competitive?" *Intereconomics* (May/June), 112–19.

Putnam, Robert, and Nicholas Bayne. 1984. *Hanging Together*. London: Heinemann.

Sato, K. ed. 1981. *Industry and Business in Japan*. London: Croom-Helm.

Saunders, Peter. 1985. "Public Expenditure and Economic Performance in the OECD Countries." *JPP* 5:1.

Sawhill, Isabel. 1986. "Reaganomics in Retrospect." In *Perspectives on the Reagan Years. See* Palmer.

Scharpf, Fritz. 1984. "Economic and Institutional Constraints of Full-Employment Strategies: Sweden, Austria and West Germany 1973–1982." In *Order and Conflict in Contemporary Capitalism. See* Goldthorpe.

Schlosstein, Steven. 1984. *Trade War: Greed, Power, and Industrial Policy on Opposite Sides of the Pacific*. New York: Congdon and Weed.

Schmidt, Manfred. 1982. "The Role of Parties in Shaping Macroeconomic Policy." In *The Impact of Parties. See* Castles 1982.

———. 1987. "The Politics of Labor Market Policy." In *Managing Mixed Economies. See* Castles, Lehner, and Schmidt.

———. 1988. "West Germany: The Policy of the Middle Way." *JPP* 7:2, 135–77.

Schmitter, Philippe. 1981. "Interest Intermediation and Regime Governability in

Contemporary Western Europe and North America." In *Organizing Interests in Western Europe. See* Berger.

Schmitter, Phillippe, and Gerhard Lehmbruch, eds. 1979. *Trends Corporatist Intermediation.* Beverly Hills: Sage Publications.

Schnitzer, Martin, and James Nordyke. 1977. *Comparative Economic Systems.* Cincinnati: Southwestern.

Schubert, K. 1987. "Politics and Economic Regulation." In *The Political Management of Mixed Economies. See* Lehner and Schmidt.

Shanks, Michael. 1977. *Planning and Politics: The British Experience.* London: Political and Economic Planning.

Shultz, George, and Kenneth Dam. 1978. *Economic Policy behind the Headlines.* New York: Norton.

Skocpol, Theda, and Margaret Weir. 1983. "State Structures and Social Keynesianism: Responses to the Great Depression in Sweden and the United States." *International Journal of Comparative Sociology* 19:4–29.

Steward, Michael. 1977. *The Jekyll and Hyde Years.* London: Dent and Sons.

Therborn, Göran. 1986. *Why Some Peoples Are More Unemployed Than Others.* London: Verso.

———. 1987. "Does Corporatism Really Matter?" *Journal of Public Policy* 7:3, 259–84.

Tsurumi, Yoshi. 1985. "Japan's Challenge to the United States." In *Revitalizing American Industry. See* Hochmuth and Davidson.

Wachter, Michael, ed. 1982. *Toward a New U.S. Industrial Policy?* Philadelphia: University of Pennsylvania Press.

Wanniski, Jude. 1979. *The Way the World Works.* New York: Simon and Schuster.

Weir, Margaret. 1989. "Ideas and Politics: The Acceptance of Keynesianism in Britain and the United States." In *The Political Power of Economic Ideas.* See Hall 1989.

Weir, Margaret, Ann Orloff, and Theda Skocpol. 1988. "Understanding American Social Politics." In *The Politics of Social Policy in the United States. See* Weir, Orloff, and Skocpol.

Weir, Margaret, Ann Orloff, and Theda Skocpol. 1988. *The Politics of Social Policy in the United States.* Princeton: Princeton University Press.

Whiteley, Paul. 1987. "The Monetarist Experiments in the United States and the United Kingdom." In *Coping with the Economic Crisis. See* Keman, Paloheimo, and Whiteley.

Wilensky, Harold, and Lowell Turner. 1987. *Democratic Corporatism and Policy Linkages.* Berkeley: Institute of International Studies.

Wilson, David. 1980. *The National Planning Idea in U.S. Public Policy.* Boulder, CO: Westview.

Woolley, John. 1978. "Monetary Policy Instrumentation and the Relationship of Central Banks and Governments." *The Annals* 434:151–73.

Yashiro, Naohiro. 1987. "Japan's Fiscal Policy: An International Comparison." *Japanese Economic Studies* (Fall), 34–59.

Zysman, John. 1977. *Political Strategies for Industrial Order.* Berkeley: University of California Press.

———. 1983. *Governments, Markets and Growth.* Ithaca: Cornell University Press.

CHAPTER 6. TAXATION POLICY

Aaron, Henry, ed. 1981. *The Value-Added Tax: Lessons from Europe.* Washington, DC: Brookings Institution.

Alt, James. 1983. "The Evolution of Tax Structures." *Public Choice* 41:181–222.

Ardent, Gabriel. 1971. *L'Histoire des Impôts.* Paris: Fayard.

Atkinson, A. B., and J. I. Leape. 1988. "The Economic Analysis of Tax Reform." *European Economic Review* 32 (March), 319–24.

Barnstable, C. F. 1903. *Public Finance.* London: Macmillan.

Barr, N. A., S. R. James, and A. R. Prest. 1977. *Self-Assessment for Income Tax.* London: Heinemann.

Beer, Samuel H. 1976. "The Adoption of German Revenue Sharing: A Case Study in Public Politics." *Public Policy* 24:127–95.

Beichelt, B. et al. 1969. *Steuermentalität und Steuermoral in Grossbritannien, Frankreich, Italien und Spanien.* Cologne: Westdeutscher Verlag.

Bellstedt, Christoph. 1966. *Die Steuer als Instrument der Politik.* Berlin: Duncker und Humblot.

Bennett, R. J. 1980. *The Geography of Public Finance: Welfare under Fiscal Federalism and Local Government Finance.* London: Methuen.

Bracewell-Milnes, Barry, and J. C. L. Huiskamp. 1977. *Investment Incentives: A Comparative Analysis of the Systems in the EEC, the USA and Sweden.* Deventer: Kluwer.

Cnossen, Sijbren. 1977. *Excise Systems: A Global Study of Selective Taxation of Goods and Services.* Baltimore: Johns Hopkins University Press.

Cnossen, Sijbren, ed. 1983. *Comparative Tax Studies.* Essays in Honor of Richard Goode (Contributions to Economic Analysis, 144). Amsterdam: North-Holland.

Esping-Anderson, Gösta. 1980. *Social Class, Social Democracy and State Policy.* Copenhagen: New Social Science Monographs.

Feige, Edward. 1982. *Observer-Subject Feedback: The Dynamics of the Unobserved Economy.* Leyden: Brill.

Gourevitch, Harry G. 1977. "Corporate Tax Integration: The European Experience." *The Tax Lawyer* 31:1 (Fall), 65–112.

Grunow, Dieter, F. Hagner, and Franz Xaver Kaufmann. 1978. *Steuerzahler und Finanzamt.* Frankfurt: Campus.

Hadenius, Axel. 1986. *A Crisis of the Welfare State? Opinions about Taxes and Public Expenditure in Sweden.* Stockholm: MiniMedia AB.

Hansen, Susan B. 1980. "Partisan Realignment and Tax Policy: 1789–1976." In *Realignment in American Politics,* by Bruce A. Campbell and Richard J. Trilling. Austin: University of Texas Press.

Hibbs, Douglas, and Henrik Jess Madsen. 1981. "Public Reactions to the Growth of Taxation and Government Expenditure." *World Politics* 33 (April), 413–45.

Hood, C. C. 1985. "British Tax Structure Development as Administrative Adaptation." *Policy Sciences* 18:1, 3–32.

Ishi, H. 1980. "Effects of Taxation on the Distribution of Income and Wealth in Japan." *Hitotsubashi Journal of Economics* (June), 27–47.

Johnson, Harry G. 1971. "Self-Assessment to Personal Income Tax: The American System." *British Tax Review* (March–April).

King, Mervyn A., and Don Fullerton, eds. 1984. *The Taxation of Income from Capital. A Comparative Study of the United States, the United Kingdom, Sweden and West Germany.* Chicago: University of Chicago Press.

McDaniel, Paul R., and Stanley S. Surrey, eds. 1985. *International Aspects of Tax Expenditures: A Comparative Study,* Boston: Kluwer.

Mennel, Annemarie. 1977. *Die Finanzverwaltungen in Europa.* Düsseldorf: Union des Finanzpersonals in Europa.

Musgrave, Richard A. 1969. *Fiscal Systems.* New Haven: Yale University Press.

———. 1980. "Theories of Fiscal Crises: An Essay in Fiscal Sociology." In *The Economics of Taxation, Studies of Government Finance,* by Henry Aaron and Michael J. Boskin. Washington, DC: Brookings Institution.

Noguchi, Yukio. 1987. "Public Finance." In *The Political Economy of Japan, Vol. 1: The Domestic Transformation,* ed. Kozo Yamamura and Yasukichi Yasuba. Stanford: Stanford University Press.

Organisation for Economic Cooperation and Development. 1976. *The Adjustment of Personal Income Tax Systems for Inflation.* Paris: OECD.

———. 1978. *The Tax/Income Composition of Selected Income Groups of OECD Member Countries.* Paris: OECD.

———. 1980. *Long-Term Trends in Tax Revenues of OECD Member Countries: 1955–1980.* Paris: OECD.

———. 1984. *Tax Expenditures: A Review of the Issues and Country Practices.* Paris: OECD.

———. 1985. "Social Expenditure 1960–1990. Problems of Growth and Control." *OECD Social Policy Studies.* Paris: OECD.

———. 1986a. *Personal Income Tax Systems Under Changing Economic Conditions.* Paris: OECD.

———. 1986b. *The Tax/Benefit Position of Production Workers 1979–1984.* Paris: OECD.

———. 1987a. *Taxation in Developed Countries.* Paris: OECD.

———. 1987b. *Revenue Statistics of OECD Member Countries 1965–1986.* Paris: OECD.

Pechman, Joseph A., ed. 1987. *Comparative Tax Systems: Europe, Canada and Japan.* Arlington, VA: Brookings Institution.

———, ed. 1988. *World Tax Reform.* Washington, DC: Brookings Institution.

Peters, B. Guy. 1986. "The Development of the Welfare State and the Tax State." In *Nationalizing Social Security in Europe and America,* edited by Douglas E. Ashford and E. W. Kelley. Greenwich, CT: JAI Press.

Robinson, Ann, and Cedric Sandford. 1983. *Tax Policy Making in the United Kingdom.* London: Heinemann.

Rodriguez, Enrique, and Sven Steinmo. 1986. "The Development of the American and the Swedish Tax System—A Comparison." *Intertax* 3.

Rose, Richard. 1985. "Maximizing Tax Revenue while Minimizing Political Costs." *Journal of Public Policy* 5:3, 289–320.

Rose, Richard, and Guy Peters. 1978. *Can Governments Go Bankrupt?* New York: Basic Books.

Rose, Richard, and Terence Karran. 1987. *Taxation by Political Inertia.* London: Allen and Unwin.

Roskamp, Karl W., and Francesco Forte, eds. 1981. *Reforms of Tax Systems*. Detroit: Wayne State University Press.

Sabine, B. E. V. 1966. *A History of Income Tax*. London: Allen and Unwin.

Sawyer, Malcolm. 1976. "Income Distribution in OECD Countries." *OECD Economic Outlook: Occasional Studies* (July).

Schmoelders, Guenter. 1970. "Survey Research in Public Finance—A Behavioral Approach to Fiscal Theory." *Public Finance* 25:2.

Shoup, Carl S. 1957. "Some Distinguishing Characteristics of British, French, and United States Public Finance Systems." *American Economic Review* 47 (May), 187–219.

Shultz, George P., and Kenneth W. Dam. 1978. *Economic Policy Behind the Headlines*. New York: Norton.

Sigelman, Lee, David Lowery, and Roland Smith. 1983. "The Tax Revolt: A Comparative State Analysis." *Western Political Quarterly* 36:1, 30–51.

Steinmo, Sven. 1986. "Taxes, Institutions, and the Mobilization of Bias: The Political Economy of Taxation in Britain, Sweden, and the United States." Doctoral Thesis, Berkeley: University of California.

Struempel, Burkhard. 1968. *Steuersystem und wirtschaftliche Entwicklung*. Tübingen: Mohr.

Tanzi, Vito. 1969. *The Individual Income Tax and Economic Growth: An International Comparison*. Baltimore: Johns Hopkins University Press.

———. 1982. *The Underground Economy in the United States and Abroad*. Lexington, MA: Lexington Books.

———. 1987. "The Response of Other Industrial Countries to the U.S. Tax Reform Act." *National Tax Journal*. 40:3 (Sept.), 339–56.

The Structure and Reform of Direct Taxation: Report of Committee Chaired by J.E. Meade. 1978. London: Allen and Unwin.

U.S. Congress. 1980. *Indexing the Individual Income Tax for Inflation*. Washington, DC: Congressional Budget Office.

Waltman, Jerold L., and Donley T. Studlar, eds. 1987. *Political Economy: Public Policies in the United States and Britain*. Jackson, MS: University Press of Mississippi.

Webber, Carolyn, and Aaron Wildavsky. 1986. *A History of Taxation and Expenditure in the Western World*. New York: Simon and Schuster.

Whalley, John. 1978. "Tax Developments Outside the United States and Their Implications for Current U.S. Reform Proposals." In *Federal Tax Reform: Myths and Realities*, edited by Michael J. Boskin. San Francisco: Institute for Contemporary Studies.

Wilensky, Harold. 1975. *The Welfare State and Equality*. Berkeley: University of California Press.

Wilensky, Harold. 1979. "Taxing, Spending and Backlash: An American Peculiarity?" *Taxing and Spending* (July), 6–11.

Willis, J. R. M. and P. J. W. Hardwick. 1978. *Tax Expenditures in the United Kingdom*. London: Heinemann.

Witte, John. 1985. *The Politics and Development of the Federal Income Tax*. Madison, WI: University of Wisconsin Press.

Woodside, Kenneth. 1982. "The Tax Revolt in International Perspective: Britain, Canada, and the United States." *Comparative Social Research* 5, 147–65.

Wright, L. Hart, ed. 1968. *Comparative Conflict Resolution Procedures in Taxation*. Ann Arbor: University of Michigan Law School.

CHAPTER 7. INCOME MAINTENANCE POLICY

Alber, Jens. 1985. "How the West German Welfare State Passed through the Recent Years of Economic Crisis." Paper presented at 13th World Congress, International Political Science Association, Paris. (Reproduced).

Alber, Jens, Gösta Esping-Andersen, and Lee Rainwater. 1987. "Studying the Welfare State." In *Comparative Policy Research. See* Dierkes, Weiler, and Antal.

Ashford, Douglas. 1986. *The Emergence of the Welfare States.* New York: Blackwell.

Baldwin, Peter. 1988. "The Politics of Social Solidarity and the Class Basis of the European Welfare State." Harvard University (Reproduced).

Bendix, Reinhard. 1964. *State and Society.* Boston: Little, Brown.

Braun, Dietmar. 1987. "Political Immobilism and Labor Market Performance." *JPP* 7:3, 307–35.

Brown, Michael, ed. 1988. *Remaking the Welfare State.* Philadelphia: Temple University Press.

Burtless, Gary. 1986. "Public Spending for the Poor." In *Fighting Poverty. See* Danziger and Weinberg.

Calder, Kent. 1988. *Crisis and Compensation: Public Policy and Political Stability in Japan, 1949–1986.* Princeton: Princeton University Press.

Carrier, John, and Ian Kendall. 1977. "The Development of Welfare States: The Production of Plausible Accounts." *Journal of Social Policy* 6:3, 271–90.

Castles, Francis. 1982. "The Impact of Parties on Public Expenditure." In *The Impact of Parties. See* Castles, ed. 1982.

———, ed. 1982. *The Impact of Parties.* Beverly Hills: Sage Publications.

———. 1985. *The Working Class and Welfare.* Winchester, MA: Allen and Unwin.

———. 1987a. "The Politics of Economic Vulnerability." *Thesis Eleven* 16:112–21.

———. 1988. *Public Policy and Economic Vulnerability.* Sydney: Allen and Unwin.

Castles, Francis, and R. D. McKinlay. 1979. "Public Welfare Provision, Scandinavia, and the Sheer Futility of a Sociological Approach to Politics." *BJPS* 9:157–72.

Collier, David, and Richard Messick. 1975. "Prerequisites and Diffusion." *APSR* 69:1299–1315.

Copeland, Lois. 1978. "Worldwide Developments in Social Security." *Social Security Bulletin* 41:3–8.

Cox, Robert. 1989. "Corporatist Competition in the Welfare State: The Development of Public Retirement Pensions in the Netherlands." *Comparative Politics.* (Forthcoming).

Cutright, Phillips. 1965. "Political Structure, Economic Development, and National Social Security Programs." *American Journal of Sociology* 70:537–50.

———. 1967. "Income Redistribution: A Cross-National Analysis." *Social Forces* 46;180–90.

Danziger, Sheldon, and Daniel Weinberg. 1986. *Fighting Poverty.* Cambridge, MA: Harvard University Press.

Derthick, Martha. 1979. *Policymaking for Social Security.* Washington, DC: Brookings Institution.

Dierkes, Meinolf, Hans Weiler, and Ariane Antal, eds. 1987. *Comparative Policy Research: Learning from Experience.* New York: St. Martin's Press.

Entwisle, Barbara, and C. K. Winegarden. 1984. "Fertility and Pension Policy in LDCs." *Economic Development and Cultural Change* 32:331–54.

Esping-Andersen, Gösta. 1985. *Politics against Markets*. Princeton: Princeton University Press.

Esping-Andersen, Gösta, Lee Rainwater, and Martin Rein. 1988. "Institutional and Political Factors Affecting the Well-Being of the Elderly." In *The Vulnerable. See* Palmer, Smeeding, and Torrey.

Flora, Peter, ed. 1986. *Growth to Limits: The Western Welfare States Since World War II.* Vol. I. New York: deGruyter.

Flora, Peter, and Jens Alber. 1981. "Modernization, Democratization and the Development of Welfare States." In *The Development of Welfare States in Europe and America. See* Flora and Heidenheimer.

Flora, Peter, and Arnold Heidenheimer, eds. 1981. *The Development of Welfare States in Europe and America*. New Brunswick: Transaction.

Flora, Peter et al. 1983. *State, Economy and Society in Western Europe 1815–1975*. Vol. I of *The Growth of Mass Democracies and Welfare States*. London: Macmillan.

Friedmann, Robert, Neil Gilbert, and Moshe Sherer, eds. 1987. *Modern Welfare States: A Comparative View of Trends and Prospects*. New York: New York University Press.

Haveman, Robert. 1988. *Starting Even*. New York: Simon and Schuster.

Hedstrom, Peter, and Stein Ringen. 1985. *Age and Income in Contemporary Society, A Comparative Study*. Stockholm: Swedish Institute for Social Research.

Hicks, Alexander, and Duane Swank. 1984. "On the Political Economy of Welfare Expansion." *Comp Pol St* 17:1, 81–119.

Jackman, Robert. 1975. *Politics and Social Equality: A Comparative Analysis*. New York: Wiley.

Jamrozik, Adam. 1987. "Winners and Losers in the Welfare State." In *Social Welfare in the Late 1980s. See* Saunders and Jamrozik.

Judge, Ken. 1987. "The British Welfare State in Transition." In *Modern Welfare States. See* Friedmann, Gilbert, and Sherer.

Kamerman, Sheila, and Alfred Kahn. 1981. *Child Care, Family Benefits and Working Parents*. New York: Columbia University Press.

———. 1988. "Social Policy and Children in the United States and Europe." In *The Vulnerable. See* Palmer, Smeeding, and Torrey.

Katzenstein, Peter. 1987. *Policy and Politics in West Germany*. Philadelphia: Temple University Press.

Kerr, Clark, et al., 1960. *Industrialism and Industrial Man*. Cambridge, MA: Harvard University Press.

Klein, Rudolph. 1980. "The Welfare State: A Self-Inflicted Crisis?" *The Political Quarterly* 51:24–34.

Korpi, Walter. 1983. *The Democratic Class Struggle*. London: Routledge and Kegan Paul.

Krieger, Joel. 1987. *Reagan, Thatcher and the Politics of Decline*. New York: Oxford University Press.

Lampman, Robert. 1984. *Social Welfare Spending*. New York: Academic Press.

Laslett, Peter, and Richard Woll. 1972. *Household and Family in the Past*. New York: Cambridge University Press.

Lee, Hye Kyung. 1987. "The Japanese Welfare State in Transition." In *Modern Welfare States. See* Friedmann, Gilbert, and Sherer.

Levy, Frank. 1987. *Dollars and Dreams*. New York: Russell Sage Foundation.

Light, Paul. 1985. *Artful Work.* New York: Random House.

Markovits, Andrei, and Jost Halfmann. 1988. "The Unraveling of West German Democracy?" In *Remaking the Welfare State. See* Brown.

Marshall, T. H. 1965. *Class, Citizenship and Social Development.* New York: Anchor.

Maruo, Naomi. 1986. "The Development of the Welfare Mix in Japan." In *The Welfare State East and West. See* Rose and Shiratori.

Miliband, Ralph. 1969. *The State in Capitalist Society.* New York: Basic Books.

Mommsen, W. J., ed. 1981. *The Emergence of the Welfare State in Britain and Germany.* London: Croom-Helm.

Muller, Edward. 1988. "Democracy, Economic Development and Inequality." *American Sociological Review* 53:50–68.

———. 1989. "Distribution of Income in Advanced Capitalist States." *European Journal of Political Research.* (Forthcoming).

Myles, John. 1984. *Old Age in the Welfare State.* Boston: Little, Brown.

———. 1988. "Postwar Capitalism and the Expansion of Social Security into the Retirement Wage." In *The Politics of Social Policy in the United States. See* Weir, Orloff, and Skocpol.

Navarro, Vincente. 1988. "Welfare States and Their Distributive Effects." *The Political Quarterly* 59:2, 219–35.

Noguchi, Yukio. 1986. "Overcommitment in Pensions: The Japanese Experience." In *The Welfare State East and West. See* Rose and Shiratori.

O'Connor, James. 1973. *The Fiscal Crisis of the State.* New York: St. Martin's Press.

O'Connor, Julia. 1988. "Convergence or Divergence: Change in Welfare Effort in OECD Countries 1960–86." *European Journal of Political Research* 16:277–99.

Offe, Claus. 1984. *Contradictions of the Welfare State.* Cambridge, MA: MIT Press.

O'Higgins, Michael. 1985. "Inequality, Redistribution and Recession; The British Experience 1976–82." *Journal of Social Policy* 14:3, 279–307.

———. 1988. "The Allocation of Public Resources to Children and the Elderly in OECD Countries." In *The Vulnerable. See* Palmer, Smeeding, and Torrey.

Olsson, Sven. 1987. "Towards a Transformation of the Swedish Welfare State." In *Modern Welfare States. See* Friedmann, Gilbert, and Sherer.

Organisation for Economic Cooperation and Development. 1981. *National Accounts of OECD Countries, 1962–79.* Paris: OECD.

———. 1985. *Social Expenditures, 1960–1990.* Paris: OECD.

———. 1988a. *Aging Populations.* Paris: OECD.

———. 1988b. *Reforming Public Pensions.* Paris: OECD.

Orloff, Ann. 1988. "The Political Origins of America's Belated Welfare State." In *The Politics of Social Policy in the United States. See* Weir, Orloff, and Skocpol.

Palmer, John, and Isabel Sawhill, eds. 1984. *The Reagan Record.* Washington, DC: Urban Institute.

Palmer, John, Timothy Smeeding, and Barbara Torrey, eds. 1988. *The Vulnerable.* Washington, DC: Urban Institute.

Pampel, Fred, and John Williamson. 1985. "Age Structures, Politics, and Cross-National Patterns of Public Pension Expenditures." *American Sociological Review* 50:782–99.

Perrin, Guy. 1969. "Reflections on Fifty Years of Social Security." *International Labour Review* 99:3, 249–90.

Polanyi, Karl. 1944. *The Great Transformation.* New York: Rinehart and Co.

Preston, Samuel. 1984. "Children and the Elderly." *Demography* 21:435–57.

Preston, Samuel, and Shigemi Kono. 1988. "Trends in Well-Being of Children and the Elderly in Japan." In *The Vulnerable. See* Palmer, Smeeding, and Torrey.

Pryor, Frederick. 1968. *Public Expenditures in Communist and Capitalist Nations*. Homewood, IL: Irwin.

Rainwater, Lee, Martin Rein, and Joseph Schwarz. 1986. *Income Packaging in the Welfare State*. Oxford: Clarendon Press.

Reynolds, Morgan, and Eugene Smolensky. 1977. *Public Expenditure, Taxes, and the Distribution of Income*. Madison, WI: Institute for Poverty Research.

Roberti, P. 1979. "Counting the Poor." In *The Measurement of Poverty*, Department of Health and Social Security. London: HMSO.

Rosa, Jean-Jacques, ed. 1982. *The World Crisis in Social Security*. San Francisco: Institute for Contemporary Studies.

Rose, Richard. 1986. "Common Goals but Different Roles." In *The Welfare State, East and West. See* Rose and Shiratori.

Rose, Richard, and Rei Shiratori, eds. 1983. *The Welfare State East and West*. Oxford: Oxford University Press.

Ross, George. 1988. "The Mitterand Experiment and the French Welfare State." In *Remaking the Welfare State. See* Brown.

Saunders, Peter, and Adam Jamrozik, eds. 1987. *Social Welfare in the Late 1980s*. Sydney: Social Welfare Research Center.

Sawyer, Malcolm. 1976. "Income Distribution in OECD Countries." *OECD Economic Outlook: Occasional Studies* 3–36.

Shalev, Michael. 1983. "The Social Democratic Model and Beyond." *Comparative Social Research* 6:315–51.

Simanis, J. G. 1980. "Worldwide Trends in Social Security." *Social Security Bulletin* 43:6–9.

Smeeding, Timothy, Barbara Torrey, and Martin Rein. 1988. "Patterns of Income and Poverty, The Economic Status of Children and the Elderly in Eight Countries." In *The Vulnerable. See* Palmer, Smeeding, and Torrey.

Stephens, John. 1979. *The Transformation from Capitalism to Socialism*. London: Macmillan.

Stockman, David. 1986. *The Triumph of Politics: Why the Reagan Revolution Failed*. New York: Harper.

Weir, Margaret, Ann Orloff, and Theda Skocpol, eds. 1988. *The Politics of Social Policy in the United States*. Princeton: Princeton University Press.

Wilensky, Harold. 1975. *The Welfare State and Equality*. Berkeley: University of California Press.

———. 1981. "Leftism, Catholicism and Democratic Corporatism." In *The Development of Welfare States in Europe and America. See* Flora and Heidenheimer.

Wilensky, Harold, and Charles Lebeaux. 1965. *Industrial Society and Social Welfare*. New York: Free Press.

Wilensky, Harold, Gregory Luebbert, Susan Reed, and Adrienne Jamieson. 1985. *Comparative Social Policy*. Berkeley: Institute of International Studies.

CHAPTER 8. URBAN PLANNING

Aiken, Michael. 1975. "Urban Social Structure and Political Competition: A Comparative Study of Local Politics in Four European Nations." *Urb Aff Q* 11:1 (September), 82–114.

Ambrose, Peter. 1986. *Whatever Happened to Planning?* London: Methuen.

Anton, Thomas. 1975. *Governing Greater Stockholm.* Berkeley: University of California Press.

Barnekov, Timothy, and Daniel Rich. 1977. "Privatism and Urban Development: An Analysis of the Organized Influence of Local Business Elites." *Urb Aff Q* 12:4 (June), 431–59.

Barrett, Susan, and Patsy Healey, eds. 1985. *Land Policy: Problems and Alternatives.* Aldershot, Eng.: Gower.

Berry, Brian. 1973. *The Human Consequences of Urbanization.* New York: St. Martin's Press.

———, ed. 1976. *Urbanization and Counterurbanization.* Beverly Hills: Sage Publications.

Boesler, Klaus-Achim. 1974. "Spatially Effective Government Actions and Regional Development in the Federal Republic of Germany." *Tijdschrift voor Econ. en Soc. Geografie* 65:3, 208–20.

Brownfield, Lyman. 1960. "The Disposition Problem in Urban Renewal." *Law & Con P* 25 (Autumn), 732–76.

Buchanan, Colin et al. 1963. *Traffic in Towns: A Study of the Long Term Problems of Traffic in Urban Areas.* London: HMSO.

Castells, Manuel. 1979. *The Urban Question: A Marxist Approach.* Cambridge, MA: MIT Press.

Cochrane, Allan, ed. 1987. *Developing Local Economic Strategies.* Milton Keynes, Eng.: Open University Press.

Cox, Andrew. 1980. "Continuity and Discontinuity in Conservative Urban Policy." *Urban Law and Policy* 3:269–92.

Drewett, Roy, John Goddard, and Nigel Spence. 1976. "Urban Britain: Beyond Containment." In *Urbanization and Counterurbanization.* See Berry 1976.

Dunn, James A. 1981. *Miles to Go: European and American Transportation Policies.* Cambridge, MA: MIT Press.

Elkin, S. L. 1974. *Politics and Land-Use Planning.* New York: Cambridge University Press.

Evans, H. and L. Rodwin. 1979. "The New Towns Program and Why It Failed." *The Public Interest* 56 (Summer), 90–107.

Falk, Thomas. 1978. "Urban Development in Sweden 1960–1975: Population Dispersal in Progress." In *Human Settlement Systems: International Perspectives on Structure, Change, and Public Policy,* edited by Niles Hansen. Cambridge: Ballinger.

Fried, Robert. 1975. "Comparative Urban Policy and Performance." In *Policies and Policymaking,* edited by Fred Greenstein and Nelson Polsby. Reading, MA: Addison-Wesley.

Gale, Dennis, ed. 1982. "Symposium: A Comparative View of National Urban Policy." Special issue of the *Journal of the American Planning Association* 48:1 (Winter).

———. 1984. *Neighborhood Revitalization and the Postindustrial City: A Multinational Perspective.* Lexington, MA: Lexington Books.

Gorham, William, and Nathan Glazer, eds. 1976. *The Urban Predicament.* Washington, DC: Urban Institute.

Gottdiener, Mark. 1977. *Planned Sprawl: Private and Public Interests in Suburbia.* Washington, DC: Urban Institute.

Greater London Council. 1984. *Planning for the Future of London: Alternatives to the Greater London Development Plan.* London: GLC.

Hall, Peter. 1966. *The World Cities.* New York: McGraw-Hill.

Hamnett, Christopher, and Peter Williams. 1980. "Social Change in London: A Study of Gentrification." *Urb Aff Q* 15:4 (June), 469–87.

Harloe, Michael, ed. 1977. *Captive Cities: Studies in the Political Economy of Cities and Regions.* New York: Wiley.

Hart, D. A. 1976. *Strategic Planning in London: The Rise and Fall of the Primary Road Network.* Oxford: Pergamon.

Harvey, David. 1973. *Social Justice and the City.* Baltimore: Johns Hopkins University Press.

Hebbert, Michael. 1986. "Urban Sprawl and Urban Planning in Japan." *Town Planning Review* 57:2, 141–58.

Heinemeyer, W. F., and R. V. E. Gastelaars. 1972. "Conflicts in Land Use in Amsterdam." *Tijdschrift voor Econ. en Soc. Geografie* (May–June), 190–99.

Kirwan, Richard. 1987. "Fiscal Policy and the Price of Land and Housing in Japan." *Urban Studies* 24:345–60.

Laska, Shirley, and Daphne Spain, eds. 1980. *Back to the City: Issues in Neighborhood Renovation.* New York: Pergamon.

Lawless, Paul. 1979. *Urban Deprivation and Government Initiative.* London: Faber and Faber.

Levine, Myron, and Jan van Weesep. 1988. "The Changing Nature of Dutch Urban Planning." *Journal of the American Planning Association* 54:3 (Summer), 315–23.

Mollenkopf, John. 1977. "The Post War Politics of Urban Development." In *Cities in Change,* by John Walton and Donald Carns. Boston: Allyn and Bacon.

Molotch, Harvey. 1976. "The City as a Growth Machine." *AJS* 82:2, 309–32.

Moor, Nigel. 1985. "Inner City Areas and the Private Sector." In *Land Policy: Problems and Alternatives. See* Barrett and Healey.

Mumford, Lewis. 1966. *The City in History.* New York: Harcourt Brace Jovanovich.

Needham, Barrie. 1985. "Local Government Policy for Industrial Land in England and the Netherlands." In *Land Policy: Problems and Alternatives. See* Barrett and Healey.

Organisation for Economic Cooperation and Development. 1979. *Managing Transport.* Paris: OECD.

———. 1983. *Managing Urban Change: Vol. 1: Policies and Finance.* Paris: OECD.

———. 1986. *Urban Policies in Japan.* Paris: OECD.

———. 1987. *Revitalizing Urban Economies.* Paris: OECD.

Pahl, R. E. 1970. *Whose City?* Harlow, Eng.: Longman.

Pempel, T. J. 1982. *Policy and Politics in Japan: Creative Conservatism.* Philadelphia: Temple University Press.

Peterson, Paul, and Paul Kantor. 1977. "Political Parties and Citizen Participation in English City Politics." *Comp Pol* 9:2 (January), 197–217.

Ratzka, Adolf. 1980. *Sixty Years of Municipal Leasehold in Stockholm.* Stockholm: Swedish Council for Building Research.

Report of the President's Commission for a National Agenda for the Eighties. 1981. New York: NAL.

Sorenson, Robert C. A. 1978. "Urban Civic Protest Groups in West Germany and

Switzerland." Paper presented at Ninth World Congress of Sociology, Uppsala, Sweden, August.

Strong, Ann L. 1979. *Land Banking: European Reality, American Prospect.* Baltimore: Johns Hopkins University Press.

Sundquist, James. 1975. *Dispersing Population: What America Can Learn from Europe.* Washington, DC: Brookings Institution.

Susskind, Lawrence, and Michael Elliott, eds. 1983. *Paternalism, Conflict, and Coproduction: Learning from Citizen Action and Citizen Participation in Western Europe.* New York: Plenum Press.

Thomas, David et al. 1983. *Flexibility and Commitment in Planning: A Comparative Study of Local Planning and Development in the Netherlands and England.* Boston: Martinus Nijhoff.

Thomson, J. M. 1977. "The London Motorway Plan." In *Public Participation in Planning,* edited by W. R. Derrick Sewell and J. T. Coppock. New York: Wiley.

Town and Country Planning Association. May 1977. *Statement on Inner Cities,* London: TCPA.

Underhill, Jack. 1980. *French National Urban Policy and the Paris Region New Towns.* Washington, DC: Department of Housing and Urban Development, Office of International Affairs.

Valderpoort, W. 1953. *The Selfish Automobile.* Amsterdam: Amsterdam Press.

Van den Berg, L., R. Drewett, L. H. Klaassen, and CHT Vijverberg. 1982. *Urban Europe, Vol. I: A Study of Growth and Decline.* Oxford: Pergamon.

Walton, John. 1979. "Urban Political Economy: A New Paradigm." *Comparative Urban Research* 7:1, 5–17.

Ward, Reginald. 1986. "Public-Private Partnerships: Role of Urban Development Corporations." In *New Roles for Old Cities: Anglo-American Policy Perspectives on Declining Urban Regions,* edited by Edgar Rose. Aldershot, Eng.: Gower.

Warner, Sam Bass. 1968. *The Private City.* Philadelphia: University of Pennsylvania Press.

Webman, Jerry. 1982. *Reviving the Industrial City.* New Brunswick: Rutgers University Press.

Wiedenhoeft, Ronald. 1977. "Malmo: The People Said No." *Scandinavian Review* 1:12–18.

Young, Ken, and Liz Mills. 1983. *Managing the Post-Industrial City.* London: Heinemann.

CHAPTER 9. ENVIRONMENTAL POLICY

Ackerman, B. A., and W. T. Hassler. 1981. *Clean Coal/Dirty Air.* New Haven: Yale University Press.

Aniansson, Britt, and Bertil Hagerhall. 1985. "Sweden, Europe, and Acid Rain." *Current Sweden* 328 (January), Svenska Institutet, Stockholm.

Ashby, Eric, and Mary Anderson. 1981. *The Politics of Clean Air.* Oxford: Clarendon Press.

Baumol, William, and Wallace Oates. 1979. *Economics, Environmental Policy, and the Quality of Life.* Englewood Cliffs: Prentice-Hall.

Berger, Suzanne. 1979. "Politics and Anti-Politics in Western Europe in the Seventies." *Daedalus* 108:1, 27–50.

Berry, B. J. 1977. *The Social Burdens of Environmental Pollution.* Cambridge, MA: Ballinger.

Boy, Daniel. 1981. "Le vote ecologiste en 1978." *Revue Francaise de Science Politique* 31 (Spring) 394–416.

Braithwaite, J. 1981. "The Limits of Economism in Controlling Harmful Corporate Conduct." *Law and Society Review* 16:481–504.

Brown, Lester et al. 1988. *State of the World 1988.* New York: Norton.

Bugler, J. 1972. *Polluting Britain.* Harmondsworth: Penguin.

Burklin, Wilhelm. 1985. "The Greens: Ecology and the New Left," in *West German Politics in the Mid-Eighties,* edited by H. G. Wallach and George Romoser. New York: Praeger.

Buttel, F. H., and W. L. Flinn. 1976. "Environmental Politics: The Structuring of Partisan and Ideological Cleavages in Mass Environmental Attitudes." *Sociological Quarterly* 17:477–90.

Cahn, Robert, ed. 1985. *An Environmental Agenda for the Future.* Washington, DC: Island Press.

Crandall, Robert. 1983. *Controlling Industrial Pollution: The Economics and Politics of Clean Air.* Washington, DC: Brookings Institution.

Dierkes, Meinolf, Hans Weiler, and Ariane Antal, eds. 1987. *Comparative Policy Research: Learning from Experience.* Aldershot, Eng.: Gower.

Downing, P., and K. Hanf, eds. 1983. *Implementing Pollution Laws: International Comparisons.* Boston: Kluwer-Nijhoff.

Dunlap, R. E., and M. P. Allen. 1976. "Partisan Differences on Environmental Issues: A Congressional Roll-Call Analysis." *Western Political Quarterly* 29:384–97.

Ewringmann, Dieter. 1986. "Discussion: The Role of Trade Unions in Environmental Policy: The German Perspective." In *Distributional Conflicts in Environmental Policy. See* Schnaiberg, Watts, and Zimmermann.

Frankel, Maurice. 1974. *The Alkali Inspectorate: The Control of Industrial Air Pollution.* London: Social Audit.

Frieden, Bernard. 1979. *The Environmental Protection Hustle.* Cambridge, MA: MIT Press.

Haskell, Elizabeth. 1982. *The Politics of Clean Air.* New York: Praeger.

Hershey, M. R., and P. B. Hill. 1977–78. "Is Pollution a White Thing? Racial Differences in Pre-Adults' Attitudes." *Public Opinion Quarterly* 41:1, 439–58.

Hirschhorn, Joel. 1984. "Emerging Options in Waste Reduction and Treatment: A Market Incentive Approach." In *Beyond Dumping. See* Piasecki.

Inglehart, Ronald. 1982. "Changing Values in Japan and the West." *Comparative Political Studies* 14:4, 445–79.

Inglehart, Ronald. 1977. *The Silent Revolution: Changing Values and Political Styles among Western Publics.* Princeton: Princeton University Press.

Jaffe, Mark. 1988. "Third World Balks on Pollution." *Philadelphia Inquirer.* (October 30), 1A.

Johnson, Stanley. 1973. *The Politics of Environment: The British Experience.* London: Tom Stacey Ltd.

Joint Economic Committee, U.S. Congress. 1980. *Environmental and Health/Safety Regulations, Productivity Growth, and Economic Performance: An Assessment: Summary.* Washington, DC: USGPO.

Joint Unit for Research on the Urban Environment/ECOTEC. (March 1982) "The

Environment Industry in the EEC: Employment and Research and Development in the Next Decade." Brussels: Commission for the European Communities.

Kasperson, R. 1980. "The Dark Side of the Radioactive Waste Problem." In *Progress in Resource Management and Environmental Planning*, edited by T. O'Riordan and R. K. Turner. Chichester, Eng.: Wiley.

Kitschelt, Herbert. 1988. "Organization and Strategy of Belgian and West German Ecology Parties." *Comparative Politics* 20:2 (January), 127–54.

Kneese, Allen, and Charles Schultz. 1975. *Pollution, Prices and Public Policy.* Washington, DC: Brookings Institution.

Knoepfel, Peter. 1986. "Discussion: Distributional Issues in Regulatory Policy Implementation—the Case of Air Quality Control Policies." In *Distributional Conflicts in Environmental Policy. See* Schnaiberg, Watts, and Zimmermann.

Knoepfel, Peter, Lennart Lundqvist, Remy Proud'homme, and Peter Wagner. 1987. "Comparing Environmental Policies: Different Styles, Similar Content." In *Comparative Policy Research. See* Dierkes, Weiler, and Antal.

Knoepfel, Peter, and Helmut Weidner. 1982. "Implementing Air Quality Control Programs in Europe: Some Results of a Comparative Study." *Policy Studies Journal* 11:1 (September), 103–15.

Knoepfel, Peter, Helmut Weidner, and K. Hanf. 1980. *International Comparative Analysis of Program Formation and Implementation in SO$_2$ Air Pollution Control Policies in the EEC Countries and Switzerland.* Berlin: WZB.

Kolinsky, Eva. 1984. "The Greens in Germany: Prospects of a Small Party." *Parliamentary Affairs* 37:4 (Autumn), 434–46.

Krauss, Ellis, and Bradford Simcock. 1980. "Citizens' Movements: The Growth and Impact of Environmental Protest in Japan." In *Political Opposition and Local Politics in Japan*, edited by Kurt Steiner, Ellis Krauss, and Scott Flanagan. Princeton: Princeton University Press.

Landy, Marc, and Henry Plotkin. 1982. "Limits of the Market Metaphor." *Society* 19:4 (May/June), 8–17.

Lauber, Volkmar. 1983. "From Growth Consensus to Fragmentation in Western Europe." *Comparative Politics* 15:3 (April), 329–49.

Logue, John. 1981. *Socialism and Abundance: Radical Socialism in the Danish Welfare State.* Minneapolis: University of Minnesota Press.

Lowi, Theodore. 1986. "The Welfare State, the New Regulation and the Rule of Law." In *Distributional Conflicts in Environmental Policy. See* Schnaiberg, Watts, and Zimmerman.

Lundqvist, Lennart. 1974. *Environmental Policies in Canada, Sweden, and the US: A Comparative Overview.* Beverly Hills: Sage Publications.

———. 1980. *The Hare and the Tortoise: Clean Air Policies in the US and Sweden.* Ann Arbor: University of Michigan Press.

Mann, D. E. 1975. "Political Incentives in US Water Policy." In *What Government Does*, edited by M. Holden and D. L. Drewang. Beverly Hills: Sage Publications. 94–123.

McGarity, Thomas. 1983. "Media-Quality, Technology, and Cost-Benefit Balancing Strategies for Health and Environmental Regulation." *Law and Contemporary Problems* 46:3 (Summer), 159–233.

Meidinger, Errol. 1986. "Discussion: The Politics of Market Mechanisms in US Air

Pollution Regulation: Social Structure and Regulatory Culture." In *Distributional Conflicts in Environmental Policy. See* Schnaiberg, Watts, and Zimmermann.

Meissner, W. 1984. *The Impact of Environmental Policy on Employment.* Paris: OECD.

————. 1986. "Implications for Environmental Policy." In *Distributional Conflicts in Environmental Policy. See* Schnaiberg, Watts, and Zimmermann.

Melnick, R. Shep. 1983. *Regulation and the Courts: The Case of the Clean Air Act.* Washington, DC: Brookings Institution.

Milbrath, Lester. 1984. *Environmentalists: Vanguard for a New Society.* Albany: SUNY Press.

Muller-Rommel, Ferdinand. 1982. "Ecology Parties in Western Europe." *West European Politics* 1:68–74.

Nagel, G. 1981. "Environmental Policy on the Hazards of Incentives and Merits of Regulation." In *Local Government and Environmental Planning and Control,* edited by Frank Joyce. Aldershot, Eng.: Gower.

Neiman, M. 1980. "The Virtues of Heavy Handedness in Government." *Law and Policy Quarterly:*, 11–33.

Organisation for Economic Cooperation and Development. 1980. *Environmental Policies for the 1980s.* Paris: OECD.

————. 1982. *Economic and Ecological Interdependence.* Paris: OECD.

————. 1985a. *Environmental Policy and Technical Change.* Paris: OECD.

————. 1985b. *The Macro-Economic Impact of Environmental Expenditure.* Paris: OECD.

Paccino, Dario. 1972. *L'imbroglio ecologico: L'ideologia della natura.* Turin: Einaudi.

Pearce, David. 1980. "The Social Incidence of Environmental Costs and Benefits." In *Progress in Resource Management and Environmental Planning.* Vol. 2, edited by T. O'Riordan and K. Turner. New York: Wiley.

Pempel, T. J. 1982. *Policy and Politics in Japan.* Philadelphia: Temple University Press.

Piasecki, Bruce, ed. 1984. *Beyond Dumping: New Strategies for Controlling Toxic Contamination.* Westport, CT: Quorum Books.

Piasecki, Bruce, and Gary Davis, eds. 1987. *America's Future in Toxic Waste Management: Lessons from Europe.* Westport, CT: Quorum Books.

Potier, Michel. 1986. "Capital and Labour Reallocation in the Face of Environmental Policy." In *Distributional Conflicts in Environmental Policy. See* Schnaiberg, Watts, and Zimmerman.

Reich, Michael. 1984. "Mobilizing for Environmental Policy in Italy and Japan." *Comparative Politics* 16:4 (July), 379–402.

Schnaiberg, Allan, Nicholas Watts, and Klaus Zimmerman, eds. 1986. *Distributional Conflicts in Environmental Policy.* Aldershot, Eng.: Gower.

Schneider, Volker. 1985. "Corporatist and Pluralist Patterns of Policy-making for Chemicals Control: A Comparison between West Germany and the USA." In *Organized Interests and the State,* edited by Alan Cawson. Beverly Hills: Sage.

Siegman, Heinrich. 1986. "Discussion: Environmental Policy and Trade Unions in the US." In *Distributional Conflicts in Environmental Policy. See* Schnaiberg, Watts and Zimmermann.

Sikora, R. I., and B. Barry, eds. 1978. *Obligations to Future Generations.* Philadelphia: Temple University Press.

Surrey, J., ed. 1984. *The Urban Transportation of Irradiated Fuel.* London: Macmillan.

Tucker, William. 1982. *Progress and Privilege: America in the Age of Environmentalism.* New York: Doubleday.

United Nations Centre on Transnational Corporations. 1985. *Environmental Aspects of the Activities of Transnational Corporations.* New York: UN.

United States Environmental Protection Agency. October 1986. "Waste Minimization Findings and Activities." *Factsheet.* Washington, DC: USGPO.

United States General Accounting Office. 1983. *Siting of Hazardous Waste Landfills and Their Correlation with Racial and Economic Status in Surrounding Communities.* Washington, DC: USGPO.

United States Office of Technology Assessment. 1987. *From Pollution to Prevention: A Program Report on Waste Reduction.* Washington, DC: USGPO.

Wams, Teo. 1987. "Environmentalism in the Netherlands: Theory and Practice—A Viewpoint." *International Journal of Environmental Studies* 30:29–35.

Wiegel, R. H. 1977. "Ideological and Demographic Correlates of Pro-Ecology Behavior." *Journal of Social Psychology* 103:39–47.

Wildavsky, Aaron. 1987. "Doing More and Using Less: Utilization of Research as a Result of Regime." In *Comparative Policy Research.* See Dierkes, Weiler, and Antal.

Wynne, Brian. 1987. "Hazardous Waste—What Kind of Issue?" In *Risk Management and Hazardous Waste,* edited by B. Wynne. Berlin: Springer-Verlag.

Zimmerman, Klaus. 1986. "Distributional Considerations and the Environmental Policy Process." In *Distributional Conflicts in Environmental Policy.* See Schnaiberg, Watts, and Zimmerman.

CHAPTER 10. POLICY CONTRASTS IN THE WELFARE STATE

Abel-Smith, Brian. 1972. "The History of Medical Care." In *Comparative Development in Social Welfare,* edited by E. W. Martin. London: Allen and Unwin.

Adams, Carolyn T., and Kathryn T. Winston. 1980. *Mothers at Work: Public Policies in the United States, Sweden and China.* New York: Longman.

Alber, Jens. 1989. *Der Sozialstaat in der Bundesrepublik 1950–1983.* Frankfurt and New York: Campus Verlag.

Arrow, Kenneth. 1963. *Social Choice and Individual Values.* New Haven: Yale University Press.

Ashford, Douglas. 1980. *Politics and Policy in Britain.* Philadelphia: Temple University Press.

Barnes, Samuel, and Max Kaase, eds. 1979. *Political Action.* Beverly Hills: Sage Publications.

Berger, Suzanne. 1981. *Organizing Interests in Western Europe.* New York: Cambridge University Press.

Beyme, Klaus von. 1982. *Economics and Politics within Socialist Systems: A Comparative and Developmental Approach.* New York: Praeger.

Beyme, Klaus, and Manfred Schmidt, eds. 1985. *Policy and Politics in the Federal Republic of Germany.* Aldershot, Eng.: Gower.

Blankenburg, Erhard, ed. 1980. *Innovation in Legal Services.* Cambridge, MA: Ohlenschlaeger.

Cameron, David. 1978. "The Expansion of the Public Economy: A Comparative Analysis." APSR 72:4, 1243–61.

Castles, Francis G. 1981. "How Does Politics Matter: Structure or Agency in the

Determination of Public Policy Outcomes." *European Journal of Political Research* 9:119–32.

———, ed. 1982. *The Impact of Parties: Politics and Policies in Democratic Capitalist States.* Beverly Hills: Sage Publications.

———. 1988. "Comparative Public Policy Analysis." In *Managing Mixed Economies,* edited by Francis Castles, et al. Berlin: DeGruyter.

Coughlin, Richard M. 1980. *Ideology, Public Opinion and Welfare Policy.* Berkeley: Institute of International Studies, University of California.

Day, Patricia, and Rudolf Klein. 1987. "The Regulation of Nursing Homes: A Comparative Perspective." *Mil Mem Q* 65:3, 303–47.

De Swaan, Abram. 1988. *In Care of the State.* Cambridge: Polity Press.

Diamant, Alfred. 1981. "Bureaucracy and Public Policy in Neocorporatist Settings: Some European Lessons." *Comp Pol* 14:101–24.

Dierkes, Meinolf, Hans N. Weiler, and Ariane Antal, eds. 1987. *Comparative Policy Research Learning from Experience.* Aldershot, Eng.: Gower.

Dogan, Mattei, ed. 1988. *Comparing Pluralist Democracies: Strains on Legitimacy.* Boulder, CO: Westview.

Dye, Thomas. 1979. "Politics versus Economics: The Development of the Literature on Policy Determination." *Policy Studies Journal* 7:652–62.

Eckstein, Harry. 1960. *Pressure Group Politics: The Case of the British Medical Association.* Stanford: Stanford University Press.

Feick, Jürgen, and Werner Jann. 1988. "Nations Matter: Vom Eklektismus zur Integration in der vergleichenden Policy Forschung." In *Staatstätigkeit: International und historisch vergleichende Analyses,* edited by Manfred G. Schmidt. Opladen: Westdeutscher Verlag.

Flora, Peter, and Arnold J. Heidenheimer, eds. 1981. *The Development of the Welfare State in Europe and America.* New Brunswick: Transaction.

Flora, Peter, ed. 1986. *Growth to Limits: The Western European Welfare States since World War II.* Berlin: deGruyter.

Freeman, Gary P. 1979. *Immigrant Labor and Racial Conflict in Industrial Societies: The French and British Experience 1945–1975.* Princeton: Princeton University Press.

Freeman, Gary P. 1985. "National Styles and Policy Sectors: Explaining Structured Variation." *JPP* 5:4 (October), 467–96.

Fried, Robert R., and Francine Rabinowitz. 1980. *Comparative Urban Politics: A Performance Approach.* Englewood Cliffs: Prentice-Hall.

Girvetz, Harry. "Welfare State." *International Encyclopedia of the Social Sciences* 16:512–21.

Gough, L. 1979. *The Political Economy of the Welfare State.* London: Macmillan.

Gustafsson, Gunnel, and Jeremy Richardson. 1980. "Post-Industrial Changes in Policy Style." *Sc Pol Stud* 3:1, 21–37.

Heclo, Hugh. 1988. "Generational Politics." In *The Vulnerable,* edited by John Palmer, Timothy Smeeding, and Barbara Torrey. Washington, DC: Urban Institute.

Heclo, Hugh, and Henrik Madsen. 1987. *Politics and Policy in Sweden.* Philadelphia: Temple University Press.

Heidenheimer, Arnold J. 1985. "Comparative Public Policy at the Crossroads." *JPP* 5:4 (October), 441–66.

———. 1986. "Politics, Policy and Policies as Concepts in English and Continental Languages." *Review of Politics* 48:1 (January), 3–31.

———. 1989. "Professional Knowledge and State Policy Variations: Law and Medicine in Britain, Germany and the United States." *International Social Science Journal*, 122 (November).

Heisler, Martin O., and Guy Peters. 1978. "Comparing Social Policy Across Levels of Government, Countries and Time: Belgium and Sweden since 1870." In *Comparing Public Policies*, edited by Douglas Ashford. Beverly Hills: Sage Publications.

Higgins, Joan. 1981. *States of Welfare: A Comparative Analysis of Social Policy*. New York: St. Martin's Press.

Hirschman, Albert O. 1982. *Shifting Involvements: Private Interest and Public Action*. Princeton: Princeton University Press.

Hood, Christopher, and Maurice Wright, eds. 1981. *Big Government in Hard Times*. Oxford: Martin Robertson.

Hood, Christopher, and Gunnar F. Schuppert. 1988. *Delivering Public Services: Sharing Western European Experience*. London: Sage Publications.

Katzenstein, Peter. 1985. *Small States in World Markets*. Ithaca: Cornell University Press.

Kelman, Steven. 1981. *Regulating America, Regulating Sweden: A Comparative Study of Occupational Safety and Health Legislation Policy*. Cambridge, MA: MIT Press.

King, Anthony. 1981. "What Do Elections Decide?" In *Democracy at the Polls*, edited by David Butler, Howard Penniman, and Austin Ranney. Washington, DC: American Enterprise Institute.

Kjellberg, Francesco. 1977. "Do Policies (really) Determine Politics? and eventually how?" *Policy Studies Journal* 5:554–70.

Levine, Robert A. et al., eds. 1981. *Evaluation Research and Practice: Comparative and International Perspectives*. Beverly Hills: Sage Publications.

Logue, John, and Eric Einhorn. 1982. *Welfare States in Hard Times: Problems, Policy, and Politics in Denmark and Sweden*. 2nd ed. Kent: Kent Popular Press.

Lundqvist, Lennart J. 1988. "Privatization: Toward a Concept for Comparative Analysis." *JPP* 8:1 (January), 1–19.

Mackay, Alfred. 1980. *Arrow's Theorem: The Paradox of Social Choice*. New Haven: Yale University Press.

Maddison, Angus. 1982. *Phases of Capitalist Development*. Oxford: Oxford University Press.

Marmor, Theodore, and David Thomas. 1971. "Doctors, Politics and Pay Disputes: 'Pressure Group Politics' Revisited." *BJPS* 2 (October), 412–42.

Offe, Claus. 1983. "Competitive Party Democracy and the Keynesian Welfare State." *Policy Science* 15:225–46.

Organisation for Economic and Cooperative Development. 1981. *The Welfare State in Crisis*. Paris: OECD.

———. 1985. *Social Expenditure 1960–1990*. Paris: OECD.

———. 1988. *Ageing Populations*. Paris: OECD.

Pempel, T. J. 1988. *Japan and Sweden: Polarities of 'Responsible Capitalism.'* Paper given at *Comparative Politics* conference at CUNY, September.

Piven, Frances Fox, and Richard A. Cloward. 1982. *The New Class War: Reagan's Attack on the Welfare State and Its Consequences*. New York: Pantheon.

Premfors, Rune. 1981. "National Policy Styles and Higher Education in France, Sweden and the United Kingdom." *European Journal of Education* 16:2, 253–62.

Rimlinger, Gaston V. 1971. *Welfare Policy and Industrialization in Europe, America and Russia.* New York: Wiley.

Rose, Richard. 1984. *Understanding Big Government.* London: Sage Publications.

Rose, Richard, and Rei Shiratori, eds. 1986. *The Welfare State East and West.* New York: Oxford University Press.

Scharpf, Fritz W. 1987. "A Game Theoretical Interpretation of Inflation and Unemployment in Western Europe." *JPP* 73 (July), 227–58.

Schmidt, Manfred G. 1988. *Sozialpolitik: Historische Entwicklung und Internationaler Vergleich.* Opladen: Leske & Budrich.

Schmitter, Philippe C. 1977. "Modes of Interest Intermediation and Models of Social Change in Western Europe." *Comp Pol St* 10 (April), 7–38.

Shapiro, Robert, and John Young. 1989. "Public Opinion and the Welfare State." *Political Science Quarterly* 103:1, 59–89.

Stone, Deborah A. 1980. *The Limits to Professional Power: National Health Care in Federal Republic of Germany.* Chicago: University of Chicago Press.

Therborn, Göran. 1987. "Does Corporatism Really Matter?" *JPP* 7:3 (July), 259–84.

Verba, Sidney, et al. 1987. *Elites and the Idea of Equality: A Comparison of Japan, Sweden, and the United States.* Cambridge, MA and London: Harvard University Press.

Wilding, Paul, ed. 1986. *In Defense of the Welfare State and Equality.* Berkeley: University of California Press.

Wilensky, Harold L., and Lowell Turner. 1987. *Democratic Corporatism and Policy Linkages.* Berkeley: Institute of International Studies, University of California.

Acknowledgments (cont'd)

Figure 8.2. From *Vallingby and Farsta: From Idea to Reality*, by David Pass. Copyright © 1973 by MIT. Published by the MIT Press. Reprinted by permission of the MIT Press.

Figure 8.3. Reprinted from *The World Cities* by Peter Hall, by permission of George Weidenfeld & Nicolson, Ltd.

Table 9.5. Reprinted from *Environmentalists: Vanguard for a New Society* by Lester Milbrath by permission of the State University of New York Press, © 1984 State University of New York Press.

Figure 9.1. From *World Resources, 1988–89: An Assessment of the Resource Base That Supports the Global Economy*, by the World Resources Institute and the International Institute for Environment and Development in collaboration with the United Nations Environment Programme. Copyright © 1988 by the World Resources Institute and the International Institute for Environment and Development in collaboration with the United Nations Environment Programme. Reprinted by permission of Basic Books, Inc., Publishers.

Figure 10.1. Reprinted by permission of Transaction Publishers from *The Development of Welfare States in Europe and the United States*, by Peter Flora and Arnold Heidenheimer, eds. Copyright © 1984 by Transaction Publishers.

Table 10.4. Reprinted from *Sozialpolitik Historische Entwicklung und internationaler Vergleich* by Manfred G. Schmidt (Opladen: Leske und Budrich, 1987) by permission.

Index

Acid rain, 312, 340–342, 364
Act to Promote Economic Stabilization and
    Growth of 1967 (Germany), 140
AFL-CIO, 109, 118
Africa, 331, 364
Agriculture, 21–22, 143, 157, 230–237,
    240, 247, 281, 285, 331
Alkali Inspectorate, 324
American Association for Labor Legisla-
    tion, 243
American Bankers Association, 118
American Hospital Association, 77
American Medical Association, 62–66, 78
Amsterdam, 125, 273–275, 280–281, 293,
    299, 301, 342
Aristotle, 7
Asia, 331
Australia, 14
    education, 38–39, 364
    health, 63, 85, 89, 364
    income maintenance, 239–241, 245–
        246, 252–253, 261–262, 364
    expenditures, 226–227, 249, 257, 262
    social insurance, 248–249, 262–263
    taxation, 193, 209–213, 365
Austria, 360–361
    economic policy, 133, 169, 172–179, 363
    health, 17
    income maintenance, 226–228, 257
    taxation, 186–191, 196–198, 212

Baden-Württemberg, 198
Bangladesh, 371
Bank of America, 149
Bank of England, 151–152
Barre Report, 114
Bavaria, 32, 35, 315
Belgium, 360
    economic policy, 133, 169, 172–174
    education, 38, 364
    environment, 320–321
    health, 364

income maintenance, 226–227, 257, 364
    taxation, 205, 211–212, 365
Bennett, William, 40
Beveridge, William, 231, 238–239
Birmingham, Britain, 295
Bismarck, Otto von, 58, 62–64, 230–231,
    235, 347, 354
Blacks, 332
Blue Cross, 63–65, 77, 94
Blue Shield, 63–65
Bolivia, 371
Bologna, 299
Bonn, 35
Boston, 289
Brazil, 331
Britain, 3, 20, 350–353, 360–362
    economic development, 335–336
    economic policy, 144–145, 154–156,
        160, 174, 179–180, 353, 363
        inflation, 133, 141–142, 152
        public/private coordination, 153–154,
            353
        strategies, 151–154, 180–181
        taxation, 151–153
        unemployment, 133, 141–142, 169,
            274–276
    education, 27, 42, 53, 354–357, 364
        comprehensivization, 43–47, 53
        grammar schools, 18, 43, 46
        higher education, 30, 48, 51–54, 357,
            361
        local government, 25, 32, 44–47
        private schools, 24, 30, 34, 44, 357
        secondary schools, 25, 29–30, 34, 38–
            42
    environment, 284, 317, 322–324, 327,
        335–336, 342–344
        businesses, 324–325
        disposal of wastes, 317, 332
        environmentalism, 319–321
        financing of, 343
        pollution, 312–314, 317

health, 59–75, 78–86, 89–96, 351, 354–356
  doctors, 64–66, 72–74, 77–79, 82, 89, 95, 351
  expenditures, 74, 77–80, 84–85, 95, 364
  financing of, 26, 61–63
  health insurance, 17, 58–65, 70, 73–77, 81–83, 87, 91–95, 355–356
  hospitals, 61, 77–79, 82
  utilization, 69, 74–75, 79, 95,
housing, 120, 127–130, 354–357
  local government, 103–105, 108–109, 113, 349
  private sector, 103, 116–117, 128–129
  public housing, 101–102, 107–113, 117–118, 349
  subsidies, 108–109, 112, 115, 122–124
income maintenance, 219–221, 224, 227–228, 235–238, 247–253, 258
  expenditures, 226, 249, 257, 364
  social insurance, 237–239, 249, 347–349, 254
taxation, 185–186, 199–204, 214–216, 362, 365
  avoidance, 204, 212
  direct and indirect, 190–196, 278
  protests and cuts, 210
  rates, 187–196, 212–213
urban planning, 271–272, 276, 284–285, 293–299, 302–303, 306
  local government, 277–278, 294–295, 305–306
  private sector, 270, 293
  and transportation, 287–289, 301
British Leyland, 153
British Medical Association, 62, 66
Brown, Jerry, 206
Buckingham University, 28
Bundesbank, 140, 158–160
Burgerinitiativen, 301
Bureaucracies, 4, 19–22, 362, 370
  in economic policy, 15–17, 146–162, 166, 175, 179
  in education, 27–28, 31–35, 40–41, 44–55
  in environment, 322
  in health, 11, 61, 65–74, 77–82, 85, 88–90, 93–94
  in housing, 97–108, 113, 120, 123–130
  in income maintenance, 228–240, 243–244, 247, 349
  in taxation, 14, 208, 213
  in urban planning, 271, 285–286, 295
Bush, George, 41, 93–94, 192, 214, 304, 345
Business, role in
  economic policy, 140–142, 145–146,

149–155, 158–159, 171–174, 177–180, 353, 361, 369
  education, 33
  environment, 309–310, 315, 320–334, 338–339, 342–343
  health, 5, 63, 85
  housing, 103–104, 109, 114–119, 125–129
  urban planning, 270, 278–284, 293–294, 300, 303–307

California, 205–207, 315, 362–363
Canada
  economic policy, 169, 174
  education, 29–30, 39, 42, 364
  environment, 340
  health, 63, 71, 80, 85–89, 364
  income maintenance, 226–227, 249, 253, 257, 348, 364
  taxation, 187–189, 193, 198–200, 203, 208–216, 365
Carnegie Foundation, 34, 64
Carter, Jimmy, 80, 155, 263, 304, 320
Catholic People's Party (Netherlands), 281
Cavazos, Lauro, 41
Centralization, 3, 350–351, 363
  economic policy, 146, 149, 153, 156–157, 172, 176, 179
  education, 24–25, 28, 31, 34–36, 46–50, 56
  health, 62, 67–71, 80–81
  housing, 104–105
  income maintenance, 233, 242
Chalandon, Albin, 113, 282
Chamat, Jean, 292
Chamber of Commerce (U.S.), 118
Chamber of Physicians (Germany), 65, 69
Chemical Waste Act of 1976 (Netherlands), 315
China, 5, 367
Chirac, Jacques, 51
Chiropractors, 66
Christian Democratic Party (Netherlands), 177–178, 337
Christian Democratic Union (Germany), 44–46, 85, 127, 159, 260
Chrysler, 155
Circular 10/65 (Britain), 44
Circular 10/70 (Britain), 44
Citizens Party (Germany), 206
Civil rights, 5, 16, 48, 106. *See also* Equal opportunity
Clark, Burton, 40
Clark, Colin, 189
Clean Air Act of 1970 (U.S.), 326–329, 332–334
Colorado, 24

Communist Party, 295, 299
   Dutch, 281
   French, 117, 292
Congress (U.S.), role in
   economic policy, 143–144, 155–157
   environment, 315, 319, 322–323, 326–328, 332–333, 338
   health, 66, 88, 92
   housing, 109, 125
   income maintenance, 263
   taxation, 153, 192, 209, 215
Conservative Party
   Britain, role in
      economic policy, 141, 151–153, 157, 180–181
      education, 25, 28, 44–47, 51–52
      health, 75, 81–82, 93–94, 117
      housing, 102, 105–108, 112–113, 116–117, 127, 357
      income maintenance, 219, 258, 349
      taxation, 188, 194, 213, 362
      urban planning, 286–288, 293, 297, 305–306
   Sweden, 280
Consumer Price Index (U.S.), 209
Control of Pollution Act of 1974 (Britain), 322
Crédit Foncier (France), 129–130
Creusot Loire, 148
Crossland, Anthony, 123–124

Dayton, 279
Decentralization, 363
   economic policy, 151, 157, 172
   education, 24, 27–28, 31, 34
   environment, 338
   health, 68, 71, 80, 84
   income maintenance, 232
   urban planning, 272, 295–296
Deferre, Gaston, 338
Democrats (U.S.), 8, 40, 70, 114, 168, 206, 264, 319
Denmark
   economic policy, 172–173
   education, 30, 364
   health, 71, 74, 80, 86, 89, 364
   income maintenance, 226, 257, 364
   taxation, 187–190, 195–198, 205–212, 365
Den Uyl, Joop, 281
Department of Health and Social Services (Britain), 91
Department of Housing and Urban Development (U.S.), 114, 279–280
Depression (U.S.), 108, 133, 137, 167, 244
Desegregation, 40–42, 105–106, 113
d'Estaing, Valérie Giscard, 147–148

Diagnosis Related Groups, 78–80, 83, 87
Dickens, Charles, 100
Dortmund, 50
Dukakis, Michael, 94

Economic policy, 14, 131, 353, 362–363
   central banks, 135–140, 150–151, 158–161, 175–177, 353
   development, 10–11, 20, 247, 340
   growth and recession, 132–135, 143–144, 148, 166, 178
   private sector, 135–136, 144, 150–159, 166–167, 170–174, 353
   strategies, 7–8, 15–17, 137–169, 181
   and taxation, 135–138, 141–145, 149–164, 175
Education Act of 1988 (Britain), 34, 51
Education policy, 3, 7, 10, 17–18, 23–28, 37, 57, 137, 350, 354–359, 363–364
   comprehensivization, 34, 37, 43–47, 53, 357
   equal opportunity, 23–26, 29, 31–38, 40–43, 48–54
   financing of, 10–13, 16, 24, 27, 30–34, 46
   higher education, 13, 24–25, 28–30, 33, 36, 48–54, 350, 357–358, 361
   local government, 25, 29, 31–32, 43–47, 53
   private schools, 16, 24–27, 30, 34, 40, 44, 357–358
   public schools, 16–18, 28–29, 33
   reform, 25–27, 31–36, 43–44, 47–48, 51, 357
   secondary schools, 13, 25, 29–30, 34–42, 47–49
Eisenhower, Dwight D., 312
Elderly, 10, 17, 363–366
   health, 13, 57–58, 62, 71, 78–81
   housing, 109–113, 276, 298
   income maintenance, 217–221, 227–229, 235–236, 241–242, 246–248, 252–264
Engineers, 26, 50, 55, 201, 325
Enthoven, Alain, 94
Environmental Party (Sweden), 321
Environmental policy, 308–309
   businesses, 309–310, 315, 320, 322–325, 332–334, 338, 342–343
   citizens' role in, 309–310, 316–318, 323
   disposal of wastes, 309, 314–317, 325, 331–332, 337, 342
   environmentalism, 164, 310–311, 318–321, 324, 329, 333–335
   financing of, 310, 315, 326–330, 337–339, 343
   legislation, 312, 315, 318–324, 329, 334, 338

local government, 315, 318, 334, 337–339
pollution, 309, 312–320, 325–332, 336–342, 351, 364
Environmental Protection Agency, 315, 320–323, 326–329, 332–334, 342–344
Equal opportunity, 10–11, 23–24, 164, 266, 367–371

Federal Housing Administration (FHA), 102, 109, 119, 296
Federal Reserve Board, 156
Federal Trade Commission, 66
Federalism, 3, 24–28, 31, 56–58, 66, 70
Feudalism, 22
Finland, 342
    education, 38–39, 42
    income maintenance, 257
Flexner, Abraham, 64
Ford, Gerald, 144, 155, 263
Fos-Etang de Berre-Martigues, 338
France, 3, 20–21, 350–351
    economic development, 146–149, 336
    economic policy, 144–145, 149–150, 154–161, 174, 179–181
        central banks, 140
        inflation, 133, 147, 148
        private sector, 140
        strategies, 140–141, 146–149, 179
        unemployment, 133, 276
    education, 24, 28, 32, 37, 364
        higher education, 28–30, 51–54
        private schools, 27
        secondary schools, 29–30, 38–39
    environment, 322, 336–338
        businesses, 325
        disposal of wastes, 317, 332
        environmentalism, 320–321
        financing of, 343
        pollution, 312–314, 317, 338
    health, 71–72, 83–84, 89–92, 95–96
        doctors, 88
        expenditures, 63, 80, 85–86, 95, 364
        financing of, 62–63
        insurance, 62–63, 95
    housing, 102–104, 108, 114–116, 129–130
        private sector, 103, 110, 116, 120
        public housing, 113–114
        subsidies, 110–116, 259
    income maintenance, 228, 235–236
        expenditures, 226–227, 257–259, 364
        program change, 233–234, 259
        social insurance, 232–236, 348–349
    taxation, 185, 200–202, 209, 216, 365
        avoidance, 191, 201–205
        direct and indirect, 190–191, 197, 278

rates, 187–191, 196, 211–212
urban planning, 272–273, 276, 286, 292, 295–298
    control of land, 282
    local government, 277–278
    private sector, 294
    and transportation, 287
    urban renewal, 301
Fraser, Malcolm, 262
Free Democratic Party (Germany), 260, 285
French Revolution, 21, 233
Friendly Societies, 61, 64, 237–238, 241

Gaullist Party (France), 113–114, 282
George, Lloyd, 187
Germany, 3, 20–21, 360–361
    economic development, 335–336
    economic policy, 132, 144, 161, 172–174, 179–181, 363
        central banks, 140, 158–160
        inflation, 133, 139–141, 157
        private sector, 158–159
        strategies, 157–160, 180
        and taxation, 158–159
        unemployment, 133, 157, 276
    education, 7, 18, 42, 354–357, 364
        comprehensivization, 43–46, 357
        Gymnasien, 37, 43, 46
        higher education, 24, 29–30, 48, 50–54, 357
        local government, 25, 29, 44–46
        private schools, 24, 30, 44
        secondary schools, 29–30, 37–38
    environment, 317, 335–336
        businesses, 325
        disposal of wastes, 314–317
        environmentalism, 319–321
        financing of, 315, 343
        local government, 315
        pollution, 312–314, 317
    health, 58, 61–65, 71–74, 83–92, 95–96, 354–357, 361
        doctors, 64–65, 69, 74, 79, 84–85, 88–89, 95, 351
        expenditures, 74, 79–80, 84–86, 95, 364
        financing of, 60–63, 77, 85
        hospitals, 59, 79, 83, 91
        insurance, 17, 59–65, 83–87, 95
        local government, 69, 85
        utilization, 69, 74, 79, 95
    housing, 102–104, 108, 120, 130, 354–356
        local government, 103–105
        private sector, 103, 109, 114–115, 127
        subsidies, 111–117, 121

income maintenance, 224, 228, 235,
249–250, 253, 259–260
expenditures, 226–227, 249, 257–260,
364
social insurance, 13, 230–232, 235–
238, 245–246, 249, 347–349, 354
taxation, 199–203, 214, 365
avoidance, 203
direct and indirect, 190–191, 278
protest, 205
rates, 187–193, 196, 211–213
urban planning, 276, 291, 301
local government, 277–278, 285, 301
urban renewal, 285
and transportation, 285, 301
Glistrup, Mogens, 205–207, 362
Gorbachev, Mikhail, 367
Government Accounting Office, 89
Greater London Council (GLC), 288–289,
294, 305
Greater Stockholm Planning Board, 106
Greece, 7, 195, 213
Green Paper on Housing (Britain), 124
Green Party (Germany), 260, 320–321,
336
Gross domestic product (GDP), 2, 15, 84–
86, 133, 165, 187, 209, 226, 240,
260–262
Gross national product (GNP), 10, 15, 18–
20, 30, 42, 62, 69, 77, 84–86, 94,
104, 134, 137, 164, 184, 187, 196,
204–206, 215, 219, 225–226, 345,
359

The Hague, 273–275
Hamburg, 35, 104, 301
Health Care Cost Containment Act of
1977 (Germany), 85
Health Care Finance Administration, 88
Health Care Insurance Administration, 88
Health insurance. See Health policy
Health maintenance organizations (HMOs,
U.S.), 80–83
Health policy, 13, 17–18, 48–50, 64, 137,
260–262, 350–364
administration, 5, 11, 61–70, 90–92
delivery, 74–80, 83, 92
doctors, 16, 26, 50, 55, 59–60, 64–70,
72–79, 82–89, 92–95, 201, 233,
350–351, 364
expenditures, 63, 74, 77–80, 83–86, 94,
364
financing of, 60–63, 68–70, 74, 78–79,
83, 95
hospitals, 16, 59–62, 65–66, 73, 76–79,
82–85, 89–92
insurance, 11, 17, 58–65, 73, 78, 81, 87,

94–95, 237–238, 242–244, 255,
261, 347, 359
and technology, 60, 64, 68, 71–73, 90–
93
utilization, 16, 67–69, 72–76, 79, 95
Health Policy Bill of 1985 (Sweden), 75
Health Systems Agencies, 81
Heath, Edward, 44
Hesse, Hermann, 12
Housing Act of 1977 (France), 114–116
Housing and Community Development
Act of 1974 (U.S.), 125, 304
Housing Finance Act of 1972 (Britain),
108, 112
Housing policy, 13, 16–18, 81, 269–273,
279, 350, 354–357
interest groups, 98–99, 103–105, 108–
110, 116, 120–121, 125
legislation, 105–107, 109, 112–119
local government, 98, 103–108, 113,
116, 349
private sector, 98, 103, 107–110, 114–
119, 125–130, 357
public housing, 100–114, 117–118, 121,
258, 349, 370
rent control, 109
subsidies, 99, 101, 107–128, 246, 259,
349, 370
and taxation, 110, 114–117, 122–125,
128, 131
HSB (Sweden), 105, 119–120
Humana hospitals, 78
Hungary, 38

IBM, 150
Immigration, 297–298
Income maintenance policy, 18–19, 122,
131, 137, 217–224, 229, 364, 367
distribution, 10, 219–221, 237, 248–256,
261, 265
expenditures, 226–227, 249, 257–263,
364
families, 246, 249–256, 259–262, 364
social insurance, 219–221, 228, 245–
250, 254–256, 263–265, 347–349,
354, 363
accident insurance, 230–232, 237,
242–243, 347
introduction of, 8, 13, 222, 228–245
pensions, 221, 227–232, 236–246,
255, 259–262, 347, 359, 363–364
sickness insurance, 221, 230–232,
237–238, 258, 262, 347
unemployment insurance, 221, 238,
243–246, 255, 258–262, 347
Independent Practice Associations, 82–83
Industrial policy
Austria, 178

Britain, 22, 145, 151–154, 180–181
France, 21, 146–149, 179
Germany, 21, 157–160, 180
Japan, 21, 142–143, 149–151, 180
Sweden, 21, 160–162, 174
United States, 22, 155–157, 180–181,
   345–346
Industrialization, 55, 58, 101, 104, 223–
   225, 228–243, 267, 271, 308
Industrial Strategy of 1975 (Britain), 152
Industry Act of 1972 (Britain), 152
Infant mortality rates, 10, 13, 95–96
Inflation, 14–15, 110, 132–145, 156–157,
   163, 166–170, 183–186, 189, 204,
   208–213, 262, 253
   strategies toward, 140–144, 147–148,
      152–154, 168–169, 173
Inland Revenue Office, 202
Interest groups, 17–22, 70, 90, 170–174,
   192, 300, 322, 351, 363, 369
Internal Revenue Service, 202–203
International Monetary Fund, 142
Insurance Doctors Association, 65
Iran, 5
Ireland, 169, 195, 211, 317, 320, 336
Italy
   economic development, 336
   education, 38–39, 48, 364
   environment, 312–314, 317, 320–322,
      336, 343
   health, 62, 71, 86–89, 364
   income maintenaance, 226, 257, 364
   taxation, 187–190, 193, 196–198, 201,
      204–205, 211–212, 365

Japan, 3, 8, 20–21, 353, 361, 366–367
   economic policy, 132–133, 144, 154,
      166, 174, 178–181, 247, 339
      inflation, 133, 142
      private sector, 142, 150, 172–173
      strategies, 142–143, 149–151, 180
      unemployment, 133, 142
   education, 24, 42, 47, 55, 358, 364
      higher education, 30, 48, 54–55
      secondary schools, 29–30, 36–39, 41–
         42
   environment, 316–317, 323–325, 335,
      339, 344
      businesses, 324–325
      environmentalism, 318–320, 339
      financing of, 343
      pollution, 312, 318
   health
      doctors, 89
      expenditures, 63, 79–80, 84–88, 95,
         364
      housing, 98, 101, 104,108
      local government, 103

private sector, 103–104
subsidies, 109, 115, 122–123
income maintenance, 260–261
   expenditures, 226–227, 257, 364
   social insurance, 241–242, 246–247
taxation, 200, 213, 217, 285, 365
   direct and indirect, 190–193, 196, 278
   rates, 187–190, 196, 211–212
urban planning, 267, 276, 286, 302
   control of land, 283–285
   local government, 274, 277–278, 283–
      285
   private sector, 283
   and transportation, 287
Johnson, Lyndon Baynes, 156, 347

Kaiser Commitee, 119
Kemp, Jack, 304
Kennedy, Edward, 73
Kohl, Helmut, 52, 213, 260
Koop, C. Everett, 93
Korea, 371

Labour Party
   Australia, 261–262
   Britain
      economic policy, 141, 145, 151–153,
         180
      education, 43–46, 51
      housing, 101, 105, 113, 117, 123–124
      urban planning, 285–288, 294, 305–
         306
   The Netherlands, 281
Laffer curve, 363
Länder, 25, 29, 35, 44–46, 52, 69, 85, 197–
   199, 202, 293, 315, 321
Landsorganization, 161
Latin America, 331, 364
Lawyers, 55, 201, 233, 324
Lekkerkerk, The Netherlands, 318
Letchworth, Britain, 271
Liberal Democrats (Japan), 193
Liberal Party
   Britain, 145
   The Netherlands, 178
Local education authorities (LEAs, Brit-
   ain), 25, 32, 44–47
Local governments, 4, 16, 263
   education, 25, 29–32, 43–47, 53
   environment, 315, 318, 334, 337–339
   health, 59–61, 69, 77, 85, 90
   housing, 103–109, 113, 349
   taxation, 184–185, 191–199, 202, 278
   urban planning, 274, 277–278, 281–
      285, 289, 294–295, 301–306
Lockheed, 155
London, 47, 93, 125, 151, 271–272, 288,
   291–295, 301, 305–306

Los Angeles, 308
Love Canal, 318
Lower Saxony, 199
Lubbers, Ruud, 337

Machiavelli, 7
Malmö, 302
Malpractice, 89–90
Manhattan, 40
Marseilles, 297–298, 338
Massachusetts, 73, 94
Medibank, 262
Medicaid, 59, 75–77, 91
Medicare, 62–63, 75, 78, 83, 88, 92–94
Mexico, 371
Michigan, 338
Militarism, 345, 349, 360, 366–367, 371
Minamata, 318
Minorities, 297–298, 332–334
Mitterrand, François, 27, 145–148, 259
Mondon, Raymond, 292
Montreal Protocol, 340
Mortgage Bankers Association, 118
Munich, 301

NAACP, 305
Nader, Ralph, 202
National Enterprise Board, 153
National Health Conference, 69, 85
National Health Service, 59–62, 65, 70,
    73–77, 81–82, 87, 91–95, 355–356
National Housing Act (U.S.)
    of 1961, 109
    of 1968, 119
Nazi Party (Germany), 157, 176, 179, 231,
    238
Nederlandse Volksunie, 298
The Netherlands, 20, 360–363
    economic development, 177, 336
    economic policy, 172–174, 177–178
        inflation, 133
        unemployment, 133, 169, 274–276,
            298
    education, 27, 354–356
        expenditures, 42, 364
        higher education, 30, 48, 50, 54
        private schools, 30
        secondary schools, 29–30, 42
    environment, 336–337, 342
        disposal of wastes, 315–318
        environmentalism, 320–321
        financing of, 328, 343
        local government, 318
        pollution, 312–314, 317, 327
    health, 68, 71–72, 79, 87, 92, 96, 354–
        357
        expenditures, 63, 80, 85–86, 95, 364
        insurance, 63

housing, 102, 108, 354–356
    local government, 103
    private sector, 103
    subsidies, 111–112, 115, 122
income maintenance, 232, 348, 354
    expenditures, 177, 226–227, 257, 260,
        364
taxation, 184, 187–189, 362, 365
    direct and indirect, 190–193
    indexation, 209
    rates, 196, 208, 211–212
urban planning, 273–276, 295, 298
    control of land, 280–282, 307
    local government, 277–278, 281–283
    private sector, 281, 307
    and transportation, 287–289
    urban renewal, 281, 301
Neue Heimat, 102–103
New Deal, 108
Newfields, Ohio, 279–280
New York, 289, 352
New Zealand, 370
    education, 38, 42
    health, 63, 85–86, 89
    income maintenance, 227, 239, 262
    taxation, 193, 211–213
Niigata, 318
Nixon, Richard M., 80, 114, 143, 155, 280,
    363
Norway, 342, 360–361
    economic policy, 133, 165, 169, 172–173
    education, 29–30, 39
    health, 63, 80, 84–85, 89
    income maintenance, 226–228, 249–
        250, 253, 257
    taxation, 190, 193, 196–198, 206

Office of Technology Assessment, 90
Oil crisis of 1970s, 2, 45, 132–133, 139–
    144, 159, 165, 173, 177–178, 261–
    262, 288
Olson, Mancur, 171
Open University (Britain), 51–52
Optometrists, 66
Oxford University, 53

Paris, 27, 35, 201, 233, 272–273, 286,
    291–295, 298–301
Parties, 8, 20, 347, 353, 357, 360
    in economic policy, 145–148, 159, 164–
        165, 168–169, 173, 177–178
    in education, 26–28, 40, 43–47, 51–52
    in environment, 319–322, 333, 336–338
    in health, 85, 90, 93
    in housing, 105, 112–118, 123, 127–128
    in income maintenance, 260, 227–228,
        231, 234–238, 244, 251, 258–264,
        349

in taxation, 192, 206
in urban planning, 281–282, 285, 292, 295, 299, 302–305
See also individual parties
People's Party for Freedom and Democracy (The Netherlands), 337
Philadelphia, 125, 278, 289
Physical Planning Law of 1965 (The Netherlands), 281
Planning Commission (France), 146
Pollution of Surface Waters Act of 1970 (The Netherlands), 328
Poor, the, 10, 264, 276, 347, 360, 364, 371
    environment, 330, 334
    health, 58–59, 62, 71, 76, 89
    housing, 97–114, 117–118, 121–122, 125, 258, 297–299, 349, 370
    income maintenance, 219, 233–235, 241, 248–256, 264
Portugal, 214
Preferred provider organizations, 83
Primary Care Networks, 83
Professional Service Review Organizations (PSROs, U.S.), 81
Propositionp 13, 205–207, 362
Prussia, 21, 27

Racism, 99, 241, 297–298
Randstad, 273–275, 281
Reagan, Ronald, 14–15, 363
    economic policy, 156–157, 363
    education, 39–41, 49
    environment, 320, 338
    health, 66, 80–83, 93–94
    housing, 107, 116–117, 131
    income maintenance, 219, 263, 347–349
    taxation, 183, 192, 207, 213, 362
    urban planning, 305–306
Republicans (U.S.), 8, 40, 93, 114, 168–169, 264, 304–305, 319–320, 338, 349, 362
Rolls Royce, 153
Roosevelt, Franklin D., 244
Rotterdam, 273–275, 281, 289, 298

Saar, 198–199
SABO (Sweden), 105, 119–120
Savings and loans, 118, 155
Schmidt, Helmut, 259–260
Scotland, 38, 194
Second Empire (France), 233
Sickness Funds (Germany), 6, 63–65
Social Democratic Party, 8–11, 14, 225–227
    Britain, 145
    Denmark, 206
    Germany, role in
        economic policy, 158

    education, 25, 43, 52
    health, 65, 117
    income maintenance, 231, 259–260
    urban planning, 285
The Netherlands, 177–178
Sweden, role in
    economic policy, 141, 160–161, 174–176
    education, 25, 34, 43, 46
    health, 70
    housing, 103, 105, 110, 119, 123
    income maintenance, 227, 236–237, 258–260
Social Security Act of 1933 (U.S.), 244
Socialist Party
    Britain, 123
    France, 27, 117, 145–149, 259–260
    Germany, 118
Spain, 75, 201, 205, 213, 299
St. Louis, 42
Stockholm, 50, 106, 121, 234–235, 273–274, 280, 287, 291, 298–299
Svenska Riksbyggen, 105, 119–120
Surinam, 298
Sweden, 3, 20–21, 350–353, 360–361
    economic policy, 144, 172–177, 363
        inflation, 133, 141, 204
        public/private coordination, 173–174
        strategies, 160–162, 174
        and taxation, 161, 175
        unemployment, 133, 141, 169
    education, 24, 27, 42–43, 364
        comprehensivization, 37, 43–46
        financing of, 27
        higher education, 48–51, 54
        private schools, 27, 30, 34
        secondary schools, 37–39, 42
    environment, 322, 335, 338–342
        businesses, 325
        environmentalism, 320–321
        financing of, 343
        pollution, 312–314, 325
    health, 58–63, 69–71, 74–79, 84–96, 361
        doctors, 69, 74, 89, 95
        expenditures, 63, 74, 77–79, 84–86, 95, 364
        financing of, 62–63
        hospitals, 59, 77
        insurance, 62–63
        local government, 61, 69
    housing policy, 102, 105, 108, 121
        local government, 103–107
        private sector, 103, 119, 125
        public housing, 102–103, 110
        subsidies, 110–115, 119–123
    income maintenance, 221, 225–228, 235–236, 247–253, 258–259

expenditures, 226, 249, 257, 364
social insurance, 234–238, 245–246, 249, 348–349
taxation, 185, 199–201, 208, 217, 365
avoidance, 204
direct and indirect, 190, 193, 197, 278
protest, 206–207
rates, 187–190, 193, 196, 206, 210–212
urban planning, 273, 276, 296–298, 302
control of land, 280
local government, 277–278
and transportation, 287
Switzerland
economic policy, 172–174
education, 29–30
health, 63, 67, 71, 79–80, 85–88
income maintenance, 226, 232, 249–250, 353, 357, 348
taxation, 187–189, 197

Taxation policy, 13, 18–19, 94, 285
assessment, 184–189, 199–203, 206, 217
avoidance, 191, 201–205, 212, 217
direct and indirect, 190–197, 278, 358
indexation, 186, 208–209, 241
local government, 184, 191–199, 276
progressivity, 185–187, 192–198, 207, 216, 250
protests and cuts, 186, 205–210, 362, 370
rates, 185–195, 210–213, 216–217, 362
and social policy, 13, 62, 110, 114–117, 183–187, 191, 214–218, 258–260, 316–365
Tax Reform Act of 1986 (U.S.), 210
Technology, 142, 148–150, 172, 179, 326–327, 339, 343–345, 369
Tennessee, 24
Thatcher, Margaret, 14, 53, 371
economic policy, 152–153, 157, 180–181
education, 25, 28, 44–47, 52
health, 81, 94
housing, 107, 116–117, 127, 357
income maintenance, 219, 258, 349
taxation, 188, 213, 362
urban planning, 297, 305–306
Third Republic (France), 233
Third World, 331–332, 340
3M Corporation, 342
Tiananmen Square, 367
Title I programs, 40
Tokyo University, 48
Town and Country Planning Association, 306
Townsend movement, 244
Toyama, 318

Transportation, 21, 97. *See also* Urban planning
Turks, 298

Unemployment, 15, 18, 54–55, 132–137, 141–144, 154, 157, 163, 166–170, 180, 183, 260–262, 273–276, 297–298, 304, 311, 335–338, 350, 363, 366–367
strategies toward, 140–146, 168–169, 173–178, 229
Unions, 8, 11, 109, 118, 362–363
economic policy, 140–146, 149–165, 169–180, 361
education, 33–35, 40, 46–47, 54
environment, 334–336
health, 65
housing, 98–100, 104, 109–110, 127
income maintenance, 225–227, 231, 234–238, 243–244
urban planning, 300
United States, 3, 15, 20, 351–352, 360–362, 366–367
economic development, 163, 335
economic policy, 132, 144, 149, 174, 180, 363
inflation, 133, 143–144, 156, 167–169, 209
private sector, 155–157
strategies, 154–157, 168–169, 180–181
and taxation, 138, 143–144, 155–157
unemployment, 133, 143–144, 157, 168–169, 274–276
education, 18, 25–27, 42, 349, 354–356, 364
financing of, 24, 31
higher education, 17–18, 24, 29–30, 36, 48–49, 54, 357–358, 361
private schools, 24–27, 30, 40, 357–358
secondary schools, 29–30, 36–42, 47–49
environment, 310, 317, 322–324, 335, 338–344
businesses, 315, 320, 324–325, 332–334, 338
disposal of waste, 315, 332, 338
environmentalism, 319, 324
financing of, 338, 343–344
local government, 334, 339
pollution, 312, 315, 319–320, 326–328, 338
health, 5, 58–84, 87–96, 354–357, 361
doctors, 64–66, 72–79, 82–83, 87–89, 92–95
expenditures, 62, 74, 77–80, 84–86, 94, 364

financing of, 62, 78, 83
hospitals, 6, 59, 62–66, 76–79, 83, 89–92
insurance, 17, 62, 65, 78, 81, 94–95, 347–349
local government, 59, 77, 90
housing, 17, 99–101, 109, 118, 128–131, 354–357
local government, 103, 108
private sector, 103, 116–119, 125
public housing, 101, 105–109, 117–119, 296
subsidies, 102, 109–111, 114–115, 122–125, 216, 349
income maintenance, 13, 219–221, 224, 228, 242, 247–254
expenditures, 226–227, 249, 257, 364
program change, 244–245, 263–264
social insurance, 243–246, 249, 254, 264–266, 347–348, 354
taxation, 185–186, 199–205, 208–209, 214–216, 362, 365
avoidance, 203, 212
direct and indirect, 190–197, 278
progressivity, 13, 192, 198, 207
protests and cuts, 205–207, 210, 362
rates, 187–196, 205, 211–213, 216
urban planning, 276, 279–280, 293, 296, 299–303
control of land, 282–285, 304–305
local government, 277–278, 284, 289, 303–305
private sector, 270, 278–284, 300, 303–304
and transportation, 287–290
urban renewal, 279
Urban Coalition, 305
Urban Development Action Grants (U.S.), 293, 304

Urban Development Corporation (Britain), 293–294
Urban Development Grant (Britain), 293
Urban Development Law of 1971 (Germany), 285
Urban planning, 3, 13, 101, 108, 116, 276, 359
control of land, 268, 280–283, 304–307
local government, 271–285, 289–291, 294–295, 299–305
private sector, 268–270, 278–282, 293–294, 299–300, 303–307
and transportation, 269–271, 279, 287–290, 297, 301–302
urban renewal, 279, 285, 298–301, 306
Urban Renewal Act of 1949 (U.S.), 303
Uruguay, 370
U.S.S.R., 176, 342, 367
Utrecht, 273–275

Veterans, 58
Veterans Administration
hospitals, 71
housing, 102
Vietnam, 132, 156, 310
Virginia, 352
Voting, 23, 57, 240, 302, 347

Wagner Act of 1937 (U.S.), 118
Whitlam, Gough, 261–262
William I, 13
Wilson, Harold, 52
Worker's Protection Board (Sweden), 322

Yokkaichi, 318
Yonkers, New York, 105–106

Zola, Émile, 100